LITERARY WAVES

A Gedenkschrift for the Literary Leviathan Dr. R.C. Prasad

LITERARY WAVES

A Gedenkschrift for the Literary Leviathan Dr. R.C. Prasad

Edited by
Dr. Samir Kumar Sharma
Dr. Gunjan

MOTILAL BANARSIDASS PUBLISHERS
PRIVATE LIMITED • DELHI

First Edition: Delhi : ***2017***

ISBN : 978-81-208-4068-3

MOTILAL BANARSIDASS
41 U.A. Bungalow Road, Jawahar Nagar, Delhi 110 007
8 Mahalaxmi Chamber, 22 Bhulabhai Desai Road, Mumbai 400 026
203 Royapettah High Road, Mylapore, Chennai 600 004
236, 9th Main III Block, Jayanagar, Bengaluru 560 011
8 Camac Street, Kolkata 700 017
Ashok Rajpath, Patna 800 004
Chowk, Varanasi 221 001

MLBD Cataloging-in-Publication Data
Literary Waves: *A Gedenkschrift for the Literary Leviathan Dr. R.C. Prasad*
Edited by Dr. Samir Kumar Sharma and Dr. Gunjan
Includes Tributes, Life and Works of Dr. R.C. Prasad, His Jottings, Reminiscences, and Articles by his colleagues, admirers and pupils
ISBN : 978-81-208-4068-3
I. English Literature II. Dr. R.C. Prasad III. Gedenkschrift
IV. Sharma, Dr. Samir Kumar V. Dr. Gunjan

Published by
Motilal Banarsidass Publishers Private Limited
www.mlbd.com • *mlbd@mlbd.com*
Printed by: Thomson Press (India) Limited

Contents

Foreword xi

Preface xiv

Acknowledgements xvi

Section I: Tributes

Former Governor of Sikkim xxi

Former Governor of Tripura xxii

Chief Minister of Bihar xxiii

Professor Emeritus George A. Shepperson xxiv

Former V.C. of Patna University xxvi

Former V.C. of Patna University xxvii

Former Principal of B.N. College xxviii

A Stroll Down the Memory Lane xxix

Section II: Life & Works of Dr. R.C. Prasad

Dr. Ram Chandra Prasad: At a Glance 3

Dr. R.C. Prasad: A Prolific Writer of English and Hindi
Prof. Sidheshwar Dhari Sinha 5

Section III: Jottings of Dr. R.C. Prasad

Letter to Shri Lali Babu 21

On Translating the Ramayana 23

The Impact of English Literature on the Indian Society 31

The Teaching of English: Illusion and Reality 35

Syncretistic Vision of Islam, Hinduism and Christianity 37

Sringivad: A Review 51

Poems by Dr. R.C. Prasad 55

Section IV: Reminiscences

Dr. R.C. Prasad: A Fond Remembrance
Dr. Kedar Nath Sharma 65

Dr. R.C. Prasad: A Unique Professor
Dr. Sister M. Carol A.C. 69

Dr. R.C. Prasad: A Good Samaritan
Dr. Indu Bhushan Sharma 71

Prof. (Dr.) R.C. Prasad: Memoirs
Dr. R.P. Roy 75

Dr. R.C. Prasad: Poetics of Experience
Mr. Rohit Ranjan 81

Section V: Articles

Preface to the Second Edition of Ram Chandra Prasad's *Early English Travellers in India*
Prof. George Shepperson 91

Tulsidas in the Global Context
Prof. Sidheshwar Prasad 93

Dr. R.C. Prasad's *Ambedkarism:* Voice and Vision of Radical Sanity
Dr. J.P. Singh and *Dr. Kalpana Sinha* 102

William Langland's *Piers the Plowman* and Dr. R.C. Prasad
Dr. Gokul Singh 112

Joyce's Narratology in *Ulysses*: A Contextual, Critical Approach
Dr. Amarendra Kumar 118

The Making of a Prince: Postcolonial Reflections on Chandragupta Maurya and Prince Hal
Dr. Jonathan B. Shaw 136

Sringara Rasa in the Early Poetry of Keats
Dr. Ratri Ray 145

E.M. Forster's *A Passage to India* as a Passage to India's Freedom
Dr. Ashok Kumar Sinha 152

Edwin Arnold's *The Light of Asia*: Buddhist Poetic Narrative and Cultural Diffusion
Dr. Shaileshwar Sati Prasad 158

Reading the Personal Essays of Mahadevi Verma in the Light of Charles Lamb's Essays
Dr. Amiya Bhushan Sharma 175

Need of Teaching Wisdom Literature
Prof. Sudha Sinha 186

A Golden Age: From Gestation to Delivery of Bangladesh
Dr. Ram Bhagwan Singh 195

A Study of Clowning in Shakespeare's Theatre
Dr. Bijay Bahadur Singh 203

A Phenomenological Study of George Bernard Shaw's Plays
Dr. Awadesh Kumar Sharma 212

Erotic Streaks in *The Rape of the Lock*
Prof. (Dr.) Radha Mohan Singh 221

Toward Skepticism as Critical Enquiry
Dr. Shanker A. Dutt 226

Ethical Understanding in the Poetry of W.H. Auden: A Study
Dr. B.P. Sinha 233

Victorian Novelists: A Critical Survey
Dr. Ashok Kumar 240

Hyperion: A Proponent of Radicalism
Dr. Samir Kumar Sharma 248

Literary Theory in Teaching Literature: The Need of Time
Dr. Gunjan 258

The Redemptive Ritual in Edward Albee's *Who's Afraid of Virginia Woolf?*
Prof. R. Saraswathi 267

Be Wise and Taste: Milton's Taming of Sin in *A Mask* and *Paradise Lost*
Dr. Ádám Bogár 278

The Use of Children's Literature to Empower Students in EFL Classroom
Dr. Leni Marlina 286

A Warrior or Not? A Comparative Study of *The Scarlet Letter* and *No Name Woman*
Dr. Quan Wang 300

Pashupati Jha: A Unique Voice in Indian English Poetry
Dr. Suresh Nath 310

Indian Ethos in the Poetry of Toru Dutt
Dr. A.A. Khan 320

Reconstructing *Ramayana*: A Texture Revisitation
Dr. Sunita Sinha 330

Chomsky's Universal Grammar (UG): An Exploration
Dr. Raj Kumar Sharma 340

Difficulties in Teaching Nominal Relative Clauses
Dr. Harish Kumar Khanna and
Dr. Satyendra Kumar 359

Dramas of Girish Karnad: Reshaping the Mind through Myth and History
Dr. D.N. Sinha and *Dr. Arvind Kumar Thakur* 367

Vijay Tendulkar as a Social Critic: A Study of *Kanyadaan*
Dr. Sweety 374

Chastity Demythicized in Karnad's *Naga-Mandala*
Dr. Anuradha Deepak 388

Isolated and Deserted Women in the Early Poetry of Tennyson
Dr. Rajni Singh 397

Of Scholarly Writing and Creative Writing: A Satirical Approach
Dibakar Pal 406

Shakespeare in Business
Dr. Rashmi Kumari 418

King Lear Revisited
Dr. Sarita Sinha 423

The Grapes of Wrath and *Kanthapura:* A Comparative Study
Dr. K.B.S. Krishna 429

English Poetry: A Journey from Obscurity to Ambiguity
Dr. Rajesh Kumar 436

Indianness as Reflected in the Short Stories of Ruskin Bond
Dr. Shrikant Singh 446

Women in Love: A Critical Perspective
Dr. Rajiv Ranjan Dwivedi 452

A Spotlight on an Indian English Poet
Dr. Bhushan Singh 460

Women at the Centre in the Novels of Anne Tyler
Dr. Ramesh Kr. Sharma and
Dr. Thirupa Thi Reddy Maru 465

Khalil Gibran: A Model of Émigré Literature
Dr. Vijay Shankar Prasad 478

Literary Intertextuality and Issues of Existence
Dr. Tanjeen A. Khan and *Dr. G.A. Ghanshyam* 486

Recreation of History and Deconstruction of Myths and Mythological Symbols in Dalit Literature
Dr. Alpana Gupta 493

Rabindra Nath Tagore's *The Home and the World:* From Feminity to Feminism
Nagendra Nathawat 505

Gender Issues in Indo-English Novels: A Study of Women Novelists
Dr. Shahnaz Begum 513

Double Crossed and Thrice Subjugated Women in Bama's *Sangati*
Mrs. Babita Mehra 522

Group Discussion as a Pedagogical Tool: Replacing the Banking Clerk Teacher
Dr. Rajan J. Barrett 529

T.S. Eliot's Theory of Objective Correlative and the Concept of *Vibhava* in Indian Rasa Theory: Some Parallels and Affinities
Dr. V.B. Srivastava 548

Indian Sensibility in Dr. Umeshwar's Poetry: A Critical Appraisal
Subodh Kr. Jha 554

The Namesake and *Namesake*: A Generic Transformation from Text to Film
Dr. R.P. Singh 564

Alice Munro as a Feminist Writer
Dr. Akhilesh Kr. Singh 569

Dialectics of the Opposites in Two of the Last Plays of W.B. Yeats
Dr. Swati Surbhi 578

The Influence of Magahi on the English Speakers of Magah Region in Bihar
Dr. Awinash Kumar Sushil 584

Multilayered Social Messages in Girish Karnad's *Hayavadana*
Dr. Niraj 595

Colonising the Child-Mind: A Study of Colonialist Designs through Pamphlets of The Great Exhibition
Dr. Shilpa D. Bhatt 601

Performance, Vernacular Cosmopolitanism and Sociolinguistics in Montreal
Kaustav Kundu 610

Structure in the Novels of Anais Nin: A Modern Approach
Dr. P.K. Sinha 620

About the Contributors 635

Foreword

The best way to remember a great scholar and teacher is to bring out a commemorative volume (Gedenkschrift) in which his brief biography and some of his writings along with the scholarly research articles and essays on different topics written by eminent scholars and young researchers are published. I am happy that Dr. R.C. Prasad Memorial Committee has done this work in an excellent way. They have not only included scholarly articles from all over the world but have also included some articles written by Dr. Prasad, who could not get them published in a book form during his life-time.

Dr. Prasad, besides being a successful teacher in the classroom, a powerful speaker and orator in the public gatherings was a great scholar who wrote many books both creative and critical in English and Hindi languages. When his *Early English Travellers in India* got its name mentioned in George Sampson's *The Concise Cambridge History of English Literature* as 'an excellent book' which is 'well served and well quoted', not only Dr. Prasad was glorified but India in general and Bihar and Patna University in particular also felt glorified and elevated. The literary asset of Dr. Prasad has catapulted him into the global hall of fame.

Dr. Prasad was an authority on almost all the important writers of English literature right from Chaucer to Stephen Spender. It was quite natural as he was a worthy disciple of the legendary scholar Dr. R.K. Sinha. Dr. Prasad had studied Hindi and Sanskrit literatures and criticism. He was honoured with the degree of D. Litt. on *Hindi Sahitya Ki Alochana Par Paschatya Prabhav.* He translated a lot of books from Sanskrit into English language such as *Vivah, Shradh, Upanayan* etc. His *magnum opus* is his translation of Tulsidas's *Sri Ramcharitamanas* from Avadhi to Khariboli Hindi and English. This translation work is so popular that five editions have already been published so far. The people of the non-Hindi belt in India and abroad have now come to know that Tulsidas was a great literary icon as were Homer, Virgil, Dante, Shakespeare and Milton. As the credit of making the importance of the Rig Veda known to the world goes to Max Muller and the credit of taking the Aryan civilization to the Southern part of India goes to August Muni, the credit of making Tulsidas known to the non-Hindi world in a forceful way redounds to Dr. R.C. Prasad. It is really a great service to the nation. It is on the basis of his writings that Dr. Prasad will remain immortal. The Shakespearean lines to express my feelings would be a handsome tribute to his immortal oeuvres.

So long as men can breathe, or eyes can see
So long lives this, and this gives life to thee

Tulsidas writes in the Ayodhyakanda of *Sri Ramcharitamanas*–

Dhanya janam jagatital tasu
Pitahin pramod charita suni jasu

(Blessed is his life upon this terrestrial globe whose father is pleased to hear of his ennobling doings) and

Putravati yuwati jag soi
Raghuwar bhakta jasu sut hoi

(Only that woman is a mother in this world who has a son devoted to Raghunatha.)

Blessed was Dr. Prasad's life as his father took pride in him and as Dr. Prasad was a votary of Lord Ram, his mother was very fortunate to have him as her son.

Dr. R.C. Prasad was such a charismatic personality who amused his parents along with the readers through his great literary exploits as a teacher, a researcher, a creative writer and a critic all rolled into one.

This commemorative volume will, I am sure, not only open up new vistas for further research on the different facets of Dr. R.C. Prasad but will also enthuse the readers to opt for new topics for seminars and researches.

Dr Bindeshwar Pathak
Founder
Sulabh Sanitation and Social Reform Movement

Preface

Literary Waves: A Gedenkschrift is published to mark the life and literary achievements of the late Dr. R.C. Prasad (Dr. Ram Chandra Prasad) who has made Patna University proud by his momentous contributions to the field of teaching, research, translation, creative and critical writings. Although he left his mortal frame at the age of sixty four, his forty five years' teaching experience, more than four dozen books and more than one hundred research articles and umpteen research guidance of about fifty scholars make him worth cherishing in our memory. Physically he is not in our midst but spiritually he is vibrant in every scintilla of Nature. This volume is a befitting and handsome tribute to this extraordinary Literary Leviathan.

Literary Waves is neatly divided into five sections. The first section has eloquent tributes paid to him by eminent personalities. The Second section focuses on life and works of Dr. R.C. Prasad. The third section Jottings contains some unpublished research articles, essays, and poems written by Dr. Prasad himself. The one epistle to Lali Babu by Dr. Prasad showcases his grave concern for upholding aloft the self respect of Indian scholars. All his thought-provoking writings tomtom the many splendoured scholarship of Dr. Prasad.

The fourth section comprises reminiscences in which Dr. Prasad's colleagues and disciples have presented different facets of his magnetic personality as a role model teacher, a ravenous reader and an erudite scholar. The fifth section zeroes in on different genres of literature from different nations such as Britain, America, India, Bangladesh, Pakistan and others. Articles related to Linguistics, English Language Teaching, New Literary Theories, Syntax and the analysis of myths in postmodernist perspectives and film adaptations make this volume an amazing read and I do hope that they will open up fresh fields and pastures new for all avid readers and researchers of Language and Literature.

A galaxy of scholars from India and abroad have contributed their thought-compelling and insightful research articles to this volume which are multi fresh flowers in this literary bouquet of Dr. Prasad. These articles will exude aroma in all times and will open up fresh avenues for all fervent readers and researchers of literature.

Acknowledgements

I am highly indebted to Padma Bhushan Dr. Bindeshwar Pathak, Founder, Sulabh Sanitation and Social Reform Movement for penning the Foreword to this volume. This long cherished dream has come true thanks to the enduring inspiration, fillip and financial assistance of Dr. Pathak. And but for his guidance *Literary Waves: A Gendenkschrift for the Literary Leviathan Dr. R.C. Prasad* would not have seen the light of the day.

I am grateful to Shri Arjun Prasad Singh, Convener, Dr. R.C. Prasad Memorial Committee for entrusting me with the onerous task of collecting and editing the articles for this commemorative volume. As he was in close association with Dr. R.K. Sinha and Dr. R.C. Prasad for more than three decades, his pieces of advice have come to fruition.

I express my gratitude to Dr. Damodar Thakur, Chairman, Department of English, Faculty of Arts, University of Sanáa, Republic of Yemen for his shower of blessings and encouragements.

I owe to all Professors, Associate Professors, Assistant Professors and research scholars who contributed their scholarly research articles to this volume. I am highly grateful to all those great luminaries who mailed messages and paid glowing tributes to Dr. R.C. Prasad and wished the publication of this volume a stupendous success.

I am thankful to all the members of the family of Dr. R.C. Prasad for their help and co-operation. I am particularly thankful to Mr. Rohit Ranjan, the grandson of Dr. R.C. Prasad for providing us some unpublished research articles, essays, book-reviews, poems, photographs, letters, diaries. of rare importance and also some research articles and stories published in the Patna University Research Journals and the Newspapers.

I am immensely thankful to Prof. Sidheshwar Dhari Sinha, Former Dean, Ranchi University, Ranchi and Prof. Radha Mohan Singh, Former Head of the Department of English, Patna University for going through the articles received for publication and their valuable suggestions. I express my gratefulness to my revered teachers Dr. Ashok Kumar Sinha, Professor of English (Retd.) Patna University and Dr.

Ram Bhagwan Singh, Professor of English(Retd.) Ranchi University who went through the entire volume and suggested necessary correction. Dr. Gunjan's unremitting toil cannot be described in words for he worked day in, day out in sending and receiving mails for this volume. And without his co-operation this Gedenkschrift for Dr. R.C. Prasad would have been an utter impossibility. I would be amiss if I do not thank my friends and colleagues.

My special thanks are due to Shri J.P. Jain of Motilal Banarsidass Publishers for their unfailing support and readiness to make this volume come into print. I'm also grateful to Shri R.K. Jain and Shri Wachaspati Pandey for their valuable editorial suggestions.

I am no less thankful to Mr. Manish Priye, Dr. Hasib and Md. Dilshad for typing the pages meticulously and error-free.

Samir Kumar Sharma
Secretary
Dr. R.C. Prasad Memorial Committee

Section I

Tributes

Former Governer of Sikkim

बाल्मीकि प्रसाद सिंह
BALMIKI PRASAD SINGH

सत्यमेव जयते
राज्यपाल, सिक्किम
GOVERNOR OF SIKKIM

राज भवन
गान्तोक-737103
(सिक्किम)
RAJ BHAVAN
GANGTOK-737103
(SIKKIM)

SKM/GOV/MESG/2013/711
18th April, 2013

MESSAGE

I am glad that the Dr. R.C. Prasad Memorial Committee is going to publish a Festschrift in the memory of late Dr. Ram Chandra Prasad, Professor and Head of the Department of English, Patna University.

Ram Chandra Babu was a distinguished scholar and an iconic teacher. He studied in Edinburgh University and did his research on – *Early British Travellers in India.* This work of his had earned him commendation from academics the world over and is mentioned in – *The Cambridge History of English Literature.* In addition to his tenure at the Patna University, Dr. Prasad also served two stints at the T.M. Bhagalpur University, initially as Professor of English and later as its Pro Vice-Chancellor for a number of years.

A renowned academic, Dr. Prasad guided more than fifty research scholars towards achieving their Ph.D degrees. An avid writer, he has to his credit more than forty books. His translation in English of Sant Tulsidas's epic work *Ramcharaitra Manas* is a prized possession in several homes in India and abroad.

I had the pleasure of knowing him and having his friendship. Ram Chandra Babu had a pleasing personality that attracted people. He was indeed a good friend, a good teacher, and a good human being. We need people like him in every walk of life in the country.

I convey my best wishes to the Memorial Committee on the publication of the Festschrift in the memory of Dr. Ram Chandra Prasad, which will surely be a great tribute to this brilliant teacher and erudite scholar and a source of inspirations to students and teachers.

(B.P. Singh)

Former Governer of Tripura

प्रो. सिद्धेश्वर प्रसाद
भूतपूर्व राज्यपाल

बी-115 त्रिवेणी अपार्टमेंट
शेख सराय फेज-1
नई दिल्ली-110 017
दूरभाष : 011-26016095
मोबाईल : 9871669133

संदेश

पटना, 2.12.2012

यह जानकर प्रसन्नता हुई कि पटना विश्वविद्यालय के अंग्रेजी विभाग के अध्यक्ष डॉ. रामचन्द्र प्रसाद जी पर एक स्मारक ग्रंथ का प्रकाशन किया जा रहा है।

रामचन्द्र बाबू अंग्रेजी के लोकप्रिय अध्यापक थे। उनकी अध्यापन-शैली विद्यार्थियों को मुग्ध कर लेती थी।

उन्होंने गोस्वामी तुलसीदासकृत रामचरितमानस का अवधी से हिन्दी और अंग्रेजी में गद्यानुवाद किया है। यह एक अनूठा कार्य है। इसके द्वारा तुलसीदासजी पर रचना सारे भारत ही नहीं विदेशों में पहुँच रही है। यह अनुवाद मानस के सभी पूर्व अनुवादों से बेहतर है। इसकी भूमिका में भी उन्होंने जो उपलिखित है उस पर भी पाठकों का ध्यान होना चाहिए।

मोतीलाल बनारसीदास ने इसका प्रकाशन कर अत्यन्त सराहनीय कार्य किया है।

मैं इस प्रयास की सफलता की कामना करता हूँ।

सिद्धेश्वर प्रसाद
2012

1/23, सेक्टर-7, हाउसिंग बोर्ड कालोनी, कंकर बाग, पटना-800 020
मोबाईल : 9693710642

Chief Minister of Bihar

CHIEF MINISTER
BIHAR

PATNA
10.7.2015

Message

I am happy to learn that Dr. R.C. Prasad Memorial Committee is going to publish a Gendenkschrift in the memory of the Late Dr. Ram Chandra Prasad, the great scholar and a brilliant teacher.

Dr. R.C. Prasad was an eminent scholar of English language and served as Professor and the Head of the Department of English in Patna University and also served as Pro-Vice-Chancellor for many years in the T.M., Bhagalpur University. He was known for his simplicity and easy accessibility.

I wish the publication a grand success.

(Nitish Kumar)

Professor Emeritus George A. Shepperson

C.B.E., B.A., M.A., Hon. D. Univ. Edinburgh,
Dr. h.c. York, D. Litt. h.c. Malawi, F.E.I.S.

15, Farleigh Fields, Orton Wistow, Pctcrborough PE2 6YB,
United Kingdom. Telephone: 01733 238772

26 May 2014

Dear Dr. Rohit Ranjan,

Ms Laura Drummond of Edinburgh University, has sent me your communication about the Gedenkschrift in memory of your late grandfather Professor Ram Chandra Prasad. I regret that I cannot communicate with you by Email because I do not use Emails. Please, therefore, when writing to me, use my postal address as above.

I should like very much to show my respect for your grandfather whom I first met in 1955. He came very often to the house of my late wife Joyce — she died eight years ago — and me during his postgraduate days at Edinburgh University, and we came to look upon him almost as a member of our family. He and I were frequent correspondents and I watched the development of his career in India with admiration.

Ram Chandra Prasad was one of the very best postgraduate student I supervised during my own academic career of almost half a century in British, American, Canadian and African universities. It did not surprise me when he went on to become a distinguished scholar, writer and administrator in his own country. I have tried to make his reputation in India better known in Britain, whose language he both wrote and spoke so well.

I am enclosing a copy of the preface which I wrote for the second edition of his book *Early English Travellers in India*. I know /

over

(2)

that this has lead many English-speaking readers to an appreciation of this work.

I hope that this preface which I wrote in 1974 may be published in the Gedenskrift, together with an indication of the deep appreciation and affection for Ram Chandra which my late wife and I had for him and which I have tried to set down in this letter.

I regret very much that I cannot write more because I am 92 years old and a very sick man. I tire very easily. I also use manual script because acute arthritis prevents my hand from using the good handwriting which I used to possess.

I was very sad to learn that Ram Chandra had died in 1993. I remember him with the greatest of admiration and affection. I learned very much from him about the culture of India in which I had spent some time — some of it in Ranchi — during my military service in South East Asia in the Second World War.

You are, I am sure, proud to have him as your grandfather. I also am proud to have helped and worked with this courteous and kindly Indian gentleman.

With every good wish,
Yours sincerely,
George Shepperson
(George Shepperson)

Former V.C. Patna University

Estd. 1917

PATNA UNIVERSITY

Prof. (Dr.) U.K. Sinha
Vice-Chancellor

Message

It is my pleasure to pay a glowing tribute to the Commemorative Volume Gendenkschrift to be published to mark the life and literary achievements of Dr. R.C. Prasad who served the Patna University and the T. M. Bhagalpur University in various capacities. Most part of his vital life was spent in B. N. College and in P. G. Department of English, Patna University. He was a stickler for punctuality and successful teacher of English. His contribution in the field of research and teaching will always be cherished by teachers and students. I wish the Commemorative Volume to be a fount of inspiration to all in all times, in all climes.

(U. K. Sinha)

Former V.C. Patna University

PATNA UNIVERSITY, PATNA

Message

Bringing out the Gendenkschrift for late Professor Ram Chandra Prasad would be a great literary achievement in the field of English literature. This would help the people, particularly the younger generation, to know the creative genius of late Professor Ram Chandra Prasad, who had created a literary genre in English, by his novels, short stories, and critical essays. Gendenkschrift, with its varied collections, by distinguished authors, would definitely bring in 'a la tradition human', in contemporary english literature, as each of the collection in it touches this aspect in different perceptions and perspectives.

Professor Sudeepta Adhikari
2/4/2013

Professor of Geography

Patna University, Patna

Former Principal of BN College

OFFICE OF THE PRINCIPAL

B. N. COLLEGE

PATNA UNIVERSITY

ASHOK RAJ PATH, PATNA-800004

NAAC ACCREDITED "B" "GRADE"

0612-2300619 (O)
2301565 (Fax)

ESTD-1889

Ref...............

Date : 02/04/13

MESSAGE

It's a matter of immense pleasure for me to learn that the Department of English is going to publish a Gedenkschrift in the memory of the late Dr. Ram Chandra Prasad, an eminent scholar of English literature in Patna University. I whooped with joy when I came to know about two months back that teachers of the English Department are going to pay true reverence to a personality who had really mesmerized the pupil by his power of knowledge for quite a longer period. It is needless to say that the role of teachers like Dr. R.C. Prasad is of paramount importance in shaping the minds of the child. We cannot imagine a society without a dedicated and doting teacher like Dr. R.C. Prasad. I can say, without an iota of doubt, that Dr. R.C. Prasad has left a rich legacy to be emulated by posterity. His acknowledged scholarship, unimpeachable integrity and impeccable touch to English literature have laid the solid foundation for creating enlightened citizens in the country. My oodles of respect to this inspirational and celebrated personality.

I personally feel very much privileged to associate myself with this pious work. On behalf of the college I extend all my support and best wishes for the publication of the Gendenkschrift.

PKPoddar 02/04/13

(Dr. P.K. Poddar)
Principal,
B.N. College,
Patna University, Patna

Principal
B.N. College, Patna

A Stroll Down the Memory Lane

Patna University basks in the glorious tradition of turning out erudite scholars of global acclaim such as Prof. Kalimuddin Ahmad, a product of Cambridge University and a researcher under Dr. F.R. Leavis. Credit redounds to Dr. Ahmad to introduce Practical Criticism to English and Urdu Studies. His work on *Psychoanalysis and Literary Criticism* is a wonderful read. And his foray into Urdu literature earned him laurels. Dr. R.K. Sinha is another literary luminary from Bihar to do research on *Literary Influences on D.H. Lawrence* under the supervision of Lord David Cecil. Had his thesis been published when it was submitted to Oxford, it would have been the maiden venture on Lawrence. Dr. Sinha beamed as the ambassador of the University of Oxford and he was indubitably an epitome of English literature.

Dr. D.P. Vidyarthi was known for his clarity and crystalline expression of his insightful ideas and thoughts in English and Hindi literature. He was also a product of the University of London. He got his Ph.D. degree on *The 18th Century Novels of Sensibility* under Prof. Geoffrey Bullough, a great scholar of Elizabethan literature.

Dr. K.P. Ambastha, a product of the University of Edinburgh was an authority on Romantic poetry and a very successful administrator also. He was an excellent teacher who was all the time available to the students.

Professor Damodar Thakur, a product of the Cambridge University was a noted scholar. He also graced the chairs of the Principal, Patna College and the Director of Education, Govt. of Bihar. His book *Constant Pursuit* is very popular among the researchers and teachers of English.

Dr. Dashrath Prasad Singh was a great exponent of modern English Literature. His D.Litt. thesis *Influence of F.H.Bradley on T.S. Eliot* is a milestone in the study of oeuvres of T.S. Eliot. Dr. Singh was full of poise and pizzazz.

Dr. Ram Chandra Prasad occupies an iconic status for his doctoral research in the University of Edinburgh on *Early English Travellers in India.* He was awarded the degree of D. Litt. on *Adhunik Hindi*

Alochana Par Pashchatya Prabhav and he has more than three dozen books to his credit.

Dr. D.P. Sen Gupta was a very popular, affable, amiable and successful teacher of English in the department of English, Patna University. Dr. Sen Gupta was simplicity incarnate. As a teacher he was a stupendous success. He was affable and amiable among teachers and students alike. His D.Litt. thesis on Irish Murdoch is an outstanding literary acquisition to all avid readers of Murdoch.

Prof. Gurudas Mukherjee who had the magic wand of making the ambiguous and grotesque stark simple and comprehensive to all and sundry. He was virtually the literary Guru of encyclopedic range. He was not Caviare to the generality. Prof. Mukerjee has become a legend who epitomizes simple living and lofty thinking: such a mentor is born once in a blue moon.

Dr. Kapil Muni Tiwary is a linguist non-pareil. His research on *Panini's Description of Nominal Compound in Sanskrit* under George Cardona in University of Pennsylvania Pa, USA in 1968 occupies a pride of place in Britannica. His work on *Dialects of Bihar* deserves kudos plethora. A number of research articles on Sanskrit, Hindi and Arabic Linguistics are to his credit. He initiated the teaching of Linguistics in Patna University and was the first commissioned Professor of English with specialization in Linguistics.

As I was closely associated with Dr. R.C. Prasad for more than three decades and knew many things about him as a man, as a teacher, as a writer and above all as an inexhaustible fount of inspiration to the students, I thought it fit to bring out a commemorative volume in his memory so that not only this generation but also the posterity may be in the know what types of teachers were in Patna University which was once the Oxford of Asia. Patna University can once again become one of the prized Universities in the world if the teachers emulate their role models in teachers like Dr. Prasad, who was a voracious reader, laborious, efficient and committed teacher, impeccable writer, erudite scholar and pious man.

In small proportions we just beauties see
And in short measures life may perfect be

These lines of Ben Jonson are very much applicable to Dr. Ram Chandra Prasad whose name resonates even today in the vast corridors of time. To translate the long cherished dream of a commemorative volume into reality, I contacted Dr. Samir Kumar Sharma, Associate Professor of English, B.N. College, Patna and convened a meeting under the chairmanship of Dr. C.N. Pandey of some eminent Professors of English such as Dr. J.P. Singh, Dr. Ratri Ray, Dr. S.S. Prasad, Prof. Sudha Sinha, Dr. Bijay Bahadur Singh, Dr. Shanker A. Dutt, Prof. Muniba Sami, Dr. Radha Mohan Singh, Prof. S.M. Ashok, Prof. Ashok Kumar, Dr. N.K. Pandey, Dr. Gunjan, Dr. Vijay Shankar Prasad, Dr. Akhilesh Kuimar Singh, Dr. Awinash Kumar Sushil, Dr. B.P. Mandal, Dr. Jawed Hayat, Dr. Ravindra Kumar, Dr. Murari Sharan Manglik and others and formed Dr. R.C. Prasad Memorial Committee of which Dr. Samir Kumar Sharma was unanimously nominated the Secretary. Dr. Sharma and his young colleague Dr. Gunjan worked relentlessly, invited scholarly articles from all over the world. And I am on cloud nine to have this delectable volume for you. Padma Bhushan Dr. Bindeshwar Pathak, founder of Sulabh International is the patron of the committee who is generous enough to bear the financial burden for its publication. I hope this volume will not be the last one rather some more volumes would come out with his financial assistance on some of the celebrated literary icons of Patna University.

Arjun Prasad Singh
Convener
Dr. R.C. Prasad Memorial Committee

Section II

Life & Works of Dr. Ram Chandra Prasad

Dr. Ram Chandra Prasad : At a Glance

1. Date of Birth : 29.07.1929
2. Place of Birth : Gorakhari, Bikram, Patna
3. Father's Name : Late Ramayan Sharan
4. Qualifications
   (a) Primary & Middle : St. Xavier's School, Patna
   (b) Matriculation : B.N. Collegiate School, Patna
   (c) Intermediate : B.N. College, Patna
   (d) Graduation : Patna College, Patna
   (e) Master of Arts : Patna University
   (f) Ph.D. : University of Edinburgh
   (g) D.Litt. : Patna University
5. Period of Service :
   (i) Lecturer in English, H.D. Jain College, Ara, 1951
   (ii) Lecturer in English, B.N. College, Patna, 1951-63
   (iii) Reader in English, 1963-73
   (iv) Professor of English, T.M. Bhagalpur University & Department of English, Patna University, 1974-80
   (v) Pro-Vice-Chancellor, T.M. Bhagalpur University, 1980-82
   (vi) Head, Department of English, Patna University, 1982-90
   (vii) Principal, Patna College, 1990-91
6. Death: 5 August, 1993
7. Works of Dr. Prasad –
   (1) *Dr. Samuel Johnson: Sidhanta aur Samiksha* (1978)
   (2) *Vimanita* – novel in Hindi (1969)
   (3) *The Mahatma* – novel in English (1978)
   (4) *Shri Krishna Sinha: A Biography.* (Co-author: A.K. Sinha). (1987)
   (5) *Shri Krishna Sinha* (in Hindi) (Co-author: A.K. Sinha) (1988)
   (6) *Ek Aur Kahani Kursi Ka, short stories* (1989)
   (7) Tenth chapter of *Hindi Sahitya ka Itihas*
   (8) Translation of *Sri Ramcharitamanas*

(9) *Udar Manjhe*

(10) *Nangi Dharti* (1991)

(11) *Shaili* (1993)

(12) *Adhunik Hindi Alochana par Paschatya Prabhav* (1973)

(13) *Early English Travellers in India* (1965)

(14) *Bihar*

(15) *The Achievement of Raja Radhika Raman: An Appraisal* – Biography

(16) *Literary Criticism* (1976)

(17) *Modern Studies and other Essays* (1987)

(18) *Upanayan* (1993)

(19) *Shradh* (1993)

(20) *"Hindi Fiction" Modern Indian Literature: An Anthology. Chief Ed. K.M. George. Vol. II, 1993.*

(21) *Mahachalisa* – last book (1994)

(22) Co-authored – *Jaishankar Pd., Surdas, Maithilisharan Gupta, Bihari, Premchand.*

(23) *Lifting the Veil* – On Acharya Rajnish's life

(24) *Nirala : Kaljayi Vyaktitwa*

(25) *Lukach*

(26) Article on *Savitri*

(27) Article on *the Gita*

(28) *Anthology of Prose*

(29) *New Golden Treasury*

(30) *Acharya Rajnish*

(31) *Mahavir: Parichaya and Vani*

(32) *Karmyog, Dharm & Gandhi*

(33) *Suli Par Saj Piyake*

(34) *Ghat Bhulana Bat Benu*

(35) *Samud Samana Bindu Men*

(36) *The Necklace and Other Stories*

(37) Felicitation Volume of Dr. R.K. Sinha.

(38) *Alok Purush:* Dr. A.K. Sen Memorial Volume.

Dr. R.C. Prasad: A Prolific Writer of English and Hindi

Prof. Sidheshwar Dhari Sinha

R.C. Prasad was born on the 29th July 1929 at Gorakhari, near Bikram in the district of Patna and died on the 5th August 1993 at Rajendra Nagar, Patna.

He was educated at St. Xavier's School at primary stage, B.N. Collegiate School at secondary stage and passed Matriculation exam. in 1945, I.A. in 1947 from B.N. College, B.A. with Hons. in English securing 2nd class from Patna College in 1949 and M.A. in English securing 2nd class in 1951.

He was appointed lecturer in English at H.D. Jain College, Arrah in 1951, He was appointed in B.N. College, Patna in 1952. He worked as Lecturer from 1951 to 1963 and as Reader from 1963 to 1973. He was appointed Professor of English at Tilka Manjhi University, Bhagalpur in 1974 and remained Professor for 18 years, including the head of the Postgraduate Department of English from 1974 to 1980 and from 1980 to 1982 as Pro Vice-Chancellor at the same University. Thereafter he returned to Patna University as head of the Postgraduate Department of English and remained on the post till he was appointed Principal at Patna College in 1990. He got retirement in 1991. After two years of his retirement he died of heart failure, leaving behind his son Biresh Ranjan, wife Sumitra, daughter Rosevita Prasad and son-in-law Col. Awadhesh Kumar. His first son Rajesh Ranjan had expired earlier. His second son Biresh Ranjan also passed away in 2014. His grandson Rohit Ranjan taught English and Mass Communication at Jamia Millia University. Now he is working at Jharkhand Central University, Ranchi. His father Ramayan Sharan, was teacher of Hindi at St. Xavier's School. His mother Mukhani Devi had died earlier.

R.C. Prasad was always smiling, very helping, popular, immaculately dressed, very regular in walking morning and evening and doing yogic practice. This charming prince, always moving in car was really a "Karm Yogi" (*Sadhak*). He had to pay the cost of sitting for hours in pursuit of his academic work. He became diabetic and died of heart failure. He was fond of all types of pens, as told by K.P. Shrivastav.

R.C. Prasad wrote both in English and Hindi having mastery over them in all genres. However, he became outstanding as a critic and mythological story writer. He wrote about 80 books and guided for Ph.D. and D.Litt. the same number of researchers.

After going through his works a colossus emerges out, who has been quoted by George Sampson in *The Concise Cambridge History of English Literature.*

Some of his books and researches that he guided for Ph.D. and D.Litt. and his critical canons, both Western and Indian, are worth mentioning. His translation of Tulsidas's *Sri Ramcharitmanas* is unique. Its introduction establishes him as an outstanding critic also. Before they are mentioned here it is appropriate to say that he was innovative and creative in criticism because he learnt all this at the feet of his guru Dr. R.K. Sinha and Dr. Nagendra in English and Hindi respectively.

His books include:

(1) *Dr. Samuel Johnson: Sidhant and Samiksha*, published in 1978 by Alekh Prakashan, New Delhi. It was dedicated to Dr. R.K. Sinha. Poetic justice and moral values that were Dr. Johnson's critical cannons, are discussed in this book.

(2) His novel *Vimanita* in Hindi was published in 1969 by Bihar Granth Academy. It is a very remarkable novel. Its introduction was written by an eminent novelist Phanishwar Nath Renu. It has thrown light on the problems of youth. Vimanita is a character in the novel who cries out not out of sorrow and suffering but out of love and overflowing affections.

(3) *The Mahatma* is a novel in English. It describes how suicide is a defeat of life and obscenity is not in the objects that are seen but in the mind of men who see them.

R.C. Prasad's *The Mahatma* is a typical example of Indian English like Raja Rao's *The Serpent and the Rope.* In it "til" and "Kashi" have been used on the first page. "Ho, Binita", here "ho" is a Hindi word, used in an English novel. "Inspector ji", "avatar", "Hai Ram" and "siddhas", "laddoos", "Ram, Ram" are such words used in conversation between Banita and her husband in the novel. Banita calls the Mahatma a fraud whom her husband reveres. *The Mahatma* exposes the so-called mahatmas who in the guise of saints do all kinds of corruption. Dr. R. C. Prasad deserves full credit for bringing the darker sides of our society in to light in a devastating way. At some places the depiction of the so called 'mahatmas' tends to be obscene and vulgar but such scenes are numerous in the novels of D.H. Lawrence and Colin Wilson. Dr. Prasad attributes it to the influence of Colin Wilson upon him and his youthful fancy. Banita, a village woman raises her voice against the evils of the pseudo religious system in which the so called mahatmas are approached for their blessings for the birth of child. Banita's experience is so traumatic that she becomes a rebel and uses harsh words for the mahatmas. She calls them 'sex maniacs'. It is a common belief that a woman's life is incomplete if she is childless. For the sake of child, especially male child, she is abused, beaten and made to sleep with sadhus. Banita reacts against this and leaves her house.

The Mahatma is an attack on fraud and superstition in Indian society in the name of religion in the novel, published in 1978 by Anupam Prakashan, Patna. The novelist's faith was shaken when he found a fraud in his guru whom he revered deeply and had written two books on his philosophy. America that also worshipped him ultimately threw him out and acknowledged R.C. Prasad as an Anglo-Indian novelist after the publication of this novel. Like other novels *The Mahatma* also bristles with wit, humour, sarcasm, arousing *vibhatsa ras.*

It is said that those English Indian novelists who ridicule their own culture are easily recognized by the West, such as, Vikram Seth in *A Suitable Boy* where "Ah, Hujur! What has brought your presence here" is used; Arundhati Roy shows how Bhim goes to Draupadi with Dusasan's bleeding intestine around his neck to wash her hair in *The God of Small Things*; in *An Area of Darkness* V.S. Naipaul shows how people defecate in the open, talking together in India and R. C. Prasad also shows the hypocrisy of the Indian Mahatma and the superstitious of Indians like Naipaul in *A House for Mr. Biswas.* However, *The Mahatma* fulfils all the criteria of a good novel, yet he seems to poke fun at his own cultural roots, he had devoted much of his time to it. It's an insider's story in the novel. So, it sounds authentic.

(4) *Ek Aur Kahani Kursi Ka* is a collection of 12 short stories in Hindi, bristling with wit and humour and it is brain-storming, touched upon by realism. It was published by Bihar Granth Kutir in 1989. Its theme is manliness that constitutes in hard work in cultivating the naked earth.

(5) The tenth chapter of *Hindi Sahitya Ka Brihad Itihas,* published by Nagripracharni Sabha, Varanasi is Prof. Prasad's unique contribution to Hindi criticism. It established him as an eminent critic of Hindi. He was a poet, a critic, a translator, a saint and wrote on travels.

(6) His translation of Tulsidas's *Sri Ramcharitmanas* is his *magnum opus.* He has translated it into both English and Hindi and added the translation of the *Hanuman Chalisa* and *Lav-Kush Kand.* In the introduction to this great book he showed how he interpreted it from the Indian and western critical canons and compared Tulsidas with Homer, Dante, Shakespeare and Milton. Tulsidas and Milton were religious poets, but the former is a saint and a seer, a lawgiver, and a liberator. Milton has Chaucer's urbanity and charity but not Tulsidas's humility. This translation is really an encyclopedia of vedant. Like Dante's *Divine Commedia* it embraces the triple worlds of Hell, Purgatory and Paradise. Milton's Paradise sweeps across Hell, Heaven and Earth. The scene of Ayodhya also extends to the forest, gods, demons and men. Tulsi's world no less than Milton's and Homer's involves great issues. Like Shakespeare and Milton he "doth glance from Heaven to Earth and from Earth to Heaven", including the role of gods in Heaven and men on earth and all actions revolve round Ram. Arnold says that a moral content makes a powerful appeal. The philosophy of the vedant and long speeches interrupt the narrative but the artistic unity of the work doesn't fall to pieces. There is a unity of sensibility. It doesn't look didactic. It abounds in similes, metaphors, and imagery. The epic represent the age allegorically and attempts to describe, "Ram Rajya", which is just opposite to the muslim misrule and integrates form and formless worship, shaivism, vaishnavism and vedantism. Shakespeare and Kalidas hardly excel the delineation of Ram Rajya. Plato's ideal republic banishes poets. So it is a picture of exclusive society. *Sri Ramcharitmanas* is inclusive. Plato's ideal republic banishes poets as they encourage emotions which should have been killed by drought but Tulsidas believes in Aristotle who thought just the other way round. The original order is brought back to the mind by the purgation of excessive emotion by arousing discordant impulses to approach and retract while encountering Ram and Ravan. Spirituality is really the source of all great poetry. This is how Ram Chandra Prasad evaluates *Sri Ramcharitmanas.* He compares and contrasts the Indian and Western poets frequently. He said that Homer's characters, like Nauseka lost her heart at the end but Sita and Manthara didn't. His characters are immoral and Tulsi's invariably moral. As Shakespeare borrowed a great deal from Plutarch, Virgil and Homer, Tulsidas borrowed from Balmiki and Vyasa, *Adhyatma Ramayan, the Gita,* the *Vedant* and the *Shrimad Bhagawat Puran.* Tulsi's idioms are rough and

colloquial. Unlike Balmiki's polished style Tulsi calls himself "the feeblest versifier". He is like Virgil but unlike Homer. Milton's fallen angels languish in Hell for ever but Tulsi's Ram kills even demons with kindness and liberates them ultimately. Milton had no generosity, yet man reads him for pleasure and profit.

(7) *Udar Manjhi* is his big Hindi story, bordering on a novel, published in 1969. There is the whole world in it.

(8) *Nangi Dharati* is a Hindi story, published in 1991.

(9) *Shaili* is a book of criticism (1993).

(10) Ram Chandra Prasad's *Adhunik Hindi Alochana par Pashchatya Prabhav* was published in 1973. It is based on his D. Litt. Degree.

(11) He wrote six revealing biographics: two on Shri Krishna Sinha in English and Hindi published in 1987 & 1988, two on B.R. Ambedkar published in 1993 and one on Karpuri Thakur published in 1992.

(12) His *Early English Travellers in India* (1965), was based on his Ph.D. degree. It is a wonderful book. He obtained Ph.D degree from Edinburgh University.

(13) *Bihar* was published in 1983. It portrays the cultural heritage of Bihar.

(14) *The Achievement of Raja Radhika Raman: An Appraisal* is his sixth biography.

(15) *Literary Criticism in Hindi* was published in 1976. It gives the history of Hindi criticism.

(16) Dr. R.C. Prasad and Awadhesh Kumar Sharma brought out a revealing book *Modern Studies and Other Essays* in 1987 which was also dedicated to Dr. R.K. Sinha, their guru.

(17) He also wrote books on Hindu rituals. *Upnayan* was brought out in 1993. It describes how Hindus perform the sacred thread ceremony. It was published by Motilal Banarsidass.

(18) *Shradh* was published in 1993 by Motilal Banarsidass.

(19) *Maha Chalisa Sangrah* is the last book, published in 1994 by Motilal Banarsidass.

(20) He also co-authored many books, edited by Dr. Nagendra, such as, *Jay Shankar Prasad* in 1989, *Surdas* in 1979, *Maithli Sharan Gupta* in 1981, *Bihari* in 1981, and *Premchand* in 1989.

(21) *Lifting the Veil* is his 24th book. It is a compendium of Rajnish's essential teachings, published in 1971.

(22) Kendriya Hindi Nideshalaya published his article titled *Nirala: Kal Jayi Vyaktitwa*.

(23) His "Lukach" was published in Ram Chandra Shukla *Granthawali*, edited by Dr. Nagendra.

(24) R.C. Prasad also wrote *Dr. Nagendra: Sahitya Sadhana ke Barahte Charan.*

(25) His article on *Savitri* was published in 1992 in *Bhartiye Mahakavya* edited by Dr. Nagendra. It's a comment on Aurbindo's *Savitri*, the longest epic in English.

Moreover, his hundreds of articles were published in different Hindi journals from time to time, such as *Jyotsana*, *Naidhara*, *Hindi Vidyapith Patrika*, Deoghar, *Hindi Granth Academy Patrika*. *Jotsna* published some lines of his poem, sent from London in 1988:

> चिर निद्रा का उनका अंतहीन इतिहास।
> उनके ही महाकाव्यों में कुंभकर्ण की कल्पना है।

R.C. Prasad's translations of the *Hanuman Chalisa*, the *Chalisa Sangrah*, the *Sri Ramcharitmanas, the Gita,* the Mantras of the Hindu wedding (*Viwah*), Sacred thread ceremony (*Upnain*) and funeral rites (*Shradh*) into plain English which is used by the English speaking people in general and of the Indian origin in particular all over the world. I doubt whether any teacher of English has such a distinction, as a translator, who fulfilled even social, cultural and spiritual needs of society.

(26) Further Prof. J.P. Singh who had researched for Ph.D. degree on Sir William Jones under him edited *An Anthology of Indian English* and *Representative Short Stories* in English with him, published by Motilal Banarsidass in 1984 and 1988 respectively.

(27) Prof. M.Q. Towheed also edited *The New Golden Treasury* with him, published by Motilal Banarsidass in 1989. Furthermore, he was a poet also as he composed two Kands (chapters) – Lav and Kush that are not in *Sri Ramcharitmanas.* His translations are being used and will be used for all times to understand indology and to practice Hinduism in the world. So, R.C.P. is a historical figure not only because his name figures in *The Concise Cambridge History of English Literature* as a writer of the "brilliant book" but also because he created the literature that crosses boundaries of countries.

(28) His second edition of *the Gita* was published in America and was praised by Swami Satyanand.

Moreover, his introduction to *Sri Ramcharitmanas* has opened up new depths and dimensions of criticism, using the critical canons of other languages also. Now, one can evaluate English literature in terms of *ras* and *alankar* also.

R.C. Prasad's some more books:

(29) *Acharya Rajnish* was published in 1969 by Motilal Banarsidass.

R.C. Prasad's edited books:

(30) *Mahavir: Parichaya and Vani* published by Motilal Banarsidass

(31) *Kamyog, Dharm* and *Gandhi*

(32) *Suli Par Sej Piyake*

(33) *Ghat Bhulana Bat Benu*

(34) *Samud Samana Bindu Me* published by Motilal Banarsidass

(35) *The Necklace and Other Stories* published by Vani Educational Books in 1985.

(36) R.C. Prasad and Awadhesh Sharma brought out a felicitation volume in the honour of Dr. R.K. Sinha.

Acharya Rajneesh used to address R.C. Prasad as Swami Anand Vitrag. He is an authority on the philosophy of Acharya Rajneesh. He recorded his philosophy in *Acharya Rajneesh* in Hindi and *Lifting the Veil* in English. He was his disciple and explained Rajneesh's concept of Yoga. But ultimately he was disillusioned.

Some of the Researches he guided:

(1) Miss Ratna Acharya did her Ph.D. on Shakespeare's tragedies in the light of Indian dramatic theories. He guided her how the dramatic theories of Bharat's *Natya Shashtra* could be applied to them. It has no tragic ending, although love is a common ingredient in both Shakespeare and Kalidas. Wit, humour, love, romance, the role of fools and clowns are common. In Kalidas, Vidushak plays the role of clowns. Style differs according to the roles of characters. Kalidas's Shakuntala in *Abhigyan Shakuntalam* uses Prakrit. They are uneducated but the educated characters use Sanskrit. The language used reflects the social status and the cultural values of characters.

(2) Shyam Sunder Agrawal's *Revaluation of Angus Wilson and His Works* was researched in 1988.

(3) Anamika's criticism on *Donne and His Ages* is very deep.

(4) Arvind Kumar's research on *Sir Gwain and Green Knight: A Critique*, done in 1989 shows R.C. Prasad's critical depths and dimensions.

(5) Moreover, Ashok Kumar's research on *James Boswel, the Man and the Biographer* is also very revealing and interesting.

(6) Bistmoi Reena researched on *The Influence of Mechiavellism on the History Plays of Shakespeare* in 1989.

(7) Chopra Rita evaluated I.A. Richards as a critic in 1982.

(8) Datta Bandana's evaluation of Daruwala in 1990 shows the trends of Anglo-Indian poetry.

(9) Hasan Syed's research shows orientation in Jame's *Etray Flecker.*

(10) Janardan Prasad Singh's research on Sir William Jones is also revealing. Sir William Jones was a Sanskrit scholar and a great admirer of Indian culture. He was an employee of the East India Company. All the researches, done under the supervision of R.C. Prasad are well-documented, very deep and revealing. New critical canons were applied to them and new dimensions of criticism were opened up.

On the basis of such academic achievements Dr. Ram Chandra Prasad's name and fame spread far and wide as a critic and a mythological story writer. His contribution to English literature has been mentioned in *The Concise Cambridge History of English Literature* on page 735: "...these early Anglo-Indian writers have a characteristic distinction which is often wanting in their successors. They have been served and well-quoted in Ram Chandra Prasad's excellent book *Early English Travellers in India* (Delhi, 1966)". Whenever he read it, tears swelled up in his eyes, as told by K.P. Shrivastav. His guru Dr. R.K. Sinha was recorded as a historical figure in *Bihar Vibhuti,* published by the Archives Directorate of Bihar Government after 46 years in 2012. So Dr. R.K. Sinha and R.C. Prasad are the historical figures of Bihar in English literature. So is Prof. Kapil Muni Tiwari. Prof. Arun Kamal is a national awardee of Sahitya Academy.

Moreover, an eminent writer of English, Holden holds that "Dr. Prasad is at home in the Shakespeare of England and equally at home in his own past."

Marquis's *Who is Who* publication also certifies that Ram Chandra Prasad is a subject of biographical record. In *Who is Who's* fifth edition 1980/1981 only those individuals are included "who have demonstrated outstanding achievements of endeavour and who have thereby contributed significantly to the betterment of contemporary society."

He was also awarded a certificate of honour for his outstanding contribution to the Ramayan by Mahatma Gandhi Institute, Moka, Mauritius in 1990. This national as well as international recognition makes Dr. Ram Chandra Prasad tower over many in literature. His criticism is individual, subtle, innovative, creative and incisive. He has applied new trends of critical canons of the East and the West. Moreover, his mythological short stories have also made a mark. His translation of Tulsidas's *Sri Ramcharitamanas* is very comprehensive. *Sri Ramcharitmanas* is itself a by-product of the comprehensive study of the vedas, the purans, and the epics like Balmiki's the *Ramayan* and Vyasa's the *Adhyatma Ramayan.* The translation of a translation is usually a pale reflection. But Prasad had grounding in background literature. So, it looks original and creative. What has made it a unique and great book is its evaluation and translation in the context of world literature. Tulsidas has been compared and contrasted with Homer, Dante, Milton and Shakespeare and also with Balmiki, Vyas and Kalidas. The early translations of *Sri Ramcharitmanas* were not so broad-based; they applied only the tools of criticism, analysis of the content, comparison, contrast and the life of the writer but R.C. Prasad also used simile, metaphor, imagery, socio-linguistics, repetition, rhyming, rhythm, tautology, phonetic net, semantic bond, metrical arrangement, new interpretations and varied sources. He took into account *ras* and *alankar* also, citing their examples from *Sri Ramcharitmanas,* Bharat's *Natya Shashtra* and Acharya Mammata's *Kanta Sammat Updesh.*

Furthermore, Arjun Prasad Singh's (well-versed in Manas) bringing Dr. R.C. Prasad into contact of his guru Acharya Girdhar Mishra, a blind bard of Chitrakut, who is a true saint and gives an original interpretation of *Sri Ramcharitmanas* and Padmbhushan Dr. Bindeshwar Pathak's Foreword to this book in which he mentioned that the lowliest of the low in society was very dear to Lord Ram made his translation creative. Ramanand was the disciple of Ramanuj and Kabir was the disciple of Ramanand and later Tulsi became his (Ramanand's) disciple. It made them vernacular versifiers. Tulsidas used Awadhi in *Sri Ramcharitmanas* which was a radical departure from the tradition. Dr. Bindeshwar Pathak quotes:

भगतिहीन बिरचिकिन होई।
सब जीवहु राम प्रिय मोहि सोई।।
भगति पंथ अति नीचौ प्रानी।
मोहि प्रानप्रिय असिमम बानी।।

It made scavengers "pran priye" to Dr. Pathak and he emancipated, liberated and rehabilitated a million of them. Tulsidas had also said पराधीन सपने हूं सुख नाहिं and जासु राज प्रिय प्रजा दुखारी सो नृप अवसि नरक अधीकारी and the picture of *Ram Rajya* was allegorically drawn to represent muslim misrule. Even a common man has become a subject of the epic, not only the banished prince of Ayodhya. So not only the language even the content was changed in the epic. Tulsidas sows the seeds of freedom and democracy in *Sri Ramcharitmanas.* R.C. Prasad gave the philosophical background of the epic. The individual talent of the poet represented the demand of the age. Not to speak of man, even an eagle like Jatayu and his doing good to others was considered superior to the prince of Ayodhya and God:

पर हित बस जिनके मनमाहिं।
तिन्ह कहिं जग दुर्लभ कछुनाहिं।।
तनुतजि त्याग जाहु मम धामा।
देहु काहि सब पुरन कामा।।

This alliteration तनुतजि त्याग reflects a new value of the age like Pope's: "Nature and nature's laws lay hid in night. God said let Newton be and there was light." It is being said, not by an Augustan poet but by a romantic poet like Tulsidas who used nature, supernatural, mystery, myths, imagination, pathos and emotion more than reason.

The tears of Ram have a dramatic effect even on birds, animals and insects, although it seemingly lacks in the objective correlative. The parting scene of Shakuntala in Kalidas's *Abhigyan Shakuntlam* and the revolt of Birnam wood at the murder of Duncan in Shakespeare's *Macbeth* also affect nature as the deep sorrow of Ram in search of the missing Sita. Tulsidas used Bhojpuri, Magahi, Brajbhasa, Awadhi and Sanskrit in the epic. T.S. Eliot's use of Sanskrit at the end of *The Waste Land* also shows the when one language reaches its saturation point other languages are also used. And verses, like, "*doha*", "*chaupai*", "*soratha*", "*sonnet*", "blank verse", and "free verse" are used.

Furthermore, Tolstoy's *War and Peace* is formless but *Sri Ramcharitmanas* shows the beginning and the end of every character. So, it has form that keeps the plot intact. It is true of R.C. Prasad's stories and novels also. A colossus in literature emerges out of all this. In every age and every human society there exists a religious sense of what is good and what is bad and it is this religious sense that is transmitted by art and literature. R.C. Prasad's literature has transmitted it in a full measure.

Every language has its critical canons. It can reveal new dimensions, if applied to other languages. Prof. Ram Chandra Prasad applied English critical canons to Hindi and Prof. Kalimuddin Ahamad to Urdu in which criticism was non-existent. It opened up new dimensions of Hindi and Urdu. Prof. Narsimhaiah applied Sanskrit critical canons to English also. Tulsi's *Sri Ramcharitmanas* was also compared with Virgil's *Aeneid.* Both dominated India and Rome four centuries later. But Tulsi is a true poet and a true saint. Such a poet belongs to the world for all ages, according to T.S. Eliot. Ram, Hamlet and Faust made Tulsidas, Shakespeare and Goethe world poets.

Furthermore, he used *ras* and *alankar* also in the evaluation of *Sri Ramcharitmanas,* for example, *shringar ras* was expressed at the meeting of Ram and Sita at the garden of Raja Janak. Comic or *hasya ras* was expressed when Lakshaman cut down the nose of Surpnakha and when the people of Lanka kicked down Hanuman and laughed at him and set fire to his ever enlarging tail. *Karun ras* was expressed when Ram weeps and also while searching Sita and asking birds, animals, insects and even plants whether they had seen the deer-eyed Sita; *raudra ras* was expressed in Kaikeyi's anger on the eve of Ram's exile, and after Surpnakha's nose was cut by Lakshman at Panchwati. She revealed her own fearsome form and it was expressed also in Ram's fight with Trishura, Khara and Dushan. *Bhayanak ras* was revealed when Meghnad showered pus, blood, bones on Ram. It also expressed *Bibhtsa ras* and *Adbhud ras* was expressed when Hanuman went on enlarging his tail in Lanka to burn it down.

All literateurs of the world can be evaluated on the touchstone of *ras, alankar* and in terms of socio-linguistics. Bhartrihari in his book *Wakyapadiye* said:

> वाक्यात् प्रकरणार्थ औचित्याय देश-कालत:
> शब्दार्थत: नप्रविश्यन्ते रूपादेव केवलात्।

Meaning can be explained by reference, context, time and space and reflected meaning as in *Natyashashtra* deepens criticism. If the languages used also use socio-linguistic social norms and cultural values of characters and use vernacular, corrupt language, Prakrit and colloquialism, their social status and education are expressed. The educated and the elite use King's English.

Moreover, meaning is not so important in poetry as sound. So, it can be enjoyed better, if one lays one's fingers on the spots, pleasure springs from. It springs from rhyming, internal and external, rhythm, repetition, tautology, semantic net and phonetic bond, irregularity, alliteration, metaphors, similes, imagery, unity of sensibility and oxymoron. Those who know British English in India are hardly aware that even Britain has recognized 12 varieties of English now. In order to describe the English language Fillmore used Panini's "case" grammar and Wilkins socio-linguistics of Bhartrihari's *Vakyapadia* but by and large Indians still hesitate to describe English language and literature on the touchstone of Indian critical canons. However, R.C. Prasad used them as Prof. Narsimehaiya did.

R.C. Prasad was primarily a critic and his mastery over English and Hindi languages and their critical analysis are really his unique contribution.

Last but not the least, is the correction of the mistakes in *Sri Ramcharitmanas*:

मरम वचन सीता जब बोली।
हरि प्रेरित लछिमन मति डोली।।

An edition of *Sri Ramcharitmanas*, published by Babu Brij Bhushan Lal Bookseller, Kachauri Gali, Varanasi in 1882 does mention the "*chaupai*" correctly. Dr. Ram Tawakeya Sharma, an authority on the epic also agrees to this form and rejects the Gita Press Gorakhpur's wrong edition.

मरम वचन जब सीता बोला।
हरि प्रेरित लछिमन मन डोला।।

At places *Sri Ramcharitmanas* seems to be the translation of the vedas, the puranas, the vedant, the Ramayan and the Mahabharat but it is really a by-product of Tulsidas's vast study of the background literature and its sources. His translation of translation is really creative and original, for example:

''जब-जब होहिं धरम की हानि'' of *Sri Ramcharitmanas* is not the literal translation of ''यदा यदा हि धर्मस्य....'' and ''ज्ञानिनामपि चेतांसि देविभगवती हि सा बलादा कृष्यमोहाय महामाया प्रयच्छति'' of the *Markandeya Puran* has not been translated literally in the "Uttar Kand" of the *Sri Ramcharitmanas* as ''जोग्या निहुँ कर चित्त अपहर ई बरियाई विमोह बस करई''. It can hardly be understood without knowing its sources and background literature. However, it can be enjoyed even without being understood as it is lyrical. Its rhyme, rhythm and alliteration make it enjoyable.

Section III

Jottings of Dr. R.C. Prasad

Letter to Shri Lali Babu

Professor R. C. Prasad
M.A., PH.D., (EDIN.) D.E.S. (EDIN.), D.LITT. (PAT.)
PRO-VICE-CHANCELLOR
BHAGALPUR UNIVERSITY
BHAGALPUR-812007
PHONE: OFFICE: 8271

March 3, 1989.

Dear Lali Babu,

Please refer to your letter No. R-57/7205 dated February 26, 1989.

If I were you, I would certainly have thrown Dr. Arya's letter into the garbage-box for the following reasons:

1. Are only Englishmen good at translating works like the <u>Manasa</u>? Not brought up in the cultural environment of the poet, can they do justice to his poem? The fact of the matter is that only competent Indians can translate Tulasi's <u>Manasa</u>, and none else.

2. I do not need a half-ignorant man like Dr. Arya to certify that I am competent.

3. I am engaged in translating scores of Hindi poems and prose pieces for Sahitya Akademi, an undertaking which has nothing to do with Dr. Arya's contention that "translations should be done in association with someone who is master of English poetic style". All those Indian scholars and writers are therefore fools who translate Indian works into English. No one has even heard of the translation Dr. Arya has recommended.

4. Dr. Arya seems to be one of those great patriots who believe that competence is the monopoly of the fair-complexioned, the white, the English-speaking. Well, I cannot now change my nationality nor beg an Indian to certify that I can translate Tulasidasa, in view of my doctorate in English (Ph.D.) from Edinburgh University and in Hindi (D.Litt.) from Patna University.

5. I can show you scores of errors of all types in the

PTO

translations of Hindi poems made by the so-called masters of poetic style.

6. If what Dr. Arya says is true, you should never publish translations - "staid,heavy,and without any poetic merit" - made by Indian authors,notwithstanding their life-long devotion to the language they teach and express themselves in.

Did Dr.Arya,by the way, care to go through some of the pages of the translation you have published ? Is he competent enough to pass such a sweeping judgment ? Does he know English ? I think - and I'm sure - he doesn't. His own letter has so many glaring mistakes. How can such an ignorant person,bereft of all sense of grammar and spelling,pass any judgment on a work lauded by such luminaries as Khuswant Singh and others? Is not Dr. Arya an excellent teacher? We Indians should learn this from him - that only "an English language poet" should translate Tulasidasa. Please tell Dr.Arya that NEITHER F.S.GROWSE NOR W.D.P.HILL WAS AN ENGLISH LANGUAGE POET. And yet their renderings are well known throughout the world. I have followed Growse and Hill and have never allowed my Indian English to spoil the sense of the original.

Please,for Rama's and Tulasi's sake,let all such people bark.

Yours faithfully,

On Translating the Ramayana

Dr. R.C. Prasad

When I was asked by a leading Delhi publisher to undertake the preparation of a new translation of Tulsidasa's popular epic, the Hindi Ramayana, I lightly accepted the task, not realizing the amount of labour involved, the incandescent symbolism of the epic, the meaning within meaning, and the vitality of which I was not quite aware. Being, as Sir George Grierson had justly remarked, "the one Bible of a hundred millions of people" of Hindustan, the work had exerted an extraordinary fascination upon me from my early childhood when I heard my parents and *gurus* recount the story of Rama, the ill-starred but irreproachable Prince of Ayodhya, and of his faithful but ill-used princess, of their magical flying monkey companions, and their implacable enemy, the ten-headed demon king, Ravana. In addition to this I had another equipment: being an Indian by birth and education I was already in the position to appreciate the cultural and religious ethos in which Tulsi's epic is rooted and to understand its meaning as one whose mother-tongue was Hindi fused with Magahi and Bhojpuri. I could, I thought, preserve through translation into English the most important property of the Ramayana: its meaning. I did not realize then that this important property of the epic is also the most difficult to preserve in another medium.

Most of the well-known reputations in the sphere of the Ramayana studies bear out my point. Whether you read a translated prose version of the epic like F.S. Growse's or the poetic version like the Rev. A.G. Atkins's, what is at once noticeable is the widely differing, and at times quite distorted, meanings of the various passages. What is so exasperating about all these translators is their refusal to settle first the authenticity of the text to be translated. It could be maintained that for sheer readability of his translation, Growse, for example, is hardly excelled by any other translator, yet the impeccable language and prose style of his narration cannot make up for its lack of reliability and failure to understand, as Douglas P. Hill has pointed out, "the meaning of some important passages." One might naturally counter this criticism by stating that since no authentic text of the *Manasa* is extant, Growse, whose errors are allegedly due to his inferior text, must be accepted without serious misgivings about the value of his translation.

It should not be thought that the Gita Press text represents the only extant shape of the Ramayana. There are scores of imperfect manuscripts and an equal number of recensions of the epic, the result, no doubt, of the loss of the original leaves of parchment. Scribes, *sadhus* and *pundits*, in fact, have a good deal to answer for the contamination that permeates the text of this great religious work. They evidently acted not simply as copyists but on their own poor poetic initiative, without the modern editor's sense of responsibility towards his material. To the copyists, the content of the Ramayana was interesting enough and of sufficient religious and spiritual relevance to persuade them of their ability to add to or make arbitrary alternations in the original. Frequently they appear to have tried to interpolate, to vulgarize, and to contaminate the text. And a work written in the Avadhi dialect of Hindi full of words from Brajabhasha, Bundelkhandi, and Bhojapuri, some sixty words even from Arabic and Persian languages, made alteration that much easier. Most of the interpolations, however, stand out so prominently that they cannot be regarded as Tulasi's own writing. There is only one important passage in the *Ayodhyakanda* – the one relating to the appearance of the unnamed ascetic – that continues to baffle modern Tulasi scholarship. According to Acharya Giridhar Mishra, a blind Tulasi scholar of uncanny critical insight, the ascetic is Tulsidas himself who met the brothers in their guise as hunters.

The multiplicity of contaminated texts and recensions of the Ramayana renders the translator's task of presenting a scientifically respectable and accurate translation very difficult. What is really deplorable is that scholars in both the east and the west have not yet determined a text acceptable for its closeness, to the poet's original. No less deplorable is the fact that the science of textual criticism, which enjoins a complete collation of all extant manuscripts, from the most complete to the most fragmentary or corrupt, has not developed in India to the extent it has in the west. Nothing less will do. In the case of the Hindi Ramayana, all editions are corrupt to some extent. Most of them are copies of copies, twice or thrice removed from reality, and have suffered, to varying degrees, from the disappearance of the original manuscript. Their original relationship, too, has become obscured by contamination, correction, interpolation and even by chance agreement in errors. A small and dedicated team of scholars expert in the area of Sanskrit epic studies is at present engaged in bringing out a densely annotated English rendering of Valmiki's *Ramayana*, kanda-wise, in seven volumes. This has been made possible, says Robert P. Goldman in the Preface to his translation of *The Ramayana* of Valmiki, by the "completion of the critical edition of the poem by scholars associated with the Oriental Institute, Baroda, in 1975" and by the co-operation extended to the translator by such scholars as Pt. T.S. Srinivas Sastri, Dr. V.W. Paranjpe, Dr. N.M. Sen, and Mr. K. Venugopalan of the Deccan College, Poona.

Tulsidas has been unfortunate in this regard. An attempt was, however, made to collate the extant manuscripts of the *Manasa* by the Kashi Raj Trust under the most competent editorship of Pt. Vishwanath Prasad Mishra. After years of unflagging endeavour, a recension, apparently based on modern editorial techniques, was prepared and published in 1961 in a low-priced edition, which forms the basis of my translation for the most part. Of the uniqueness of the Kashi Raj edition there is no dearth of evidence. The text strictly observes the rules governing compounds or *samasa* and nasalization called *chandrabindu*. Such usages, to which must also be added the frequent use of outlandish spellings and rhymes, compel one to question its value as a reliable text or its much vaunted closeness to the poet's version. Aside from these factors that lessen the value of this edition, there are its numerous departures from the texts which have already been accepted by the lovers of the *Ramayana*, who have been reciting it for hundreds of years now in *kirtan mandalis, Ramalilas* and in gatherings at sacred places and on auspicious occasions.

The Ramayana Translation Project in the United States owes its success to "the most generous, consistent, and vital support" provided by the National Endowment for the Humanities under its Translation Project Grant Programme. To the American Institute of Indian Studies, to the Centre for South and Southeast Asian Studies of the University of California, Berkeley, and to its director, Dr. Bruce R. Pray, it is especially indebted. In the absence of such translation projects and vital support from centres of Indian studies in India and abroad, we must still await the appearance of "a scholarly, readable, and densely annotated" English translation of the Tulasi Ramayana like that of Valmiki or even like the most well-known and scholarly seven-volume Hindi edition called *Manasa-piyusha* edited by Pt. Anjaninandan Sharan.

So far I have spoken of the non-availability of a reliable, standard, corruption-proof text of the Tulsi Ramayana. When I was called upon to render this work into English, this was the first major problem that exercised my mind. Considering the inaccessibility of manuscript materials, I depended on the Kashi Raj and, to some extent, on the Gita Press editions, and, only where they differed or sounded rather implausible, on my own meagre intellectual resources.

The translator, I discovered, has to adopt "a procedure of pairing a sentence in one language with those sentences in another language which share *as many as possible* of their properties with the sentence being translated." I cannot pretend to have the ability to pair Tulsi's verses with my English prose sentences, nor, generally speaking and, naturally, does English share the properties of Avadhi, Bhojapuri and Brajabhasha. When the actual work on the rendition began, I also realized, somewhat as Goldman did before undertaking the translation of the Valmiki Ramayana, that "in view of the size of the text and the translator's obligation to give his audience the benefit of the varied and copious tradition" of medieval and modern commentary on the Ramayana, "it would be impossible for one person to do the translation alone." Goldman sought the help of a small and dedicated band of scholars expert in the area of Sanskrit kavya literature; I had to do the translation alone, which accounts for many of its imperfections. I wish, in the words of Dryden, that, "instead of three years, which I have spent in the translation.... I have four years more allow'd me to correct my errors, that I might make my version more tolerable than it is."

"A translation to serve its purpose," says S. Radhakrishnan in the preface to his translation of *The Bhagavadgita*, "must be as clear as its substance will permit. It must be readable without being shallow, modern without being unsympathetic. But no translation of the *Gita* can bring out the dignity and grace of the original. Its melody and magic of phrase are difficult to recapture in another medium. The translator's anxiety is to render the thought, but he cannot convey fully the spirit. He cannot evoke in the reader the mood in which the thought was born and induce in him the ecstacy of the seer and the vision he beholds." These words of the philosopher-translator apply not only to the *Gita* but also to the *Manasa*, in which the poet surrounds his subject with every possible association of native beauty or grandeur, often culled from the *Prasanna-raghava* of Jayadeva, the *Raghuvansha, Kumarsambhava* and *Meghadoota* of Kalidasa, and from the *Adhyatma Ramayana*, Valmiki's *Ramayana*, the *Hanuman-nataka*, etc. He refines on the passages taken from others, loading sweets on sweets, till they become what in Indian poetics is called *rasatmaka*, and raises his images, whether of beauty or of terror, to a gigantic elevation which no translation can accurately represent or convey.

One can easily cite passages which can be appropriately translated in the thought-preserving way. Indeed, such a translation is probably to be preferred in the absence of one that is also spirit-preserving and ecstacy-inducing. Take, for instance, the following *dohā* from the *Balakanda*:

> *basai nagara jehi lachi kari kapata nari bāra*
> *besu tehi pura kai sobhā kahata sakucahim*
> *sārada sesu*

A literal though-preserving translation of this *dohā* would be:

> The magnificence of the city wherein Lakshmi dwelt in the charming disguise of a mortal woman made even Sharda and shesha shrink from describing it.

Those familiar with the Indian puranas will doubtless find the translation appropriate and the intent of the poet well captured. But to others such a translation will probably be inadequate and will demand an explanation of the mythological references to Lakshmi, Sharda and Shesha. Such words as *bitgnu* and *bandanivare* are translated as *canopy* and *festoons*, but the English equivalents do not convey the cultural and ritual associations with which to an Indian *mandapa* and *bandanavara* are invested. Then take this couplet:

> *caukaim bhāti aneka purāim*
> *simdhura manimaya sahaja suhāim*

The appropriate translation of this would be:

> squares of all sorts, naturally exquisite, were drawn on the ground and filled with elephant-pearls.

But "caukaim" are not just squares. The word, I feel, cannot be adequately translated into English. To a Hindu familiar with his own marriage customs and rituals, it has certain properties and values which fail to be recaptured in English unless we are able to explain them. This is also true of the words "kāvari" and "kahāra" in

dadhi ciura upahara apara
bhari bhari kāvari cale kahārā

In Hill the line, rendered into English, becomes

porters came, too, with baskets laden with curds
and rice and countless offerings.

My version is slightly different:

a train of porters marched with their loads of
curd and parched rice and presents of endless
variety slung across their shoulders.

Neither version brings out the spirit of what is encoded in the words"kāvari" and "kāhārā" or even in "dadhi" and "ceura". As a norm, Tulsidas expresses his thought exactly, generally embellishing it with tropes and figures, especially alliteration; as a norm, too, the translator fails to communicate the entire range of the poet's meaning. The ambiguity or vagueness inherent in all translations of passages describing a situation that is unique in that it relates to an aspect of India's cultural tradition, certainly acts as a communication hindrance.

To illustrate more concretely this approach to the translators' inability to capture the entire gamut of the poet's meaning, let us focus on some of the verses which describe the nuptial scene in the *Balakanda*:

cha rasa rucira bimjana bahu jātī
eka eka rasa aganita bhāmtī
jevata dehim madhura dhuni gārī
lai lai nāma purusa aru nārī

Even this translatable direct description cannot be adequately represented in another language without explanatory comments on "garī" ("scandalous jests"?). When a native reader comes across the word "janavāsā", as in

> *dei pāna pūje janaka dasarathu sahita samāja*
> *janavāsehi gavane mudita sakala bhupa siratāja*

or in

> *ati sumdara dīnheu janavāsa*
> *jaham saba kahum saba bhāmti supāsa*

He conjures up images of a pretty large number of wedding guests, old and young, dressed up in all their finery, assembled at one place with a large embroidered canopy over them. Further, the English expression "With due honour Janaka offered *pan* to Dasharatha" would also require an explanation so that it could be clearly understood by one not familiar with the Hindu custom of offering betel leaves to guests, these leaves being symbols of auspiciousness and are believed to have certain hygienic properties.

There are hundreds of words in the Hindi Ramayana for which we have, in English, no appropriate equivalents. In his essay on "Some Logical Problems in Translation" E. Keenan speaks of the "adequacy criteria for exact translation" and maintains that

> For two sentences in different languages to be exact translations they must of course have the same meaning. Hence the criteria we use to determine exact translationhood are basically the same as the ones needed to determine whether two sentences in a given language are paraphrases. .... if two sentences fail to share one of these properties we may conclude that they are not exactly the same in meaning....

If what Keenan says is true, then none of the existing translations of the Ramayana can claim to be a hundred per cent exact. Being unable to share all the properties of the poet's language and style, they are not exactly the same in meaning as the original.

Of numerous words the exact equivalents of which with all their wide-ranging cultural and religious properties are rarely available in non-Indian languages. A few can be listed here: they are *kohabara, bhāmvari, javāsa, samadhi, parichana, dhenudhuri bela, caranodaka, sumirana, gunamaya, gīvanamūri, cakavas, mainās, jāvakajuta, katisutra, janeu,* etc. Most difficult to recapture, however, are the poetic embellishments and music of the original. No translator has done justice to the verses like:

kamkana kimkini nūpura dhuni suni
kahata lakhana sana rāma hrdaya guni
manahu madana dumdubhī dīnhī
manasā bisva bijaya kaham kīnhī

My translation of these mellifluous lines is completely void of all flavor: "Hearing the tinkling of her bangles, the small bells on her girdle and the anklets, Rama thought within himself and then said to Lakshmana, it sounds as though Cupid has sounded his kettledrum, ambitions to conquer the universe." And Atkins's rendering is not unexpectedly distorted:

At the sound of the tinkling of anklet and bangle,
Said Rama to Lakshman, as thoughts 'gan to mingle,
"I hear sounds that seem 'tis the Love-god who comes,
With world-conquering cymbals and beating of drums."

Expressions like gan to mingle, "It is the Love-god who comes" and "with world-conquering cymbals" border on the absurd and, insofar as the meaning of the text is concerned, are absolutely irrelevant, imposed as they are upon it from outside. But why blame Atkins alone? None of the translators has been able to bring out the meanings most deeply embedded in some of the chaupais:

aruna parāga jalaju bhari nīke
sasihi bhūsa ahi lobha amīke

The Impact of English Literature on the Indian Society

Dr. R.C. Prasad

When our authorities try to establish that English literature has had a tremendous impact on the Indian society, they have, no doubt, inklings of it, but no real evidence. The common man in India never came under the spell of this literature, though some of his poets did come. K.R. Srinivasa Iyengar considers it, legitimate to look upon "Indo-Anglian Literature" as a "minor tributary of English Literature" and asks: "Does it take its riches (such as they are) to the main stream, or does it rather – like a canal – draw its continuing inspiration from the parent river?" His answer is: "Indian writing in English (not in English alone, but all Indian writing) is greatly influenced by writing in England, and we have had our own "Romantics," "Victorians," "Georgians," and "modernists," Prof. Iyengar is right in asserting that Indo-Anglian literature is a minor tributary of English literature – minor, that is, auxiliary and complementary. The impact of English literature on it may be great, but this literature itself is an infinitesimal part of India's long literary tradition. I say "infinitesimal," not "unimportant." Our own Romantics and Victorians, Georgians and Modernists are merely those cultivated Indians who constitute a special class rather than the Indian society in general. They are not its true representatives. They are, in the words of Jawaharlal Nehru, "an English-knowing caste separated from the mass of our people". To this mass, English still smacks of the British Raj in India when, as Nehru remarks in his *Autobiography*, the alien rulers "seized her body and possessed her, but it was the possession of violence. They did not know her or try to know her. They never looked into her eyes, for theirs were averted and hers downcast through shame and humiliation. After centuries of contact they face each other, strangers still, full of dislike for each other."

There is no denying the fact, however, that there are hundreds of English words which even the common man in India uses today either as they are in their original forms or as their vulgarized mutations. But English literature is not all words and syntax; it is something one reads and enjoys. The common man, still vastly illiterate, has no idea whatsoever of English literature as he has of his own literary and cultural heritage, of, say, the *Ramayana* and the *Mahabharata.* He thinks of the English language and, perhaps, of English literature as a school and university subject. Given the opportunity, he would certainly have read and admired the English writers, but whether he would have enjoyed them we cannot certainly tell, for even the majority of our university students, who opt for English either as a compulsory or as an elective subject, do not show much interest in, or understanding of, English literature. They are often fascinated by the exotic sounds used by men of education and learning, the English teacher, the upper-class intelligentsia, but they are hardly, if ever, receptive to their nuances.

How English literature came to be introduced in India and how it influenced its readers, however limited in number, is an interesting chapter of modern Indian history. The story of this influence begins in 1800 with the foundation of Fort William College in Calcutta and of the Baptist Mission Press in Serampur, near Calcutta. Dr. John Gilchrist, a professor of the college, along with William Carey, his indefatigable associate, and a band of dedicated scholars, produced textbooks, translations from the Sanskrit classics as well as from European literature, and dictionaries and grammars. In the second half of the nineteenth century India witnessed an upsurge of nationalism which, as Percival Spear has put it, "was "caught" by the new Indian intellectuals, especially in Bengal, by the joint effect of observing the habits of the British and studying their literature. Mother India, a new secular goddess, was created." The appearance, for the first time in India, of newspapers and the printing press made its own contribution to the changing scene, as a result of which Hindi literature was led towards new directions palpably different from those that had characterized the medieval literary effort. The British impact on these developments was so great that Western science and history gradually made their way into the curriculum, and the whole range of Western ideas and attitudes began to be conveyed through English and European literatures.

After about 1857 we find the Indian literary scene showing all signs of a change in poetic themes and styles and new elements emerging, one of which is the fervent patriotism of the poets which is seen to have taken dual forms. One of these is their effort to glorify the past, while the second is their effort to reject blind insularity. They become open-minded towards continental, especially British, ideas which enabled them to derive considerable inspiration from the rich storehouse of patriotic poems existing in English literature. Shridhar Pathak, for example, was so enamoured of Goldsmith that he translated his *Hermit* and *The Deserted Village* into Hindi in 1886 and 1889 respectively. Nor can we forget Bharatendu Harishchandra in this context, for his vigorous moral personality at times gives an edge to episodes purporting to be only the harvest of an enlightened young writer who is widely read in India and English dramatic literature. In fact, there appeared a school of writers who, in addition to translating the Sanskrit classics into Hindi, rendered a number of Bengali and English plays of Michael Madhusudana Dutta, Manomohana Basu, Rajakishore De, Dwarkanath Ganguly, Shakespeare and Addison. Bharatendu's essay titled "Natak", written in 1883, embodies some interesting views on Western dramatic rules of construction and dramatic theory, and thus reflects his tendency to harmonize Eastern and Western principles of dramatic criticism. The book-reviews published in Balakrishna Bhatt's *Hindi Pradeep* (1877), Badari Narayan Chowdhary Premghan's *Anand Kadambini* (1881), Sadanand Mishra's *Sarasudhanidhi* (1878), etc. and the publication of these and other journals itself show the growing impact of English literature and an exciting literary situation reminiscent of the early eighteenth-century world of *The Spectator, The Tatler* and *The Rambler.* The old critical terminology, the reviewers felt, was inconsistent with the changed literary environment and something more than the theories of *rasa, alankara* and *dhvani* was needed for the proper appreciation of the new works. The new terminology was derived from English literature while new modes of criticism – comparative, historical, descriptive, etc. – appeared and new literary forms were forged under its impact, the Indian novel being one of them. Richardson, Goldsmith, Fielding, George Eliot, Thackeray, Dickens, Hardy, D.H. Lawrence and scores of others began to leave a lasting impress upon the Indian mind. James Joyce and Virginia Woolf, too, have their literary disciples here, disciples who model their novels on their stream-of-consciousness technique and fill their pages with epiphanies of all sorts. The novels of crime and detection, ghost stories and narratives of mystery and adventure are not all indigenous in their basic inspiration. Textual criticism being written in India today owes considerably to the English practitioners of this mode.

Around 1918 there appeared in Hindi literature a new manner of experiencing reality and a new literary vision that gave prominence to feeling and imagination and initiated a revolt against the essentially matter-of-fact, moralizing attitude of the writers of the Age of Dvivedi. The poets of this mystico-romantic school regarded themselves as explorers of Nature, revealers of beauty, and harbingers of a new-social order. They *loosened* upon the world of Nature not only as a wild landscape but as a vital spirit that informs the soul of every living human being. The poets of the *Chayavad* school – Jaishankar Prasad, Nirala, Mahadevi Verma, Ram Kumar Verma, et al–are unforgettable examples of the impact of English literature on the Indian mind. The influence of Omar Khayyam, derived through Edward FitzGerald's English translation of the *Rubaiyat,* is to be felt throughout Harivansharai Bachchan's *Madhusala* (1935), *Madhubala* (1938) and *Madhukalasha* (1938).

The history of the Post-Chayavad period is essentially the history of the flowering of Nirala's and Pant's creative genius, and of the emergence of certain new trends which the historians of Indian literature group under three heads: progressivism, experimentalism and new writing, all of which bear unmistakable traces of the impact of English literature. As a traditionalist, Acharya Ram Chandra Shukla, the great Hindi critic, was highly suspicious of the various poetic movements which had swept the whole of Europe in general and England in particular. Movements such as expressionism, imagism, impressionism, surrealism and neo-classicism appeared to him as nothing but short-lived flashes arousing partisan emotions. Those of our writers who fell under the influence of these movements are indeed indebted to English literature. The exponents of what is called Nakenvad – Naresh, Keshari Kumar and Nalin Vilocana Sharma – the new writers of the Tara Saptaka school, even such scholarly Acharyas as Nand Dulare Vajpeyi and Dr. Nagendra, all Indo-Anglian poets, including Sarojini Naidu, Tagore and Aurobindo, all imagists, progressives and experimentalists, including Ajneya, are carriers and transmitters of the impact of English literature on the Indian creative mind and, indirectly, on the Indian society.

The Teaching of English: Illusion and Reality

Dr. R.C. Prasad

We in India not only like to befool others but are seldom aware of the subtle ways in which we befool ourselves. We pretend to be lovers of our native languages but are keen on educating our children in English-medium institutions. Even our simple village folk have caught this infection and try their outmost to ape their urban counterparts. Numerous so-called English medium schools have sprung up in remote villages, schools with meager or no provision for the kind of education the parents want their children to be imparted. The kind of English spoken in those schools is hardly, if ever, English, Indian or British. Distorted intonations, faulty grammar, indecorous composition brimful of incorrect usages and incorrigible howlers plague such systems of "English" education.

Let us not deny the vogue of instruction through the English medium, its widespread appeal to all except a few diehards. A recognition of this popular practice, to which even the proponents of education through the vernacular are subject, will help us face the reality of the situation in a pragmatic manner. We know in our heart of hearts that no nation, howsoever advanced, can do without English which is now a language of international communication. All technological advancement we plan to make in the years to come shall have to take into account the importance of English. The English speaking world is witnessing an incredibly large, spectacular production of English books almost every day, books containing relevant scientific and technological information which must be made available to our own native scientists and scholars. Unless English is efficiently taught and thoroughly mastered by the educators in India, an interminably large proportion of that information will be denied to our countrymen. The window on the world will remain shut. The plea that the native experts will make all knowledge contained in English books available to our readers in India through translations in the Indian languages does not sound tenable, for the number of books published in English every day will outweigh all effort to implant that knowledge on the Indian soil.

The illusion that Indian English must approximate British English in form, spirit and tone must be dispelled. India has already evolved its own English which has come to stay and will certainly witness greater efflorescence in the years to come. Let us not fight shy of our English but let this English be free from stupid howlers and incomprehensible idiosyncratic usages that would jar on the listener's ears. It must possess communicability and effectiveness. The teacher of English must see to it that what he teaches as English enables the student to comprehend an English text and to render his ideas and experiences into his "second" language. English is no longer a foreign language, nor should it be treated as such. Acknowledgement of this vital truth will help us improve our modes of teaching the English language and our knowledge of its idioms and usages. In order that we may acquire a fair degree of competence in learning and teaching English, nothing short of a movement is the need of the hour. We must be awakened to the irrefutable popularity and mass appeal of the English language. The illusion that making English compulsory will be detrimental to the growth and advancement of the native languages must now be dispelled once and for ever. One cannot pull out with patriotic pincers the deep-rooted belief in the common psyche that English-medium schools produce brighter pupils who have brighter prospects. Even a semi-literate or illiterate commoner is well aware of this, though we know that this is but an oversimplification and a superstition.

Syncretistic Vision of Islam, Hinduism and Christianity

Dr. R.C. Prasad

Answering what seems to be an oft repeated question, what is Islam?, Md. Mazharuddin Siddiqi finds occasion to dilate on the transgressers which the muslims today are guilty of. Accusing them of adopting un-Islamic behavior and of performing actions contrary to the teachings of *the Quran,* Siddiqi, shocked and grieved beyond measure, makes the following observation:

> The whole life of an average muslim in these days is a flat denial and repudiation of those ideals for which Islam stands. When did Islam teach submission to evil and injustice? When did it permit muslims to love and choose un-Islamic ways in preference to those approved by Islam? The whole world is filled with un-Islamic ideas and modes of living. What are the muslims doing to counteract them and to bring the world back to right ideals and modes of life? Even those Muslims who have some relic of the religious spirit left in them, think that prayers, fasts and social duties exhaust the essentials of Islam. While it is sure that these things do form a part of religion, they do not cover the whole ground. Islam is much more than prayers, fasts and social duties.

The questions are expressive of a lament and a latent exhortation. Choosing un-Islamic ways in preference to those approved by Islam is certainly sacrilege, an offence contrary to the teachings of the prophet. The instruction and exhortation employed is that muslims all over the world have a religious duty to perform – to give impetus to "the world movement for moral and spiritual regeneration" of mankind and to let the humans realize, wherever they are and whosoever they are, that spiritual values in Islam have a close connection with secular and material aspects of life. M. Siddiqi puts a pertinent question:

> What are morality and spiritualism for, if they do not transform men's material and secular life? Prayers, he holds, become meaningful when they create in the praying soul that firmness of spirit and strength of faith which shrinks from no sacrifice in upholding religious and moral values in the daily political and economic life of man and woman. Religion is not an apparel that can be put on or taken off at will. It is the pivot, round which man's entire life should move. Islam was an affective force when it formed the pivot of the muslim's life. But what is the present position? Individual selfish ends, promotion in official career, successes in business, maintenance of social status, family ends and political ambitions, these are the pivots on which the life of the muslims moves.

What Siddiqi then says is no less significant: He wants us to "cease talking of belief in God and of our attachment to Islam, unless we revolutionise our own life and shape it in the manner required by our creator, and, then proceed to change the whole world." Impelled by an extremely noble purpose and a pious aim in view, Siddiqi, while advocating a psychological and moral mutation to which every believer must subject himself, wants Islam to "become an effective force in human affairs." Thus, he says, will the dark course of modern western civilization be "lifted," and thus will the way be paved for a nobler and better type of living in conformity with the fundamentals of the Islamic teachings enshrined in *the Quran.*

Siddiqi's lament is reasonably worded and is a reason itself. It is not only muslims, however, who have astrayed into un-Islamic ways; death of the religious spirit is more or less a universal phenomenon, a process of decline in which muslims and hindus are alike involved. The true religious spirit, the edifying, enabling faith in God, have given way to the ignorance of the Zealot. The false crusading spirit of the fundamentalist, bellicose, postures of the conceited propagandist of baseless dogmas, half baked truths, the distortions and mutilations of historical facts are resorted to by the quasi-world of researchers whose claim to historical objectivity is based on myths and hearsay.

In its praise of righteous action – doing work rightful to do – Islamic teachings shows a remarkable affinity with those contained in the following verse of *the Geeta*:

Therefore, who doeth work rightful to do,
Not seeking gain from work, that man,
O Prince!
Is sanyasi and yogi – both in one!
And he is neither who lights not the flame of
Sacrifice, nor hand to ask.

One of the verses in *the Quran* is reminiscent of these lines:

> Those that have faith and do good works, attend to their prayers and pay the alms-tax, will be rewarded by their Lord and will have nothing to fear or to regret.

One of the divine assurances recurrent in *the Quran* and its central motif is expressed in the phrase "O what is right." Right dress, whosoever they may be, are assured of a reward from their Lord and of living without any fear or regret. It is on this account (of resemblance and on account of many other similarities, often hidden from the unperceptive eye, that it is shocking as well as painful to find the upholders of the injunctions enshrined in *the Quran* and *the Geeta* engaged in endless squabbles and mutual hostility. If Krishna gave to Arjun, and through him to all mankind, all manner of precepts, and instructions concerning all things, the Lord revealed His mind through the prophet – revealed to the world in divine injunctions, inscribing them upon tabulates. What Krishna directed Man (Arjun) to do the Lord called upon Moses to disseminate among the believers:

> Observe these steadfastly, and enjoin your people to observe what is best in them. I shall show you the home of the wicked. I will turn away from My signs the arrogant and the unjust.

As in the *New Testament* and *the Geeta*, so in *the Quran* God is spoken of as a perfect being in the closest intimacy with man, yet there is at the same time something mysterious about him in all these books. What St. John or St. Paul says of the Lord is not far from how *the Quran* and *the Geeta* represent the Supreme Lord. To all the prophets and seers and patriarchs the Lord is an inexplicable mystery, a being who is fully invisible and yet visible, inaccessible and accessible. Both *the Geeta* and *the Quran* no less than St. Paul speak of God as eternal, all knowing and omnipotent, and this concept is latent in all the thought of these scriptures in their concept of the divine nature, the holy scriptures leave no room for mutual contradiction or opposition. There are nevertheless zealots and ignoramuses who misinterpret the fundamental concepts of the two major religions and add to the chasm that divides the one from the other for no obvious rhyme or reason. It is the irrational and irreligious, purblind to the basic similarities underlying Hinduism and Islam, who widen the chasm instead of bridging it.

In so far as God's attributes are concerned, all believers, whether Hindu or Muslim, hold anthropomorphic beliefs and describe the Supreme Being as creator, sustainer and destroyer. He is the source of all life and controller of our inmost thoughts and feelings. *The holy Quran* describes Allah in terms not very different from those used by the seers of the *Upanishads* in "The Confederate Tribes," one of Allah's attributes is said to be His omnipotence, which includes his power, not subject to any external influence but voluntarily exercised, to lead the devotery from darkness to the light, for He is, *the Quran* repeatedly asserts, merciful to believers. All prophets are, in fact, not more or less than witnesses and bearers of good news. *The Quran* is explicit in describing the prophet as a warner as well and as one who shall call men to Allah by His leave and guide them like a shining light. Like shining lights have the Hindu Incarnation been, the incarnation of Vishnu and the great Hindu seers, rishis and acharyas. If the Hindu gods and goddesses reward the believer for all acts of charity and compassion, Allah, too, has bounteous blessings in store for him. It is not just accidental, a matter of chance and coincidence that the two great religions of the east exhort the faithful not to yield to the unbelievers and hypocrites but to disregard their insolence. But unequivocally they call upon the devotees to put their trust in God – in Allah, says the Quran, for Allah is all sufficient guardian. In "The Confederate Tribes" *the Quran* also lays down marriage laws for men and women, especially for the protection of the latter, of their honour and chastity.

> Believers, if you marry believing women and divorce them before the marriage is consummated, you are not required to observe a waiting period. Provide well for them and release them honourably.

This is the Quranic style of saying succinctly, without mincing word what the Hindu Laws, *Karama-kalaps* and *Karma-kandas*, say so elaborately in chapters extending to hundreds of pages. *The holy Quran* is, in fact, a poetical collection of sutras and parallels the *Braham Sutras* in brevity and in the richness of meaning. *The Holy Quran*, if we may say so, is Allah's *Sutras*.

All sutras, whether this sutra or that, whether Quranic or Upnishadik, describe God's omniscience in unambiguous terms and aver that whether one hides or reveals what one feels or thinks, Allah has knowledge of all things. "Mighty is Allah and wise" – this is one of the recurrent motifs of the Quran. "Allah is wise and all knowing." "Allah was watching over all your actions." "He is Allah, the one, the Almighty?" "He is the Mighty, the Benignant one." "Such is Allah, your Lord. His is the Kingdom, there is no god but Him." "He knows your inmost thoughts."

No heresy or apostasy is ever tolerated or pardoned by either religion. The unbeliever is destined to be punished and thrown into a blazing hell fire. If Allah's is the kingdom of the heaven or the earth, Ishwar's is the kingdom of the *trilokas*, the three worlds. In the principal attributes possessed by Allah and Ishwar, they are almost identical; they are identical also in judging human action, a man's virtues and transgressions. Their attributes are an amalgam of contradictions: they are merciful and stern, considerate and erratic in granting grace, though masters of the universe yet extremely compassionate even to their erring votaries. If the Quranic view of the role of the prophet is closely examined the difference from the Hindu view of Krishna becomes apparent. Neither Allah nor the prophet gives any evidence of being sportive, of performing what is commonly known as *leela*. Krishna's dalliance with the Gopis is absolutely alien to the prophet. He is the true messenger of Allah, an impeccable medium, a perfect recipient of Allah's message. No Hindu incarnation is as sternly serious as either Allah or His Prophet.

Whenever or wherever Allah's attributes are mentioned, the seriousness of tone and texture becomes apparent. Allah must take things seriously, judge all actions with stern impartiality, and pass His judgement unequivocally. He speaks like an immovable and unbending judge, whose justice knows no seasoning with mercy, and whose every word is law. But this is a fleeting impression for the very next moment we realize how merciful He is. As the bestower of everything needed by man, He's all compassion and benignity, a perfect model of charity without any equal, the very quintessence of loving compassion. To describe Allah, therefore, merely as a judge, unshakable and merciless is to mutilate evidence and distort fact, which is that in Allah all attributes naturally meet, some of which conflict with one another. From Allah emanates all mercy, all light, all blessings, all grace, all beauty and what not. He is the fountain head of all perfection, the absence of which, so universally extensive and cosmic proportions, is the imperfection of created beings. The transgressing creation being Allah's own, is to the materialist an evidence of Allah being the creator of the opposite, the attributes enumerated above. The absence of light is darkness; that of beauty ugliness. One cannot be oblivious of the aspect of Allah, constantly reminded of by the prophet, according to which He is an ever ready granter of rewards and blessings. He is as ready to meet out punishment to his erring humanity, sunk deeply in the mere disbelief as is ready to dole out bounties and rewards. Of this rewarding Allah showering his choicest blessings on the believer examples are legion, examples with which the pages of *Quran* are strewn. This reveals the difficulty inherent in all scriptural writings, who speak of Allah or Ishwar he is to speak in paradoxes, without which no description of Supreme Being is possible. All mystics throughout the world have spoken of the ineffable only through a language of paradox, and have admitted in essence that He is not nor can he ever be a subject of thought when He Himself is the thinker. All speech syllables, words and sentences, rhythms and rhymes, accents and emphasis belong to Allah and flow from Him. It is He who speaks in the *Quran* which is a symbolical evidence to show that utterance is only divinely possible by Allah's grace.

It is true, as most thinkers and mystics believe, that though divine nature cannot be properly known or expressed, *the Quran* is a living revelation of the divine consciousness. Islam is as mystical as any living faith, such as Hinduism and Christianity and yet it goes beyond them in representing through Quranic revelations, Allah, Allah's countless attributes, His so seemingly inexpressible, indescribable and mysterious nature. Even while admitting that the divine nature is beyond all verbal description, an attempt is made to describe Him. Even the mystical formula *Neti-Neti* is covert, indirect description of the transcendental reality. The *Quran* reveals the ultimate reality in all Its sublime glory. It reveals Itself. It does not depend on any human revelation. it alone can reveal Itself. In this sense the recognition that none can know or express. It is worthy of note. The revelations in the

Quran are a living testimony to Allah's transcendence to the fact that he is beyond the reach of human speech. He can be expressed only by Himself, in his own words, through His own paradoxical *Ayats*, through His own metaphors. Such pronouns as "He," "It," "This," "That," "She," "Her" etc. do not apply to Allah. He is all beyond any part of speech used by mankind to designate Him or describe Him. Yet we cannot do without the nouns or pronouns, the verbs and the adjectives when writing about Him. This is where all human speech fails. Allah's speech alone can describe Allah. Allah's revelation of Himself can reveal Allah.

It is for this reason that the mystics realizing the limitations of human speech use paradoxes when articulating their mystical experiences and giving utterance to their intuitive realizations. Instead of knowing Him – human beings can know Him – they experience Him and instead of seeing Him with their materialized, they see Him in their purified, immaculate souls, though they realize full well that the seer is He Himself. None can see Him unless the seer is Himself. Ultimately, therefore, only He is, or else is an emanation from Him – Himself. In the book called "Yasin," it is said:

> Glory be to Him who made His creatures male and female: the plants of the earth, mankind themselves, and the living things they know nothing of.
> The night is another sign for men. From the night we lift the day – and they are plunged in darkness.
> The Sun hastens to its resting-place: its course is laid for it by the Mighty One, the All knowing.
> We have ordained phases for the moon, which daily wanes and in the end appears like a bent and withered twig. The Sun is not allowed to overtake the moon, nor does the night outpace the day. Each in its own orbit runs. We gave them yet another sign when we carried their offspring in the laden Ark. And similar vessels we have made for them to voyage in. We draw them if we will: none can help or rescue them, except through our mercy and unless we please to prolong their lives a while.

Here the implication is that since no human being, howsoever mighty and potent he may be can force his language to describe the all transcendent Allah, He for once reveals His omnipotence in His own words. Let not any mundane agency dare attempt a description; it simply cannot describe Him. This is what He is to Himself though the language is human, the representation Anthropomorphic, there is a divine sublimity in the words uttered. Allah's omnipotence includes power to represent, to articulate, to express what is unrepresentable or unexpressable. Man, limited, imperfect creature, cannot describe His transcendent glory, His radiant glory but He certainly can. He is the source, the fountain head of all speech and of all silence, things yet unformed and beings insubstantial and invisible as well as material bodies and visible objects all owe their existence to Him. The audible, invisible speech also flows from the source-head of all speech.

Allah's sovereignty extends to an encompasses the entire universe in the heavens and the earth alike. It is an unchallengeable sovereignty, eternally established, so firm that none could invade or destroy it. It brooks no indiscipline and insecurity for evenly the Sun's course is laid for it and the moon's phases ordained: "We have ordained phases for the moon .... daily wanes and .... withers a twig." Symbolically, Allah is Islam; He is Peace and Order; He stands for Justice and order and security, all of which are visible in the waning and waning of the moon in all sunrises and sundowns.

It is well known that the *Holy Quran* was given to mankind to confirm and not to abrogate those books of God which were before it, which were revealed by His prophets and His apostles, affirming the teachings embodied in those early writings. There is therefore no contradiction. Nor is there rejection of what is contained in the earlier revelations, be those revelations bequeathed to mankind in the form of *Vedas* or in that of *Bible.* The *Quran* is a confirmation of those earlier revelations. Iskander Jadeed rightly observes that:

> This is a clear testimony which admits of no other interpretation or interpolation because confirmation cannot agree with abrogation which, in effect, is to invalidate.

It is unfortunate that such commentators on *the Quran* as Iskandar Jadeed limit the spirit of the *Quran,* its meaning in order to defend *the Bible* which, they say has not been abrogated by the Prophet. Nor have any of the early books been abrogated, including the *Vedas, Upnishads* and *the Geeta.* Just as the *Quran* does not refer to the *Bible* – the *Old Testament* or *the Gospel* – by name, so does it leave out the old Hindu scriptures. This absence of any reference to the *Vedas* was necessitated because of the certain historical and geographical reasons, by the people and the place for whom the *Quran* was delivered. The intervening period between the appearance of *the Vedas* and that of the *Quran* had already witnessed the incarnation of the world; God had become fresh, and Christ had delivered the News. The Prophet abrogated neither *the Bible* nor *the Vedas.* He confirmed the scripture of the Hindus as well as those of the Jews – Tura and the Christian – *The Bible.*

Just as the Upanishadic seers do not abrogate the teachings of the *Vedas* or of the *Geeta,* so are the *Vedas* not abrogated. The early scriptural writings catered to the spiritual needs of the ancients and where they rose to their spiritual growth and intellectual attainment. The ancient symbols and icons and imagery had lost their meaning with the appearance of new spiritual values as natural outcome of the unseizing evolutionary process. True there is no reference, remote or close at hand, to any of the Indian revelations, but the reason is obvious. The Prophet's listeners were hardly aware of their existence. The Prophet makes innumerable references to scriptures familiar to the people. But there is certainly no abrogation of the earlier teachings which should be considered as referring not only to *the Bible* but to every other scriptures, Indian or Jewish, Hindu or Hebraic. If God reveals Himself, He does so not to any favoured country or nation. He cannot and must not. This is evident from the behavior of the planets, the cosmic laws regulating the being and working of the natural forces-operating in the universe. If the *Quran* has been revealed to the Meccans it is not because they were to Allah the only people He loved. Since Allah must speak through a human prophet the latter must belong to a place somewhere in the world. The perfect medium chosen by Allah happened at that time to be a Meccan. But the Prophet belonged not only to Mecca but symbolized all mankind, spoke for all mankind and became the receptical of Allah's message for all mankind.

Moreover the *Quran* being a revelation – Allah's own message – it incorporates into its sacred body all the teachings enshrined in all the holy books of the world may be in an embryonic form.

In so far as pure bhakti is concerned, the *Quran* leaves bhakti hymns far behind in many of its recurrent emphasis on devotion, on unwavering faith in Allah, in total surrender to the divine will, in asserting and repeating "In saying thy will be done." It is essentially a glorification of Almighty Allah made in anthropomorphic terms as most of the world scriptures tend to represent the Lord. In *the Vedas,* the most ancient scripture of the Hindus is worshipped under different names and titles, not as so many gods distinguished from one another. The same God appears sometimes as Indra, Agni, Atma, Pran and at other times as Rudra, Narayan, etc. The following excerpt from the *Vedic Experience* is notable in the present context:

> At the end of the path there cannot but be a loving person, a personal deity, for love is essentially personal. At the end of the path of knowledge there will be total reality, absolute truth. Every human tradition has given different means to these three goals. Yet in one way or another the three goals, or rather that which stands at the end of the pilgrimage, must be ultimately equivalent: heaven is the vision and enjoyment of God, the love of God is communion with him, and God is only another name for absolute truth and supreme reality. God is here used as a universal symbol. But the unity or oneness of the three goals is only a postulate of our thinking and the fact that they somehow seem to coalesce should not be interpreted in the light of any of the three systems. It is here that the discourse on the Lord becomes relevant and the message of the Upanishads important. Let the Karmakandins, the men of action–even if the action is the performance of sacred rites and the offering of sacrifice– assume that the final goal is the building of a perfect work; let the bhaktas, the devotees of any kind, aver that there is nothing higher than a personal deity, and let the Jhanins, the sages of the various schools, claim that God must be transcended in favour of an ineffable Brahman or absolute void. Let them all follow their own paths. At the end they will all find the goal, the aim or their efforts, or of their love, or of their thoughts, the Lord who is not a concept or reality in the sense in which all other things are such; the Lord is at the end of every action, wish, desire, longing, tendency, thought, will, and is the end of them all. He is not necessarily a state or a Person or a Being. He cannot be circumscribed, and there is no discussion on this point, because the discussion has meaning only inside a concrete system. But the Upnishads, which are at the source of so many systems and schools, cannot be interpreted exclusively

> in favour of any one of them; the Upanishads are the Vedanta, the end of the *Vedas*, in the double sense of the world: they stand at the end of the *Vedas* as their culmination but they also represent the end, the surpassing, of them.

The Vedic experience should not be interpreted as something unique, something that the followers of other religions have not experienced or have not had. The Hindu scriptures by naming so many gods do not ignore the fact or are oblivious of it that the Lord is one indivisible, omnipresent, transcendent, omnipotent and omniscient. The Lord of the universe, the creator of that is – isness itself, pure existence, ineffable and interminable. The Quranic God should not therefore be alien or incomprehensible to the orthodox Hindu who is already familiar with Him in spite of this different religious background which admits of a multiplicity of gods. To the enlightened Hindu there is but one God, the Supreme Lord of all creations, compassionate, and an unmoved mover, when the *Vedas* and the seers declare that He is beyond human speech – Neti, Neti – the Quranic Allah would not refute it or deny it. It is within Allah's power, but beyond human competence, to enable any creature or thing, living or non-living to endow it with the power of expressions. The speaker is ultimately Allah. It is a fact recognized by the *Quran* itself as also by the Vedic and Upanishadic seers. The human speech and all the sounds with which nature is vibrant belong to Allah, the only Lord of the universe.

In *Katha Upanishad*, the recognition that Brahman is unknowable is expressed in clear terms. The seer describes the unborn one as follows:

> Of the Unborn One, whose consciousness is unflickering, there is a city with eleven gates.
> Meditating (on Him), one does not grieve and, becoming freed, one becomes emancipated.
> This is that.
> As the moving (Sun) He dwells in heaven, (as air) He pervades all and dwells in interspace; as fire. He resides on the earth, as soma He stays in a jar; He lives among men; He lives among gods; He swells in space; He is born in water; He takes birth from the earth; He is born in sacrifice; He emerges from the mountains; He is unchanging; and He is great.

> All deities worship that adorable one, the seated in the middle, who pushes the pran upward and impels the apāna inward.

These verses contain evidence of the seer's belief in the immanence of God who pervades the universe in one form or another visible or invisible in spite of this indwelling, immanent spirit and its countless manifestations, It is One. If the seers perceived and described it anthropomorphically they made no error nor did they commit any spiritual transgression. If a votary creates his God in his image, this is the only way he has ever created Him; and if ever he feels that he cannot do without such a creator, an Almighty and Alseeing one, the latter cannot also do without him. Both man and God are interdependent. God's Being is perhaps related to the sentient, the creation which alone can experience or feel the necessity of Him. One worships Him so long as one is living in a bodily form. God seizes to be after one's death.

The scriptures would not therefore encourage a believer to invite questions on any of the texts Ayats and Sutras, for to invite question is to invariably provoke ambiguous answers. If, for example, it is said that God does not need man's praise, a man's skeptical mind might say, "How do you know He does not? Have we not told at one time or another that human praises are God's food. How does one know what God's needs are? The fact is that God needs nothing – neither praise nor blame, neither this nor that, for to have a need is to suffer dearth. God is plenitude perfect, full of everything and in need of nothing. Why should we isolate praise in particular and say that He does not need our praise. Let us repeat; He needs nothing. If at all He needs anything He needs man to say what He needs and what He does not. Whosoever talks about God's needs, talks gibberish – anthropomorphically, as all scriptures must. The Prophets in all the religions throughout the world have made God in their own images and use human tongues of flesh and blood and human sounds to express their own needs and experiences" – they have to All talk about God is anthropomorphic.

The myst therefore is silent. The inexpressible and infinite as God is, efforts are made to define and limit Him, to see Him in a human image or in an idol. To thus circumscribe the infinite by assigning it a form, verbal or material is an act of sacrilege, a blatant denial of Allah's inexpressibility and infinity. But human beings, in dire need of His grace and healing touch, cannot do without speaking or writing about Him. That accounts for the birth of religions, of the organized church, and of the Tomes of commentaries and exegeses. The *Quran* is in certain places a bitter denunciation of idol worship and of polytheism – of the tendency to set other gods against Allah or to allege them to be his partners. To the zealots professing other religions, especially to the orthodox Hindu, ignorant of the essential teaching enshrined in the shastras and their symbolic meaning, not only objects to the Quranic view of their idols, but rejects it outright and upholds their idolatory and continue to practise their age old idol worship. It is here that Islam and Hinduism part-ways. Let not ignorance whether of the Hindu worshipper or of the Muslim critic complacently assume that an idol is not more than an idol. Neither of them knows the true meaning of the symbol, the enlightened among the two communities know that there is more behind the idols than keeps the eye. The Puranas describe how the Ultimate Reality sanctified all the elements, all nature, all existence and each being, animate or inanimate by incarnating itself as almost every conceivable being. The entire universe is thus bathed in a cosmic holiness, is sacred, apotheosized by the countless incarnations of Brahma and Vishnu. It is the indwelling spirit in every object, small or big, God behind the gods who is worshipped. The so-called idol worship should not, therefore, alienate enlightened person a true believer, from the mass of those worshippers who reverence an idol even without knowing what their idols stand for. He who worships an idol is just because it is an idol is stupid but he whose reverence for an idol is for the god it represents must be regarded as a believer. Superstition and ignorance assume the existence of so many gods who are in reality like the so many organs of a single body. The multitudinous duties of the Hindus are but the attributes of the one Ultimate Reality. Vishnu's thousand names are all His attributes. But this is perhaps a wild shot, a piece of speculation or misrepresentation. To assert that this interpretation alone is correct or that whatever has been written about idol worship by our predecessors or what is being written about it by our contemporaries is all trifling nonsense is not our aim. What we want to assert is that superstition, wherever it is and in whatever form it exists, must be denounced. Even if its idols are many and so are the gods but all of them are one, simply the images are different.

We can make idols but we cannot divide the Almighty Allah. He will always remain one – without partners, without anyone to share his glory and challenge His Sovereignty.

No god, was, is, shall be Allah's equal:

On that day He will call out to them, saying: "Where are the gods whom you alleged to be My partners?" From every nation we will bring a witness, and we shall say to them: "show us your proof." Then they shall know that the truth is Allah's and the gods of their own invention will forsake them.

Sringivad: A Review

Dr. R.C. Prasad

Sringivad is a book of staggering ingenuity, perhaps most fascinating when it is most stirringly imaginative and expressive of the writer's spiritual cravings. There is in Dr. Shreenivas an artist, great and versatile, whose brilliant gift for self-expression finds a felicitous complement in his formulation of memorable spiritual and metaphysical theories. His faith in God and science has nothing ancient about it; it sees beyond his age, to a future of progress through reason, in which a distinctly modern ideal is outlined. While *Sringivad* by no means provides any evidence that he has given up orthodox Upanishadic or Advaita views, it must be admitted that his belief is not a little tinged with what will be the scientific Hinduism of the next centuries.

With a remarkable power of lucid analysis and logically developed explanation, Dr. Shreenivas pushes Sir Thomas Browne's *Religio Medici* farther, showing in full detail how God is neither elusive nor elusory, how the "space speaks of Him and announces the ultimate subtlety of His manifest aspect with éclat and elan and in sprucy sprightness." But his temper is more complex than Browne's, and successive aspects of it are revealed as the book progresses, especially where he drifts into many memorable generalizations, and says, "Religion and godliness, the linchpin of rural peace, progress and prosperity, have been smashed. They have succumbed to rapid modernization, and to the enormity and anonymity of breaking families and drifting population, in the wake of industrialization, and as the scourge of social insecurity and slanderous standards." From the theme of the tenebrous evening setting in and the high banks of Balan weaving the river's brink into dark and serpentine pleats, of the creeking car singing a serenade, fear, Mathematics, Maya, non-existence of symmetry in nature, efficiency of natural progression, space, God, consciousness, etc., the subject broadens out to a full systematic *examen* of the Arrow of Time, Love that is the Absolutely Absolute, laws of Karma, Ecstasy, egolessness, etc., etc. For the most part these varied themes are developed with the nicety of touch and the lucidity of expression which characterize genuine art. Thus it pays to read the author for edification alone, though, of course, he has other and more precious rewards in store.

In spite of the wealth of his ideas, Dr. Shreenivas's imagination and illimitably wide reading do not fail to correlate them, to educe from them a common system, spiritual or idealistic, in the nature of things. He has, he claims, seen the immensity of that immanence, the mysterious and mystic opulence of the One, God in toto. At the level of his discerning mind and intellect he finds Him as the Super Saturated Space, the Empty Void; at the level of awareness and transcendence he recognizes Him as the Absolutely Absolute Abstraction, the Cosmic Consciousness. "We discover Him," he maintains, "manifesting as the selfless LOVE of the mother – the creator and the sustainer, the protector and the provider, the bestower of gifts – and the immortality of genetic LIFE." People in general have a tendency to look upon God as invisible, abstract, indescribable. Such a tendency Dr. Shreenivas does not share; the "Omniscient Consciousness lets ITSELF be limited by the brain-mind-psyche triumvirate of the individual truth-seeker," he says, and descends when the triumvirate ..... have reached ..... a proper degree ..... of excellence and "wave-length" for the Divine communication ..... His attitude towards God reflects the traditions of both mysticism and rationalism. Like Browne, he loves to lose himself in a mystery, to pursue his reason to an *O attitude.* The rationalism of his science, which, he observes, has taken up only the threads, of the middle and woven a "drama of ideas," leaving the two ends as unknown as ever, mounts to the mysticism of his Divinity. Creation and the Creator are for him "equivalent and invariant in their mutual relationships. And there is one final law of conservation which depends on nothing else but itself and which is the First Fundamental Fulcrum of manifestations and their laws, the End-point of Equilibrium, Inertia and Equivalence, the Original Conservation Law – equivalent to *Space.*"

It is obvious that Dr. Shreenivas's rationalism is a step towards his mysticism; upon the subtlest science's alter stairs he appears to mount through space up to God. The altitude of his mysticism (like Browne's again) can be taken from the vantage of his science. The God whom we behold as quaint, whose brightness is adumbrated in light, and who is "the everlasting, changeless, omnipresent, omniscient and omnipotent Immortal Being," has an essential kinship to Dr. Shreenivas's magnetic monopole, his Intelligent Universal Ecosystem or Cosmic Consciousness. His God never imposes His will on the Free Will of man but tethers it to Maya or the mere good of mankind.

"The dim glimmer of sentience," he remarks, "has evolved into the effulgent conflagration of the rational mind – both powered by the "energy" of the consciousness .... Which is the Absolutely Absolute Abstract Being, the omnipresent, omniscient, omnipotent, as the One-without-the-Second, Life-Consciousness–Bliss entity, the Truth-Benevolence-Beauty, the suchness of Existence." This mystical element in Dr. Shreenivas should, of course, not be underestimated. He knows, as the seers and mystics did, that a very tiny replica of God resides within us and that a dive into meditation leads to the experience of transcendence like that of a dip into the holy Ganga. He recognizes within himself the germ of that indwelling Spirit which is the source of man's transcendental consciousness and link with the Being of God. In deepest recesses of his spirit, in that abyss where selfhood ceases to have meaning, and the individual soul touches the life of the All, distinction vanishes and he sees God in a point. Such an experience is highly characteristic of mysticism. The German mystics, temperamentally miles asunder from Dr. Shreenivas, describe it as the attainment of the "still wilderness" or "lonely desert of Deity." What is necessary for transformation is God's love, the "enzyme" of faith. Thus the characteristic theme of Dr. Shreenivas's *Sringivad* is that a "Life lived fully in righteousness is its own reward" or that "through Fog and Mist, Instinct and Illusion, Smoke and Storm, Loss and Gain, Sobs and Smiles, God must be loved and pursued to the very End."

Dr. Shreenivas has ceased to be a searcher but continues to be a mystic who describes in many a beautifully tempered and measured word his encounter with Truth. The spirit and cadence of such passages remind us of the great mystics, Meister Eckhart, Blessed Henry Suso, John Ruysbrock, Nicolas of Cusa, Walter Hilton, St. Catherine of Siena, etc. He has no patience with those zealous co-religionists of his who seek God in the scriptures alone. God for him is the Absolute Anchor to which all the conservation laws will be found to be anchored and at which they converge to be annihilated and from which they diverge to be created. He is the unmanifest AAA, the Origin, the Source, the Essence, the Ultimate, the All abiding ITSELF, the Life – Existence – Consciousness – Bliss-Truth – Benediction Beauty "nature" of the Supreme Self.

This is not just consummate phrase making; it has the resolute vigour of a thoughtful man who knows man and God and Nature and Consciousness, peace, tranquility, bliss, compassion, radiance, beauty, immortality, limitlessness and freedom through and through, and though no doubt it shows profound scholarship born of wide reading, it has the thrust of a shrewd eclecticism and original thinking, which Dr. Shreenivas takes no pains to conceal, and which is the more telling, in the end at least, for his evident modesty. Hundreds of years earlier, Benjamin Whichcote, the first Cambridge Platonist, wrote, "How much easier is it quietly to enjoy, than eagerly to contest! How vastly wiser!" The two men think alike. Both have loyalty to truth, and both are capable, at the proper challenge, of defending it, but both know the difference between blind partisan strife and that search for truth which, as Bacon says, is "the love making or wooing of it."

How can one sum up Dr. Shreenivas's religious qualities or his view of what he calls "the Art and the Science of the Creator called God?" Let us not forget that he combines the believer and the scientist, the acute intellect and the propensity to faith. He makes a synthesis which is the result partly of a great overweight of learning and the ability to see all related facets at once, partly of an inborn power to formulate general principles, and of a great assimilative talent. His is the strength of a powerful, solitary mind, always sensitively aware of the infinite resourcefulness of the Almighty and always alive to the "clever craftsman in disguise," to the inter conversions of physical energies, to the Will of God, to the harmony and the law-governed system of the universe, and to its spiritual meaning.

This book, I am sure, will do good to anyone and everyone who reads it. It has the clearness and depth of uncontaminated mystical vision through which Dr. Shreenivas's knowledge moves with sureness and insight. It seeks to draw together a variety of trends, scientific and religious, which are too often considered in isolation. In so doing it should help to stimulate thought and action in regard to the particular problems and opportunities which face mankind in this last quarter of the twentieth century. I commend it wholeheartedly as a textbook for the student and general reader and to all whose prayer is "Lord, I believe; help Thou mine unbelief."

****

Poems by Dr. R.C. Prasad

Disconsolation

On that monument of sorrow sat Patience and Disconsolation,
Arguing and brooding, in converse engaged,
"She is my subject;" cried Patience, amazed
At Disconsolation's havoc, "worth all attention;
A Sita of fortitude, envy of all creation,
Yet a mountain of sorrow, by sorrow's utterly razed".
She'll annihilate all, when enraged;
This, take it, is for your information.

I'm Fate's lackey, said the other,
"A principality he has, usurping, enslaved;
Grace and compassion his edicts do not cover,
Though in one point he has certainly failed.
Having me subdued, she caused him many tremors
And lest he under her curse be laid," he fears.

7 Feb. 1988

*****

British Library

Pray look at it
Look at this dome
This womb
Sarasvati's own shrine
And these mystic oblations.

"We're decaying," a musty volume cried,
"We're dying," another said.
I wondered what all this insolence was about
When yet another batted in "Get away, you senseless lazy lout."
I said, "Not me, I won't,"

"Don't you see," the volume added,
"That this stream is all stagnant
Dried up and unresponsive to environment?
Yet touch me not I'm still a maiden,
Though Dedication is my husband,
Industry handmaiden."

6 Feb 1988

*****

Children in the Museum

It's now a commonwealth
Of flowering newtons
An eden of odorous chrysanthemums.
Wherefore should you lament
The loss of a few distant regions?
Each of them is a domain
A realm of Golconda diamond
Vaster than the ocean,
Each a womb
Filled with promises,
A pyramid of puissance
In creative speculation
An everest.

7 Feb. 1988

*****

In the British Library

Myriads of mountains of letter'd gold
Harems of glittering burkas
Humble me from the bluish dome
The round earth's true replica
With all the sketches and scribblings of the masters

Their accusing tongues
Reprimand me, shut me down:
"How puny you look," they say,
Here Sarasvati's valiant votaries
Dwell rapt in mystic silence
Brood absorbedly with scholarly mien
Each a Socrates, each wondrous keen

Myriads of experiences and imaginings, tearful, vapturons, responses
Negative positive assertions flow out
Flooding all Fitzroy street
Drowning us all in ancient wisdom?

6 Feb. 1988

*****

Love and Amity

You've riches, riches,
Riches to hoard and riches to waste
To fly in the clouds, to parley and play;

You've a spouse dear, dear,
Spouse that loves you, bashful and tender,
A source of comfort, Mansarovara of Joy;

You've a positional covet, covet
Position to command and position to brag,
Position to slaughter and behead;

Yet all these are futile fertile,
All is variety, verity of variety,
Save "Thou art That," love and amity.

7 Feb. 1988

*****

Mother and Reality

When with pain
The trivialized womb had rejected me
Bleeding and blistered,
You cushioned me soft
And your breasts suckled me sweet
And your hands rocked me in delicate drowse
Elate with stale motherhood's joy.

Yet you were cruel, mother,
Cruel as Love's dread death,
Breeding gloomiest numbness and hopeless tear;
You led me to nothingness
To sheer futility you banished,
And I cried
Not for you but,
Nor for the nectar of the sagging nut.
I cried,
For the tough cool
Death to whom you delivered me.

6 Feb. 1988
London.

*****

YMCA

When on first February I reached London
Straight from Heathrow, I met Mr Patro,
"Aha," he cried, prying into a chart, eyes aglow,
"I've no room vacant, no, I say without reservation,
YMCA's no kennel, for racial hybridization.
It's a hostel, India's cultural stream to flow,
To ripen in the U.K., mature, mellow,
Not to encourage terrorism or foster phoney fusion."

But this is what I see YMCA doing;
It's all oblivions of India's glory,
It's neither asserting nor diffusing,
It's culpably hybrid, ingloriously showy,
With an avowed aim – to keep up appearances
To get Anglicized, to obliterate her hallowed traces.

7 Feb. 1988
YMCA, London

*****

Detachment and Love

Nine and twenty years have passed,
twenty-nine slow, withering years
Crammed with events of variegated hues,
Births of grandsons, deaths of parents,
Births and deaths of hopes and fears
And foreheads marked with furrows,
Only the living have changed
Flowed and fluxed,
On the surface have the unliving
Remained transfixed, immuted.
"I'm with thee," said a tree
Despite its autumnal numbness
In the frost-beaten Russell Square,
"I'm aged as thou art,
Aged but wise,
In perpetual communion entranced,
With realization grown a Buddha
With spiritual beauty adorned;
Now I know what one of my luminaries knew,
The negative capability, the beauty of age,
Detachment and love
And that I am He the real, Not the mirage."

*****

Section IV

Reminiscences

Dr. R.C. Prasad : A Fond Remembrance

Dr. Kedar Nath Sharma

Shakespeare in *Julius Caesar* speaks of noble Brutus in these words:

> His life was gentle, and the elements
> So mix'd in him that nature might stand up,
> And say to all the world "This was a man"!

These lines may be very appropriately adopted to outline the life and personality of late Dr. Ram Chandra Prasad. Remembering him is like experiencing a whiff of fresh air in a small stuffy room. Memories of all sorts come in crowding, too difficult to manage in a short space like this.

At first glance, the most noticeable aspect of Dr. Prasad's life is his meteoric rise to eminence from a modest beginning. Hailing from a remote village (Gorakhari) of Patna district in Bihar, he graduated to the highest post in the university, which was the main field of his occupation. He started his career in 1951 as a lecturer in English at H.D. Jain College under Magadh University. In 1952 he joined B.N. College, Patna. After a doctoral degree from Britain, he shifted to the post-graduate department of English of the Patna University. My acquaintance with him dates back to that very time. My initial impression of him was of a well-dressed handsome young man; but very soon I discovered in him an inquisitive scholar with unquenchable thirst for knowledge. He read widely and wisely, always noted down his impressions of whatever he read. Thus, by dint of labour and perseverance, he distinguished himself as a well-informed sincere teacher, respected and loved by the students. He also caught the attention of Dr. R.K. Sinha, who was then the Chairman of the department of English, Patna University. His sincerity and hard work won him the full confidence of Dr. Sinha, and Dr. Prasad fully justified the trust reposed in him. In Dr. Sinha's absence, Dr. Prasad managed the department most efficiently, so much so that when some teacher was on leave, or was late in coming, Dr. Prasad used to rush to the class, if he was free. He continued to do so when he became Chairman of the department. His unique devotion to the job of teaching endeared him to the students as well as to the colleagues.

Dr. Prasad got me transferred from B.N. College to the post-graduate department in 1987, which brought me in closer contact with him. I was greatly impressed, rather inspired by his promptness and punctuality. He saw that no class went unengaged. He held that a teacher should be always ready to go to class, if some one was absent. His advice to his colleagues was that one should keep in reserve a few well-prepared lessons, to be used at the moment of urgency. Thus one could engage unscheduled classes at a moment's notice. It happened once that I was slightly late for the class, and as usual Dr. Prasad rushed to my class. I showed up at the door and signalled him to come out and let me teach, but he rather preferred to continue till the end of the period. This worked as a corrective measure against those who came late for the class. Of course, in most cases, the delay was due to the traffic jam on Ashok Rajpath, which according to Dr. Prasad could be avoided by starting for the class well in advance. All this shows that Dr. Prasad was a valued colleague for his juniors and seniors alike.

Dr. R.C. Prasad was sweet-tempered, soft-spoken, he was never acerbic or indecent in his words or action. Fault-finding was not his forte. He always conducted himself gracefully. There was not even a grain of artificiality in him, he was exactly as he appeared, although he was very punctilious in his dress and address. If not by birth, but by temperament, he was an aristocrat.

Some teachers are outstanding in their performance in the class but fight shy of putting pen to paper, or opening their mouths at seminars and symposia. But Dr. Prasad always participated in them enthusiastically and productively, distinguishing himself with his scholarly deliberations. I remember having attending a literary function in the Patna Medical Association Hall presided over by Dr. R.C. Prasad. Dr. Namwar Singh, a noted critic of Hindi literature, was the chief speaker. I wondered what Dr. Prasad would say in his presidential address. As usual, Dr. Singh's presentation on the Marxian approach to the contemporary Hindi literature was nicely conceived and delivered. When Dr. Prasad stood up to speak, he took the audience by surprise with his scholarly speech delivered in chaste Hindi. When he finished, the big hall resounded with applause. Then I came to know that he was also a well-known figure among the scholars of Hindi.

Dr. Nagendra, another great scholar of Hindi, was then preparing a book on modern Hindi literature, comprising English translation of the selected pieces from the masterpieces of different genres of Hindi. Dr. R.C. Prasad was associated in this venture as the Co-ordinator. Dr. Prasad encouraged his colleagues in the department to contribute some pieces to this publication, and they did it enthusiastically. I too contributed two translation pieces, one from *Saket* and another from *Shekhar Ek Jeevani.* The book was published by Hindi Grantha Academy. Dr. R.C. Prasad gradually published several books and articles in English as well as in Hindi. But his monumental work is the English translation of *Sri Ramcharitamanas* of Tulsidas, containing the rendering of the voluminous text in the Roman script, the paraphrase, and the meaning in English. On its publication it was acclaimed as a great achievement.

Academically, too, Dr. R.C. Prasad rose to the apex. In quick succession he was appointed Chairman of the English department of Bhagalpur University, then of Patna University, the Pro-Vice-Chancellor of Bhagalpur University, and finally the Principal of the prestigious Patna College, from where he retired. He left his mark on all these posts. Unfortunately Vice-Chancellorship which he deserved eluded him, may be because of political machination. But Dr. Prasad did not feel frustrated. He was happy wherever he was. He had learnt to deal with the vicissitudes of life. There is a blend of pains and, ups and downs, profits and losses in everybody's life, and it is very difficult to maintain equanimity. But Dr. Prasad went on his way happily and merrily.

On the side line it may be mentioned that Dr. Prasad's is familial life, was not enviable in many respects – he was bereft of the motherly affection early in life, his elder brother fell a victim to the village politics, his elder son died in a suspicious circumstance; Dr. Prasad seemed to inhabit the house of Atrecus. He found some solace in his daughter who stood First in First Class at M.A. (English) Examination. But she left him after her marriage. The only pillar of strength and inspiration was his father, a very successful man in life. He loved Dr. Prasad very affectionately. His death in the nineteen eighties was an irreparable loss to him. Despite all this Dr. Prasad sailed on and on merrily. He was neither a stoic, nor a cynic. Nobody could fathom his fortitude, nobody could discover the secret of his inner strength.

There is a saying, you cannot serve both God and Mammon. For his aristocratic way of living and for his craze for buying books Dr.

Prasad was always in need of money. But he never earned money by dishonest means. He supplemented his income from salary and examinership from several universities and by writing books. Still there was no dearth of his critics who raised doubts as to his probity and morality. In most cases the criticism originated from their jealousy. Actually Dr. Prasad was a prolific writer, an avid researcher and an excellent performer in the classroom. Whatever topics he taught, he taught excellently and mesmerized the classroom. Seeing his qualities his critics found themselves dwarfs before him.

There is another side of Dr. Prasad's personality which needs to be mentioned here – the lighter side. Every morning at six o'clock he went to Moinul Haque Stadium for walk. There was a good number of morning walkers who joined him. There he was a different man, very jolly and jovial, with an abundant sense of humour. With his jokes and humorous anecdotes he kept the pleasant company roaring with laughter. In that mood he did not hesitate to crack rustic jokes verging on vulgarity. Once while returning from a *Baraat* along with some friends and colleagues, he was waiting for the steamer at Pahaleza on the other side of the Ganges. Someone amongst them proposed that they should bathe in the Ganges. Dr. Prasad along with them jumped into the river and enjoyed swimming, poking fun at each other. Dr. Prasad was at his on such occasion too.

Unfortunately this noble soul did not enjoy a long life; he died soon after his retirement from principalship of Patna College in nineteen ninety three. It was an irreparable loss to Bihar as well as to the whole of north India. The country lost an excellent scholar, a dependable friend, a versatile writer, and above all, a good man. I will ever cherish his memory for whatever he was. Burus rightly says, "A man's a man for a' that." And Henry Newman says about man:

> O man, strange composite of heaven and earth!
> Majesty dwarfed to baseness! fragrant flower.
> Running to poisonous need! and seeming worth
> Cloaking corruption!

Dr R.C. Prasad: A Unique Professor

Dr. Sister M. Carol A.C.

In the early 1960s, Patna University was really a place of learning, far from what it is now. It could compare with the best universities in India and could even confidently send students to Oxford. Those were the days of learned professors, like Dr. R.K. Sinha, Dr. R.C. Prasad, Dr. S.D. Singh, Fr. B. Haas S.J. and others. They maintained a high standard of teaching and learning. Lectures were well prepared and interesting, and professors dropping classes was unheard of. When I see what has happened to the university since those days and the sorry state in which it is today, I thank God that I was lucky enough to do the M.A. in the heyday of Patna University and I feel sorry for the present day students.

The professors were all interested in the progress of the students and weekly essays and other assignments were required of us. One of the professors from whom I profitted the most was Dr. R.C. Prasad. My sister companion and I soon found out that he would, not only, like the other professors, correct our work, but would take immense trouble to give us many extra tips, so that we really progressed. There was a difference of attitude between his correction of our work and that of other professors. I might call it personal interest in the individual student.

The dissertation in lieu of two papers for the M.A. examination was the domain of the Head of the Department, Dr. R.K. Sinha. He would help us select the subject and require us to see him at intervals, but for the doubts and difficulties that turned up along the way, we would automatically turn to Dr. Prasad. He would go painstakingly through our work and give us many valuable tips, which gave us a real push forward. What he possessed was knowledge combined with, what I have mentioned above, as real zeal for the student's progress. You felt free to ask him for help in difficulties, whenever they turned up. We were in awe of the other professors, but not of him. Though he kept his dignity, he was approachable. When the dissertation was complete, it was understood that he would do the preliminary correction, before the Head of the Department took it up. So, he was not only knowledgeable and approachable, but also very hardworking – hundred per cent dedicated to his profession.

When I was doing the Ph.D on G.K. Chesterton, Dr. R.K. Sinha was my guide. But the procedure was the same as with the M.A. dissertation. Occasional visits to the guide and the rest of the work done by Dr. R.C. Prasad, because I chose to ask him for help and because Dr. R.K. Sinha had no objection. There are many things I learnt from him during these years that showed me how well-read he was, and some of his tips helped me in my college teaching. He would even go further than was needed. He helped me to get my thesis published.

Some years later, I wrote a biography of the founderess of my religious congregation, who was English and very much connected with the Oxford Movement. Because I had so much faith in Dr. Prasad, I asked him to read it and give me his opinion on it, before I got it published. His opinion was that I should present it for the degree of D.Litt. in Patna University – which I did.

Dr. Prasad remains in my memory as a rare academic person – learned, dedicated, human, a person for his students. I can never thank him enough for all that he has done for me.

Dr. R.C. Prasad: A Good Samaritan

Dr. Indu Bhushan Sharma

I have seen Dr. R.C. Prasad in many roles on the stage of life. I would like to share some of my chosen reminiscences which throw light on the versatility of Dr. Prasad as a great scholar, teacher, writer, administrator, orator, guardian and father figure – all par excellence.

Dr. Prasad was a great Samaritan in the true sense of the term. He always did good to others in the best of his capability. I belong to the session which at its close witnessed the retirement of the great legendary intellectual Titan Dr. R.K. Sinha, and the arrival of his worthy student Dr. R.C. Prasad as the new succeeding Head of the Department of English, Patna University.

What distinguished Dr. Prasad from others was his simplicity and humility in his behavior with those who came to him. Although an aura of awe-evoking grandeur and dignity always surrounded him, yet within him there was a generous and benevolent stream of inexhaustible compassion that magnetically attracted everybody who came in contact with him. Very often he helped his close students even out of his way.

In 1980 I appeared before the Interview Board of Bhagalpur University for the appointment of lecturer in English. Dr. Prasad being the Pro-VC of the University was the Chairman of the Interview Board. The subject – experts asked me questions about Metaphysical Poetry, which I answered to the satisfaction of the Interview Board. One of the experts wanted to grill me by asking some tricky and irrelevant questions. Dr. Prasad sensing some trouble for me interrupted by questioning me about the comparative study of English Literature and Sanskrit Literature which was one of my Pass Course subjects at B.A. Thus he saved the situation for me.

I had been a boarder at Saidpur PG Hostel No. 3. I remained there a bit longer as a guest of one of my juniors. In December, 80 I was taking rest on the bed in the morning. In a semi-conscious state I heard some voice whispering into my ears: "You sleep, and in Bhagalpur they are about to finalise the Panel." Suddenly I got up, took bath, dressed up, and reached Patna Junction Railway Station.

The train, Vikramshila Express started. I had no time to buy the ticket. I started running after the moving train. I reached the Guard's cabin. The guard allowed me to board inside his cabin. I reached Bhagalpur University Guest House where Dr. Prasad stayed. He was inside his room, and nobody was permitted to knock his door. It was his instruction to the caretaker of the Guest House that the visitor should either wait for Dr. Prasad to come out or he should visit another time. I waited and in the evening Dr. Prasad came out for his usual walk. When I greeted him, he asked me the cause of my visit. I said, "I got intuition in the morning today that the Panel is getting ready, and so I came." He smiled, and replied, " Your intuition is really very strong. Now you know that there are two ranks of lecturers: Junior and Senior. Which rank do you expect to get?" I said, "I don't know. Do as you please." When the Panel was announced, I found my name in the Senior Grade and got posted at Godda College.

After this meeting at the Guest House was over, I wanted to take leave. Like a guardian he asked "Where are you putting up?" I said that I would stay at any hotel near the railway station, and tomorrow afternoon I would take the train for Patna. Very compassionately inwards but with subtle indifference in tone he said, "Even here at Guest House there are some rooms for visitors. If you want, you can talk to the caretaker." The caretaker Mr. Bhattacharya was a lean Bengali gentleman. Very sternly and curtly he said that he would provide me accommodation with meals. Next day at noon I asked him about the Bill. He said that the Bill has already been paid by "Sir" (Dr. Prasad).

When I got the appointment letter from Bhagalpur University, I went to Dr. Prasad to show the Panel and take further instruction. He said, "Go to Godda, see the place, meet the people and then join there if everything satisfies you." I did accordingly and finally joined there. Sometimes I had to face adversity at Godda College which had a hospitable but headstrong Principal. Once I visited the Guest House to share my problems with Dr. Prasad. He said, "Life is full of problems but this doesn't mean that people should commit suicide. Learn to cope with adversity, and struggle for survival. Excess tension leads to physical and mental disorder." My Panelmates of Bhagalpur University had to struggle a lot for the regularization of services because our initial appointment was temporary in nature. Dr. Prasad, the Pro-VC acted as per establishment rules of the University in his office but when we met him at the guest house, he always advised us to struggle for our cause. He kept a balance within him between the two contrary roles of an administrator of University, and guardian of students. But when the decisive moment came, the guardian element in him superseded the administrator element. As a result, we got our services regularized.

When I was in Godda College, I sometimes went to Patna via Bhagalpur. Sometimes Dr. Prasad also travelled by the same train. I remember once he had a bundle in his hand. He had a reservation in the upper class of Vikramshila Express. When the train reached Patna Junction, I accompanied him at the platform and overbridge. I wanted to take the bundle from his hand. He said, "No, thank you. I can't give you this. This bundle carries University Examination papers. They are 70, and I checked them all in the train." He was a born guide to teach youngsters how to spend time and all its moments creatively.

He was a deeply religious man devoted to Lord Ram and Sri Hanuman. He translated *Hanuman Chalisa* and *Sundarkand* into English when he was a school student at St. Xavier's High School, Patna. Later he translated *Sri Ramcharitamanas* into English. The translation was widely acclaimed, and the book was released at Haridwar by Sri Ramanand Sagar who had brought the Ramayan – renaissance worldwide through the small screen. Dr. Prasad was fond of Milton's poetry – Milton's high sense of Liberty and Religion. When he came back to P.U. as Head of English Dept., he found that Milton's *Paradise Lost* was taught by Dr. K.N. Sharma, a good experienced senior teacher of the Department. One day Dr. Prasad called him and very humbly requested to take up any other poet because he himself would like to teach Milton whom he considered his "grand father." Dr. Sharma wittily replied: "A grand father has many grand sons. Why do you want to monopolise him?" But he conceded and took up Tennyson's *In Memoriam* instead.

Dr. Prasad as a teacher realized the difficulties and problems faced by the Indian students in learning English as second language. In order to help them improve the English language at the initial stage he wrote an anthology of stories based on the *Ramayan*, the *Mahabharat, Panchtantr, Hitopdesh* and *Jatak.* The title of the book is: *When the World Was Young.* It was prescribed in all the universities to be taught at 2-year Intermediate course. I taught it in the class for many years. The Indianness of thought, lucidity and originality of expression embedded with fresh similes and metaphors are the uniqueness of the book. He maintained a tight schedule routine morning to evening. It was very difficult for the visitors to get him at home. His father scolded them because he wanted his son to spend time in academic pursuit. Dr. Prasad wrote many books and supervised hundreds of research works for Ph.D. and D. Litt. degrees. And he gave credit of his achievements to his father who helped him get time for creative work at home. In the early hours of morning he could be seen walking and jogging in Rajendranagar Stadium when in Patna or TNB College field when in Bhagalpur. At home he also practised yoga everyday.

When Dr. Prasad was the Head of the Deptt. of English, P.U. a UGC-sponsored Seminar on The Art of the Novel was organised in 1979. The venue was PU Central Library. Many luminaries of India participated. Dr. R.K. Sinha was the star attraction. Dr. Prasad, a devoted student of Dr. Sinha expressed his gratefulness to his teacher with utmost humility, "Dr. Sinha is not only a great scholar but also a big librarian. He reared us and taught us. Whatever we learnt, we learnt at the feet of Dr. Sinha."

Such a towering personality like Dr. R.C. Prasad has left a deep imprint on the minds of his admirers. Now he is physically not present before us but his memory will remain as fresh and live as ever. He will always stand as an ideal especially today when in an era of the commercialization of education the distance between a teacher and the taught is increasing day by day.

Prof. (Dr.) R.C. Prasad: Memoirs

Dr. R.P. Roy

I feel pleasure to write from my memoirs about the Late Dr. R.C. Prasad, who had been a renowned scholar and Professor of English.

As a Head:

After Dr. N.K. Banerjee, Dr. R.C. Prasad, who had come from Patna University, assumed the chair of the Head of the Post Graduate Department of English at T.M. Bhagalpur University, Bhagalpur. When a short time, he brought a big change in the academic activities; and, of course, the academic environment of the Department appeared to be changed. The students who had been straying here and there in the campus, began to take interest in attending classes regularly.

Dr. Prasad ran the Department amicably, behaving with the juniors as friendly and the seniors as brotherly. He even called the seniors "Badey Bhai." He motivated almost all the teachers of the Department for doing research work; and consequently, they did and got Ph.D. degrees.

The Muhalla in which he lived at Bhagalpur, was quite near the Department. So he always went to the Department on foot as he felt no need of any rickshaw or car. I always saw him bear some books in his hand while he was going to the department.

As an Organizer:

He was not only a scholar and a professor but also a good organizer. From time to time he organized departmental seminars to improve the knowledge and information of the students and their careers and qualities. In 1976, it was a good opportunity for T.M. Bhagalpur University when he organized the orientation course in English. I was very fortunate to get an opportunity to attend it. I got a lot of experiences and information of academic activities. I was very much benefited.

A number of highly illustrious scholars, professors from different Universities of the country, were invited; and they participated in it. May I cite a few of them who delivered their lectures? Dr. R.K. Sinha from Patna University, Dr. Amalendu Bose from Calcutta University,

Dr. Shishir Kumar Ghose from the Central University, Shantiniketan, Dr. D. Thakur from Lucknow University, Dr. Tulsi Ram from Pilani and Dr. K.K. Khemkar from Bombay University and others. Such a grand and successful organization of the orientation course could be possible only Dr. R.C. Prasad's effort.

As a Teacher:

I saw Dr. R.C. Prasad for the first time in 1975, when I was a student of English Honours at T.N.B. College Bhagalpur. He was then the Head of the P.G. Department of English, T.M. Bhagalpur University, Bhagalpur. He used to come and take honours classes at T.N.B. College twice a week. He taught us Pope's *The Rape of the Lock* in the most interesting manner. One line from the book that is "Belinda smiled and the world was gay," he repeated twice-thrice and gave emphasis on it to create interest in students. Since the day, this cherished line is vivid in my memory. I often utter this line on some occasions even now.

When I was a student of M.A. English he taught us Milton's *Paradise Lost,* Chaucer's *The Canterbury Tales*; Langland's *Piers the Plowman* and Brown's *Religio Medici.*

To my mind, he was a powerful teacher. He was good at teaching indeed. He was an experienced and perfect master of literature and language. He used simple words and sentences to make the language lucid, while imparting lectures in the class-room. He made difficult passages easy to understand. He sometimes expressed a sentence twice or thrice, so that students might easily follow. They were alert and spell bound.

He was a good motivator also; he motivated students for studies, hard labour, a good result and a good job. A teacher must be a good psychologist to understand the mood of the students. Such a quality I observed in him. Whenever he found their minds wavering here and there or their vacant looks, he drew their attention telling some interesting things. Once, some students were yawning in the class and some had vacant looks, he, all of a sudden, stopped teaching and asked us a question. We were replying one by one. When my turn came, I stood up to reply and began to speak. I might have spoken two or three sentences when he interrupted and said "Oh! Don't smile and speak in a dialogue like Devanand."

At this, all my friends burst into laughter. I stopped speaking. He further said, "Do you think, you are an evergreen hero like him?"

They burst again into a thunderous laugh. At this I shrank in shyness. Then he smiled and beckoned me to sit down. I smiled and sat down looking left and right. After that, there was a silence for a while. None of us but he broke the silence first. We felt at ease and were ready to listen to the lecture. He resumed the lecture after entertaining us.

In another class he was delivering his lecture on Chaucer's *The Canterbury Tales*; he was explaining the satirical tone of Chaucer's, referring this line; "Nuns' Love Locks on their foreheads." He repeated this line. We were alert to listen to him. He smiled. We were silent. He took us in a hilarious mood. He then said jestingly, "I see your all activities."

"Yes, I see. You are talking about me. Aren't you?" We were silent and grave. He said smilingly, "You call me sir on the campus. But I know, you would be speaking outside simply R.C.P. Wouldn't you?" "No sir, no sir! Never!" we said repeatedly. "Well, not always, but at times R. Cipia too?" "No sir, no sir!" we repeated in a hilarious tone. "Yes, yes! sometimes R. Cipia too," said he smilingly. At this remark, we all burst into laughter. He kept on staring and smiling at us. For a few minutes the environment of the class-room echoed with laughter.

Then there was silence. He began the lecture again.

As a City Personality:

Dr. R.C. Prasad was a popular personality of Bhagalpur. The people of Bhagalpur knew him and loved him in different ways. He was magnanimous and co-operative. He helped so many persons of the city. He produced a number of scholars and made the career of so many students.

In his conversational talk, he used four languages with local dialects. He used English while imparting lectures, Hindi with Hindi speaking people, Bhojpuri and Magahi with Bhojpuri and Magahi speaking people.

He was a scholar, Professor and Pro-Vice-Chancellor of T.M. Bhagalpur University. But above all, he was a nice gentleman. The people of Bhagalpur still remember him.

His personal life was very fashionable. He ever looked smart. He wore beautiful and costly dresses made of printed cloth. He went to the department everyday in a changed dress. He put on a costly platinum-coated, big framed spectacle with a distinct look.

He wore on his wrist a beautiful watch with a golden chain and on his fingers some coral, moon and diamond rings. His curly hair tumbled in a style that gave him a persuasive look. His face had glaze and gleam that he had developed by yoga. To all appearances, he was a persuasive personality.

As a Writer:

The most important thing about him is that besides being a scholar and voracious reader, he was an arduous writer. He was a man of pen and paper. He was fond of a good pen and paper and worked with them as friends. This was his unique quality. A writer is always in search of a good pen; he, therefore, had a number of good pens that always decked the upper pocket of his shirt or coat.

He had written a number of books including novels and translations. But his two books earned him name and fame. *Early British Travellers in India* is his research work, for which his name has been referred to and a few lines have been quoted in *The Concise Cambridge History of English Literature.* His next striking book is the English translation of the *Sri Ramcharitamanas*, a great Hindi epic by Goswami Tulsidas, which also earned him name and fame. The Publisher of this translated book, Motilal Banarasi Das loved him much; and, therefore, told him to let the book remain on the royalty basis; but he considered if its royalty would be more profitable than the selling of the manuscript. He had some doubt about getting full royalty. He therefore, sold out the manuscript perhaps for seventy five thousand only. He was very much happy to get a lump-sum heavy amount. But when orders for its supply before it was published, reached the publishing firm, from many Manas Societies of Asian countries, and as Dr. Prasad was informed about the orders for its supply; he repented for committing a big mistake of selling it.

As a Sadhak:

A very few people must be knowing that Dr. R.C. Prasad was not only a Professor and writer, but also a *sadhak.* He devoted his particular time in *sadhana. Sadhana* was the part of his routine life. Once I went to see him, I found him doing *pranayam.*

He lived a bachelor's life in Parwati Muhalla of Bhagalpur which was near the P.G. Department of English. He had sufficient time for reading and writing. He wrote articles and research papers.

He spent his surplus time in *sadhana.* To him, reading and writing also were *sadhana.* He had achieved his goal in this discipline also.

Besides all these, he practised everyday meditation. Yoga (breath-controlling) and *sirshasan* (standing on the head).

He must have learnt such *sadhana* by joining Acharya Rajanish; for, he had joined the Acharya's *ashram* for some time. He liked the philosophy of the Acharya and wanted to practise it in his life.

Another source of his interest in *sadhana* was his meeting Dr. Ram Khelawan Rai, a Professor of Hindi at B.N. College, Patna. Professor Rai also practised yoga. He had contact with some *yogi* or *tantrik*. To a great extent, Dr. Prasad must have been motivated by Professor Rai. Both were then the teachers of Patna University.

I cannot say exactly, but perhaps in 1970-71, Dr. Ram Khelawan Rai went to Muzaffarpur for some work; he stayed for one day at my residence in Khabara road. Then I was a student at Muzaffarpur, and lived in Khabara road, together with Professor Siya Ram Rai.

Professor Ram Khelawan Rai talked to us, about *sadhana*. I saw him the next morning, doing *pranayam*; as when we talked together, he often talked about Dr. R.K. Sinha and Dr. R.C. Prasad.

In summer, not regularly but sometimes Dr. Prasad went to take bath in the Ganges. One day, he was sitting on the bank of the Ganges and watching the view. In the mean time, a stranger who had applied the Ganges soil utterly over his body from head to toe suddenly and surprisingly appeared before him. As soon as Dr. Prasad's eyes fell on the stranger, he was startled and dismayed. The stranger folded his palms and said to him, "I am Parma Sir! But he was silent and was looking at him." The stranger repeated, "I am Parma Nand, Sir! Parma Nand!" I am the student of sixth year English.

"O! it's you!" he said.

"Yes, Sir."

"What an awful look you have made! I thought, some ghost has stood before me", he said. "No, Sir! Just as that!" the stranger said and smiled. He further said, "Sir! I have come to tell you something." "Yes, you may" he permitted him.

The stranger said, "Sir! whenever I go to see you at your residence, a teacher does not let me see you. I have returned several times disappointedly. Have you permitted him not to let anyone meet you, Sir? Am I not your student? May I not see you? May I not tell you my problems?"

He heard him patiently and said, "It's his bad habit. It's his habit. He has no right to prohibit my students from meeting me. I don't like his such dirty habit. You may come and see me. Nobody can disturb you now."

The stranger felt a relief getting assurance and consolation. He went away to have bath. After his going, he took bath in the immaculate water of the Ganges. With every dip he felt himself afresh. Such an experience, I heard him while he was giving a talk on Acharya Rajnish's philosophy.

R.C. Prasad: Poetics of Experience

Mr. Rohit Ranjan *

A man's life of any worth is a continual allegory.

—John Keats

Ram Chandra Prasad also known at various stages in his *bildung* as Swami Anand Vitaraga, R.C. Maxwell, or simply by his initials as RCP was a towering and formidable figure at home in Rajendra Nagar, Patna during my formative years in the 80's and early 90's. As far as my memory goes back in time to the mid 80's, I was fortunate enough to have witnessed the critical years of Dr. Prasad's growth as an erudite scholar of literatures in English and Hindi, both as a grandson as a precocious initiate into the pleasures of literature. As I reminisce, we were all at awe of his overall personality, a significant part of which was his impeccable *modus vivendi* – a lifestyle bulwarked by a strict regimen of Yoga and assiduous studies. The way he used to synthesize personal decorum, style and fashion (e.g. his wardrobe consisting of innumerable suits, shoes, watches, pens, ties et al which he would don for office reminds one of the figure of the literary Dandy in the early 19th century London, Paris and Berlin, famous among whom were Wilde, Swinburne, Pater, Baudelaire, etc.) with a very modernist mind and body controlling routines such as yogic exercises and long hours of diligent scholarly study of the vast collection of books in his personal library was not only awe-inspiring for me as a kid but it was exemplary to see a polymath like granddad at work. If dandies were sometimes celebrated in revolutionary terms: self-created men of consciously designed personality, radically breaking with past traditions and Baudelaire wrote about them as having "no profession other than elegance...no other status, but that of cultivating the idea of beauty in their own persons.... The dandy must aspire to be sublime without interruption; he must live and sleep before a mirror," in RCP's case it was not a dandyism and scholarship that broke with tradition but it was more on the lines of what Holden Furber said about him in Journal of Asian Studies commenting on his *Early English Travelers in India* (Doctoral dissertation at Edinburgh University first published in 1965, MLBD): "As a university teacher of English, he is thoroughly at home in Shakespear's England; as an Indian, he is equally at home in his own past..." In his personality and his writings RCP tried to combine qualities that could be as diverse and yet close in same ways as in Sanskrit and Western poetics and epistemologies. His thin, handsome framework and scholarly mien, a broad furrowed head and impeccable sartorial style matched by his wide scholarship and incredible writing style (both in English and Hindi) would make him look no less than a *rishi, tapasvi* or a sage towards the end of his life.

I can clearly recall how in the mid-80's while translating what many consider to be his magnum opus – Tulsidasa's Ramacharita-manas, Prof. Prasad would shut himself like a hermit from all of us and be engrossed in studies for hours on end for almost two years. He would at best devote around 8-10 hours in a day to reading and writing almost all his life which in consequence swelled up his oeuvre to a considerable extent, leaving behind him a large body of work including critical books and essays on literature and history, novels, short-story collections, numerous scholarly articles and translations, compiled anthologies of poetry, comparative literary monographs, course-books, etc. During the late 80's till his retirement from a post of Principalship of Patna College, Head of Department English, Patna University in'90 I have early memories of granddad waking up early in the morning to go for a brisk walk around the peaceful environs of the local stadium and then after returning home follow it up with Yoga at home. During his sabbatical years and the years following retirement Dr. Prasad would hardly meet anyone and devote his time to finishing off work at breakneck speed like a Trojan. Until I became his amanuensis on a couple of books (*Ambedkarism, A Preface to Ambedkarism*) in 1991-92, I would often get a chance to take a glimpse of his sage like isolation in our first floor study-room, bringing refreshments for him off and on. Surrounded by a sea of books, dressed in pristine white *dhoti* and *kurta* (his usual home wear which was a complete antithesis to his public personal) I saw him sometimes ensconced on a sofa or writing with his Mont Blanc pen on the tall upright desk newly gifted to him by his students. No wonder he could complete a score of books in such a short span of his life marred by diabetes mellitus. He was to undertake the translation of *The Mahabharata* before his untimely demise.

Though I could not attend any of his lectures during his lifetime, I was fortunate enough to hear him on a few occasions outside the University. I succinctly remember the piquant brilliance of his talk on the History of Ideas, Faith and Religion at the local Bahai faith centre in Rajendra Nagar, Patna. It was a breathtaking display of philosophical oratory which lasted almost three hours, during which Dr. Prasad seemed possessed as if by Goddess Saraswati herself, sweating profusely at the end of the lecture. On a couple of occasions I heard him give a talk on All India Radio too – once it was in English and another time it was in Magahi! Later, I got to know from the members of the family that he used to give talks on various literary subjects on the radio for a long time and granddad himself told me once that his expertise extended in reading Old and Middle English, Latin, French, Sanskrit, Braj, Avadhi, Magahi, besides modern Hindi and English. He added that his spoken French was not so good any more because of desuetude.

Often I would eavesdrop on Prof. Prasad's expatiating on a wide range of various literary and non-literary topics to his students in his study room or in the living room at home: from Latin Poetics, Homer, Virgil; Horace and Longinus to his medieval favorites like Chaucer and the epic poet of Stuart England John Milton. The Bible, Lawrence, Hindi poetry and criticism, myth, political history of Bihar and India were his other preferred topics for speaking about at length. On many occasions I accompanied him with other students during his frenetically fast paced evening walks to the Moinul Haq Stadium where he would like Aristotle incarnate a peripatetic philosopher declaim to his students trailing him all around the circumference of the basketball court, his comparative views on the writings of Maithilisharan Gupta, Jayashankar Prasad, Dinkar, Nirala, Surdasa, Virgil, Dante, Milton, Shakespeare and the lives of great political personalities of Bihar such as Sri Krishna Sinha; contemporary politics, etc.

Since this is only a reminiscence of my grandfather Ram Chandra Prasad, I would refrain from commenting on the nuances of his scholarship and his critical and fictional corpus here. It is also beyond the scope of this essay to attempt anything beyond a mere sketch of his personality as I remember it, as I believe a life such as his genuinely deserves a monograph or a detailed biography of sorts. As I now sift through his published books and scattered essays and stories, I can discern a journey of an artist/critic and his dispersal of the self in the books and the essays that he wrote and the traces that he left behind through an art of living itself. Prof. Prasad wrote in his article "Art and Experience" (1976) while he was the Pro-Vice-Chancellor Bhagalpur University:

> One of the many perennial problems of aesthetics is the interaction of art and experience. The aesthetic aspect of the problem lies not so much in the artist's mode of experiencing as in his dealing with his experience in terms of art. All great artists, all creative geniuses, have only one aim and purpose, namely to express the actual sensation of life as they themselves experience it. They are beings who convey through their art the felt intricacy of their existence and who know that no part of life must need be barred as inartistic, that nothing in mature experience is too sublime or too sordid, too remote or too commonplace to serve as material for art... The artist's sensibility is of a special sort; it is as T.S. Eliot says in another context, "a finely perfected medium in which special, or very varied, feelings are at liberty to enter into new combinations." It is the poet's special sensibility as well as the unifying power of his imagination that enable him to amalgamate disparate experience and distinguish him from ordinary men. Whereas the ordinary man's experience, says Eliot, is chaotic, irregular, and fragmentary, the poet's experience is not. When the former falls in love, or reads Spinoza, the two experiences do not combine with each other, or with the noise of the typewriter or the smell of cooking. In the mind of the poet, Eliot continues, these experiences are always forming new wholes... Experience for Henry James is also ability and power, such cluster of gifts as the power to guess the unseen from the seen, to trace the implication of things, to judge the whole piece by the pattern etc. Experience in this sense is just another word for imagination, but it is not with "never limited" experience that the artist is concerned. He has to unify this cluster of gifts into an experience, into vital, creative experience...The artist not only transmutes ideas into sensations and experience or "takes in more every minute than his duller companion," he also clarifies his sensations though some conscious and explicit pattern and gives them a sequence and development. Our fantasies and dreams, our

> love and hate, are all brought under the discipline of some deliberate, logical and practical pattern...

Digging deep in the "lake" of the chronology of the work that Prof Prasad has left behind (37 works in 98 publications in 4 languages and 1,108 library holdings as WorldCat Identities lists on the Internet), one can also discern a deliberate design and a logical pattern emerge which alludes to the subtle traces of his self scattered around like "a heap of broken images" in a portrait gallery consisting of travellers, outsiders, preachers, saints, conmen, litterateurs, mythic figures (esp. in his novella *Udar Majhe and* short story collections *Nangi Dharti and Ek our Kissa Kursi Ka)* and finally the supreme hero Lord Rama. As I look systematically now at not only the man I knew but what essentially he has left behind beyond personal fond memories – *his works* – lucid and distinct phases of his life emerge and coalesce together in an interesting manner – as a flamboyant reader of English Literature in the early 50's, as a student and traveller in Edinburgh and England looking back at the nation though the lens of obscure travelogues written by early English travellers; returning back to India and writing his complex treatise in Hindi called *"Adhunika Hindi alocana para Pascatya prabhava"*; like a Beat poet and a counterculture figure (one thinks of Allen Ginsberg, Gary Snyder, etc. here) taking part in "Rajneesh Religion of Experience" and writing on zen, mysticism, sex and super-consciousness; emerging out of the atmosphere of the commune and ending it with a satirical novel called *The Mahatma;* writing about the history of Bihar (NBT) and great political personalities like Karpoori Thakur, Shri Krishna Sinha, Ambedkar etc; a final phase market by what one can call his Bhakti period – the translation of Tulsidasa's *Ramacharitmanasa* and other vedic texts on Hindu Samskaras. As Prof Prasad would write in his book *Literary Criticism in Hindi 1976* about *rasa* theory and the rise of the *Dhvani* school:

> According to Anandavardhana, all good poetry has two meanings, the direct or the expressed and the suggested or the unexpressed. The unexpressed or the suggested part, which is distinctly linked up with the expressed and which is developed by a peculiar process of suggestion (*vyanjana*), is regarded as the "soul" or essence of poetry.

When I was in my teens in the late 80's grandfather used to say that I may not understand the meaning of what he was writing about at that stage of my life and that I would fully grasp it's import when I grow up. Now as I go through his writings, I can sense a similar "*vyanjana*" expressed subtly and strewn across his works. It requires scholarly work worth thousands of pages to understand the significance of the journey and progress of an artist critic and it is surely beyond the scope of this fragment. At the same time, his positions on literature and criticism open up problematic areas on what constitutes modernism. As a student of literature myself, I am also amazed at the fact how Prof. Prasad would completely ignore the latest developments in "knowledge" in the west after New Criticism – namely Structuralism, Post-Structuralism, Postmodernism, Post-Colonialism etc., clinging to his own version of a Comparative criticism between Eastern and Western canons and a sort of "artistic self-purging" being immersed in *Bhakti rasa* that the work of Tulsidasa's afforded. That was also the only recorded music I ever heard with him – the verses from the *Ramacharitamanasa*. (Television and recorded music being almost banned in his presence! Although he was fond of classic cinema and early film music, in retrospect I can sense his bafflement at the cultural industry of the 80's which was peddling a major chunk of trash. I remember him laughing at the inanity of a song *Tu tu tu Tara* when some local loudspeaker or TV at home would blare it out!) Although he was familiar with the works of novelists like Hesse, Hamsun, Mann, John Barth, Henry Miller, Sartre, Camus (I was really fortunate to have their works lying in our home library) and other modern writers, he chose not to write on them instead encouraging his students to undertake research work on them. When in Class 10th I picked up "Topic of Capricorn" by Henry Miller from his library – a book considered to be the Bible of the Beats, full of dissident behaviour and explicit language, *baba* did not disapprove of it, but when I started rattling off words like "cosmococci" learnt from the book he asked me not be a "pedant". I succinctly remember him asking me to find a book called "History of Western Morals" written by Crane Brinton from among his huge private collection, a few days before his death. Michel Foucault having not made it to the shelves till then and many an author out-shelved by the Bhakti poets, one can discern a life lived according to the principles of Indian philosophy albeit constantly supplemented by philosophical discourses concerning sexuality and morality in the West.

As I dwell in grandfather's fond memories now, it is difficult to separate the man from the scholar that he was and for me his persona as a writer/teacher always overshadows that of his role as a grandfather – a loving one that he was! I was blessed to have him as my first teacher at home and perhaps the best one I ever had. Although it is difficult to ascertain his influence after about 20 years of his demise, his students all across the world would not have remained untouched by his life which seems in retrospect to me to be an exemplum of many intricate modernist strands that Dr. Prasad was trying to synthesize: style/fashion/aristocratic decorum vs. regimented disciplinary hard work and intellectual labour; ethical living vs. aristocratic sensuality (with his Lawrencian outlook on life Dr. R.K. Sinha, his guru whom he was really fond of, is often seen as it's prime personification). Many of these strands require unraveling by his students and contemporaries alike. A glimpse of his views on the university, where he was an able administrator for a long time, can be seen in the introduction to his book on Bihar Kesari *Shri Krishna Sinha: A Biography:*

> ...many of his contemporaries, acknowledged readers, politicians and thinkers assigned to the university a purely intellectual function. Shri Krishna Sinha pondered over this vexing question of the role of the universities and came to the conclusion that in a static society, a university may well limit its activities to the intellectual sphere alone, and become a placid, isolated centre of learning. A university worth its name shall have to play a different role altogether in a society which is in ferment and in which all values, moral and social, are in the melting pot. With the foresight of a mature thinker, intelligent and insightful, he could apprehend how the human race was threatened with self-annihilation through nuclear weapons and was groping for a way out of this grave impasse. In such a situation a university cannot lead an isolated existence and devote itself solely to the pursuit of knowledge, shutting its eyes to what is happening around it.

Likewise, the fond memories of my grandfather come to me in the guise of his many voices, somewhat akin to Stephen Deadalus in Jayce's Ullysses. Besides knowing him as a great human being, trailblazing personality and scholar, an irrepressible writer and enigmatic teacher, his persona emerges from the scores of books he wrote in many guises as a traveller, an outsider, a mythic hero, a sage, a seer. A day before his death on 5th August '93 (I was about to become his chosen amanuensis!) he dictated me an article on the Theosophical Society of India. We could not complete the note that day and I was to join him the next day. The note remains incomplete to this day but I could see a closure not only mortal – of his life – but also one which was profoundly spiritual – traversing many a rigorous intellectual phase to a final ablution in the Holy Lake of the acts of Rama.

Works Cited

Prasad, R.C. "Art and Experience." *Indian Philosophical Quarterly*: Volume 4, No3, (Ed.) S.S. Barlingay, Rajendra Prasad (April 1977): 275-288.

—. *Literary Criticism in Hindi.* Meerut: Sarita Prakashan,1976.

Prasad, R.C.; Sinha, A.K. *Shri Krishna Sinha: A Biography.* New Delhi: N.K. Enterprises, 1987.

* Mr. Rohit Ranjan is the grandson of Dr. R.C. Prasad.

Section V

Articles

Preface to the Second Edition of Ram Chandra Prasad's *Early English Travellers in India*

Prof. George Shepperson

> And up from India glances
> The silver sail of dawn. —A.E. HOUSMAN

This preface to the welcome re-publication of Professor Ram Chandra Prasad's fascinating book is written four centuries after Francis Drake, the Elizabethan seaman, set off in 1577 on his famous voyage which was to make him the first Englishman to sail round the world, and thirty years after the British left India in 1914. It is a happy accident that this preface should be written at the time of these two anniversaries because they indicate the long sequence of years which has witnessed the rise and decline of British interest in and influence upon the Indian sub-continent.

It is usually considered that the British period of Indian history begins in 1757 with the battle of Plassey. But the interest of individuals from England in the problems and prospects of India began almost two centuries before this. It is, therefore, appropriate that Professor Prasad's book should start with an engaging study of the first Englishman known to have settled in India: the Jesuit priest, Father Thomas Stephens, who made an important contribution to literature in the Marathi language.

T.S. Eliot once said that the aim of the introducer of a book "should be to arouse the curiosity of a possible new reader." I can imagine no better way of arousing the curiosity of a potential reader of this book than that of drawing his attention to the unique career of Father Thomas Stephens who was, as Professor Prasad declares, "the greatest English poet to write in an oriental language." Since the first edition of Professor Prasad's book appeared in 1965, Stephens has not ceased to interest those fortunate enough to learn of his remarkable career. For example, Dr. M.F. Chamberlain of the University of Wales, in a book entitled *Britain and India: the Interaction of Two Peoples* (Newton Abbot, 1974) to which the reader may be referred for a succinct description of the whole four centuries of British-Indian relations, also feels the fascination of Father Stephens and notes that he "may have been a Jesuit priest who left his country for conscience's sake, but his father was a leading London merchant." How, then, did such a man come to write a classic of Marathi literature? The reader who wishes to know should turn to Professor Prasad's perceptive account of him. This is not the only valuable service that Professor Prasad performs for the understanding of the first half-century of the interaction of the Indian and the British peoples. Through a scholarly and sympathetic but, very properly, unsentimental study of the significant English travellers in India between 1579 and 1630, he reveals the many strands, some in glowing colours and others in darker hues, which are interwoven into the ties that have bound and still, in many ways, bind the great and ancient civilisations of the Indian sub-continent with the smaller and shorter civilisations of the British Isles. He combines the skills and resources of the historian, the literary critic and the student of comparative literature and languages to demonstrate what we may learn of these two countries from the often idiosyncratic but always rich prose of Englishmen abroad in the ages of Queen Elizabeth I and King James I. I, too, was an English traveller in India – but during the Second World War, three and a half centuries after the period which Professor Prasad examines in this study. How I wish that his book had been available to me in those days! It would have helped me to understand better than I did then my own countrymen abroad, their virtues and their faults, in the dusk of the Raj; and it would have assisted me in my appreciation of many of the multi-faceted problems of India, with their roots deep in the past. I grew to appreciate them better, however, when, ten years after I returned to Britain from India, I had the privilege of observing and learning from the eagerness and energy which Ram Chandra Prasad, representative of the dawn of the new India, threw into his study of the origins of the British and Indian connection. With the late Regius Professor of rhetoric and English literature at the University of Edinburgh, W.L. Renwick, I acted as supervisor of his doctoral dissertation from which this book has grown. I know that Professor Renwick would have been as pleased as I am to see it in print again. It is a notable contribution to the understanding of two cultures; and I commend it warmly to my own countrymen as well as to Professor Prasad's.

August, 1977

Tulsidas in the Global Context*

Prof. Sidheshwar Prasad

In India many Professors of English have written in Indian languages, too. We have examples of Prakash Chandra Gupta, Harivansh Rai Bachchan, Raghupati Sahay Firaq, Ram Vilas Sharma – all English Professors, who wrote either in Hindi or Urdu. Dr. Kalim Ahmad, Head of the Dept. of English, Patna University, besides writing a book, *Psycho-Analysis and Literary Criticism* in English wrote two other books on Urdu poetry and Urdu prose, and thus gave a new height to Urdu criticism just as Ram Vilas Sharma an eminent English Professor did the same to Hindi literary criticism by writing many critical books in Hindi.

Prof. Ram Chandra Prasad, Professor and Head of the Dept. of English, Patna University has added a new dimension to the tradition of Prof. Kalim Ahmad by translating *Shri Ramcharitmanas* of Goswami Tulsidas from Awadhi into Hindi and English simultaneously. It's a daring work because unlike in the European tradition, translation work is not considered very respectable in India. The English translator of Dante's *Divine Comedy*, Lawrence Bunyan enjoys immense respect. An American poet, Siarde produced a new translation of Dante's work after 23 years of relentless effort. How is it possible to have the taste of world literature without translation?

There is need to appreciate this translation by Prof. Ram Chandra Prasad from this viewpoint. The success and popularity of this translation is evident from the fact that after its second edition in 1990, it underwent many reprints in 1994, 1999, 2005 and 2006. Now it has occupied the rank of the hitherto best translation of *Shri Ramcharitmanas.*

In his well thought and well-expressed 12 pages of Introduction, Prof. Prasad has deeply meditated on presenting the background of Tulsidas in the light of the devotional cult (*Bhakti Andolan*). Here I would like to mention one point. Madhusudan Saraswati was a contemporary of Tulsidas and he also used to live in Kashi. He was the last commentator on *the Gita* in the tradition of Shankaracharya and was held in great esteem. Today very few people will be found When Gandhiji went to Kingsway camp to meet the refugees in 1947, there could be found nobody familiar with the name of Akbar. But every body knew Tulsidas, and thousands of them used to recite *Shri Ramcharitmanas* and *Shri Hanuman Chalisa* everyday.

In order to evaluate *Shri Ramcharitmanas* in the global context, the writer Prof. Prasad has presented the facts after making a comparative study of the works of Tulsidas with those of Homer, Virgil, Shakespeare, Milton, Goethe and Dante. He has also considered the opinions of the critics and commentators of these great poets of the European tradition. At the end of his Introduction he quotes from the essay of T.S. Eliot entitled *Goethe as the Sage.* By this quotation the readers will come to know that in the Indian tradition a poet is considered a sage, and this attitude has been very strong in the literary and religious tradition of India. Although Eliot always considered Dante as a greater poet than Shakespeare in the western tradition, yet he used the epithet "sage" only for Goethe because Goethe not only innovated the first world epic but also became himself an embodiment of world poetry. Cirtius in his *Essays on European Literature* considered Goethe the topmost point of the European tradition in which Homer, Virgil, Shakespeare, Milton and Dante–all get assimilated. Goethe's house became a cultural pilgrimage of Europe.

In the literary criticism of Ram Chandra Babu, Tulsidas occupies the same place as Dante has in the criticism of Eliot, Goethe in the criticism of Cirtius and Shakespeare in the criticism of Herald Bloom. On the interpretation and evaluation of Literature, I tried to answer the basic question about criticism, and wrote (Bihar Rashtrabhasa Parishad, Patna) that at every stage the basis of our judgement always ought to be value-based. And literary criticism is its magnified and purified form. Man's basic values are determined by the place, time and action/situation in which he lives. North India, especially the contemporary India of Tulsidas demands from him a Saviour whom he presented in *Shri Ramcharitmanas,* and the presentation was so dignified that his epic took the place of Valmiki's *Ramayan* (Valmiki became Tulsi: *Valmiki Tulsi Bhayo,* वाल्मीकि तुलसी भयो and even today the readers prostrate before this Saviour hero. Ramchandra Babu has translated the epic with the same depth as Tulsidas had composed it. It is obvious from the Introduction of the book that Tulsidas is not only his ideal but his devotional centre as well, and with this he was able to reach Ram successfully.

Tulsidas was a devotional poet – a devotee as well as a poet. Kabir, Soor, Mira, Nanak, Dadoo, Raidas were all devotional poets.

The specific characteristic of Tulsidas was that he made the Saviour Ram his hero who was born to reestablish right consensus (*Dharm* धर्म) after killing the demons. Tulsidas was not a devotee of the flute-player Shri Krishna but of the bow-holder Shri Ram (Tulsi will bow his head only when you hold the bow and the arrow in your hands: *Tulsi mastak tab nave dhanush ban lo hath* (तुलसी मस्तक तब नवै धनुष बाण लो हाथ). Tulsi's Ram always holds the bow and the arrow even when he is in the sitting posture(*Kar kamlan dhanushayak pherat* कर कमलन धनुसायक फेरत) always alert to safeguard righteousness, always in his garb of a warrior hero.

Tulsi's Ram despite getting incarnated in the human form, is able to make Brahma, Vishnu and Shambhu dance at his tune (*Vidhi hari shambhu nachavan hare*) – not formless but in the form. In his Introduction Prof. Ram Chandra Prasad has referred to that *Advait* which is the joint form of Tulsi's *Nirakar* and *Sakar,* and which is always instrumental in punishing the unjust raising his hands. He pleaded to make the earth free from demons (*Nishicharhin karaun mahi, bhuj uthai pran kinh* निशिचरहीन करौं गही भुज उठाई प्रण कीन्ह)

Such a devotional attitude of Tulsidas is as per the *Vedas.* It is said in *Vrihadaranyak Upanishad* that there are two forms of Brahma – formless and with form. When Acharya Ramchandra Shukla objected to the devotion to the formless, Poet Jay Shankar Prasad referred to this observation of his *Vedas* in support of his viewpoint. Actually speaking, Tulsidas was not only a devotee and a poet but also a literary creator and that is because his relevance in the mass community is undoubted even today. It is in this light that Dr. Grierson had declared Tulsidas as the greatest mass-leader of Northern India. Here it is proper to consider the view of Chanakya that one who knows the world and masses is all-knowing. Tulsidas was on the highest pedestal of devotions. From that peak point of poetic vision he observed the actions of Ram in the world, and he expressed the same in *Shri Ramcharitmanas.* This is the basis of his vision and faith, the power of his devotion.

Acharya Ram Chandra Shukla's critical analysis of Tulsi literature is chiefly based on his observation of the sentiments with which the poetry of Tulsidas used to be recited in every village and every household. This critical approach is still in vogue today.

Dr. Ram Chandra Prasad has given a global context to this study by-ranking the poetry of Tulsidas with the chief epics of the Western tradition and also by giving his comparative observation.

The Indian tradition of literary criticism is not only different from its Western counterpart but also more enriched, and that is because T.S. Eliot had to use the epithet of Indian tradition, "sage" for a poet. It is the place of "sage" at which the voice of the poet becomes the voice of the Age. In the Indian tradition Valmiki, Vyas, Kalidas, Tulsidas and Jayshankar Prasad became such poets whose relevance was as much in their respective age as it is today and it will remain so in future.

At the end of his Introduction Prof. Ram Chandra Prasad has briefly said that the Ramayan of Tulsidas gives inspiration to everybody – be he rich or poor, urbanised or villager – to live a peaceful life and it enables him to morally and spiritually elevate himself. For this there is need for the empathetic Ram, not brutal savage aggressors like Ravana, Tamurlaine, Alexander or Napoleon.

In the Introduction the writer has observed that the importance of Tulsidas is not based on *Shri Ramcharitmanas* alone but on the totality of all his works as it is found in the context of Shakespeare, Goethe and Dante.

Tulsidas like Goethe, has variety, abundance and unity. If there is no unity (of place, time and action) along with variety and abundance, then the work remains as one like Chaucer's *Canterbury Tales.* Aristotle considered unity as an essential characteristic of Drama. From the Indian view-point, if there is no unity, then the aesthetic taste can never be enjoyed.

Kush and Lav used to recite *the Ramayan* of Valmiki at the hermitages of sages, and finally they sang it at the conference Hall of Shri Ram, with the result that everybody's heart, even the heart of the washerman melted at the injustice meted out to Sita. *The Ramayan* of Tulsi of the middle stage, and so it has the acceptability of both as read and heard poetry. People have been reciting it in solitary seclusion, and it is also the subject of discourse at social gatherings. It is a strong band of socialization. Although this tradition is weakening, yet the popularity of *Ramayan* is intact. The latest example is late Ramanand Sagar's TV serial of *Ramayana* which became so popular that the crowd of audience at the discourse of orators shrank too much.

In his Introduction the writer has also said that Tulsidas was a saint with the foresight of vision. Tulsidas understood well the needs and aspirations of his Age, and the impact of Kaliyug on them. He had full faith in chanting the name of Ram. He considered it the panacea for all sorts of ailments. So he wrote that Valmiki changed his name of Ram in the reverse order, and as a result, became Brahm like. When the bridge was being constructed on the sea, the stone that Ram himself threw got sunk but the stone-pieces that monkeys and bears threw after inscribing the name of Ram on them, started floating on the sea-surface, and thus the bridge was constructed. So Tulsidas has written that the name of Ram is greater than Brahm Ram himself.

If man has full faith in the name of Ram, he can cross the sea of worldly life, and attain never ending bliss.

Tulsidas says, *kalp bhed haricharit suhaye, bhakti anek munisan gaye,* (कल्प भेद हरि चरित सुहाए, भक्ति अनेक मुनीसन गाये). In every age Ram takes incarnation, performs various actions and poets sing about him. So Tulsidas says again that God (Hari) is endless and so are His stories: *Hari anant hari katha ananta.*

Dr. Ram Chandra Prasad has compared *Sri Ramcharitmanas* of Tulsi with the epic of Italian poet Virgil (BC 70-19) in which the aspirations of the age have got expressed. Virgil made Rome the hero of his epic but Tulsi made Ram the hero of his Age. Just as Virgil's epic *Aenid* influenced the education and literature of Rome, so the poetry of Tulsidas influenced the society and literature of India.

It is the straightforward comment of Prof. Ram Chandra Prasad that whereas the gods of Homer do not hesitate to commit unnatural offences, Tulsi's gods are morally flawless. It is the specific feature of Indian tradition which has been upheld by Tulsidas.

Just as Dante was the inheritor of the tradition of Roman poets and the Bible, so was Tulsidas of the tradition of the Valmiki Ramayan and the Puranas. The fullness of the epic Age was prevalent in the works of both Dante and Tulsidas. Both had full command over their language and with their poetic power they brought it to the climax. Neo-Italian language could never again attain the fullness of Dante nor could Awadhi that of Tulsi.

In the comparative study of Indian tradition and the western tradition, it is often ignored that in the former the moral value which is borne by the creation is called *Dharma.* In the *Rigveda* it is said that the wrong-doers cannot cross the path of the world (*Anritasya pantha na taranti duskritas* Rig. 9.73.6 (अनृतस्य पंथा न तरन्ति दुष्कृत्ः)

In *the Gita* the same has been expressed as *Vinashaya cha duskritam* (to destroy the evils). Tulsidas upheld the same by saying *Jab jab hoyi dharam ki hani* (जब-जब होहिं धरम की हानि). If the European tradition lacks such an intact consciousness about the form of Righteousness, how can it be found with Homer, Virgil and Shakespeare? Dante accepted the explanation of Christianity by Thomas Acquinas (1225-1374) in *Summa Theology* (1265-1321) and made unembodied righteousness embodied in his epic. So he got a respectable place with both epic-readers and truth-seekers. Tulsidas besides upholding the Indian tradition of righteousness established the power of the name of Ram in the mind of everybody in such a forceful way that the lines of Tulsi's poetry have become an inseparable part of everyday life. Europe didn't have such a mass poet who could also be accepted as an Acharya of Righteousness.

In Dante we have Chaucer's narrative power, Shakespeare's dramatization and Milton's religiousness. If we include Homer and Virgil to this unity, it will become a greater unity, and such a greater unity is very easily perceived by the readers in the poetry of Tulsidas.

In the following poem composed by Mahatma Gandhi, Father of the Nation, righteousness befitting the age presents devotion in a new garb:

Prayer of a Servant

O! the ocean of humbleness
Dweller in the wretched cottage of a poor
in the beautiful country watered by the sweeper
Ganga, Yamuna and Brhamputra
help us to feel your presence everywhere
Give us receptiveness and open heart
Give us your meekness,
ability and aspiration to be
one with the people of India
O Lord! You come to help
Only when man negates his own self and surrenders to you
Bless us that we never get alienated from the people
whom we want to serve as servants and friends
Fill us with sacrifice, devotion and humbleness so that
We can understand and love this country more and more.

Valmiki's Ram appeared as Tulsidas's Ram, and the Ram of both took the incarnation as Mohandas in the modern age not as Lord but as a servant and this is the climax of non-dualism ("Advait"). So here I have quoted his full poem in which he offers his prayer as a servant because virtually he is the modern edition of Tulsi's Ram. Tulsidas wrote that sages make efforts for many lives but at the time of death the name of Ram doesn't come to their lips (*Janam janam muni jatan karahi ant Ram kahi avat nahi* जनम-जनम मुनि जतन कराही अंत राम कही आवत नाहीं). But this Gandhi was such a devout devotee of Ram that despite getting shot with three bullets in his chest, the name of Ram came from his lips twice. There is a line in Narsinh Mehta's song: *Ram namshu tali lagi, sakal tirath tena tanma re* रामनामशुं ताली लागी, सकल तीरथ तेना तनमां रे (When the mouth is locked with the name of Ram, all pilgrimages enter the body.). The same happened with Gandhiji. But what can be said about the person who doesn't want to open his eyes?

In the Introduction Prof. Ram Chandra Prasad has written that the "Advait Vedant" which Tulsidas has upheld in *Shri Ramcharitmanas* is the best possible explanation of this principle. Tulsidas accepted the "*Advait*" philosophy of Shankaracharya in which "*Maya*" plays an important role. Shankaracharya called it "Vivart." In the works of Tulsidas the playful actions of "*Maya*" are quite obviously seen. A great sage like Devarshi Narad getting overpowered by *Maya* wants to live a worldly life. Only Shiva, Hanuman and Bharat remain untouched by *Maya*. Lord Shiva is the Lord of Lords, and so He is an exception because He forms a part of triumvirate along with Brahma and Vishnu. Hanuman is such a staunch devotee of Ram that Maya is afraid of even his sight. Tulsidas has placed Bharat at a greater height than Ram. Ram says about Bharat that if Bharat were not born in the world, the entire righteousness of the earth world have met the dust (*Jo na janam jag hot Bharat ko, sakal dharma dhur dharani dharat ko* जो न जनम जग होत भरत को। सकल धरम धुर धरनि धरत को). In the whole of *Manas*, Bharat is the only ideal personality who dares to reject the suggestion of Kulguru Vashishtha. When he comes back to Ayodhya from his maternal place, Vashishtha asks him to accept the throne of Ayodhya after the demise of King Dasharath. Bharat calls Vashishtha a conscientious saint in whose hands all the intellect of the world is like a plum fruit. To Bharat, time is adverse and so Guru Vashishtha asks him to rule Ayodhya. Ram got victory over Lanka by the grace of Vashishtha, and Bharat disobeys Vashishtha because the latter has no devotion to Ram. And Tulsi had advised Mira who was tortured by Rana to take refuge at the feet of Ram. Bharat didn't see anything worthwhile in the world other than Ram. He is a symbol of *sevak* dharma (*Sab te sevak dharm kathora* सब ते सेवक धरम कठोरा).

No form of devotion (which has nine forms) can exist without dualism. Tulsi's devotion was the devotion of slavery to Ram. How can non-dualism (Advait) remain true? So Kabirdas said, " When I was, Hari wasn't. When Hari is, I amn't. I get submerged in Hari as a drop of water does into the ocean." जब मैं था तब हरि नहीं, जब हरि तब मैं नाहीं।

What Kabir means is the end of dualism. The path of Advait is the path of Intellect, which is called a sharp edge of blade in Uttarkand. So Kakbhusundi says to Garud that it is impossible to cross the ocean of worldly life without the devotion of slavery to Ram.

Today what we call moral path is actually the modern form of the "Rit" path mentioned in the Puranas. Ram is the moralistic ideal of the Indian tradition. Tulsi's Ram leads both men (of the world) and gods together. So he says repeatedly, *Lok hu ved na Jan upayu.* लोक हु वेद न जान उपाऊ) Morality is above both the world and Vedas, and it is called the "Rit" path, which is universal and can't be bypassed. Ram is established in this universal tradition even today. The ancient kings of Egypt used to be called Ram-1, Ram-2, Ram-3 etc. in 3000 B.C. Ram-charit (the action of Ram) is prevalent in South-East Asia in different forms. So Ram-charit by virtue of its morality has the same relevance in the modern age.

The Indian tradition believes in three types of world – "Bhuh", "Buvah", "Svah". भु:, भुव:, स्व: These three worlds are actually symbolic of three levels – physical, moral and spiritual. They are the worlds of demons ("danav"), men ("manav") and gods ("dev") respectively. Those who are bereft of morality and are mindful of the bodily pleasures only are demons. Men are those in whom moral consciousness has awakened. The gods are those who have attained the conscientious consciousness of the spirit. The Upanishads explain this classifications in different ways. *Kathopanishad's* Nachiketa has become a synonym of godhead because he developed the sense of the Absolute.

If man negates his self-consciousness, then he generates from the state of manhood to demonhood. But if he wants, he can attain godhead by his relentless efforts, preference and spiritual aspiration. By the truthful vigour and pursuit Yudhisthir attained Heaven with his physical body. *Na hi satyat paro dharmah* (न हि सत्यात् परो धर्मा:). There is no religion or righteousness above truth.

In the human society morality has developed because of the adherence to righteousness. No creature has the sensitivity concerning morality as man. Man sacrifices even his own life at the urge of morality.

In the modern age Mahatma Gandhi accepted Ram as an ideal for morality which is synonymous to truth. To uphold and safeguard the truth Dasharath sacrificed his life, and Ram made himself a live example of the highest degree of morality by establishing the truth for which even today people talk of Ram Rajya. In his Introduction Prof. Ram Chandra Prasad has laid considerable emphasis on this aspect to present Tulsidas in the global context.

Dr. Ram Chandra Prasad has written his Introduction keeping his foreign readers in mind; so the analysis, interpretation and evaluation of *Sri Ramcharitmanas* have all been done taking these readers into consideration. The way the work (analysis, interpretation and evaluation) has been done to globalize the whole context was never done before. The translation work is of the same standard as Fitzegerald's translation of Omar Khayam's Rubais which has been included in Palgrave's collection of poems, *Golden Treasury*.

Surdas has said that one who takes to the path of devotion has to relinquish both house and family. But in the devotional path of Tulsi, there is duty consciousness ("Karam Yog") which is rare in world literature. Tulsidas has said explicitly that one should perform one's duty with hands, and keep one's mind with Ram (the abode of compassion); *Kar so karm kariye vidhi nana, man rakhiye jah kripa nidhana* (कर सो कर्म करिय विधि नाना। मन राखिये जंह कृपा निधाना).

The "Triveni" like confluence of Devotion, Dutifulness and Intellect that Tulsidas has created gives the opportunity to the readers of every class for self-elevation. Dr. Ram Chandra Prasad has done a commendable job by presenting *Sri Ramcharitmanas* on the stage of the world literature in the global context.

* This essay was originally written in Hindi. It was translated by Dr. Indu Bhushan Sharma, Associate Professor of English, S. Sinha College, Aurangabad, Bihar

Dr. R.C. Prasad's *Ambedkarism*: Voice and Vision of Radical Sanity

Dr. J.P. Singh
Dr. Kalpana Sinha

Ambedkarism 1993 as an analysis of the vision of Baba Saheb B.R. Ambedkar is the voice of "Radical Sanity". Elizabeth Wurtzel in her book *Radical Sanity* just echoes the eternal "*mantra*" of any revolutionary radical change: "Always ask...... Freud, Marx, Einstein asked questions however debatable." (Wurtzel, intro.) Dr. R.C. Prasad's *Ambedkarism* is, in fact, a searching analysis of a revolutionary social ideology that asked questions, demolished toxic assumptions of oppressive Hinduism which had virtually forced generations of the Dalits to go braindead down the millennia without asking questions. The following blazing words – an outright rejection of the repressive architecture of Hinduism – underline the vision of this "Radical Sanity:"

1. "I shall have no faith in Brahma, Vishnu and Mahesh nor shall I worship them."
2. "I shall have no faith in Rama and Krishna who are believed to be incarnations of God nor shall I worship them."
3. "I shall not allow any ceremonies to be performed by Brahmins."
4. "I renounce Hinduism which is harmful for humanity and impedes the advancement and development of humanity because it is based on inequality, and adopt Buddhism as my religion." (IBA, p. 86)

The above-mentioned fiery "Negatives" like flaming Biblical injunctions are just four of the 22 historical vows of Baba Saheb B.R. Ambedkar. It was on 15 October, 1956 that Dr. Ambedkar had a mass religious conversion ceremony at Deeksha Bhoomi, Nagpur, Maharashtra. Possibly it was the largest religious conversion the world has ever witnessed. The total number of persons who had undergone the conversion to Buddhism was about 800000 (eight lakhs) in number. It was here in this conversion assembly that Dr. Ambedkar prescribed 22 vows for his followers as a form of directive guidelines to mark a complete severance of bond with Hinduism. These vows were aimed at liberating converts from superstitious wasteful and meaningless rituals which had supposedly led to pauperization and degradation of the masses down the ages. These 22 vows lead us back to Ambedkar in 1935 when he had, with agony in his soul and a gritty stamina in his voice, announced his resolution at least not to die as a Hindu. On October 13, 1935, ten thousand people had assembled at Yeola, a town about 35 miles from Nasik to attend the Bombay Presidency Depressed Classes Conference. Ambedkar presided over the Conference and in his speech lasting over an hour and a half he underlined the failure of the depressed communities in India to secure even elementary rights and a semblance of equality in the Hindu fold:

> Because we have the misfortune of calling ourselves Hindus, we are treated thus. If we were members of another faith, none would dare treat us so. Choose any religion which gives you equality of status and treatment. We shall repair our mistakes now. (IBA, p. 86)

The climactic point of his speech was his personal dramatic resolve to cut off the umbilical chord with the Hindu fold. Possibly it was a decision triggered by years of alienation and hostility experienced in the Hindu fold:

> I had the misfortune of being born with the stigma of an untouchable, because I had no control over it. However, I can assure you .... that I will not die a Hindu, for this is in my power.(Moon, p. 206)

In fact, the plaintive but the disillusioned angry thunder of his voice recalls the satirical denunciation of revolutionary *KABIR* who, in one of his poems, preferred to glorify himself with the traditional epithets of abuse and indignity which the Brahminic monolith of the yore had heaped upon the poor in means and low in caste. Addressing the Maya – the goddess of Illusion – Kabir reprimands her to seek out those who are high in caste and mighty in power, for what would she get in a pauper outcaste's household:

> *tun ghar Jahu hama:r behna: vish Lage tohar naina:*
> *tahan Jahu Jahan pat patambar, aradh chandan ghas lina:*
> *a:i hamare ka: karogi, ham tou Jat Kameena:*

(तूं घर जाहू हमार बहना, विष लागे तोहार नयना
तहाँ जाहु जहाँ पाट पटम्बर, अगर चंदन घस लीना
आई हमारे का करोगी हम तो जात कमीना।) (Dwivedi)

It is against this background of revolutionary socio-cultural upsurge that Ambedkarism as a conceptual ideological tool became as popular as Marxism, Maoism, Vedism or Islamism. During the last two decades of the 20th century analysis of the ideological components of Ambedkarism as a revolutionary philosophy of social restructuring gradually caught the fancy of social activists, academics and justice fraternity. If justice V.R. Krishna Iyer stands with his *The Dalit Future* on one end of the spectrum, Dr. R.C. Prasad with his *Ambedkarism* and *A Preface To Ambedkarism* along with Dr. Bindeshwar Pathak with his concrete action plans cover the other end of that spectrum. The duo hailing from Bihar, it needs to be underlined, have sought to set forth certain prominent tendencies in Ambedkar's writings as well as to highlight their socio-political implications. It is as a part of egalitarian radical social re-structuring and "shaping humanitarianism into a militant mould" that "Ambedkarism" as a concept can be appreciated in the right perspective. For V.R. Krishna Iyer the term "Ambedkarism" underlines, denotes and suggests "Group Justice" that implies a structured social architectural design based on justice and equality. (Iyer)

For Dr. R.C. Prasad, "Ambedkarism" as an ideological philosophy is a "militant"s technique of waging his struggle for the uplift of the untouchable Dalits of Society." (Prasad, p. ix) No wonder, he coins this expression "Ambedkarism" meaning thereby a radical activist and ideological Ambedkar who possesses the "non-negotiable quality of matchless courage and prodigious intellectual energy supportive of his value system." (Prasad, p. ix)

However, Dr. Prasad's definition of Ambedkar's radicalism modifies V.R. Krishna Iyer's assessment of Ambedkar as a "constructive politician and a compromising meliorist." (Iyer, p.102) Nonetheless, his academic conviction stays unimpaired when he affirms that a true "Ambedkarian" like the "Icon" himself would even remain a swordsman of social justice and a demolisher of *status quo ante* which denied even the recognition of human identity to a vast segment of Indian population.

Rejection of Hinduism as a suffocating poisonous gas chamber for the millions of so-called sub-castes and Dalits naturally led to Ambedkar's quest for an alternative. This alternative was Buddhism that had rejected Hinduism and its caste-ridden Brahminic elitism. Buddhism flashed with a magnetic pull on Ambedkar's consciousness as a philosophy, as a doctrine of worth in opposition to the doctrine of birth. Down the centuries all Upanishadic spiritual insights had degenerated into a hereditary theology of Brahminic elitism.

Courage, conviction and incisive clinical dissection were the hallmarks of Baba Saheb Ambedkar as a militant social revolutionary. No wonder, his comments on the Vedas, Manu, the oppressive caste hierarchy and on all the overt or covert protectors of the rotten stinking system sometimes grew bitter and pungent. He was virtually shattering the old icons and whether it was Gandhi or Jinnah mattered little to this swordsman. His following comments both on Gandhi and Jinnah reveal the underlying truth of his outspokenness:

> Politics in the hands of these two great men have become a competition in extravaganza. If Mr. Gandhi is known as Mahatma, Mr. Jinnah must be known as Qaid-I-Azam. If Gandhi has the Congress, Mr. Jinnah must have the Muslim League. If the Congress has a Working Committee, the Muslim League must have its Working Committee. The session of the Congress must be followed by a session of the League. If the Congress issues a statement, the League must also follow suit. If the congress passes a resolution of 17,000 words, the Muslim League's resolution must exceed by at least a thousand words. If the Congress President has a Press Conference, the Muslim League President must have his. When is all this to end? When is there to be a settlement? There are no near prospects. .... Never has there been such a deplorable state of bankruptcy of statesmanship as one sees in these two leaders of India. (Moon, p. 123)

The analysis of "Ambedkarism" as a philosophical ideology underlines Dr. Prasad's logical positivism – a naked exposure of the inconsistency and untenable illogicality of some of Hinduism's theological assumptions. The inconsistency of religious assumptions is reflected in Hinduism's two spiritualized mythical formulation. "*Aham*

Brahmasmi" (I am that Divine) and "*Tat Twam Asi*" (You, too, are the some). The illogical absurdity and inconsistency of this wonderful formulation lie in the total amnesia of the Brahminic Hindu mind in not practising the latter when it comes to interact with the Dalits in day to day practical life.

The analyst – the perceptive Ambedkarite in Dr. Prasad – naturally inclines him to echo the Dalit icon and repeat his haunting puzzle:

> Is there any society in the world which has *unapproachables* and unseeables ?.... The tragedy is that they have to be counted in millions, millions of untouchables, millions of criminal tribes, millions of Primitive Tribes ! One wonders whether the Hindu Civilization is Civilization or Infamy ! (Moon, pp. 219-20)

This questioning denunciation of Hindu inconsistency is naturally born out of Ambedkar's critical response to this dichotomy between "*Aham Brahmasmi*" and "*Tat Twam Asi.*" Ambedkar's questioning is repeated, re-echoed by the writer of *Ambedkarism.* He quotes and requotes Ambedkar: If all persons are parts of Brahma then all are equal and all must enjoy the same liberty which is what democracy means. And Ambedkar's bewildering puzzle keeps rolling on and on:

> But how could they support inequality between the Brahmin and the Shudra, between man and woman, between casteman and outcaste ? (Prasad)

It was this radical questioning mind of Ambedkar that propelled him all the time to keep on condemning Hinduism that had sanctified the downgrading and marginalizing of the untouchables as some sort of sub-human species. It was this approach to Hinduism that set him poles apart from Mahatma Gandhi, an approach more radical in content and more modern in vision than the one Gandhi expounded. Ambedkar's essay entitled "Gandhism: The Doom of the Untouchables" is a standing testimony to his aggrieved sense of disappointment with Gandhi's traditional approach. This essay forms a part of his larger work entitled *What the Congress and Gandhi have done to the Untouchables.* No wonder he could see through Gandhi's bundle of contradictions:

> Gandhism is a paradox. It stands for freedom from foreign domination, which means the destruction of the existing political structure of the country. At the same time, it seeks to maintain intact a social structure which permits the domination of one class by another on a hereditary basis which means a perpetual domination of one class by another. (IBA, p. 78)

Dr. Prasad at this stage veers round to Ambedkar's radicalism because as an analyst he believes that this neo-Buddhist iconoclast was more aggressive and more radical than Gandhi.

Naturally Ambedkar contemptuously sneered at band-aid approaches to softening the caste rigours through intercaste dinners and stray examples of intercaste marriages:

> Caste is a state of mind. It is a disease of mind. The teachings of the Hindu religion are the root cause of this disease. We practise casteism and we observe untouchability because we are conjoined to do so by the Hindu religion. A bitter thing cannot be made sweet. The taste of anything can be changed, but poison cannot be changed into nectar. (IBA, p. 83)

The writer of *Ambedkarism* has successfully analyzed and traced Ambedkar's suspicion of Gandhi's democratic credentials to his faith in *varnasram* ideals. On Gandhi's support for the Hindu caste system, albeit devoid of untouchability, no reader, however objective and pro-Gandhian he may be, can ignore Ambedkar's logic. "For whether one takes for comparison caste or varna both are fundamentally opposed to Democracy." (IBA, p. 78)

In the final analysis as a critique of *Ambedkarism* one can only say that the work offers a fascinating insight into the multiple layers of socio-cultural and political ideology of an Icon who radicalized the Indian thought-process in the first half of the 20th century. The sparks caught on but the garbage heap in a recycling revolutionary process is still smoldering. It is true, the "varna" demon still remains unslain throwing up *tantrums* in a delirium of convulsion. Dalits are still being burnt, their children are still being hampered and their daughters still being trafficked, one can corroborate this dark dismal revolting scenario with the latest screaming headline in one of our National Dalies:

> After the attack Dalit students discriminated against in schools. Caste Hindu students keep away, even sit separately in classes. (Hindustan, 17.11.12)

"It was on Nov. 7, 2012 that Dalits were attacked and houses burnt in Natham, Kondampatti and Anna Nagar Dalit Colonies in Dharma Puri and subsequently Dalit children had to be carried to schools in Police vehicles." (The Hindu, 17.11.12) Analyzed in terms of Ambedkar and as analyzed by Ambedkarites like Dr. Prasad this is not an accidental rivalry or feud between scattered groups, but a problem of untouchability which is actually a residue of the lingering vestiges of caste and class struggle. It is here in such contexts that Ambedkar's analysis of the conjoined forces of class and caste struggle sheds light on this perpetual curse of the Hindu society. In fact, his agony that he expressed about six years before his death has morphed into an agony of our lame, lurching and lumbering democracy. Hemingway had raised the question "For Whom the Bell Tolls"?. In fact, his subsequent answer is an answer for all of us; "It tolls for us all." This tolling of the bell may be heard as a prophesy in Ambedkar's words:

> To put it straight, it can be said that struggle between the Hindus and the Untouchables is a permanent phenomena. It is eternal, because the religion which has placed you at the lowest level of society is itself eternal, according to the belief of the Hindu caste people. No change, according to time and circumstances is possible. You are at the lowest rung of the ladder today. You shall remain lowest for ever. This means the struggle between the Hindus and Untouchables shall continue for ever. How will you survive through this struggle is the main question... For me it is not difficult to answer this question. Those who have assembled here will have to agree that in any struggle one who holds strength becomes the victor. One who has no strength, need not expect success. This has been proved by experience, and I do not need to cite illustration to prove it.
>
> (IBA, pp. 95-96)

In the process of focussing on the multiple dimensions of Ambedkarism as a militant revolutionary strategy of social emancipation two central nodal points of committed engagement have been referred to right in the beginning. On the one side of the spectrum stands Dr. Prasad who has sought to explore, analyse and project the academic efflorescence of Baba Saheb's philosophy. At the other end of the spectrum stands Dr. Bindeshwar Pathak who, with his ethico-socialist commitment, has sought to and succeeded in giving a concrete form to Ambedkar's dream. In fact, Dr. Pathak presents a unique and sublime convergence of Gandhi-Ambedkar action plans which had possibly been debated as two sharply contrasted personalities during the Freedom Struggle. The plans and subsequent benefits can be summed up as follows:

(A) Liberating millions of scavengers and rehabilitating them in other professions.

(B) Making concrete action plans for the education of the disadvantaged groups in various skills like embroidery, handicraft, tailoring etc. or else they would have relapsed into their age old profession under economic pressures.

(C) Launching a sanitation crusade with the Sulabh International climaxed today with one Dalit Mahila (Mrs. Usha Chaumar) now holding office as President of this Organization.

(D) Executing a climatic socio-judicial event wherein the Supreme Courts of India calls upon Dr. Pathak to do something for thousands of abandoned widows in Vrindavan Ashrams. (Sulabh India)

This Supreme Court call on Dr. Pathak's Sulabh International was as a sequel in response to a P.I.L. filed by National Legal Services Authority drawing the court's attention to the pathetic condition of Vrindavan widows. The P.I.L. stated:

"After death they (widows) could not be cremated for lack of funds. The widows who die are cut into pieces and put in gunny bags and then disposed of."

The Supreme Court felt shocked, pulled up the Governments concerned and lashed at the National Commission for Women and at the Uttar Pradesh State Women's Commission. Finally, the court asked the petitioners to approach the Sulabh International which had "set up Public toilets all over the country to find out whether they could come forward to help the 1,790 old widows living in deplorable conditions in the four government shelters at Vrindavan."

Inspired by a holy spiritual and revolutionary confluence of Ambedkar-Gandhi cascading streams Dr. Pathak stepped forward honouring the court's wishes. So the steps taken can be summed up as follows:

(A) The Sulabh International has started giving Rs. 2000/- per month to each widow living in five Govt-run shelters in Vrindavan.
(B) Besides, they have opened a centre to provide proper healthcare and last rites to these abandoned widows.
(C) The Sulabh has provided five well-equipped ambulances for the medical emergencies to these Ashrams.
(D) Planning has been initiated and undertaken to motivate the orphans and able-bodied widows to acquire skills in tailoring, handicrafts and embroidery. (Sulabh India, July:2012)

In the final analysis one feels that Ambedkar's inspiration is still alive, still triggering off the process of evolutionary ideas and meliorist dreams. As a writer expounding his philosophy he had an impetuous ferocity in his pen, a supreme talent for dialectics in his logic and a clarity in his socio-economic ideology that hit his targets and nailed the dead and moribund traditions in the coffins. It was all because he had the first-hand experience of the plight of the Dalits or of the Depressed classes and was fired with an inveterate non-conformist vision of radical sanity. There can be no better tribute to Baba Saheb Ambedkar than to remind ourselves of his apocalyptic words of warring to our sick and caste-splintered society:

> Caste cannot be abolished by intercaste dinners or stray instances of inter-caste marriages. Caste is a state of mind. It is a disease of the mind. The teachings of the Hindu religion are the root cause of this disease. (IBA, p. 83)

The part of the Constitution that aimed at abolishing untouchability was approved on Nov. 29, 1948. The final draft of the Constitution was accepted on Nov. 26, 1949. Dr. Ambedkar, however, had a deep insightful perception of the complex play of contradiction between our political and economic existential realities. The contradiction, for him was between "one man and one value." His words still remind us of our national hypocrisy and political illusions of a free fair sovereign state:

> On January 26, 1950 we are going to enter with a life of contradictions. In politics, we will have equality and in social and economic life we will have inequality. In politics, we will be recognizing the principle of "one man one vote" and one vote one value." In our social and economic life, we shall by reason of our social and economic structure, continue to deny the principle of "one man one value." How long shall we continue to live this life of contradictions ? ... or else those who suffer from inequality will blow up the structure of democracy which this Constituent Assembly has so laboriously built up.(IBA, p. 54)

Works Cited

Dwivedi, Acharya; Prasad, Hazari. *Kabir.* New Delhi: Raj Kamal Prakashan, 1999.

Illustrated Biography of B.R. Ambedkar. Delhi: R.B.C International, 2004. (In short form: IBA)

Iyer, V.R. Krishna. *Dr. Ambedkar and the Dalit Future.* New Delhi: B.R. Pub. Corp., 1990

Moon, Vasant.(ed.) *Dr. Babasaheb Ambedkar: Writings and Speeches.* Bombay: Department of Education, Government of Maharashtra, Vol. I, 1979.

Prasad, Dr. R.C. *Ambedkarism.* New Delhi: Motilal Banarssi Das (1993), Preface & Introduction, p. IX .

Sulabh India, July, 2012 and October, 2012.

The Hindu, 17th November, 2012., 2nd September, 2012 and 4th August, 2012.

Wurtzel, Elizabeth. *Radical Sanity.* N.Y. Harcourt Brace, Introduction.

William Langland's *Piers the Plowman* and Dr. R.C. Prasad

Dr. Gokul Singh

(A Humble Homage)

Much before I came in contact with Dr. R.C. Prasad for my research work, I had heard a lot of his multi-colored personality, his depth of encyclopedic scholarship, his wide range and the variety of his inter-disciplinary interests, his being a widely acknowledged authority on medieval English literature, and to crown all or his child-like simplicity and warmth of humanity.

It is in the light of his guidance on *A Sociological Study of Langland's Piers the Plowman*, a subject for which he was already in search of a suitable candidate, that I am inclined to render my humble homage to my revered guru and guide. Somehow or the other he had a mind that I was Marxist-minded so he prompted me to undertake this study but made it clear that it would be naive for me to think that Langland's opus magnum *Piers the Plowman* would respond to any simple process of analysis, because of its vastness, richness and varied significance. I was asked to go to the streams of Philosophy, Theology, Sociology, Political Science, History and Economics in order to have a sociological study of the poem. I had read Langland and Chaucer in M.A. classes, and Political Science and Economics at the B.A. level. My special interest in the study of socialism and communism also helped me.

As directed, I kept myself buried for a pretty long time in books and articles housed in his own library, and in the process, I also consulted relevant materials available in Patna University and Patna College libraries. Some recently published indispensable books were also managed directly from London, all by the grace of Dr. Prasad. It was his overwhelming affection and care that kept me attached to this work. Whenever I met and talked to him about my problem, I could never help being inspired by the aura of his scholarship that flowed from him always.

He led me kindly and I moved forward through the B-Text of the poem and found significant socio-economic and political ideas that agitated the medieval mind, and even modern ideas shooting forth through very many important lines of the poem. I was simply delighted.

Among medieval English poets I always admired Chaucer for "God's Plenty" but loved Langland (1332-1400) the most for the simple reason that he had chosen a plowman for the title of a very long and difficult poem in Three Texts, and elevated him to the status of Christ at a time when the peasantry was rising in revolt. I loved Langland the more as I saw in the image of his plowman who "swonken ful harde" the image of my own farmer-father who "delved" his few acres of land as "Adam delved." Surely, Langland was giving the answer to the burning question of John Ball:

> When Adam delved and Eve span
> Who was then the gentleman?

But the question remains unanswered even today. Even the so-called communist or socialist world could not answer this question. Who is then the gentleman? The modern world has not changed very much for the poor and the needy slum-dwellers.

Langland has developed the image of plowing with great conviction to express the value sense of what the good life really is and who is really the gentleman. The poet won't reverence "Lords and ladies" and persons in "fur and silver." It is the Plowman who:

> In setting and sowing swonken ful harde' that grips his imagination and this very plowman grows into Christ "In a pore mannes apparaile."
> Many times God hath been met among needy people,
> When never man him saw in company of the rich.

Describing the poorest folk, his "neighbor" Langland writes with a depth of understanding and unshakable hold on social realism:

> The most needy aren aure neighbours and we ryme good heed
> As prisons in putts and poure folke in cotes
> charged with children and chief lord's rente. . . .
> And also hymsilue suffreren much hunger

And wo in winter time, with wakynge a nyghtes.
To rise to the ruel to rock the cradles.
Bothe to Karde and to Kembe to Clouten and to wasch.
. . .
The wo of these women that wonyth in cote
And any other men that much wo suffreren. (CXTI.84)

No modern poet has ever surpassed Langland for conveying the sensuous impact of cold, discomfort, hunger:

For whan he streyneth hym to streche,
The strawe is his schetes. (XIV. 233)

At times he is inclined to be sensual enough:

the lyme that she loued me fore and leef was to feel
Whan we naked were (XX. 104)

Such lines are present in abundance in the novels of D.H. Lawrence. But the lines quoted above cannot lead to any adverse criticism of Langland who can go even to the extreme point to expose the naked realism. Both the rich and the poor slept naked in the medieval world with the great difference that the rich slept under woolen cover and fur coat while the poor slept under the sheet of straw. These lines make Langland more than a mere religious minded poet, more secular and sociological.

The finest passages of the poem bear the eternal stamp of the social, political, and economic as well as religious ferment of the time, and at times, the poet expresses thoughts germane to social revolution.

In this poem there are many manifestations of rebellion against the old order of things suffering the birth-pangs of the new. His words and phrases are so apt that they were used as electrifying watchwords in the Peasants Revolts of 1381. The poet is inclined to justify a life even of stealing to provide the starving one "at great need" (XX-20) for the basic needs of food, clothing and drink. Holy Church also says that God commanded the earth to produce in "comune three things" (I.20).

When hunger and poverty plagued the land and the "comune," religious pilgrimage was relegated to the background and Langland even gave up pilgrimage to Canterbury for ploughng the field and growing corn. His very first vision takes place on Malvern Hills:

> In somer sesoum whan softe was the sonne,
> I saw a fielde ful of folke,
> Workehying ful harde...

This makes a difference between *Piers the Plowman* and *The Canterbury Tales.* Langland's strong sense of social realism grows out of and away from allegory, throwing a real challenge to purely religious literature.

Apart from Malvern Hills, only the "citi of London" provides the physical landscape of the poem, but what interested the poet most was the social, economic, and political landscape. Westminster is a place where Lady Meed reigns and where even the King is impressed by her argument. It is a place where worshippers of money live and where law is both used and abused (B XX. 282 ff).

There is much of medieval politics in the Rat Fable which takes us to the political world of the old king Edward III and the boy king Richard II. Conscience reminds the king that he should "reule the rewyn in resoun" and the "comune will assent" (IV. 182). The poet wanted the king to rule with reason and with the assent of the people. What a bold advice, indeed!

Of late, there has been a lot of hue and cry outside and inside the Indian Parliament over rampant corruption in private and public life. India, at the very present moment, needs a poet like Langland to expose Lady Meed and proclaim to all world "for conscience sake" that Wrong will not get off so lightly and that Meed shall not guide the course of law in any way: Shalnes more mede be maistre (III.228)

Langland is as much agitated by the way Meed can and does suppress justice in the case of Peace Vs Wrong as any Marxist or reformer can be in the very many cases of cancerous corruption eating into the vitals of our country. Meed is very much alive to this day and the case against Meed is still pending in several courts of law. Langland's trenchant criticism of Lady Meed's role in Passus II, III, & IV reflecting upon King Edward's attachment with Alice Perres identifiable with Lady Meed is a very bold attempt on the part of the poet. Such ladies enjoy a good deal of social freedom and political influence in the socio-politico system of all times. We have not grown wiser than the medieval poet to deal with such problems.

Langland's preoccupation with hypocrisy and formalism has a direct bearing on modern times. The endless struggle of good over evil continues. Modernity is, thus not a question of date but of outlook. On several counts we have not grown more modern than Langland.

Even the common place medieval theme of salvation has been related in this poem to "tresoure." The prologue is chiefly concerned with "tresoure." how to get it and how to spend it. Wealth and salvation are not incompatible for Langland. He is keenly conscious of the "kindered points of heaven and earth but it is what" passeth on the earth (I.8) that evokes the best in him. His Dowel, Dobet, and Dobest' the thride' and none otherwise but as thei thre assented, (VIII.98 ff) will guide both the people and the king and take care of both the world, the heaven and the earth. There is, thus, in this poem, a passionate concern with proper ordering and running of socio-politico life of the people, to see how human beings run their divinely organized world. The poet is, indeed, dealing with the sociological problems of the times.

Langland's views on the ethical problems of wealth, inheritance, hierarchy, love and marriage are as mixed and complex as those of any liberally minded modern man. In the apocalyptic vision at the end of the poem also the poet sees his vision of spiritual renewal of the world. The endless struggle of Good over Evil continues to the last in the poem. The poet is confident enough that the new age will witness the triumph of Truth and Love:

> I, conscience know this mother with me it taught,
> That reason shal reign and realms goveryn..
> Meed shal no more be master as she is now,
> but love and lowlinesse and loyalty together,
> These shal be masters on earth, Truth to save (B III.282ff)

Behind the naked dance of the Seven Deadly Sins in Passus V (the dance that we see today in our times) the ideals of Truth and Love are also shown alive and functioning. All is not lost for Langland and Milton. Though deserted and almost defeated at the end, Conscience makes a promise to go out once more in search of Piers, the same piers in "pore man's apparaile:"

I wil bicome a pilgryme,
and walken as wide, as al the worlde lasteth (XX.378-9)

While a poet can go even beyond the sun, what to speak of as al the worlde lasteth, I find no space to move any farther, though much relevant "matter" is left behind. Anything useful this "matter" contains, a matter which has really grown out of my long and fruitful association with such a loving, inspiring, and lovely great man like Dr. Prasad is prayerfully, dedicated to the departed soul:

Twadeeyam vastu Govind
Tubhyamev samarpayet!

Joyce's Narratology in *Ulysses*: A Contextual, Critical Approach

Dr. Amarendra Kumar

The novel form is so vast and varied in its scope that sometimes its apparent formlessness comes to be an elusive norm to judge it as an aesthetic whole, in the organic unity and intimacy of its tissues hanging loose like threads in a worn or torn web, knit together or recomposed by the kind of reading desired. A simple classic conception of the form by Dorothy Van Ghent shows its vital function in a lucid light: "... novels have their primary interest in the illumination they cast upon life, not life somewhere else and at another time but immediately here, immediately now..."(Ghent, p. vii) by being "coherent" and an "aesthetic whole." Further, the critic quotes Lionel Trilling from his essay on "Manners, Morals and the Novel": "It can be said that all prose fiction is a variation on the theme of Don Quixote."(Ghent, p.viii) Evidently, this is a critical conjecture above the ingredients of parody and paradox on which *Don Quixote* (1605-1615) is built as a satire in its hallucinatory texture.

In Cervantes' novel fantasy operates at the physical level that is rocked by the convulsions of a sick, book-fed imagination till its eventual collapse through shattering encounters. But fantasy may also be exploited at the level of technique to subvert fictional conventions by the use of innovative structural and stylistic devices, disruptive and diffusive but still narrative in function in some way to sustain the story and evolve an epic form. In fact without resorting to myth, fantasy and imaginative conjury no novel can transmute the crude material of life's reality into a metaphor in the light of the author's vision, so that an autobiographical novel is anything but a novel if it is merely an organized pattern of biographical details. James Joyce's *A Portrait of the Artist as a Young Man* (1916) is an outstanding work in this genre, and *Ulysses* (1922) and *Finnegans Wake* (1939) are innovatively designed as novels on a biographical base in different narrative patterns and styles, one a modern epic of exquisite and complex workmanship and the other a fantastic apprehension of the local and personal as the universal, recurrent and perpetually renewable life cycle.

In the middle of the eighteenth century Laurence Sterne's novel *The Life and Opinions of Tristram Shandy, Gent.* (1759-1767) places the narrator's consciousness at the centre of the work in a time scheme both temporal and atemporal and shows how the associative chain flows above the contingencies and constraints of the passing time. The narrator hero takes a long time to be born and his father and uncle consume six chapters by their talk while coming down a staircase, presumably needing one chapter for each step taken. In Marcel Proust's seven-part monumental novel *Remembrance of Things Past,* originally published in fifteen volumes in the first two decades of the twentieth century, the timeless time also defies the dictates of clock time with perfect ease, so that a dinner takes one hundred and fifty pages to be depicted, irrespective of the limits imposed by the normal flow of time. Edouard Dujardin, James Joyce and Virginia Woolf conceive time in their fictions as the flow of experience and thought and depict the psychological reality of the living world beneath the surface of existence chiefly by the technique of the stream of consciousness.

Joyce uses "immense intellectual industry to distort the structure of language"(Storm, p. 73) and indulges in a "[w]ilful sabotage of coherence," (Storm, p. 45) in *Ulysses* and *Finnegans Wake* in the latter particularly. But this charge, though partly tenable, needs to be seen in the light of the author's attempt to intensify the enjoyment of the textual difficulties by a rather matching mode of reading, patient and penetrating. With a rebellious will to be daringly different he plays a language game in an experimental vein to mystify common perceptions by omission, ellipsis, indirection, verbal permutations and combinations, and above all by a sort of disintegration of conventional techniques for a new integration of the shaping forces at work in his mind and art. However, his new technique in *Ulysses* is parody-prone for an ironic exposure of the contemporary muddle and malady and makes use of various narrative and dramatic devices and styles as a playful exercise in storytelling by incorporating conventional methods like description, straightforward narration, dramatic dialogue, teasing catechistic procedure, cataloguing, scientific inquiry and exposition.

Simple objective storytelling has been in vogue ever since stories began to be told and written, as the basic natural medium of the art for hypnotic or moving conjuries in words. The novel form uses its methods with a sustained care to build up an integral effect more by telling than implying to bring out its dramatic and discursive purposes. Despite its universal vision and immense scope Tolstoy's *War and Peace* (1862-69) unfolds a pattern of plot and character in a historical setting that imparts a certain meaningful consistency to its inherent diffusiveness. On an enormous symbolic canvas Gabriel Garcia Marquez's novel *One Hundred Years of Solitude* (1967) depicts the founding of civilization and its ultimate dissolution in individual dramas by the inner natural forces of decay, death and annihilation at work in the human and natural world, aided by a maiming, perverse will. The insidious, destructive process is powerfully evoked as it swallows the human endeavour to live, thrive and survive through an indefatigable quest for material means as well as scientific and ultimate knowledge. Of course the finely evolved magic realism doesn't obstruct readerly perception with its fidelity to the conventions of novel writing plain narrative style and communicative language medium.

Similarly Jean-Paul Sartre's modern historical novel sequence *Roads to Freedom* (1948...), set in the backdrop of the second world war, synchronizes the characters' feelings and thoughts and their evasiveness and the apprehensive mind of Europe under the looming threat without disrupting the channels of communication. Later, in *Midnight's Children* (1981) and *The Satanic Verses* (1988) Salman Rushdie magicalizes the story dramas in broad, colourful sweeps of narrative detail with the flavour of a bilingual style or music, rather like and unlike Joyce and Mulk Raj Anand, with an exuberance and gaiety typically his own. *The Satanic Verses* opens with the two protagonists Gibreel Farishta and Saladin Chamcha falling down from a great height after an aircrash, in the icy night air of London and the Thames under an alabasterlike moon. Gibreel sings in an incredible mood of levity and defies the impending doom, while Saladin Chamcha snappily asks him to stop the infernal noise. "To be born again," sang Gibreel Farishta tumbling from the heavens, "first you have to die. Hoji ! Hoji ! To land upon the bosomy earth, first one needs to fly. Tat-Taa ! Takathun ! ..."

Anand conversely breathes local colour and vivid, vibrant life with his bilingual expressions in a neorealistic vein. Joyce is however bafflingly multilingual in the European context and occasionally bilingual in the Indian, much more in *Finnegans Wake* than in *Ulysses*, with some Hindi and Sanskrit words alluding or referring to myth, scriptures, Buddha and Buddhism. Although he accuses T.S. Eliot of having stolen *The Waste Land* (1922) from his *Ulysses* and is critical of some of his Sanskrit quotations in the long poem, he himself relies on the effectiveness of this transtextual practice on the language level. After his intelligible storytelling in *Dubliners* (1914) and *A Portrait of the Artist as a Young Man* he intellectualizes the novel form with daring experiments to the extent of earning a sort of notoriety as a disintegrator of coherence.

Besides the fragmentation of the form and the language Joyce conceives character and situation in an idiosyncratic manner, by a process of unfoldment lacking consistency and firmness, on purpose though. His characters appear to be madeup wholes before presentation in a life drama. According to Vladimir Nabokov, "Joyce takes a complete and absolute character, God-known, Joyce-known, then breaks it up into fragments over the space-time of his book. The good reader gathers the pieces and gradually puts them together."(Nabokov, p. 217) Indeed, Stephen grows or changes less except his torment at his refusal to pray for his dying mother in silent ungodly pride and attains an essentially cerebral individuality with literary and philosophical ideas and witty utterances. But the portrayal of Leopold Bloom and his wife Molly approaches a mark of perfection in character creation by an unravelling of their complex, conflicting impulses, feelings and thoughts, impregnating them with the stirring mystery of a rich, manysided, strong individuality through their sex obsessions and perversities. On reading *Ulysses* Carl Jung felt intrigued and baffled by Joyce's intuitive, revealing grasp of female psychology, Molly's, as discernible in her long unpunctuated monologue climactically. To him, only "the devil's grandmother knows so much about the real psychology of a woman. I didn't."(Tindall, p. 323)

In *Finnegans Wake* Joyce probably hits back at Virginia Woolf and Leonard Woolf for their delicate taste that was outraged by his coarse, obsessive, "biological" phraseology, unabashedly frank and hurtful to them for which *Ulysses* earned their rejection as publishers and owners of the Hogarth Press. His tuneful mockery in neologistic fervour comes in a veiled way in *Finnegans Wake*: "Dood and I dood. The wolves of Fochlut ! By whydoyoucallme ? Do not flingamejig to the twolves ! (*Finnegans Wake*, p. 479)" This is of course an interpretative insight into the lines that appear to register his reaction to sensitive Mrs. Woolf's smarting blow. If *Ulysses* provoked her so much, she couldn't even endure flipping through *Finnegans Wake* that offends refined taste with its appalling abandon of sex imagery and insinuations of perverse, incestuous sex as well as recurrent references to urination, defecation and bowels gas release.

Ulysses works out its flowing design with a consummate craftsmanship of a dual focus that welds together story, myth and metaphor into a shaping force, fraught with moral implications. Within the frame of the conventional narrative the novel gains a rare fluidity and flexibility to interiorize the story drama in the mind flow of the three protagonists in particular whose gross physical existence glints with meaning more when irradiated by the pulsations of their inner life, their instincts, emotions, intuitions, imagination and fancy, dreams and adaptation to the harsh realities of life and the world, visions, philosophical, moral and metaphysical ideas. The submerged irony of the parallelism of the fantastic voyage and adventures of Odysseus in Homer's epic and the physical and mental rambles of Stephen Dedalus (named Dedalus to suggest in his case his vision and artistry like that of the mythical maker of a labyrinth and wings in ancient Crete), a Jew advertisement solicitor Leopold Bloom and his singer wife Marion Bloom in Dublin on a single day implies the aching void between the glorious heroic past and the sordid present. Also the lyric intensity and unity of a short story given an epic scope in the image of a limitless stretch of time in the orbit of a cyclic mobility, a psychic reality of multiple dimensions. The eventful day of small or significant epiphanic encounters is Thursday, 16 June 1904, between early morning and predawn time of Friday, perhaps redolent of Joyce's memory of his meeting Nora whom he married later.

Originally planned as a short story, the novel acquires an epic dimension by the intricacies of a complex technique that seeks to capture the drift of the human consciousness in a perpetual quest for self-realization in appalling or fancifully elevating conditions. Stephen is alienated from his father Simon Dedalus and his sisters in a self-imposed exile, in a state of smouldering rebellion against rigid religious norms, ignorance and philistinism. He is a poor, low-paid teacher at Mr. Deasy's school, apt to waste his little money on distractions, still rapt in his scholarly and creative pursuit. On the other hand, Bloom is a man of material quest, a cuckold, unfretfully resigned to his buxom, luscious wife Molly's infidelities. Himself a sex-hunter, he seems to swim in a blurred mist of illusions, in a subliminal search of a son after his son Rudy's death in infancy.

In a way Molly is the centre of the giddy circle, a voluptuous singer, younger in mind than her daughter Milly by her wild fancy and yearning and real hunt, quite an adulteress but still a loving wife. She is true to Bloom at heart above the sins of the flesh and the haunting memory of her first love Lieutenant Mulvey and her flirtations with her concert agent Blazes Boylan. Amidst the tangle of the tense relationships and conflicting quests the vein of "serious gaiety" or the notion of the "joking Jesus" animates the panorama where nothing like a central dramatic crisis actually happens. Of course the talks, discussions, visits and encounters on the shifting scene of physical location at Martello Tower, the cemetery, the newspaper office, the brothel, the city outside and Bloom's house on his return with Stephen have the scintillating charm of a lively drama of slow revelations, simple or banal but meaningful as a manifestation of the author's vision in his carefully evolved design. As a tragicomedy of cross purposes the novel takes the shape of a traumatic, titillating tour of the landscape of life in the real world by its unfoldment of the reality of death and the torment and horror bred by it, of the complexity of human nature and conflicts of opinions and even a physical assault, along with fantastic, nightmarish episodes.

T.S. Eliot's comment on the continuous parallelism of contemporaneity and antiquity in the novel clinches the author's impulse and design in his artistic choice of the "mythical method" instead of the plain, straightforward, progressive narrative technique: "It is simply a way of controlling, of ordering, of giving a shape and significance to the immense panorama of futility and anarchy which is contemporary history."(Rogers, p. 386) However, Vladimir Nabokov quietly warns against any painstaking endeavour to establish the analogy and the allegorical import of the mythical method in the novel, belittling its significance by an emphasis on Joyce's omission of the Homeric titles of the chapters after the serial publication of *Ulysses* on a mature judgement.

As a writer Joyce has a European mind, for he derives much inspiration from Zola's naturalism and Mallarme's symbolism and depicts reality with an unerring eye, keenly alive to its form, colour and texture, even if trivial or distasteful, and relies on the evocative music of the words, suggestion and implication in a self-reflective vein. He seizes the "ineluctable modality of the visible" and of the "audible" as well and sees beyond the "signatures" of all things into the timeless and unknown, like Stephen in *Ulysses*, "walking into eternity along Sandymount strand." In fact he laid his Dublin scene on a mental map with a vivid memory and a Dublin Directory. Basically, his is an art of intellectual imagination and multilingual response to experience, harnessing new fictional techniques and the devices of music and the cinema. In this respect, his later fictional work comes to be a fantasia of the conscious with their thematic content of fun and fantasy and novelties of technique.

In *Ulysses* Martello Tower in Dublin is an "omphalos," a centre of life's vigour and joy as well as its poetic, prophetic and creative potentialities, in its seaside setting. Its chief occupant Stephen, a poet, scholar and teacher, lives here with a medical student Buck Mulligan, an epitome of vigour and buoyancy, and an Englishman Haines in sojourn there. Old jolly Mother Grogan's voice is mimicked by Mulligan in a rumbustious lighter vein – "When I makes tea I makes tea... And when I makes water I makes water (p.14)." The air of conviviality and witty crosstalk in the opening tower episode assumes a flippant tone when Buck asks Stephen whether the old lady's tea and water pot figure in "the Upanishads". Whereas Stephen is a quiet visionary, gay and eloquent in his company, Buck is apt to burst into song and a recitative frenzy, pouring out poetry, any moment. Stephen's reply to Bloom later about why he left his father and home sets the tonal key of the novel with a luminous touch of ambiguity, light but deeply suggestive "to seek misfortune". His mother's death haunts him with the horror of its painful paroxysm and of his refusal to kneel down in prayer for her out of an inner revolt against Catholicism and its afflictions during his early educational career. In fact he seems to be a thinly disguised projection of the author and is prone to gather dust and dirt, not only by walking and wandering but also by not caring to have a bath for eight months. He may be said to live a life of art and literature with his sensations and ideas, in the light of his poetic eye and receptive ear in his lonely quest. His conscientiousness is synonymous with his quaint phrase "agenbite of inwit."

Bloom is also a wanderer, not on a misty horizon but on the palpable plane of a search for distractions, for pleasure. By nature he is kind and gentle and noble, though he has a wrong wife with the right body in seductive bloom and is resigned to his fate as a horned man. To Molly however he is a goading bull. But she endures him and loves him despite her defiling fancies and betrayal of the marital bond. Simon Dedalus, Milly, Lynch, Lenehan, the strange sailor with his boozing and yarns and others make the novel a bristling canvas, each one integral to the comedy of the cyclic Dublin voyage.

In this fantastic prose epic of Greek and Arabian resonances of *Odyssey* and *The Arabian Nights,* messy webs of instincts and passions, walking-wandering and talk-discussion motifs, mind monologues, sudden mysterious events and encounters devise a choppy meandering course of unheroic action with hints of meaning at the core. The first three episodes at the Martello Tower at the beginning come off as a slow exposition of the book's mind in broken bits of talk and eating and walks around the central figure Stephen whose consciousness gives a momentum to the story at the inner level. Subsequently twelve episodes enlarge and thicken the plot of things happening or imagined by a shifting spotlight on the death and burial of Patrick Dignam, a recurrent unifying thread in the novel, on visits, talks and confrontations. Outstanding among the places depicted besides the graveyard are a newspaper office, a brothel, a city street witnessing the viceregal cavalcade and a physical attack, a beach where Bloom flirts with Gerty Mac Dowell and a maternity hospital where he meets Stephen. His homecoming with Stephen and Molly's wild uninhibited flow of erotic memory and yearning and love emotions constitute the organ swell of the music of the minds interwoven with talks, events and fantasies in the book.

The conflicting preoccupations and thought streams of the three major characters don't affect them inwardly to provoke a clash, rather they embody the psychic forces that intertwine in their destinies as partners in a slow, mysterious dance as complementaries to something within them yet incomplete. Stephen's intellectuality, rootlessness and emotional solitude, Bloom's frustrations and libido play and love fancy and Molly's eroticism and love yearnings may resolve the dilemmas of their internal solitudes into a homecentric relationship if not subjected to perversions and the afflictions of separateness any more. In his romantic escapade Bloom reveals his masculine and feminine traits that bring about a fantastic climax in his authorial conception as a man-woman, big with child, delivering babies on bodily pressure at Bella Cohen's brothel in a lurid, disgusting, surrealistic, saturnalian mind drama moulded by the author's imagination.

But his soaring fancy of self-aggrandisement makes him an emperor, popularly hailed and adored. And then the colourful baloon is punctured and he is on the verge of meeting the fate of a condemned man, as a public nuisance to the city, and earns a graceful deliverance through a doctor's intervention as a male mother to the baby to be born. Obviously, Bloom's fancy as it soars and subsides comes as a nightmarish projective beam from the author's mind. Molly's fantasy however springs from her memory, taste and longing on a firmer ground. All this is sharply different from Stephen's eloquent scholarly expositions of the suffusion of Shakespeare's personal life and family history in his dramas. But there is a physical side to his scholarly pursuit in his visit to the brothel and in his obsessive concern with the breach in Shakespeare's conjugal life as he sees it.

This infinitely complicated muddle is a mockery of Ulysses' adventures and Penelope's passionate devotion to him and the filial bond of the legendary father and his brave loving son Telemachus. But the irony is the implied moral drama, a shaft of redeeming light in the gloom. Beneath the complex web of "cohesive" deviations and the opacity of the innovative strategies lies Joyce's will or design to bring into play the art of writing as a self-conscious shifting agency of verbal and formal devices for a multifocal exposure of his vision and philosophy, of the innate regenerative possibilities of the human drama presented. Here the plain narrative technique used happily blends with the blur of the minds' streams that flow and interfuse very often as natural thought flashes and present a poetic conjury of synthetic perceptions and associated ideas and images, imparting depth and richness to the texture. Besides, the parodies of various nonfictional forms vary the narrative mode to achieve an ironic and comic impact: of newspaper headlines in Chapter 4 of Part Two, of music in Chapter 8 and mystical and slapstick plays in Chapter 4 and 8 of the same part, respectively. Examination type of questions and answers in a catechistic manner occur in Chapter 2 of Part Three and reinforce the comical impact as they interrupt or distort the narrative flow with an odd recurrence.

Also notable elsewhere are the parodies of literary styles and authors of various periods, of lady magazine writing or journalese affecting elegance. Scientific inquiry and objective description in elaborate and minute details, blown out of proportion in dramatic situations, reflect a conscious enjoyment of the fun of doing it. Riddles and puns all over the book produce a mirthful intellectual appeal as in journalist Lenehan's riddle or pun: "What opera resembles a railway line ?" ... Answer : "The Rose of Castille (rows of cast steel)p.125." Portmanteau word coinages like "strandentwining" and "syphilisation" and wordclusters, short or very long, one of them eliminating the time space between some facial expressions and a head gesture "smiledyawnednodded," abound in the novel and are both funny and meaningful. Water as a source of life in its infinite variety, humanity as a whole, the sea link of global contact and communication, etc. are the implications of the first coinage ("strand...") and a rotten, evil, syphilitic civilization is what the other implies, probably connoting the Irish rage over the tyrannical British rule in the country. This proliferative or expansive verbal device shows the author's ingenuity in manipulating words and their music to force sense into their shapes and sounds for producing striking effects beneath their apparent oddness.

Joyce's novelties of technique are manifold, as noted. But the focal point of his strategies in this novel is his attempt to interiorize the plot-character development process by the depiction of the stream of consciousness and the association of ideas that accompanies it. This is intended to refract his omniscience by its intuitive identity with others' subjective experience and thought behaviour. To him this is a more realistic approach to the inner life that the narrative art should seize and depict. Besides, the Ovidian cross-metamorphoses occurring in the brothel comedy, at the mental level, in vivid form and colour, though, anticipate the process of melting, merging and crosstransference of the identities of the characters in the baffling pantomime of *Finnegans Wake.*

Joyce's astonishing craftsmanship also saves *Ulysses* from being romantically or cloyingly lyrical. He is basically a Homeric poet of the whole truth that incorporates the tragic truth of life. He tends to be comical and even farcical in his wide charity of acceptance of human frailties or fallibility. It may be said that he comicalizes the novel form with an implicit faith in the creative norm of conception of story in terms of the motifs of wandering, search or exploration for an intuitive tapping of the mind to dig out its mineral wealth. He sharply registers the mind flow in thought, memory, associative imagery, impressions, emotive response, introspection, etc. by the use of matching stylistic devices. In *Ulysses* Stephen has a seasoaked sensibility or mind that is stirred by Mulligan's evocative phrase from Swinburne "a great sweet mother" for the sea and his alliterative and onomatopoeic play on it through "mummer" and "murmur" as he accuses him of having killed his mother by not praying for her at the time of her death. Then, images and sounds merge in Stephen's mind in memory flashes that turn the sweet sea into a bitter bowl of water, calling forth the bowl in which his mother poured out her rotten liver's green fluid vomiting and groaning. Mulligan's shaving bowl in this situation and the white china bowl with the green bile at her bedside fuse together with the image of the bay and its "dull green mass" of water in Stephen's heaving inarticulate agony.

Recurrent phrases like "dogsbody" for poor forlorn Stephen and "softbodied cat" for Bloom and "white mackintosh" for the author's disembodied presence in his work are unifying threads in the elusive flux of the mind and the diffusive episodes of talk, discussion, riddle games, witty exchanges and unemotive, extensive, scientific and objective descriptions in an interrogative frame. A strange similarity of dreams occurring to Stephen and Bloom about a voluptuous oriental beauty projects the Molly image foreshadowing their mutual involvement in the tragic triangle that rankles in Bloom's mind. The young poet, musiclover and teacher, a son figure to him, could teach his singer wife Italian pronunciation and improve her mind and also supplant gaudy, uncultured Boylan as her lover. He could marry his daughter Milly as well. Conversely, Molly's agony over Bloom's rage of lust comes up in a powerful poetic line "... all the poking and rooting and ploughing he had up in me..." In her erotic yearning and narcissism she echoes his kinky lovemaking by kissing her bottom in her image of that part as the "cheeks of my bottom."

But the memory of his marriage proposal to her draws forth a fine phrase from her about a woman's body being a "flower," simple, sensuous, redolent of self-love with a sense of touch. It seems to soften in a redeeming light the oppressive phantom of his animal lust and behaviour in trying to milk her for making tea. Both the Blooms swing between poetry and sheer animality, with Bovarysme as a common factor between them, true to each other at heart in the light and shadow play of Donne's image of a twincompasslike connectivity, untorn by vagrancy. On the other hand, Stephen wittily conjectures about Shakespeare's wife Ann Hathaway whose intrigue with his brother Richard Shakespeare he has no means to prove. Shakespeare, a recurrent link in the exchanges of views and expositions, provides a thematic base to the intellectual atmosphere of the story in a creative context, reflecting the intricacies of the tensional love relationship of the Blooms obliquely.

As already noted, Homer enlarges the scope of the novel for the underlying myth to dissolve into a life drama by an ironic inversion.

In the parallelism evolved or implied the wandering mysterious sailor, Odyssean and Arabian by thematic association, and the circus clown who desperately and amusingly falls upon Bloom claiming that none but he himself was his missing father reinforce the father-son theme with a poignant irony, corresponding to the Bloom-Stephen relationship. In their funny, embarrassing or sad situations this ironic motif is a muddle on the surface with an embedded layer of meaning in a maze without an outlet, just promoting a quest as the only way out. Fanciful, symbolic, though funny, a fresh lemon cake sings in a fantastic episode: "We're a capital couple, Bloom and I;/He brightens the earth, I polish the sky (p. 404)." In the newspaper office Bloom's mild but emphatic suggestion for a business ad to appear in the Telegraph, to win Mr. Keyes' favour, provokes a wild sally of annoyance and agitation from the Editor Myles Crawford: "Will you tell him he can kiss my arse ? (p.137)." Stephen whom Crawford had seen with a good pair of boots on that day was more interesting and pleasing to him as he had seen him last in shoes showing his heels. Bloom's wistful plea after a pause is greeted by another howl: "He can kiss my royal Irish arse... Any time he likes ..." Bloom a wanderer like Stephen, Molly a daydreamer, and others of the mobile, articulate or fantasying bunch emanate from the author's mind like a cinematic beam on the screen forming images, frame by frame, in a montage sequence, in a disorderly or orderly manner. In the novel there is an air of conviviality rung by laughter, louder than the sobs.

Even the Irish political struggle for freedom from the British regime wavers between violent resistance and acquiescence and produces a species of gallows humour in the violent erection of a hanged man's penis on the gallows, sending forth a gush of sperm on the cobblestones, with elegant, elevated ladies rushing ahead to sop it up. It may of course be seen in a suggestive, symbolic light as well. In another ghastly episode of the execution of an Irish freedom fighter a sudden startling turn shows the wailing ladylove on the scene readily accepting an Oxford graduate's offer of marriage, reminiscent of Petronius's tale "The Widow of Ephesus" and Christopher Fry's play *A Phoenix Too Frequent* dramatizing a similar switchover from lament to a frenzy of new love. During a fantastic political debate of conflicting opinions Stephen says "... You die for your country... Let my country die for me... Damn death. Long live life ! (p. 494)." Unmistakably, Stephen epitomizes the loneliness of a genius, and he cuts below the surface of existence for things of a deeper and abiding value.

Defecation and urination, central to Joyce's conception of life, are appallingly pronounced in *Finnegans Wake*, but *Ulysses* also has its whiffs of the Swiftian odour. With an absurd funny accuracy it records the volume, quantity and trajectories of Bloom's and Stephen's urine flow, showing how Bloom's jet differs from that of the younger person on account of his age and its natural effect on the discharge. In fact the Woolfian reactions to this indelicacy or vulgarity stand rather unmollified, though not quite unrelieved in the author's comic vision of life. Obviously, the novel employs absurdity and disproportionate emphasis as technical means to depict reality amusingly, in order to provoke mirth even at the cost of delicacy. On the other hand, all the deliberative "seances," the elaborate cataloguing of facts and figures, of the topics of discussion, the question-answer formulation of story, and the irritating volume and accuracy of scientific knowledge provided cause a deliberate narrative fragmentation or obstruction. However, the unfictional strategies tap the potential of pause as a perceptual process, obliquely related to the story flow by its illuminating, titillating wealth of information despite its accumulative density and interruptive character. This new strategic approach to storytelling may therefore be designated as a structural and stylistic discovery of the comicality at the core of the novel.

One authorial question – "What proposal did Bloom, diambulist, father of Milly, somnambulist, make to Stephen, noctambulist? (p. 583)" makes a suggestive use of a simple method of interrogation to bring out individual traits with humour or to attribute them to the characters with gaiety. Besides, the absurd accuracy of the scientific delineation of the sleeping postures of Bloom and Molly in bed is notable for its inner layer of mirthful humour: "Listener (Molly), S.E. by E. Narrator (Bloom), N.W. by W.: on the 53rd parallel of latitude, N., and the 6th meridian of longitude, W.: at an angle of 45 degrees to the terrestrial equator (p. 620)." In sharp contrast to it Bloom is depicted in his sleep as "the manchild in the womb," to be reborn in the life cycle after a refreshing sleep, innocent as an unborn baby or a baby just born, or a baby in his angelic infancy. Now the irony of the babies born to him in the nightmare fantasy at the brothel neither tickles nor bites. Fun or farce is resolved here in the divine, human or primal state of sleep. This quiet dramatic touch has a great narrative value with its connotations of a return to the secure fold of relationships and homely comfort in spite of the taint and gnawing pain of infidelities. With its poignancy, depth and silence it comes as a lovely metaphor of reticence in the discursive form of the novel that is loud in its multiple tones and peals of laughter.

Bloom is back home like a sailor after his voyage or sea adventures, a mind-time traveller in repose, recaptured vividly and resonantly by a verbal and musical shuffle with an explosively funny *Arabian Nights* refrain:

> He has travelled.
> With ?
>
> Sinbad the Sailor and Tinbad the Tailor and Jinbad the Jailer and Whinbad the Whaler and Ninbad the Nailer and Finbad the Failer and Binbad the Bailer and Pinbad the Pailer and Minbad the Mailer and Hinbad the Hailer and Rinbad the Railer and Dinbad the Kailer and Vinbad the Quailer and Linbad the Yailer and Xinbad the Phthailer.
>
> When ?
> ... Darkinbad the Brightdayler.
> Where ? (p. 621)

The proliferative, variational word-and-sound game is boisterously funny, though oddly repetitive on an alphabetic base. It treats time as a dark tunnel with light at the end through the coinage "Brightdayler," a silver lining in itself. But the place is left unlocated because this is all in the sleeper's mind under an authorial focus, a nowhere with the conflicting urges of the couple still unresolved.

Ulysses with its entire gamut of modern fictional, unfictional, epic, poetic and musical devices sounds postmodernistic in its accent of self-conscious artistry, refracting the authorial omniscience in manifold ways rather unobtrusively. Although a vivid stamp of intellectuality marks the progress of the work through learned, multilingual allusions and references entailing an explicatory reading, the poetic, associative, impressionistic narrative mode is superbly evocative and unfolds itself at its best through condensation and suggestion and intertextual or transtextual echoes without overt reference. Stephen's mind moulds the visual image of the sea scene early in the first part of the book with nuances and resonances worth noting. "Inshore and farther out the mirror of water whitened, spurned by lightshod hurrying feet. White breast of the dim sea. The twining stresses two by two. A hand plucking the harpstrings merging the twining chords. Wavewhite wedded words shimmering on the dim tide (p.11)." By a vibrant focus of eye and mind on the stirred surging sea the poetic verbalization subtly seizes the tonal shades of the tremulous surface woof as it heaves under the breeze and conjures it up as a verbal or musical phrase. The lovely sea view in its finer pulsations smoothly merges into the Greek pagan, literary and mythical contexts of sea, song, harpmusic and handplay on the strings, all twining together in a verbal or phrasal form, waves become words in a rhythmic pattern.

For Joyce's articulate and perceptible mode of thinking in a philosophical mood, the following lines from *Ulysses* are strikingly notable: "Creation from nothing. What has she in the bag ? A misbirth with a trailing navelcord, hushed in ruddy wool... The cords all link back strandentwining cable of all flesh... Put me onto Edenville. Aleph, alpha: nought, nought, one (p. 38)." Stephen thinks as he walks on the Sandymount Strand about nature, life, birth processes, the Biblic Creation, the swarming scene of humanity, the void and nothingness at the core of worldly existence, with the intermingling of the Hebrew, Biblic and Greek contexts in "Edenville" and "Aleph, alpha." The climax seems to come off in a dim apprehension of a divine centre of unity in the zeroic reality of things through a small verbal shuffle at the end, in "one." In the mindstream the interminable chain of life and death takes shape as a "Bag of corpsegas sopping in foul brine," a seascape of creation and dissolution, through an acutely vivid and sharp metaphorical fusion of the senses of sight and smell. The thought resonates reflectively: "God becomes man becomes fish becomes barnacle goose becomes featherbed mountain. Dead breaths I living breathe, tread dead dust, devour a urinous offal from all dead (p. 49)." In Joyce's stream of consciousness technique in the novel, a thought wave is thus a suggestive, half-formed grammatical or ungrammatical syntax, sensory, visionary or philosophical, associatively interknit by rapid shifts from one idea or object to another in an emotive and reflective key. This flowing mind matter amalgam is essentially poetic in nature and function, relevant to the narrative art by its movement on the plane of the inner reality of life.

Molly's predawn long reverie in bed occurs in an unpunctuated mind monologue in pure native English, simple, rhythmic, rippling, natural and naked in content. Sharply receptive to the surge of memory and feeling, erotic urges and fancies in the most intimate details, this silent soliloquy is a masterpiece of a penetrating portrayal of female psychology. Molly bares her love and sex impulses with a yearning for fulfilment so overpowering that it seems to be an orgy of self-indulgence in which narcissism and nymphomania mingle like a cocktail of intoxicating potions. But her seething senses and fancy flight don't tear her off her roots : her love for Bloom and domestic care, her birdlike instinct to feather her nest fine, her anxiety about his hunt for pleasure outside, his prodigal waste of money and her natural sense of economy. She seems to have the strength to cut through the messy agitation of mind and body with a true feeling, deep and intense; "I'd rather die 20 times over than marry another of their sex of course had never find another woman like me to put up with him the way I do ... (p. 628)." Her reverie trails off into a memory flash in a mood of ardent surrender "...his heart going like mad and yes I said yes I will yes (p. 663)."

Contrarily, Bloom's Dublin rambles conclude with a cool calculation about the day's failures, particularly about his failure "to certify the presence or absence of posterior rectal orifice in the case of Hellenic female divinities... (p. 614)." This is an irreverent sally of coarse humour, reflecting the comic spirit of the novel, unmodified by canons or considerations of moral delicacy. Joyce also uses here Sanskrit words for male and female sex organs at play with the same ease, with no inhibition for a pause to tone it down by a softer substitute. At heart Bloom is still a caring, loving husband in his quiet tragic, dramatic choice of Stephen as a lover for Molly for her intellectual elevation and refinement.

All this is perhaps a symbolic portrayal of Joyce's empirical and searching mind that deeply probes the divine manifestation as a visible and audible phenomenon, engulfed by the overwhelming presence of aberrations and evils. Here the couple embodies the flawed nature of man in the redeeming light of the psychic split between their frailties and perversities and their emotional attachment to each other. To the author it may be a variation on the Biblic theme of Adam's cognate creation of hell and heaven in the warring forces that constitute the world of his progeny, fallen, falling, rising to seek grace in some form and measure. William Blake's not-so-serious critical remark on Milton's *Paradise Lost* and *Paradise Regained* may throw light on this aspect of the creative impulse and work of the novelist; "The reason

Milton wrote in fetters when he wrote of Angels & God, and at liberty when he wrote of Devils & Hell is because he was a true Poet and of the Devil's party without knowing it."(The London magazine, p. 4)

In *Ulysses* Joyce forges in his smithy many styles to render the reality of the living world and of the mind's stream of images and ideas. Like a Concrete poet he also plays upon the spelling and sound of Leopold Bloom's name by a permutational mode of ordering in an anagram :

Leopold Bloom
Ellpodbomool
Molldopeloob
Bollopedoom
Old Ollebo, M.P. (p. 568)

Of course Concrete poetry is as old as George Herbert and William Blake, even older in the pictorial management of physical space for poetic composition, acknowledging the value of extraverbal devices in the outbringing of the meaning to be made. Its later development in typographical, alphabetic designs and crossfertilized forms produces some good and valuable work of visual dimensions with minimal word sets. But here this alphabetic play anticipates Joyce's ultimate form of fragmentation and disintegration of both the language medium and the novel form in *Finnegans Wake*, on a flimsy plotground of a dramatized philosophy of history and ideas, after Vico and Bruno, in permutational episodes of a family history, emblemizing all people and places at all times, in an onomatopoeic, alliterative musical medium.

Ulysses has however a story to tell, a narrative, dramatic pace of an unconventional sense of direction, through characters with individual traits, and a structural pattern in an ascending scale of dramatic interest despite the tangible effects of Joyce's literary nonconformity on the work. But between his two colossal works of fiction of the later phase there runs one thread of life philosophy as a connecting link – the possibilities of the present to be explored by the pursuit of elevating ideals, by a regenerative reliance on the "Adya" or "Vartman" in the image of the "Padma" (Lotus) of the Hindu and Buddhist scriptures. "Padma, brighter and sweeter, this flower that bells, it is our hour or risings. Tickle, tickle. Lotus spray. Till herenext. Adya (*Finnegans Wake*, p. 598)." In the darkness of sins and evils creative endeavor or artistic creativity, or hopeful, joyful, purposeful action is a valid norm to live by, to impose order on the chaos of experience and of the world outside.

Works Cited

Davies, Peter. "Poet vs. Preacher: Milton's Dichotomy in Paradise Lost." *The London Magazine.* London: October - November 2011: 4.

Ghent, Dorothy Van. *The English Novel : Form and Function.* New York: Harper and Publishers, 1961 (reprint).

Jameson, Storm. *Parthian Words.* London: Collins and Harvill Press, 1970.

Joyce, James. *Ulysses.* Delhi: Jainco Publishers, (reprint).

—. *Finnegans Wake.* London: Faber and Faber Ltd., Reprint, 1971.

Nabokov, Vladimir. *Lectures on Literature.* ed. Fredson Bowers, London: Weidenfeld and Nicolson, 1980.

Rogers, Pat. (Ed.) *An Outline of English Literature.* Second Edition, Oxford University Press, 1998.

Tindall, William York. A *Reader's Guide to Finnegans Wake.* New York: Syracuse University Press Edition, 1996. (reprint)

The Making of A Prince: Postcolonial Reflections on Chandragupta Maurya and Prince Hal

Jonathan B. Shaw

During the heyday of colonization when Macaulay declared with aplomb and flourish that the entire literary output of the Orient did not amount to the cultural worth of one single shelf of European civilization, he might have honestly believed in the immense superiority of Western literatures. But who knows, it might well have been a cool calculated ploy to justify the colonization of the Orient, for after all it was "the White man's burden" to educate and civilize all others. The Europeans in general, and the British in particular, had already proved their supremacy in arms and diplomacy. However, they were well aware of the fact that in order to consolidate their hold on the Indian peninsula, they needed not only to win Plassey and Buxar, but also subdue the natives intellectually and culturally. Literature has traditionally been regarded as providing an index of cultural superiority(Boehmer, p. 358), as such it was necessary to assert the superiority of their literature and denigrate the literary output of the Indian subcontinent.

That they did succeed fair and square in their objective is clearly reflected in the attitude prevalent among the average Indian as well as the intelligentsia during the 19th and 20th centuries. The colonial mind-set, founded upon Macaulay's education policy was further augmented by blind idolatry and servile imitation of the West. The cliché that Kalidasa was the Shakespeare of India and Chandragupta Maurya/Samudragupta was the Alexander of India are classic examples of such subaltern approach. The postcolonial approach, on the other hand, is clearly reflected in Shashi Deshpande's short story, "Why a Robin?" (2003). As a matter of fact, so far as creative writing is concerned, postcolonialism can be traced back to Kalidasa's Yaksha (Meghadutam), Shakespeare's Caliban (*The Tempest*) and Shylock (*The Merchant of Venice*) as also to the *Asterix-Obelix* comics. But as a theory of literary criticism, postcolonialism came in vogue only by the 1980s. However, it was during the late 1960s when the author was studying the History Plays of Shakespeare with Dr. Ram Chandra Prasad (R. C.

P) as the mentor, that he was counseled by the latter to examine the plays specifically from the Indian perspective. The term, postcolonial criticism was yet to gain currency and, as such, it was not applied. Today by hindsight, it becomes evident that what was meant by R.C.P., was a postcolonial fresh look at the History Plays. (Shaw:2010)

The present paper which happens to be a sequel to the dissertation, elaborates the same postcolonial approach to Prince Hal and, is therefore an academic tribute to the critical acumen and vision of Prof. Ram Chandra Prasad.

One of the chief tenets of essential unity underlying all literatures, as we know, is logical credibility or a willing suspension of disbelief. As such a major task faced by any author especially if he/she is dealing with characters and plot with unexpected and fantastic contours of development, is to dispel the lurking disbelief from the minds of his readers/audience. And it is true, no less of historical literature than of imaginative, for facts may at times turn out to be stranger than fiction. When such is the case the task becomes all the more demanding. A well known instance is Shakespeare's treatment of the unexpected development of Prince Hal from a profligate in *Henry IV : Parts I and II* to a national hero in *Henry V.* The only extant Sanskrit historical play, *Mudra Rakshasa* by Vishakhadatta, depicting the growth of King Chandragupta Maurya, provides an interesting study in comparison and contrast.

To consider the historical facts first, King Chandragupta Maurya occupies the same venerable position in Indian history as does King Henry V, the victor of Agincourt in the history of England. The former vanquished the Greek in India, founded the famous Mauryan empire and extended its territory to the western most parts of the then India (which included not only the present day Pakistan, but also Afghanistan), the latter defeated the French and succeeded in extending the English territory – though for a brief spell to France. In both cases, victory culminated in matrimonial alliance, rewarding the victor and, honouring the vanquished, Chandragupta Maurya was a usurper not unlike Bolingbroke (Henry IV) and, although Prince Hal inherited the crown, the issue of usurpation continued to haunt him right through his growing up from princehood to kingship. In the case of Chandragupta Maurya, he was not only a usurper, but also a subaltern – the bastard son from a *Shudra dasi* (a fact generally ignored/twisted or underplayed perhaps deliberately by the historians), which made his credentials all the more suspect.

Now let us analyse the treatment of the basic material by the two playwrights without colonial or anticolonial prejudice. From the historical facts it follows that both the Sanskrit playwright and the English bard were faced with a somewhat similar situation as well as problem, viz., to provide logic for the "figs growing on thistles." Vishakhadatta portrays a national martial hero in Chandragupta. So does Shakespeare in Prince Hal. The crux of the problem before both the playwrights, however, is that the national hero to be projected wants legitimacy. Further byproducts of this central problem are the threats to the national hero – the intrigues, the challenges, the unacceptability as well as the apparent lack of moral sanction behind certain acts of the national hero – and how to make the crown secure despite the usurpation and illegitimacy.

Shakespeare tackles the problem by using the Prodigal Son-motif and by letting his Prince adopt a mock-playboy image consciously in order to distance himself from his usurper father, so much so that the latter is constrained even to wish disowning "my young Harry," seeing just "riot and dishonour" on his brow. Thus deliberately distancing himself from his father as well as statecraft, mingling freely with Falstaff and the likes of Poins, Peto and Bardolph, and using/misusing the "sweet wench," Mistress Quickly, Prince Hal, as part of his elaborate game-plan, imitates the sun, allowing:

> the base contagious clouds
> To smother up his beauty from the world.
> — but only for a while.

In *Mudra Rakshasa*, on the other hand, at the instruction of Chanakya, Chandragupta play-acts a mock quarrel and distances himself from his revered guru for a while in order to project his image as an independent sovereign. Just as in the case of Prince Hal it is the Prince himself who unravels the plan through the soliloquy quoted above, in the case of Chandragupta too, it is he who discloses the mock quarrel plan in a soliloquy:

> *Kritkalhan Kritwa Swatantren Kinchit*
> *Kalantaran Wyabhartavymityardeshah*
> (It is the command of my percepter that I should manage independently for a while after picking up a mock quarrel with him.)

Both the princes are in the process of growth, but the expositions of their growth are diametrically opposed. While in the case of Prince Hal the first projection of his image is deliberately negative, in the case of Chandragupta the first projection itself is positive. However, in both the cases the purpose is to hoodwink the enemy as well as the people. In *Mudra Rakshasa* the people in general, and Rakshasa in particular, are completely taken in by the diplomatic mock quarrel, culminating in Chandragupta's declaration:

> *At prabhrityanadritya Chankyam Chandraguptah swayamev Ranyam Krishyateeti Kriyanatam prakrityah* (Act III)
> (Let the subjects be informed that henceforth ignoring Chanakya, Chandragupta himself will rule.)

In immediate reaction the Chamberlain soliloquizes:

> *Katham niruppadmev Chanakyamiti, naraychankyamity. Hant, sangrihitoadhikarah*
> (He says "Chanakya", not "noble Chanakya". Alas! Authority has been withdrawn.)

And the arch rival of Chanakya, Rakshasa is delighted at the reported "*apkrista*" (alienation) of Chandragupta from Chanakya.

In case of Prince Hal, the regality, the rebels, the rioters, all are convinced of his alienation from the king and kingship. To the extent, the king is disappointed, Falstaff and the revelers are hopeful of the golden time "When thou art king," for when thou art king, "old father antic the law" would be banished the shores of England and, gallows would become a thing of the past. And to the extent the Prince is alienated from the king and bears the image of a mere "sword-and-buckler Prince of Wales" (Act I Sc iii.230), he becomes safe and out of range of the rebels.

Hotspur: But that I think his father loves him not
And would be glad he met with some mischance.
I would have him poison'd with a pot of ale.

Even at Shrewsbury, when the two Harries meet, Shakespeare does not let Hotspur forget this bleak background of Prince Hal, a factor which adds to his cockishness :

.... would to God

Thy name in arms were now as great as mine! (V iv. 69-70)

— and contributes to his defeat.

Thus the apparent adversity of the situation is turned into an advantage by both the Princes, who emerge stronger through their calculated mock behaviours. Both Chandragupta and Prince Hal offend — the former sham offends his Guru and father-figure, Chanakya (although at his instance), the latter offends his father, Bolingbroke, but

so offend to make offence a skill. (I.i. 209).

What is more, in both the cases in order to reinforce the regality of the Prince as also to highlight the tussle between the regality and the rebels, the dramatists press well known cosmic images into service. In keeping with the Elizabethan concept of the world order, Shakespeare consistently employs the sun image for the Prince. Hence when Prince Hal chooses to divulge his elaborate strategy, the sun-image comes up quite naturally:

Yet herein will I imitate the sun (I.i. 190)

At the same time in the Henry IV plays Shakespeare also exploits the moon badges of the Percies, and in sharp contrast to Prince Hal and his sun-image, allots the moon-image to Hotspur:

.... sweet fortune's minion and her pride (I.i.82)

Hotspur. "By heaven, methinks it were an easy leap

To pluck bright honour from the pale fac'd moon" (I.iii. 109)

It is interesting to note that in a similar way, Vishakhadatta finds the moon-image handy, though in this case for describing not the rebel but the Prince himself, for "*Chandra*" is moon. As per the convention of Sanskrit Drama, when the play is introduced by *Sutradhara* (the stage manager), the plot of the play is also invoked. In *Mudra Rakshasa* when the *Sutradhara* enquires of his wife as to the occasion of the festivity.

Kthay kasminninte?
(Tell, what is the purpose?)

Her reply is :

Ovarjjadi kil bhauvam Chandotti. (Act I)
(For the moon (i.e. Chandragupta) is going to be eclipsed.)

That the moon-image is consistently ascribed to Chandragupta Maurya, is also confirmed by his keen interest in the *Kaumudi* festival (the festival of the full moon of the autumn), which is cancelled by Chanakya owing to reasons of the State. In the opening *Shloka* (verse) of the VI Act, we hear *Sidharthaka* applauding Chandra gupta in the following words:

Jaddi ajandithi Chandmachandantto.
(Glory to Chandragupta also the moon to eyes of the people.)

— and yet again, after a few lines, using the epithet; "*Chandsirino*" (Moon-like) for Chandragupta.

The image of the lunar eclipse in respect of Chandragupta, is therefore, not unlike the image of the sun-under-cloud in respect of Prince Hal. The lunar eclipse image is further expanded when the manager refers to *Malayketu,* the *malech* (alien), Prince, being propped up by *Rakshasa*:

Krurgrahaha sketushrichandram sampurnmandamidanim Abhibhavitumichati balat..... (Act I)
(The malignant planet, *ketu* (*Malayketu)* wishes forcibly to eclipse the orb of the moon (Chandragupta).)

Thus while taking the advantage of the names of Chandragupta and order to underline the threatened attack on Chandragupta by Malayketu, he lets Chanakya take up the cudgels on behalf of his protégé:

Tamektwamupagatam dyutimiv Prahladyantim jagata kaschrondradiv Chandraguptanriptch kartumwaywasa – yat prithaka (Act-II)
(Who dares to separate Chandragupta from sovereignty, like moon-light from the moon?)

It is logical that while *Malayketu* is associated with the malignant planet *ketu,* and Chandragupta Maurya with *Chandra* (Moon), the sun-image, the prerogative of the king in the Elizabethan context, is used here for Chanakya, the Guru and the father-figure:

> "*ghamnatishayayati*"
> (surpassing the splendour of thousand-rayed sun)

And finally to get back to the question of morality, while both Vishakadatta and Shakespeare adopt an amoral stance, the former does so more blatantly and categorically. There is no question of the expiation of the sin of deposition and liquidation of the *Nanda* dynasty, no publicised Holy Wars (as in 1 and 2 *Henry IV*) nor even foreign wars (as in *Henry V*), no haunting of the conscience by the ghosts of those liquidated (as we find in the crucial moments right from Promfret castle to Agincourt). The only question that engages the mind of Chanakya is how to make the crown safe and secure for his Prince, and the only test that Vishakhadatta appears to apply to his Prince is administrative acumen.

To the central moral question of usurpation, both Vishakhadatta and Shakespeare add a further dimension by introducing the question of the individual conscience versus blind obedience of the subjects, and both come up with the same answer. Despite the long-laboured exposition of the Selic Law by the Archbishop justifying Henry's claim to the French throne, we are not allowed to forget its dubiousness, and the issue crops up again in the debate among the soldiers on the eve of Agincourt. It becomes apparent that the average soldier is far from convinced of his (i.e. the king's) "Cause being just and his quarrel honourable." The general attitude of the soldiers is voiced by Bates:

> ....We know enough if we know we are the king's subjects. If his cause be wrong, our obedience to the king wipes the crime of it out of us. (*Henry V*, IV.i. 130-32).

This amounts to a willing suspension of morality. It is interesting to note that faced with similar issue, Vishakhadatta too comes up with the same solution so much so that Bhagurayan, one of the minor characters in *Mudra Rakshasa,* appears to confirm and surmise the verdict of Bates:

> *Tadagram Kurvano hitamhitmithdeddhuna*
> *vichartikrantah kimiti partantro vimrishati* (Act V)
> (A man in dependent position need not debate the question of moral or immoral while executing a command.)

It is a pity that only one historical play of Sanskrit is extant. Nevertheless as demonstrated above, a comparative analysis, essentially postcolonial, of the making of the two princes – Chandragupta and Prince Hal – enriches our understanding of Sanskrit as well as Shakespearean historical drama. What is more, it demonstrates that Vishakhadatta had succeeded in resolving a grave aesthetic problem centuries before Shakespeare faced and resolved the same precisely in similar fashion. As a matter of fact no nation can claim any monopoly in the domain of literature. All great literature transcends time and space. No wonder therefore that classical Sanskrit literature provides characters and episodes which can be placed with pride beside the best of their counterparts in Western literature. So much for Macaulay's vainglorious "shelf". It is about time we discard the myopic colonial glasses and remember the following words of Walt Whitman about his song (as also about all great literature):

> These are really the thoughts of all men in all ages and lands, they are not original with me,
> If they are not yours as much as mine they are nothing, or next to nothing.

Works Cited

Boehmer, E., "Postcolonialism", *Literary Theory and Criticism(ed.)*. Patricia Waugh: Oxford, 2011.

Boehmer, Elleke. "Postcolonialism" in Patricia Waugh (*ed.*), *Literary Theory and Criticism.* Oxford University Press 2006.

Keith, A.B., *The Sanskrit Drama in its Origin, Development, Theory and Practice,* Oxford, 1924.

Lucas, F.L., *Tragedy, Serious Drama in Relation to Aristotle's Poetics,* London, 1957.

Shakespeare, W., *Henry IV, Part I* (Arden Edition)

———, *Henry IV, Part II* (Arden Edition)

———, *Henry V* (Arden Edition)

Shaw, J.S., "The Sun and the Moon: Structural use of the Images in *Henry IV. Part I*", *Journal of the Bhagalpur University Humanities,* Vol. XI, No. 2, 1978.

———, *Shakespeare's History Plays: A Revaluation.* New Delhi: Atlantic Publication, 2010.Revised edition,

Spurgeon, C., *Shakespeare's Imagery,* Cambridge, 1965.

Tillyard, E.M.W., *Shakespeare's History Plays,* Penguin, 1962.

Vishakadatta, *Mudra Rakshasa,* (*ed.*) J.C. Misra, Varanasi, 1972.

Winternitz, M., *A History of Indian Literature,* Vol. III, Part I (*Tr.*) S. Jha, New Delhi, 1977.

Walt Whitman, "Song of Myself", 17. ll. 355-60. W. J. Fisher and Others (*ed.*) *American Literature of the Nineteenth Century: An Anthology.* New Delhi: Eurasia, 1964.

Sringara Rasa in the Early Poetry of Keats

(*Homage to Dr. R.C. Prasad*)

Dr. Ratri Ray

Come back into memory, like as thou wer't
in the day-spring of thy fancies, with hope
like a fiery column before thee....

Lamb ends this famous invocation with the words: "..... Samuel Taylor Coleridge; Logician, Metaphysician, Bard." Let me end the sentence with the words; "Dr. R.C. Prasad; scholar, academician, mentor." You will find that the prose rhythm does not suffer.

Our gurus, or mentors, make us what we are. People tell me that I know a bit about *Rasavada,* but whatever I know about it is because of my mentor, Dr. Prasad. It was he who inspired me to study *Rasavada* at the time when I wanted to do something new, which yet would not be totally new. It was only Dr. Prasad who could have fulfilled this paradoxical demand by introducing me to this age-old theory which would be a completely new thing in the late 1970s if applied to English literature; I can best pay my homage to him by presenting a brief exposition of the evocation of *sringara rasa* in the early poetry of Keats.

It will be but scant justice to Keats to take up any of the pre-*Endymion* poems. *Calidore* is but a fragment about a medieval knight-errant and cannot be taken really seriously. It contains a passage in which *sringara rasa* would seem to be present:

He feels a moisture on his cheek and blesses
With lips that tremble and with glistening eye
All the soft luxury
That nestled in his arms. (Keats, p.10)

This seems to be a case of *sambhoga sringara,* for it describes love in union. Seems to be, yet *sringara* is not undoubtedly present. Let me clarify why I think so, for many readers may easily find *rasa* here.

As such, *sambhoga sringara* has not inspired the Sanskrit acharyas much. They become eloquent when discussing the heroine's capacities in this direction, but *sambhoga* in its theoretical aspect has not been productive of much analysis. Keats' passage goes on, describing "soft dimpled arms" and their disastrous effect on the young knight. The trouble is, all this sensuous paraphernalia does not seem (to me at least) to generate *sringara*.

Methinks the poet doth protest too much. The lines do not ring with authentic passion. *Bhava* is definitely there, but does it condense into *rasa*? The reader has but to remember the touchstone of just one line evoking true *sambhoga sringara* to realize the hollowness of this passage:

> If it be love indeed, tell me how much? Or turning to lyric poetry:
> For God's sake hold your tongue and let me love.

(N.B. This is a scholarly article, meant for scholars. So I am not supplying references for such obviously known lines as these. No doubt this is being defiantly unscholarly, but there it is.)

Here indeed we are overwhelmed by the swell and surge of *sringara*. All the lipping about in the passage quoted above fails to achieve the effect of these single line utterances. Such comparisons are neither fair nor proper, but these touchstones are used merely to point out that in this passage, as I personally feel, *rasa*-experience does not occur. What is the *rasa*-experience like? Visvantha Kaviraja tells us:

> *Vedyantara sparsasunyo brahmasvda-sahodarah*
> *Lokottara camatkara prana kescit-pramtrbhih*
> (Free from contact of aught else perceived, akin as a uterine brother, to the ecstatic contemplator's perception of God, the life whereof is hyper-physical wonder, is enjoyed by those competent.) (Babu, p.115)

When such an experience really occurs, the reader is not left in any doubts whatsoever. I am rather finicky about *rasa*-experience. Such an event, I feel, does not occur very easily. One has to sweat blood over it. Keats is young yet, he has not yet learnt to load every rift with ore. Let us possess our souls in patience.

Turning to *Endymion* one finds *sringara* welling up again and again. Before taking up the relevant passages, let us talk about a few more details about the treatment of the theme of love in this poem. Keats describes the effect of love upon Endymion in many isolated passages. He is shown groaning under love's yoke in the most classically approved manner, whether Sanskrit or Petrarchan. According to the *rasa* theory there are eight states of *sattvikabhava,* give or take one or two. Dhananjaya gives them in this order:

> *Stambha-pralaya-romāricam svedo vaivarna-vepathu*
> *Asru-vaisyaryam iti astau*
> (The eight involuntary states are : paralysis, fainting, horripilation, sweating, change of colour, trembling, weeping and change of voice.) (Hass, p.108)

Some of these are quite clearly to be found in our hero:

> But in the selfsame fixed trance he kept
> Aye, even as dead-still as a marble man
> ....
> His footsteps slow
> From stumbling over stumps and hillocks.(Keats, p.56)

These would be, respectively, the states of *pralaya, stambha* and *vepathu.* Later he faints at a touch from his Goddess and that too, in a dream:

> Methought I fainted at the charmed touch
> ....
> I sighed
> To faint once more by looking on my bliss.
> ....
> Ah, my sighs, my tears
> My clenched hands.(Keats, pp. 61-62)

In other words, both *pralaya* and *asru* are here. This may seem to be hyperbolical and unrealistic today. Perhaps that is because, in this permissive age, we have become inoculated against this deadly disease. In all classical literature however the first attack of love was a particularly virulent one. Even stalwart heroes had to take to their couches under its devastating effects. The Sanskrit scholars do not include sighs in their list, clearly because it is too elementary a state. Usually the lists begin with *asru*–sighs would be rather tame a beginning. Be that as it may, Keats' description of Endymion in the throes of love tallies with the prescribed descriptions in Sanskrit poetics.

Let us take up now the passages in which *sringara rasa* has been generated. The first such passage occurs when Endymion describes a dream to Peona in which he had met Cynthia. There is nothing far-fetched in this, for according to Sanskrit poetics dream is one of the five ways in which love of the *purva-raga* kind can be generated. As a matter of fact Endymion in every way, including the process of falling in love, acts exactly like a *dhira-lalita* hero, but that is rather irrelevant. In this dream the Moon Goddess comes to him. There is a long description of her beauty:

> She had
> Indeed, locks bright enough to make me mad.
> ....
> Such a paradise of lips and eyes
> Blush-tinted cheeks, half smiles and faintest sighs
> That when I think thereon my spirit clings
> And plays about its fancy.(Keats, pp. 60, 612-613, 618-621)

Then he describes how she came to woo him:

> Towards me like a very maid
> Came blushing, waning, willing and afraid
> Willing and afraid the hand: Ah! twas too much
> Methought I fainted at the charmed touch.
> (Keats, p. 61, 364-67)

This dream is recounted in no less than a hundred lines. There can be no question that the emotions involved are intense ones, but, most unfortunately, there are certain impediments to a truly flawless *rasa* experience. First of all, Cynthia's beauty is described in great detail and secondly, Endymion's intense love is described too many times. Even without following the *rasa* theory, it can be said that the very length of the passage renders it diffuse and ineffectual. The *rasavadi* will take a look and pronounce it to be a case of *rasa-vighna.*

Rasavighna occurs when, due to certain reasons, *rasa* cannot be experienced properly. There are no less than ten such reasons as given by Mammata. Two of them are relevant for us: "*dipti punah punah*" and "*angasyapayati*". (Dwivedi, pp. 357-58)The first of these occurs when the same *rasa* is evoked again and again with little interval in between. Anandavardhana has called it *"paunah-punyena dipanam"* and has given the famous example of "*parimlana-kusuma parimala*" which was later repeated by almost every *acarya.* Just as a flower, if crushed repeatedly, loses its fragrance, so *rasa* if evoked too frequently cannot be enjoyed. Endymion's love loses by this flaw of excessive repetition.

The second reason for *rasavighna* is *angasyapayati,* or too long a description of those elements that help create *rasa.* Cynthia's beauty, being *uddipana,* generates love, but the descriptions are so long that they minimize the effect of the *rasa* itself.

Here therefore in this long passage *madhura rasa* of the *sambhoga* variety could easily have been created but *rasavighna* occurs and the reader is prevented from enjoying the ineffable pleasures of *rasa*-experience. Such an unsatisfactory state, however, cannot endure forever and later when Endymion meets the Indian Maid we have *sṛngara rasa* that at first seems to be *kusumbha raga* and finally develops into the *manjaistha* variety. Acarya Visvanatha Kaviraja has classified this *rasa* into three categories (a) *nitiraga* is enduring but undemonstrative love *(b) kusumbha raga* is intense, beautifully expressed but evanescent love (c) *manjaistha raga* which is beautifully expressed and enduring love – "*manjaistha –raga mahustada yannapaityati sobhate.*" This is a curious instance of love of the second variety turning into the third. We know that Endymion's true devotion is to Cynthia and his attitude to the Indian Maid seems to be superficial (*kusumbha raga*). But as we know that the Maid is actually Cynthia in disguise, his love for her would, in the light of this knowledge, seem to be the true devotion of *manjaistha raga.*

Not only does the moon shine on the lovers but *ujjvala rasa* (another name for *sṛngara*) itself bathes the whole scene with its gentle radiance. Here we have the young *dhira-lalita* hero as the *saraya*(recipient) of the *rasa* and the Indian maid as the *alambana* (fundamental determinant). Her beauty and youth, the lovely forest glade, Endymion's own ability to accept this earthly love – all these are the *uddipana*(excitant). Endymion's joy, his admiration of the maid's charm and grace, his realization of the precarious beauty of this mortal love – all these are the *anubhava*(consequences). *The sthayi bhava* of course is *rati* and pleasure, doubt, hesitation etc. are the *sringara*(transitory emotions). Everyone, irrespective of time and space can experience this *rasa* because all these factors get universalized (*sadharani karana*) as the reader identifies (*tadatmya*) himself with either of the characters. The permanent emotion (*sthayi*) of love as depicted here is not the love of Endymion for the Maid, or of the reader for the Maid, or of the reader for his own beloved (*nija-kanta-smrti*). It is love in a liberated form.

It is difficult to resist pointing out another aspect of this passage. This entire speech is more than a hundred lines long and full of attractive phrases:

> See, through the trees a little river go
> All in its midday gold and glimmering,
> Honey from the gnarled hive I will bring
> And apples, wan with sweetness, gather thee,
> Cresses that grow where no man may them see
> And sorrel untorn by the dew-claw'd stag. (Keats, p.130)

Keats has already started to load his rift with ore. Arnold will call it natural magic and what will the *Rasavadi* say? This lovely description definitely produces the effect of *camatkara. A* disquisi-tion into this quality will be irrelevant, but I would like to tell the reader that acarya Ksemendra has listed ten varieties of *camatkara.* The first of these is *avicarita ramaniya,* translated by S.K. De "as it appeals without much thought". (De: 1365) With one's brains to appreciate the beauty of the passage, we experience the enchantment of *avicarita-ramaniya.*

Much more, indeed, remains to be said, but let us bring our reading of Keats to an end here. At the end, I once more bow down in homage to my *guru,* Dr. R.C. Prasad, who had revealed this wonderful world of *Rasavada* to me. Requiescat in pace.

Works Cited

De, S.K. *History of Sanskrit Poetics.* Calcutta: Firma K.L.M. Pvt. Ltd., 1365, Bengali year.

Dwivedi, R.C. (Tr.). *The Poetic Light: Kavyaprakasa of Mammata.* Patna: MLBD.

Haas, C.O. *The Dasarupa.* New York: Columbia University Press, 1912.

Keats, John and P.B. Shelley. *Complete Poetical Works.* The Modern Library edn., New York: Random House.

Mittra, Babu P. and Ballantyne, J.R. (*Tr.*). *The Sahitya Darpana or Mirror of Composition.* Calcutta: Bibliotheca Indica,1861.

E.M. Forster's *A Passage to India* as a Passage to India's Freedom

Dr. Ashok Kumar Sinha

Preamble

E.M. Forster visited India in 1912-13 and, encouraged by Syed Masood, the original for Dr. Aziz, began his first draft of the novel *A Passage to India.* After a second visit to India in 1921-22, he finally completed and published *A Passage to India* in 1924.

It is important to note that E.M. Forster's second visit to India and the final drafting of the novel coincided with increasing activity for political independence, the Amritsar Massacre 1919 and Mahatma Gandhi's passive resistance movement and imprisonment from 1922-24.

Though such significant movements are referred to only obliquely in the text of the novel, E.M. Forster's political concern can not be denied.

It is also worth noting that this English Traveller in India shaped his novel *A Passage to India* using his experiences in Bihar as his main inspiration. Bankipore (modern Patna, the capital of Bihar in India) became metamorphosed into Chandrapore. Barabar caves (near Gaya) became Marabar caves. Modern Gandhi Maidan of Patna became Oval Maidan. Bankipore Club (in Patna) became Chandrapore Club.

The aim of this paper is to throw some light on an aspect of the novel which perhaps has not drawn the attention of other literary critics. This aspect is basically concerned with the subtle way in which the novel gradually builds up towards a climax which specifically states how India will surely make a passage towards freedom very soon. Published in 1924, the novel takes only twenty three years to fulfill what it has forecast, because it is 1947 when India finally gets its freedom.

This paper tries to give an in-depth analysis of the major characters and the important events which go to form the essential fabric of the climax. So this paper tries to trace how, from the very beginning of the novel, Forster has plotted his major thematic concerns and the socio-cultural backgrounds of the major characters in such a way that India's freedom in the near future seems to become inevitable.

The major characters belong to various segments of the pre-independent India society and even the British who are ruling the country have various shades in their attitudes. Dr. Aziz is an Indian Muslim Doctor who begins with dancing attendance to the British but later becomes anti-British. Mahmoud Ali is an Indian Muslim lawyer, a friend of Dr. Aziz, who harbours feelings against the British. Hamidullah, also a friend of Dr. Aziz and a distant relative educated at Cambridge, is positively anti-British.

The Indian Hindus are represented by Godbole who is an insensitive superstitious teacher non-committal about his stand for or against the British. But Amritrao is an anti-British Hindu lawyer.

On the other hand, the British themselves have different shades of responses. Cyril Fielding, the Principal of the local Government College, begins with soft feelings for the Indians, specially Dr. Aziz. But later he changes his point of view. Miss Adela Quested who has come from England to marry Ronny Heaslop, and Mrs. Moore who has accompanied Adela to meet her son Ronny are the two British tourists who have come to see the real India and start with a fondness for the Indians which gradually changes its colour. Ronny Heaslop is the British Magistrate who is biased against and intolerant of Indians. The boastful Major Callandar is the British Civil Surgeon who is definitely anti-Indian. Mrs. Callandar hates the Indians as "uncultured inferiors." Mr. Mc Bryde, the Superintendent of Police and Mr. Turton, the Collector also hate the Indians. So the major characters carry within them the sparks of emotions which are gradually going to ignite the main battle of wills of the novel.

The novel begins with the following description:

> Except for the Marabar caves – and they are twenty miles off the city of Chandrapore presents nothing extraordinary ... Inland, the prospect alters. There is an Oval Maidan, and a long sallow hospital. Houses belonging to the Eurasians stand on the high ground by the railway station. (Forster, p.1)

Interestingly enough, the Marabar caves which will play an immensely dramatic role in the forging of the climax of the novel, has been presented right at the very beginning. And the Eurasians have been already presented on "high ground" in the very opening paragraph of the opening chapter.

Chapter Two presents Dr. Aziz visiting his friend Hamidullah, and the impossibility of any friendship with an Englishman is already highlighted. Mahmoud Ali, a lawyer tells his friend Dr. Aziz:

> The red-nosed boy has again insulted me in Court, I do not blame him. He was told that he ought to insult me. (Forster, p. 3)

Such a reference made to the insult meted out to the Indian lawyer in the Court subtly hints at the way in which racial prejudice and misunderstanding have already permeated in the very "justice" being carried out by the British in pre-independent India. And Hamidullah comes out here as positively anti-British.

Even Dr. Aziz is already conscious of a net when it is observed in Chapter Two:

> But at last he was rattling towards the civil lines, with a vivid sense of speed. As he entered their avid tidiness, depression suddently seized him. The roads named after victorious generals and intersecting at right angles, were symbolic of the net Great Britain had thrown over India. He felt caught in their meshes. (Forster, p. 7)

Dr. Aziz already feels "caught in their meshes."

Chapter Three presents the English Club, and the British attitude towards the Indians becomes obvious. Indians are not allowed into this club even as guests. When Adela voices her desire to see the real India, the British people gathered in the Club make fun of the very idea. Mrs. Callandar observes that the kindest thing one can do to a native is to let him die. The natives of India give her the creeps.

Chapter Five tries to bridge the gap between the British and the Indians by throwing a Bridge Party which turns out to be not a success. The Indians are constrained and the English are arrogant. Mrs. Turton's attitude is just disdainful. Mrs. Moore and her son Ronny have a heated exchange of words in which the different shades of their attitudes come out. When she tells Ronny that his sentiments are of a god, her son hits back by retorting that Indians like gods. When Mrs. Moore concludes by saying that Englishmen like posing as gods, Ronny observes:

> There's no point in all this. Here we are, and we're not going to stop, and the country's got to put up with us, gods or no gods. (Forster, p. 34)

But there is yet another shade of emotion presented by Cyril Fielding who is a liberal broad-minded Englishman who has travelled widely and does not fit into the narrow minded and arrogant world of the English community. Fielding and Dr. Aziz take to each other immediately.

Let us now look at the Marabar caves which have been introduced to us in the very first sentence of the novel. The visit of some major characters to the Marabar caves can be interpreted and understood as the central part of the novel which is going to change the equations between the characters and the turn of events in such a dramatic way that the gaps between the British and the Indians will be exposed making the readers conclude that if the winter of India's bondage has become so deeply entrenched, then the Spring of India's freedom is not far behind.

Dr. Aziz has planned meticulously for this visit to the Marabar caves in which he has invited Adela Quested and Mrs. Moore as his guests (primarily because he does not want them to visit his own shabby household). Fielding and Professor Godbole unfortunately miss the train to Marabar caves. So Dr. Aziz alone dances attendance to the British visitors paying through his nose to make them comfortable. Yet the Marabar expedition proves to be a huge failure because, Adela comes out accusing Dr. Aziz of having tried to molest her inside one of the caves.

This accusation becomes the spark which ignites the fire of racial hatred of and for the British in India. Dr. Aziz is arrested and imprisoned. The British come out with group hysteria against Dr. Aziz and all the other Indians. There come out absurd over-reactions from the British against the Indians. And the Indians themselves rally around Dr. Aziz to form a tough alliance. Fielding resigns from the English Club and joins his new allies.

The day of Adela's trial arrives. The court and the entire Chandrapore are buzzing with anti-British feelings among the Indians. And the English community covers up Adela and is full of hatred for the Indians. Mr. McBryde questions Adela "with agreed words."

You went alone into one of those caves.... The prisoner followed you, didn't he?

Adela asks for half a minute before she replies to that question. And then she blurts out:

> I'm afraid I have made a mistake.... Dr. Aziz never followed me to the cave. (Forster, p.170)

Adela withdraws the charge and the Superintendent of Police Mr. McBryde gazes at his witness as if she was a broken machine. The flimsy framework of the court breaks up, the shouts of decision and rage culminate, people scream and curse, kiss one another and weep passionately. Miss Quested has renounced her own people. She is swept away from the English by the crowd and Fielding puts her in his carriage for her own safety.

It is from this point of the novel that events start building up in a specific direction hinting that the days of the British in India are numbered. After the victory feast, Fielding and Dr. Aziz talk under the stars on the roof of the Nawab Bahadur's house Dr. Aziz is calm and gracious, but bitter. He plans to leave Imperial India to work in some modern state far away from the British. Strains have already developed in the friendship between Dr. Aziz and Fielding. Racial division, suspicion and resentment over Adela cause a rapid cooling of the intimacy between Dr. Aziz and Fielding. So Fielding makes a passage to England and is described as returning to the familiarity of the Mediterranean with relief. The European summer at last brings hope and a sense of renewal for him.

But this is not the end of the novel, for, in Part 3 entitled Temple the entire criss-cross of attractions and revulsions suggested in the earlier two parts reaches a crescendo. Dr. Aziz has settled in Mau with his children, and he has already broken with Fielding pre-supposing that he (Fielding) has married Adela in England. Now Fielding arrives on an official visit to Mau with his wife and her brother, and Dr. Aziz is determined to avoid him. Later, Dr. Aziz discovers that Fielding has actually married Stella Moore, Mrs. Moore's daughter by her second marriage, not Adela Quested. But that does not change the human equation between the friends.

The novel ends with the final ride of Dr. Aziz and Fielding which marks their final separation from each other. When Fielding mocks at

Dr. Aziz's dream of nationhood, Dr. Aziz tells him that they will only remain friends when the English are thrown out of India:

"Fielding mocked again"

And Aziz in an awful rage danced this way and that, not knowing what to do, and cried:

> Down with the English anyhow. That's certain. Clear out, you fellows, double quick. I say, we may hate one another, but we hate you most. If I don't make you go, Ahmed will Karima will, if it's fifty five hundred years we shall get rid of you, yes, we shall drive every blasted Englishman into the sea, and then ..... you and I shall be friends.
>
> (Forster, p. 242)

Thus it is evident that there is a subtle progression of human interactions and events in *A Passage India* which makes the novel predict that the day of the freedom for India is not very far away. Indeed *A Passage to India* can be certainly interpreted as a passage to India's freedom.

Work Cited

Forster, E.M., *A Passage to India,* Sana'a University, Sanna, Republic of Yemen, 2006.

Edwin Arnold's *The Light of Asia*: Buddhist Poetic Narrative and Cultural Diffusion

(In Memory of Prof. Ram Chandra Prasad)

Prof. Shaileshwar Sati Prasad

Do not think there is any distinction,
(says Saraha, the Buddhist poet)
Yet it possesses no single nature,
For I know it to be quite pure,
Do not sit at home, do not go to the forest,
But recognize the mind wheresoever you are.
When one abides in perfect enlightenment,
where is samsara and where is Nirvana?

(Sarahpa)

Sir Edwin Arnold's *The Light of Asia* or *The Great Renunciation (Mahabhinishkramana) Being The Life and Teaching of Gautama Prince of India and Founder of Buddhism (As told in verse by an Indian Buddhist)* was published in 1879 and "led to quite a widespread interest in Buddhism among the middle classes in England and America, and aided the Buddhist renaissance in Sri Lanka." What is significant that this narrative poem in blank verse inspired the colonized from India and the writers, poets and artists from both USA and Great Britain. In India this poem was an inspiring *mantra* for a spiritual leader like Vivekananda, the father of the nation Mahatama Gandhi, the young radical activist Jawaharlal Nehru and the great philosopher Dr. S. Radhakrishanan.

On February 2, 1900, Vivekananda delivered a speech at the Shakespeare Club Pasadena, California, USA, and said:

> Almost all of you, perhaps, have read Edwin Arnold's poem on the life of Buddha, and some of you, perhaps, have gone into the subject with more scholarly interest, as in English, French and German, there is quite a lot of Buddhistic literature. Buddhism itself is the most interesting of subjects, for it is the first historical outburst of a world religion.

He writes that in India during the days of Buddha the Brahmins debarred the masses from all knowledge and severely punished those who wanted to learn the Vedas:

> If just a word of the Vedas entered the ears of a man, terrible punishment was visited upon him. The priests had made a secret of the Vedas – the Vedas that contained the spiritual truths discovered by the ancient Hindus!
>
> At last one man could bear it no more. He had the brain, the power, and the heart – a heart as infinite as the broad sky. He felt how the masses were being led by the priests and how the priests were glorying in their power, and he wanted to do something about it. He did not want any power over any one, and he wanted to break the mental and spiritual bonds of men. His heart was large. The heart, many around us may have, and we also want to help others. But we do not have the brain; we do not know the ways and means by which help can be given. But this man had the brain to discover the means of breaking the bondages of souls. He learnt why men suffer, and he found the way out of suffering. He was a man of accomplishment, he worked everything out; he taught one and all without distinction and made them realize the peace of enlightenment. This was the man Buddha.

In this context in order to emphasize the admiration of Buddha he refers to Edwin Arnold's *The Light of Asia:*

> You know from Arnold's poem, *The Light of Asia,* how Buddha was born a prince and how the misery of the world struck him deeply; how, although brought up and living in the lap of luxury, he could not find comfort in his personal happiness and security; how he renounced the world, living his princess and new-born son, behind; how he wandered searching for truth from teacher to teacher; and how he at last attained to enlightenment.

Similarly Gandhi and Nehru both were deeply impressed by Arnold's poem. C.D. Narasimhaiah in his autobiography *N for Nobody* informs that Gandhi and Nehru were first introduced to *the Bhagavad Gita* and the Buddha story through Edwin Arnold's *Song Celestial* and *The Light of Asia.*

Gandhi himself refers to this book in his *Autobiography* which was recommended to him by two theosophist friends which he read with greater interest and pleasure than Arnold's translation of *the Gita.* Like Gandhi, Dr. S. Radhakrishnan, too, had studied *The Light of Asia* very deeply and critically. In his English translation of *The Dhammapada,* he quotes from *The Light of Asia* in his note to *Yamakaraggo* – the Twin-Verses.

The Buddha's teaching is a way of life, not a way of talking. We are what we love and care for. Some modern existentialists affirm that man is a self-creating, self-maintaining, self-fashioning will. The importance of human effort is stressed in this chapter. Every moment the course of our life is being decided. The raw material out of which life is made takes its form and sets by our thoughts and deeds. As it does so, the unknown future becomes the irrevocable past. Our freedom can operate only within limits.

The Buddha does not support the cynical view that nothing really matters. For him every act has significance. He criticizes Makkhali Gosala's teaching that all action is the foundation of all serious living.

> Seek nought from the helpless gods by gift and hymn
> Nor bribe with blood, nor feed with fruits and cakes,
> Each man his poison makes. *(The Light of Asia)*

While translating "Jaravaggo – Old Age" 153 and 154, Radhakrishnan comments on these and cites the translation of the allegory done by Edwin Arnold:

> 153 and 154 represent the words which Gautama the Buddha is said to have uttered at the moment of his enlightenment. In the commentary on the *Brahmajala Sutta,* this verse is said to be the first utterance of the Buddha, his last being the words in the *Mahaparinibbana Sutta*: "Life is subject to age, strive in earnest."
>
> The builder of the house is craving, *tanha.* It is the cause of rebirth. If we shake off craving there is nothing to bind us to the wheel of existence.

kama janami te mulam, sakalpat kila jayase
na ivam samkalpayisyami tato me na bhavisyasi.
(Desire, I know thy root; from imagination art thou born:
no more shall I indulge in imagination, I shall have no
desire any more.)

Sir Edwin Arnold renders the allegory thus:

Many a house of life
Hath held me – seeking ever him who wrought
These prisons of the senses, sorrow-fraught;
Sore was my ceaseless strife
But now,
Thou builder of this tabernacle – Thou!
I know Thee! Never shalt Thou build again
These walls of pain,
Fresh rafters on the clay;
Broken Thy house is, and the ridge-pile split!
Delusion fashioned it!
Safe pass I them – deliverance to obtain.

Arnold's contribution to the strengthening of India's cultural nationalism through his *The Light of Asia* is a very remarkable contribution of a person belonging to the hegemonic ruling race and deserves more serious academic attention and focus. In this context Elleke Boehmer rightly lauds Arnold's contribution on the cultural level:

> Colonization in many cases involved a translation between cultures. Edwin Arnold, the Victorian colonial headmaster, poet and later diplomat, presents a case in point. While promoting Empire in his leaders for the *Daily Telegraph*, Arnold was also the author of a verse biography of Buddha, *The Light of Asia* (1879), which T.S. Eliot read, and the translator of *the Bhagavad-Gita* into English in which form Mohandas Gandhi encountered the poem.

However, Boehmer raises a vital point to ponder:

> Edwin Arnold, who differed from many in regarding Indians as "civilized" none the less can imperial rule as a task of improvement committed "by providence to English race."

The impact of Arnold's poem on those Indians who were fighting against the British imperial rule, was not only the result of cultural dimensions but also rooted in Buddha's concept of compassion and non-violence.

Jawaharlal Nehru understood this well and after independence it still became "A conviction that non-violence can serve to lessen world's tensions." Michael Brecher writes about the "legacy of India's ancient tradition, the principle of Ahimsa and non-violence" and very perceptively comments:

> In the land where Buddhism originated non-violence as a method of social action is deeply rooted. More recently in the hands of Gandhi, it became the creed of Indian nationalism and left an incredible mark on the generation which now rules the state.

Jawaharlal Nehru due to his reading of Arnold's poem became attracted to Buddhism and it was due to Buddha's "stress on free-will, its contempt for superstition and the message for non-violence." In his *Discovery of India* Nehru writes about Arnold's impact on him:

> The Buddha story attracted me in early boyhood and I was drawn to young Siddhartha who after many inner struggles and pains and torments was to develop into the Buddha. Edwin Arnold's *Light of Asia* became one of my favorite books.

Due to his admiration for Buddha, Nehru assents:

> Some words of the Buddha or of the Christ could shine out with deep meaning and seen to be applicable as much today as when they were uttered two thousand or more years ago. There was compelling reality about them, a permanence which time and space could not touch.

Due to this in 1955 he narrated the story of Ashoka to Nikita Khruschev who was elated on Soviet scientists' achievement of perfecting "a terrifying weapon of mass destruction." He told Mr. Khruschev "You know, Mr. Khruschev, more than two thousand years ago a great warrior ruled over India. His name was Emperor Ashoka. Through frequent wars he extended his dominion throughout the land. His generals were victorious everywhere, and after every battle they would report thousands killed and many taken as slaves. Ashoka became troubled by this slaughter, and in time was converted to Buddhism." Nehru further said that when Ashoka was informed that thousands had perished and his enemies were victims of untold destruction, he got up from his throne, took out his sword and broke it in two and thundered:

> Enough violence and carnage. There shall be no more. Peace will reign over the land.

Raja Rao, the eminent Indian novelist in English has compared Gandhi to Buddha and Nehru to Buddhisatwa. He writes about Gandhi's voyage to England:

> He left behind his widowed mother, his weeping wife, his first son – much like Gautama, the Buddha, unbeknownst to himself, this was the ride out from Kapilavastu.......

Moreover, in the great city of London:

> Just as the Buddha had, on the banks of Ganges wandered among the Yogis and the ascetics, questioning philosophers and practising severe austerities, Gandhi wandered among the Christians, the contraceptionists, the Fabians, living like a monk, for his habits of economy and his study of Hindu thought were begun in London.

If Gandhi is like Buddha for Raja Rao, Nehru is Buddhisatwa. He writes "Pandit Jawaharlal was the Buddhisatwa. Lord, Mayst thou have a halo round thy auspicious face!"

The comparisons of Gandhi and Nehru with Buddha and Buddhisatwa is important but what is more significant is the eternal presence of Buddha in the consciousness of a creative writer of India who writes in the English language of the colonizers and it is here that the far reaching impact of Arnold's *The Light of Asia* on the Indian psyche directly or indirectly is discernible.

It was Arnold's impact that was not only felt in India but also in the English speaking western countries. Rev. Wm. H. Channing wrote to a friend "*The Light of Asia* is a poem in which the effort is made to bring before our modern age, in the western world, that sublime embodiment of the finest genius of the orient, in its prime, whom we call BUDDHA, in living form, and to sketch this outline of his speculative and ethical system in vivid pictorial representation......"

Never has the image of the serene and heroic and saintly and gently sage been more beautifully portrayed than in this poem.... "...... Buddha lives and moves and speaks again in these pages, as he lived and moved and taught amid the sacred groves of India." Channing praises the poem and rightly comments:

> One of the chief charms of the poem is the singularly vital reality with which the very scenery and climate, the people and the communities, the manners, dwellings and actual society of Hindustan, two thousand years or more ago, is made to pass, as if in palingenesia, before and around us.

What is more he has a point when he says that Arnold "has found a fit sphere for his poetic genius in this representation of Buddha, in which he has embodied his own highest ideals and aspiration." Dr. Ripley in his review of the poem in the *New York Tribune* praises Arnold's affluence of imagination, splendor of diction, and virile descriptive power, which focus on Buddha's personality and as Arnold himself said "Not a single act or word is recorded...." which marks the perfect purity and tenderness of this Indian teacher, who united the truest princely qualities with the intellect of a sage and the passionate devotion of a martyr? He concluded that Arnold is a genuine profit of the soul as his imagination is combined with acute historical sense and rare perception of harmonies. He rightly comments that this poem forms a grave ethical treatise, shadowing forth in the legendary life of Siddhartha some of the deepest mysteries and loftiest experiences of the human soul. The great doctrine of renunciation, so earnestly insisted on by Goethe and Carlyle, is in fact the key-note of the poem, and the evolution of character from an exclusive devotion to self to a tender charity for our kind, which is so lucidly set forth in the philosophy of Herbert Spencer, is illustrated with all the charms of a fascinating narrative and the enchantments of melodious verse. As an exposition of the religious system of Buddha we reckon this poem as no more successful than the numerous similar attempts in prose. We have no sufficient data for the solution of the problem. But as a magnificient work of imagination, and a sublime appeal in the interests of the loftiest human virtue, we tender it the sincerest welcome, and grasp the author by the hand as a genuine prophet of the soul.

It appears–Arnold's own spiritual quest for self-realization, tranquility and peace in the intellectually volatile Victorian period where various dilemmas, Darwin's evolutionism, cross individualistic capitalism, all coalesced together and had a negative impact upon the general western consciousness. He had been a witness to the British tyranny during the first war of Indian independence in India. He was an inquisitive and enlightened person and found Buddha's rationalism and his advice of "Attho Dipobhava" self liberating. Therefore his soul stirring *The Light of Asia* influenced writers, poets and thinkers of various countries and cultures. A good example is that of the American novelist Dreiser. In his well researched paper "Some impressions of the Buddha: Dreiser and Sir Edwin Arnold's *The Light of Asia"*, Douglas C. Stenerson points out that "Dreiser drew heavily upon Arnold's poem for his knowledge of Buddhism. Some time between 1900 and 1916, he preserved nine substantial excerpts from it in his scrapbooks more than from any other single work."

This was due to the fact that the poem's major things were similar to "his own most deeply held feeling and conviction". These themes were "love of nature, Darwinian struggle, the power of sex", hence he was himself a seeker and wandered and appreciated what the Buddha's six year quest for enlightenment cost in suffering and self-sacrifice. On the philosophical level Dreiser along with his contemporaries faced a crisis of faith which prompted them to look beyond Christianity to Buddhism.

Stenerson points out that Arnold used the English translation of the Chinese of the *Abhinishkramanasutra* in which Arnold discerns and Arnold found compassion for every life and deep spiritual and mental evolution. The lines which influenced him are the following:

1. See the pleasurance of spring
   ....
   And all the Jungle laugh with nesting-songs
   ....
   Pleased at the spring time. (The Light of Asia *I: 12,13*)
2. How Lizard fed on ant. And snake on him ....
   Mutual murder from the worm to man. Who himself kills his fellow..... (I, 13-14)
3. Buddha says to Yashodhara
   Nay, though we locked up love and life with lips so, close to that night and day our breaths grew lips one, Time would thrust in between to flinch away
   My passion and thy grace. ..... (III, 40)
4. Oh suffering world; ......
   Of all its best, the anguish of its worth (III, 40)
5. How hath it steadied man to pray, and pray .....
   Tithes of the corn and sit, to chant the charms, ...
   Ascending day by day, like wasted smoke (IV, 62)
6. To search for truth ......
   The road would open for his painful feet..... (IV, 64)
7. Eyes lighted within love flames, alluring smiles ......
   And all the world was given in one warm kiss (IV, 105)
8. Final selection – "Arnold's interpretation of the Buddha's vision of an ordered universe." All things both great and small which suffer life. (VI, 109-110)

Thus, Stenerson rightly concludes that for Dreiser "the contrast between the materialist of modern west and the spiritual of the ancient east was one of those polarities between conflicting energy that demanded a greater degree of equation." In fact Dreiser approach was akin to the European artists and intellectuals because "When Buddhism arose in the West in the middle of 19th century, Western culture had in a sense been preparing for sometime...."

The fathers of the Enlightenment asserted that if there was God, he was like "the good watchmaker," he had made a mechanically perfect world and then withdrawn to let it tick away of its own accord. Edwin Arnold's poem is a synthesis of verbal art and spirituality, therefore, it directly contributed to the growth of a Buddhist poetic tradition in the contemporary world. As is natural in our globalised context and cultural diffusion, Buddha, his philosophy and the various sects have been utilized by Eliot, Ginsberg, from the west and K.K.N. Daruwala, Srinivas Rayaprel, and Meena Alexander from India who have utilized the English linguistics medium to correlate their quest to find inner poise in the Buddha path. The "karmakshetra" of Buddha was Magadh, Vaishali, Sarnath, the modern Hindi speaking states of Bihar and U.P., therefore, it is but natural that poets like Amarendra Kumar from Hazipur and Raj Kamal Shiromani from Patna have rendered their faith in Buddha's philosophy and "Nirvan" in their poetry.

But on the other hand it would be erroneous to think that Buddha inspired only those writing in English. His influence was on various cultures, languages and different art forms and literary genres through the ages. But in a short paper like this these various influences of Buddha on man's creativity, his aesthetic ideas and moral quest cannot be encompassed in the totality. Therefore while focusing on English poetry and Buddhism which achieved popularity and a sound cultural base due to Arnold's *The Light of Asia* this paper also examines Arnold's impact upon Hindi poetry as well as makes references to other Indian languages, too.

In the third section of *The Waste Land* entitled "The Fire Sermon" T.S. Eliot reinforced Arnold's Buddhist views on the intellectuals and poets, not only in the west but also in the English speaking different cultures. Eliot writes:

> Burning burning burning burning
> O Lord Thou pluckest me out
> O Lord Thou pluckest
> Burning

It would be helpful to note that "The Fire Sermon" was preached by the Buddha against the fires of passion, hatred and infatuation. In his notes to *The Waste Land* Eliot informs the complete text of the Buddha's fire Sermon (which corresponds an importance to the Sermon on the mount) from which these words are taken, will be found translated in the late Henry Clarke Warren's *Buddhism in Translation* (Harvard Oriental Series). Mr. Warren was one of the great pioneers of Buddhist Studies in the occident.

While commenting upon Eliot's notes F.O. Matthiessen writes that "some of the general references to the notes help to sharpen the outlines of Eliot's structure. The self consuming ferning of sterile passion which is the theme of "The Five Sermon" receives added emphasis from the pertinent reminder of the expression of that name by Buddha and St. Augustine....."

Eliot had read Arnold's poem and was well versed in Hindu and Buddhist writings. In *The Cocktail Party,* a poetic play, he has accentuated Buddha's last words to "unravel" the problems of lives tangled by mind created illusions of human attachment, the psychiatrist who is the central character advises his patients, they must "work out their salvation with diligence." These last words of Buddha are repeated three times in the play. Similarly these are the echoes of Mahayan doctrines in the following lines in his *Four Quartets.* He writes:

> The inner freedom from the practical desire,
> The release from action and suffering, release from the inner
> And the outer compulsion, yet surrounded
> By a grace of sense, a white light still and moving,
> Erhebung without motion, concentration
> Without elimination, both a new world
> And the old made explicit, understood
> In the completion of its partial ecstasy,
> The resolution of its partial horror.... (Burnt Norton)

Cyril Moore in his scholarly article "Buddhist Ideas in English Poetry" has not only raised and analysed the above ideas but also mentioned the influence of Mahayana on Eliot. Like this great poet Allen Ginsberg too was influenced by the Buddhist thought and this Eastern philosophy was a significant shaping influence on him. He quests for tops of the concept of Nirvana; one has to liberate himself from the body in order to get "Nirvana." But it cannot be attained, one has to get control over one's desire for the liberation, and it is possible only through enlightenment. Ginsberg writes:

> Desire that created me. Desire surprising the Babylonian possible world. That makes my flesh shake orgasm of thy name.
> *Ginsberg's quest always needed a spiritual Guru and in 1971 he met Tibetan Lama Chogyan Trungpa who rejected the conventions and American way of life and initiated him to "Vipasana" and finally took shelter in Vagrayana. He writes about these experiences with "ecstacy:"*

I seize the tablets of the law,
the spectral Buddha and the spectral
Chirst turn to a stick of shit the void, a fearful Idea,
I take the Crown of the Idea and place it on my head,
and sit a king beside the reptile Devas of my Karma.
(Television was a Baby Crawling toward that Death chamber.)

Broken bones O Buddha!/ Take my skull today/ Or take back my skull someday Birdbrain realized he was Buddha by mediating (Birdbrain).

In India T.S. Eliot made a great impact on the poets of different languages. Vishnu De and Muktibodh wrote poems on him and the Indian English poets too developed an interest in Buddhism and his philosophy. As discussed earlier Eliot's use of the "Fire Sermon" was utilized by Keki N. Daruwala, himself a zoroastrian fire worshipper having an encyclopedic reading into various schools of philosophy through his "Fire Sermon" a poem which he gives the title in Pali and calls it "Agni Sutta" and uses the English translation within brackets.

Srinivas Rayaprol has written two poems for Buddha. In the first one he follows the sonnet form and describes the mental state and the clash of feelings in Siddhartha before setting out on his quest for enlightenment "To seek the love that man has lost to find a foe." In the second poem he describes a conversation between Buddha and the Bodhee Tree.

And the Bo-tree rustled a leaf of sound
And said: This love, this incident will repeat
For other men and other trees. Why, my, friend.
For time will end no out?
And he
Not against time
For I contain that within this beaten body
And the green that shouts through your shoots
Through this flesh and bone
Not against Death
I am the man tomorrow and you.

Meena Alexander in her *Deer Park at Sarnath* describes the "flowering mustard" trees, clouds, soil and dirt of Sarnath where Buddha gave the Sermon and concludes:

There is no grief like this
The origin of landscape is mercy.

Vaishali and Patna have been closely linked with Buddha and in folk beliefs, rituals, way of life and the general consciousness of the people Buddhism has made a great impact. The English educated middle class academicians have also come under Buddha's influence. Dr. Amarendra Kumar, a professor of English at Hazipur and a significant poet in English has written poems on Buddha and related themes. His "Lord Buddha," "Caveman" and "Great Buddha Statue" are artistic creations. In "Lord Buddha," he writes about Buddha's spiritual experiences :

Footsore pilgrim In wood and valley endures the penance of a boundless quest

On vague horizons

....

The hungry emaciated hermit eats Sujata's sweet food......
No new phantom of Yashodhara gleaning golden mean

Under the Bo tree
The resplendent beam
Of a sublime ethical norm
annihilates the travails
of the interminable chain.

Spirit of regulate
The ascending circle
Of inner life,
In action;
Compassion to nourish
And heal.

Selfless focal trance
To breathe eternal bliss
Beyond the barren fire
And wheel.....
Nirvana.

Thus, Amarendra Kumar not only talks of "Nirvana" but also its impact on Ajanta caves, too. He describes his experiences watching the superb aesthetic creators:

> Image arch from
> Bodhisattva to Buddha
> Still halo ring –
> More sad than still.
>
> Pristine pieties
> Of the ogre's den
> In the sanctuary shift –
> Paranoiac selfish rift.
>
> . . . .
>
> . . . .
>
> Granite altar veg vow
> My holy mythical bow
> To break
> How.

Amarendra Kumar himself comments upon the poem that it is the result of "the inner gaze," "sense of wonder, mystery and curiosity" at Ajanta's "enigma of the eternal creative principle." The ironical discovery of the Buddhist caves during a tiger hunt is a strange amazing coincidence that sets off a train of conflicting images. The poet accepts "Buddha's salvation in self conquest and compassion – a healing balm to humanity." His "Great Buddha Statue" is a tribute to Daibutsu Buddha Statue in Bodh Gaya. "The Lotus Seat," "Dhyan Mudra" and the "Seated Buddha's," "Half Open Tranquil Eyes" and "The Sharp Sculptured Nose" all evoke mixed feelings in his heart.

Rajkamal Shiromani's *You and my Haiku* has these words:

> Surrender to Buddha
> Buddham sharanam gachchami
> Surrender to Sangha
> Sangham sharanam gachchami
> Surrender to dharma
> "Dhamman sharanam guchchami!"
> And that is SALVATION.

The Preface tells us that some of Shiromani's Haikus speak of the contemporary issues, torturing humanity and also of materialistic tendencies vanquishing men who treat everything as object in the 21st century. He writes thus:

> Which civilization
> We're heading to and for what
> money, terror, lust.
>
> Living with all fear
> A smiling face will become
> An archive's possession
>
> It's a world of fear
> Man is all afraid of man
> faking love and smile
> Death all around, death
> Of all morals and ethics
> Laughter in graveyard!
>
> Are we moving or
> turning turning all around
> reaching nowhere lost?

Arnold's contribution can best be evaluated if one examines his poem's unifying role not only among the various religions but also between the national culture of India and its subcultures. Assamese, Bengalis, Biharis, Uttarpradeshis and Kannadas all have accepted Buddha's path as a possible solution to the agonies and conflicts of our age. To take the example of the Hindi subculture region Ramchandra Shukla was sad to notice the absence of Buddha's memory in the masses therefore he translated *The Light of Asia* in Brajabhasha in 1922 and initiated a new trend. He did take liberties with the narrative and interpreted some of the western concepts of Arnold in his own way which is opponent in his *Buddhacharit.* The narrator says in Shukla's translation towards the end:

> चरित भयो यह पूर्ण, कहयों मैं जो कछु गाई
> तो यह साहस मात्र भक्ति बस जानो भाई

and ends with

बुद्धं शरणं गच्छामि
धम्मं शरणं गच्छामि
संघं शरणं गच्छामि

Shukla's translation led to Pt. Anup Sharma's *Siddhartha* which was modelled on Arnold's *The Light of Asia* but followed the Sanskrit's classical Mahakavya tradition. On the other hand Jagdish Kumar's *Nirvan* was published in 1977. He writes in his preface that there are two parts in Buddha's legend "Marganveshan" and "Margakhyan" and his poem is based upon the first one. He has based the biographical facts of Buddha's life on the ancient Buddhist texts like *Lalitvistar(s), Nidankatha; Buddhacharit* but has also taken good help from Arnold's poem. In fact he has quoted lines from him too:

Which seeing, Prince Siddhartha took the bird
Tenderly up, rested it in his lap
Or
I think I shall not lose my love for such as these.

Apart from the focus on Buddha's life and renunciation as well as his quest for man's salvation Arnold sensitively portrayed his wife Yashodhara's noble character which reinforced Buddha's humanism and the intensity of his psychological dilemmas. Maithilisharan Gupta's Hindi poem *Yashodhara* has echoes of Arnold's sensitivity and her role in the Buddhist tradition. The acceptance and portrayal of a woman's psychology adds pathos to the *The Light of Asia* and Yashodhara's questions inspire a sensitive contemporary Hindi poet Anamika to ask questions from the Dalai Lama from a female perspective:

The Dalai Lama continued to laugh
addressing a large audience
....
The Dalai fame was expounding
On the Four Noble Truths of Buddhism
....
How do those noble truths
Connect with

Such random bits
The ignoble truths of life
Does truth too have hierarchies
A caste system?
Brahmin truths at the top
And then the Shudra truths at the bottom?
....
Dalai Lama, you tell me, please
If the truth is like these mountain ranges —
high and low.
I prefer living in the deep cave of a small truth
Occasionally coming to you
To learn the nobler truths of life;
"Dalai Lama"
(Translated from Hindi by Ariene Zide & the poet)

Like Anamika we have to ask questions, seek our own salvation but surely owe to Buddha to know the path in the present day neocolonial globalized context.

Reading the Personal Essays of Mahadevi Verma in the Light of Charles Lamb's Essays

Amiya Bhushan Sharma

(*Remembering Ramchander Babu*)

We called Professor Ramchandra Prasad or Ramchander Babu or RCP. Chandrabhushan, my youngest brother had been a student of T.N.B. College at Bhagalpur in 1975-76 where RCP used to deliver lectures at the intermediate level. He was his favourite student. I was pursuing my master's in English at Ranchi. Those were the years of JP-movement and we were uncertain about the MA examination. So I decided to take the union civil services examination of 1975. However, a state of emergency was imposed on India and Ranchi University held its examination that year at which I did not appear. So I decided to sit for the examination for the 1972-74 session from any other University. Chandrabhushan talked about it to Ramchander Babu and he advised Chandrabhushan to call me to Bhagalpur. Ramchander Babu was the Professor and Head of the Department at the then Bhagalpur University. This was the immediate reason for my meeting RCP.

Ramchander Babu was enormously supportive and encouraging. He advised me to attend some of his lectures, not necessary for a private student. These lectures were profoundly learned and yet clear and lively. Frequently I used to show my answers to him. He read them with great care. Ramchander Babu was a painstaking writer. If my writing can count for anything, Ramchander Babu's influence has to be acknowledged needless to say that the shortcomings are my own and, I'm not at all as disciplined or hard working as Ramchander Babu.

Ramchander Babu had a magnetic personality. He was very polite, cheerful even in adverse situations and concerned about others. Owing to these qualities and in spite of his medium height he could not be ignored in a crowd. Ramchander Babu took great care of his health and personal appearance. He was an early bird and took regular yog exercise apart from his morning walk at Bhagalpur and Patna. On the first floor of his house at Rajendra Nagar, Patna, he had his office or study next to his bedroom where he had a large portrait of

Gorakhnath close to his bed on the wall. He told me that it was an imaginary portrait. He came from Gorakhari, a village close to Patna. They were all followers of Gorakhnath, disciple of Matsyendranath. Legend accords Gorakhnath a period well before the tenth century.

Ramchander Babu was a great scholar of both the Western and Indian traditions and combined in himself the best of both the worlds. His doctoral work on the early English travellers in India is an acknowledged monumental piece of research. I had the privilege of meeting him a few times at Patna when he was working on Tulsidas's *Ramcharitmanas,* updating the late nineteenth century District Magistrate and Collector successively of Mathura and Bulandshahar F.S. Growse's translation for Messrs Motilal Banarsidass. It came out as *Shri Ramcharitamanasa or the Holy Lake of the Acts of Rama.* This is another great work which will keep Ramchander Babu's memory alive. Ramchander Babu translated and annotated texts on Hindu rituals of Upnayan and Shraddha and wrote on subjects as diverse as Bihar, Shri Krishan Sinha and Dr. B.R. Ambedkar.

Ramchander Babu was among those very few teachers of English in Bihar who could write ably both in English and Hindi and was also equally at home in the literatures of both these languages. Those were not times though when students of English paid much attention to American, African or New Literatures in English and Ramchander Babu's field was English Literature – medieval to modern, poetry, prose, drama and criticism. I had attended his lecture at Bhagalpur on Sir Thomas Malory's *Morte d' Arthur.* However, he edited an anthology of Indian English writings for the undergraduate students with Prof. J.P.Singh, his former student and close friend till the end of his life.

Ramchander Babu was a creative writer also. He had written a novel in English called *The Mahatma.* He told me that it was based on his own life as a student at Patna University. He gave me the manuscript of this novel when I was a lecturer at T.N.B. College and was keen to hear my views. With my anti-humanistic puritanical outlook on life in those days I found the novel too loud. What impressed me, however, was RCP's brilliant ability to handle English prose.

In 1979 Ramchander Babu moved to Patna University. He succeeded Prof. R.K. Sinha as the Head of Department of English. However, in 1980 he was back at Bhagalpur as the PVC . Prof. M.Q. Towheed was the V.C. I got married in April that year. In August I was offered the National scholarship for Study Abroad by the Ministry of Human Resource Development, Government of India and the

British Council Scholarship. I opted for the latter and decided to go to Aberdeen. The MA students, Ram Pratap and others organized a warm send off party at which both the VC and the PVC were gracious enough to come to bid me adieu for the farewell the postgraduate students had organized for me. Ramchander Babu had been at Edinburgh; I was going to Aberdeen, further north in Scotland, to do my doctorate on Samuel Johnson. The research had begun under the supervision of Ramchander Babu. Then the proposed title was "Samuel Johnson: His Mind and art." Finally my thesis turned out to be on *Dr Johnson: An Economic Perspective.* His pieces of advice proved to be very useful to me and I acknowledged his contribution in my dissertation which pleased him very much when I showed it to him and Dr R.K. Sinha in 1984.

In 1986 I moved to Visva-Bharati and from there in 1987 to Indira Gandhi National Open University. Thereafter I only read and heard about the great man that Ramchander Babu was. Many people like me will read him and hear about him in the years to come. He is for me a role model as a teacher of English and perhaps the like of him will not be seen very soon.

Ramchander Babu was interested both in English and Hindi literatures and wrote in both the languages angelically and I would humbly like to offer a paper on Mahadevi Verma and Charles Lamb which I had an opportunity of presenting at the MLA conference held in Chicago in 2007 to the festschrift on Ramchander Babu, the many faceted and magnetic personality that he was.

Mahadevi Verma (1907-87) was an academic administrator and teacher by profession, personal essayist, memoirist, lover of animals and above all a poetess. She was one of the four pillars of the Romantic Movement in Hindi literature known as Chhayavad (1920-35). The other three were: Jai Shankar Prasad (1889-1937), Suryakant Tripathi "Nirala" (1899-1961) and Sumitranandan Pant (1900-77). It is generally accepted by historians and critics of Hindi literature that the poets of Chhayavad Movement in Hindi literature were influenced in some measure by the English Romantic poets: William Wordsworth (1770-1850), S.T. Coleridge (1772-1834), George Gordon Byron (1788-1824), P.B. Shelley (1792-1822) and John Keats (1795-1821), and in prose by William Hazlitt (1778-1830) and Charles Lamb (1775-1834). Mahadevi won the highest award for literature in India, the Gyanpeeth Purashkar.

Great art, by common consent, is an expression of the artist's deepest feelings and quite opposed to propaganda no matter how genuine or great the cause. An artist is in love with life and the expressions of the same all around her. However, she secretly weeps when she finds that all is not well and that life could be better if it had been somewhat otherwise. "Our sweetest songs" said Shelley, "are those that tell of saddest thought." An artist, notwithstanding, is not a judge, religious leader or social reformer. Her suggestions, if at all, may or may not come even as *obiter dicta.* She is content to portray the incongruities, inconsistencies and injustices. Mahadevi Verma, like her contemporary poets, seems, in her essays, merely to portray the common people – domestic servants, porters, hawkers, a widowed daughter-in-law, poor children eager to learn, village folk, fortitude of people trapped in riots, etc. but in doing so she goes quite beyond the "artistic" purpose and affects us emotionally. Perhaps it was in this sense that Shelley had called poets "the unacknowledged legislators of the world". It is not one of the aims of this paper to explore each stance and instance in her essays where she has directly or indirectly pleaded for social justice – as she never does so – but to identify her attitude as reflected in her style, what may be called after Helene Cixous, *l'ecriture feminine.* In this respect a comparison of her writing with the style of Charles Lamb is expected to prove very helpful and fruitful. With these prefatory remarks we may examine Mahadevi Verma's *l'ecriture feminine* and compare her with Charles Lamb's style.

In the first of her brief twin-essays on her career as a literary artist Mahadevi Verma makes an attempt to characterize her work in prose, especially essayistic writings. She never attempted fiction. She rejected the old Sanskrit belief in prose as the whetstone of poets – *gadyam kavinam nikashah vadanti.* She equates prose with logic and argument, poetry with the soul. She considers the memoir to be closer to the spirit of poetry than the "nibandha" which, according to her, is not the same as the essay because she holds that while the essay has a loose structure the "nibandh" demands a logical development with a beginning, a middle and an end, an opening introduction, followed by a development of the topic and finally a conclusion derived from what has gone before. Mahadevi did not like to call her memoir "sketches" as her contemporaries such as Ramvriksha Benipuri did. Sketches, according to her are neutral in character, detached and disinterested, whereas her memoirs are just like her poetry an extension of her being, a fragment of her consciousness, a part of her mind, body and soul.

There is no expression in Hindi which could stand for the personal essay in English such as those of William Hazlitt and Charles Lamb in English and in the case of Mahadevi we find in her *Atit ke Chalchitra* (1941), and *Smriti ki Rekhayen* (1943).

Personal Essays are different from Autobiographical essays examples of which are, E.B. White's (1899-1985), "Once More to the Lake" (1941), George Orwell's "Shooting an Elephant" (1936) and Virginia Woolf's "A Sketch of the Past" (1940). The personal essay is not above the self but as Alfred Kazin pointed out, about "the self thinking".

Mahadevi's essays are about people she had known, not about herself. However, she is present everywhere in them. She appears in an essay on her servant Rama who worked in their family when she was a child or in an essay on old maid servant she called Bhaktin, stubborn and aggressive and yet tragic and funny. Bhaktin, her maid servant in later life appears again and again in several of her essays in *Smriti ki Rekhayen.* At one point of time she is seen resisting Mahadevi's plans of *Kalpavas* in one of her essays on Thakuri Baba and fighting on her behalf on one of her visits to Arail, a village near Allahabad in the essay on Munni's mother.

Bhaktin did not like Mahadevi's idea of spending a month on the banks of the confluence of Ganga, Yamuna and Saraswati at Prayag at Allahabad in cold *Magh.* Bhaktin's work was going to increase. The idea of living away form the safety and security of a well built house appeared impractical to her. She protested with a grin in Bhojpuri – "When the proper age for *kalpavas* arrives then that too would get done. I wonder if you have taken a vow to perform all religious austerities in one day."

Mahadevi narrates that although she did not respond to Bhaktin's protests and gentle jibes, the latter knew that the former would do as she would want to. Mahadevi sojourned for a month (*kalpavas)* on the banks of the confluence at Prayag not in the hope of some spiritual enlightenment but to know life with greater intimacy than she could do at her home in the city. She tells us "And ever to know about life is my nature." Mahadevi was a humanist but not by rejecting tradition, scorning age old values or going against a way of life that has found its way into the present day by the acceptance by the people, old and young, educated, semi-educated and illiterate but for that reason not uninformed.

In the fourth essay in *Smriti ki Rekhayen,* on Munni's mother, we see Mahadevi, a dignified lady, finding satisfaction in Bhaktin's defense of her from attack of Dubri's daughter-in-law. Mahadevi's anger finds vent in her graphic description of the daughter-in-law's appearance:

> Of her dirty, dingy and dishevelled hair some lie sticking to her cracked lips. Her dark body wrapped in layers of dust, look so dusty that they appear to be of the same hue as her dirty dhoti which has gained the colour of dust. All her fingers colored by the henna of cow-dung hide many inscrutable signs of fight. Her condition for friendship is – defeat me in a battle and I'll be your friend – for she considers it below her dignity even to talk to a person who has not defeated her in a duel of words. If someone does not accept her invitation for a fight she considers her unfit for friendship.

Mahadevi's essential humanity responds in tacit approval of Bhaktin's volley of attack.

When Mahadevi asked "Whose house is this?" Dubri's daughter-in-law responded "Why should you wish to know that? Women from the cities have no work and they go about walking here and there." To her angry and insulting response Bhaktin caustically rejoined, "It is the talk of the town that the mistresses of this village pick cow-dung and make cow-dung cakes; so we decided to come and see them perform such chores with our own eyes."

Perhaps the classic case of the ubiquitous presence of the personal essayist in his writing are *The Essays of Elia* (1823), first published between 1820 and 1823 in the *London Magazine* and *The Last Essays of Elia* (1833). Lamb wrote from behind the mask of Elia, a former Italian clerk at the South Sea House. However, we notice him as Elia and his sister Mary in the person of Bridget in his essays quite frequently. A new tea set in "Old China" becomes an excuse for Bridget to feel nostalgic about the good old days when they were poor but young, when in order to buy the plays of Beaumont and Fetcher they had to postpone the purchase of a pair of suit for Elia in place of the brown suit that had become threadbare.

In his "Dream Children" (1822) Lamb passionately remembers Ann Simmons, his first and probably last love, in the guise of Alice

Ann Simmons later married Mr. Bartram, a pawn broker of Price Street, Leicester Square. In the essay Lamb bemoans, "the children of Alice call Bartrum father." After Lamb had narrated the stories of the great grandmother Field and Uncle John Lamb, John and Alice want to know about their "pretty dead mother." Lamb goes on:

> Then I told how for seven long years, in hope sometimes, sometimes in despair, yet persisting ever, I courted the fair Alice and as much as children could understand, I explained to them what coyness and difficulty and denial meant in maidens – when suddenly turning to Alice the soul of the first Alice looked out at her eyes with such a reality of representment, that I became in doubt which of them stood there before me, or whose that bright hair was; and while I stood gazing, both the children gradually grew fainter to my view, receding and still receding till nothing at last but two mournful features were seen in the uttermost distance, which, without speech, strangely impressed upon me the effects of speech: "We are not Alice, nor of thee, nor are we children at all. The children of Alice call Bartrum father."

This is not poetry, it is song, with rhythm and pulse, something connected with the body, not the Cartesian mind alone; it is not representational language – so many ideas in that many words, the idea of the Royal Society – but words standing for dancing, heaving, singing, caressing, fondling and all that the body, rather being (to use a word from Metaphysics), can do.

This language is a constant in all Lamb's essays. Even when he decides to speak of "Some sonnets of Sir Phillip Sydney" he offers not an intellectual, logical, argumentative fare but a caressing and an emotional repast. Milton (1608-74) had called Sidney's (1554-86) *The Arcadia* (1581) "vain and amatorious" but "full of wrath and wit." Sidney's sonnets according to Lamb are "a sort of after time or application" of the same method. Lamb's metaphor for Sidney's sonnets is a "Courtier" not the "commonwealthsman." Significantly he thinks of the Cavaliers and Roundheads, Charles I and Oliver Cromwell. Sidney's sonnets like Milton's masques – *Comus* (1637) and *Arcades* (1645) – are the courtier and not the commonwealthsman. "Milton was a courtier when he wrote the masque at Ludlow Castle and still more a courtier when he composed the Arcades" writes Lamb.

Lamb's contemporary and friend William Hazlitt (1778-1830) rejected "formulas of criticism" and wanted "to feel what was good" and this was exactly what Lamb was doing. His method won him A.C. Bradley's (1851-1935) applause for him as the greatest critic of his century.

In her essay on Thakuri Baba, the fifth essay in *Smriti ki Rekhayen* Mahadevi bemoans the loss of emotion in common life especially among the city-dwellers. Towards the end of the essay Mahadevi describes a religio-cultural evening, deeply emotional, and full of piety, at which the village folks staying on the 8 feet wide verandah of her recently erected palace of reeds sang devotional songs. She discovered why all common people in Krishna's life received nothing but insult. She keeps the discovery all to herself. However she goes on,

> "The pictorial quality of their song waves (swar lahiri) made me aware that words can also create curves and fill those with color. Old and young, men and women, we were all permeated by the same emotion, vibrated alike and the hair on our bodies bristled with the same vibration.
>
> "I cannot tell you what they sang and for how long, for when the *aarti* took place at the end of the session I awoke as if from a trance. Each one spread one's linen on the verandah and lay on it. I sat in front of my brass lamp in my room, lost in thoughts.
>
> "The Sahuain first peeped inside, then half stepped in and uttered modestly, the gist of which is the lamp should be told good-bye for her mother must be waiting for her.
>
> "A smile rising from my heart stopped at my lips. If everything is living for them then why shouldn't they imagine the lamp's mother expecting her daughter back home. When I assured the Sahuain of putting it off, she rushed in and blew it with the gush of air coming from her pallu lest I should clumsily extinguish it by blowing air from my mouth.
>
> "I do not remember for how long I kept thinking but when I came out of my *parna kuti,* reed house, night was fading away. Moonlight meshed with silence, like a silk wrapper, was coiled in the waves and spread on the sand of the bank.
>
> "The verandah of my parna-kuti on two sides was washed in moonlight. I was haunted by the thought of the chasm between the external appearance and the inner self of the creation that was sleeping on cold ground, hay, or a bed linen

> on the verandah? Why did the culture of their heart, their natural gentleness, their aesthetic sense, their ability to work indefatigably was considered so valueless that they could not gather the barest necessities of life for themselves?"

"I care not who makes the laws of my nation I'm content to write her songs", says the poet. Mahadevi's stance is that of a poet, not a moralist, much less a legislator. Her meditations on her night's rapturous religio-poetic experience made her bring to mind her experiences of so-called "civilized" and "cultured" people who having forsaken their natural goodness pretend to display the same by artificial methods.

Mahadevi and Lamb could be seen as kindred souls. Lamb could not afford a marriage owing to his poverty and probably a spurt of insanity in 1795-96. Mahadevi, while a child, got married to Swarupnarayan Verma, one evening after she returned from her play and did not know what was happening. She and her husband never lived together as man and wife, their education and the non-vegetarianism of her husband's family coming in the way. This must have caused a terrible absence in their lives notwithstanding the fact that Lamb as a clerk at India office and Mahadevi as the principal of Mahila Vidyapeeth at Allahabad were very busy indeed. The boredom could have been relieved by Mary, Lamb's sister and in the case of Mahadevi by her domestic servants, flora and fauna, apart from her writing that was of prime interest to her, as to Lamb.

Women, Cixous believes, can most accurately tell their stories by writing through their bodies. This means, as Cixous opines, that they should abandon the linear and orderly characteristics associated with male writing. Cixous uses the word "voler" the French word for flying in order to characterize women's writing. However, "voler" also means "stealing" and Cixous opines that if women are ever to fly, then they must steal from men their right to speak their body which is theirs. Such according to Cixous is *l'ecriture feminine.*

However Cixous admires male writers such as James Joyce and Jean Jenet who wrote antiphallogocentric texts. For "woman", Monique Wittig points out "does not exist for us; it is only an imaginary formation, while "women" is the product of a social relationship. This meant that *feminite* was not unique to women. It was a state of consciousness. The left-outs of our civilization among whom would number, according to Cixous, apart from Joyce and Genet artists such as Hoffman, Kleist and Poe also. Hence *feminite* is a social construct and not a biological fact which can and should be assumed as a stance as much by men as by women.

In his preface to the *The Last Essays of Elia*, Lamb introduced Elia thus:

> He herded always while it was possible with people younger than himself. He did not conform to the march of time, but was dragged along in the procession. His manners lagged behind his years. He was too much of the boy-man. The *toga virilis* never sat gracefully on his shoulders. The impression of infancy had burnt into him and he resented the impertinence of manhood.

And Lamb concludes, "These were weaknesses; but such as they were they are a key to explicate some of his writings". How well Lamb spoke for himself. "[T]oga virilis", "impertinence of manhood", "boy-man" are significant expressions that explain his antiplallogcentric texts, to use Jacques Derrida and Cixous term.

In one of his letters (November 10, 1803) to William Godwin (1756-1836) Lamb had admitted:

> Ten thousand times I have confessed to you, talking of my talents, of my utter inability to remember in any comprehensive way what I read. I can vehemently applaud or perversely stickle, at parts; but I cannot grasp at a whole.

This is a confession of the boy-man who has found himself unable to catch up with his age, who shudders at the thought of a *toga virilis* and resents the "impertinence of manhood."

Compared with him, paradoxical as it might sound, Mahadevi is mature as a principal of a women's college, a political activist of sorts, an extrovert who never hesitates to participate in and chair literary conferences. So she is in control all the while she is in public view but within herself she is a woman, an Aditi (boundless freedom) the mother of the gods, as she would see herself, not Diti, the mother of demons, cribbed and confined, or an Aphrodite such as Luce Irigaray (1932-) would wish to see women as, not a Persephone, mother of Proserpine, a construction of men.

"Poetry" opined Tzvetan Todorov in his Bateson Memorial Lecture at Oxford "must certainly please, but it must also instruct and, at the same time it must imitate nature." How does poetry and for that matter a personal essay does that? By being itself, inartificial, close to nature, close to its source of inspiration, by its *L'ecriture feminine* which suppresses to a large extent our drive for power. Mahadevi Verma as Charles Lamb before her were writing themselves, their bodies and wrote personal essays that would make societies more humane such as some of the French feminists – Helene Cixous, Julia Kristeva and Luce Irigaray – have dreamt of.

Acknowledgment: This paper was presented at the MLA conference held in Chicago (December, 2007). The writer of this paper owes a debt of gratitude to the members of the Travel Grant Committee of and to IGNOU for the grant and would like to thank them for the same.

Works Cited

Cixous, Helene. "The Laugh of the Medusa," *Signs1*(1976): 875-93.

Irigaray, Luce. *Thinking the Difference: For a Peaceful Revolution*(*Tr.*). Karin Montin, New York: Routledge, 1994.

Jones, Ann Rosalind. "Writing the Body: Towards an Understanding of *L'ecriture Feminine" Feminist Studies.* Vol. VII, No. 2, Summer 1981, pp. 247 - 263.

Lamb, Charles. *The Essays of Elia.* (*ed.*) Alfred Ainger, London: Macmillian, 1887.

— *The Letters of Charles Lamb.*(*ed.*) Alfred Ainger in 2 volumes, London Macmillian, 1891.

Obaldia, Claire De. *The Essayistic Spirit: Literature, Modern Criticism and the Essay.* Oxford: Claredon Press, 1995.

Schomer, Karine. *Mahadevi Verma and the Chhayavad Age of Modern Hindi Poetry.* Delhi: OUP, 1998.

Todorov, Tzvetan. "Poetic Truth: Three Interpretations" F.W. Bateson Memorial Lecture, *Essays in Criticism.* Vol. XXXVIII, No. 4, April, 1988. pp. 95-113.

Verma, Mahadevi. *Mahadevi Sahitya Samagra.* in 3 volumes. (*ed.*) Nirmala Jain, New Delhi: Vani Prakashan, 1969, 2000.

Wittig, Monique. "One is not Born a Woman" *Text of the Speech Given at the City University of New York Graduate Center,* September 1979.

Need of Teaching Wisdom Literature

Prof. Sudha Sinha

Dr. Ram Chandra Prasad was our English teacher in the real sense of the term. I don't think I am paying a tribute to a great soul but showing my lasting admiration, respect and affection.

He strode the English literary world of Bihar like a colossus. He had a disciplined attitude to everything he touched. He was methodical, humble, and polite with a penetrating vision and a deeply philosophical mind. *A Comprehensive Survey of Bihar* is a book he wrote about the importance and the glory of Patliputra, the seat of three great religions of the world, Buddhism, Jainism and Sikhism. It is one of the most authentic and much sought after books today.

The translation of *Sri Ramcharitamanas* into English was taken up by him at a time when translation as a genre was not only in its infancy but also had not become the interdisciplinary approach as has today. As I sit here to write, an incident comes to my mind, anxious as I was, while preparing for my M.A. previous examination, I sought his help in a special paper – W.B. Yeats.

I still remember his comparative approach and analysis of W.B. Yeats, Eliot and Indian Philosophy. Was he influenced by the oneness of God "*Tat twam asi*" "Thou art that" and the "being and becoming" come to be correlated to the "ancestral darkness" of the "winding staircase" of W.B. Yeats. Dr. Prasad thrashed out each and every point in both Indian philosophy and the materialism of the West which fell short of "Realization" of

> *Datta. Dayadhvam. Damyata.*
> *Shantih Shantih Shantih* (The Waste Land)

At a certain stage in his life he was influenced by Acharya Rajnish. He was suffused with the writings of the Acharya and sought refuge in his spiritual beliefs, ideas and emotions which had saturated his mind and heart. He was serious and labored everyday of his life, beginning his life as a lecturer in one of the colleges in Aarah, now V.K.S. University. In 1952 he joined B.N. College, Patna. In 1979 he moved to the Department of English Patna University. He succeeded

Prof. R.K. Sinha as the Head, Department of English. However, in 1980 he was back at Bhagalpur as the Pro-Vice-Chancellor.

In fact, I thought while delivering the lectures on Wisdom Literature and the *Book of Job*, as Resource Person in one of the Refresher Courses in Patna University English Department how the ways of men are all the same, all over the world. *The Mahabharata* and *The Ramayana* are full of examples of the moral aspects dealt with by Lord Krishna who explained the meaning of action to Arjuna against his own kith and kin when the latter hesitated. The meaning and the suffering of Job, the Do well, Do better and Do best, of Langland's pilgrim in *Piers the Plowman,* all speak of good life of a good man. They coalesce in my mind. Ideas in the western philosophical concepts come very close to "realization" or the *Anubhuti* of the Supreme being which has been so well expounded in *The Bhagavad Gita.* How men must be like the lotus above the muck and mire of the world, be granted the old man's frenzy to live this life again yet be pure in heart and thus be close to God.

In essence, Dr. Ramchandra Prasad, our English teacher, continues to live in each one of his students and is quintessentially modern in his thoughts and feelings in the "One World Concept" which he followed throughout his life. He is the essence of the *Man of Today* and it is this beginning of a New World, a new philosophy that Dr. Prasad tried to usher in all his thoughts and ideas, in the books he wrote, and the life he led. Dr. Prasad's creativity as a writer can be seen in the novel in English called *The Mahatma.*

This article is an outcome of my reminiscences and works of Dr. R.C. Prasad which attract my interest in this area of socialization which is badly needed at this time because of the steady decline of moral and social values among the human beings today.

The study of Wisdom literature has recently become a subject of growing scientific interest, although the concept of wisdom is ancient. This article focuses on the conceptualization of wisdom in *The Bhagavad Gita,* and *The Book of Job* arguably the most influential of all ancient philosophical/religious texts. Knowledge of life, Emotional Regulation, Control over Desires, Decisiveness, Love of God, Duty and Work, Self-Contentedness, Compassion/Sacrifice, Insight/Humility, and Yoga (Integration of personality) etc. are the characteristics of wisdom literature.

Wisdom literature is the genre of literature common in the Ancient Near East. This genre is characterized by sayings of wisdom intended to teach about divinity and about virtues. The key principle of wisdom literature is that the techniques of traditional story-telling are used, books also presume to offer insight and wisdom about nature and reality. Wisdom is really an approach to life, a way of looking at the world, a way of living out in very deliberate, rational ways and their commitment to God. Wisdom's roots go back to the early days of history of India and the western world.

Wisdom is concerned with everyday life, how to live well.

1. Wisdom is concerned with the issues facing humanity in general, the typical and recurring aspects of life that face human beings on a daily basis. Much of the Scripture is concerned with those unique events in history in which God reveals himself.

2. Little interest is there in history, politics. It is God who acts, and performs and condones sins and offers forgiveness to guilt; these things are not discounted, only that the concern is focused on daily living on what might be called the mundane aspects of life, such as raising children, providing economic security, finding the appropriate wife, etc.

3. The world view is not mythical or cyclical, but it is concerned with stability and order, *the status quo,* especially in the social arena; the goal is to live in a harmonious relationship with God, others, and the world.

4. The perspectives of wisdom are not unique to Israelites, although in Israelite Wisdom, commitment to God is simply assumed.

5. The focus is on interpersonal relationships, as well as reflective questions about the meaning of life and how to live it.

Domains of Wisdom Described in the Gita

For each domain, I begin with an illustrative quote from *The Gita* and then summarize its description as given in the text.

Knowledge of life

Who so possesses wisdom's eyes sees indeed (Ch.15 v.10).

Knowledge is regarded as a great virtue, but *The Gita* assigns different qualities and importance to different types of knowledge. The highest level of knowledge equated with wisdom is the ability to differentiate between the perishable (worldly or material) and the imperishable (sublime) things.

Emotional Regulation

Anger, desire are the Wise man's eternal foes; By this is wisdom overcast (Ch. 3, v. 39).

The Gita considers equanimity as an essential virtue. Wise people are characterized by lack of negative or extreme positive emotions. Wisdom implies that events of joy or sadness are treated similarly. However, satisfaction with a job well done is considered appropriate.

Control over Desires

> Whose senses are withheld from objects proper to them... firm-stabilised is the wisdom of such a man (Ch. 2, v. 68).
>
> A man of faith, intent on wisdom, his senses all restrained, will wisdom win... (Ch. 4, v. 39).

A lack of preoccupation with sensual pleasure is highly valued. Various nuances of this quality – self-restraint, moderation, detachment from desire, and renunciation of attachments and of material ties are elaborated in various sections. A "yogi" is described as one who is free of material ties and is moderate in his actions and reactions.

Decisiveness

> And so, take up the sword of wisdom, cut this doubt of thine, unwisdom's child still lurking in thy heart: Prepare for action now. Stand up! (Ch. 4, v. 42).
> No part in this world has the man of doubt, nor in the next, nor yet in happiness. (Ch. 4, v. 40)

A wise person is one of steadied thought and certain in his understanding. Lack of ambivalence is equated with decisiveness, and differentiated from a deluding self-conviction. It is also equated with an understanding of the absence of duality and dichotomy in the world.

Love and Faith in God

Let him (a wise man) sit intent on Me (God)... (Ch. 2, v. 61)

Being a religious text, *the Gita* dwells on the close relationship between wisdom and faith in God. Meditation with concentration and spiritual exercise are described as a way of controlling the mind and promoting several qualities discussed in this section. Emphasizing the spiritual dimension, regular meditation is recommended as a tool for achieving as well as maintaining wisdom.

Duty and Work

For men of action wisdom is the yoga of work. (Ch. 3, v. 3)

Also called "karma," *the Gita* describes a wise man as one who is committed to his or her duty in the society. A commitment to work and maintaining discipline with respect to work constitute an important component of wisdom. An integral element of "karma" is doing work for the sake of work. According to *the Gita,* a wise person works in order to discharge his/her responsibilities to the society, and not for the sake of its material rewards. Different types of work are described in terms of caste-appropriate roles; however, these descriptions need to be viewed within the socio-historical context of the period. *The Gita* stresses that no work done in order to keep a person appropriately productive should be considered "bad."

Self-contentedness

Detached from contacts with the outside world, in self he (a wise person) finds his joy (sukha). (Ch. 5, v. 21)

A wise person is described as one who is self-assured, and demonstrates non-dependence on others.

Compassion and Sacrifice

Steadfast in the yoga of wisdom, restrained and open-handed, performing sacrifice... (Ch. 16, v.1).

A wise person is compassionate. Sacrifice, for the sake of sacrifice, and not for its material rewards, is also an element of wisdom. Helping others, acts of kindness and charity, and doing no harm to others are tied into this as well.

Insight/Humility

Let him (a wise man) give up all thought of "I", force, pride...
(Ch. 18, v. 53)

A wise person is aware of his/her own limitations including mortality and relative unimportance in the broader realm of the universe at large. Humility and a lack of narcissism are, therefore, critical elements of wisdom.

Yoga (Integration)

> Perfection found, is wisdom's highest goal;
> Let a man be integrated by his soul...restrain himself with constancy...
> abandon things of sense...passion and hate cast out...
> (Ch.18, v. 50-52)

The ability to integrate multiple other components of wisdom (described above) and to practise these to the benefit of those around is regarded as the most valued component of wisdom. Yoga includes practising what one preaches, illustrating a lack of hypocrisy. (Hypocrisy is described as a virtue of fools.)

Components of Wisdom can be taught and learned

An important and noteworthy concept in *The Gita,* usually not considered in the modern literature, is that wisdom (or at least some components of it) can be improved through teaching. *The Gita* itself constitutes an example of how wisdom may be taught and learned, as the narrative of *The Gita* is a lesson in wisdom taught by Lord Krishna to Arjuna. While Arjuna already possessed several elements of wisdom such as knowledge, compassion and sacrifice, insight/humility, he was markedly ambivalent about fighting with his family members even though he knew that they had evil motives and methods. Krishna helped Arjuna solve his moral dilemma by emphasizing duty over feelings. In the process, Krishna also sought to teach Arjuna various other facets of wisdom in everyday life. *The Gita* stresses that active effort is required to learn wisdom. Any person, irrespective of gender or caste, can become wiser, and no case is considered hopeless from this perspective. ("For whosoever makes Me (God) his haven, base born though he may be; Yes, women too, and artisans, even serfs – Theirs it is to tread the highest way " – Ch. 9, v. 32).

The Book of Job, one of the wisdom books of the Bible, deals with two issues crucial to every person: the problem of suffering and the sovereignty of God.

Job (pronounced "Jobe"), was a rich farmer living in the land of UZ, somewhere northeast of Palestine. The key question *The Book of Job* asks:

"Can a favoured, righteous person hold on to his faith in God when things go wrong?"

In a conversation with Satan, God argues that such a person can indeed persevere, and points out his servant Job as an example. God then allows Satan to visit terrible trials upon Job to test him. In a short period of time, marauders and lightning claim all Job's livestock, then a desert wind blows down a house, killing all of Job's sons and daughters. When Job keeps his faith in God, Satan afflicts him with painful sores all over his body. Job's wife urges him to "Curse God and die." (Job 2:9, NIV)

Three friends show up, supposedly to comfort Job, but their visit turns into a long theological debate over what caused Job's suffering. They claim Job is being punished for sin, but Job maintains his innocence. Like us, Job asks, "Why me?"

A fourth visitor, named Elihu, suggests that God may be trying to purify Job through suffering. While Elihu's counsel is more comforting than that of the other men, it is still only speculation.

Finally, God appears to Job in a storm and gives a stunning account of his majestic works and power. Job, humbled and overwhelmed, acknowledges God's right as the Creator to do whatever He pleases.

God rebukes Job's three friends and orders them to make a sacrifice. Job prays for God's forgiveness of them and God accepts his prayer. At the end of the book, God gives Job twice as much wealth as he had before, along with seven sons and three daughters. After that, Job lives 140 more years. *The Book of Job* is a book that refutes retribution theology. We don't get punished on an individual basis for what we do. All humanity gets punished for what all humanity does.

Job 7:9 As the cloud is consumed and vanisheth away:

So he that goeth down to the grave shall come up no more.

Job 14:10 But man dieth, and wasteth away:

Yea, man giveth up the ghost, and where is he?

14:11 As the waters fail from the sea, and the flood decayeth and drieth up.

14:12 So man lieth down, and resteth not: till the heavens be no more, they shall not awake, nor be raised out of their sleep.

Job 20:7 Yet he shall perish for ever like his own dung: they which have seen him shall say, where is he? Be grateful to the Lord for what you have.

Elihu : In *The Book of Job,* Elihu is a prophet God speaks through in the storm. He probably wrote the book. (In Job 33:8-11 he reads back his notes on what Job had said.)

His humility in not giving himself credit as the prophet has made it difficult to see his contribution. Job and his three friends each spoke at length to find confirmation in God's voice, which never came because they were stuck in righteousness, or rigid religiousness. Young Elihu came along and his soliloquy, being closer to God's holiness and truth, resulted in God's conversation and speech happening through him.

JOB : Lesser teachings conclude *the Book of Job* says that we will never understand God. Therefore, lesser teachers say, the sum is Job 13:15, "Though he slay me, yet will I trust in him.... I will maintain mine own ways before him." And so the errant church maintains its own ways before God! After more scourging of pride (which is leviathan, not some dinosaur), Job finally gets it and sees with spiritual eyes how wrong he was to be rigidly righteous, in effect, enthroning the self to be God because of pride in, knowledge in, God. The scourging finally worked to demolish the pride of position and God's knowledge which finally made Job close to the true God. Job said, "Now mine (spiritual) eye seeth thee." And he repented. So far we have not seen the popular church or so-called body of Christ do this yet. Therefore we see that with amazing strategy, God tricked Satan into pushing Job out of his comfortable yet disconnected from God righteousness and into the excruciating pride-removing overcoming into holy fellowship and friendship with God! By the way, preachers stuck in righteousness cannot see this or teach this because they are not yet in holiness and cannot and do not believe in it...yet! So they are stuck in the loop of Job 13:15a.

Righteousness and Holiness : Righteousness is good and so is holiness. But there is a big difference between the two. When we begin with God we must learn righteousness, which is learning, loving and obeying God's rules. A lot of people get stuck there in major pride-of-religion. And they really, like it. They are the Christian Cops! They believe what they have achieved. Period! However, the saints break the rules of righteousness. Well, holiness is that relaxed, close fellowship with God. It lets Jesus pick corn and heal on the Sabbath. It lets David eat the forbidden temple show bread. Righteous people are God's servants; holy people are His friends. Righteous people can't hear God's voice very well. Holy people hearken unto the voice of the Lord, which really upsets the righteous people. Righteous people are rigid, holy people flexible. Righteous people might do a wrong thing in an emergency, holy people might do the perfect and creative thing because God might tell them and they might hear instantly. Righteous people have an extremely hard time understanding how to break the chains of rigidity and become flexible with God, who may be the most flexible entity in the universe. After all, God has to deal with six or so billion of us poor creatures, right? He is of course flexible, and our stiff-necked rigidity problem is pride. Righteously proud teachers say the book of Job says we must endure trials because we can never really know God. Holy teachers say the book of Job tells us we must endure great tribulation to get rid of our rigidity and pride-of-religion so we can hear, obey and really know God.

Studies of wisdom literature would seem to have considerable relevance for psychiatry. While it may be challenging to develop interventions aimed at promoting a multi dimensional construct such as wisdom, it is reasonable to suggest that interventions aimed at improving specific dimensions of wisdom may enhance outcomes in mentally ill persons. The concept of wisdom may indeed be useful to psychiatry as an "umbrella" under which several novel approaches for improving the outcome in mentally ill persons can be grouped and used as a foundation for creating integrated models of remission and recovery.

Finally, studies of cross-cultural comparisons of concepts of wisdom would be particularly helpful, as they may have implications for developing possible interventions to enhance wisdom as a means of facilitating successful restoration in a culture-specific manner. Additionally, combining elements of wisdom literature from various cultures could yield a more comprehensive and effective means of promoting wisdom literature.

Works Cited

Avari, B. *India: The Ancient Past.* London: Routledge, 2007.

Baltes, P.B.; Kunzmann, U. *Wisdom Psychologist.* 2003; 16:131–133.

Baltes, P.B.; Staudinger, U.M. Wisdom: A Metaheuristic(pragmatic) to Orchestrate Mind and Virtue toward Excellence. *American Psychologist.* 2000; 55:122–136.

Bhat, A.K.; Dhruvarajan, R. "Ageing in India: Drifting Intergenerational Relations, Challenges and Options." *Ageing & Society.* 2001:21:621–640.

Blazer, D.G. "Successful Ageing," *American Journal of Geriatric Psychiatry.* 2006.

Boyatzis, R., *Transforming Qualitative Information: Thematic Analysis and Code Development.* Thousand Oaks, CA: Sage, 1988.

Bryant, E.E. *The Quest for the Origins of Vedic Culture: The Indo-Aryan Migration Debate.* New York: Oxford University Press, 2001.

Prasad. R.C. *Tulasidasa's Sri Ramacaritamanasa.* New Delhi: Motilal Banarsidass, 2009.

Perdue, Leo G. *Wisdom Literature.* Westminster: John Knox Press,U.S.

Radhakrishnan, S. *The Bhagavad Gita.* New Delhi: Harper Collins Publishers india, 1973.

Singh. Dr. T. *The Book of Job.* Bareilly: Student Store, 2003.

A Golden Age: From Gestation to Delivery of Bangladesh

Dr. Ram Bhagwan Singh

Tahmima Anam's *A Golden Age* is her first novel and a first major Bangladesh novel about the travails the new nation has to undergo until its delivery. It covers the nine months' period from March 1971 to 16 December, 1971. It is a chronicle of pre-independent Bangladesh – the story of people's thwarted aspirations, political subjugation, economic exploitation and cultural asphyxia. The people of East Pakistan were disillusioned as the religious tie was too weak to hold together incompatible linguistic and cultural divergences. In just two decades of its separation from India the eastern wing had seen untold tyrannical oppression and injustice. Even after Sheikh Mujibur Rahman's Awami League had won the election, General Zia was not ready to hand over power to them. Naturally people, especially the youth rose against the discrimination of West Pakistan and were demanding a separate Bangladesh.

The novel revolves round the heroine Rehana, her son Sohail, daughter Maya and their freedom fighter group Joy, Aref and Partho. Sohail tells Mr. Sengupta, it's been two months since Mujib won the election. They should have convened the national assembly by now and made him the Prime Minister, but they kept delaying. Some of the students were urging Mujib to take more drastic action. (p.28) Regarding exploitation he says further:

> ...West Pakistan is bleeding us out. We earn most of the foreign exchange. We grow the rice, we make the jute, and yet we get nothing– no schools, no hospitals, no army. We can't even speak our own bloody language.... What we have is an emergency. There is no possibility of reconciliation now. Mujib should have declared independence. (p. 29)

The general impression is that East Pakistan has been given a step-motherly treatment by the government. Students at the Dhaka University are up against this ill-treatment and are protesting vehemently. Even Rehana sees no sense "having a country in two haves, poised on either side of India like a pair of two horns". She ruminates ever since" the Pakistani authorities had ruled the eastern wing of the country like a colony. First they tried to force everyone to speak Urdu instead of Bengali. They took the jute money from Bengal and spent it on factories in Karachi and Islamabad. One general after another made promises they had no intention to keep." (p. 33)

Almost every day they take out procession on the streets and shout slogans like, "Joy Bangla!" "Death to Pakistan!" "Death to dictatorship!" (p. 42) Strikes and martial law are the order of the day. It is for this reason that when Rehana's husband dies, Faiz wants to take her children away to Lahore for safety. Police atrocities are increasing day by day. Indiscriminate killing of women and children has created an aura of fear and uncertainty. Unmarried girls in particular are not safe. In such a situation Mrs. Chowdhury wants to marry her daughter Silvi then and there to Lieutenant Sabeer.

Curfew has become more frequent. People hear the rat-tat-tat of the machine guns and shrink away from the streets. On trucks the army through the megaphone threatens, "Bengalis, take down your flags. Take down your flags. Take down your flags. Take down your flags. Flag-bearing is illegal. You will be arrested. Take down your flags, you bastard traitors." (p. 61)

However, the protestors, the freedom fighters are undaunted. They have joined the Mukti Vahini and are consolidating their positions in every town and locality. And one day on their secret Bangladesh radio the announcement comes:

> I, Major Zia, provisional Commander-in-Chief of the Bangladesh Liberation Army, hereby proclaim on behalf of our great national leader Sheikh Mujibur Rahman, the independence of Bangladesh. I also declare we have already formed a sovereign, legal government under Sheikh Mujibur Rahman. I appeal to all the nations to mobilize the public opinion in their respective countries against the brutal genocide in Bangladesh. (p. 65)

Wild rumours circulate in the quiet. The army has dug a mass grave to hide the bodies. There is a warehouse, somewhere on the outskirts of the town, where they torture the prisoners. The animals in Alipur zoo, even the Bengal tiger, have all died of fright. But no one seems to know anything for sure. In the situation the butchers, the tailors, the milkmen, the rickshaw pullers, the boys who painted cinema actresses on the back flaps of rickshaws and even the younger boys who made tea in rusting kettles on pavements – all leave silently, snaking out of the city with bundles on their shoulders, children cradled against their backs.

Mrs. Akram had become so hysterical, screaming about Kayamat, the end of the world that they had to tie her to the bed posts. (p.70)

The newspapers were mostly blank because of the censorship. Giant banner advertisements for Tibet soap and Brylcream framed empty spaces. However, the protests went on. And one day they heard "there is a resistance across the border. All the Bengali regiments have mutinied." (p. 79) The movement is gaining momentum day by day with more and more people joining the Mukti. Aref, Joy and Partho irrespective of religious considerations have reinforced the freedom struggle. Even college girl students have jumped into the fray. The Dhaka University is the epicentre of the struggle. Maya is determined to fight for her country like her brother Sohail. Even her mother Rehana after initial hesitation allows her house Shona to be used by the freedom fighters. They dump rifles and explosives digging the earth beside the rosebushes. Very soon Shona becomes the headquarters of guerilla operations. Sohail's friends are engaged in destroying communication links and power installations to obstruct the Pakistani army from looting and killing civilians. It is learnt that Sharmeen was gangraped and later killed by the soldiers of Tikka Khan. People are leaving their homes and crossing the border into India. Free Bangla Radio reports that the number of refugees flowing into West Bengal has reached one million. The International Red Cross has stated that the refugee camps along the border between India and Bangladesh are overcrowded and suffer from a lack of clean water, sanitation and proper medical facilities. The Indian Prime Minister Indira Gandhi has pledged her support for the people of Bangladesh, stating that the freedom loving Bengalis would soon triumph over the fascistic regime of the Pakistani dictators. (pp. 98-99)

Maya has volunteered to serve in the Refugee Camp at Calcutta. She is the incharge of a group of refugees and works day and night unmindful of her own comforts. She stays in a dingy hovel in a slum area. When her mother visits her she is overcome with grief to see her condition in that hovel. But the Refugee Camp has a sobering effect on her and reinforces her nationalism. She offers to sew mattresses and blankets out of old clothes for the refugees. Rehana calls Mrs. Rahman and Mrs. Akram to co-operate in sewing Kathas for the refugees. She also makes pickles for the war effort. Later she joins her daughter and helps the refugees. When she is suggested to go to Lahore and live comfortably with her husband's brother barrister Faiz, she declines. She is determined to live and die for her own country. Dr. Rajesh calls her "a true nationalist." (p.142)

> The Pakistani army had let loose a reign of terror. Throughout June, Tikka Khan's soldiers made their way across the summer plains of Bangladesh. They looted homes, burned roofs. They raped. They murdered. They lined up the men and shot them into ponds. They practised old and new forms of torture. They were explorers, pioneers of cruelty, every day outdoing their own brutality, every day feeling closer to divinity because they were told they were saving Pakistan and Islam may be even the Almighty Himself, from the depravity of the Bengalis... (p.129)

The Bengalis resist but their resistance is weak and sporadic. They just blow up a bridge here and have an army-convoy ambush there or capture a railway station. But they have undaunted courage and determination. The Pakistani army tortures Lieutenant Sabeer as he is suspected to be in support of Bangladesh. He is sent to jail where they beat him, break his ribs. They make him stare at the sun for hours, days. They burn cigarette holes on his back. They hang him upside down. They make him drink salt water until his tips crack. And they tear out his finger nails. (p. 215) Sabeer is totally crippled. When Rehana gets him released, the man is unable to walk because of his broken ribs. He is carried like a luggage on to a rickshaw. Mentally and emotionally too, he is totally broken. He dies after a few days.

Despite the army atrocities they revolutionaries fight with their back to the wall. Strangely enough, the Pakistani government does nothing to diffuse the crisis perhaps because the time is over now. The people have rejected the government in favour of Sheikh Mujibur Rahamn's Awami League. Rehana's entire family is fighting for the independence of Bangladesh – Sohail by forming a group of guerrilla fighters, Maya by joining the Mukti and Rehana herself by serving the refugees and nursing the wounded Major in her house.

The freedom struggle comprises Hindus and Muslims alike. In the novel we see dedicated Hindu freedom fighters like Partho, Senguptas,

Dr. Rajesh and Dr. Rao, Mrs. Supriya Sengupta helps and nurses the needy in the refugee camp. She has lost her husband and son Mithun in the freedom struggle. The fact is that a counter nationalism has emerged based on linguistic and cultural integrity. The much cherished "Our golden Bangla" is an epitome of the public aspirations and a secular identity. Politics there is, no doubt, but mellowed with democratic norms. People want respite from the exploitative and autocratic government. India supports the freedom fighters and gives shelter to the millions of refugees. They have high hopes from India. BBC World Service rightly says, "...if Indira Gandhi intervenes, the war will surely be won for the people of Bangladesh."(p. 212) People are optimistic enough. Sohail says, "We're outnumbered, outgunned, outmanned. But sometimes we can beat the hell out of them. ...I can taste the end. The modhu-roshogolla-honey-end."(p. 236)

Towards the end Col. Jabeer comes to Shona to arrest Joy, Partho and Sohail. He tells Rehana, "I have to bring those Bengalis back. I have to arrest them. And then I have to shoot them."(p. 262) While searching for the three boys the Sergeant catches hold of the unknown Major who is trying to escape. No doubt, he is not Sohail. But Rehana suggests in the affirmative. The wireless message confirms that the other two boys, Joy and Partho have been arrested in Comilla. Barrister Faiz is brought with hands and feet cuffed. He begs Rehana to get him out of captivity. With folded hands he implores her, "one word from you and they would let me go" (p. 272) but Rehana doesn't forgive him.

At long last the Pakistan army surrenders. And Rehana addresses her dead husband, "The war will end today. Niazi will sign the treaty and I will walk into the streets. Your daughter will hold my hand. There will be a pressing crowd on the pavement but Maya will elbow us to the front. A boy will sell flags for two taka and everyone will wave and crane their necks to see the road. Coloured paper will sail from buildings; fists will wave in the air; there will be dancing, a man on a flute, a woman beating a dhol slung across her shoulder."(p. 274)

Tahmima Anam's *A Golden Age* is multi-dimensional. It reads like a historical novel, a family story and a romantic tale. As a historical novel it has recreated Bangladesh's struggle for freedom and as independent identity the novel covers the time span from March 1971 to 16 December 1971 – the crucial period of Bangladesh war of Independence. It recounts the gradual progress of the mass movement, the involvement of the students particularly of the Dhaka University.

Even the housewives take part in processions and slogan-shouting against Pakistan. Though they are all in favour of Sheikh Mujib, it is remarkable to note that there is no mention of Awami League at any point in the novel. This is probably because the novelist wants not to glorify any political party. To her what matters is the cause and the man who champions it. Hence, Mujib occurs at places in the novel to show what people want of him. However, Mujib does not appear in person as Gandhi appears in R.K. Narayan's *Waiting for the Mahatma* or the great Indian leaders address the people in Amir Ali's *Conflict*. Again, though there are references to the Pakistan Army's atrocities on Bangladesh, the novelist has refrained from particularising them and giving them historical authenticity. Even the commonly known killing of Dhaka University teachers and intellectuals has been quietly bypassed. Similarly, there is a sweeping reference that the Bengali regiments have mutinied, no more than that. Likewise Rehana says, "This isn't war. It's genocide."(p. 79) and leaves it to the readers' imagination to elaborate. The genocide is not substantiated with factual details. Again, Faiz alleges that Hindus don't treat East Pakistan as their own country – they were never a part of Pakistan but the allegation is not corroborated.

A most remarkable point is that the novelist has neither bouquet nor brick bats for India which is apparently intriguing. At one point she accuses India, rather Mujib, for getting fat on his "pay check" from India. In fact, Pakistan authorities called India expansionist and imperialistic in its design. Even Sheikh Mujib's contribution is not adequately acknowledged. There is no reference to Mujib's imprisonment in an unknown place and his final release. The novel ends saying that the war will end today and people will rejoice themselves.

A Golden Age relates the story of the Bangladesh War of Independence from the perspective of a woman, a mother. In a way, it is a personal story of Rehana's doting husband, his tragic death and later her separation from her two children as the court entrusts the children to their uncle for safe upbringing in the troubled times. When the children are restored, they indulge themselves in the freedom struggle and the mother has to take all possible steps to protect them. Out of her sense of nationalism Rehana herself becomes a party to the mass movement and makes her house Shona the centre of guerrilla operations. Though she herself does not take the gun, she collects donations for the war effort and sews blankets out of old clothes for the freedom fighters. She also helps the refugees in the Refugee Camp. She becomes instrumental in securing the release of Lieutenant Sabeer who is imprisoned and tortured in jail for supporting Bangladesh. It is also the story of her circumstantial infatuation for the wounded Major and later sacrificing him. Thus, the novel is the story of Rehana, her grief and concern for her children and her involvement in the nation's struggle. Again and again, she turns towards her dead husband to share in her troubles. She also invokes his memory to share in the joy of the triumph of the independence struggle.

Being a woman's narrative by a woman, it has the natural delicateness, smoothness, softness and serenity. The novelist has chosen not to delineate the horrors of war, the thundering, bombing and devastating aerial sorties, not to speak of the booming guns. Tahmima Anam has maintained deliberate aloofness from any controversial or inflammatory details. Granted too much historical facts might have told upon the fictional sobriety and the evenness between history and fiction. As a romantic tale, the novel has in its core the conjugal love of Rehana and Iqbal Haque which sustains even after the husband's death. Whenever faced with a crisis, she recalls him for national support. In fact, the novel begins with a letter addressed to the late husband. The wife addresses him whenever she is confronted with shaky situations. Then, there is the love of Sohail and Silvi, the daughter of Mrs. Chowdhury. Silvi is married to Lieutenant Sabeer and Sohail's love remains unfulfilled. But the novelist makes Sohail rationalize it. She hardly delves deep into the recess of the lover's heart. Rehana's love for the wounded unknown Major is born out of pity and compassion. Precisely for this reason when the occasion comes, she sacrifices this new found love to save her son. She rather extracts the price for saving him and nursing him in her house. In her letter to late Iqbal Rehana admits, "And yes, I loved him. For the smallest fraction of those ninety six days, I loved him." (p. 274) But when Major Jabeer of Pakistan Army comes to Rehana's house in search of her son Sohail, Rehana points out to her lover of ninety six days who is captured by them. Rehana says, "I let them think they had Sohail. That is what I chose. To let that man pay my debt." (p. 274) Rehana's offering her lover to the Pakistan Army to pay her debt reminds one of Porphyria's lover in reverse. Porphyria's lover strangles his beloved at a moment of highest emotional pitch of love to perpetuate and immortalize their love. But in the case of Rehana it is making the lover pay the price of loving her which trivializes her love.

The novel has the slow, smooth pace of a ghazal and the tenderness of a loving mother and wife. A golden age has dawned for Bangladesh.

Work Cited

Anam, Tahmima. *A Golden Age.* Euston Road, London: John Murray Publishers, 2007.

A Study of Clowning in Shakespeare's Theatre

Dr. Bijay Bahadur Singh

"Clowning" as an art form or distinguishable sport was probably best personified in the years directly preceding Shakespeare's works by the famous clown Dick Tarlton. Tarlton's universal appeal was due largely to the "rural and cultural unity of the time" (Weimann, 186). Tarlton was "the favorite of laborer, city-burgher, and Queen alike" (Weimann, 186). Tarlton was so famous in London that during his lifetime he was named "Queen Elizabeth's first jester" (Wiles, 23). He became increasingly well known for his jests (which were published posthumously), his jigs, and for his universal appeal:

> His comedy cut across barriers of class, proving acceptable both at court and in the tavern, because most people could accept the proposition that beneath every human exterior there lurks a coarse anarchistic peasant. (Wiles, 23)

"Clowning," and the use of the oral and physical traditions by the clown, is not only a response to the cultural intermingling, but from the need therein for a unifying figure. This clown fits into the "Hodge Podge" that the audience had become by sampling from it. Building on the physical tradition, he became a patchwork of convention: topical reference, Shakespearean prose, and physical honour. The "mingle mangle," the "trafficke and travell" described by Lyly indicates an undeniable change in culture that mandates a figure such as Tarlton or, later, the Gravediggers of Hamlet. They epitomized the diversity of the "now" – an important element in the Elizabethan drama. Robert Greene of the University Wits, a group of Londoners far more educated than Shakespeare and frustrated by his success, directly chastised Shakespeare in the pamphlet "Greene's Groats Worth of Wit..." for being a "Johannes factotum" (Jack of all trades) when, in actuality, Shakespeare (and his clowns) could not have been anything but the early modern city clown, then, picked up where the pre-modern clown left off, as a liminal figure in a now representational drama. This is the liminality Victor Turner describes in *The Anthropology of Performance,* where liminality is the blurred line between the worlds of ritual and "represented" performance. This clown, who is more sophisticated than his predecessor, still retains many of the qualities of, for example, the Vice figure in Mankind. The early modern clown in the drama continues to occupy the non-representational performance space of the platea, creating the distance from the stage and audience rapport that is again essential to the art of clowning. The clowning scene was one which pleased the groundling contingency of the audience while being favorably observed by the members of the upper class in the same audience (Gurr, 86). The theatre was a major unifying force in this new English society. For the first time:

> people from the whole social gamut...attended plays ...citizens and artisans joined with gentlemen and prostitutes, porters and household servants, gallants, lawyers, and soldiers on leave. (Gurr, 217)

The clowning scenes used in *Hamlet* and *Macbeth* are some of the finest examples of the incorporation of the city clown and its ramifications. The functions of these scenes are, then, to provide an alternate viewpoint by interrupting the main action of the play and playing specifically to that "mingle mangle". The clowns used the oral/ physical tradition to create diversity and to provide a more complete understanding of the theme by employing a "mingle mangle" of their own. This popular technique was to spread into the Shakepearean play, where it would undoubtedly be accepted by the audience as a whole, just as Tarlton had been accepted by the full class spectrum of England. This method of enhanced understanding and entertainment in the theater through the "buffoonery of clowning" (Lowers, 89) was certainly a wonderful development of Shakespeare's time. Joseph Hall's Virgidemarium acknowledges the presence of this heterogeneity, stating "...a goodly hotch-potch! when...vile russetings are matched with monarchs..." and of the success of this phenomena: "comes leaping a self- misformed lout [into the Prince's place] then doth the theatre echo all aloud...." Hall's statements (1597) were both insightful and foreshadowing: for not only did the clowning scene sit well with the entirety of the crowd, its importance grew as Shakespeare used the clown as a tool for the shift in focus necessary to convey more effectively the theme of the dramas. These scenes can also be viewed in *The Two Gentlemen of Verona* in the character of Launce, and in *As You Like It,* the famous clown Touchstone.

The use of these universal, identifiable figures provides a shift in focus from the subject matter of the play. By using recognizable references from contemporary times, the clown can, through the use of the oral tradition, make the audience understand the theme being played out by the court-dominated characters in the play. The clown at this point utilizes what M.M. Bakhtin calls "hetero-glossia": another's speech in another"s language – engaging not only in his own intention (i.e. digging a grave), but in the "refracted intention of the author" (i.e. critiquing the Reformation in England) (Bakhtin, 324). The clown uses colloquial speech; playing to the common man with the permission of the nobility – for laughter is a powerful tool, and everyone loves a clown. This alternate viewpoint is helpful when combined with the remainder of the thematic content of the play, for it solidifies the ideas present by reiterating them through the eyes of a distanced (if not disinterested) third party. The synthesis of all the perspectives used ends in a greater comprehension of the play as a whole.

One clear example of these elements can be observed in Act V, scene I of Shakespeare's *Hamlet,* known as the Gravedigger's scene, where Shakespeare identifies the two men who dig the grave of Ophelia as Clown One and Clown Two, giving them as well the physical humour associated with the clowning rituals of the pre-modern. These two "clowns" open the scene by throwing skulls up out of a grave and singing a little song; extremely humorous in the light of the pervasive seriousness of the play until this point. The clowns likely received what would today be labelled obvious or gratuitous laughter; this lightness seems appropriately placed to contrast the forebodingly "heady" nature of the first four acts of this play. The topical, cultural themes are introduced immediately by the gravediggers: these men are by no means royal. They speak in the informal and make references that clearly have nothing to do with Elsinore, or even Denmark. The First Clown is digging the grave of Ophelia, who is to be buried in Denmark (if one is "playing along" with the representationality of the drama). And yet this clown calls out to his counterpart to: "go, get thee to Yaughan, fetch me a stoup of liquor" (V, i,18-19), simultaneously breaking the represented reality of the drama and creating an audience rapport through the humour implicit in his statement. As the playgoing audience would certainly have recognized, Yaughan was a pub around the corner from the London Playhouse where *Hamlet* was playing (Weimann).

This likely warranted as much raucous laughter as did: "... [insanity] will not be seen in [Hamlet] there [in England]; there the men are as mad as he" (V, i, 18-19).The importance of these references is twofold: they give the audience a much-needed laugh, and provide the proper distance from Elsinore to view what the clowns say as discreet parallels, not direct commentaries: the clowns, though they speak with Hamlet, are assuredly not his contem-poraries. The subsequent incongruities of intellectual argument are the real theme of the scene – the "seriousness through buffoonery" for which these scenes are famous. The clowns begin to engage in what appears to be a serious, philosophical discussion but which ends in hilarity, even going so far as to mock the classical Latin and Aristotelian studies of the Italian-influenced Humanists. The first clown, when speaking on the nature of Ophelia's death, describes it as "in self defense," then proceeds to misquote the Latin in labelling it "se offendendo" (self offense), then changing the word "ergo" into "argal". These references would certainly have been recognized by the Shakespearean audience – if only the parts of the audience that had studied Latin. The clowns also delve into complex Aristotelian logic, saying that "...if I drown myself wittingly it argues an act, and an act hath three branches: it is, to act, to do, to perform..." (V, i, 10-11). Clearly the argument is incongruous and wholly inapplicable to the situation at hand; he really has no point. But the comic element lies in the confidence with which both parties continue the conversation, delving into a religious discussion which, given the circumstances of the Reformation and the unresolved religious dissention in England at the time, was likely to have been a hot topic. The clowns take a Protestant viewpoint, discussing whether Ophelia is to have a Christian burial, going so far as compare themselves to Adam to prove that they are indeed gentlemen capable of such a discourse and decision:

> First Clown: There is no ancient gentlemen...
> but ditchers and gravediggers: they
> hold up Adam's profession.
> Second Clown: Was he a gentleman"
> First Clown: ...what, art a heathen?...the Scripture
> says Adam digged...

That the clowns discuss the Scriptures on the stage during a time of heated religious tension is a brilliant theatrical choice on Shakespeare's part. Who better to discuss the most serious topics than those characters who appear to be complete idiots? The threat of blasphemy, disrespect, or other negative connotations decrease. Macbeth thinks he might actually be insane and says that he has murdered sleep. This scene is necessary to maintain the thematic focus: to equate Macbeth's sins with the sins of the London townspeople both distanced the audience from the main traumatic action of the play and made them think about it on their own terms. Once again, the synthesis of these diversified parts leads to a greater understanding of the play as a whole. This scene is another example of Bakhtin's heteroglossia: while the Porter's discourse is with MacDuff and Lennox, Shakespeare's "refracted intention" (Bakhtin, 324) is to refer to the Gunpowder Plot in order to bring the tragedy of Macbeth down to a realistic level.

The placement of the clowning scenes is extremely important: the appearance of the clowning scene usually occurs just as the shock or trauma level of the play has reached a point when the minds of the audience members begin to become desensitized. The clowning scenes "give spectators a chance to catch their breath and mentally prepare themselves for what follows" (Epstein, 306). These scenes provide a break from the murder, treachery, and death of the plays while still remaining focused on the central themes of the play. They give the audience a "breather" of sorts, and allowing the necessary time to process the copious, complicated information just presented.

Both *Hamlet* and *Macbeth* are set in countries other than England, yet in both plays the audience is temporarily returned to England, if only for "a stoup of liquor" or to consider the "tailor's hose." Each time the play leaves the main action, the audience returns better able to grasp the entirety of the theme and to synthesize the alternate viewpoints into one cogent, unified theme. The clowning scenes in these plays are excellent examples of the alternate perspective caused by distance. These scenes support Lyly's theory of the "mingle mangle" that was the composition of the Elizabethan audience: this diversity is reflected in everything from the dramatic structure to the discourse and is prevalent in the clowning scenes. Indeed a mingle mangle of dramatic conventions are used in these plays. All, however, yield the same conclusions as to the function of the clowning scene. Primarily, identification is extremely important to the understanding of the fundamental scenes of the play. What cannot be understood when expressed by the Prince of Denmark makes logical sense when simply outlined by the gravedigger and put into contemporary terms, as transcription into a different idiom facilitates understanding and comprehension. The clowning scenes, through the use of cultural topicality, interrupt the main action of the play to provide a diversity of perspective, or an alternate viewpoint. This necessary shift of focus allows the audience to stay focused on the main theme of the play, and must be placed at some time before desensitization of the audience occurs, hence the timing of placement is also critical. The audience of Shakespeare's time had indeed become a "Hodge-Podge:" the sophisticated drama that Shakespeare's Hodge-Podge audience were witnessing had evolved from their own social mobility and advancement: it was through the clown that it both spoke and understood.

In her book *Renaissance Revivals,* Wendy Griswold studies the history of revivals in an attempt to understand the ongoing, mutually influential relationship between a society and its cultural products (Griswold, 5). The theatre is an effective convention through which we can view this relationship – that the theater and its symbolic figures shift along with the society and reflect as well as influence it is readily apparent, as we have seen. The clown in this period is usefully studied as a cultural object, its staying power directly dependent upon its ability to distill the humor from an increasingly complicated world and still function as a repository of shared significance embodied in form, where:

> Significance refers to the object's incorporation
> of one or more symbols, which suggest a set of
> denotations and connotations, emotions, and memories.
> (Griswold, 6)

Thus, a Shakespearean clown could be easily identified by his incorporation of the time honored tradition of physicality and familiar speech – breaking the tension as well as interrupting the represented reality to make some familiar and useful jokes. This clown samples from the society to suggest the appropriate set of connotations and denotations for whatever topic he addresses. In *The Two Gentlemen of Verona,* for example, the character of Launce appears in a variety of scenes, almost always as the comic relief. But it is in his several monologues where we begin to see him as this cultural object, using the familiar symbols and placed in the proper area, thus meeting the criterion of the clown. In one especially effective moment, Launce appears after a touching "parting of the lovers" scene (which is soon to be forgotten by Proteus, one of the lovers in the play), performing a parody of the scene with a cast of characters which includes his dog, his shoe, his hat, and a broom, all of whom he speaks with and for, ending the speech with a comparison of his mother's breath to the scent of his shoe. This scene is an excellent example of the "mutually influential relationship" between society and its art; while maintaining the qualities of his ancestor the pre-modern clown, Launce impersonates the "parting of the lovers scenes" popular in the tragedies of the 1590's. Later in the play, Launce will ask his dog Crab: "when didst thou see me heave up my leg and make water on a gentlewoman"s farthingale?" (IV, iv, 37-39). Again, physical comedy, this time in the form of bathroom humor used as a cultural reflector, here of the class structure in *The Two Gentlemen of Verona* (and in Elizabethan England); not only does Launce, a commoner, have no idea how to perform in the house of Sylvia, an upper-middle class lady, but Proteus has misjudged his ability to perform an important errand, sending a clown to do a man's job.

The clown which evolved as a response to the many influences of the Renaissance and the self-development that followed retained from its pre-modern ancestors elements of the familiar and universal. This clown, which was enormously popular during its time, influenced the many forms of theatre which ensued, including the outlandish, satirical physicality of the Harlequin, and the tradition of the English pantomime.

Shakespeare's clown was, nevertheless, lodged in a specific cultural context, and as time moved on, this luminal figure, however useful, was to be short lived in the evolution of the "modern drama" in England. For, however effective as a theatrical convention, the clowning figure, in fact the phenomenon of clowning, was to be stifled by a 17th-century action known as the "expulsion of the Harlequin (Weimann)." In this period, prominent religious leaders decided that the time and place for ritual tradition was at an end, and took it upon themselves to rid the stage of this "menace." In an act appropriately named "The Reform of the Stage," the ritual figure was excluded from new dramas.

Traces of this art form were to reappear in the form of vaudeville, slapstick, or today, the postmodern Archaos clowns, whose leader

Pierrot Bidon is quoted as saying: "To survive, the clowns have to mutate and re-use the scraps of society's refuse" (Jenkins, 64). This was the same method used by the pre-modern clown to survive in the newly modern world. The Renaissance clown is effectively studied as a cultural object responding to a period of intense change – change which necessitated the clown as well as providing it with a plethora of material on which to draw, and which forced the clown from the stage. The clown figure is a seminal theatrical convention in the society and will continue to "mutate" and to be present in some form as long as the theatre has a society with which to interact.

To study the Renaissance and its effects on the development of the conventionality of clowning is only useful to a point; it is the application of this study to contemporary thinking and practical application to the theatre that is the ultimate focus of my work. The repository, the archive of which Griswold speaks is evident in the nameless clowns of the pre-modern, in Shakespeare's clowns, and in the comic influences on every kind of theater following them. However, it is the "action" – the magic of live, contemporary theater done well – that is the real life's blood of these clowns. This fall, was seen in Robert Cohen's production of *As You Like It,* and the true meaning of my studies come to life. Michael Thomas Holmes brought Touchstone to life in contemporary readings of the famous clown's monologues; interpretations that, would have made Shakespeare proud. Holmes included references to Arnold Schwarzenegger's Terminator movies, Elvis Presley, Jack Nicholson, and Robert Deniro, to name a few. Combined with the physicality he brought to the performance, he was the overwhelming favorite of the audience, which came alive every time he took the stage. It was then that the clown figure was most evident as an actual sponge – immersed in a culture, soaking it up, extracting the humour, and giving it to the audience in the form of laughter.

Works Cited

Bakhtin, M.M. *The Dialogic Imagination.* Austin: University of Texas Press, 1981.

Boyce, Charles. *Shakespeare A to Z.* New York: Bantam Doubleday Publishing Group, Inc. 1990.

Brody, Allen. *The English Mummers and Their Plays.* Philadelphia: University of Pennsylvania Press, 1983.

Griswold, Wendy. *Renaissance Revivals.* Chicago: University of Chicago Press, 1986.

Gurr, Andrew. *The Shakespearean Stage, 1574-1642.* Cambridge: Cambridge University Press, 1992.

Jones, Louisa E. *Sad Clowns and Pale Pierrots: Literature and the Popular Comic Arts in 19th Century France.* Lexington: French Forum Publishers, 1984.

Kaula, David. *Shakespeare and the Archpriest Controversy.* The Hague: Mouton & Co. N.V. Publishers, 1975.

Kittredge, George Lyman (ed.). *The Complete Works of Shakespeare.* Boston: Ginn, 1936.

Lowers, James K. *Notes on Hamlet.* Lincoln: Notes Inc. 1971.

Pearce, Richard. *Stages of the Clown.* Carbondale: Southern Illinois University Press, 1970.

Taylor, Gary. *Reinventing Shakespeare: A Cultural History from the Restoration to the Present.* New York: Oxford University Press, 1989.

Weimann, Robert. *Shakespeare and the Popular Tradition in the Theater: Studies in the Social Dimension of Dramatic Form and Function.* Baltimore: The Johns Hopkins University Press, 1978

Weimann, Robert. "Performance Theory" and "Shakespeare and His Theatre." *UC Irvine.* Winter/Spring 1994.

A Phenomenological Study of George Bernard Shaw's Plays

Dr. Awadesh Kumar Sharma

The present study may, to a certain extent, be considered to be based on my desire to understand the principles and postulates underlying George Bernard Shaw's (1856-1950) plays. In the search for these principles and postulates it was necessary for me to start with a revaluation of Shaw's plays themselves. But that was not enough. It was also necessary to know about Shaw's socio-political ideas, his approach to the problems of women and, above all, his iconoclastic attitude. This led to an examination of his numerous speeches, essays and pamphlets, some of which came before the publication of his plays, while others were published side by side with his plays. Although in different kinds of writing Shaw may seemingly appear to be speaking in different voices, the truth, nevertheless, is that these different voices are the manifestation of a single reality which is based on the overall understanding and perception of the author.

Before Shaw came from Dublin to London in 1876, at the age of twenty, he had memorised a number of operas and oratories by the great European masters. It is also to be noted that it took Shaw nearly sixteen years in London to publish his first play, but this period was formative and of crucial importance in the life of Shaw, as he kept struggling experimenting with various kinds of intellectual exercises and political ideas. He had been in constant search of a vocation ever since he heard the famous speech of Henry George on the "liberative war of humanity." He tried his luck as a music and drama critic, wrote novels, but success remained away from him. He joined the Fabian Society and became a leading member of its executive committee, acting as propagandist and thinker. It was during this period when he realized that writing on socio-political themes was his forte and reaching out to the masses his ambition. He wanted both to be heard and to be read and that is why he chose public speaking and drama writing to be his means to reach out to the masses.

My submission in this study is that the complete oeuvre of Shaw's speeches and writings constitutes one single text. The difference between his political and literary writings and speeches is one of medium, some of them have a greater amount of literariness while others have that in a lesser degree, and not of content. In other words, the conceptual structure of his plays is nearly the same as that of his political writings. Drama for him was not an end in itself, it was rather a means to a socio-political end. His main concern was to be heard. He himself said, "In order to get a hearing, it was necessary for me to attain the footing of a privileged lunatic, with the licence of a jester. My method is to take the utmost trouble to find the right thing to say, and then to say it with the utmost levity. And all the time the real joke is that I am in earnest." Drama for him was only "an extension of his more overtly political work." He was a writer with a palpable design and didactic end, not at all ready to write for art's sake alone. Even though he was charged with "the damnable vice of preferring rhetoric to truth," he constantly held that "Effectiveness of assertion is the Alpha and Omega of style."

He was essentially a reformationalist who wanted to reform humankind both from inside and outside – the inner reformation was possible by changing the human nature and the social institutions like marriage and family whereas the outer reformation could be achieved through changing the socio-political structure of the world. He darted his glances around and did not allow anything, howsoever big or small, to escape his attention. The range of his critical corpus spanned widows, widowers, prostitutes, labour, housing, education, religion, love, marriage, war, peace, family, wealth, social class, agriculture, governance, human life and world order. He addressed himself to these and many other subjects both in his plays and essays and speeches. He treated all his subjects morally, intellectually and realistically.

As Shaw kept changing his views, his ideas kept evolving. He started as a Fabian socialist and then grew to be a Marxist socialist followed by Shaw as a democrat and unorthodox feminist. His views on war and peace and love and marriage as well as family and society kept evolving and changing with the passage of time. The writer of *Plays Unpleasant and Pleasant* is not intellectually and aesthetically the same as the writer of *Man and Superman, Major Barbara, Saint Joan* and *Back to Methuselah.* He evolved not only as a social thinker and a philosopher but also as a mature dramatist and an artist. When we compare the Shaw of the 1880's with the Shaw of the 1920's or 1930's, we find a sea change between the two attained not only through the external influences but also through inner contradictions and compulsive intellectualism. In the development of his political thought we notice a marked change from his Fabian socialism to his political pronouncements in *The Guide* and *Everybody's*. Their pronouncements were largely related to his mature views on economics, education and democracy. It can also be noted in passing that the two World Wars and the rise of Sovietism and Fascism forced Shaw to change many of his early political views. These changes in his socio-political views are very aptly evidenced in his plays. For example, Blenkinsopp in *The Doctor's Dilemma* speaks on behalf of the weaklings of the middle class, and says about his poor patients that "patients are all clerks and shopmen. They daren't be ill: they can't afford it." Two other plays of the same period, namely *Getting Married* and *Misalliance*, also depict the bourgeois mentality. In *Man and Superman* also he takes the capitalists to task and is implicit in the claim that "we must either breed political capacity or be ruined by democracy."

The changes in Shaw's outlook in the middle period were postulated in *The Perfect Wagnerite*, a critique of Wagner's *Ring Cycle*, which revealed Shaw's own moral and philosophical outlook. It was a natural successor to *Quintessence of Ibsenism*. Both of these were the forerunners of the philosophy of life force which Shaw presented in *Man and Superman* and in *Back to Methuselah*. Shaw was of the view that majority of human beings were averse to progress and therefore we should try to create new ones instead of torturing the old ones. That is why he announced:

> The majority of men at present in Europe have no business to be alive, and no serious progress will be made until we address ourselves earnestly and scientifically to the task of producing trustworthy human material for the society. In short, it is necessary to breed a race of men in whom the life giving impulses predominate, before the New Protestantism becomes politically practicable. (Shaw 1932, Major Critical Essays, p. 215)

It is true that Shaw's concern for eugenics kept changing over the years, his moral concern about the conduct of the individual remained deeply ingrained in all his writings. In *The Guide*, he pronounced very emphatically and consequentially, "The working classes, the business classes, the professional classes, the propertied classes, the ruling classes, are each more odious than the other: they have no right to live." (Shaw 1949, *The Guide*, p. 490). Such provocative statements only express his growing concern for morality and uprightness in both private and public life. Both in his essays and speeches as well as his plays, he rejoiced contradicting his own arguments, particularly his arguments related to the science of marriage. In the preface to *Man and Superman*, for instance, he suggested that "Being cowards, we defeat natural selection under cover of philanthropy: being sluggards, we neglect artificial selection under cover of delicacy and morality." But the debate in the play has something different to posit:

> Beware of the pursuit of the Superman: it leads to an indiscriminate contempt for the human. To a man, horses and dogs and cats are mere species, outside the moral world. Well, to the Superman, men and women are a mere species too, also outside the moral world.
>
> (Shaw, *Man and Superman, Act III,* p.129)

A number of his masterpieces deal with Shaw's sense of doubt and despair. The long unpleasant arguments of the social democrats in Act III of *Man and Superman* is a case in point. In *Major Barbara* also the radical forces were deeply affected by the powers of capital and convention. We cannot believe that Cusins and Barbara will ever be able to deal with the mounting pressure exerted by Andrew Undershaft and Lady Britomart, although the closing scene of the play is a bit encouraging. In *John Bull's Other Island* where Father Keegan's vision of a new commonwealth was only a dream, the sense of uncertainty becomes even more prominent. The advocacy of violence in *Major Barbara* and the vision of the decline and fall of the European civilisation show Shaw's politics of desperation caused by his awareness of the failure of Fabian gradualism. In the preface to *Major Barbara* also he admitted that his preaching and pamphleteering were ineffective: "We paper apostles and artist-magicians have succeeded only in giving cowards all the sensations of heroes whilst they tolerate every abomination, accept every plunder and submit to every oppression."

A perspective on his views on the working class could be gained from his "class war" articles in *The Clarion* and the dramatic test of *Major Barbara*. As a moralist, he sought to transform consciousness by developing a new and positive sense of responsibility. As a socialist, he was interested in efficient management by a hierarchy of experts, with responsibility being understood in a negative sense. In this way, he undermined the means by which his republican vision of emancipation might be realised, because the experience of responsibility required for the development of character was divorced from day-to-day lives of ordinary working people. In the play the emphasis was on strict hierarchy in working relations. Undershaft, quite cynically speaks about his workmen, "Of course they all rebel against me, theoretically. Practically, everyman of them keeps the man just below him in place. I want a power simple enough for common men to use, yet strong enough to force the intellectual oligarchy to use its genius for the general good." *Major Barbara* cannot be taken as conclusive evidence of Shaw's views, which, taken as a whole, offer conflicting possibilities for the young and the poor. Turning again to the evidence of the plays for a moment, the last act of *Major Barbara* rings with such militant assertions as "the ballot paper that really governs is the paper that has a bullet wrapped up in it." Shaw's Fabianism was the respectable face of socialism and as such it had "drawn the teeth of insurgent poverty." His plays of this period, namely *Getting Married, The Doctor's Dilemma* and *Misalliance* were not as much the works of a moral revolutionist as those of a respectable gadfly operating within the confines of bourgeois society. That is why Shaw needed to revise the foundations of his social realism in order to find out a unifying doctrine that might dispel the mounting tensions of his argument.

Another important aspect of Shaw's consciousness and understanding was his concern for women and his discovery of "the new woman," which is popularly known as "Shavian woman." A Shavian Woman is conscious of her socio-economic and educational conditions and is eager to acquire upward socio-economic and educational mobility and finally stability in life. These "new women" are at once strong and dynamic as well as intelligent and realistic. Shaw expressed very loudly and clearly both in his plays and essays and speeches his idea of "the new woman." In fact, Shaw and the Woman's cause were inseparable. Critics like F.C. Burnaud, Wilma Meikle, Lady Rhondda and many others spoke in the superlative about Shaw's concern for women. However, there were those also who castigated Shaw for his overemphasizing the women's cause. Whether a "patron saint of the women's movement" (Watson 1977:114) or an anarchist for bringing "an unmarried mother on to the stage" (Marcus 1983:20), the fact is that he was genuinely concerned with the lot of women and sincerely wanted their emancipation. He was critical of the Victorian view of women:

> I do not regard women as animals of another species, I have no difficulty, as a playwright, in making female dramatis personal as easily as male ones: and I conclude that I could not do this if I had not a first-hand knowledge of both, being my mother's son as much as my father's. The sexes wear different boots and bonnets, not different souls.
>
> (Shaw 1920, *Women Since* 1860)

Such statements support the view that Shaw's reflections on women were based on an androgynous principle. When the actress Margaret Holston asked him to write a short speech for her on "The Women in Shaw's plays," he said quite categorically:

> There are no women in Bernard Shaw's plays. Don't think that I mean they are untrue to life. I mean exactly the contrary. For I will tell you another secret. There are no women in the real world. Believe me, ladies and gentlemen, woman, of whom we hear so much is a stage invention, and to me at least, a very tiresome one.
>
> (Shaw 1985, *Collected Letters* 1911-25)

He always assumed that men and women were alike, and his radical feminist view was that human nature was neither exclusively masculine nor feminine, but a mixture of the two; "a woman," he once said, "is a person exactly like myself." The essence of Shaw's radical feminism was to be found in the chapter on "the womanly woman" in *The Quintessence of Ibsenism,* where he held that the apparent dissimilarities between the sexes were the product of convention.

The portraits of women in Shaw's plays often expressed the complications involved in the process of emancipation. Louka and Raina in *Arms and the Man,* Blanche in *Widowers'* Houses, Julia in The Philanderer, Vivie in *Mrs. Warren's Profession,* Mrs. Clandon in *You Never Can Tell,* Eliza in *Pygmalion,* Candida in *Candida,* Ann in *Man and Superman,* to name only a few, are the examples of spirited women who represent their sex in the world of Bernard Shaw.

Shaw is until today a renowned socialist feminist and *The Guide* remains a landmark text in this context. In his philosophy of the life force also women play the pivotal role.

Another important area which forms part of Shaw's socio-political and literary oeuvre is war and peace. Between romance and marriage he rejected romance and upheld marriage, and in the same way between war and peace he rejected war and upheld peace. To Shaw, war was a romantic notion which did not provide solution to any problem. In *Arms and the Man,* the professional soldier carried chocolate creams instead of bullets. *The Devil's Disciple* portrayed war as a bloodless pastiche of gentlemanly manoeuvrings. In *Heartbreak House,* which was written during the World War I, the promise of violence was all pervasive, symbolizing ultimately the destruction not only of lives but also of values. The great war posed many dilemmas of a personal and doctrinal kind for Shaw and these can be linked to the tension between realism and moralism in his outlook. He viewed war as "a far lower form of villainy than commercial exploitation" (Shaw 1965, *Collected Letters 1874-1897*). For Shaw, the state was not only necessary for the efficient management of society, it also had a wider historical role to play as a moral force promoting humanitarian values. However, his attempt to bring the morality of peace to bear on war is open to many interpretations. The fact, nevertheless, remains that the war left an indelible mark on Shaw. When his wife died in 1919, he said that he hoped it was not the war that killed her: "A good many people have died of simple horror, mercifully without quite knowing it." He described the war as "four years of mud bath and blood bath, of intellectual and spiritual looting." And that showed his reaction to the war.

When all is said and done, George Bernard Shaw was a great intellectual thinker and writer in whose thought and writing are encompassed ideas related to nearly all the domains of human life, in particular the domains which are directly or indirectly related to the betterment of human life. His prose style, his sense of wit and humour, his provocative statements and iconoclastic thoughts and, above all, his concern for improving the quality of human life in the world are some of the inimitable aspects of his thinking and writing and his popularity as a fabianist, socialist and dramatist. I would like to conclude with an excerpt from an unsigned article published in the *Manchester Guardian* as a tribute to Shaw on his death in 1950:

> The degree to which he was an original thinker is probably negligible, but he was so admirable a verbal artist, so brilliant in controversy and satire (the greatest master since Swift), so

ready to invert the conventional view and trust to what might happen, that there can be few forward-thinking minds for two generations that have not been at some period affected by his influence.

Works Cited

Bentley, E., *Bernard Shaw.* 2nd edn, London: Methuen, 1967.

Bernstein, E., *My Years of Exile.* London: Leonard Parsons, 1921.

Chesterton, G.K., *George Bernard Shaw.* London: John Lane, 1910.

Clarke, P. , *Liberals and Social Democrats.* Cambridge: Cambridge University Press, 1978.

Ellis, R.W. (*ed.*), *Bernard Shaw and Carl Marx: A Symposium.* New York: Random House, 1930.

Evans, T.F. (*ed.*), *Shaw and Critical Heritage.* London: Routledge and Kegan Paul, 1976.

Grccn, N., *Bernard Shaw: A Critical View.* London: Macmillan, 1984.

Henderson, A. *Table Talk of G.B.S.*, London : Chapman and Hall, 1925.

___________ . *George Bernard Shaw-Man of the Century.* New York : Appleton/Century/Crofts,1956.

Holroyd, M. *Bernard Shaw: Volume I – 1856-1898, The Search for Love.* London: Chatto & Windus, 1988.

__________ .*Bernard Shaw: Volume II – 1898-1918, The Pursuit of Power.* London: Chatto & Windus, 1989.

__________ . *Bernard Shaw: Volume III – 1918-1950, The Lure of Fantasy.* London: Chatto & Windus, 1991.

Irvine, W. *The Universe of G.B.S.* New York: Russell & Russell, 1968.

Jackson, H. *Bernard Shaw.* London: Grant Richards, 1909.

Joad, C.E.M. (*ed.*). *Shaw and Society.* London: Odhams Press, 1953.

Kilroy Silk, R., *Socialism Since Marx.* London: Allen Lane & The Penguin Press, 1972.

Morgan, M.M. *The Shavian Playground.* London: Methuen, 1974.

Ohmann, R. *Shaw: The Style and The Man.* Middletown: Weslayan University Press, 1962.

Pease, E.R. *The History of the Fabian Society.* London: Frank Cass, 1963.

Pimlott, B. (*ed.*). *Fabian Essays in Socialist Thought.* London: Heinemann, 1984.

Rosenblood, N. (*ed.*). *Shaw: Seven Critical Essays.* Toronto: University of Toronto Press, 1971.

Shaw, G.B. (1920 b) *Women Since 1960.* Time and Tide, 8 October: 443-45.

________ . *Major Critical Essays.* London: Constable,1932 .

________ .*Collected Letters 1874-1897.*(*ed.*) D.H. Lawrence, London: Max Reinhardt, 1965.

________ . *Selected Non-Dramatic Writings.* (*ed.*) D.H. Lawrence, Boston: Houghton Mifflin, 1965.

________ . *Collected Letters 1898-1910.* (*ed.*) D.H. Lawrence, London: Max Reinhardt, 1972.

________ . *Collected Letters 1911-1925.* (*ed.*) D.H. Lawrence, London: Max Reinhardt, 1985.

________ . *Collected Letters 1926-1950.* (*ed.*) D.H. Lawrence, London: Max Reinhardt, 1988.

_______ . *The Complete Plays of George Bernard Shaw.* London : Constable, 1931.

Turco, A. *Shaw's Moral Vision.* Ithaca and London: Cornell University Press,1976.

Weintraub, R. *(ed.). Fabian Feminist: Bernard and Woman.* London: Pennsylvania State University Press, 1977.

Whitman, R.F. *Shaw and the Play of Ideas.* Ithaca and London: Cornell University Press, 1977.

Strauss, E. *Bernard Shaw: Art and Socialism.* London: Gollancz, 1942.

Erotic Streaks in *The Rape of the Lock*

Prof. (Dr.) Radha Mohan Singh

The perennial appeal of *The Rape of the Lock* has varied from age to age. In other words, every age unearths new dimensions of the poem according to its own preoccupations and preponderant thoughts or its code of morality. The eighteenth century acclaimed it though like Dennis, there were trenchant critics of it as a work of sweet satire on the flippancy and frivolity of its aristocratic echelons. The nineteenth century found in it an evidence of adroit poetic craftsmanship. "A bit of filigree work" as Hazlitt called it, though the poem as a whole was marginalized.

The twentieth century, however, has embarked on the insightful exploration of *The Rape of the Lock* much more than another century could even dream of. This has been possible thanks to the startlingly revolutionizing discoveries in the domains of Sociology, Psychology and Anthropology. These discoveries have enhanced our understanding of human psyche and of works of art which are concerned with the analysis of human nature. The uncovering of the sexual imagery and implications in *The Rape of the Lock,* one most responsible impact has been the discovery of the unconscious by Sigmund Freud. A creative work is partly the product of the conscious mind but mostly of the unconscious mind. A plethora of things lying embedded in the unconscious manage to seek their outlet to the conscious mind get mixed with its ideas, thoughts and feelings under different garbs and find articulation in the work. And an understanding of these is desideratum to understand the work in its totality.

If a twentieth century critic or reader envisions clearly sexual imagery and symbolism, it is not at all due to his blind faith in Freud's revolutionizing work. In 1715 Pope himself published a pamphlet called *A Key to the Lock* under a pseudonym E. Barnivelt known as Barnivelt Pamphlet. Apparently, this pamphlet is a parody on the superficial comments made on *The Rape of the Lock* and explicates in humorous vein underlying the poem, which furnishes a launching pad for unfurling sexual implications in the poem.

Stanley Edgar Hyman, a celebrated twentieth century critic has described the poem as "one vast comic defloration," that is a comic treatment, of the loss of virginity. After the anthropological discoveries of James Fraser and Jessie Weston, he considers the hair to be a fertility or Sex Symbol, the hair being employed to ensnare birds, hook fish and arrest men. Hyman also points out that the word "Lock" is a pun on Freud's description of the female organ as the locks that all keys fit, and again, this is abundantly clear also from Barnivelt Pamphlet. This being so, the shearing off the lock is to be taken for a sex act of defloration, in the light of which Belinda's shrieks for restoring the lock are nothing but absurd.

Hyman, however, himself goes to an absurd length in his anxiety in almost everything of the poem a sexual implication. In the line, "And maids turned bottle, call aloud for corks" perhaps the sex symbol is of course crystal clear. In fact, the image smacks of cynical streaks too. But to see in the sneezing-spout of the Baron, a symbolism of sex orgasm is certainly going too far. Again, in Belinda's remark to the Baron:

> Oh, hadst thou, cruel been content to seize,
> Hairless in Sight, or any hairs but these!

The joke may lie in the pun on the pubic hair and private hair, but to Hyman, it is starkly suggestive of sex.

It may be necessary for a twentieth century perceptive critic to hammer home this point, for this is an aspect which had never been noted before. But Hyman is not alone in laying bare the sex elements informing *The Rape of the Lock.* G. Wilson Knight leaps to the same conclusion, though in a modified form, by analyzing its poetic resources, imagery, rhythm, diction too. He finds that its sex is "juxtaposed with religion" in his own words:

> The religion of Post-Renaissance literature is based fundamentally, on Eros Cult. So in blending religious tonings with feminine vanity, Pope makes a synthesis of the Christianity-Eros conflict on a comparatively superficial, but delightfully human plane, the rich humour being both the measure of a relation and the resolving of a conflict.

And in this juxtaposition, Wilson Knight finds the source of the humour of *The Rape of the Lock.* "A synthesis of the sexual and the religious" is organic to the humour of *The Rape of the Lock.*

Earl R. Wasserman, in this connection gives more cogent and convincing arguments. He pinpoints that the sexual implications in the poem are Pope's conscious work, and that the readers of the time fully understood these implications. Of course, Freud wrote his classic works more than hundred and fifty years after Pope, but the reading public of the time did not require Freud to get the hang of these implications. Wasserman argues that the very title *The Rape of the Lock,* in a word, "The Rape" Pope has deliberately built in "ambiguous social nuances." It is not sheer bathetic, to arouse laughter or to mock at the quarrel over the cutting off the lock or again, merely to furnish some seeming justification for Belinda's tantrums.

Cleanth Brooks, a more thorough critic, believes that "a pervasive sexual symbolism informs almost everything in the poem" and that is his use of sex symbols Pope anticipates both Fraser and Freud. In other words, Brooks believes that Pope made a conscious use of "the Sex Symbolism" and this makes for the complex design of the poem. He analyses the game of cards to show that, this is a symbol of the war of the sexes. Every move in the game, the name of the card of the card, the manner of playing it all suggest sexual game. And it is not merely that the card game is a sexual symbol, but a pervasive game sexual symbolism informs, not only the description of the card game, but almost everything else in the poem. We are not forced to take the poem as either sly bawdy or as delightful fantasy. But if we are to see what Pope actually makes of his problem we shall have to be alive to the sexual implications which are in the poem.

The poem unfolds with an apostrophe to the Muse in which the sexual implications are underscored:

> Say what strange motive, goddess! could compel
> A well-bred Lord assault a gentle *belle* ?
> Oh say what strange cause, yet unexplored
> Could make a gentle *Belle* reject a *Lord*?

True, we can take *assault* and *reject* in more general meanings not in their specific Latin senses but the specific meanings are there just beneath the surface.

The sexual implications become quite specific after the "rape" has occurred. Thalestris, in inciting Belinda to take action against the Baron, cries:

> Gods! Shall the Ravisher display your hair
> While the Fops envy and the ladies stare!

Even if we take *ravisher* in its more general sense, still the sexual symbolism lurks just behind Thalestri's words. Else why should honour be involved as it is? Why should the Baron desire the lock and why should Belinda object so violently, not as to an act of simple rudeness, but to losing "honour" and becoming a "degraded Toast?" The sexual element is involved at least to the extent that Belinda feels that she cannot afford to suffer the Baron, without protest, to take such a "liberty." But a profound sexual import is emblemized by the whole incident. Belinda's anguished exclamation :

> Oh hadst thou Cruel! been content to Seize,
> Hairs less in sight, or any Hairs but these!

carries on unconsciously, the sexual overtones, the lines betray, primarily, of course, Belinda's exasperation at the ruining of her coiffure.

Sexual implications are inevitable in a poem which was written primarily to reconcile an undeclared war between two families arising out of flirtations between a young sophisticated lady and a young romantic lord.

The explicit suggestive images are galore such as "soft bosoms," "lap dogs," "giving themselves rousing shake." Ariel laying his "winning lips" to Belinda's ear, "the melting maids," "midnight masquerades," "shock," "waking his mistress with his tongue," "white breast," "wearing, a cross," "third bodies half dissolved," "the charge of the petticoat," etc. Besides the card game as Brooks has pointed out, is symbolic of the sex game between man and woman. After the lock is clipped, Belinda's "screams of horror" and the Baron's "exultation in joy" are suggestive of the sexual game between man and woman. "The conquering force of unresisted steel" is suggestive of the male overpowering the willing female.

In the fourth canto describing the visit to the cave of spleen the sex symbols are gathered as though in a dream fantasy. In the following lines:

> Here living teapots stand on arm held out,
> And maids turned bottles, call aloud for corks.

Nearly most suggestive of Freudian symbols occur "living teapots," "A pipkin," "walking," "a Jar," "sighing and eventually," "the maid turned bottles," "calling aloud for corks."

All these sexual implications foreground Pope's own take on sex; spinsterhood, according to *The Rape of the Lock* is an abnormality, as frivolous indulgence, sex is an abnormality. Pope pillories these abnormalities in the sex relationship.

Belinda's rejection is abnormal in so far as she rejects for the sake of carrying on her sex adventures and intrigues, with other young men or she rejects because she refuses to marry at all, and is willing to stay a virgin. The whole poem scorifies the idea of virginity. And even when one is able to retain virginity, it is to no purpose. And Clarissa in her moral harangue, clarifies:

> But since alas! Frail beauty must decay
> Curled or uncurled, since locks will turn grey;
> ....
> And she who Scorns a man must die a maid
> And keep good humour still whatever we lose.

Clarissa's speech enunciates Pope's moral lesson which espouses a natural, socially useful and healthy and salutary relationship between man and woman through love and marriage. Foucault has justly observed:

> Since the eighteenth century, sex has not ceased to provoke a kind of generalized discursive (dimension). And these discourses on sex did not multiply apart from or against power; but in the very space and as the means of its exercise.

The erotic streaks in *The Rape of the Lock* make the poem an engrossing read.

Works Cited

Tillotson, Geoffrey. *Pope's The Rape of the Lock: The Twickenham.* London: Methuen & Co. Ltd., 1962.

Rousseau, G.S. *Twentieth Century Interpretations of The Rape of The Lock.* New Jersey: Prentice-Hall, INC, A Spectrum Book.

Toward Skepticism as Critical Enquiry

Dr. Shanker A. Dutt

(This piece of writing is dedicated to the memory of Dr. R.C. Prasad who fondly ignited my interest in Seventeenth Century critical thought.)

While the renaissance had privileged individualism and occasionally appropriated constitutive elements of the classical canon, the neoclassicists saw advantage in classical values of objectivity, impersonality, decorum, balance, harmony, proportion and moderation (Habib 274) each of which structured the preferences of the Enlightenment. The crafting of literature was to be rational and disciplined with the recognition that humans could attain a degree of perfection within reasonable limits of their potential.

Neoclassical literary creativity in theory and praxis focused on imitation and nature. The first reaffirmed objectivity. The second emphasized balance, harmony, propriety, hierarchy, both social and political, while indicating the timelessness, universality and immutability of human nature. Hierarchic harmony was deeply coveted because of a bloody civil war and the priority lay with the reconsolidation of a shaken social order. Hence the neo-classical notions of lesson, nature, order and propriety were key virtues that literature required to embody and represent (Eagleton 15).

In seventeenth century England the scientific movement comprised a few major principles: first was the demand for a skeptical mind, freed from all preconceptions and maintaining a critical attitude towards all ideas presented to it. Second, observation and experimentation were insisted upon as the only trustworthy means of securing sufficient data. And third, the inductive method of reasoning was to be employed on these data. (James 42) The establishment of experimental science necessitated the overthrow of the still dominant principles of authority, those of Aristotle and the other Ancients. Thus anti-authoritarianism as a principle was incorporated into the movement. In order to achieve this with any degree of success, it was necessary to oppose the prevailing theory of nature's decay. This theory strongly claimed that modern times represented the geriatric phase of the universe and the last stages of the decay of nature in which human powers had declined to a level far below that of the Ancients who lived when nature was at its prime. The chief exponent of this theory, a clergyman, Godfrey Goodman in *The Fall of Man* (1616) held that corruption was introduced to all nature through the fall of man. The argument in support of this hypothesis was drawn from two theories: (a) that the farther a creature departed from the first mould, the more imperfect it becomes accompanied by the analogy of a stream that becomes more defiled the farther it goes from its source and (b) since parts of the creatural world passed through various stages to the decay of old age, so that nature must partake of the nature of its parts and experience decrepitude, drawing this time the analogy or infancy, prime and decay – the stages in a man's life. (Jones 11-12)

Such attitudes and ideas plus the value of liberty to investigate truth coalesced to form the scientific movement that culminated in the formation of the Royal Society. Francis Bacon who had been its beacon light had asserted that inquiry must begin "from hard data gathered by precise observation that remains uninfluenced by our beliefs and theories about the world." This was opposed to the Aristotelian method of inquiry. In Book 7 of the *Nichomachean Ethics,* Aristotle cites his method:

> Here as in all other cases, we must set down the appearances (phenomena) and, first working through the puzzles, in this way to go on to show, if possible, the truth of all beliefs we hold (endoxa) about these experiences, and if this is not possible, the truth of the greatest number and the most authoritative. For if the difficulties are resolved and the beliefs are left in place, we will have done enough showing. (*Nussbaum* 383)

The method is devoted to and circumscribed by the appearances or phenomena interchangeable with collective beliefs (endoxa). If the puzzles and contradictions therefore are resolved while preserving as true "the greatest number and the most authoritative of those beliefs," the work is satisfactorily accomplished. The methodological reform pronounced by Bacon – his method involved a natural history, composed of data gathered over a wide field by means of direct observation and experiment; the application of an inductive method of reasoning to these data; and insistence upon a doubting attitude of mind and upon the necessity of experiments until all doubts should be removed, had been unreservedly adopted by the Royal Society which gained distinction not only because of its scientific achievements but also in their ability to popularize certain methods of thinking and writing. This is aptly exemplified in the motto of the Society ÌNULLIUS IN VERBAÎ (take nobody's word for it) and correspondingly the method "assent to a proposition had to be suspended until the evidence was examined" ushered an attitude of skepticism as a means of ratiocination.

Paralleling the rapidly developing scientific movements with its aggressive defense of modernity as opposed to the authority of the ancients was a literary movement which comprised values and attitudes quite different to that of science. Neo-classical criticism which was based on the twin principles of imitation of nature and the moral purpose of art maintained that the proper models of writing were to be found in Greek and Roman literature (Homer and nature being the same) and that the modern writers ought to scrupulously follow those models. This was "a critical philosophy which upheld the principle of authority (though many critics tried to equate it with reason or common sense), limited the freedom of the poetic imagination, and rendered impossible beyond the achievements of the past." (Jones 44) Neo-classical criticism, in effect, lent support to the "theory of nature's decay, which indeed became one of its major theses." It does not require much perspicacity to observe that the views and attitudes in criticism were exactly antithetical to those of the scientific movement.

A representative critic of antithesis, as well as one who intersects between these attitudes was John Dryden, who when able to overcome "the shadow of the French neo-classical critic" was tentative and skeptical in his approach to literary criticism. It was a characteristic of which he was fully aware, for, in speaking of his translation of Lucretius in the Preface to Sylvae (1685) he says, "I laid by my natural diffidence and skepticism for a while, to take up the dogmatical way of Lucretius." (Ker 260) But if this skeptical, undogmatic attitude of mind was his by nature, it was also, perhaps, fostered and encouraged by his contacts with the scientists of his day. The Royal Society which existed as an informal association of like-minded individuals since 1645 was formally founded in the year of the restoration of the monarchy and received its royal charter two years later. The first members were men of diverse occupation and talent: Robert Boyle – the only authentic scientist, John Webster – a puritan chaplain, Joseph Glanvill – a rector in the Anglican Church and Thomas Sprat (later the historian of the society) – a preacher; the others being John Evelyn, Samuel Pepys,

Sir William Petty and the distinguished architect Sir Christopher Wren. They were united by a common thread of classical education, and implicit acceptance of the humanist culture and interest in the new inquiries. One of the early books published with the support of the Society was *Silvia* by Evelyn which was an elegant discourse on the art of planting and gardening "for the benefit and diversion of gentleman and persons of quality." Among the poets were Denham, Waller, Cowley and Dryden. Dryden joined the Society in 1662 and is on record for having served in two committees and praised and defended it in his poetry. The skeptical and critical attitude which the Royal Society had preserved and promoted derived from Bacon, could hardly have escaped his notice or been without influence upon him. In the "Defence of An Essay of Dramatic Poesy," prefixed to *The Indian Emperor* (1668) he explains the method of *The Essay:*

That my whole discourse was skeptical, according to that way of reasoning which was used by Socrates, Plato, and all the Ancients of old..... which is imitated by the modest inquisitions of the Royal Society in vindication of the charges of dogmatism (Ker 124) writes of his own "natural diffidence and scepticism" or "sceptical" way of reasoning and contrasts it with "majesterial" or "dogmatical" manner, the word "sceptical" is being used to describe a mode of inquiry, a "way of reasoning." It is a method of modest inquisition which "consists in investigating a question in an open and unbiased manner in letting the reader make up his mind for himself." This mode of inquiry was adequately described by Joseph Glanvill in *Plus Ultra* as a procedure which renders them wart and modest, diffident of the certainty of their conceptions, and averse to the boldness of the peremptory asserting. So that the philosopher thinks much, and examines many things, separates the certainties from the plausabilities, that which is presumed and that which proved, the Images of Sense, Phansie, and Education, from the dictates of genuine and impartial reason. This he doth before he Assents or Denies; and then he takes with him also a Sense of his own Fallibility and Defect, and never concludes but upon resolution to alter his mind upon contrary evidence. Thus he conceives warily, he speaks with as much caution and reserve, in the humble forms of so I think, and In my opinion, and perhaps 'tis so with great (deference) to opposite persuasion, candour to dissenters, and calmness in contradiction, with readiness and desire to learn, the great delight in the Discoveries of Truth, and Detections of his own mistakes.

This was published in 1668 the very year in which Dryden was describing his way of reasoning in *The Essay* in fairly similar terms and likening it to the "modest inquisitions of the Royal Society." The opposite of such a mode of investigation and reasoning was, according to the members of The Royal Society, was that of the Ancients, especially Aristotle which consisted in "a haughty confidence in one's own opinions and an arrogant attempt to impose them upon others." Critics have been disturbed by the use of the word "Inquisition" in Dryden's explanatory passage in *The Essay*. The word in common usage would mean severe judicial or official investigation conducted with little regard to individual rights, and perhaps conjures up a mental picture of the former Roman Catholic tribunal for the discovery and punishment of heresy. Dryden who was conscious of "the propriety of thoughts and words" could hardly have penned such a word without adequate consideration. It is rather unlikely therefore that it was an act of carelessness. An examination of the context would perhaps explain Dryden's use of "inquisition." The whole discourse of *The Essay* was skeptical, which we accept in spite of the subtle technique of infiltrating the minds of his readers and the skeptical method is in accordance with the method of inquiry adopted by the Royal Society. Dryden was critically aware of the connotations of "inquisition." Hence, an adjective (modest) is prefixed to it, in order that the method of scientific inquiry espoused by the Royal Society may carry force but that the pejorative and perhaps jagged connotations may be suitably moderated, in a sense smoothened. Yet the word without the accompanying adjective would be applicable to the authority of the ancients. An illuminating parallel to Dryden's habit of mentioning skepticism as contra distinct to dogmatism is offered in Glanvill's earliest book. When it had appeared for the first time in 1661, he had entitled it *The Vanity of Dogmatizing* which was subsequently changed to *Scepsis Scientifica* and dedicated to the Royal Society in reference to the method espoused in the book. He urged his readers to adopt "the scepticism which consists in freedom of Inquiry" for "Scepticism, that's the only way to Science." Distinguishing his "scepticism" from "endeavouring to discourage philosophical inquiries, by introducing a despair of Science" in the manner of the ancient skeptics – or Pyrrhonist – Glanvill declared "I desire it may be taken notice of one for all then, that I have thought to do with that shuffling Sect, that love to doubt eternally, and to question all things. My profession is freedom of inquiry, and I owe no more scepticism than what is concluded in the motto which the Royal Society have now adopted for their Nullius in Verba." Like Glanvill, Dryden's scepticism is "the confident affirmation of the powers of the human reason. When unexamined opinion is accepted as a substitute for honest investigation, Dryden believed, reason is betrayed and truth made captive."

Not only is the skeptical attitude of the scientific movement endorsed by the Royal Society perceptible in Dryden's criticism, but its corollary the inductive way of reasoning also can frequently be discovered there. "The method of reasoning employed by the dogmatic critics of his day was essentially deductive or syllogistic. They reasoned from general principles established largely from authority. Dryden, on the other hand, gathers his data from literature and from these data draws his conclusions." (Jones 45)

An example that Richard Foster Jones provides, sufficiently illustrates this point, indicating Dryden's independent spirit of inquiry and freedom from dogma. For a dogmatic critic, Jones argues, poetry is an imitation of nature (such a premise resting upon the authority of Aristotle); the supernatural is not an imitation of nature; therefore poetry containing the supernatural is not correct poetry. Dryden opposes the narrow rigidity "I will ask any man who loves heroic poetry... If the ghost of Polydorus in Virgil, the Enchanted Wood in Tasso and the Bower of Bliss in Spencer could have been omitted, without taking from their works some of the greatest omitted, without taking from their works some of the greatest beauties in them, and asserting critical independence in opposition to narrowness of attitude he draws a general principle that an heroic poet is not tied to a bare representation of what is true... but he may let himself loose to visionary objects and to the representation of such things as depending not on sense, and therefore not to be comprehended by knowledge, may give him a freer scope for imagination." While for Sprat and the Royal Society, the last perfection constituted restoring language to "the primitive purity, and shortness, when men delivered so many things in an equal number of words" bring all things "near the mathematical plainness" preferring the "language of artisans, countrymen, and merchants before that of wits and scholars" (Daems 45), Dryden was crucially aware of the role of literature to provide a just and lively image of human nature (Ker 110) that would provide profit and pleasure.

Challenging received authority, Dryden wrote in *Defence of the Epilogue,* "I hope I shall not be thought arrogant when I inquire into their errors. For we live in an age so skeptical, that as it determines little, so it takes nothing from antiquity on trust, and I profess to have no other ambition in this Essay, than that may not go backward, when all other arts and sciences are advancing." (Ker 162-163)

Thus it may be concluded that neo-classical criticism led by Dryden, who with nuanced flexibility, nursed a desire to transcribe the progress that the scientific movement was making into the making of literature.

Works Cited

Daems, J. *Seventeenth Century Literature and Culture.* Chennai: Viva Continuum Edition, 2008.

Eagleton, Terry. *Literary Theory: An Introduction.* Oxford: Blackwell Publishing, 1983.

Habib, M.A.R. *A History of Literary Criticism.* Oxford: Blackwell Publishing, 2005.

Ker, W.P. (*ed.*) *Essays of John Dryden.* Vol I. Oxford: Clarendon Press, 1900.

Jones, R.F. *The Seventeenth Century.* NY: Stanford University Press, 1951.

Jones, T.B & B.D. Nicol. *Neo-Classical Dramatic Criticism* 1561-1770. London: Cambridge University Press, 1976.

Nussbaum, M. in T. Jones Luce (*ed.*) *Ancient Writers.* New York: Charles Scribber's Sons, 1982.

Watson, G. *The Literary Critics.* London: Penguin Books, 1962.

Wykes, D. *A Preface to Dryden.* New York: Longman, 1977.

Ethical Understanding in the Poetry of W.H. Auden: A Study

Dr. B.P. Sinha

"Of all the poets," J.W. Beach records,

> of the thirties and forties, it is Auden, who returns most often to the image of the journey, and it is for him the symbol of different types of seeking. (Beach, p.187)

This is true. Whatever interpretation we might give to Auden's poetry, one thing is clear that it represents his profound concern with truth. In the early writing of the thirties in which the object of the journey is not very clearly envisaged, the underlying motive is of the search of some regenerating pattern of truth for the lonely and the sad individual, who is member of diseased society. In the course of the development of Auden's thinking, we see that the social and spiritual meaning of the quest transforms into metaphysical and religious ones.

Auden's poetry is linked with the Marxian ideas of progress and the principle of evolution. One may see the image of the wanderer, the figure of a political revolutionary seeking for a qualitative change. Auden and his contemporary poets were convinced of the urgent need of a radical change in the structure of the society. In *Dog Beneath the Skin* for instance the successful end of the search of the missing Baronet, ultimately turns to be the quest for a new political and social organization. In the poem entitled *The Love Letter,* one finds a more poetic and suggestive picture of the wanderer who has been from the very rst coming down in a new valley experiencing complete alienation.

> Nor question over much the nod
> The stone smiles, of this country God
> That never was more reticent
> Always afraid to say more than it meant.
>
> (Collected Shorter Poems, 1933)

The realization of human values is of primary importance throughout Auden's poetry, and he has ever since stressed the need of a personal change of heart. It is in term of human beings that he sees the political issues and in terms of human values that he sees the solution. Thus, his quest is founded largely on the idea of moral evolution and spiritual growth. The individual, if at all he wishes to survive, has to identify himself with the will of evolving life force; as otherwise, he has to face automatic extinction:

> Means that I wish to leave and
> To pass on
> Select another, form, perhaps you
> Son. (Collected Shorter Poems, 1933)

In his early works, Auden shows compassion and sympathy for the man, who accepts the challenge of active life and leaves his house with firm determination to proceed on a voyage of quest. Such a man is impelled by a strong urge of his will and is determined to face the difficulties and deviations involved in the journey. He cannot be deterred from his mission by family bonds and emotional attachments:

> No cloud-soft hand can hold him,
> Restraint by women;
> But ever that mangoes
> Through place-keepers, through
> Forest trees,
> A stranger to stranger over un-dried sea.
> (Collected Shorter Poems, 1933)

The Poem-II of *Poems* from which these lines are quoted is a representative example of Auden's early treatment of the theme of quest.

It is evident that the self-willed exile of this wanderer represents a step of migration from a dead past into a new future, and the wanderer seems to be one of the explorers of new worlds of thoughts and conduct. Auden's interest in the idea of journey is motivated by his constant concern with man as an evolving animal, and in this respect the journey symbolizes the varied experiences of life the old experience always evolving a quest at every step of life. Auden discredits the inert life of a man, who lies idle in contentment, tied down to a dead past and living an uncertain present. For him the solution lies in the direction of the past towards a brighter future.

As Auden is interested in the order and harmony of life, he pictures his voyager as a man of earnest will determined to come out of his unhealthy state of existence and move on in quest of better conditions, of greater moral freedom and spiritual harmony. The harmony of the spirit can be achieved only when a requisite social order has been attained and the ailment of the human psyche bred by the frustrating convention of the earlier social order has been cured and tension released. Thus, in this pattern we find Auden's effort at a synthesis of social, psychological and spiritual ends. The actual journey takes place inside the heart of man – the heart being both the subject and object of the voyage in quest – as it is suggested to begin and end with a change of heart.

Temptation described in the sonnets written by W.H. Auden, deal with the inner dilemmas of the exceptionally gifted human beings, who, evidently, are in quest of a principle of self-gratification rather than spiritual resurgence. Their position is beautifully summed up in the Sonnet IX, entitled *The Tower* in which there is clear indication that the tower that embodies the unique attainments of the exceptional men, may turn into an ivory tower for their isolation and escape, in whose spell they are to be miserably caught. The poet says:

> The desert glared into his
> blood shot eyes;
> the silence roared displeasure;
> looking down,
> He saw the shadow of an Average Man
> Attempting the Exceptional, and ran.
>
> (Collected Shorter Poems, 1933)

By the time, Auden came to write these sonnets, he seems to have reached the frontier of his quest and it remains a moment's task for him to declare his entrance into a new territory. In *The Age of Anxiety* Auden returns to use the quest symbolism, for depicting the ordinary people from real life, who have lost grips with the meaning of life. Lost and lonely, the four wanderers are shown suffering from a tormenting sense of emptiness, and, therefore, they are engaged in searching out the cause of their hollowness, as also the meaning of life. And in this fact alone, that they know their dilemma and are also conscious of the guilt and anxiety of their life lies the earnestness of their desire to get out of their cursed life. No matter, whether they achieve it or not, the course of movement of their journey is obviously from guilt to innocence. In fact, Auden is seeking now, an eternal order in the timeless, in the temporal one bound in time, and the earlier image of false city is assimilated in that of the authentic city, which is the end of all quests.

J.B. Beach rightly observes that,

> the sense of guilt and the longing for innocence are perhaps, along with fear and anxiety, the dominant emotions of the period in which we live. (Beach, p. 307)

The cause of the general unhappiness of man is that today "loneliness" is man's real condition. Auden earnestly felt that in the literary works of the writers, there should be a clear and straight moral and ethical order for the disturbed and anxious society. Historically, it is the modern age of science and materialism, which has bred widespread restlessness, frustration and self-contempt. The whole situation of Auden's age, besides being symbolic of the anxiety-ridden world, is quite realistic of our life, in the mid-twentieth century, with the Second World War in the background. The point, which Auden intends to bring in his ethical views, that there is absolute futility of a world without faith in God.

In this connection we can mention *The Age of Anxiety* where, Auden like Eliot in *The Waste Land* went to show the emptiness of life without faith. Throughout his work, we find a moving appraisal of our age, which has witnessed two world wars, and in which forces of dehumanization and disintegration have been working with an ever-increasing strength. We notice that mood of despair is given a place of prime importance and the enormous disappointment, which accompanies anxiety both as its cause, and its manifestation, is depicted with great concentration. Although in the final analysis, such a brooding on personal malady or on human existence is a kind of intellectual flight from their actual surroundings, it is obvious that they are also trying to see their own individual situation in the larger perspective of the eternal truth of human existence.

Beneath the apparent layers of psychological and pathological meanings in the *Age of Anxiety* we can easily discover the poet's religious outlook of seeking how man can be happy. The ultimate and sought after is always the condition of man's happiness, which is denied to him, because of his willful negation of the religious truth – the faith in Divine Grace. Man himself is responsible for his alienation from God. We can say that the final impact of Auden's poetry is usually one of intellectual appeal and greater awareness of one's self and environment. His ideas, be it political or clean ethical, closely related to his personality. W.H. Auden seems to stand outside the experience which has resulted in the detachment of the poet from the object of treatment. His poetry makes us consciously receptive of the truth.

Auden's Marxism was simply another dimension added to his interest in human psychology. The varying concepts of love, which are related directly to the different stages of his intellectual development, point also to the poet's common interest in love as a healing and reintegrating principle. At every stage the idea of true love has been contrasted with false love. Similarly, through the frequent use of archetypal images of voyage and quest, Auden presents human life in terms of a journey, undertaken for the attainment of certain positive ends of inner and outer transformation. His concern with the psychological dangers of the journey in the thirties and the spiritual temptations in the poetry of the forties, relates his poetry with a common interest in the dangers and problems of the journey in both the stages. In the treatment of all these ideas, Auden shows an abiding interest in the problems of necessity and freedom. He exhibits a profound concern about the human condition and brilliant capacity to present man both in the perspective of the contemporary and the universal order of existence. Poetry according to Auden has to produce the excitement of new awareness, which can be achieved through the unique expression of illuminating ideas.

The basic concern of the poet is love in its various aspects. Like Shelley, Auden seems to believe in the efficacy of love as a key to both individual and social happiness and well-being. We have noticed that the quest for the good place or just city in other words for a happy society is deeply related with Auden's treatment of love. A.S. Collins, writing on Auden, stresses this point very effectively.

> In the modern darkness, when hatred, fear, death were in the air and men are sick of soul, feeble, selfish, despairing, it was time to seek redemption, and to learn in suffering the way, the truth, and the life, no more turning our backs upon the vision.
>
> (Collins, p.124)

Frustration, dissatisfaction and unsettlement hung over the world, when Auden made a mark as a poet in the early thirties. Such a world,

Auden felt, needed a change of heart. In the age of violence and hatred, he looked for the opposite values of peace. In his poems, he established hopeful faith in Love and Peace.

> About Auden John Hollander has justly remarked that the poet has spoken not for national affairs or victories, but on events and crisis in the world of the moral imagination.
>
> (Hollander, p. 84)

The whole world of Auden is an integral whole, but at the same time it would be wrong to comment that it is religious thought, which accords continuity to Auden's poetry. While it is difficult to reconcile Auden's early and later poetry on the basis of religious thoughts, his search for the growth of healthy love can be logically shown to have led him to Freud, Marx and Christianity successively.

For Auden love is a way of life. For mankind love is the means of survival in the modern society. For Auden love is finally great, greater than all. The poet begins with earthly love, describing firstly the love of one's own interest, then we find love in a higher form i.e. the love of one's neighbour in the pursuit to fulfill the second commandment.

The erotic or romantic love is considered to be inadequate in the world of thirties. In *As I walked out one evening*, we get the idea that Auden finds personal or romantic love, inadequate:

> The glacier knocks in the cupboard,
> The desert sighs in the bed,
> And the crack in the teacup opens
> A lane to the land of the dead. ('As I Walked out', p. 115)

This grim reality reminds the lovers to be aware of such a love. For Auden, it is time to reject the erotic love as a complete answer:

> ......the word is love,
> Surely, one fearless kiss would cure,
> The million fevers, a stroking brush
> The insensitive refuse from the burning core
> Was there a dragon, who had
> closed the works
> While the starved city fed it
> with the Jews?

Then love would tame it with
his trainer's look.
(August for the People and their favourite Island, p. 156)

We find that Auden's life long quest for unraveling the nature of love, finds a fitting culmination beginning with Freudian and Marxian overtones. Auden moves to Christian theology but ultimately he relies on its broad and universal meaning to find a fulfillment of his ideas in a calm mood of acceptance and atonement.

Auden is, from first to last a moralist with deep serious ethical values, who wants his poems to arouse his audience into critical self-awareness and to incite them to reform. Yet, he rejects all attempts, including some of his own early sermonizing to tell the reader exactly what the moral truth is, what the ethical value is.

Works Cited

Auden, W.H. *Collected Shorter Poems.* London: Faber and Faber, 1933.

__________, *As I Walked Out.*

__________, *August for the People and their Favourite Island.* August 1935, E.A.

Beach, J.W. *Obsessive Image.* London.

Collins, A.S. *English Literature of the Twentieth Century.* London: University Tutorial Press, 1969.

Hollander, John. *Auden of Sixty.* The Atlantic, Vol. 220, No. 1, July 1967.

Victorian Novelists: A Critical Survey

Dr. Ashok Kumar

Absorbing into itself a very large part of the creative energy of the time, the Victorian novels became a vehicle of ideas as well as a means of amusement. Writers of different schools of thought employed it to embody their general criticism of life. While it was found to lend itself equally well to the purpose of those who, having any special thesis – and there were so many in that age of confusion – to expound, desired to reach the largest body of readers whose number had suddenly increased. It was inevitable that it should thus come to reflect all the forces which were shaping the complex Victorian world. The spread of science made it realistic and analytical; the spread of democracy made it social and humanitarian; the spirit of religious and moral unrest, of inquiry and criticism, was often uppermost in it; often, too, it revealed the powerful influence of the romantic revival. In its very variety of matter and treatment, therefore, the Victorian novel is the index of many-sided interests and conflicting elements of the age. At this point the well-marked tendency towards specialization in fiction should also be noted. Some Victorian novelists aimed to give a fairly comprehensive picture of the contemporary society. But, as a rule, aspects of life were picked out for separate treatment, and sub-division of labour and interests was the result. Thus, for example, we have novels of the sea and of military life, of high life, middle class life, criminal life, industrial life, political life, artistic life, clerical life, and so on. Frequently, the sub-division follows geographical lines, as in the fiction which concerns itself with Irish life, or Scottish life, or even, it may be, the life of different English counties. It is largely through the free development of these sub-dividing tendencies that prose fiction in the Victorian age expanded on all sides until it came to be practically extensive with all the aspects and the activities of the age.

A detailed consideration of all the aspects of Victorian novel is neither possible nor necessary. The broad characteristics of the important novelists may be touched upon.

First to mention Charles Dickens, whose fiction suffered in proportion to its popularity. Instead of refining the tastes of his thousands of readers, Dickens appealed to their weaknesses. He gave them what they wanted, and they wanted melodrama, theatricality, episodic plots, fantastic characters, and sobs of sentimentality. He distrusted the intellect; he distrusted science. The result is that his novels represent a *laisseze-faire* of emotionalism. They are characteristically structureless and undisciplined; and characters in them do not have depth.

But Dickens had in abundance an extraordinary creative vitality because of which characters, incidents, and situations tumbled from his pen. The characters are abnormally exaggerated – they are largely grotesque, dwarfs, and giants – but they are intense and vivid, the situations are contrived but they are vastly entertaining; the dialogue needs pruning but it is as close to the condition of heard speech as one could wish.

One fascinating aspect of Dickens, the novelist is his preoccupation with evil. He is the master of the weird and the horrible; dark mystery and nightmare existence. Fagin, Bill Sykes, Monks and Magwich move us more surely and terribly than the cherubic old philathropists and virtuous young ladies. The Dickens' universe, in the long run, is monstrous, evil, thrilling, satanic. Even such an apparently innocuous piece as the Christmas story of old Scrooge and cripple Tiny Tim is too terrifying for many children. Living in a world of twisted minds, warped bodies and triumphant terror, we are sometimes led to think that the secret mind of Dickens charmed itself with the awful music of despair. His humour and pathos are not to be sharply differentiated; laughter and tears lie closely together in his writings and frequently invade one another's territory –"something are of that nature as to make one's fancy chuckle while his heart doth ache." There are no great depths to his imagination as there are in Shakespeare and Milton, no such subtleties as in Meredith and Thomas Hardy, but for acute sensibility he has no peer in English letters. Dickens is, as has been said, in no sense a psychologist. His work is impressionistic, not analytical and when he elaborates his potrait, it is not to show the quality of motives so much as the quality of whistcoat buttons.

The most representative novels of Charles Dickens are: *David Copperfield* (autographical), *Bleak House, Hard Times, Little Dorrit,* and *Great Expectations. A Tale of Two Cities* (a historical novel about the French Revolution) is not at all typical of Dickens.

We cannot miss the attitude of a satirist and moralist in the novels of William Makepeace Thackeray. As a novelist Thackeray tried to do what Dickens did not; he set out seriously to represent life, to give a picture of the contemporary society emphasizing the tragi-comedy of wordliness. An amazing prober of social sin, he wrote several of the finest novels of the century, chief among which are *Vanity Fair*, a novel without a hero, and the *History of Henry Esmond.*

At its best, Thackeray's fiction has rare distinction. His style is urbane, charming and reserved; he admirably alternates humour and satire; has a penetration into human motives is almost breath-taking; he has a fine sense for form (*Vanity Fair*, for example); he has the poet's ability to evoke the past, and suggest cycles of changes of life waxing and waning, of flowers unfolding and withering. But he lacks the vitality of Dickens, as also his warmth and expensive geniality; and his mood, constitutionally melancholy, does not yield itself readily to the readers. He unfortunately allowed his own sentimentality to cloud and dim his pictures of characters. Compton Rickett points out, "Thackeray's style appeals to our intelligence, Dickens' to our heart and imagination. Thackeray excels as a painter of manners, as an artist of conventions, as a draughtsman of civilized man with all his merits and limitations. And he did the same service for English fiction as Ben Jonson did for English drama; and just as Jonson, Shakespeare with his deficiencies and his danger as a model to writers with less genius, so did Thackeray realise the imperfection of Dickens and the danger attaching to young writers who should slavishly follow in his wake."

George Meredith may also be mentioned in the list of the great novelists. A poet-pagan, he was a green-field sacramentalist who believed that nature and all things natural are holy and sanctified. He even modified the doctrine to fit his system of purified naturalism. His position was that though the evolutionary process had operated mechanically in the past, it had now achieved a directive intelligence in the minds of responsible thinking of men and women who are therefore obliged to co-operate with the impulses of nature if there is to be a better tomorrow. Everyone (man, more than woman, for man is the arch-egotist) must purify himself from self-love and learn to live in the service of others. The love of a woman will infallibly redeem a man from his selfishness, because woman is instinctively better than man, more generous in her life, since she is less absorbed in the contemplation of her own image. Another indispensable aid to self-betterment is the Comic Spirit which helps a man to laugh at his vanity, affectations and pretensions, and this helps him to rid himself of anti-social and anti-natural evils.

In fact, every Meredithian hero is made to face an "Ordeal," a conflict between nature and some falsification or distortion of it. Practically every male character is put in some situation whereby he is forced to overcome some defect of "blood" (sense), "brain" (reason) and "spirit" (the hallowing principle of life). Snobbery, egoism and sloth are the vices singled out for study. We read his novels like *The Ordeal of Richard Feverel, Rhoda Fleming,* or *Egoist* not for the "blood" and glory of brave deeds simply narrated but for the subtle play of the author's brilliant intellect.

Skipping over the novels of Hardy which serve as an epilogue to the Victorian age, we may mention some lesser Victorian novelists to conclude this survey. More remarkable of these lesser writers are: Lord Lytton, the author of memorable *Last Days of Pompei* and sensational *Pelham,* George Borrow, the author of *The Bible in Spain, The Gypsies in Spain, Lavehgro* and its sequel *The Ramany Rye.* With Charles Read social purpose is generally dominant (e.g., *Foul Play, Put Yourself in His Place*); but the best of his books is *The Cloister and the Hearth.* Charles Lever is remembered today for *Harry Lorrequeer* and *Charles O'Mally* – two books of rollicking fun. Mrs. Gaskell may be mentioned here as a humanitarian novelist (e.g., her pathetic story of factory life in *Mary Barton*), though for most readers she lives as the author of the quaint and charming village idyll, *Cranford.* Then there is the voluminous and realistic novelist Anthony Trollope who has given us photographic picture of early Victorian provincial life in *Barchester Towers* & *Dr. Thorns.* He was at his best as a novelist of clerical life (e.g., *The Warden, The Framley Parsonage*). Wilkie Collins was a maker of ingenious plots, and a master of thrills and chills. He wrote two novels which have become classics for mystery *The Woman in White* and *The Moonstone.* R.L. Stevenson wrote an immortal adventurous story "Treasure Island" which is not likely to lose its cherished place on the reading lists of the young in age and heart. Profoundly interested in the problem of evil, including the fall of families and dualism of personality, he wrote *Kidnapped, Dr. Jekyll and Mr. Hyde* and *Master of Ballantrae.* Stevenson's prose is exceptionally flexible and musical, the narrative movement is sure, and the atmosphere is one of realized powers. Out of fifteen volumes of his collected works only one of Samuel Butler's books, namely, *The Way of All Flesh,* stands out with shocking power. This book may be taken as voicing a radical protest against the narrowness of Victorian morality. Its intensity is personal. It is a document drenched with hate. If Butler can be said to have less passionate interest one of them was his deification of Life-Force and his advocacy of the doctrine of evolution. He has also written two utopian novels: *Erewhon* and *Erewhon Revisited.*

A special mention must be made of the Bronte sisters. Like a flash of chain-lightning the fire of genius illuminated a small parsonage in the town of Haworth on the fringe of the Yorkshire Moors. At least three children of Rev Patrick Bronte reached literary heights. Anne Bronte's gentle talents are less dramatic than those of her two other famous sisters, but her *Agnes Grey* and *the Tenant of Wild fell Hall* are good prose narratives. Her sister Charlotte Bronte was far more intense and subjective. Out of the web of childhood consciousness and adult emotional yearnings, she composed a fiction which is amazingly frank, articulate and emotionally disturbing and which tells us about her hidden and possibly sub-conscious life. Most of it has been done in an autobiographical manner and most of it has the shock of a confessional revelation. Her heroine is invariably a governess who, beneath her prim, proper and plain manner, has the soul of a passionate woman. In the range of subjective and romantic fiction there are few more dynamic and volcanic books than *Jane Eyre, Villette,* and *The Professor.*

But more challenging and violent is Emily Bronte's *Wuthering Heights.* Remarkably objective and dramatic in its rendering of materials, this novel seems at first sight to be an astonishing triumph of gothicism. Later analysis shows that it is far more than a gothic novel. One may think that it has a cosmical significance. Trushcross Grange and Wuthering Heights, are not isolated areas in geography; they are the symbols of world forces, respectively the dynamic and the quiescent. The novel is an integrated work of art. The story of Heathcliffe and Cathy, of the successive generations of Earshaws and Lintons is as nearly perfect as one could desire. Dramatic and lyrical, it has a unique place in world literature. Charlotte Bronte in her novels revolted against the tradition of Jane Austen, Dickens and Thackeray and her novels are not of manners but of passion and the naked soul. Emily Bronte is fiercer than Charlotte but her fierceness is strongly accompanied by numerous strokes of intuitive illuminations.

George Eliot, the third great novelist of the period, followed the pattern set up in the novels of manners written in the 18th century by Fielding and Smollet. Sprawling, vigorous, colourful, her fiction presents large scenes and multitude of characters seen in their externalized attitudes. With her a new kind of novel came into existence. Both psychological and sociological; it studies characters in their inwardness and relates political and social movement to the total mental and moral lives of people.

George Eliot belonged to a group of avante-garde thinkers which included Herbert Spencer and John Stuart Mill; she affirmed a belief in Naturalism and held that the universe functions according to inevitable moral laws. Her intellectual dialectics works throughout her fiction, even in the idyllic *Scenes from Clerical Life, Adam Bede, The Mill on the Floss,* and *Silas Marner.* The last novel preaches Auguste Compte's "religion of humanity." In the later works the intellectual design is clearer. *Romola* and *Middlemarch* bear the mark of the application of her doctrine of naturalism and necessitarianism. Here she tests her characters for sin with the painstaking technique of an expert laboratory analyst. But the sternness of her moral and philosophical outlook is softened by her gentle humour, her kindliness, and her poetic idealism. Her rustic characters are as large as life; her settings are memorable and her style is flowing, serene, calm and picturesque. George Eliot stands at the gateway between the old novel and the new, no unworthy heir of Thackeray and Dickens and no unworthy forerunner of Hardy and Henry James. At her worst George Eliot is laboured, self-conscious, and didactic, never trivial or shallow. At her best she is rich in mellow wisdom and in sympathetic insight. She was a sort of Moses to the Victorian age, leading it to the promised land of full intellectual, moral and political freedom, even though the results of its entering upon that inheritance have been similar to those that overtook the Jews after entering over Jordan and "her imagination is not like a distorting glass like Dickens, vitalising her figures by accentuating their personal idiosyncrasies, nor is like Charlotte Bronte, a painted wisdom suffusing them with the colour of her own live temperament; it is an X-ray, bringing them to life by the clearness with which she penetrates to the secret main spring of their actions."

Mrs. Elizabeth Gaskell, who used novel as an instrument of social reform, is well known for her novels, *Mary Barton* and *North and South.* These novels dramatise effectively the life of the working-class in an industrial town – a contrast of industrial England with rural England. Mrs. Gaskell had no political theory or affiliation like Disraeli and nothing of the passion and frustration of the Bronte Sisters. W.L. Cross says, "She did not possess the clearness of vision, the equipment of knowledge, and the breadth of horizon required for completely satisfying the definition of the psychological novel. What she did in part was fully accomplished by George Eliot." Compton-Rickett points out, "Mrs. Gaskell had neither the intellectual equipment nor the artistic power of George Eliot, but she was a shrewd observer, with a tolerant sympathy and a strong sense of humour."

Thomas Hardy's work may be considered under three aspects – descriptive artist, analytical artist and philosophic artist. His novels were marked by humour and pathos for the creation of which he had a natural capacity. As Chesterton points out, he was not a conscious critic, but he intuitively perceived social injustice, cruelty and inhumanity which he exposed in his novels. For the sake of comedy he had to exaggerate and overstate, but the final effect was always a healthy kind of realism. Artistically his novels were not perfect like those of Jane Austen but they certainly had much more life. They also differ from George Eliot, with whose psychological methods his work shows certain affinities. Hardy, a versatile and prolific novelist, wrote a number of novels – *The Return of the Native, The Mayor of Casterbridge, Tess of D'Urbervilles* and *Jude the Obscure.*

Thomas Hardy's novels have appealed to successive generations of readers. Nature, which to Wordsworth and the Romantics had seemed stimulating and benign, appeared to Hardy as cruel and relentless. Hardy was read with pleasure as one who had the courage to portray life with the grimness that it possessed, portraying it not to lose pity. His profound awareness of man's futile struggle with fate or destiny is an imaginative rendering of the invincibility of the natural forces which man in vain tries to conquer.

Hardy, a scientific as well as poetic observer, has a sensitive brooding imagination, impulses of pagan feeling, sexual devotion, pity, courage, endurance and proves himself an analytical artist, an interpreter of life and a philosophical artist. Randall Williams observed, "Hardy's art was the art presenting the tragic struggle between human will and cosmic forces," whereas Lionel said, "In Hardy's novels the strongest thing is necessity, the wisest is time, and the greatest is the heart of man."

The Victorian novels provide a wealth of experience and an untiring and triumphant zeal of men to help one another and reflect all the complex forces which influenced the contemporary age. Large sympathy with children is one of the chief contributions made by the Victorian England to real civilization. Hudson remarks:

> The spread of science made it realistic and analytical; the spread of democracy made it social and humanitarian; the spirit of moral and religious unrest, of inquiry and criticism was uppermost in it; often too, it revealed the powerful influences of the Romantic Revival.

Works Cited

Alexander, Michael. *A History of English Literature.* New York: Palgrave Macmillan, 2000.

Ricket, Arthur Compton. *A History of English Literature.* New Delhi: Universal Book Stall, 1990.

Cecil, David. *Early Victorian Novelists.* Ludhiana: Kalyani Publisher, 1972.

Hyperion: A Proponent of Radicalism

(*In Memory of Dr. R.C. Prasad*)

Dr. Samir Kumar Sharma

John Keats is the high priest of truth and beauty as is William Wordsworth, a votary of Nature or Gandhi, is an apostle of truth and non-violence. Every writer especially a poet is a product of the age to which he belongs and wants to make the world a better place to inhabit. A true poet serves humanity in general and his nation in particular. He raises his voice against the tyranny of the administration and crusades for liberty, equality and fraternity. To regulate the social system he also suggests some measures or lays the foundation of such ideas that cross the boundaries of time and space and the whole human society gets inspiration and light from them. Romantic poets, in general, had a deep interest in nature, not as a treasure trove of beautiful and dappled images but as a balmy and spiritual influence on life. It was as if frightened by the onslaught of cross industrialism and nightmarish, tentacles of trades and commerce they turned to nature for soul touching serenity or as if, with the declining strength of traditional religious beliefs, men were making a religion from the spirituality of their own experiences. They saw life steadily with new sensibilities and fresh vision. They are the men who suffered and out of their suffering they created great works of art. Sometimes personal agonies and sufferings are metamorphosed into something rich and universal in the artistic form. John Keats is such a poet who died in the prime of his life. He was the last born of the Romantics and the first to become a morsel for the mouth of death. He occupies a very important place in the history of English poetry. His *Hyperion: A Fragment* popularly known as *Hyperion* is an artistic exploit shaped by the social and political contexts.

Some unusual events of time, periods of radical, rapid and violent change expect their poets to record and analyse those events and provide history in literary flavours to mankind so that posterity may imbibe lessons. Milton was the one such poet in the seventeenth century, which was the century of violent and radical change in England. Keats admired *Paradise Lost* and wished to mark his age in a similar way. He began to write *Hyperion* and divided it into books as Milton had divided his epic. But after writing two and a half books of 357, 391 and 136 lines respectively, he abandoned it. *Hyperion* has the same unrhyming iambic pentameter lines as Milton had employed in *Paradise Lost.* Keats also dealt with the theme of war as Milton had done in his epic and the techniques of speeches are also the same as Milton's but the message is different because Keats thought "into the human heart" so he elected Wordsworth as his more relevant model because Wordsworth had lived through the French Revolution and its aftermath.

The theme of *Hyperion* is war between two orders of gods — the Titans and the Olympians. In Greek mythology the centre of power changes frequently. The giant Titans replaced their parents and now they have been dethroned by the Olympians. The story of the epic starts in *medias res.* i.e. in the middle of things. The war between the Titans and the Olympians is over. We have a picture of the fallen Titans, with their leader Saturn sitting alone defeated and bewildered:

> Deep in the shady sadness of a vale
> Far sunken from the healthy breath of morn
> Far from the fiery noon, and eve's one star
> Sat gray-hair'd Saturn, quiet as a stone.*(Hyperion,* Bk I, 1-4)

The entire atmosphere seems to be motionless. Even the dead leaves remained at the place from where they fell. Thea, the wife of Hyperion, the only one undefeated and potentially active, leads Saturn to the other Titans. They discuss different reasons why they were defeated and what course of action they should take. Most of the Titans are in favour of recovering "the old allegiance once more." Hyperion, who is himself doubtful whether he would be able to retain "the cradle of his glory" and "haven of his rest" and sees only "darkness, death and darkness" opines :

> Over the fiery frontier of my realms
> I will advance a terrible right arm
> Shall scarce that infant thunderer, rebel Jove
> And bid old Saturn take his throne again.
> (*Hyperion,* Bk I, 247-50)

"Sad sign of ruin, sudden dismay and fall" have filled in the Titans "fear, hope, and wrath; actions of rage and passion." It is perhaps in the human nature that defeat is not easily accepted and Satanic ideas "all is not lost" abounds in men even when they are badly wounded, exhausted and almost dead. Keats favours the idea of acceptance. The second book of *Hyperion* describes the council in which the Titans are discussing their future plan. Oceanus, the god of the seas opines that change is natural and it is by the law of nature that they have been supplanted by the more beautiful Olympians :

> We fall by course of Nature's law, not force
> Of thunder, or of Jove. (*Hyperion*, Bk II, 181-82)

He further says that they were not the first powers and so cannot think to be the last. They were neither the beginning nor can they suppose to be the end. He appeals to the Titans that they should accept the eternal truth. In the beginning there was only chaos and darkness and light came from them and then the Heavens and the Earth came into being. If we look at the "Hymn of Creation" in the *Rig Veda*, we find :

> At first there was only darkness wrapped in darkness
> All this was only unillumined water
> That one which came to be, enclosed in nothing
> Arose at last, born of the power of heat.
> (A. L. Basham's translation in *The Wonder that was India*)

The giant Titans ruled over the new and beauteous realms. Now their turn is over and some new "power more strong in beauty" is fated to excel them:

> .... for't is the eternal law
> That first in beauty should be first in might:
>
> (*Hyperion, Bk II,* 228-29)

Clymene, a nymph tells of her experience when she tried to make music to soothe her grief at defeat. A new, unfamiliar, more beautiful music overpowered her with grief and joy. Through that "new blissful golden melody," she heard Apollo's name being called out:

.... grief overcame
And I was stopping up my frantic ears
When, past all hindrance of my trembling hands,
A voice came sweeter, sweeter than all tune
And still it cried, "Apollo! Young Apollo!"
The morning-bright Apollo! Young Apollo!
I fled, It follow'd me, and cried "Apollo!"
(*Hyperion,* Bk II, 289-95)

Among the Titans Enceladus is warlike. He disagrees. He favours the idea of war and undefeated Hyperion is his hope. He is ready for revenge and to get back the lost joy of power.

Book II of *Hyperion* establishes this epic as a poem of evolution, of the supersession of lower forms by higher ones and the successors are to prevail because they are superior in beauty. Oceanus represents the enlightenment belief that the world progresses naturally in a straight line towards perfection. Enceladus and Hyperion represent those aristocrats of the ancient regime, who were not really to accept change. Clymene represents intuitive, non-rational knowledge as well as the idea that a new era paves way to new art forms.

Book III of *Hyperion* takes us to the sacred island of Dilos, the birth place and home of Apollo and his twin sister Artemis. Apollo has never been outside Delos and so is not exposed to the outside world. But he does not pretend that he knows everything rather he knows that he is ignorant of the natural laws and the suffering of the world. Mnemosyne, mother of the muses and goddess of memory gives him "knowledge enormous" of the suffering of others. When he is enlightened with the knowledge of suffering, ignorance within him dies and great knowledge is born within him. He is ushered from darkness to light – *tamaso ma Jyotirgamaya.* Then he goes through a physical convulsion like labour pains. The metaphor of birth suggests that Apollo dies into life and wisdom is linked with female activity. It is the female deity that gives him a new life, a life of wisdom. Female deities and forces are the sources of wisdom, according to the Romantics. And this idea is also unfurled in *Sri Durga Saptashati,* a holy book of *mantras* written hundreds of years ago:

Adharbhuta jagatas twameka
Mahiswarupen yatah sthitasi
Apang swarupsthitya twaitat
Dapyayate krishnamalanghya virya

> (O Goddess! You are the mother and protector of the universe. You are the ruler of all that is moving and unmoving the sole substratum of the world because you subsist in the form of earth. You are inviolable valour.
>
> (*Sri Durgasaptashati, XI,* 3)

Apollo's knowledge makes him superior to the ignorant Titans, who have questions but no answers. Therefore they have to make room for Apollo. Here the story comes to an end making the message very clear in favour of change.

Critics observe that *Hyperion* is an unfinished epic. John Keats, too wrote to Reynolds on September 22, 1819 from Winchester:

> I have given up *Hyperion* – there were too many Miltonic inversions in it – Miltonic verse cannot be written but in an artful, or, rather, artist's humour. I wish to give myself upto other sensations. English ought to be kept up. It may be interesting to you to pick up some lines from *Hyperion* and put a mark X to the false beauty preceding from art, and one // to the true voice of feeling. Upon my soul't was imagination – I cannot make the distinction – every now and then there is a Miltonic intonation but I cannot make the division properly.

The critic in John Keats is aware of the weaknesses of the poet in John Keats. Dr. R.C. Prasad was of the opinion that the greatest critic of John Keats, the poet is John Keats himself. *Hyperion* is unfinished, therefore it is "a fragment" but we have to enjoy the poem and take the message from it on the basis of what it is and not on the basis of what it would / should have been. Conjectures create hindrances in the better understanding of the poem. Technically the epic may be incomplete but so far as the message is concerned, it is complete and crystal clear. The gems of ideas that we glean are that the Titans and the Olympians represent the old regime and the new regime respectively. Hyperion takes the side of the old one. He is like a selfish aristocrat or politician whose main concerns are his comforts. He has nothing to do with the sufferings of others and Hyperion forfeits divinity. Apollo gains it for he is like a saint who suffers for others. Christ suffered for others and there is no dearth of saints and great men like Gandhi who suffered for others. In *Sri Ramcharitamanas,* Tulsidas writes :

Sibi Dadhichi Harichanda naresha
Dharam hetu sahe koti kalesha
(Shivi, Dadhichi and King Harishchandra endured
countless afflictions for duty's sake.)

(*Sri Ramcharitamanas, Ayodhya Kanda,* 94.2)

At another place Tulsidas searches for the image to describe the nature of saints. The image of "butter" conjures up in his mind because other poets have used it :

Sant hridya navanit samana
Kaha kavinha pai kaha na mana
Nij paritap dravai navanita
Pardukh drawahin santa supunita
(Poets have said that the heart of a saint is as soft as butter,
but they have missed the essential truth; for butter melts of
its own heat, but the most holy saints melt at others' trials.)

(*Sri Ramcharitamanas, Uttarakand,* 124.4)

Keats experiences the same Indian feel in *The Fall of Hyperion* (1819) which is a reformulation of *Hyperion* as a dream vision. Keats believes that real poetry can be composed by the real saints:

To whom miseries of the world
Are misery, and will not let them rest.

(*Hyperion: A Vision,* 148-150)

Apollo gathers this knowledge that life would be meaningful only if he is helpful to others and this knowledge makes him superior to Hyperion and John Keats has made Apollo the hero of *Hyperion.*

Keats' originality consists in the fact that he had realized that the job of a poet is to write about the truth of experiences in life and in order to fulfil this social function, a poet has to say good-bye to the older forms of poetry and a variety of new forms should be created. It is again the job of the poet to make the readers receive the new art forms emerging from radical changes. In Keats time radical changes were taking place not only in the social ethos but also in art and literature. Through Enceladus' speech the poet has made us mentally, physically and spiritually prepared for accepting the law of change which the Titans are not willing to accept. Although to accept the change is like a perilous spiritual odyssey from ignorance to wisdom (knowledge) which is accompanied by pain but this pain becomes pleasure and makes us spiritually stronger and stronger. Life is not roses, roses all the way but is paved with the thorns and thistles of experiences and the only truth of life is to know "the agonies, the strife of human hearts" and "the weariness, fever and fret" of life. Sometimes we are in the vale of sorrow when we think of them:

"Where to think is to be full of sorrow." Keats thinks that artificial beauty perishes whether it is love or youth or seasons because they are the slaves of time but truth remains the same, simply the circumstances and situations change. He finds no difference between truth and beauty:

> "Beauty is truth, truth beauty" – that is all
> Ye know on earth and all ye need to know.
>
> (*Ode on a Grecian Urn,* 49-50)

This idea is romantic, no doubt, but the Romantic movement was not a phenomenon limited to English literature but was part of the European Movement which was swayed by the study of Indian literature and philosophy in which Beauty, Truth and Welfare are integrated. What is Beauty is Truth and what is Truth is for the well being of all – *Satyam Shivam Sundaram.*

It is only through a clear perception of Beauty that Truth can be felt. To have feelings for the things which seem to be mute like the mountains, the rivers, the woods one has to realize that they have life in them. The insects, the autumn season and many other things that have traditionally been considered unimportant are very important to Keats, because "the poetry of the earth is never dead." Keats takes everything in his stride. There is nothing repugnant to his sensibility. "Let your mind be a thorough for all thoughts" is the clarion call of Keats. Keats suggests that we should look into the heart of the matter which is Truth. Where there is Truth there is Beauty. And if we become one with the natural things we will realize that the objects of Nature are speaking to us and they have a lot of ideas to communicate to us. Here Keats is like those *Vedantis* who give importance to the soul i.e. internal beauty and then say *tat twam asi* – thou art that or *soham* – I am that. Keats feels nature through all the senses and prefers a life of sensations rather of thoughts. And this feeling makes him realize :

> A THING of Beauty is a joy for ever:
> Its loveliness ever increases, it will never
> Pass into nothingness; but still will keep
> A bower quiet for us, and a sleep
> Full of sweet dreams, and health, and quiet
> breathing. (*Endymion,* I, 1-6)

Although there are some similarities between *Hyperion* and *Paradise Lost* such as the council of the fallen Titans (Book II) offers parallels with council, between Satan and his followers in *Paradise Lost* (Book II) etc. and Keats admired *Paradise Lost,* imposed by Milton's evocative compression and grandeur. But it also departs from Milton in a intriguing way. His story does not encompass a cosmic clash between good and evil; rather it centres on the fact of the evolution of a progressive movement from one order of things to another that is more developed from the rule of the Titans to the Olympians.

Although *Hyperion* contains an epic list (the roll-call of Fallen Titans in Book II) and an address to the Muse (III), it does not make use of supernatural machinery as it is concerned with gods who are preoccupied with their own affairs, not with humans whose affairs are shaped by acts of divine intervention. Another example of Keats' Romantic displacement of epic conventions is that the invocation of the Muse occurs at the beginning of the third book and not at the commencement of the poem. French Revolution is known for the new ideas like – equality, liberty and fraternity. It is also known for the struggle between the powers old and new. The old power wants to hold power while the new one wants to dethrone it. Hyperion is motivated by self-interest. He represents the aristocrats who enjoy all comforts and luxuries of life. Once they lose power, life will become very hard for them. It is this searing and gnawing anxiety from which Hyperion suffers :

> Saturn is fallen, am I too to fall?
> Am I to leave this haven of my rest
> This calm luxuriance of blissful light,
> These crystalline pavilions, and purefanes
> Of all my lucent empire (*Hyperion,* Bk I, 234-39)

Hyperion can be also interpreted in terms of political allegory. Those who know the situations before and after the French Revolution can easily find a number of possible historical comparisons. The relationship between Saturn and his son and conqueror, Jove, could be paralleled with that between George III and his son the Prince Regent. The exiled, melancholy Saturn stands comparison with the iconic Napolean Bonaparte finally defeated at Waterloo in 1815 and exiled to the remote island of St. Helena where he met his death in 1821. In addition, the theme of regime change echoes the reshaping of the post-Napoleanic Europe that was taking place in 1810s, a process being thrashed out by the victorious powers, including Britain, at the congress of Vienna. The reactionary nature of the post-Napoleanic settlement raises possible questions about the nature of Jove and his new regime. One of the unseen figures in the epic, the new king of the Olympians remains a mystery, as does the nature of the rule he will impose. Will it be better than what has gone before, the same, or worse?

Apollo is the god of music, harmony, beauty, knowledge and champion of change. His victory indicates that Keats is in favour of the radicals. His poem is about the replacement of an old regime, written at a time when Europe was trying to resolve a post-Napoleanic political settlement and when England was beset by internal conflict. The concluding sections of Book III reveal that *Hyperion* is also a poem about the process of becoming. It figures forth the painful coming into being of both a poet (Apollo/Keats) and a poem *(Hyperion* itself). By implication, then, Keats' epic is about the replacement of an old poetry by a new poetics. This new regime is boiled forth in Apollo, destined to defeat Hyperion and become a new god of sun and of poetry. It is also enshrined in Keats' fragmentary epic, a poem whose ending – suspended halfway across the page – enacts something that is, on going, inevitable, and "Celestial."

Works Cited

Basham, A.L. *The Wonder that was India.* New Delhi: Rupa & Co., 1981.

Bromwich, David. "Keats's Radicalism," *Studies in Romanticism.* Summer, 1986.

Bush, Douglas. "Keats and His Ideas," *English Romantic Poets: Modern Essays in Criticism.* ed. M.H. Abrams, New York: 1960.

Dickstein, Morris. "Keats and Politics," *Studies in Romanticism.* Summer, 1986.

Hough, Graham. *The Romantic Poets.* Bombay: B.I. Publications, 1967.

Keats, John. *Complete Poems.* London: The Softback Review, 1993.

Matthews, G.M. *Keats: The Critical Heritage.* London: Routledge, 1971.

Muir, Kenneth. "The Meaning of Hyperion." *Essays in Criticism II*. 1952. Rpt.

Muir, Kenneth. (*ed.*). *John Keats: A Reassessment.* Liverpool: 1958.

Prasad, Dr. Ram Chandra(*ed. & tr.*), *Sri Ramcharitamanas,* Delhi: Motilal Banarsidass, 1989.

Roe, Nicholas (*ed.*). *Romanticism.* New Delhi: OUP, Indian edition, 2005.

Shastri, Sri Ram Navayan. (*tr.*) *Sri Durga Saptashati.* Gorakhpur: Gita Press, 2010.

Literary Theory in Teaching Literature: The Need of Time

Dr. Gunjan

The Present era is the age of Science and Technology, Trade and Commerce, Business Management and Computer Science. Even the Faculty of Humanities is paying more attention to the communicative skills than literature. And the main focus is on teaching/learning how to communicate effectively. So it is quite natural for the students to ask this question: "Why should we study literature?"

To answer this qustion first we have to understand what Literature is. Literature, in general terms, is writing which expresses and communicates thoughts, feelings, emotions and ideas towards life but this definition of literature is not enough for the students of literature. Literature must have the following essential qualities:

a) Permanence.
b) "Life enhancing" or "a criticism of life."
c) Originality.
d) Technical skill or craftsmanship.
e) Moral consciousness and high seriousness.

We should study literature if we want to understand the other countries and their people. The identity of a nation or society is projected in its literature. Ancient Indian culture, Greek culture, Egyptian culture, Roman culture, Arabic culture, are projected in their literary works of art like *The Vedas, The Mahabharata* and *The Ramayana, Iliad, Odyssey, the Arabian Knights* English literature right from Chaucer to T.S. Eliot describes the contemporary society very well. So do the literatures of other countries. History also describes society but there is a difference. History depends on the factual description whereas literature describes the external facts and internal psychology as well as it describes each detail quite minutely not only physically but also psychologically.

The other reason why we should study literature is that we feel "cultured" or "well read." In most civilized countries people are proud of being well educated and knowledgeable.

Literature from the ancient times serves the society and instills culture and makes man humble, honest, knowledgeable, pious and decent. Reading is an important form of enjoyment for literate people even in the age of television and computer. Literature helps us towards a better understanding of ourselves and our fellow human beings. By studying literature we learn more about human problems and difficulties. It helps us during the days of stress, sorrow and frustration. Sometimes these problems become so acute that people are driven to suicides. But if one is fond of reading literary books, one gets the power, the capacity, and the courage to sustain in this world. History is witness that when England enslaved almost the entire globe and people were made to suffer, the suffering people could sustain themselves only with the help of their great literature.

Indian political history reflects the importance of literature and only due to the literary insight Mahatma Gandhi, J.L. Nehru, Indira Gandhi and Atal Bihari Bajpai were accepted as the pagoda tree of Indian politics. Professor Sidheshwar Prasad, a grand oldman of Bihar who held various positions such as Central Minister and HE the Governor of Tripura opines that the growth of America is due to literature. *Leaves of Grass* is a collection of poems by Emerson which develops a democratic and national feeling in the hearts of the Americans. He further remarks that Indian people in general and politicians in particular do not pay importance to literature resulting in rank corruption, terrorism, molestation and various other kinds of evils in our society. Because once devoid of literature, most of the so called educated people have lost their passion for others as they have become so self centred that the others' emotions have no room in their hearts. They hardly care what they speak and how they use the words.

In this materialistic and mechanical world it is not possible to learn/teach literature in old traditional ways because feelings and sentiments are dead in our hearts. To develop and make study interesting we need the help of theory or scientific way of teaching/ learning literature. Twenty first century is regarded as the age of globalization, transnationalism and telecommunication. Education today is focused to prepare people to be flexible, multi-skilled, dynamic problem solvers, and creative explorers of resources with the ability to interpret reality from multiple perspectives and bring harmony between knowledge and creativity. Therefore, the traditional approaches to teaching literature have been replaced with modern approaches. The modern approaches were introduced at the turn of twentieth century. Initial efforts were made by Formalists and the New Critics who assigning primary importance to the text set up the tradition of close reading. The structuralist approach was replaced by post-structural approaches in the second half of the twentieth century which brought the reader to spotlight and support him/her to hold the centre stage. Today Reader Response, Deconstruction and other deconstructive reader-based interpretative theories such as New Historicism, Post-Structuralist Marxism, Cognitive Poetics, Feminism, Postcolonialism and Postmodernism are considered major interpretive methods. The present paper evaluates both traditional approaches and poststructuralist literary theoretical approaches to the teaching and interpretation of literary texts in the light of research on twenty-first century education and teaching literature.

"Literary theory" has become a cover-term for an increasingly diffuse trend away from a concern with the individual text toward a concern with the general conditions of literature or "literariness." Twenty first century is the age of globalization, multiculturalism, telecommunication and digital technology. Education today is considered as an important mechanism and effective means to develop creative and effective human resource. The theory recognizes a pre-existing object or concept and proceeds to formulate the correct description of that object. On the contrary, the object or concept is in a very real sense constructed by the theory. So "literature" is a different entity depending on what theory constructs the concept, whether "it" is theorized by Roman Jakobson, by Northrop Frye and so on.

The formalist approach regards literature as "a unique form of human knowledge that needs to be examined on its own terms." All the elements necessary for understanding the work are contained within the work itself. Of particular interest to the formalist critic are the elements of *form* – style, structure, tone, imagery, etc. – that are found within the text. A primary goal for the formalist critics is to determine how such elements work together with the text's content to shape its effects upon readers. More specifically, the Formalists were interested in analyzing literature into its component parts and in describing its principal devices and modes of operation. The Formalists noticed that narrative literature consisted of two major components: the plot, by which they meant the story as narrated within the pages of the book (with all the attendant arrangements of chronological sequence, point of view, etc.), and the story, by which they meant the sequence of events in the order and the actual duration in which they ostensibly occurred. Once this simple distinction is made, one can begin to analyze all of the features of story-telling, the many devices such as point of view, delayed disclosure, narrative voice, and the like that go into the creation of the imaginary story through the manipulation of plot or story-telling devices. One can, for example, begin to study a novel like *The Scarlet Letter* for its narrative strategies instead of for the ways in which it depict the Puritanism epoch to another. The Formalists account for such change in two ways. They claim that literary evolution is the result of the constant attempt to disrupt existing literary conventions and to generate new ones. And they argue that literary change is the result of the autonomous evolution of literary devices

The New Criticism was "new" because in the decades of the 40s and 50s when it was championed by its most influential exponents (W.K. Wimsatt, Cleanth Brooks, Randall Jarrell and John Crowe Ransom, among others) it represented a set of critical practices that were proposed to replace an earlier critical tradition that had emphasized the biography of the writer, the historical or theological contexts for particular works, the moral and ethical enlightenment conferred upon readers, and the highly impressionistic and "appreciative" accounts of the aesthetic and ethical features of literary works. The New Criticism was a formalist criticism because it emphasized the formal features of a literary text. It treated the text as an artifact, something constructed and subject to objective, scientific description and then to an evaluation based on observable features. It is no accident, I think, that formalist literary criticism emerged most forcefully in the 1950s simultaneously with formalist or descriptive linguistics, which sought to provide scientifically accurate accounts of the workings of specific languages.

New Critics were inclined to forego discussions of an author's biography and the background for literary works in favor of a discourse that honored the "integrity" of a literary text, its coherence as a unified artifact whose every detail must be regarded as meaningful, whether consciously intended by the artist or not.

Psychological approach reflects the effect that modern psychology has had upon both literature and literary criticism. Fundamental figures in psychological criticism include Sigmund Freud, whose "psychoanalytic theories changed our notions of human behavior by exploring new or controversial areas like wish-fulfillment, sexuality, the unconscious, and repression" as well as expanding our understanding of how "language and symbols operate by demonstrating their ability to reflect unconscious fears or desires;" and Carl Jung, whose theories about the unconscious are also a key foundation of Mythological Criticism. Psychological criticism has a number of approaches, but in general, it usually employs one (or more) of three approaches:

1. An investigation of "the creative process of the artist: what is the nature of literary genius and how does it relate to normal mental functions?"

2. The psychological study of a particular artist, usually noting how an author's biographical circumstances affect or influence their motivations and/or behavior.

3. The analysis of fictional characters using the language and methods of psychology.

Mythological criticism emphasizes "the recurrent universal patterns underlying most literary works." Combining the insights from anthropology, psychology, history, and comparative religion, mythological criticism "explores the artist's common humanity by tracing how the individual imagination uses myths and symbols common to different cultures and epochs." One key concept in mythlogical criticism is the *archetype*, "a symbol, character, situation, or image that evokes a deep universal response," which entered literary criticism from the Swiss psychologist Carl Jung. According to Jung, all individuals share a "collective unconscious," a set of primal memories common to the human race, existing below each person's conscious mind – often deriving from primordial phenomena such as the sun, moon, fire, night, and blood, archetypes according to Jung "trigger the collective unconscious." Another critic, Northrop Frye, defined the archetype in a more limited way as "a symbol, usually an image, which recurs often enough in literature to be recognizable as an element of one's literary experience as a whole." Regardless of the definition of archetype they use, mythological critics tend to view literary works in the broader context of works sharing a similar pattern.

Reader-Response theory takes as a fundamental tenet that "literature" exists not as an artifact upon a printed page but as a transaction between the physical text and the mind of a reader. It attempts "to describe what happens in the reader's mind while interpreting a text" and reflects that *reading*, like writing, is a creative process. According to reader-response critics, literary texts do not "contain" a meaning; meanings derive only from the act of individual readings. Reader-response criticism, then, emphasizes how "religious, cultural, and social values affect readings; it also overlaps with gender criticism in exploring how men and women read the same text with different assumptions."

Deconstructionist approach "rejects the traditional assumption that language can accurately represent reality." Deconstructionist critics regard language as a fundamentally unstable medium – the words "tree" or "dog," for instance, undoubtedly conjure up different mental images for different people – and therefore, because literature is made up of words, literature possesses no fixed, single meaning. The methods of this approach tend to resemble those of formalist criticism, but whereas formalists" primary goal is to locate unity within a text, "how the diverse elements of a text cohere into meaning," deconstructionists try to show how the text "deconstructs," "how it can be broken down ... into mutually irreconcilable positions." Other goals of deconstructionists include (1) challenging the notion of the authors' "ownership" of texts they create (and their ability to control the meaning of their texts) and (2) focusing on how language is used to achieve power, as when they try to understand how some interpretations of a literary work come to be regarded as "truth."

Sociological Criticism "examines literature in the cultural, economic and political context in which it is written or received," exploring the relationships between the artist and society. One influential type of sociological criticism is Marxist criticism. Marxist literary theory develops a critical attitude in the readers and enables them to recognize and question the authority of hegemonic groups which set exploitative structures for class in a society through literary texts. A Marxist interpretation of the text takes the reader beyond the facade of neutrality and draws their attention to class affiliation and ideology of the author and his representation of social and economic issues. Similarly postcolonial theory informs readers about racial issues through literary texts. Critical reading strategies such as that of colonial discourse analysis, Orientalism and contrapuntal reading encourage the learners to read canonical texts from a different lens which calls into question the universality of the text through a highlighting of the text's complicity with the ideology of imperialism.

Poststructuralist literary theory being the outcome of Derrida's theory of deconstruction has brought the reader and the interpreter onto the centre stage and made him the co-creator of the text. The poststructuralist literary theory assigns the responsibility of meaning making to the reader in a variety of contexts including the cultural context, postcolonial context, post modern context and feminist context. Feminist literary theory aims at developing a critical consciousness in the readers about the operation and functioning of oppressive structures of patriarchal ideology in the text. It enables the readers to actively engage with the text to unearth the ideological and political configurations of textual representation in order to understand the cultural processes in which gender roles are constructed. In the process the readers deconstruct the ideological binary opposition set up between male and female genders in male dominated patriarchal culture. Gender approach "examines how sexual identity influences the creation and reception of literary works." Originally an offshoot of feminist movements, gender criticism today includes a number of approaches, including the so-called "masculinist" approach recently advocated by the poet Robert Bly. Feminist criticism attempts to correct this imbalance by analyzing and combating such attitudes – by questioning, for example, why none of the characters in Shakespeare's play *Othello* ever challenge the right of a husband to murder a wife accused of adultery. Other goals of feminist critics include "analyzing how sexual identity influences the reader of a text" and "examin[ing] how the images of men and women in imaginative literature reflect or reject the social forces that have historically kept the sexes from achieving total equality."

New historicism helps the reader see silences and gaps in recorded histories and critically investigates the established discourses of history. Drawing their theoretical concepts from a variety of disciplines, the above mentioned critical approaches instill an attitude of reflexivity which encourages the readers to call into question common-sense traditional notions of gender, race, history, class and culture.

Literary theory as a pedagogical tool employs the principles of modern approaches to learning and, thus serves to nurture the cognitive processing of students, helps them connect the classroom with the world outside the classroom and be active learners. Students are not encouraged to treat a text as sacred and follow the traditional assumptions and interpretations introduced by teachers or other literary critics. Reader-based poststructuralist approaches provide an effective cognitive learning framework. Literary theory working on the principle of cognitive learning engages readers independently in the process of meaning making. Students reading literature with literary theory see literature as a part of larger society outside the text and the classroom. They are trained to read a text in connection with the social and cultural realities and institutions. This helps them take reading of literature a meaningful activity. Literary theory making students active and independent readers destabilizes the unchallenged authority of teacher in the classroom. Discussion and dialogue replace lectures and the teacher becomes the facilitator to promote inquiry and investigation in the classroom. Students do not see text as a source to find the author's belief but a world to be reconstructed and interpreted in the light of their beliefs and experiences. They become co-creators of the text. Literary theory acknowledges the social function of literature. Reader-based approaches outlined above establish a meaningful link between literature and society. Feminist, Marxist, New historical and postcolonial literary theories are all interdisciplinary and transdisciplinary and they promote intertextual readings. Students are trained to cross the boundaries of other disciplines and see how different texts correspond with one another. This leads them to have an understanding of the society, its structures and institutions. One of the important objectives of the twenty-first century education is developing the critical and the creative thinking skills of the students. Students engaged in transdisciplinary intertextual reading through literary theory are actually engaged in creative experimentation. They are set on a quest to explore new avenues and investigate how effectively the meaning of a text can be drawn through exploring the world of other disciplines. This experimentation opens up ways to creating new categories of knowledge. Thus students become creators of knowledge not the storehouse of information. For example, postcolonial theory enables students to reexamine and reevaluate literary masterpieces such as Conrad's *Heart of Darkness* and Forster's *A Passage to India* which were previously perceived as critiques of imperialism. Feminist literary theory and New-historicism have also generated new readings of Shakespeare showing how his theatrical masterpieces such as *Hamlet* and *Othello* were reinforcing misogynist and racist attitudes. Reader-based approaches to interpreting literature are actually an exercise in creative thinking. Students are encouraged to restructure plot, characters and events, and give innovative interpretations to the texts.

This provides them training to become an effective and creative work force as well as active agents to challenge established social hierarchies in order to bring change.

Literary theory as discussed in this paper also encourages and trains students to generate new and innovative meaning of the texts by utilizing their real world experiences and their beliefs. It being multidisciplinary it prepares informed students who have the ability to approach texts from multiple directions and become mature critical thinkers and problem solvers. As it provides central position to the students, so the teacher becomes a facilitator to promote dialogic inquiry and investigation in the class. Thus teaching literature with literary theory can help to achieve the major objectives of twenty-first century education. Literary theory now a days enjoys the place of prominence in the curriculum and acts like a lifeline of teaching/ learning literature or we can say it is the need of the time.

Works Cited

Culler, J. *Literary Theory: A Very Short Introduction.* Oxford: Oxford University Press,1997

Eagleton. T. *Literary theory: An Introduction* (2nd ed.). USA: The University of Minnesota Press, 1996.

Feden, P.D.; R.M. Vogel. *Methods of Teaching: Applying Cognitive Science to Promote Student Learning.* New York: McGraw-Hill, 2003.

Guerin, W.L; E. Labor. *A Handbook of Critical Approaches to Literature*(5th ed.). New York: Oxford University Press, 2005.

Lynn, S. *Texts and Contexts: Writing about Literature with Critical Theory.* New York: HarperCollins,1994.

Showalter, E. *Teaching Literature.* Oxford: Blackwell, 2004.

The Redemptive Ritual in Edward Albee's *Who's Afraid of Virginia Woolf?*

Prof. R. Saraswathi

Although the methods by which the argument of a play is communicated are never really separable from the argument itself, it may be convenient to discuss the structure of *Who's Afraid of Virginia Woolf?*, at least initially, in terms of such a distinction. We may begin by referring to Albee's declaration that all his plays are "political" in a broad sense, that in any play that's worth its salt at all, "the situation is a microcosm of larger values".* We may perceive the larger concerns of such a play by understanding the immediate situation as a metaphor leading to other levels of concern (as well as, of course, being of interest dramatically in its own right). Albee's material springs from a concern with his country and its spiritual and political health, but there is a continuing push to greater universality. Peter in *The Zoo Story* is afflicted with the spiritual decay of American suburban life, but he is also the Everyman in us that prefers the security of blindness to the terror of insight.

This technique of "message by metaphor" is also the basis of *Who's Afraid of Virginia Woolf?*, but the scope of material brought in is much broader than in the earlier plays and the number of levels of metaphor is greatly increased.

An indication of the complexity of *Who's Afraid of Virginia Woolf?* may be seen in the variety of roles George plays. On the most immediate level, the "realistic" level, George is a domestic failure who must fight to break out of the roles he has trapped himself in, who must re-assert himself as the "pants-wearer" in the family. This level is complemented by a series of "psychological" suggestions in the play. On this level, of course, the examination of George and Martha's marriage leads to an examination of Nick and Honey's marriage and ultimately becomes an exploration of all human relationships.

If man can examine the past to understand and alter the present then man is a free agent, not a fated one; his traps are of his own making. Albee seems to be saying that the power of faith derives not from God but from man. In *Who's Afraid of Virginia Woolf?*, this faith in man involves two levels. First, as a historian, George must assert his fatih in the importance and value of man's history. If man can examine the past to understand and alter the present then he is a free agent, not a fated man; his traps are of his own making. The content of this faith, though intellectually presentable, is inadequate by itself. Even George has lost his faith in history at the beginning of *Who's Afraid of Virginia Woolf?* In order to lead himself and others out of their self-created hells, he must turn not only to the facts of history but even more importantly to the larger meaning of religion. Religion leads to salvation by leading man into communion with man. Religion becomes a metaphor for man's faith in himself, a faith which George must rediscover to assert himself in his marriage and to free himself and Martha from the illusions which bind them.

The success of *Who's Afraid of Virginia Woolf?*, involves such a large number of levels as this must finally depend on the ability of the play both to lead the audience from the specific situation to more universal concerns, while at the same time sustaining a sense of unity among the levels to produce a resonance among them in which they strengthen rather than distract one another. In *Who's Afraid of Virginia Woolf?* mythology and ritual are used to help bridge the gap between private experience and public significance and understanding. Albee's final choice of a title for the play (it was originally to be called *The Exorcism)* suggests the importance the mythology will have in it. As the four little pigs move through the evening, they describe their present and their pasts in terms of mythologies ranging from Oedipus to D.H. Lawrence to Bette Davis. This use of mythology in the creation of the characters helps move them from the realm of purely private individuals to characters whose communal import becomes an important element in the dramatic experience of the play. It enhances the symbolic potential of the characters, while at the same time, the familiarity of these mythologies makes the characters more accessible to us on an immediate level.

The second method which Albee uses to make us aware of the significance of what is happening is to ritualize the action. If the ritual may be defined as a formal act by which private emotion is made communal, then we may perhaps view the starting point of ritual as the process of formalization itself, with the success of the ritual being determined by its power to communicate. Seen in this light, the progress of the play may be viewed in part as the quest of a successful ritual.

The formalization of the play's action can be seen in the use of repetition, folklore and story-telling devices, and various kinds of ritual. The repetition of certain phrases and patterns increases the intensity of their effect and helps us move from the level of individual action to the level of ritual significance. The patterns of profanity and blasphemy that greets us with Martha's opening "Jesus H. Christ" leads us to the final ritual of expiation and redemption.

The use of story-telling as a method of communication adds to the "formality" of the play. The stories of the characters' pasts are never entirely realistic, but they do communicate what we need to know. As a formalizing process, story-telling operates in much the same way as other rituals – stories are a vehicle for communicating private emotions and secrets to make them "public," Martha's opening story about the Bette Davis picture is an expression of her own discontent. The details suggest the frustrations she wishes to communicate to George. Similarly, Martha humiliates George by telling Nick and Honey the story of George's ignominous defeat in "the boxing match we had," and closes out the first Act by telling Nick and Honey the story of her "rapport" with her father, her Lawrention sexual initiation, her marriage to "contemplative" George and this "FLOP! " as "heir apparent."

Like other rituals, stories are repeatable, often with quite different purposes and results. In Act II, the dissatisfied husbands George and Nick exchange personal confessions. George tells Nick the story of the death of his parents, but disguises his confession as the story of another boy he knew at school. Nick confesses to George that he married Honey "because she was pregnant." He follows this admission with the story of Honey's "hysterical" pregnancy and details about her preacher father's wealth – the factors which led him into a sterile union with an infantile partner.

Although both men are prompted by a desire to air their private frustrations, George warns Nick:

You realize, of course, that I've been drawing you on this stuff, not because I'm interested in your terrible lifehood, but only because you represent a direct and pertinent threat to my lifehood, and I want to get the goods on you. (111)

As it turns out, both men's stories are repeated. Inspite of George's furious protests, Martha tells George's story as it occurred in his aborted "novel," but reveals the punch-line as well: "George said . . . but Sir, it isn't a novel at all . . . this is the truth . . . this really happened

. . . TO ME!" (136-137). George follows this exposure with one of his own – the story of his "second novel." George's second novel – "it's an allegory really – probably – but it can be read as cozy straight prose" (142) – is the story of Nick and Honey, with a "flashback" to "How They Got Married." This "second novel" exposes Nick and almost exposes Honey as well, for she fears George may have guessed about her secret abortion: ("hysteria: WHAT . . . and then, WHAT?")

The death of the imaginary son is also linked to a series of stories. Martha's mention of "their son" to Honey violates his "secret" nature "you broke our rule, baby . . . you mentioned him to someone else" (136). What has been done cannot be undone, and the full consequences follow. In the final "party game," "Bringing Up Baby," the imaginary son is brought to full public exposure as George and Martha vie with their stories about him. George kills off his "son" with a new story, a story concocted at the end of Act II, but not made public until the end of Act III. The story of the son's accident is an ironic echo of the accident in which George killed his father, and whose "secret" was revealed by Martha. It is not the veracity of the story, but the public confirmation which spells a death blow to private illusions. Martha protests violently but it is too late; Honey, an outsider, publicly confirms George's explanatory story about "Crazy Billy" and the eaten telegram: "I watched you . . . you ate it all alone" (234-35).

The gradual revelation of the murderous secrets and fears hidden in the characters' stories and actions is central to the play's action. The characters have been caught between the horror of what they are or have done, and the fear of exposure. Their stories and actions (George's novel, Honey's vomiting) are covert gestures of guilt, but the exorcism of their fears and atonement for their guilt are possible only when their confessions are made public. It is not the stories themselves, but the process of explanation by other characters which brings about public understanding ("Jesus Christ, I think I understand this."). Public confession and communal understanding permit the final gesture and spirit of communion which follows the son's death.

This communal understanding is further facilitated and enhanced by allusions to a variety of religious and cultural stories. These allusions broaden the scope of the stories and increase their contact with our "public" experience. This interweaving of stories and meanings should also, of course, lead the audience to an appreciation of the entire play as the playwright's story, fraught in its own right with meaning to be communicated.

The ritualization of action occurs on many levels in *Who's Afraid of Virginia Woolf?* In one way, the play may be viewed as the movement from Martha's chanting of "Who's Afraid of Virginia Woolf?" to George's recitation of the mass for his son. Martha attempts to exorcise her fear by rejecting it, by treating it as a joke. She tries to get the others to join her, but only Honey will join in. Like her subsequent fertility rites, Martha's chanting is ineffective. She is still afraid of Virginia Woolf at the end of the play, though George has helped her find the strength to acknowledge her fear.

The final movement of the play is an affirmation of the power of human involvement leading to self-discovery and understanding. The audience must become involved to recognize this power on an emotional, as well as intellectual level, since the impact of a play is the product of the development of the intellectual content interacting with the emotions unleashed in the characters as they build up to an explosive force. We must look to the characters, then, to examine the tensions which give the play its vitality and purpose and the rhythms which may bind its diverse elements into a unified and satisfying whole.

The "Saturday night orgy" from which George and Martha are returning at the beginning of the play has in fact been a "get acquainted" party for Nick and Honey: "We're a close-knit family here ... Daddy always says so ... Daddy wants us to get to know each other ... that's what he had the party for tonight" (164).

Martha's justification for inviting them over for a drink afterwards is "Because Daddy said we should be nice to them, that's why" (10). George is already suspicious before their guests arrive; to Martha's description of Nick as "thirty, blond and . . ." George adds "good looking." George resents Martha's motives in "springing" the party on him ("and try to keep your clothes on, too. There aren't many more sickening sights than you with a couple of drinks in you and your skirt up over your head, you know" [17], and refers to open the door to the guests until he has infuriated Martha sufficiently. (Her "SCREW YOU" is aimed at George but seems to greet the guests – a significant opening for the action to follow.) George adds to the inhospitality of the evening by undercutting Martha's attempts at hospitality. He succeeds in making Nick feel unwelcome ("I told you we shouldn't have come") and attacks Nick's attempts at conversational openers ("jostling" him about the abstract painting). He begins by attacking Nick, and then settles down to interrogate the new comer. He asks Nick's age, weight, and Department, and then recognizes Nick as "the one's going to make all that trouble... making everyone the same, rearranging the chromosomes, or whatever it is. Isn't that right?" (37) George is "very mistrustful" and, without giving Nick a chance to reply to the question whether "people learn nothing from history," launches an attack on eugenic science. After further interrogating Nick about "kids," George continues: "You think you're going to be happy here in New Cartharge, eh?" Nick can only reply "I hope we'll stay here," but not necessarily "for ever" (40-41). Honey's fear of adulthood has led her to "secret little murders the stud-boy doesn't know about." The doctors have announced that there is nothing wrong with Honey "organically;" hers is a failure of the spirit and must be dealt with as such. Her conversion is crucial, for it is she rather than Martha who still retains the potential for fertility, and it is George, of course, who must finally provide the faith necessary to overcome their shortcomings. The movement of the play requires that George and Martha, Nick and Honey come to a new understanding of themselves.

Martha is the central force of the sexual comedy in *Who's Afraid of Virginia Woolf?* She describes her sexual initiation as a "kind of junior Lady Chatterley arrangement," complete with a latter-day huge power lawn mover. Her days at Miss Muff's Academy for Young Ladies ended with her being "revirginized" which was "a laugh . . . because theoretically you can't get an annulment if there's an entrance" (78). Martha attempts to find an answer to her fears in hedonism and sex. The sexual comedy, however, is a failure. Performance falls short of potential. Martha, the sex goddess, is barren, Nick, the "stud," is impotent. Honey, the character most in need of transformation, is merely repelled and decides that she won't remember anything: "Don't remember, not can't." Animalism falls short of humanity; Martha is a "sub-human monster" who can never win George. Nick's failure with Martha is much the same as his failure with Honey; his sexual "potential" is "dandy," but he lacks the compassion which could humanize his relationships. And Martha points out that the "only one man in my life who has ever . . . made me happy" is not the gardener who initiated her, but George, her husband. She is lacking in any faith which could help her transcend her fears. She declares herself "an atheist," George corrects her: "Not an atheist, Martha, . . . a pagan . . . Martha is the only true pagan on the eastern board" (73). On a "pagan" level, the action of the play becomes the enactment of a Dionysic ritual awash in alcohol, sex, and blood. Dionysus, god of wine, is associated with the ecstatic, emotional and dark nature of mankind. His worship is characterized by drunkenness, sexual frenzy, and violence. Part of the conflict in the play may be understood as a conflict between Dionysic and Apollonian forces, with Martha acting the role of Dionysic priestess and Maenad. Her "Sunday Chapel dress" is designed to reveal her at her "most voluptuous," and alcohol is a central and continuing element in the social interaction in the play.

The Dionysiac "revel" becomes most explicit in the dancing scene in Act II. Honey announces that she wants "some dancing." George attempts to divert the action from the course he sees it taking by putting on Berthoven's 7th Symphony, which Honey accepts quite uncritically. Martha puts on some jazzy dance music and leads into "mixed doubles" with Nick, while George and Honey observe: "It's a very old ritual, monkey-nipples . . . old as they come" (131). Martha then begins to recite, in rhyme, the story of George's novel while she and Nick dance around the others like a Greek Chorus. The action becomes more frenzied as Martha's recitation drives George to a point of fury and loss of control: "I will not tolerate this! . . . STOP IT, MARTHA! . . . DESIST! DESIST!" (134-135). Even Honey is caught up in the frenzy ("[happily] Violence! Violence!") and joins the others in attacking George ("Honey joins in the laughter, not knowing exactly why"). The violence culminates with George's attempt to strangle Martha, but the sexual frenzy continues:

> George: . . . How about Hump the Hostess? (To Nick) You wanna play that one? You wanna play Hump the Hostess? Hunh? Hunh? (139)

The Bacchanalia does not end with the ensuing lull, but is a continuing element of the action. The forces unleashed are unstoppable. George warns Martha; "I'll rip you in pieces" (158). The violence aroused will be played out "to the death," a death Martha neither anticipates nor desires.

The inexorable movement towards the death of the imaginery son, a movement which begins with George's first "warning" to Martha not to mention the son, provides an ever-deepening tragic tone for the play. Even as George conceives the death of his son as his final move in his "total war" with Martha, his "soft" laughter of triumph is mixed with the tears of his own pain. At the same time, George's struggle to assert his own identity and maintain faith against despair and personal suffering, a struggle underscored by a complex interweaving of religious allusions, gives him a tragic nobility and provides a seriousness of tone which enhances the power of his faith and permits it to transcend even the irony of the imaginary slaughter.

The play draws much of its strength from the tension between the wisdom, insight, or faith gained by George and the catastrophic price George must pay in suffering and death. In *Who's Afraid of Virginia Woolf?*, both the wisdom and the death are essential. Faith is the wisdom the characters must accept to confront the threat of meaninglessness; the son's death is the sacrifice necessary to cure the characters of their delusions.

The movement towards a redemptive religious ritual – George's movement from stagnancy and despair to faith is accompanied by various movements which help enlarge the significance of his struggle and communicate that significance to the other characters and to the audience. There is the movement from the personal sacrifice of a "somewhat more private portion of the anatomy," George's manhood, to the public sacrifice of the imaginary son complete with the Latin mass of the dead. Along with this we see George move from being "a blank, a cipher" at the beginning of the play to asserting himself as "a Doctor, A. B. . . . M.A. . . . Ph.D. . . . ABMAPHID!," a sort of culture priest, to acting the role of a religious priest in the final scene. We also see George shift from being a pacifist and a failure (he not only refuses to fight Martha's father but is even knocked down by the novice Martha) to challenging Martha to "total war."

George's movement towards a successful ritual is accompanied by a series of religious allusions. Although the religious philosophy of *Who's Afraid of Virginia Woolf?* is not merely the sum of its religious imagery, religious archetypes and religious references abound in the play and add strength to the movement away from George's personal entrapment and towards a redemptive religious ritual. A second major element of classical religious imagery is connected with the figures of Dionysus and Apollo. We have already seen the connections between the "comedy" and the Dionysic revel. Against the "dark" forces of the revel, however, are suggestions of the Apollonian forces of order, reason and light. These are not, by the way, polar opposites of good and evil, but forces which are both necessary in the life of man.

The second major source of religious imagery in *Who's Afraid of Virginia Woolf?* is the Christian imagery. Christian imagery is used not only to enhance the religious symbolism of the characters, but also to structure the interaction among the characters and the development of the play's meaning. Both George and the imaginary son are identified with Christ. This overlapping permits Albee to achieve some unusual effects. The components of Christ's struggle, the temptation and the passion, enhance the power of George's quest for faith, while the death of the son is transformed into a "crucifixion" which can redeem all the characters.

George is associated with Christ both through imagery (his exits and entrances are usually connected with someone exclaiming "Jesus" or "Jesus Christ") while the play's action serves as an ironic "Easter Pageant." Though George's faith is not so much in Christianity *per se,* his defense of his moral principles is built on a model of the temptation and passion of Christ. Christ's crucifixion assumed its significance not simply through his role as victim, but through his affirmation of faith in the face of temptation and suffering before the crucifixion itself. In his defense of his humanistic principles, George is not only defending himself, but also becomes a kind of saviour for the others: "I'm trying to give you a survival kit. DO YOU HEAR ME?" (115). The faith George discovers is not faith in the power of an external God to save him, but faith in the potential of man to change things and take control of his own destiny. George's progress in assuming control over his own destiny is seen in his recognition of the need for action, for a fundamental change in their situation:

> When people can't abide things as they are, when they can't abide the present, they do one of two things . . . either they turn to a contemplation of the past, as I have done, or they set about to . . . alter the future. And when you want to change something . . . You BANG! BANG! BANG! (178).

The battle must indeed be "to the death." Only the death of the imaginery son is capable of producing the change necessary to get past the labels to "something inside the bone . . . the marrow . . and that's what you gotta get at." In getting at the marrow, George must recognize that if we would have miracles we must create them. After announcing the son's death, George tells Martha: "I'm not a God. I don't have the power over life and death, do I?" (233). Yet in a universe in which "all truth [is] . . . relative," man must create and assert values; in a universe devoid of God, it is man who must become God, who must make and accept the responsibility for the decisions which affect and direct his own life. In moving into battle, George has finally been forced to exercise his most divine attribute, his free will, to cast out the illusions which have separated him from reality. His faith has given him the strength to face life without illusions, but it is only through action that he can alter and improve it.

The final element in the "religious" level of *Who's Afraid of Virginia Woolf?* is Honey's development. It is with her that the success of the fertility ritual rests. Honey is gradually brought into the revel by George, in the spirit of the Bacchanalia. When George does finally guess the truth about Honey's "secret little murders," we see the first hint of a transformer. Her first response, "I want my husband! I want a drink," are followed by a more ambiguous, "I want . . . something . . ." (177). When she is brought in to observe the final game, she announces; "I've decided I don't remember anything" (211). During the game of "Bringing Up Baby", Honey breaks into Martha's "recitation" to exclaim: "I want a child. I want a baby" (223), but then the "perfection" of the fantasy shifts to reveal the ugliness underneath. Only when George comes to the announcement of the son's death does Honey face the fact that she does remember and she tries to stop it. She fails to stop George, but she does join him in the communal healing of the litany: *"Et lux perpetua luceat eis"* (237). Only now can we believe in the reality of Honey's conversion. As George and Martha send them "home to bed," Nick and Honey echo the spirit of faith and regeneration: "Yes . . . Yes . . . Yes."

For George, however, the assertion of faith, even with the disappointments attendant upon it, can carry him through.

Martha (pleading) : Truth and illusion, George; you don't know the difference.

George: No; but we must carry on as though we did. (202)

George's faith gives him the strength to cast off his illusions and move past his failures. As we have seen, the ritualization of action occurs on many levels in *Who's Afraid of Virginia Woolf?* In one way, the play may be viewed as the movement from unsuccessful private games to successful ritual. At the beginning of the play, George is trapped in a private game of refusing to talk to Martha. Though this game does reveal George's hostility, it is ineffective in communicating the sources of his discontent. Seen in this light, the movement to the viciousness and violence of the party games represents a considerable advance. The games may hurt, but they do communicate. In the void of the absurd, violence communicates more effectively than silence and cruelty is kinder than indifference. These games also represent a step in the direction of overt ritual. They are given names to emphasize their significance and are governed (to some extent) by a set of rules. Though these games do communicate and lead to new understanding, they are still rituals of hostility. It is only with the final ritual, a ritual of faith and forgiveness, that we may take the final step from communication to communion, from private fears to a sustaining faith in man himself.

Works Cited

* "Albee Gives Insight to Drama," *Daily Texan.* 6 Oct. 1972.

Albee, Edward. *Who's Afraid of Virginia Woolf?* New York: Atheneun 1972.

Adler, Thomas, P. "Albee's Who's Afraid of Virginia Woolf?: A Long Night's Journey into Day," *Educational Theatre Journal.* 25: 66-70.

Falk, Eugene, H. "No Exit and Who's Afraid of Virginia Woolf?: A Thematic Compriser," *Studies in Philology.* 1970, pp. 406-17.

Hilfer, Anthony, C. "George and Martha; Sad, Sad, Sad," Whitebread, Thomas *Seven Contemporary Authors.* pp. 119-39.

Mc Donald, Daniel. "Truth and Illusion in Who's Afraid of Virginia Woolf?," *Renascence.* 23, 1971, pp. 159-67.

Be Wise and Taste: Milton's Taming of Sin in *A Mask* and *Paradise Lost*

Dr. Ádám Bogár

One can only understand the things that one tames.
Antoine de Saint Exupéry: *(The Little Prince,* p.78.)

In John Milton's *A Mask* and *Paradise Lost* the ample presence of temptation is obvious. The scenes involving Comus and Satan as trying to seduce the Lady and Eve are turning points of the plots and are in the focus of attention for both readers and critics. Besides other expressions, the words "wise," "wisdom," and "taste" are of key importance in these scenes, and I am to argue that a consideration of Milton's use of these expressions, changes in their meanings and their relation throughout these temptation scenes reveals a pathway that leads to a recognition and taming of sin through getting to know its nature.

The *OED*'s definitions of taming generally associate the idea with animals and their domestication.[1] If we extend the scope of this expression, then we can say that not only wolves and other animals can be tamed, but also ideas.[2] What I suggest is that in the course of the mentioned works sin is subjected to an extended act of taming in order to turn it into something that may be reckoned with, something that can be controlled. The taming of sin as I see it is a process the phases of which are traceable in *A Mask* and *Paradise Lost.* In trying to avoid damnation, life may become a tough struggle with pain to be endured and temptation to be resisted. But although this endurance and resistance can be considered truly meritorious, they have their repercussions as well since they make life a constant fight against evil's temptation with no possibility of rest. Although he was a stalwart advocate of the Puritan case, Milton[3] at times seems to have considered this task a burden, which may have contributed to his widely discussed sympathy for negative characters.[4] I argue that in these poetic works Milton tries to identify the very nature of sin as the main cause of the struggle of life in order to facilitate the handling of this struggle and the resistance to temptation. I regard the temptation scenes in the three works as case studies he presented throughout his analysis, the footsteps of which lead from *A Mask* to the 1674 edition of *Paradise Lost*.[5]

The order of the publication dates for the works under consideration (1637 and 1674) is the inverse of their plots' setting in human chronology. Although masques are usually placed in a mythological, pagan, and pre-Christian environment, there are hints suggesting that the plot of *A Mask* takes place after Christ's death and resurrection,[6] while *Paradise Lost* is an account of, among other things, the very beginning of all human chronologies, the creation of Man. The reverse order of publication dates and that of the plots' chronologies suggests that looking back in human history is essential for the taming of sin. We are to follow here the order of publication dates, so we start our consideration with *A Mask* of 1637.

The temptation scene of *A Mask* offers a way to get rid of the practice of temperance. The text seems to stage Milton's internal debate on whether it is possible to keep God's ways without what Comus terms the "lean and sallow Abstinence" (l. 709). Through Comus' tempting words, the Lady is faced with the possibility of living on without the burden of a moderate conduct of life. By drinking Comus' "cordial Julep" she would be free to feel relief on bodily terms,[7] but along with this bondage her hopes for spiritual salvation would be gone as well: virtue, chastity, and purity are the prices to be paid for such an easy life. Comus argues that the Lady "harshly deal[s] like an ill borrower" (l. 683), and by conducting such a temperate life she is actually acting against the will of nature. Finally the Lady rejects him with the help of Virtue and retains her ways against Comus' temptation.

If we consider *A Mask* as a part of this sequence of works aiming at the taming of sin, then the verbal battle between the Lady and Comus is Milton's first analytical step towards this aim. Their debate sketches a theoretically possible way to deal with the constant struggle of life, namely the way of forgetting. Comus' "be wise" (l. 813) is about forgetting and getting rid of something that has already been achieved, it is about expelling the standard of virtuous Christian temperance from oneself, and by doing so, being quit of the burden of necessity to comply with God's ways. Without this coercive force, one could live the Comusian easy life.

This option however leads astray, since without the program of temperance it is impossible to stay with God's ways. Through *A Mask,* Milton seems to present the first hypothetical recipe for enduring difficulties of life deriving from living in accordance with the Christian or rather puritan norms by raising the idea of the rejection of temperance. In Comus' language the expression "be wise" is used in a way to imply that such an erasure of temperance indicates the state of wisdom. This kind of wisdom however is of no use for the Christian, as the only adequate scenario for avoiding damnation is temperance (cf. e.g. 436–440, 762–767, 1018–1023). *A Mask,* Neil Forsyth remarks, contains passages that are "magnificently anti-puritan" (41), and one may add that the masque as a form of theatrical entertainment does not conform to the puritan tendency to oppose "the entertainments of the period" (39), which suggests that Milton then was not the "militant puritan" (39) he is often thought to become later. In the end the Lady, and therefore chastity, proves victorious, still the debate between the Lady and Comus could not reach its end due to the inrush of the two Brothers and the Attendant Spirit. Moreover, Comus's charms could only be broken by Sabrina, a supernatural being, thus the fable is terminated by *deus ex machina,* an instrument already criticized by Aristotle (cf. *Poetics* 1454a-1454b). We never learn how long the Lady would have been able to resist Comus' temptation, which may indicate fear of the evil party as well as an obscure sympathy towards it, a predecessor of the widely discussed sympathy Milton could have felt towards Satan in *Paradise Lost.*[8] Obviously, the possibility of such a smothering up of puritan ideals for the sake of convenience would be impossible for the Milton of the decades to come.

I view the revised and finalized version of *Paradise Lost* of 1674 as the ultimate resolution of the quest for taming sin. Its plot takes place at the very beginning of human chronology, as it retells – among other things – the creation of the world, the war in Heaven, and the fall of Satan and his crew, and last but not the least, the fall of Man, events which occurred well before the Redemption. The temptation scene of *Paradise Lost* is categorically different from that of *A Mask,* since it ends with the complete success of the tempter, Satan. This fact that results in Adam and Eve's expulsion from Eden, and the appearance of Sin and Death in the world, adds a tragic tinge to the end of the epic, still this tragic event provides the key to the resolution of the dilemma under consideration.

As I see it, for both Comus and Satan "being wise" is a kind of euphemism for comitting sin against God's actual word. Both of them are proposing that their targets have misunderstood the will of the superior power they are applying to (cf. e.g. *A Mask* ll. 682–684 and *PL* 9.692–697). They hint that this misunderstanding might be rooted in their state of not being wise, and consequently, being wise is essential to the complete understanding of the ways of living life as prescribed by the superior powers. Wisdom and tasting become once again closely related to each other in the temptation scene of *Paradise Lost.* Satan refers to the Tree of Knowledge as "Sacred, Wise, and Wisdom-giving Plant,/Mother of Science" (9.679–680), meaning that the fruit of the tree can make one wise if tasted, and he encourages Eve to do so (see 9.732) to be wise and to have the possibility of "participating God-like food" (9.717). The summary of Satan's tempting speech can be read as "taste and be wise." These words can be parallelled with line 813 of *A Mask* where Comus ends his argument "[b]e wise, and taste." It can be observed that the order of the cause and effect is reversed by the time of the revised version of *Paradise Lost* was published. This reversed structure implies that Satan's "be wise" is the way of acquisition, that of acquiring something that was by then unknown, in contrast with Comus's "be wise," which is chiefly about forgetting.

John Tanner reads *Paradise Lost* as a text that is meant to "obscure and attenuate the etiology of evil," he nevertheless says that "[t]o the question "Whence cometh evil?" the muse supplies, in effect, the entire complex poem as answer" (45). As to my reading, here Milton depicts the circumstances of the Fall of Man, and finds answers for questions such as what the exact source of original sin was, when it came into existence, and what form it took. These answers enabled him to circumscribe sin, and by doing so, he got a grasp of its very nature. This argument is supported by the fact that *Paradise Lost* has actual allegorical characters called Sin and Death. Their appearance in the epic is puzzling in many ways and has evoked substantial criticism through the ages. Joseph Addison for example notes in issue 273 of "The Spectator" that bringing "two Actors of a shadowy and fictitious Nature, in the Persons of sin and death" into the poem is a serious mistake, because "I cannot think that persons of such a chymerical existence are proper Actors in an Epic Poem" (123), and Samuel Johnson went as far as stating that "Milton's allegory of sin and death is, undoubtedly, faulty" (258). Other critics however have evaluated these characters differently, e.g. lately Mindele Anne Treip argued that "the poem is in fact written in a consistently figurative mode, with nuance, metaphor and symbol passing [...] into allegory" (251). Milton took hold of sin and employed it for his own ends in his epic. Regardless of how fearful they are, Sin and Death were turned into toys in Milton's hands. The poet commanded them, he made them do and say everything they actually did and said throughout the whole epic. Milton brought them under his control, that is, he managed to tame them.[9] From this point on, sin and death (and the struggle of life, since it mainly originates from these) was something that – at least in an allegorical sense – had a quite well-defined shape, and, therefore, changed from something to be feared, yet not known, to something that can be faced, and with Gadamer, something that can be dealt with (see footnote 10). From this point on, sin did not show its natural fierceness to man.[11]

Works Cited

Addison, Joseph, and Richard Steele. *The Spectator.* Vol. 4. London, 1712. Print.

Blake, William. "The Marriage of Heaven and Hell." *The Complete Poetry and Prose of William Blake.* Ed. David V. Erdman. New York: Anchor Books – Random House, 1988. 33–45. Print.

Forsyth, Neil. *John Milton: A Biography.* Oxford: Lion, 2008. Print.

Gadamer, Hans-Georg. *Truth and Method.* 1960. New York: Continuum, 2004. Print.

Gallagher, Philip J. "Real or Allegoric: the Ontology of Sin and Death in *Paradise Lost.*" *English Literary Renaissance.* 6.2 (1976): 317–335. Print.

Gimelli Martin, Catherine. *The Ruins of Allegory: Paradise Lost and the Metamorphosis of Epic Convention.* Durham: Duke UP, 1998. Print.

Johnson, Samuel. *The Lives of the Most Eminent English Poets: with Critical Observations on Their Works.* Vol. 1. London, 1781. Print.

Lewalski, Barbara Kiefer. *The Life of John Milton: A Critical Biography.* Oxford: Blackwell, 2003. Print.

Luxon, Thomas H., (*ed.*) "The Milton Reading Room." *Trustees of Darthmouth College.* Nov. 15, 2011. Web.

Milton, John. *A Mask Presented at Ludlow Castle. 1634.* 1645. Luxon "A Mask [Comus] (1645)."

—. *Paradise Lost.* 1674. Luxon "Paradise Lost (1674)." de Saint Exup Èry, Antoine. *The Little Prince.* 1943. Trans. Irene Testot-Ferry. *Hertfordshire: Wordsworth,* 1995. Print. Tanner, John S. ""Say First What Cause:" Ricoeur and the Etiology of Evil in *Paradise Lost.*" *PMLA* 103.1 (1988): 45–56. Print.

REFERENCES

[1] Although *Paradise Lost* was originally published in 1667, I rely on the 1674 edition here, because I suggest that besides many other possibilities, the unconscious endeavor to tame sin may have been an important motive of Milton's rearranging the epic. This claim may be supported by the fact that the 1674 edition has the names of the characters Sin and Death italicized "to conform to the usual practice in referring to the characters" (Lewalski 338). This may suggest that by 1674 the allegorical yet person-like representation of Sin (and also of Death) became more important for Milton than it was at the time of writing the 1667 version.

[2] Despite the fact that most of the personae are taken from pagan mythologies, the positive characters exhibit basic Christian virtues like chastity, temperance, faith, hope, charity (cf. 1 Cor 13:13) to such an extent that they may be considered Christian; towards the end, the Attendant Spirit even speaks of "Heaven lend[ing] us grace" (l. 938). Bearing this in mind, we may say that if the Lady had the possibility to rely on mercy (cf. l. 695), supposedly on God's universal mercy, which was made available to mankind only after the redemption, then we must presume that Christ's sacrifice has already been fulfilled, ease after pain" (l. 687), and what he proposes and keeps praising is a hedonistic way of life, in the name of which he scandalizes the lack of culinary (cf. e.g. 710–714, 720–721) and sexual pleasures (cf. e.g. 679–681, 739–747, 752–755) in the Lady's life.

[3] One of the first and most well-known proponents of this view was William Blake, who described Milton as "a true Poet, and of the Devil's party without knowing it" (35).

[4] Cf. my extended definition of taming above, as well as e.g. Hans-George Gadamer's *Truth and Method,* where he writes about the existence of an established and well-working tradition for the mediation of hermeneutic experience through human language, a tradition of dealing with problematic experiences by wording

them. According to his observations, "[w]e know how putting an experience into words helps us cope with it. It is as if its threatening, even annihilating, immediacy is pushed into the background, brought into proportion, made communicable, and hence dealt with" (450).

[5] Interestingly, Catherine Gimelli Martin's conclusion is quite the opposite of what I propose here. She argues that "the poem's allegorical machinery can no longer "confine" even overtly allegorical personae like Sin and Death, whose sting can no longer simply be purged in a ritual House of Holiness. Instead, both the reader and the poet must experience the psychological effects of a sin against which they can never be externally inoculated" (27).

[6] Lee Quinby also expresses the similar view,"In *The Woman Warrior*, she promotes "new forms of subjectivity" by refusing the totalizing individuality of the modern era" (125). Likewise, Roger Bromley maintains, "[Ö] my "aunt crossed boundaries not delineated in space," "she" becomes, for a hypothetical moment, the active subject of her own verbs or actions—"she looked"; "she liked" " (31).

[7] "For, as our good Governor Winthrop was made an angel this past night"(*Scarlet Letter* 124). Cindy Weinstein informs us that, "It is significant because this gives us the dates of the novels, 1624-29, and calls attention to the strategic ruse of making Bellingham governor" (Introduction to *Scarlet Letter* xxix).

[8] In Shu's understanding, the narrator has assumed "the position of a privileged first-world woman" and speaks for the third world aunt because as the subaltern, she "cannot represent herself and has to be represented by the first-world feminist writer" (208).

[9] E.D. Huntley has provided a different but very convincing interpretation of her silence: a courageous "act of will." "no name aunt maintains total silence throughout the months of her ordeal: she does not cry out when the villagers ransack her home; she refuses to identify the father of her child; she gives birth without a sound; and she dies without a word. Her silence is an act of will, while by contrast, the wordless Chinese American girl displays the silence of inaction, of an overprotected and weak woman who depends on others to speak for her" (87).

[10] Weinstein clearly points out the magic transformation of "the meaning of the "A" from Adultery to "Able" and even "Angel"" (Introduction xxvii).

[11] For Smith, this symbolic description of vastness of the black sky suggests the potential possibilities of female identity undefined by patriarchal society: craving but also fearful. "While the endless night proposes limitless identities being the confining borders of repetitious patriarchal representations, it promotes the "agoraphobia" attending any move beyond the carefully prescribed boundaries of ancestral, familial, and community paradigms of female self-representation" (154).

The Use of Children's Literature to Empower Students in EFL Classroom

Dr. Leni Marlina

A. Introduction

One of the most challenging tasks constantly facing English language teachers is how to empower or enable their students in studying. Besides, the teachers are expected to capture the interest and to stimulate the imagination of their students so that they will be more motivated to learn. Oura (2010), states that there is currently a wide array of teaching materials available to ESL (English as Second Language) or EFL (English as Foreign Language) teachers to accommodate student's various study needs and empower them in studying. Many of these materials are commercially produced. They can be authentic teaching materials.

Nunan (1999) defines authentic materials as spoken or written language data that has been produced in the course of genuine communication, and not specifically written for purposes of language teaching. One of authentic materials which can empower students in studying English is children's literature.

Brown (2004) states that typically, in an EFL/ESL context, literature is associated with advanced university students or other high level adults. However, children's literature is an important part of English language literature as a body of work, and using it for EFL/ESL teaching at middle schools has many benefits for students. Teaching English as a first language through authentic children's literature has been used for teaching English as a first language in many English speaking countries such as New Zealand, England, Canada and the United States. Then, integrating authentic children's literature either wholly or partially became a reality in teaching English as a second language. In addition, many researches have shown that the use of authentic children's literature is an effective and motivating in ESL classroom strategy. How about integrating children's literature in Indonesian EFL classroom?

Using literature especially children's literature in teaching English at Indonesian schools is quite little, if not neglected. Even though present curriculum has given much proportion to functions, experience and observation as well as research shows that EFL classrooms in Indonesia still emphasizes on forms. School textbooks in middle schools tend to include many conversational skits and there are not many literary works as teaching materials. The use of literature in English learning in school does not go further to discussions on language use or cross cultural understanding. If literature is presented, it is usually to model a generic structure for a narrative text. So, teaching English like nowadays at most of schools in Indonesia is not optimal enough to enable students in understanding English and having critical thinking.

The aim of this paper is to discus three main points. They are (1) the importance of utilizing children's literature, (2) the types of children's literature which can be used in teaching English, and (3) the implementation of integrating children's literature into EFL classroom.

B. The Importance of Utilizing Children's Literature

There are four main reasons which lead an English teacher to include children's literature in foreign language class (Hismanoglu, 2005). They are Valuable Authentic Material, Cultural Enrichment, Language Enrichment and Personal Involvement.

a. Valuable Authentic Material

Children's literature is authentic material. Most of children's literatures are not created for the primary purposes of teaching a language. Thus, in a classroom context, learners are exposed to actual language samples of real life or real life like setting. In reading children's literary text, middle school students have also to cope with language intended for native speakers. So, the students become familiar with many different linguistic forms, communicative functions and meanings. In addition, since children's literature is teaching authentic material, it is good to expose learners to this source of unmodified language in the classroom because the skills they acquire in dealing with difficult or unknown language can be used outside the class. In line with this, Bertens (2008) states that "Literature offers the most profound insights into human nature and the human condition that are available to us. Because of its profundity and its authenticity it offers us a vantage point from which to criticize the superficial, rationalized, and commercialized world we live in."

b. Motivating Material

Children's literature is more likely to motivate the students than artificial teaching inputs because it is generated by some genuine impulse on the part of the writer and deals with subjects and themes which may be of interest to the students as readers. Besides Metcalf (2009) states that childern's texts are obviously easier and therefore less intimidating for a student to tackle. Yet, the texts are still genuine, they have not been written specifically for English students but for native speakers. This combination of simpler but authentic texts is more motivating for a student than ploughing through a text pitched too high or reading a text so obviously written for EFL purposes.

Furthermore, Rass and Holzman (2010) in their research show that authentic children's stories could be very motivating, enjoyable and a very effective source for foreign language learning. Moreover, they conclude that using children's stories in EFL classrooms could be a very motivating and encouraging tool for achieving a positive attitude among the learners as well as their instructors. In short, children's literature could be used as a stimulus for increasing the learners' participation in EFL classroom language learning activities.

c. Cultural Enrichment

Children's literature facilitates understanding how communication takes place in the country in which English is spoken. Though the world of tales, short stories or novel is an imaginary one; it presents a full and colorful setting in which characters from many social or regional backgrounds can be described. The students can discover the way the characters in such literary works see the world outside such as their thought, feeling, custom, tradition, possession, belief, fear, how they speak and behave in different settings.

d. Language Enrichment

Children's literature provides learners with a wide range of individual lexical or syntactic items. The students become familiar with many features of written language, reading a substantial and contextualized body of text. Thus, the students can enrich their writing skill. Furthermore, Chen (2006) states that children's literature can be suitable material for literacy development due to its simple language style, embedded cultural information, and comfortable length.

Smallwood (1998) states that children's literature is important for students at elementary and middle schools for their developing language and literacy skills. Indonesian Junior High School students as adolescent learners can benefit in many ways by studying children's literature. Carefully chosen children's literature can offer educational benefits for English language learners.

Hafiz (2002) states the use of literature in the language classroom to provide students with examples of language used at its best, the wide use of literature making up for what is lacking when language teaching focuses on grammar, vocabulary and syntax as it is actually only through continued contact with writing aimed at native speakers that non-native students can acquire the connotations of words used.

Smallwood (1998) states that children's literature is important for students at elementary and middle schools for developing language and literacy skills and content knowledge. In addition, because high quality children's literature is characterized by economy of words, stunning illustrations, captivating but quickly moving plots, and universal themes, carefully chosen children's literature can offer educational benefits for adult English language learners as well as for children.

In addition, to improving reading and writing skills in general, children's literature presents an excellent source of vocabulary. Students take advantage of the sophisticated words found in books by using them as a source of explicit vocabulary activities, which resultes in a significant increase in vocabulary.

e. Personal Involvement

Children's literature can be useful for students' personal involvement. Once the students read the literary texts, they begin to inhabit the text. They are drawn into the text. The students become enthusiastic to find out what happens as events unfold via the climax. They feel close to certain characters and share their emotional responses. Furthermore, children's literature can train the readers' mind and sensibility.

Children's literature also has a significant role because it evokes critical discussion since literature presents problems faced by human beings. In doing so, students are expected to be aware of not only how to use English correctly and appropriately, but also engage their minds critically (Clandfield, 2010). In addition, it is significant for junior high school students because of its memorable contents.

Children's literature can be used in learning English because literature especially poetry, song lyrics, short stories are memorable. They can be a memorized archive of linguistic usage.

Generally, empowerment means the development of know-ledge, skills and abilities of students to control and develop their own learning. In addition, Harvey and Burrows (1992) states that teachers can empower students by giving them more control over their own learning. There are two dimensions of student empowerment (Sullivan, 2010): intrapersonal and interpersonal. The former is the ability and capability of students to pursue appropriate and complementary social and achievement goals through the establishment of agendas and the latter is the pursuit of goals by students who are not in conflict with peers or the teachers.

How can the teacher empower the students in the classroom? First, she should give them lots of opportunities to succeed in the course. Then, she should encourage all students to participate in classroom discussions and appreciate all contributions. If students are struggling in her class, she will give them additional instruction or help them find someone who can help them. In addition, she encourages her students to work in groups and to help each other with the material. Besides, students become empowered when they feel some ownership of the material which they have for learning. Furthermore, the teacher helps them to gain a theoretical and working understanding of the material which she presents to them. All of these ways can be done by utilizing children's literature in the classroom:

1. Students' Language Skills Empowerment

Students' language skill empowerment means to enable the students to gain language skills. They are reading, writing, speaking and listening.

a. Reading

Children's literature, compared to adult literature, has arguably simpler language, fewer lengthy stories, fewer abstract ideas, less complicated themes and offers just as a wide variety of stories. All of these features are encouraging, especially in boosting reading confidence. In reading children's literary text, middle schools students have to cope with language intended for native speakers. It is good to expose learners to this source of unmodified language in the classroom because the skills they acquire in dealing with difficult or unknown language can be used outside the class.

The natural convergence between literature, language, and culture suggests the use of children's literature in the EFL curriculum. In an EFL classroom where mastery of linguistic and cultural literacy becomes the main attention, children's literature can be suitable material for literacy development due to its simple language style, embedded cultural information, and comfortable length (Chen, 2006).

b. Writing

Children's literature encourages students to reflect on what they read and to share their thoughts in writing, thus developing their writing skills.

c. Speaking and Listening

When students read literature, they are exposed to "horizons of possibility." They raise questions, recognize problems and look for causes and solutions, reflect on ideas, and make connections. Literature encourages students to talk, thus developing their listening and speaking skills.

2. Students' Language Areas Empowerment

This means enabling students to gain language areas. In terms of vocabulary, the language used in children's literature shows some characteristics (Martin, 2009). They are (1) simple but creatively-built, (2) used in daily casual interaction, and (3) rhythmical in productions. These features can be represented in various linguistic forms dominantly found in the three texts, prominently, (a) registers specific to children and (b) onomatopoeias; registers are vocabularies which are identified specific for children users and onomatopoeias are those derived from the imitation of the real objects' sound.

Children's literature presents an excellent source of vocabulary. Students take advantage of the sophisticated words found in books by using them as a source of explicit vocabulary activities, which result in a significant increase in vocabulary.

3. Students' Critical Thinking Empowerment

Children's literature helps to provide stimulating materials for peer interaction, fosters cooperation, opens up avenues for free individual expression and critical thinking, encourages the faculty of imagination and creativity in drama, and increases multicultural exposure (Hai-yan, 2008).

Texts in children's literature are often rich in multiple layers of meaning, and can be effectively mined for discussions and sharing feelings or opinions. This evokes critical discussion since literature presents problems faced by human beings. In doing so, students are expected to be aware of not only how to use English correctly and appropriately, but also engage their minds critically.

C. The Types of Children's Literature Which Can be Used in Teaching English at Junior High Schools

Children's literature can be divided in many ways. Basically, children's literature can be classified into four categories. They are books written by children, books written for children, books chosen for children and books chosen by children. The most suitable definition of children's literature for junior high school students are books written for children. In addition, children's literature can be also categorized based on its genre. They are picture books, traditional literature, fiction, book series, and poetry. Furthermore, Hunt (1994) states that children's literature encompasses stories, rhymes, poetry and plays. Stories are the most popular ones used in EFL classroom.

The most appropriate of children's literature for the beginners at middle schools are picture books, because pictures can speak louder than words. As stated by Putri (2007), "... picture books are outstanding ones that can carry the reads beyond the plain and the literal sense towards the more intangible and visible concepts and ideas." Both picture books and other types of children's literature with fewer pictures or without picture at all are suitable for junior high school students for different levels of students'ability.

According to Pardede (2010), short stories are the most suitable literary genre to use in middle schools due to its shortness. They are practical as their length is long enough to cover entirely in one or two class sessions. In addition, they are not complicated for students to work on their own. Furthermore, short stories have a variety of choice for different interests and tastes. They can be used with all levels (beginner and advanced), all ages (young learners to adults) and all classes.

The short story is very useful to improve the students' vocabulary and reading. It also can be a powerful and motivating source for writing in EFL, both as a model and as a subject of subject matter. In addition, the short story can be a powerful and motivating source for teaching both speaking and listening. Tseng (2010) states that the choice of the short stories is the most students' favorite literary genre among other genres such as novels, poems, and plays. Furthermore, folktales are good units to study for middle schools because they are predictable. In addition they include stock of characters. And they are loaded with adventure humor and rich language.

There are two kinds of stories that can be used in EFL classroom. They are tales and fictions.

1. Tale

Tales are the oldest spiritual companions of people. Long ago tales have been short and with simple structure but with time passing they have become longer, richer, complicated stories. They have always been a source of moral values, a kind of religion, philosophy, and science. They have always enchanted and fascinated children as well as adults. There are many kinds of tale such as:

a. Fables: animal stories
b. Folktales of the sea
c. Starlore: tales of the night sky
d. Story feast: folktales about food
e. A garden of stories: folktales about plants
f. Folktale heroes
g. Myths from around the world
h. Folkales of feathered friends (bird stories)
i. Gender and story (strong women/men)
j. Tales of the supernatural (ghost stories)
k. The flowing story (water in myth, legend, sea stories)
l. Geographical studies through folktales (India, Arctic, Africa, Asia, America, etc.)
m. Rites of passage (tales of childhood)
n. Tales of peace & war
o. Journeys: folkloric travel
p. Tales of clothing (magical shoes, caps of invisibility, changing clothes)
q. Big and small: stories about size (giant tales, miniature characters)
r. Topography tales such as frost and fantasy in Arctic,

jungle expedition in the global tropic, and the story of the desert.

2. Story

It can be classified into: science fiction, crime story, horror story, love story and realistic story. **First,** science fiction generally explores ideas like space travel, cloning, time travel, or aliens. Fantastical things happen but all have a scientific explanation. No use of magic. Settings often include other planets, space ships, or futuristic cities. These may be described in detail. Characters often include robots, aliens, astronauts, or scientists.

Second, crime story is also called mystery. Its plots always involve characters trying to discover a vital piece of information which is kept hidden until the climax. Solving crimes by the use of clues is common in this genre. Characters usually include detectives, criminals, or the police.

Third, horror story has a plot which is always a horror experience and it usually involves the intrusion of a supernatural element into everyday human experience. Characters are often ordinary but vulnerable people, such as children and women. Settings vary but they are usually secluded and isolated places. Atmosphere is often created by description of the setting.

Fourth, love story is also called romance. Plots of romance revolve around two people as they develop romantic love for each other and work to build a personal relationship. Both the conflict and the climax of the story are directly related to that core theme of developing a romantic relationship. There is often a happy ending.

Fifth, realistic fiction is usually set in modern times. It can also have a historical setting, event usually have something to do with an important historical event. Characters are ordinary, believable people. Stories may be funny or serious dialogue is realistic.

D. The Implementation of Integrating Children's Literature into EFL Classroom

1. Selection of Children's Literature

Tseng (2010) states that to maximize the benefits of literature teaching in language classrooms, selection of literary text is a crucial issue. Selection of literary texts should partly depend on the target students' needs and preferences. Criteria for literature selection generally involve two aspects: students and the text itself. Regarding the students, the literary text selected should cater to the students' tastes, interests and hobbies, and should take into consideration their linguistic proficiency, cultural and literary background.

Chen (2006) states when a teacher faces numerous literature resources, selection becomes the first and foremost issue. To choose appropriate materials for EFL students, generally we need to take three important factors into consideration: language, content, and length.

First, the language of literature text should not be stylized, dialectal, or otherwise difficult. This does not mean simplifying the text by limiting the length of sentences or the number of words within the text. The text should be simple.

Second, the good content of literature should involve the reader at three levels: personal, cultural, and universal. Priority must be placed on stories that enable students to relate their own experiences and feelings to reading. Students' interests and backgrounds may influence their responses to and comprehension of the stories. **Third,** length is another important element in choosing children's literature. The story should be short but long enough to stimulate students' interests and feelings.

2. Implement Model of ITB (Into, Thought and Beyond)

Once children's literature has been selected, the teacher, supplied with strategies and methods, begins lesson planning. The model of teaching by using children literature can use a certain format suggested by Richard-Amato and Snow (2005), it is framed as a sequence of *Into, Thought, and Beyond (ITB).*

a. Into

It is the step that occurs before reading. During *Into*, the teacher draws upon many resources to be prepared and make students interested in the text. There are some activities that can be done such as using illustration, pre-teaching vocabulary, introducing theme and talking about cultural background. During *Into,* the teacher may need to explain and justify the use of tale or story. The story is then briefly introduced, key vocabulary is previewed, and some key illustrations or characters may be highlighted. Students are invited to predict the story from the illustrations and other clues. These motivational strategies involve students in the story and help connect it to other experiences, literary or real-life.

b. Thought

Thought is the step when students are ready to read the work. The way to engage a class in a story is to read aloud with expression. The teacher can also use the following strategies: move slowly around the room; take time to show the pictures; modify the language of the text as needed to facilitate comprehension; and pause occasionally for dramatic effect, to highlight new words or concepts, or to check for comprehension. These are some activities during reading such as using a variety of ways to read, sustaining reading, doing total physical response, following characters and their voice, and giving vocabulary help. During *Thought*, neither independent reading nor being read to is a passive activity but an interactive one. To comprehend and appreciate a work, students need to be able to follow an event sequence, recognize foreshadowing, distinguish flashback, visualize the setting, analyze characters and motive, experience the mood, comprehend the theme, and the use of irony and symbols. Students need activity to aid them in this task. The teacher may select passages for in-depth discussion and analysis, helping to draw attention to what is significant in the work.

c. Beyond

Beyond is the step where students can do activities to extend the appreciation of the work. In this step called post-reading activity, student can do check quick comprehension, make a poster/ illustrate story, do stimulus for writing, do role play or acting out. During *Beyond,* students traditionally write to clarify their thinking and deepen understanding. The students recall the plot of the short story, identiy the process that furthers the plot. To become successful in writing, students need opportunities for conferencing and comments on the content of their writing peer revision activities, and comprehensible feedback on their attempts to use the new language in academic ways. Other *Beyond* activities include comparing a text with its film representation or preparing a dramatization based on scene or ideas from work. In *Beyond,* the teacher may give different tasks depending on the story and on our aims. The task may be: multiple choices, true or false, guess the meaning, write the sentences in the correct order, and answer the questions.

3. Implementation by Using Literature Circle

The teacher has to ask the students to read children's literature-story or text as homework and then come to the class to discuss the story. Sometimes the students are often very resistant to this type of assigned reading and whole class discussion. To anticipate this condition, it is needed to introduce Literature Circle to the students.

According to Furr (2010) Literature Circle is a small student reading group which provides a specific framework allowing EFL students to have real, meaningful discussions about literature in English. It is fun, focused classroom-based student reading and discussion group which naturally combines the skills of reading, writing, speaking and listening. Successful EFL Literature Circles will contain most of the following features. First, the teacher selects reading materials appropriate for her students. Then, small temporary groups are formed. Different groups are usually reading the same text. After books are finished, readers may prepare a group project. Next, groups meet on a regular, predictable schedule to discuss their reading. To make this effective, a **Role Sheet** is needed. The Role Sheets break down the skills of a reader into smaller, manageable parts so that each member of the group is responsible for one aspect of what a reader does naturally. The role of students consists of Group Discussion Leader (GDL), Summarizer, Connector, Word Master (WM), Passage Person (PP) and Cultural Collector (CC).

GDL is to act as a facilitator in the group and to keep the discussion flowing. **Summarizer** presents the summary early in the discussion so that everyone can remember the plot of the story. It's important to emphasize that the summarizer gives a brief, but complete summary of the plot. **Connector** is to try to find connections between the text and the real world in which she lives. For example, the Connector may make connections between the thoughts, feelings or actions of characters in the story and family members, friends or classmates. While GDL and Summarizer need to read the text and prepare to discuss the story from a global standpoint, **WM** focuses on single words or very short phrases; thus, the WM is doing a very close reading of the text. **WM** may choose only five words which he believes to be the most important words found in a story. **PP** is asked to make a very close reading of the text and to look for well-written or key passages in the story. **CC** is to work with the cultural and historical backgrounds of some of the stories which they had read.

E. Conclusion

Integrating children's literature in EFL classroom gives some challenges for the teacher. The main challenge is to select suitable children's literature. The most appropriate children's literature to be used in Junior High School are stories especially tales. To empower the students in learning English, the teacher should apply ITB model at the classroom and ask the students to run Literature Circle outside the classroom also.

Works Cited

Bertens, Hans, *Literary Theory.* New York: Routledge, 2008.

Brown, Eowyn, 2004. *Using Children's Literature with Young Learners.* TESL Journal, Vol. X, No. 2, February 2004. (Online). http://iteslj. org Techniques/Brown-ChildrensLit.htm. Retrieved on July 14th, 2010.

Chen, Yuh-Mei, 2006. *Using Children's Literature for Reading and Writing Stories.* ASIAN EFL Journal. Volume 8. Issue 4. (Online). www. asian-efl-journal.com/Dec_06_ymc.php. Retrieved in January 2010.

Clandfield, Lindsay, 2010. *Teaching Materials: Using Literature in the EFL/ ESL classroom.* (Online). http:www.onestopenglish.com section.asp? docid=146508. Retrieved on November 4, 2010.

Furr, Mark. *How and Why to Use EFL Literature Circles.* (Online).http:// www.eflliteraturecircles.com. Retrieved in November 2010.

Hafiz, Zahedah bt Abdul, 2002. "*Children's Literature and Language Learning.*" IPBA International Conference 2002 Proceeding: English as the Lingua Franca of the 21st Century. International Languages Teacher Training Institute, Kuala Lumpur. *(Online).* Retrieved on July 2010.

Harvey, L and Burrows, A.1992. *Empowering students.* ***New Academic,*** Vol.1, No. 30. (Online) http:www.qualityresearchinternational.com glossary/ empowerment. htm. Retrieved in January 2010.

Hunt, P., 1994. *An Introduction to Children's Literature.* Oxford : Oxford University Press.

Hismanoglu, Murat, 2005. *Teaching English Through Literature.* Journal of Language and Linguistic Studies. Vol. 1, No. 1, April 2005. (Online). Retrieved in November 2010.

Martin, Laily. *Children's Literature in EFL Classroom: The Stylistic Considerations.*(Online). http://cotefl.blogspot.com/2009/05/ childrens literature-laily- martin. html. Retrieved on July 27, 2010.

Metcalf, Emma. *Using Literature in the EFL Classroom with Specific Reference to Children's Literature and Literature and Film.*(Online). http:// www. developingteachers.comarticles tchtraining /litemma2. htm. Retrieved on July 27th, 2010.

Nunan, D. *Second Language Teaching and Learning.* Boston: Heinle and Heinle Publishers, 1999.

Putri, Desi P., *Picture Speak Louder Than Words.* Journal Polygot. Vol.1 No.2. January 2007.

Rass, Ruwaida Abu and Holzman, Susan 2010. *Children's Literature in Traditional Arab Schools for Teaching English as a Foreign Language.* English Language Teaching. Vol.3 No.1. (Online) Retrieved from www.ccsenet.org/elt on July 14th, 2010.

Richard-Amato, Patricia and Snow, M.A (eds.), *Academic for English Language Learners.* New York: Pearson Education, Inc. 2005.

Smallwood, Betty Ansin, 1992. *Children's Literature for Adult ESl Literacy.* ERIC Digest. (Online). Retrieved from http: www.ericdigests.org / 1993/adult.htm on July 14th, 2010.

Sullivan, Anna M., *Pursuit of Goals in Partnerships: Empowerment in Practice.*(Online). http://www.aare.edu.au/02pap/sul02098.htm. Retrieved in October, 2010.

Tseng, Fan-ping, *Introducing Literature to an EFL Classroom: Teacher's Presentations and Students' Perception.* Journal of Language Teaching and Research. Vol. 1, No. 1, pp. 53-65, January 2010. (Online). http:/www.academypublisher.com. Retrieved on July 27th, 2010.

A Warrior or Not? A Comparative Study of *The Scarlet Letter* and *No Name Woman*

Dr. Quan Wang

In the interview with Paula Rabinowitz, Maxine Hong Kingston expects her readers to read "No Name Woman" in *Woman Warrior* in comparison with Nathaniel Hawthorne's *The Scarlet Letter*, implying sufficient similarities. "When I was writing "No Name Woman," I was thinking about Nathaniel Hawthorne and *The Scarlet Letter* as a discussion of the Puritan part of America, and of China, and a woman's place" ("Eccentric" 182). Although two novels are both centered on adultery, is there a Hesterian warrior spirit in the no-name woman, "my aunt," albeit in different degrees? According to Sidonie Smith, the nameless aunt is a "truly transgresssive and subversive" figure (154), who strives to mark "female identity and desire" (153). However, this paper, based on the comparative study of *The Scarlet Letter* and *No Name Woman*, argues against the fighting spirit of the titular heroine in the latter story.

First of all, an exploration of the respective backgrounds will shed light on our comprehension of the two stories. "The grass-pot before the jail, in Prison Lane, on a certain summer morning, not less than two centuries ago, was occupied by a pretty large number of the inhabitants of Boston" (*The Scarlet Letter* 41). Hester moves from the Old World of Europe to the New World of America, and settles down near Boston. Severing herself completely from a sophisticatedly interconnected hierarchical system, Hester arrives at a new world of potential possibilities. Annette Rubinstein has beautifully recaptured this nirvana-like transformation after the trans-Atlantic spatial movement. Unlike the Europeans who "lived in communities where their families had known each other for many generations and their sense of social gradations, relationships and organization was a very strong one," it was a totally different story for new settlers in America in Hawthorne's times. "Thus many areas were settled by individuals of different backgrounds, customs, religions and even languages. Nor were these new communities very stable when settled" (Rubinstein 7). Separating themselves from the convoluted hierarchy, these immigrants were roughly on an equal footing with each other, and different cultural backgrounds and geographical isolation produced individualism and democracy among them. "Individualism is a mature and calm feeling which disposes each member of the community to sever himself from the mass of fellow-creatures;" what is more, Alex de Tocqueville wrote in *Democracy in the United States:* "Thus not only does democracy make every man forget his ancestors, but it hides his descendants, and separates his contemporaries from him; it throws him back forever upon himself alone, and threatens in the end to confine him entirely within the solitude of his own heart" (qtd. in Rubinstein, 3).

Hawthorne also deliberately describes this land as a Utopian place in *The Scarlet Letter,* suggestive of the potential individual experiments on the new soil. "The founders of a *new colony,* whatever *Utopia of human virtue and happiness* they might originally project, have invariably recognized it among their earliest practical necessities to allot a portion of the *virgin soil* as cemetery, and another portion as the site of a prison"(Emphasis mine, 39). We can recapitulate the essential points mentioned in the very beginning of the story: on the one hand, this promising land is full of various unlived possibilities of life; on the other hand, no matter how ideal the paradise is, two negative things are indispensable: death and crime, which are concretized in Dimmesdale's decease and Hester's adultery. However, unavoidable as the crime is, there is great room for people's potential new attitudes towards life, because of the overemphasis of the *New* World.

But it is a completely different story in *No Name Woman.* In the Chinese villages in the 1920s, the whole villagers, in the possession of the same surname, are structured like a big family. "All the villagers were kinsmen, and the titles shouted in loud country voices never let kinship be forgotten" (*No Name Woman,* 11-12). In some cases, there are three or four surnames in a village. However, after intermarriages, they are soon linked together as the members of the same family. "Marriage promises to turn strangers into friendly relatives – a nation of siblings"(12). One's identity is measured and defined by this collectivism. In addition, its time-honored cultural inheritance is so comprehensive that it is ready to assimilate any odd and aberrant exceptions. People have long been accustomed to their established cultural and moral standards, and any transgression and aberration will stir up their uneasy psychological percussions. Anyone determined to struggle against its overwhelming power is doomed to fail. Any aberration, let alone the temptation to alter its deep-seated order, will be tantamount to, if not insurmountability, extreme difficulty.

Apart from the settings, the roles of men in the stories also deserve our further consideration. As the husband, Chillingworth, despite his efforts in searching for his wife, has not provided any iota of assistance to Hester during the past years. This is clearly shown in the text: "I [Chillingworth] have met with grievous mishaps by sea and land, and *have been long held* in bonds among the heathen-folk, to the southward, and am now brought hither by this Indian, to be redeemed out of my captivity"(*Scarlet Letter*, 50). Hester, all by herself, a lonely woman struggling independently for survival in a totally alien land, wins certain excusable sympathy towards her transgressive behavior from the readers.

In contrast, the husband of "my aunt" seems to be a very responsible man. In order to support the family, he had to leave home to earn money "in starvation time" (*No Name Woman,* 6). "[...]your aunt's new husband sailed for America, the gold Mountain." "All of them sent money home"(3). Also implicitly suggested in the text is the fact that it is the hard-earned money by her husband as a coolie in gold mining field that has spared the aunt the horrible labor work commonly suffered by other fellow village women: "More attention to her [the aunt's] looks than these pullings of hairs and pickings at spots would have caused gossip among the villagers" because her care-free sensual dressing is sharply contrasted with their humdrum drudgery: "Women looked like great sea snails – the corded wood, babies, and laundry they carried were the whorls on their backs," which will inevitably lead to the "bent back[s]" (10). Economically secured, "my aunt" is also emotionally nurtured by the family members. The daughters-in-law in Chinese families usually have very intimate relationships. And this is especially true during the absence of men who are out to make a living for the family. The sisterly solidarity unifies with the members left in the family, sharing their weal and woe, unbosoming their secrets to each other. However, the economical and emotional support does not seem to satisfy her needs, "my aunt" decides to season her life with a lover: "such commonplace loveliness, however, was not enough for her," and "she dreamed of a lover for the fifteen days of New Year's , the time for the family to exchange visits, money, and food. She plied her secret comb"(10). On the one hand, her husband is risking his life earning every possible penny to send it back home to support the wife. Apart from the long-hour menial labor and ingrained cultural prejudice, Chinese miners often died during their work because of the unsafe security measures. Even worse than that, the anti-Chinese activities generated in numerous persecutions on these poor foreign workers. For example, *Alta California* reported a typical case, "An American yesterday attacked a Chinaman, beating him shamefully. [...] The assailant held the unfortunate Celestial by the queue and kicked and beat him until he was tired, and when the poor fellow got loose and was going off a policeman came up, saw by his bloody face that he had been in a fight and arrested him" (Mccunn, 27). Ironically, the wife at home, living on the toil money of the husband, is pursuing her sexual pleasure. Nora from *A Doll's House* provides a striking example for her: to pursue one's own new life, above everything else, one must not crutch upon others and must try to be independent by oneself in the first place.

Besides the husbands, another interesting contrast can be seen in the two lovers. As the adulterer, Dimmesdale, as is suggested by his symbolic name (a dim dale, something could not be exposed to the public), has not revealed his inner shadowy secret to the villagers until the denouement of the story. However, by employing an omnipotent third person narrator, Hawthorne enables the readers to have access to his inner sufferings and thus share with his gnawing consciousness. Tortured by Chillingworth's secret revenge, this formerly energetic figure is reduced into ghostly pale inactivity. "His [Dimmesdale's] nerve seemed absolutely destroyed. His moral force was abased into more than *childish weakness.* It groveled *helpless* on the ground" (Emphases mine, 125). Thus Dimmesdale becomes the desirable object of the war-of-tug between Chillingworth and Hester, and the feminist warrior image of Hester is unambiguously revealed in reversing the classic literary tradition: the weak and passive princess, captured in some remote castle, is waiting for the rescue of some brave and vigorous knight. "Strengthened by years of hard and solemn trial, she felt herself no longer so inadequate to cope with Roger Chillingworth as on that night." With the newly gained warrior courage and power from the past hardship, "She [Hester] resolved to meet her former husband, and do what might be in her power for the rescue of the victim on whom he had so evidently set this gripe" (131). Apart from this physical battle of rescuing Dimmesdale, Hester also serves as his spiritual guide to see the truth: with her care, love and encouragement, Hester plays an indispensable role in enabling him to be honest with himself and the public: to declare his secret A Letter to the mass. As is acknowledged in his confession to Hester, "Oh, if this be the path to be a better life, as Hester would persuade me, I surely give up no fairer prospect by pursuing it! Neither can I any longer live without her companionship; so powerful is she to sustain, – so tender to soothe!" (157). Her love and guidance also enable him to experience a transformed new life; "Do I feel joy again?" Cried he, wondering at himself, "Methought the germ of it was dead in me! O Hester, thou art my better angel! I seem to have flung myself – sick, sin-stained, and to have risen up all made anew [...]"(158).

On the contrary, the information of the adulterer in the *No Name Woman* only discredits the aunt as "a warrior." The narrative structure of the short story only provides the readers with the bits-and-pits speculations of the unknown man. As a cautionary tale to educate the daughter, the mother narrator is "powered by necessity:" the indispensable background information, the detailed description of the raid on the house, and only very brief and indirect mentioning of the aunt's pregnancy. The bulk of the whole story is the daughter's (who is living in a different American context) speculative reconstruction of the narration told by the mother, full of uncertainties. The most natural reason to explain her pregnancy in such a seemly lawless and barbaric land is rape. "Some man had commanded her to lie with him and be his secret evil"(6). "If you tell your family, I'll beat you. I'll kill you. Be here again next time"(7). If we follow this version of the interpretation of her pregnancy, we can only sense a sympathetic victim, who does not dare expose the name of the brutal violator, even at the moment of her death, too timid to deserve the title of being a warrior: "my aunt, my forerunner"(8). After the suspension of rape, the daughter narrator provides another more plausible and also more feminist-like explanation: love, and thus the story becomes her courageous pursuit of her beloved man despite the traditional shackles. Thus "she often worked at herself in the mirror, guessing at the colors and shapes that would interest him, [...]." "Then she pulled the thread away from her skin, ripping the hairs out neatly, [...]"(9). However, a question of principle should be asked at this moment: is it a pursuit of happiness through the faith of love or just a flirtation for sensual pleasure? As a girl from an economically better-off family, she has enjoyed some inaccessible privileges denied to other women. "[...] her four brothers went with her father, husband, and uncles "out on the road" and for some years became Western men"(11). In the

1920s, if some Chinese had relatives in USA, it was greatly admired and they were actually much more affluent than other villagers. Also "his [grandfather] Western-style great coat" implicitly indicates his unusual economic status. Besides, "she may have been unusually beloved, the precious only daughter, spoiled and mirror gazing because of the affection the family lavished on her"(10). The pampering and indulgence on her fantasy is further reinforced by the unbridled fondness of girls of the grandfather, the most influential patriarchal figure in the family, as is narrated in the text, "he [grandfather] had traded one of his sons, probably my father, the youngest, for her [a baby girl]. They must have all loved her [the aunt]"(8).

The economic superiority and lavishing affection have fostered her vanity and her increasing attention to her sexual appeal, also tantalizing her pleasure-seeking desire. "[...] her desire delicate, wire and bone"(8). Instead of letting "dreams grow and fade," she "went towards what persisted." "She offered us for a charm that vanished with tiredness"(8). The seeking for sensual pleasure is further revealed in the text, "It could very *well have* been, however, that my aunt did not take subtle enjoyment of her friend, but a *wild* woman, *kept rollicking company. Imagining her free with sex doesn't fit,* though"(8 Emphasis mine). The situation is even worse than that: her excessive sensual dressing has already stimulated the sexual disturbance within the family, shaking the very fundamental patriarchal order of incest taboo: "Uncles, cousins, nephews, brothers would have looked, too, had they been home between journeys. Perhaps they had already been restraining their curiosity, and they left, fearful that their glances, like a field of nesting birds, might be startled and caught." To avoid this incestuous love, the men had to leave the home, as is suggested, "But another, final reason for leaving the crowed house was the never-said"(10). In short, neither of the possible reasons of her pregnancy – the passive victim of a rape or the audacious pleasure adventurer – could crown her the title of a woman warrior.

The different ways of punishment in the two novels are also very instructive. In the opening chapters of *The Scarlet Letter,* Hester, standing on the scaffold, is suffering the "Public Execution" to be humiliated for her individual crime, but also as a cautionary example to teach young girls a lesson. Then, in order to make her repent upon her rebellious misdeeds, she is separated from the civilized world and expelled into the wilderness of the forest, a symbolic place suggestive of her moral degeneracy. However, after her personal confrontation with the public resentment for seven years, Hester is able to throw a magical spell upon the mass, that is, her pioneering spirit has gradually transformed the public opinion: the shift of the meaning of *A* letter from the shameful Adultery to the virtuous Angel image, as the story narrates, "many people refused to interpret the scarlet *A* by its original signification. They said that it meant Able; so strong was Hester Prynne, with a woman's strength" (127). In fact, even the most severe moral and political guardians of the original meanings of *A* letter have gradually changed their views: "Day by day, nevertheless, their sour and rigid wrinkles were relaxing into something which, in the due course of years, might grow to be an expression of almost benevolence" (127).

In contrast to the legal punishment on Hester, the devastating ransack on the aunt's house seems to suggest barbarism and violence. To understand the meaning of "the mischievous, inhuman, and irrational" raid of Chinese peasants, Yuan Shu argues that the rationale behind the surface is very much in demand. She situates the story into its broad political background, domestically and internationally, rather than limits it to the narrow village setting. Invaded by Western countries and Japan, Chinese government was on the edge of collapse, and people were burdened with unbearable taxes. Under this circumstance of "the restless feudal and colonial society," the villagers' attack is symbolic of directing "its own energy of confusion and frustration towards anything accessible, rather than as a premeditated moment of Chinese patriarchal practice or a ritualistic pattern practice at the village level in China" (Shu 29). But, I would interpret the episode from the perspective of cultural differences. Fundamentally different from Western individualism, the Chinese culture essentially believes in collectivism. The village, instead of consisting of individuals, is structured like a big family in which every one is just a member whose fate is tightly linked with and inseparable from each other. Personal misdeed is not just an individual behavior, rather, according to the Chinese superstition, as an ominous breach of normal cycle of cryptic nature, which would invite endless troubles to all the members in this community. "But one human being flaring up into violence could open up a black hole, a maelstrom that pulled in the sky" (*No Name Woman* 12). Since the villagers "depend on one another" (3), the aunt's infidelity of breaking up the "roundness" "had already harmed the village." Like the Western concept of the scapegoat archetype, the villagers must sacrifice something to pacify the angry gods who are in charge of the "roundness" order, therefore they destroyed her house to teach her a lesson, and massacred the pigs and sheep to offer them to the furious gods so that they could cleanse the evil and avoid the misfortune that is supposed to befall. Thus instead of taking her life away ("her husband's parents could have sold her, mortgaged her, stoned her"), they just killed the domestic animals – a gesture already merciful enough. The attack on the family house also conveys another explicit message: a warning to the family who fails to carry out its due and proper accountability of educating their children, as is succinctly expressed in Chinese proverb: "........................." (it is the parents who are responsible for the misbehaviors of their children).

The family punishment further dissipates the heroic flavor of the nameless aunt. Disgraced by her shameful behaviors, the family also inflicts its own punishment upon the nameless aunt. "Don't tell anyone you had an aunt. Your father does not want to hear her name. She has never been born" (15). In other words, the nameless aunt is relegated into the obscure corner of the family: disappearance, silence and non-existence. Michel Foucault has a wonderful explanation of this repression: there is nothing to say, nothing to see, and finally epistemologically, nothing to know (4). In short, publicly she is regarded as a great violator of the mysterious order of "roundness" and, privately she comes into oblivion of the memory of the family members. Therefore, we cannot help asking what kind of influence she had exerted upon the villagers? Unlike the gradual but miraculous transformative power of Hester, "my aunt" has only reinforced and sharpened the traditional awareness of the patriarchal system whose gruesome authority makes it more dreadful to be transgressed.

The final death scene is also pregnant with symbolic meanings. "The black well of the sky and the stars went out and out and out forever; her body and complexity seemed to disappear. She was one of the stars, a bright dot in the blackness"(14). The daughter narrator seems to crown her as a bright feminist star in the suffocating darkness of patriarchal culture – the feminist flavor is revealed to the fullest degree. Despite the overwhelming suggestive tone of feminist awakening, intended by the narrator, some contradictory details could not escape the careful readers: "Sometimes a vision of normal comfort obliterated reality: she saw the family in the evening gambling at the dinner table, the young people massaging their elders' back"(14). What she is much hungrier for is a name remembered in the family tree: “No one would give her a family hall name.” If we define her feminism as transgressing the patriarchal conventions concretized in the traditional family life, her longing for “a family hall name” at the dying hour is symbolic of her acknowledgement of the mainstream value and her past “wrong deeds.” A scrutiny of the textual details will make the point more salient. “Don’t tell anyone you had an aunt. Your father does not want to hear her name. She has never been born” (15). Not to be mentioned in the discourse is a frequently employed patriarchal way to relegate the challenging behaviors to the obscure corner of silence. Therefore, if the aunt desires her name to be carved in the “family hall,” she has to be a “virtuous woman”(meeting the patriarchal expectations), the very thing she is short of and regrets for. In this sense, her innermost craving for “giv[ing] her a family hall name” at the dying hour has totally erased the seemingly feminist awakening. The final denouement is always of supreme importance in interpreting the significance of the protagonist’s behaviors. Sula, until the very last moment of her death, still maintains her rebellious belief against the conventions; Hester Prynne, on her tenacious persistence to her own belief of faith, has transformed the villagers’ reading of *A* letter from shame to virtue. On the other hand, Moll Flanders, towards the end of the novel, repents her previous challenging behaviors. In this line of thinking, no-name woman’s longing for conventional family comfort and her desire for the recognition in the “family hall name” suggests an implicit acknowledgement and repentance of her improper behaviors, a further indicator of her non-warrior spirit.

Works Cited

Bromley, Roger. *Narratives for a New Belonging: Diasporic Cultural Fictions.* Edinburgh: Edinburgh University Press, 2000.

Defoe, Daniel. *Moll Flanders: Fortunes and Misfortunes of the Famous Moll Flanders.* Boston: Houghton Mifflin, 1959.

Deleuze, Gilles and Felix Guattari. *A Thousand Plateaus: Capitalism and Schizophrenia.* Trans and foreword by Brian Massumi. London: The Athlone Press, 1988.

Foucault, Michel. *The History of Sexuality.* Trans. Robert Hurley, Vol.1. New York: Pantheon Books, 1978.

Hawthorne, Nathaniel. *The Scarlet Letter.* Intro. Cindy Weinstein. New York: Oxford, 1962-2007.

Huntley, E.D. *Maxine Hong Kingston: A Critical Companion.* Westport,

Connecticut and London: Greenwood Press, 2001.

Ibsen, Henrik. *A Doll House in The HBJ Anthology of Drama.* Ed. W.B. Worthen. Harcourt Brace College Publishers, 1993.

Kingston, Maxine Hong. *The Woman Warrior: Memoirs of a Girlhood Among Ghosts.* New York : Knopf, 1977.

—. "Conversation with Maxine Hong Kingston," Laura E. Skandera Trobley. *Critical Essays on Maxine Hong Kingston.* New York: G.K.. Hall & Co.,1998. 33-50.

Lim, Shirley Geok-lin (*ed.*). *Approaches to Teaching Kingston's the Woman Warrior.* NY: The Modern Language Association of America, 1991.

Ling, Amy. "Maxine Hong Kingston and the Dialogic Dilemma of Asian American Writers." *Critical Essays on Maxine Hong Kingston.* Ed. Laura Skandear-Trombley. New York: G.K. Hall & Co., 1998. 168-81.

Mccunn, Ruthanne Lum. *An Illustrated History of the Chinese in America.* San Francisco: Design Enterprises of San Francisco, 1979.

Morrison, Toni. *Sula.* New York: Alfred A. Knopf, 1975.

Quinby, Lee. "The Subject of Memoirs: *The Woman Warrior*'s Technology of Ideographic Selfhood."*Critical Essays on Maxine Hong Kingston.*Ed. Laura Skandear-Trombley. New York: G.K.Hall & Co.,1998.125-45.

Rubinstein, Annette T. *American Literature Root and Flower: Significant Poets, Novelists & Dramatists 1775-1955.* Volumes I. Beijing: Foreign Language Teaching and Research Press, 1988.

Shu, Yuan. "Cultural Politics and Chinese-American Female Subjectivity: Rethinking Kingston's *Woman Warrior.*" MELUS (Summer 2001). Vol. 26 Issue 2. 199-223.

Skandear-Trombley, Laura E. (*ed.*) *Critical Essays on Maxine Hong Kingston.* New York: G.K. Hall & Co., 1998.

Smith, Sidonie. *A Poetics of Women's Autobiography.* Bloomington and Indianapolis: Indiana UP, 1987.

Rabinowitz, Paula. "Eccentric Memories: A Conversation with Maxine Hong Kingston." *Michigan Quarterly Review* 26.1 (1987): 177-87.

Weinstein, Cindy. *Introduction to Scarlet Letter.* New York: Oxford, 1962-2007. lx–xxxii.

Pashupati Jha: A Unique Voice in Indian English Poetry

Dr. Suresh Nath

> What remains embedded in the reader's mind in most of his poems are the concluding lines which, like Urdu couplets, are pithy, poignant, memorable and have a stunning effect, like the stroke of a hammer – a trait one can find in abundance in the poetry of Robert Frost and Nissim Ezekiel.
>
> —*Prof Ramesh K. Srivastava*

The above comments by a famous writer-critic point to the excellent poetic craft of Pashupati Jha's three widely read and reviewed collections – *Cross and Creation* (Prestige Books: New Delhi, 2003), *Mother and Other Poems* (Creative Books: New Delhi, 2005) and *All in One* (Adhyayan Publishers: New Delhi, 2011). His poems have been regularly coming out in reputed literary journals for the last seventeen years. Although he is a senior Professor at I.I.T., Roorkee and Chairman of the Indian Association for English Studies (Jan. 2006 to Dec. 2011), he rigidly keeps his academic side away from his poetry – there is hardly any obscure allusion or myth in his lines to give any deliberate cosmetic touch of high complexity. What he prefers rather is a lucid poetry that can directly touch the core of the readers' heart without obstruction from scholarly allusions. And yet, because poetry has to take into account some amount of craftsmanship, so he balances delicately the elements of art with artifice, without letting the other disturb the essential harmony. Prof. M.R. Verma points out: "Although Jha applies the poetic tools of alliteration, irony, comparison and contrast at appropriate places, his poems are refreshingly free from intellectual claptrap...he trusts the sincere language of emotion much more than the conscious sophistication of intellect."

Another literary critic, Prof. A.N. Dwivedi, opines, therefore, that the poetry of Jha is "a delight to read, a feast to the hungry poetic hearts." In addition, his poems are highly inspiring too. Mr Jackson, a British poet-critic, during the course of appreciating the poetry of Jha, has expressed his views thus: "We are faced here with the inspired writings of an enlightened intellectual, a man of passion, whose verse is imbued with clarity of style and concept." Because of his total involvement in poetry, he has taken up this art quite seriously, without turning this seriousness into difficult lines full of ancient mythical references as Yeats, Eliot, Pound, Auden and similar others quite frequently do, turning poetry into a strictly class-room exercise.

What strikes one in the poetry of Jha is his wide variety of themes, such as creative process, love with its various faces, the exploitation of women like widows, housewives, prostitutes, riot victims, maidservants in Indian society, crass commercialism affecting the mindset of the people, and an overall lack of emotion in modern life. Jha is perhaps the first Indian English poet to write the largest number of poems, about eighteen, on the creative process involved in writing poetry. Although he is aware of all the theories, he never reflects them in any of his poems. His concept of creativity is completely his own. Poetry needs years of intense feeling and suffering as a prelude to its birth; as he himself writes in his poetic preface to *Cross and Creation*:

> After years of
> reading
> teaching
> and suffering,
> now I dare
> the dangerous plunge
> and taste the forbidden fruit;
> fully well aware
> that a fall would be
> the only outcome.
> But who is not tempted
> by the trap of creation? (*CC*, p.7)

While, because of the hovering clouds of the Second World War, Auden had lost his faith in the meaningful function of poetry in his poem "In the Memory of W.B. Yeats" ("For poetry makes nothing happen"), despite things going awry around him, Jha still finds the relevance of it, provided the human heart is ready to accept the poetic breeze. So in "Poetry makes a lot to happen," Jha writes:

Then, in a flash,
we are transported into another world,
transformed into a different creature
than a nagging woman
or a short-tempered man;
every other thing recedes into oblivion,
even for a few moments
we listen to a different music
altogether. (*CC*, p.10)

For poetic sensibility to be productive, one has to wait for that special moment when some inspiration triggers the chain reaction, resulting into the creation of a poem, such as the morning sun bursting through the crack of a wall, giving a new hue to the photograph of a woman, listlessly hanging in the private room of the poet. The falling rays of the sun on the face of the woman set a series of emotion resulting into the birth of a poem: "But till that rare moment comes/ the blank space silently waits/for words to appear" (*CC*, p.12). This long wait for the appropriate time of final creation is equated with a mother's nine-month wait in "The Birth": "Lastly life stirs off her girth/poetry has a difficult birth"(*CC*, p.18). The suffering, struggle and agony involved in the creation of poetry is again expressed by Jha in "Creation II" and "No Romantic Agony This." In the first, the poet recounts the various challenges that a poet must face as an apprentice of the Muse, before he can think of composing a poem. But once that price is paid, the process goes on undeterred: "The waves intensified their fury/and the storm uprooted many a thing/but the sheet went on increasing." (CC, p. 44). In "No Romantic Agony This," he clears the romantic aura associated with the writing of poems; the process involves searing pain searching for an outlet which, when unbearable, breaks out in flashing words because "you cannot earth a volcano/ for long":

This red-hot sizzling lava
has to explode and surface
someday into molten words
itch-burning on the virgin page—
as sperm long nourished and stored
finally bursts out a crying baby

after breaking the womb-walls
with blood, broken flesh and amniotic fluid. (*CC*, p. 55)

Jha is averse to the high profile manner and method highlighted so much as the source of poetic inspiration, such as falling in love, the dressing and behaving abnormally, reading great masters to imbibe poetic spirit, or attending poetry workshops to learn creativity. For him, creativity can be spontaneously activated by any deeply moving natural sight – he himself has tried all worn-out methods of becoming a poet, but could not move further than a few lines.

Then:

Years later I saw the primal scene
of a young mother breast-feeding her babe
unmindful of the public gaze
affection flowing to the child
satisfaction flowing back to her
and the thaw in my ink
melted with the milk
and for days my pen had no respite. (*MOP*, p. 47)

Like the variety of emotions expressed in poetry, there are various sources of poetic inspiration. But common to these poetic sources is a deeply-felt experience that overwhelms the mental consciousness of the poet, generating highly sensitive, almost an agonized, expression where loss of serenity leads to divine frenzy, which leads further to the creation of Poetry. As Jha explains in "Muse's Mystique":

Emotions stir and implode
striving for an outlet;
a blank sheet virgin white
sneaks near to be seeded,
I want my youth back again.

Forget my thick, embossed papers
I have a wild side too;
when I am alone, utterly denied
bent down and writhing in pain,

the sea rages within with leaping tides
when everything is eaten, embers remain,
to tell of another loss, another gain. (AIO 3)

"The Only Option" talks of the compulsive need of a poet to write as an escape from ugliness, deception, and assaults all around. When there are hovering dark clouds of hopelessness, the only way out of this labyrinth is the cathartic soothing that comes out of creating a beautiful imaginative world: "I then only wait for words/ to create afresh my very own world/free from dirt, free from hurt" (*MOP*, p. 53). But the best lines on the rationale of writing, almost with Shakespearean shades, is in "Phoenix-Love" where the intense feeling of the poet for his dying beloved, makes him to permanently enshrine her in his lines, thus almost defying death:

As an ultimate act of love
I imprison everything of yours
on pages – your eyes, your smiles
your words and events —
so that whenever I feel utterly alone
I may easily go to them
and experience you whole
without any moral and social qualms.
I have loved you more than love
and would not let you fade away
and die, my dear. (*MOP*, p. 54)

But his love is not confined to his wife/beloved; he seems to love his children and other deprived ones with almost the same intensity. " 'Dear Daughter' is a very touching poem on the parents" love for the girl child; the feeling gets quite poignant because she would have to leave her birthplace for nurturing another home, for creating and sustaining another set of life – far away from her parents. Though the parents are sad at her departure, yet they seem to bless her on her new journey:

Now she is leaving us, leaving behind
a gaping hole in our home and hearth
she would soon become the mother earth
and grow her own garden, begin a new birth. (*CC*, p. 49)

In "Our Son Going to College," the same feeling of sadness juxtaposed with the parents' prayer for the son's future life, is presented with all delicate feelings. When departure leads to a meaningful new beginning, it is given a poignantly artistic welcome by Jha; so he concludes the poem with this rhyming couplet: "We forget our grief in their vive/may lord keep their zest alive!" (*MOP*, p. 55) This placing together in a poem of naturally flowing unrhymed lines with rhymed ones is common in Jha; while this strategy breaks the monotony, this also gives him ample opportunity to play with internal music by applying occasionally poetic tools like alliteration and assonance at apt places.

Jha's love spreads to deprived children in "Birthday" and "A Visit to the School for the Deaf." In the first, a poor child, who cannot afford the bash of a birthday party, is consoled finally by the love of his mother; her song inducing him to dreamy sleep, making him float with fairies in "the land of moon and stars/my dream lighted many times/more than mere bulbs and candles." (*MOP*, p. 36) In the second poem, a casual visit to the school meant for disabled children, changes the poet's mindset completely; while he expected sullen-faced children cursing their fate there, he found them bubbling with future dreams, thus transforming the poet's mind from sadness to enthusiasm:

> One look at you
> gives me so much of life—
> efforts extending to the limits of possibilities—
> there is yet something to strive for,
> there is yet something to hope for. (MOP, p. 49)

In "Night in a City," the poet talks not only of the poor child but also of the deprived section of the society as a whole, struggling for existence on day-to-day basis. While coolies stare at the starry sky because they did not have money to go back home and see their families; prostitutes, on the other hand, have to barter their bruised bodies for a few bucks all through the night. In another street, a maidservant hangs herself to death because she is impregnated by her master and so cannot face the world now. But the worst is the case of hopelessly poor parents, who cannot afford the medical treatment, nor can they see the daily suffering of their child:

> In the nearby slums, the shriek of a child
> shreds the silence of midnight,
> his head – smashed by hapless parents
> to cut-short the pang of slow death—
> looks like a cracked watermelon
> thrown casually on the roadside. (*CC*, p. 21)

But Jha never ends on a note of unmitigated pessimism; there are always possibilities for a better future in his poetry, at times with divine intervention: "The limit of limit is crossed, and the stake/ stirs again, for another Resurrection."(*CC*, p. 21)

This social concern expressed poetically without any political overtones, is quite common in Jha – this is evident in his poems on women and communal violence too. The pathetic plight of Indian women, despite the scriptural veneration assigned to them, is described tellingly in "An Indian Woman," and "Widow's Woes." In the first poem, her situation is one of relentless exploitation in all the roles assigned to her – daughter, wife and mother. So, this poem, amid all such secondary positions given to her, concludes quite ironically: "I am a mirror/to this ancient culture/where woman is always worshipped."(*CC*, p. 30) In the second poem, the suffering of a young widow is pathetically presented; when the simmering discontent wants to surface, she has to suppress her voice: "But I am a widow/I must keep my mouth shut." (*CC*, p. 35) Similarly, the poet's heart goes to share the agony of a virgin, who is gang-raped during a communal riot. Shouting the name of their gods, the rioters first butcher her father and then ravish her till she becomes mad. As her tormentors did this crime in the name of religion, so she has almost forgotten her god, allowing her tormentors to taunt her further: "Since then, however I try, I fail/to utter the name of God, how sad/they leer at me, and call me mad" (*CC*, p. 59).

Being an experienced person, who has seen many ups and downs in his life, Jha has developed a philosophy of facing life's odds with strong vigour and not yielding to the various frustrations. This is often expressed in his poems like "The Flickering Flame," "Spring from Stone," "Seeking Life in Death," "A Thing of Beauty," "A Grammar of My Life" from *Cross and Creation,* in "Pages of My Life," "Waiting for the Lotus," "All the Difference," "Creative Optimism," "The Only Option," "Eternal Wait" and "Instinct and Experience" from *Mother and Other Poems* and in "History Will Not Repeat", "Happiness", "Death and Life" and "Autobiography: Short and Simple" in *All in One.* But this philosophy is first to be transmuted in poetic feelings and then shaped into beautiful expressions – Jha is a great master in poetically wording his concept. Even when he has seen life to the fullest, his humanism goads him to live further for others:

> I have already burnt my boat,
> I do not have a life of my own;
> yet I live with hundred smiles
> and thousand tears when I am gone. (*CC*, p. 36)

Even if he has burnt his life's boat, he has not yet exhausted his life's possibilities; he does not want to be lost to the oblivion of death – he wants to be reborn and re-experience life in another birth:

> But I am not tired of the movement
> I am not bored with thc cyclc
> I do not want the final freedom;
> life is a movement from
> moment to moment
> from experience to essence. (*MOP*, p. 41)

Thus life may have bitter-sweet experiences, yet it is worth-living; the joy is in enjoying the various experiences, irrespective of its sweet or sour taste. As optimism amid pessimistic predicaments is key to his life's final attitude, so Jha has even devised a way out of successive losses by giving more importance to gains:

> When I make
> my balance sheet
> of life lived and love lost,
> I bank on the gains
> and leave out the losses;
> then hike the price
> of what I have –
> this is the way
> I do survive. (*MOP*, p. 60)

What makes Jha unique then? Commenting on the wide variety of themes in his first collection itself, Prof B.S. Naikar comments:

> The thematic concerns of the poems in this collection range from birth to death; from identity/ego to cosmic consciousness; from family to the world; from science to art and religion; from pain to love, and from suffering to acceptance and resignation, thereby capturing the irony and paradox of human experience itself. (Naikar, p. 245)

Apart from such a variety, the other special features are "the sanity and the emotions" that "intersperse the poems and lend a distinct life and tone" (Mishra, p. 126) to them. Critics have found in Jha intense emotion controlled by excellent craftsmanship, passionate lines flowing without breaking the barriers, because, as pointed out by Patricia Prime about his poems:

> Passion and creation work hand in hand, but it is creation that has the last word. (Prime, p. 172)

Besides, there are other qualities in Jha's poetry as pointed out by Prof B.N. Singh:

> One of the striking qualities of these poems is the smooth fluency and surprising directness conveyed by the rhythms and diction.... These lines have the lucid gleam of the morning dew and liquid clearness of the limpid stream that runs glittering in open sunshine. These poems are remarkable for their clarity, chiseled beauty and inevitable poetic afflatus.(Singh, p. 111)

It is time, therefore, that this unique poetic voice should be heard, enjoyed, and appreciated by all poetry lovers for its novel freshness, its simple and yet profound philosophy of life based on love, tough optimism, and pervasive humanism.

Works Cited

Dwivedi, A.N. "Review of Mother and Other Poems," *The Indian Journal of English Studies.* Vol. 44.

Jackson, Bernard M. *The Commonwealth Review.* Vol. 15, No. 1, p.168.

Mishra, Prajya. "Review of Mother and Other Poems," *Poetcrit.* Vol. 20, No. 1.

Naikar, B.S. "Review of Cross and Creation," *The Indian Journal of English Studies.* Vol. 41.

Prime, Patricia. *The Commonwealth Review.* Vol. 15, No. 1.

Singh, B.N. "Not Tempted by the Trap of Creation," *The SPIEL Journal of English Studies.* January, 2006.

Srivastava, Ramesh K. "Review of Cross and Creation," *The Journal of Indian Writing in English.* Vol. 31, No. 2.

Verma, M.R. "Review of Cross and Creation," *Points of View.* Vol.10, No.1.

Indian Ethos in the Poetry of Toru Dutt

Dr. A.A. Khan

Toru Dutt was the first Indian poetess to give Indian ethos an English voice. Today, when Indo-Anglian poetry has come to be recognized as a genuine Indian voice, time is ripe to hark back on its tradition which can be traced back to the first quarter of the nineteenth century and was developed mainly through the writings of four poets Toru Dutt, Rabindranath Tagore, Sri Aurobindo, and Sarojini Naidu. These four may aptly be christened as the four wheels of Indo-Anglian poetry. Since independence, Indo Anglian poetry has moved to pastures of new thematic glories and stylistic finesse. Yet, it remains essentially Indian whose roots are anchored in the works of its pioneers. The present paper outlines the expression of Indian ethos in the poetry of Toru Dutt.

Though Toru's personality and genius were moulded by Western influence, she never lost touch with India and Indian traditions. After all, she was an Indian woman writing in a foreign medium. Like Sarojini Naidu, who followed her, Toru was perfectly "autochthonous." In her work there is no room for "artificiality or stimulated hot-house efflorescence." After the premature demise of her sister Aru in 1874, Toru passed through a period of immitigable grief relieved only by her single minded devotion to the study of Sanskrit. Soon, she acquired a considerable mastery over the language and announced her intention to bring out a "sheaf gleaned in Sanskrit fields," following the pattern of the earlier sheaf. But death intervened, and the "sheaf" could only be published posthumously in 1882 under the title *Ancient Ballads and Legends of Hindustan.*

After Toru's death, her father Govin Chunder Dutt found the manuscript of *Ancient Ballads* among her papers. However, since there were only seven instead of nine ballads as originally planned by Toru, Govin Chunder chose to include two verse stories which had earlier appeared in Calcutta based journals and thus completed the total of nine. These two verse renderings are those of the "Legend of Dhruva," and "The Royal Ascetic and the Hind," both adapted from the *Vishnu Purana.* Other ballads and legends included in the volume are: "Savitri," "Lakshman," "Jogadhya Uma," "Buttoo," "Sindhu,"

"Prahlad," and "Sita." Seven poems of non-mythological character are also included in the volume. The book was hailed as a rare literary attempt which marked the "beginning of a new phase since the development of Toru's genius, namely, her desire to give expression to her intense love of her own land and its traditions." The legends recounted are stories recollected in moments of tranquillity amid personal agonies, from childhood memories. Thus an aura of nostalgia surrounds these narratives. By vigorous and pleasing narration, Toru has struck a genuinely Indian note and has conveyed to the West the intellectual and philosophical traditions of this ancient land. Though Toru's range of selection is limited, yet her poetic vision encompasses the whole religious culture of ancient India. Each legend exemplifies a few of the immortal values of life as conceived by sages of yore. Toru accepted Soul and God as main themes in her poetry and the retold legends are a quest after the ultimate truth that lurks behind the maya of man's relation with the universe and its creator.

The longest legend in the book is "Savitri." The immortal story of Savitri and Satyavan taken from the *Mahabharata* illustrates the triumph of pure love and courage over the forces of death. Savitri's extraordinary constancy and sacrifice are the bywords for the highest standard of wifely devotion even today. Toru recounts the story of Savitri in five parts illustrating – love, marriage, devotion, sacrifice, and fulfillment. The ballad is greatly merited because of its successful recreation of the immortal character of Savitri. It needs to be pointed out that Toru's rendering of the well-known legend does not agree in minute details with the original in the Mahabharata. Divergences may be noted at such points such as when the king expressed to the queen his desire to find a perfect husband for their daughter. Also, the arrival of Narad at the king's palace and the first meeting of Savitri and Satyavan are not faithful to the original. However, such divergences bear the stamp of Toru's originality and are a sign of her strength rather than weakness. A short consideration of the poem will bring out the exposition of Indian philosophy as attempted by Toru.

Savitri, the only child of the king of Madra, lived in those far-off days when daughters were not pent in closed zenanas. Beautiful of face and form, with nature pure as snow, as Savitri approached womanhood, her father pondered over the question of her marriage, but could think of none fitting for one so pure. One summer morning, on her way to the hermitage, Savitri saw a number of youth intent on sport. Among them was one "tall and lithe," and "royal in port." She inquired about the youth and learnt that he was Satyavan, the only son of Dyoumatsen – the rightful king of Salva, who deposed by his enemies, old and blind, was living with his wife and son as a hermit. For Savitri, it was love at first sight. Returning home, Savitri confided her feelings to her mother. Not long after, Narad Muni, the venerable sage, came to the palace of Madra, to the dismay of the king, Narad became strangely troubled when told about Savitri's choice. On being insisted, the omniscient sage declared that Satyavan was doomed to die within a year. He also tried to persuade Savitri to choose for herself another husband, but to no avail.

Her mind firmly made up, the marriage was solemnized with great rejoicings. Savitri was graciously welcomed to her new home by Dyoumatsen. Months of quiet happiness passed by in fulfillment of homely duties. Savitri was however troubled deep inside by the remembrance of Narad's prophecy. When the fateful day arrived, Yamathe God of death himself came to take away the soul of Satyavan. As Yama did his work and moved towards his own dominions, Savitri followed him despite Yama's instruction to go back and perform the funeral rites as enjoined in scriptures. Heedless of Yama's warnings, Savitri told him that wifely duty bids her to be with her husband in woe or weal, whether he went somewhere on his own or whether someone else carried him. This was followed by a philosophical discussion between Savitri and Yama. Savitri spoke in terms of Vedantic philosophy:

> I know that in this transient world
> All is delusion, – nothing true;
> I know its shows are mists unfurled
> To please and vanish. To renew
> Its bubble joys, be magic bound
> In Maya's network frail and fair,
> Is not my aim! (p. 19)

Pleased with her, Yama granted Savitri three boons, the first two with a condition that she did not ask for Satyavan's life and the third without any condition attached. Seizing the opportunity, Savitri asked for Satyavan's life. Satyavan rose from his death-sleep and the two returned to the hermitage where old parents awaited them in anxious anticipation. Yama's other boons came to be fulfilled in due course of time. The name of Savitri is invoked to this day at every Hindu marriage.

Critics have lavished the poem with undiluted praise. Even Harihar Das, who considers the poem a failure, is of the opinion that the poem seems to augur "great future possibilities in development of Torus genius." Lotika Basu avers that "Savitri is the finest of the poems dealing with epic legends [. . .]" The story of Savitri captivates the reader as he anticipates with breathless anxiety the final victory of love over the forces of death.

The next poem, "Lakshman," is in the form of a conversation between Sita, and Lakshman, Lord Rama's wife and brother respectively. Lord Rama had incurred the wrath of demons by rebuffing the advances of Soorpnakha – one of the sisters of Ravana the demon king. To avenge her wrong, Ravana commanded Maricha to assume the form of a golden deer and come roaming to the hermitage where Rama, Sita, and Lakshman dwelled. Deeply moved by the beauty of the deer, Sita begged Rama to get it for her, and despite Lakshman's warning – for he suspected it to be a trick played by the demons, Rama went off in pursuit of the deer leaving Sita in charge of Lakshman with a strict injunction not to leave her alone at any cost. After a long pursuit, Lord Rama shot an arrow which pierced the deer's heart and with a terrific bound it sprang up in the air and fell to the ground dying, assuming its true form. While dying, Maricha's piercing cries, "Oh Sita! Oh Lakshman!" resounded the jungle. The poem opens at this point.

Sita heard the cry and is urging Lakshman to go to Rama's help. Lakshman tries to convince Sita of Rama's might and advises her not to be disturbed by the cries which she just heard for they must be due to some trick of magic by the foe. But Sita is adamant and orders Lakshman to at once leave the hermitage and go in search of Rama. She also taunts Lakshman and accuses him of disloyalty to his brother and goes so far as to say that Lakshman and Bharat desire Rama's death so they may take possession of his wife and kingdom. Unable to bear her insults any longer, with a heavy heart, Lakshman goes out in search of Rama. But before he leaves for the forest, Lakshman draws a magic circle around the hermitage with his arrow and asks Sita not to step beyond it. The poem presents an insight into the strength of the bond that binds the members of an Indian family. Harihar Das fittingly remarks, "nowhere, we think, outside Indian thought, could we get so perfect a picture of brotherly loyalty."

The story of the ensuing ballad "Jogadhya Uma," was told to Toru by her old nurse Suchee, of whom Toru and her siblings were very fond. A peddler of shell-bracelets was trading his wares along the road to Khirogram early in the morning. Few heard his cry in that early hour. A bend in the road brought him to a tank shadowed by fruit trees. On one side of the tank, facing the morning sun, sat a lovely maiden with large eyes and dark hair. The peddler stopped by to display his wares to the maiden. An indescribable air of nobility radiating from the maiden filled the peddler with awe. Tossing aside stray curls of hair from her brows, the maiden asked the price and then bade the peddler seek payment at home. She directed the peddler to a temple whose gilded spire appeared at a distance, saying that the temple priest is her father to whom he should ask for money. She also said that should her father say that he does not have so much money, he (the peddler) should ask him (the priest) to open the vermillion streaked box kept at the shrine where the money would be found.

On reaching the temple, the peddler spoke to the priest of his errand. When the priest laughed saying that he had no daughter, the peddler repeated the story and the maiden's direction concerning the vermillion streaked box. The priest fetched the box and on opening it found the exact sum. In a flash he realized that the simple peddler had beheld the Goddess herself. The old priest and the peddler swiftly ran for the tank where they were disappointed, for all was quiet. A hush seemed to envelope nature over which a solitary heron stood sentinel. They received no response to their repeated calls to the divine maiden. As they turned to depart with saddened heart, the chime of temple bells pealed out and the two beseeched the Goddess for some sign of their presence, in response to their prayers:

> Sudden from out the water sprung
> A rounded arm, on which they saw
> As high the lotus buds among
> It rose, the bracelets white, with awe.
> Then a wide ripple tost and swung
> The blossoms on that liquid plain,
> And lo! The arm so fair and young
> Sank in the waters down again. (p. 41)

Ever since that day, descendants of the peddler have annually paid shell-bracelets of old design as a tribute to the Goddess who on that eventful day crowned their ancestral industry with success.

In composing the ballad, Toru shows creative originality of the highest order. It is difficult to accept Lotika Basu's assessment verbatim that the "Indian atmosphere of the poem is sometimes split by the rather jarring introduction of the priest's house which is anything but Indian." It is true that certain English associations have crept in the poem, but the content, the setting, and the treatment are essentially Indian. Harihar Das rightly considers the ballad "a gem of art among the Ballads of Hindustan."

The next ballad, "The Royal Ascetic and the Hind," centres round the matchless asceticism of king Bharat of Saligram and his apparent failure when he developed a strong attachment for a foundling deer fawn. King Bharat left his royal abode and went to the forest where he practised penance and underwent privations to gain mastery over the soul. A change however came over him when one day, while sitting by the river bank, engaged in his prayers, he saw a beautiful pregnant hind jump to her death into the river on hearing the roar of a lion. Its offspring tumbled from her womb and struggled for life in swirling waters. Deeply touched, the hermit-king rescued the new born creature and took it to his hermitage. Thenceforth, he developed a deep attachment for the foundling, caring little for his devotions. After many years, when on the death bed, the king was filled with anguish at leaving the fawn and not on the question of death and eternity as befitting an ascetic. Toru misreads the implications of the original and infers that by yielding to his love for the orphaned deer fawn, king Bharat failed in his path of asceticism and hence her spirited defense of the king's conduct:

> Not in seclusion, nor apart from all,
> Not in a place elected for its peace,
> But in the heat and bustle of the world,
> Mid sorrow, sickness, suffering and sin,
> Must he still labour with a loving soul
> Who strives to enter through the narrow gate. (p. 45)

In the above lines, we discern a pronouncedly Christian note to have intruded upon her diction. However, such comments are rare and Toru largely stands up to her task of narrating the ancient legends.

Like the previous legend, "The Legend of Dhruva" is also taken from *Vishnu Purana* (Book I, Chapter XI). It relates the story of a prince who being denied of father's love because he was the son of the less favoured queen, spurns worldly love and seeks spiritual glory instead. An interesting aspect of Toru's interpretation of the legend is the introduction of "Karma theory." While consoling her son, Suneetee expounds the doctrine of Karma:

The deeds that thou hast done, The evil, haply, in some former life, Long, long ago, who may alas! annul, Or who the good works not done, supplement The sins of previous lives must fruit. (p. 47)

She also held Dhruva the prospect of future rewards should he live his present life with humility. The young prince however found little consolation in his mother's words and declares his unalterable resolve to seek the highest goal of life – spiritual enlightenment. He left his father's palace to live among the sages in the forest and in due course, fulfilled his resolve by attaining the highest place in the heaven, where he still "shines a star" (p. 49), and where men behold him in their nightly walks. Here, we witness another aspect of morality presented by the poetess – that of the assertion of individual worth and a stout refusal to wait for somebody's mantle to fall on one's shoulders. The greatest strength of the poem is in effective synthesis of the old world morality with the dynamism and the confidence of the new world order.

The story of "Buttoo," is taken from the *Mahabharata.* Buttoo, otherwise known as Ekalavya, the son of a low-born hunter, was rejected and humiliated by Dronacharjya the incomparable master of archery. Glowing red with shame, Buttoo bade a proud farewell. At this point, Toru gives a modern twist to the ancient tale, no doubt, an impact of the European exposure on the young poetess's mind. As Buttoo resolved to learn the art of archery on his own, he muttered to himself:

My place I gather is not here:
No matter, – what is rank or caste?
In us is honour, or disgrace,
Not out of us, 'twas thus he mused,
The question is, – not wealth or place,
But gifts well used, or gifts abused. (p. 51)

Resolving to attain perfection, Buttoo retreated to the forest, built a hut and an earthen statue of Dronacharjya, and taking the statue to be his master, Buttoo commenced his practice. Resolute and steadfast, Buttoo's training ultimately bore fruit and in time he learnt all the secrets of archery.

One evening, while intent on practice, much to Buttoo's dismay, his weapons failed him again and again, and at the same time, he heard the howling of a dog portending ill-omen. He let a magic shaft fly which silenced the dog without hurting it, but it proved to be his undoing. On that very day, Dronacharjya and his disciples, the Pandava and the Kuru princes were in the woods hunting. While hunting, Pandava prince Arjuna chanced upon the dog. He sought Dronacharjya and accused him of betrayal, as the great master had promised that none beside him shall learn the secret of magic shaft. Dronacharjya assured Arjuna that he had not betrayed his trust, and together they went in search of the marksman who had shot the shaft and reached Buttoo's hut. On being asked by Dronacharjya, Buttoo revealed the story of his perseverance and mastery over the craft and credited the great master to be his sole inspiration. Listening to this, Dronacharjya, demanded from Buttoo his right-hand thumb as his due – the "guru-dakshina." Buttoo's loyalty towards his professed master did not waver even at this cruel demand and in a flash his severed thumb lay at the master's feet. Structurally, Buttoo is a neat piece of poetry and technically the poem is "one of the happiest and least affected" of Toru's poetry.

The "Karma" theory has also been presented in the ballad "Sindhu." It is the story of a son's devotion to his parents and his untimely death as he is killed erroneously by king Dasarath. Sindhu is killed as a result of his past "karma" of killing one of a pair of doves. The king too dies broken-hearted, pining over the loss of his son as a result of the sin he incurred by killing Sindhu, the only stay of old sage couple. The ballad is composed in a simple language, though stylistically it is distinctly inferior and can be placed with Toru's earlier attempts like "The Legend of Dhruva," and "The Royal Ascetic and the Hind." "Prahlad" is the story of a young prince's unparalleled devotion to God and the ultimate victory of good over evil. King Heerunkasyapu, father of Prahlad, was a tyrant; he tore the Vedas into shreds, forbade the worship of gods, slew the holy men, and ordered that he alone should be worshipped. The king appointed for his children a tutor who was to teach them all they needed to know, but was strictly forbidden to teach anything about the soul or God. One day, the four princes were summoned to the king's court for a test. When Prahlad's turn came, he was asked to explain the "cream of knowledge" (p. 74). The boy's reply, which was full of devotional fervour, enraged the king beyond reconciliation and he ordered Prahlad to be executed. However, the young prince could not be executed divinely protected as he was. Prahlad was once again summoned to the king's court where he proclaimed God's omnipotence and omnipresence:

> I fear not fire, I fear not sword,
> All dangers, father, I can dare;
> Alone, I can confront a horde,
> For oh! My God is everywhere! (p. 79)

Hearing this, the king mockingly asked Prahlad if God was present in the crystal pillar against which he leaned, when Prahlad replied in a affirmative, the king gave a mighty blow to the pillar. The pillar came tumbling down and out sprang a warrior of immense stature with a lion's head and a human body. With a terrible roar, it struck the tyrant and ripped him down. It then hailed Prahlad as the king of all realms and vanished in a thunder clap. The story of Prahlad is successfully told. Written in eight-lined stanzas, the technique of the poem is "far in advance of that of the earlier poems:"

"Sita" is the final ballad in the volume. Short in length as compared to other ballads in the volume, it recounts the tale of Sita's unmerited suffering at the hands of Rama who exiled her on the flimsy ground of a slanderous rumor. Artistically, the poem is the best among the legends of Toru. The picture of Sita, sad and forlorn in the hermitage of sage Vashishtha, along with her children is a deeply moving one:

> Not in vain
> She weeps, – for lo! At every tear she sheds
> Tears from three pairs of young eyes fall amain,
> And bowed in sorrow are the three young heads. (p. 81)

The poem is rich in pathos and has a strong autobiographical touch. The above lines recreate as much a scene from the mythical past as it does of the Dutt household, when in their childhood, Toru and her siblings gathered near their mother in the twilight hour to listen to the sad old story of Sita. The seven "Miscellaneous Poems" in the end of the volume display Toru's creative genius at its best. They span the whole of Toru's creative period from 1870-1877. Autobiographical in vein, their quality has led the scholars to comment that but for her short life, Toru might have written "beautiful lyrics" or "powerful sonnet-sequence or poetic tragedy."

Taken as a whole, Ancient Ballads displays Torus fine understanding of the cultural tradition of her race and country. It further appears from a study of the volume that deep philosophies and pathetic aspects of life moved Toru the most, while light, joyous aspects of life hardly appealed to the poetic sensibilities of this "fragile exotic blossom of a song:" This is obviously an offshoot of the tragedies the young poetess had to witness in her own short, tragic life. Her sad life reminds us of the great romantic poet Keats. Despite certain shortcomings pointed out by critics, the ballads do no injustice, neither to the originals nor to the language in which they are rendered.

Works Cited

Basu, Lotika. *Indian Writers of English Verse.* Calcutta: The University Press, 1993.

Das, Harihar. *The Life and Letters of Toru Dutt.* London: Oxford University Press, 1921.

Das, Harihar. "The Classical Tradition in Toru Dutt's Poetry," *Asiatic Review.* October 1931.

Dutt, Toru. *Ancient Ballads and Legends of Hindustan.* Preface by Raja Rao. Calcutta: Writer's Workshop, 1972.

Gosse, Edmund. "Introductory Memoir," *Ancient Ballads and Legends of Hindustan.* London: Kegan Paul & Co., 1882.

Jha, Amamath. "Introductory Memoir," *Ancient Ballads and Legends of Hindustan.* Allahabad: Kitabistan, 1969.

Lyengar, K.R. Srinivasa. *Indian Writing in English.* New Delhi: Sterling Publishers Pvt. Ltd., 1999.

Mukherjea, S.V. *Disjecta Membra.* Bangalore: The Indian Institute of World Culture, 1959.

The Bengal Magazine. October, 1876

The Calcutta Review. January, 1877.

Reconstructing *Ramayana*: A Texture Revisitation

Dr. Sunita Sinha

All acts of communication are acts of translation.
—George Steiner

Wherever literature exists, translation will surely exist. The very concept of literature would be unimaginable without translation. Goethe believed that without external influences national literatures rapidly stagnate. The entire history of literature is enlightened by a process of transmission; a great work of literature is able to adorn itself by originating new meanings as it enters new contexts. Translation could be visualized in this context as the inherent metaphor of all literary communication. Hence, translation remains the most significant aspect of all scholarly researches but perhaps most importantly for an Indian who from very childhood has had to learn how to manoeuvre across the domains of our mother tongues and English. Earlier, schools compulsorily prescribed the "retranslation" of Bengali and Sanskrit passages into English. However, my focal interest lies in pursuing the *Ramayana* through varying domains of language and culture and analyzing the textual transformations in various versions of the *Ramayana* in the changing social milieus.

The Ramayana remains one of the greatest epics of world literature – a story rich in characters and drama. It is one of the most celebrated works of the Indian literary heritage and focuses on the power and nobility of Prince Rama, his bride Sita, and brother Lakshmana, as they encounter the evil king Ravana. The world of the *Ramayana* is peopled by wise sages and spiritual masters, evil demons, supernatural deeds, and great accomplishments. But above all else, it is also a story relevant to the modern world – a story of family relationships that defines the ideals of love, fidelity, loyalty, and honour. India's foundational epic, *The Ramayana* continues to influence social, religious, cultural, and political life of modern South and South East Asia and is a source of inspiration not only to devotees but scholars who have given translated as well as adopted versions in different languages. Brought to textual life in Sanskrit by the legendary "first poet," Valmiki, over the following centuries the tale has been recycled with extraordinary adaptability and diversity through the different cultural heritages of India and other parts of Asia and the diversity of its retellings suggests that *The Ramayana* holds different meanings for different audiences. The basic tale of *The Ramayana* is continually adapted to new contexts, forms, and media. It is read, recited, sung, danced, and acted in one form or another, and renewed so constantly by changing times and values that it demands constant revaluation.

Valmiki's Ramayana, in the Sanskrit literature known as Adikavya or the first poem and was composed between around 2nd century *b.c.e.* and 2nd century *c.e.*, by Sri Valmiki Muni known as Adikavi or the first poet. Generally taken to be the foundation of all subsequent versions Valmiki Ramayana is the source of many other versions of *Ramayana* such as *Adhyatma Ramayana* (Sanskrit), *Kamba Ramayana* (Tamil), *Tulsidas Ramayana* (Hindi), *Ezhuttachan Ramayana* (Malayalam) and other Ramayanas in all the languages of the states in India and also in the South East Asian languages. As Tulsidas, the author of *Ramcharitamanas* said, "Ramakatha kai miti jaga nahi" – It is impossible to keep count of Ramakathas (Ramayana versions) in this world (Sundaram, 2002) Swami Ranganathanda pays his tribute to great Adikavi:

> *Kujantam rama rameti madhuram madruraksaram;*
> *Aruhya kavita sakham vande valmiki kokilam*
> [*Trans:* "I salute Valmiki, the cuckoo, who, perching on the tree of poesy, melodiously sing the sweet syllables – Rama, Rama."]

In one of his much discussed essays, A.K. Ramanujan raises a pertinent question, "How many Ramayanas? Three hundred? Three thousand? At the end of some Ramayanas, a question is sometimes asked: How many Ramayanas have there been?" (Richman, 1991). Ramanujan's supposedly controversial essay "Three Hundred Ramayana's: Five Examples and Three Thoughts on Translations" from the Bachelor's of Arts (BA) course. The essay was introduced in 2006 and was strongly opposed by the ABVP from the very start. In 2008, several ABVP workers vandalised the History Department building with heated exchanges with professors and students being reported. BJP leaders like Vijay Kumar Malhotra as well as ABVP members have since justified their actions. Malhotra has gone on to say that Ramanujan has done a great disservice to the nation. The Hindutva brigade terms Ramanujan's essay controversial and blasphemous for two reasons. One, because it details the several "tellings" of the Ramayana across and beyond the Indian subcontinent and questions the assumption that Valmiki's Ramayana is the original or authentic one. Two, the essay also speaks of versions of the Ramayana in which Ram and Sita are siblings and in certain others where Sita was Ravana's daughter. This did not go down well with the generation brought up on Valmiki's Ramayana. As a young ABVP member pointed out, "I grew up watching the Ramayana as shown on the TV (produced and directed by Ramanand Sagar). There can be no other version of it."

I shall concentrate on Ramayana versions of northern and eastern India – the region, where Valmiki Ramayana is believed to have originated. The narrative structure and the mainplot elements of the Valmiki Ramayana remain the same in these later versions, and their authors not only confess their indebtedness to the adi kavi but suggest that their works are reliable interpretations of Valmiki's poem. However, they do differ from Valmiki's script in rendering the details of a few episodes, some invented ones, and more significantly, in their moral and religious postulations. These conceptual variations are so deeply entrenched and their principles are so besetting that they come forth as narrative interventions, such as changed emphases and even absolutely new episodes. In the process, they almost reform the Ramayana. Some chiefly retell Valmiki's narrative, while others concentrate more on peripheral stories and/or philosophical expositions. For instance, *Adhyatma Ramayana* or spiritual Ramayana is extracted from the Brahmananda Purana, traditionally ascribed to Vyasa which is considered to be the inspiration for Tulsidas' *Ramcharitmanas* in Awadhi. While the Valmiki Ramayana emphasizes Rama's human nature, the *Adhyatm Ramayana* tells the story from the perspective of his divinity. Vasistha *Ramayana* – a dialogue between Vasistha and Rama in which Vasistha advances many of the principle tenets of Advaita Vedanta includes many anecdotes and illustrative stories, but does not recount Valmiki's story of Rama in detail. Though traditionally attributed to Valmiki and the traditional story of Rama, *Ananda Ramayana* is mainly composed of stories peripheral, though related, to Valmiki's narrative. These include Ravana's abduction of

Kausalya and Rama's instalment of the Shiva Lingam at Rameswaram. [*Ananda Ramayana*, Parimal Publications, 2006.] *Adbhuta Ramayana*, includes related stories of Rama but it focusses on the role of Sita, the circumstances of her birth as well as on the story of her defeat of Ravana's older brother, also known as Ravana but with 1000 heads.

Valmiki's *Ramayana* declares the virtue of dharma and its ultimate victory over evil. Rama himself delivers this message on various occasions. For instance, in the Ayodhyakanda, Rama says to Lakshmana:

> *dharmo hi paramo loke dharme satyam pratist hitam/*
> *dharmasam Britam etac ca pitur vacanam uttamam//*

Dharma is paramount in the world and truth is found in dharma. This command of Father's is based on dharma and is absolute. (VR.2.18.34)

Further, in the Kishkindhakanda, the entire episode of Rama's killing of Vali raises questions about right action. To vindicate Rama, Valmiki avers that the principle of dharma is higher than that of a fair fight, which is accepted by Vali himself:

> *mam apy avagatam dharmad vyatikrantapuraskram*
> *dhramasamhitaya vaca dharmajna paripalaya//*

You understand dharma. Therefore, with words consonant with dharma, comfort even me, known to be a flagrant violator of dharma. (VR.4.18.44)

Towards the end of the Lankakanda, occurs a far more dramatic and shocking instance of Rama's commitment to dharma, when Sita is brought to Rama after her long captivity. At this point in the story the audience expects a joyous reunion. However, contary to everyone's expectation, all that Rama has to say to Sita is that he has done his duty as a warrior king and has fulfilled his dharma as a husband, but now as the ruler of Ayodhya he has to fulfill the dharma of casting out a wife who might be perceived as an unchaste woman. Rama forgets that he is God, when he disowns Sita and compels her to enter the burning pyre. To the assembled deities he says, "I think of myself to be a human being, by name Rama, the son of Dasharath." The deities then remind him that he is the avatar of the Supreme God. When Sita emerges from the flames Rama says that though he knew that Sita was pure the Agni Pariksha was essential to prove her fidelity before the society at large. Despite the rationalization attempted the morality of the act can still be questioned. One cannot compel someone to undergo torture in the guise of exoneration by the society. The values conjured here are openly social and political, with no moralistic motives. These crucial episodes present Rama centre stage as human hero. It is only in medieval Ramayanas that the celebration of Rama as God becomes the main concern of the story. The aim of Valmiki's story is not to declare that Rama's deed is integral to the divine scheme of creation, which is carried forward by Rama as the living god. On the contrary, it is a battle story that signifies and upholds absolute dharma, a term that is to be taken in its social and practical proportions. Rama is of course idealized and his deeds are celebrated, but not because he is God; rather, he is the perfect man and his perfection is represented in terms of his absolute commitment to the masculine force, soldierly determination, dynastic dignity and aristocratic duty. Leadership qualities and a warrior ethic remain the central issues. Retelling this story truthfully into other languages of India, together with its conceptual underpinnings, should not have been difficult. However, no such faithful translation was done until modern times even though there was no dearth of poets who did undertake the mammoth task of retelling Valmiki's story. Though, they did relate the same story, but their versions assumed tones and colours different from Valmiki's and presented absolutely different dimensions.

The major difference is the apotheosis of Rama from Man to God, as is evident in the clear and persistent presentation of Rama as Vishnu. While Valmiki tells us that Vishnu took human form to combat evil, his Rama is not worshipped as God. On the contrary, in the two most important north Indian versions, Krittivasa's 15th c. Bengali version and Tulsidas's 16th c. Hindi one, Rama's divinity is always the prime concern of the story. He is worshipped as God, rather than as warrior prince and his deeds are extolled as manifestations of divine power. What is more remarkable is the changeover from praise to devotion in retelling Rama's deeds, to the extent that both in Tulsi and Krittivasa the narrator assumes the position of total surrender to Rama. The story is thereby situated unavoidably within the bhakti culture. In that light, the divinity glorified is not merely the upholder of dharma but the source of such ecstasy that the worshipper has no option but to seek union with that divine being through complete surrender. Seen from this aspect, issues of social relations and political necessities do not vanish but they appear primarily as openings for declaring the glory of the deity.

In both Tulsi and Krittivasa, bhakti overpowers dharma. This reorientation demands recurrent reminders that Rama is God. For example, as the royal parties take leave from one another at the culmination of Rama and Sita's wedding, Tulsi offers a hymn of praise through Janaka's mouth in accordance with the spirit of bhakti (RCM.1, 340.4b-342.3a). In Valmiki's original, Janaka's concern is exclusively with social relations when he tells Rama: "*iyam Sita mama suta sahadharmacaritava*" (VR.1.63.26b-27a). Here he is reminding Rama of the responsibilities dictated by dharma. The most acclaimed remake of the Ramayana of our time, Ramanand Sagar's 1987 TV version, upholds rather the spirit of bhakti and prapatti or devotion and submission, and follows Tulsi, not Valmiki. In Sagar's Ramayana, Sita tells Rama "*ajna kijiye, main apki dasi hun*" (Command me, I am your handmaiden) (TVR. II. 148), her rhetoric of submission reflecting the spiritual idiom of bhakti as aptly as the politics of gender that epitomizes the world for which the film was made.

The culture of submission is not, however, quite consistent and Tulsi's absolute bhakti is not always visible in other poets in the bhakti tradition. His older contemporary, Krittivasa of Bengal, makes similar effort to project Rama as God in the audience's mind, and yet he cannot keep uncomfortable questions from coming up. In some ways, Krittivasa pushes the bhakti line even farther than Tulsi. For instance, when his Ravana lies dying on the battlefield, he admits that he considers Rama as the eternal Brahman (Brahma sanatana) at whose feet he seeks a place as a devotee (ciradin ami das carane tomar). Some of the rakshasas are devout vaishnavas who have chosen rebellion against virtue as the fastest way to get noticed by Rama. Nevertheless, Krittivasa's Sita accuses Rama of acting like a low-born, dishonorable man when he discards her after his victory. True, her accusation comes to nothing but the fact that it is included into the text, gives Krittivasa's work a degree of uncertainty unimaginable in Tulsi.

This ambivalence within the bhakti tradition seems distinctive of Ramayanas from both eastern and southern India. A close contemporary of Krittivasa was Shankaradeva of Assam, whose Sita says in the uttarakanda:

sabe bole enuvaramaka bhala bhala/
maito jano mora ramesa yamakala/
svami hena nidaruna kaita ache suni/

All speak well of Rama but I know that for me he is like Death itself. Tell me where there is so cruel a husband. (Smith, p. 99)

A much later poet, the very popular too, Dasu Ray follows Krittivasa and makes the raksasas devotees of Rama. When Hanuman enters Lanka, he is struck with wonder and he says:

ki ascarya mari mari/
raksasete bale Hari//

How astonishing, upon my life! Demons utter the name of the Lord. (Pancali, p. 51)

Yet, Dasu Ray injects a sharp note of doubt when he makes Agni comment on Sita's agni pariksha fire ordeal in these terms:

dekhilam eito a karya,
je din habe ra maraajya,
diner prati to emni bicar habe/
Now I see how it works:
The day Rama's reign begins
This is the justice that the powerless will get!
(Pancali, p.114)

In general, these retellings in the bhakti mode replace Valmiki's practical representation of the ethical fabric of a warrior culture with the values of a settled and conservative society. But at the same time, even within the apparently flawless belief system of bhakti, cracks do appear that suggest considerable discomfort with the brutalities of battle narratives and produce undercurrents of criticism against the dominance of bhakti.

The translation of Man into God replaces moralistic following with surrender as the conceptual epicentre of the Ramayana. This is not the place to think why this should have happened but we may note that it is part of a larger movement. Effective manifestation can be quoted from the Bhagavadgita, which remains perhaps the most significant and certainly most direct, moralistic work within that movement. When Krishna preaches Arjuna, "*sarvadharman parityajya mamekam sharanam vraja,*" (Bhattacharya: 18.66) he is demanding from Arjuna prapatti or surrender and asking him to place prapatti above his understanding of dharma. Contemporary Hindu beliefs and practices formulate for the devotee the ideal of bhakti, in which prapatti or surrender is the main concept and one that governs the religious and social world of that time. Not only the re-formed Ramayanas but the burgeoning avatara fables establish Rama as an accomplished God in place of Valmiki's warrior prince who is not God but god-like. Thus, Rama is seen as the absolute truth himself, and therefore, nothing he does can be challenged. For Tulsidas, Rama's reliability and compassion are so absolute that his Sita no longer remains the sahadharmini of Valmiki's tale but a devotee of Rama.

Readership and audience keep changing through time. Valmiki composed the epic *Ramayana* in Sanskrit which restricted his work for an elite group who could follow the language of the privileged class. It was meant to be heard and comprehended by them. They received instructions on ethical and moral problems through this epic, by the example of Rama's adherence to dharma. With the emergence of bhakti as a belief system particularly approachable to the masses in medieval times, the need for stories narrated in regional languages became strongly felt. The poets who took up the task of re-presenting Valmiki's *Ramayana* were clearly aiming at making it attainable to the mass audiences. They no longer attempted to produce "a warrior tale" preaching righteousness, and Rama ceased to be accepted mainly as a righteous and devout man. Rama was installed as "God" himself and moved ahead from being considered merely a part of Vishnu to full fledged Godhead by the time the first regional version was written. People were encouraged to surrender to the God Rama, who cannot be questioned. It was easier for people to identify with this mode of bhakti, which had soon achieved mass appeal. With the influence of a vast range of bhakti literature like *Harivamsha, Bhagavatapurana* and *Gîtagovinda* on the Vishnu/Krishna culture, and the influence of Sivabhakti and Vishnubhakti in Andhra, Tamilnadu, and Maharashtra, people were receptive to the concept of Rama as Brahman. The appeal of the Ramayana as a tale of bhakti was then a necessary and obvious reformation of a warrior tale into a dharmic tale.

Thus, we can conclude that writers and poets have not translated this effective tale, written by Adi-Kavi (the first poet) Valmiki in

Sanskrit, in their respective languages but have rewritten or recreated it according to the cultural influences of the times. When we try to deliver into our own idiom a narrative as huge as the Ramayana long after the social world that produced it has passed by, its narrative structure remains much the same but its conceptual substance and ideological core get lost. They are replaced by concepts and ideologies that are begotten out of a different world and sustain a different world. The history of the Ramayana exemplifies the manner in which the travels of a text through time, space and cultural forms test the limits of translation and thrust upon that text, new forms of thought, feeling and expression.

In his introduction of the book, *The Ramayana Revisited*, Mandakranta Bose makes a pertinent remark:

> The Ramayana has developed into a text of cultural hegemony affecting a wide array of modes of expression from academic articles to folk-art, sculptures, music and theatre and adapting in industrial age to film, comic books, and T.V. across the continents.

Works Cited

Bose, Mandakranta. (*ed.*) *The Ramayana Revisited.* New York: Oxford University Press, 2004.

Bhattacharyya, Shyamaprasad. (*ed.*) *Srimadbhagavadgita.* Calcutta: Nirmal Book Agency. (n.d)

Krittivasa. *Ramayana.* (*ed.*) B.Sil. Calcutta: Akshay Library,1954 [bangabda 1361].

Lutgendorf, Philip. *The Life of A Text.* Berkeley: University of California Press, 1991.

Pauwels, Heidi. *Only You: The Wedding of Rama and Sita, Past and Present.* In Bose, ed. The Ramayana Revisited, 2004.

Ranganathanda, Swami. cited in Subramaniam, K. *Ramayana* (8th ed.) Mumbai, India: Bharatiya Vidya Bhavan, 2003.

Ray, A. (*ed.*) *Dabrathi Rayera Pañcali.* Calcutta: Mahesh Library, 1997.

Richman, Paula. (*ed.*) *Many Ramayanas.* Berkeley: University of California Press, 1991.

Smith, William. *The Ramayana Tradition in Eastern India*. Stockholm: University of Stockholm, 1988.

Tulsidas, Goswami. *Sri Ramacharitmanas.* (*ed.*) H. Poddar, Gorakhpur: Gita Press, 1942/1990.

Valmiki. 1960-75. *Valmiki Ramayana,* 7 vols, general editors, G.H. Bhatta and U.P. Shah. Baroda: Oriental Institute.

Chomsky's Universal Grammar (UG): An Exploration

Dr. Raj Kumar Sharma

Introduction

Noam Chomsky, as the proponent of cognitivism in the second half of the 20th century, brought forth some novel ideas about the knowledge of language that revolutionized the whole corpus of linguistic studies. He proposed that all the human beings are endowed with innate language learning capacity. Our brain has a separate language faculty that is equipped with the grammar of all the human languages. The existence of this universal grammatical system located in the language faculty with potential to account for all the linguistic operations taking place in human languages is termed as UG. Depending on the response from the society in which we grow and use language, the grammar of that language gets activated. This external linguistic stimulus, that is technically called triggering experience, picks up that grammar which accounts for the sentences used in this language. This proposition is principally based on the observation that the properties of individual languages are extractions from a broad set that contains all the linguistic properties together in one whole. Each language of the world contains some of these properties with the help of which it functions. This broad whole consisting of all the linguistic properties exists as something hardwired in the language faculty of human brain. The exposure to the linguistic items of an individual language provides the natural stimulus for the learners which helps them in picking up the items of their mother tongue very fast as the rules governing this language already exist in their brain. The concept of UG is based on this principle. Chomsky, thus, considers UG as a system of principles, conditions and rules that are elements or properties of all the human languages.

The Basis of UG Theory

The advent of UG theory invoked a serious debate among the linguists who construed it as an extreme view. Hence, Chomsky provides a logical basis to his UG theory through the introduction of cross-linguistic data or evidences along with reliable laboratory operations. He says that a child uses sentences which he/she never hears. Technically, it is called poverty of the stimulus argument. A child produces unheard sentences only because of the subjection of the input (items of the mother tongue) to some mental operations, i.e. this input stimulates the hardwired linguistic apparatus, that is also called Language Acquisition Device (LAD), which processes it leading to the new kind of output (unheard sentences). This processing becomes possible only due to the innate linguistic endowment. Chomsky considers language faculty as a faculty independent of all other faculties of brain that contains the exclusive software for individual's linguistic affairs. This language faculty is the seat of UG which has a set of principles and parameters that determine the properties of human languages. He finds these principles as universal properties of languages such as, structure dependency, movement of Noun Phrases, embedding of clauses, etc. whereas parameters as the properties that vary from one language to another (discussed below). These language specific features in the form of principles and parameters are unique to the domain of language faculty which establishes its autonomous identity among all the faculties of the human mind. This set of principles and parameters may account for all possible grammatical constructions in all the human languages. Because of this set, a native speaker of a language intuitively understands the acceptable and deviant expressions of this language. Several researches conducted on children with a view to testing their native language ability approved the idea that they easily distinguish between correct and incorrect expressions without having grammatical ability to explain the nuances involved. This also lends credence to the theory of UG.

Further, several researches conducted in medical sciences have shown that some children suffer from certain linguistic disorders like aphasia, dyslexia, etc. which are directly associated with the deformities in the nervous system or genotypic traits. It supports the view of existence of separate language faculty as Chomsky claims. Apart from this, a corpus of research has proved that the growth of language among children takes place at a uniform pace without the role of conscious effort or external factor, i.e. cascade effect. Those children, who are brought up in a multi-lingual environment, pick up more than one language with equal dexterity or on a par with the children growing in monolingual settings. It indicates that the existence of UG facilitates the learning of many languages even at a very early stage. The researches conducted on establishing the relationship between language learning ability and IQ levels have proved that this ability is not directly related to the IQ levels. It has been seen that many children have astonishing language learning capacity despite low IQ and vice-versa. Children suffering from "Specific Language Impairment" show normal cognitive development. This dissociation between intelligence and language learning ability reinforces the biological endowment of UG. Various researches conducted on the language learning ability of animals have shown that they cannot learn discrete linguistic items like human beings regardless of the intense effort. Our much developed organs of speech also hint at the biological endowment of language. Moreover, the identification of speech control area inside the brain (Broca's area) supports the view of innateness hypothesis. All of these largely substantiate the relationship between human brain and linguistic manifestation that gives a strong basis to UG theory. Dobzhansky, a biochemist, found out in 1970 that "each individual's genotype determines the potential range of functional adaptations to the environment". This may rightly be applicable to the linguistic genotype of human beings that gets reflected as UG. The triggering experience provided by the environment sets the ball rolling resulting into the gradual development of linguistic faculty, the phenotypic manifestation. Much research is underway in neurolinguistics and many findings till date strongly support the Chomskyan view of UG as a reality.

The Notion of Principles and Parameters

Chomsky's theory of principles and parameters is very significant in the framework of Universal Grammar. This theory suggests that the knowledge of language that is innately endowed among human beings has a set of two kinds of linguistic features separately termed as principles and parameters. Those linguistic features which are common to all the languages, are universal principles, whereas those which vary from one language to another, are called parameters. These principles and parameters constitute the fundamental basis of UG that is accounted for the linguistic competence a child is born with, i.e. UG is present in a child's mind as a system of principles and parameters. The principles are fixed and constant elements marking the universal features of languages, and the parameters are some highly restricted variable elements specific to individual languages. It is important to have a look at some of the important principles and parameters observed in natural languages.

Major Principles of UG

Structure Dependency – It is a principle that proposes that all languages are structure dependent, i.e. the change in sequence of phrases that constitute sentences will alter the meaning or make the sentences ungrammatical. But it does not imply that all the languages have the same grammatical structure. We have "subject + verb + object" in English, whereas "subject + object + verb" in Hindi and Japanese. In order to produce different kinds of sentences in a language, we have a set of rules regarding structures that account for the grammaticality of sentences. Likewise, each language is structure dependent and any deviation from the rule bound structure will produce ungrammatical sentence. Chomsky says – "All known formal operations in the grammar of English, or of any other language, are structure-dependent" (1971).

Headedness Principle – This principle advocates that each phrase has a head word without which a phrase cannot exist. As we have seen earlier in the chapter syntax that a sentence consists of phrases and each phrase has a head word after which this phrase is named. For instance, a Noun phrase has a noun as the head word, a prepositional phrase has a preposition as the head word, etc. Look at the sentence "His son is at the gate" which has "son" as the head word of noun phrase, and "at" as the head of the prepositional phrase. Likewise, in the Hindi sentence "uska beta darwaje par hai" "beta" and "par" are the head words of noun and prepositional phrases.

Embedding Principle – It is a principle which states that subordinate clauses are embedded in languages in general. Look at these sentences of English and Hindi respectively – "He went when it was raining" and "*Wah gaya jab warsha ho rahi thi.*" The cases of embedding are commonly observed in French, Arabic and many Indian languages. This shows embedding as a universal principle which is applicable in natural languages.

Projection Principle – It proposes that the properties of words of a language determine the syntactic features, i.e. the structure of a sentence depends on the semantic feature of words used in it. As for instance, a verb like "give" will take a subject, a direct object, and an indirect object, for completion of a grammatical and meaningful sentence. A sentence "He gave a book to me" contains all the items given above, and so, it is a complete sentence. Look at these expressions:

He gave to me. (what)
He gave a book. (to whom)
He gave. (what)

All of these structures are incomplete syntactically as well as semantically that is because of the semantic property of the word "give". Likewise, there are words like "prefer" "buy" "weep," etc. which have semantic features that condition the structure of sentences accordingly. Such words are found in all the languages. In Hindi, the words like "*pitna*"(beat), "*dena*"(give), "*kharidana*" (buy), etc. have semantic features which determine the structure of sentences.

Maine use pita. (I beat him)
Usne mujhe ek kitab di. (He gave a book to me)
Usne ek kitab kharidi. (He bought a book)

These examples clearly show that the structures of these sentences are conditioned by the semantic features of the verbs used in them. All the words given above have semantic projections that need to be accommodated in syntactic frames permissible in a language.

Locality Principle – This principle states that grammatical operations are usually local in nature, i.e. these operations take place among the words which are physically close to each other in a sentence. An English sentence like – "He has been living in Delhi for ten years" has "has been" as auxiliary verb. When it is changed into an interrogative sentence, "has" is fronted, not "been". We say "Has he been living in Delhi for ten years"? We don't say "Been he has living in Delhi for ten years"? It shows that the auxiliary that is close to the subject is fronted conforming to the locality principle. Likewise in Hindi, a sentence like – "*Ram bhat aur Sita roti kha rahi thi*" (Ram was eating rice and Sita was eating bread), the verbal ending (feminine) is controlled by the subject (Sita) that is closer to the verb. It approves the locality principle.

Major Parameters of UG

Head Parameter – All the phrases that constitute a sentence have head words like noun for noun phrase, verb for verb phrase, preposition for prepositional phrase, etc. These head words have complements either before or after them varying across languages.

For example, in English, these complements appear after the head words and so, it is considered as head first language. Look at these constructions:

the book on the table ("on the table" complement of Noun)
prefer syntax ("syntax" complement of Verb)
in college ("college" complement of Preposition)

All these examples show that English is a head first language because heads appear before the complements. But Hindi is a language in which heads come after complements in expressions like – *table par* (on the table), *kamare me* (in the room), *Aman ka ghar* (house of Aman). So, Hindi is a head last language. On this basis, it is generalized that a language can be either head first or head last. This is called head parameter as it varies from one language to another unlike principles.

Pro-drop Parameter – There are some languages in which pronouns used as subjects are dropped in declarative sentences and a sentence starts with a finite verb. The languages like Arabic, Italian, Chinese, etc. have such structures. Since this phenomenon is language specific, it is a parameter. In Arabic, we say – *yathadat^h anlogalarabia* (He speaks English). In this expression of Arabic, there is no pronoun equivalent of "he" of English. It is different in English/Hindi where a pronoun used as a subject of a formal sentence can't be dropped. We can't say – "Am a teacher" in the place of "I am a teacher". Likewise in Hindi, we can't say – "*ek shikshak hun*" in the place of "*main ek shikshak hun*".

On the basis of the examples cited above, the difference between principles and parameters can be understood. Moreover, the principles are different from the traditional concept of rules in the sense that a rule is specific to a particular kind of construction of a language, whereas a principle is applicable to the constructions across the languages. The principles are the broadest constructs that subsume rules. Chomsky says, "The basic assumption of the Principle and Parameter model is that languages have no rules at all in anything like the traditional sense, and no grammatical constructions (relative clauses, passives, etc.) except as taxonomic artifacts" (1995). He does not view a language as a set of rules rather as a set of specifications in terms of parameters evolved in the light of the invariant principles. As for instance, the structure dependency is a principle that provides a broad framework inside which the system of language specific parametric variations like "s+v+o" or "s+o+v," etc. are introduced.

UG and Language Acquisition

The process of language acquisition holds a very significant place in the framework of UG. Actually, Chomsky's concept of UG derives its sustenance from some concrete observations and findings drawn from the domain of language acquisition only. The theory of UG foregrounds the process of language acquisition through which Chomsky convincingly extends his arguments of innate endowment. As per the conventions of UG, the language faculty of a child has a computational system along with principles and parameters that interacts with the input (external stimulus), i.e. the linguistic item of the mother tongue, and transforms it into something quite new (unheard sentences). Apart from this, there is space for lexicons that get activated with the listening of words of the mother tongue. When a child starts getting exposure to the items of his/her mother tongue, the computational system of the UG gets activated and starts acting upon this external stimulus. It gradually sets the parameters for this mother tongue as they vary across languages, whereas principles contained in this mother tongue stand in tune with invariant universal principles already existing there in the language faculty. Further, Chomsky talks of "fixed principles governing possible sound systems" and "a rich and invariant conceptual system" as the contents of UG that may reasonably be considered as parts of the universal principles (1988). All of these principles and parametres work in coordination in the course of interaction with the external stimulus which results into the creation of a core grammar of the mother tongue that helps a child produce grammatical sentences.

Here, acquiring a language, thus, means setting the values for all the parameters such as, for English, head first, non-pro-drop, etc. and for Hindi, head last, non-pro-drop, etc. which we have already seen earlier in this chapter. The vocabulary items are acquired with the help of principles governing sound systems that deal with pronunciation, and projection principles that introduce syntactic restrictions depending on the properties of words. Likewise, the different aspects of the mother tongue are taken care of by different kinds of principles and parameters resulting into its complete acquisition. At this stage of acquisition, a child develops the grammatical competence (core grammar) that is fully determined by the governing principles, parameters and vocabulary items that account for the properties of his/her mother tongue. But it doesn't mean that all aspects of a language are fully covered by UG. For instance, in English, irregular verbs, concepts of plurality in certain words (sheep, cattle, man) etc. are the aspects which go unaccounted by UG. Chomsky defends it by bringing forth the concept of core and periphery grammar, in which, the core accounts for all the features covered by UG, whereas periphery accounts for those which are not covered by it. Therefore, the acquisition or learning of such irregular verbs of English appears to be challenging for native children as well as the non-native adult learners who learn it as a second/foreign language. Since the domain of language is very vast, UG can't be held responsible for non-inclusion of such peripheral aspects of languages which can be seen as gradual additions to linguistic repertoire resulting from sociolinguistic interactions.

Thus, we see that UG provides a logical account of language acquisition. The linguistic competence of a child consists of the activation of the principles, setting of the parameters and creation of the core grammar. This competence enables the native speakers of a language to make distinction between grammatical and deviant structures intuitively. The goal of linguists working in Chomskyan tradition, who are called generativists, is to enquire about the nature of this intuitive linguistic competence. They are entrusted with the task of bringing out theories regarding language acquisition in different languages which may determine the principles of UG along with parametric variation in the language in question on the basis of the input (linguistic items) and creation of the core grammar as a result of interaction among these components. A theory that clearly outlines all such aspects of a language is supposed to have attained explanatory adequacy according to Chomsky.

Some Major Theories of UG

Since UG intends to encapsulate the universal attributes of languages and tries to formulate theories that may account for the linguistic operations in all the human languages, Chomsky has evolved certain theories in the framework of principles and parameters that help us understand the universal grammatical features from a different perspective. He suggests that different theories working within the domain of principles and parameters, are involved in the construction of sentences, and each theory may be independent of others, which is technically known as the modular approach. Here, each theory is regarded as a separate module and a sentence is viewed as a product of complex networking of these modules. Now, let us have a look at these theories.

X-bar Theory – This theory deals with the phrasal structure/ constituents of sentences in human languages. The theory claims that each sentence of a language is a combination of phrases (Noun phrase, Verb phrase, Adjective phrase, Prepositional phrase) which have head words belonging to the same lexical categories, i.e. a noun will be the head word of an NP, a verb will be the head word of a VP, and so on. This can be represented as phrasal constituents in English sentences in this theory in the same way it is represented in syntax. All the constituents of a phrase can be shown at the same level. The following diagram makes the idea more clear.

a. a book on the table (NP)

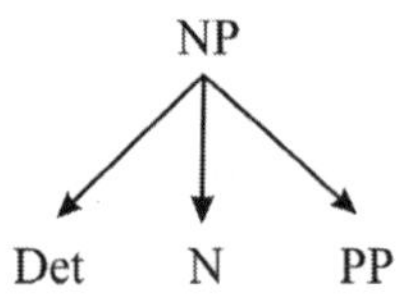

b. Bought a book from a shop (VP)

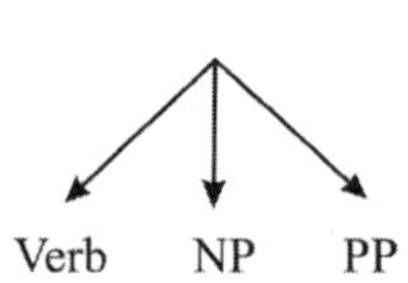

Both of these examples show that all the constituents of NP and VP have been kept at the same level as they are all sister nodes. This representation doesn't show the hierarchical relationship among the sister nodes due to which we cannot understand the degree of closeness existing among these constituents. For example, in "a" the relationship between "det" and "N" is not the same as is the relationship between "N" and "PP." Likewise, in "b" the relationship between "Verb" and "NP" is different from the relationship that exists between "V" and "PP." The above representation fails to capture such differences in the relationship of the different constituents which is considered as an inadequacy. The X-bar theory proposes a hierarchical structure of phrases that introduces an intermediate level which clearly shows the relationship among the constituents, and adds to the explanatory adequacy of sentences across the languages in the framework of principles and parameters theory.

Chomsky says "Phrases typically consist of a head and an array of complements determined by the lexical properties of the head" (1986). The implication is that a head stands in a very close relationship with that phrase which functions as its complement compared to other phrases which function like adjunct. To make it more clear, a complement is a complete phrase in itself that makes the meaning of the head complete in terms of its lexical projection. A complement in this sense can be an object (NP), a prepositional phrase, etc. depending on the requirement of lexical projection. An adjunct on the other hand gives extra information in a sentence and does not remain strongly bound to the head like complements. According to Chomsky, an X-bar structure is composed of projections of heads selected from the lexicon (1993). He talks of maximal projection shown as X" (with double bar), intermediate projection shown as X' (with single bar), and minimal projection shown as X (without a bar). The structure of a phrase in the scheme of X-bar theory appears as follows.

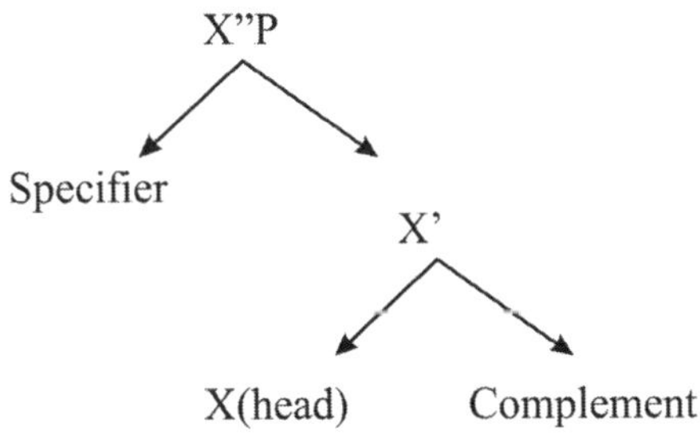

This structure is the basic frame of X-bar structure through which the different elements of a phrase are represented. Here, X stands for any lexical phrase like Noun, Verb, Adjective, Preposition. A specifier comes in the place of determiner which is a functional category as this structure takes into account functional categories except the head for which lexical category is used. A specifier is that word which precedes the head of its containing phrase. Determiners are specifiers as they appear before the head words of the phrase of which they are parts. The specifiers are much inclusive and so, it becomes convenient to present distinctive features of phrases with their help. The X" is the intermediate level which is the sister node of "specifier." A complement is the sister node of the head (lexical category). Since this structure includes lexical (formal) as well as functional categories into account, it is called cross categorial representation of phrases as the head represents the lexical category (noun, verb, adjective, preposition) and other items represent functional categories (complement, specifier, adjunct). In this structure, an adjunct appears as the sister node of X", the intermediate level if it is a part of the phrase. Let us see some examples.

a. "a book of English"

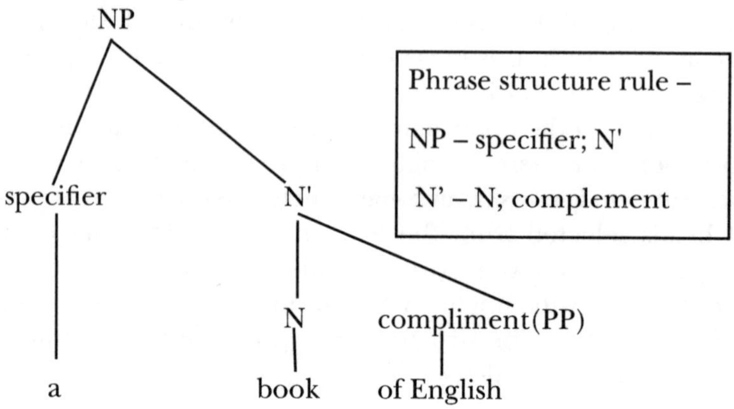

b. "very mad after cricket"

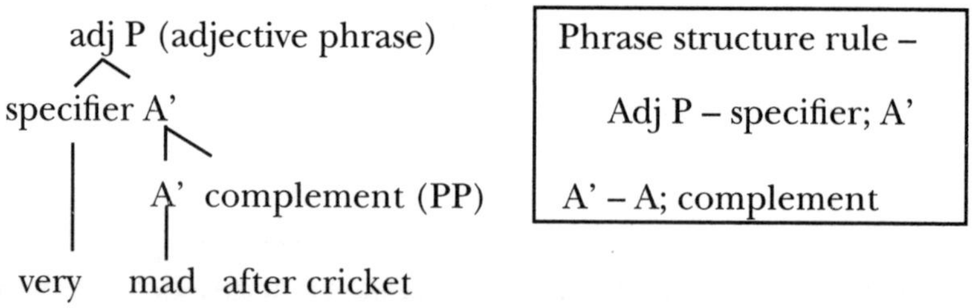

c. " read a novel in the class "

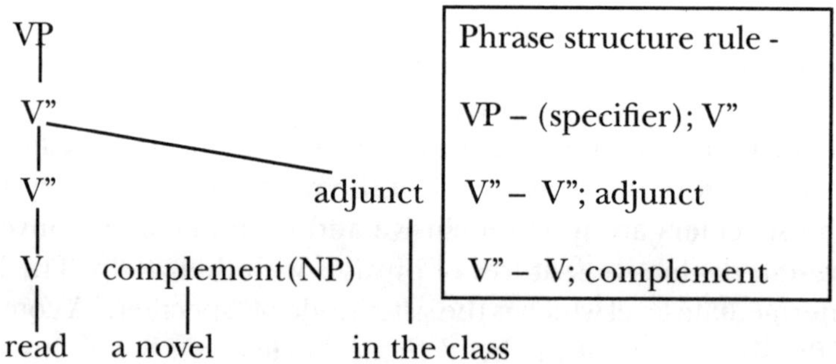

Thus it is seen that X-bar structure clearly shows the hierarchical relationship existing among the constituents of various phrases. It is very clear from the given diagrams that a complement is the sister node of the head, whereas an adjunct is the sister node of single bar level above the head. It represents the degree of relationship between the head, its complement and adjunct which was a major inadequacy of the flat tree diagrams in which all of these constituents were represented at the same level.

In terms of phrase structural rules, X-bar theory does not propose any order of occurrence between the constituents, i.e. a complement may come before a head or after a head depending on the nature of a language. Since English is a head first language as it has been seen earlier, the head comes before the complement. In Hindi, a phrase like – "*Sudhir ki kitab*" (Sudhir's book) will be represented as follows.

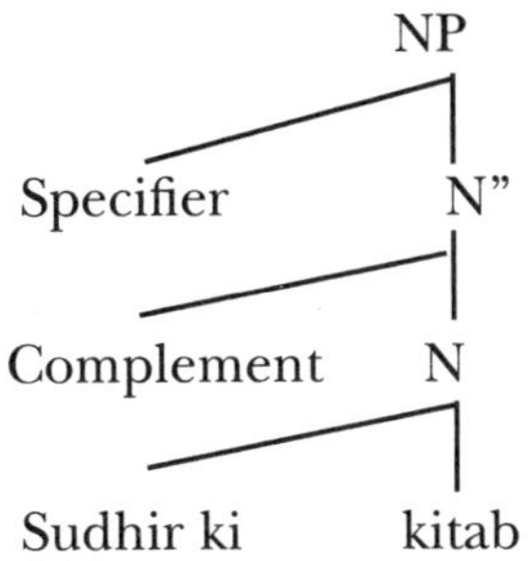

Phrase structure rule –

NP – N"; specifier

N" – N; complement

Here, it is seen that the head is preceded by the complement reflecting head last feature. Thus X-bar theory attempts to capture the universal feature of hierarchical structure of phrases in human languages as a principle and gives space for the accommodation of parametric variation across them conforming to the principles and parameters theory.

Theta (Ø) theory – This theory proposes a systematic explanation of the lexical projections of grammatical entities that determine the syntactic features of a sentence across the languages in the framework of principles and parameter theory. It states that the semantic range of grammatical entities like verbs, prepositions, adjectives, etc. play a very important role in the construction of a sentence. Let us look at some sentences.

a. Ram sent a letter to his father.

b. She wrote a book.

c. I smile usually.

We see that lexical features of the verbs in all of these sentences determine the structure of these sentences, i.e. "send" needs a sender, something (letter) to send, and a receiver. Thus, a sentence with "send" as the main verb will be complete and acceptable only if it has got all the constituents given above. Likewise, we find that "write" as a verb needs a writer and a product (book) that is written. A verb like "smile" needs someone to do the act of smiling. These are the minimum requirements of such verbs to produce a meaningful sentence. All such grammatical entities that largely determine the structure of a sentence are technically called predicates. This concept of predicate is not to be confused with the traditional concept of predicate of a simple sentence. A verb like "send" thus, is a three place predicate as it essentially needs three elements, a verb like "write" is a two place predicate that needs two essential elements, and a verb like "smile" is a one place predicate as it needs one essential element. All these essential elements are called the arguments of their predicates, i.e. the verb "send" has three arguments and likewise the case with "write" that has two arguments, and "smile" has one argument. These arguments are the referring entities realized as persons, things, etc. and can rightly be considered as parts of lexical projections of the predicates.

The theta theory advocates that a predicate assigns certain roles to its arguments which are called thematic roles. These thematic roles are identified as an agent (doer of an action), a patient (receiver of an action), a theme (thing affected by an action), a goal (beneficiary of an action), etc. For instance, in sentence "a" given above "Ram" is the agent (subject argument), "letter" is the theme (NP argument), and "his father" is the goal (NP argument). In sentence "b" "she" is the agent (subject argument), and "book" is the theme (NP argument). In sentence "c," there is only an agent that is subject argument. All of these arguments emanate from the lexical properties of their respective predicates. As regards the relationship between arguments and theta roles, each argument of a predicate is assigned one theta role, and each theta role is assigned to only one argument. This is called theta criterion. A sentence can be a grammatical construction only if this criterion is fulfilled. Let us see a sentence with an adjectival predicate.

He is jealous of me.

In this sentence, the adjective predicate "jealous" has two arguments "he" and "of me" because someone has to practise jealousy, and for this act to be practised, a stimulant (me) is required. These two arguments assign two theta roles (each argument one theta role), "he" as the agent and "of me" as the theme. This fulfils the theta criterion and the sentence becomes complete as an expression like "he is jealous " cannot be considered complete unless the cause of jealousy is given, i.e. jealous of what. In the examples discussed above, we see that a predicate has arguments to its left (before the predicate) and right (after the predicate), if there are two arguments of it as is the case with "jealous." In this case, "he" is considered as external argument (subject argument), and "of me" as internal argument (complement argument). In English language, the position of these two kinds of arguments is to the left and right of the predicate, i.e. subject argument appears to the left and complement argument appears to the right. Now, let us look at these Hindi sentences.

Usne ek kitab likhi (He wrote a book).

Maine use pita (I beat him).

In the first sentence, the subject argument for the verbal predicate "*likhi*" is "*usne*" and the complement argument is "*ek kitab.*" This subject argument is assigned the theta role of agent, and complement argument is assigned the theta role of theme. Likewise, in the second sentence, the subject argument is "*maine*" for the verbal predicate "*pita,*" and the complement argument is "*use.*" These two arguments assign the theta roles of agent and patient to "*maine*" and "*use*" respectively. Thus, the theta criterion is fulfilled in both the sentences. Further, we see that both the arguments appear to the left of the predicate, subject argument is followed by the complement argument. This feature which varies across languages is captured by parametric variations.

Government and Case Theory – The theory of government talks about the relationship among different constituents of a sentence basically in terms of the governor and the governed. We see that certain features of some constituents of a sentence restrict the choice of some other constituents in the same sentence. The constituents that impose such restrictions are governors, and the constituents that are realized as resultant forms of such impositions, are governed. This relationship between governor and governed can be understood in a better way with the illustrations of grammatical cases in sentences.

In English sentences, the object of a verb is realized in the accusative case, while its subject is realized in the nominative case. Look at the sentence – "He called me" in which the case features of "he" (nominative case) and "me" (accusative case) are determined by the verb "call." Hence, this verb is the governor, and its subject and object are governed. This verbal constituent restricts the choice of grammatical case, as we cannot use "him" or "I" in the place of "he" and "me" respectively. Likewise, a preposition governs its object as its accusative form can only occur after it. In a sentence like – "They talked about me" we cannot use "I" in the place of "me." A preposition, thus, restricts the choice of case of its object. So, this preposition is a governor, and its object is governed.

The case theory in the frame of UG proposes that in any sentence some constituents are case assigners and some are the receivers of cases. For example, verbs and prepositions are case assigners as they assign accusative cases to their objects as we saw in the examples given above. We have already seen in the previous chapters that tense is an integral part of a finite verb and it conditions the choice of a subject. So, it is assumed that this tense assigns nominative cases to subjects, whereas the lexical verb assigns accusative case to its object in English sentences. There is physical proximity between the constituents in case assignment, i.e. the assigner and the assigned are immediate constituents, as a tense assigns case to its immediate left (subject position), and a verb assigns case to its immediate right (object position). A preposition occurs just before its object. Government and Case theory is part of universal principles found across the languages. The diversity observed in the direction of case assignment and the physical proximity among the constituents of sentences of a language is subject to parametric variation. Look at these sentences of Hindi.

> "*unlogon ne use mara*" (They hit him.)
> "*wah mere sath gaya*" (He went with me.)

Here, "*unlogon*" has nominative case and "*use*" has accusative case. Both of these words are assigned cases from the finite verb that has tense as an integral part. The lexical verb "*marana*" assigns accusative case to its object "*use*," and its past tense assigns nominative case to the subject "unlogaon." Thus the case assigners are governors that determine the cases of subject and object like English sentences. Further, the preposition "sath" assigns accusative case to its object "mere," and the tense of intransitive verb assigns nominative case to the subject. It is relevant to mention that an intransitive lexical verb does not assign case as it has no object. So, a preposition is a governor that assigns accusative case to its object.

In both of these sentences, we find that the proximity as well as the direction between the assigner and the assigned is different from what we found in English. Because of the structural difference between Hindi and English sentences, here, tense assigns nominative case to the subjects but they are not immediately left to the tense. Further, the verb, in the first sentence, assigns objective case to its object which is to its left unlike English where the object comes immediately after the verb. Moreover, preposition in Hindi is preceded by its object unlike English where the object of a preposition succeeds it. These differences are accommodated under the heading parametric variations in the frame of UG.

Binding Theory – This theory deals with the relationship existing between noun phrases and some forms of pronouns like reflexives (himself, myself), reciprocals (each other, one another), and pronominals (him, them), in a sentence. The term "binding" implies syntactic and semantic bonds of such pronouns with noun phrases they refer to. Technically, reflexives and reciprocals are also called anaphors as they refer to specific nouns in a sentence, and such nouns are known as antecedents. The nouns or pronouns which occupy the subject positions are called referring expressions. Let us look at these sentences.

a. They praise themselves.
b. We like each other.
c. Pratyush beats him.

In the first sentence, "themselves" refers to "they;" in the second sentence, "each other" refers to "we;" but in the third sentence, "him" does not refer to "Pratyush." The pronominal "him" refers to an entity outside the domain of the given sentence. The binding theory attempts to explore the dimension of such relationships in a sentence with an eye to the grammaticality involved in the framework of UG. The anaphors and their antecedents are co-indexed that is represented with the symbol (i) in a sentence. Now consider these sentences.

Ram said that his friend killed himself.
I like my students to study themselves.

Here, "himself" refers to "his friend" not to Ram, and "themselves" refers to "my students" not to "I." It establishes that the concept of binding operates in a local domain, i.e. the anaphors and the antecedents exist within the same clause as is the case in the given sentences. On the basis of these observations, it is deduced under the heading binding theory that –

a. Anaphors are bound as they refer to their antecedents in a sentence.
b. Pronominals are free as they refer to the entity outside the domain of the sentence.

c. Antecedents / referring expressions are also free like pronominals. Let us see its implications in Hindi. Look at these sentences.

> *Ramesh apni prashansa karata hai* (Ramesh praises himself.)
> *Ramesh uski prashansa karata hai* (Ramesh praises him.)
> *Ramesh ne kaha ki uska dost apni prashansa karata hai* (Ramesh said that his friend praises himself.)

In the first sentence, "apni" is anaphor with Ramesh as its antecedent. In the second sentence, "uski" is the pronominal referring to an entity outside the domain of the sentence. In the third sentence, "*apni*" refers to "*uska dost*" not to Ramesh, which indicates the operation taking place in a local domain, i.e. inside a clause, as we saw in the case of English sentences. It shows that this theory is applicable across the languages. Certain structural differences in sentences of different languages may be explained in terms of parametric variations.

Thus, we see that all these theories mentioned above corroborate to the concept of UG, as they are applicable across the languages. Each of these theories is independent of others but they interweave a pattern that accounts for almost all the grammatical operations with the help of which a language works. For instance, the implications of theta theory, projection principles, case theory, etc., are always there in the production of a grammatical structure but there is ample scope of autonomy with which each one of these theories can be looked into. This view justifies the modular approach adopted to interpret linguistic phenomena under the framework of UG.

Minimalism: The Latest Innovation

Chomsky has been modifying his theories of UG since the inception of cognitivism. After having realized the complexities, and to some extent, inadequacies of the principles and parameter theory in interpretation and analysis of the true nature of language, he shifted his focus towards economy and precision in presentation and derivation of universal features of languages under the concept "minimalism." He lays emphasis on phonetic and semantic components of language in minimalism and considers them to be sufficient to account for various linguistic phenomena. Chomsky puts it like "Each language can be regarded as a particular relationship between sound and meaning" (1972). Any language basically operates with sound-meaning interface.

We listen to sounds of a language that are transformed into meanings by certain mental operations making the act of communication possible. The physical realization of the phonetic component of a language undergoes a computational system inside the mind that changes these signals into meanings, the semantic component of a language. The response of mind to the phonetic component is governed by sensorymotor system, whereas its transformation into semantic component is governed by conceptual-intentional system. Both of these systems work at the point of interface, i.e. at the point of interaction of PF and LF with the computational system. The sensorymotor system responds to the external stimulus (sound) and modifies it according to the requirement of the computational system for further processing. The conceptual-intentional system integrates the modified linguistic input with the object (concrete) or idea (abstract) that this input intends to refer.

This process can be seen in this figure.

Phonetic Form (PF)	Computational System (application of principles and parameters)	Semantic/ Logical Form (LF)
(sensorymotor system)		(conceptual-intentional system)

The semantic form is realized in a logical form as meaning is derived based on logic with the application of syntactic rules in computational system. Actually, syntax plays a very vital role inside the computational system. For instance, look at the sentence "That boy is intelligent." Here, the sounds of the words that appear in a sequence are interpreted in terms of syntactic rules operational inside the computational system resulting into the logical derivation of the meaning. Because of this, the semantic component represents a logical form. This logical form represents that partial meaning which is determined by the syntactic structure. This meaning undergoes contextual interpretation leading to the final semantic component. The syntactic structure plays a central mediating role between the physical form (phonetic component) and abstract meaning (semantic component). This computational system applies the theories of principles and parameters, such as structure dependency, projection principles, theta theory, etc. on the input, i.e. phonetic component. This application transforms the phonetic data into meaningful units.

As regards the system of computation, Chomsky talks of mental lexicon. Each individual has a set of lexical entries (words) inside the mental faculty that contains lexical properties of these items as well. These lexical items realized in phonetic form are subjected to syntactic operations that take into account their projection properties. For instance, a word like "help" has to be tested in terms of its lexical projection, that is to say, whether it has a subject and an object. This word "help" needs someone as a helper and someone to be helped as we have already seen in projection principles. The computational system sets the order of the words depending on the information it has about these words in the mental lexicon. The sequence of words so evolved becomes an acceptable grammatical structure leading to a logical meaning.

Chomsky's emphasis on mental lexicon in minimalism as a concept draws our attention towards his relentless effort made in the direction of establishing a concrete link between the linguistic manifestation of human beings as living entities and our mental faculties. He points out, "Current understanding falls well short of laying the basis for the unification of the sciences of the brain and higher mental faculties, language among them" (2005). Much research is underway in the area of mental lexicon today which is largely inspired by the Chomskyan ideology. Minimalism as the latest theoretical advancement in the tradition of UG, is truly an extension of his previously advocated principles and parameters theory which has been adequately and reasonably accommodated in the computational system of the current theory.

Works Cited

Chomsky, N. *Syntactic Structures.* NY: Mouton de Gruyter, 1957.

Chomsky, N. *Aspects of the Theory of Syntax.* Massachusetts: MIT Press, 1965.

Chomsky, N. *Current Issues in Linguistic Theory.* Paris: Mouton, 1970.

Chomsky, N. *New Horizons in the Study of Language and Mind.* Cambridge: CUP, 2000.

Chomsky, N. *Minimalist Programme.* Massachusetts: MIT, 1995.

Haegeman, L. *Introduction to Government and Binding Theory.* Oxford: Blackwell Publishers, 1991.

Radford, A. *An Introduction to English Sentence Structure.* Cambridge: Cambridge University Press, 2009.

Difficulties in Teaching Nominal Relative Clauses

Dr. Harish Kumar Khanna
Dr. Satyendra Kumar

INTRODUCTION:

The use of relative pronouns is one of the ways to bring coherence in a piece of writing. There are overt as well as covert Relative Pronouns/adverbs in languages. It is often seen that in context the *nominal relative clauses* are preferred to relative clauses in general.

1. WHAT IS A RELATIVE CLAUSE?: A relative clause is a part of a complex sentence which describes a noun/pronoun, it follows. In other words, when two or more sentences are combined, the second identical noun/pronoun is replaced by a relative pronoun(RP). See the following examples:

1. **I have a** shirt. **John brought** it **for me. = I have** the shirt that **John brought for me.**

2. He teaches different subjects. It is good for the department.
= **He teaches different subjects, which** is good for the department.

In (1),"***a shirt***" and "**it**" are identical. The RP "**that**" replaces "**it**" referring to "***a shirt,***" the object of the matrix clause which is its antecedent, whereas in (2), "**He teaches different subjects**" and "it" are identical. The RP "**which**" replaces "it" referring to the whole matrix clause which is its antecedent.

2. A NOMINAL RELATIVE CLAUSE: In general an RP is controlled by its antecedent(noun/pronoun/clause) preceding it. Generally, the antecedent is adjacent to the RP. "When it is difficult to refer to something by using a noun group, a special kind of relative clause called a nominative relative clause, Collin Co-build English Grammar(1990). In other words, the nominal relative clause is the one which has its antecedent (in context) outside the sentence or clause. The nominal relative pronoun WHAT being more self contained (merged with its antecedent) is preferred to a regular relative pronoun(RP, such as that/which) in context.

See the following examples:

3. a. I will give you **the thing** (that) you want. (Relative Clause)
   b. I will give you **what** you want. (Nominal Relative Clause)
4. a. Burger is **the fast food** that children like. (Relative Clause)
   b. Burger is **what** children like. (Nominal Relative Clause)

"What" in 3 refers to its antecedent in context whereas in 4 "burger," its antecedent in the main clause inside the sentence. The clause containing "wh-element" is termed as "Nominal Relative Clause" (as mentioned above) since they come in nominal positions and modify some noun in context and the "wh-element" WHAT is termed as "Nominal relative pronoun."

3. Preference: The use of Nominal relative clauses is preferred over relative clauses in general as the expression looks natural and conveys the exact meaning intended in context, moreover, the nominal RP brings logical coherence in the meaning. The sentences 3b-4b are more natural than the sentences (3a-4a).

4. Grammatical Functions and Nominal Relative Pronouns: The Nominal Relative pronoun "WHAT"occupies the positions of all grammatical functions namely, as subject, object, object complement, and object to preposition as shown below:

5. This is **what** made me angry.

Subject

6. He gave me **what** you gave him.

Object

7. You are **what** he is.

Complement (subject)

8. We are **what** our parents made us.

Complement object

9. Listen to **what** he is listening to.

Object to preposition

5. Anaphoric and Cataphoric references of the Nominal Relative Pronoun: The examples given above are evident that the RPs need their antecedents overtly and nominal RPs need their antecedent present outside the clause or in the context. Following are the examples proving that the nominal relative pronoun WHAT obligatorily needs its antecedent.

10. **Computer** is **what** he sells.

11. Patience is **what** I need to have.

The nominal Relative Pronoun has both anaphoric as well as cataphoric references. In(10-11) WHAT has an anaphoric reference. It has its antecedent as "**computer**" and "**patience**" respectively in the subject position, whereas in (12-13), below, the nominal relative pronoun has cataphoric references.

12. **What** he sells is computers.

13. **What** I need to have is patience.

In (12-13) WHAT has its antecedent "**computers**" and "**patience**" respectively in the complement position.

6. POTENTIAL AND LONG DISTANCE ANTECEDENTS OF THE NOMINAL RELATIVE PRONOUN: In the examples above the nominal relative pronoun WHAT has its anaphoric/cataphoric reference, which is outside the clause but within the sentence. Let us see the following sentences:

14. He teaches **English**. **This** was **what** I hate.

15. A: **He comes late**. B: **This** is **what** makes me angry.

In (14-15), there seem to be two antecedents of WHAT, namely potential and long distance. In (14) "**this**" is a potential antecedent, not the logical(real) one as far as semantic account goes. In fact, in (14), "WHATî refers to **this** and in return this refers to ambiguously either to "**English**" or the whole sentence "**He teaches English.**" On the other hand, in (15), WHAT again refers to "**this**" and in return **this** refers to the whole sentence "**He comes late.**" It means **what** (in 14-15) may sometimes depend on its long distance (logical) antecedent for the complete meaning as the potential (grammatical) antecedent in the above examples fails to do so. We can conclude that in general the antecedent of WHAT is always outside its clause. Whether it is a potential one (near) or logical (near/distant). Let us see what kind of antecedent WHAT has in the following sentences:

16. **What** he gave me was nice.
(= **The thing that** he gave me was nice.)
17. I brought **what** I like.
(= I brought **the thing that** I like.)
18. I will follow **what** you say.
(= I will follow **the thing that** you say.)

It was observed in (14-15) that the antecedent of WHAT is overtly present in the sentence. But in (16-18) above, there is no overt antecedent of WHAT, rather an abstract element referring to something/someone = the thing/the one, in general, but it is not clear at all what exactly something/someone refers to, which is purely implied.

7. SEMANTICS OF WHAT: As discussed above the nominal relative pronoun "what" has its antecedent outside the clause or in the context (abstract), but "what" has different semantic interpretation in different contexts as shown below:

WHAT as a nominal relative pronoun is used when the speaker/ listener

a	b	c	d
doesn't want to DISCLOSE to others what he is telling/asking the speaker/ listener (to do).	does/doesn't do THE SAME AS the speaker/ listener says/ does/likes etc.	mentions the thing which is VISIBLE/ CLEAR.	mentions something (exclusively) as a whole completely (=all).

Let us see the following examples:

19. I didn't see **what** you told me. (a)
20. He will eat **what** you have cooked. (a)
21. We will eat **what** you all eat. (b)
22. Do **what** he does. (b)
23. **What** I brought is this. (c)
24. **What** he taught was this. (c)
25. **What** he had in the shop is this. (d)
26. **What** you will have to do is this. (d)

We can reach at the conclusion that the use of nominal RP "WHAT" is context based where there can be an overt or covert antecedent of "what" as discussed above.

8. NOMINAL RELATIVE CLAUSES AND WH-CLEFT CLAUSES: In discourse it is common to lay emphasis on certain words/phrases in the sentences to highlight it as far as semantic interpretation goes. For the same purpose the Nominal Relative Clause in Embedded clauses can be fronted in order to focus the thing that you are talking about or to introduce a new topic or to correct a question, statement or assumption. This fronting is known as (regular) *wh*-clefting. It is important to note that this is possible only when the meaning of WHAT is the same as mentioned in (7 c-d) above (otherwise it is not possible, see below, reverse wh-clefts), the sentences (23-26) are examples of *wh*-clefting.

9. THE REVERSE WH-CLEFTS: The examples (23-26) show the cases of clefting. What has to be noted is that the wh-clause in the sentences (23-26) can be reversed, that is, the embedded clause moves to the complement position of the main sentence, which is termed as reverse wh-clefting as shown below:

27. This is **what** I brought.
28. This is **what** I taught.
29. This is **what I** had in the shop.
30. This is **what** you will have to do.

The sentences containing *wh*-clefts and reverse *wh*-clefts can be represented as shown below:

Regular wh-clefts – XYZ(where X = *wh*-cleft clause, Y= nite verb, Z = complement) ↓

Reverse wh-clefts – ZYX

31. **What** I hate is English. = English is **what** I hate.
    X Y Z Z Y X
32. **What** he said was that he didn't like the play. = That he didn't like the play was **what** he said.
    X Y Z Z Y X

(Angela Downing and Philip Locke, 2006) But every time *wh-* cleft clause cannot be reversed. Note that WHAT can be a part of cleft clause or reverse cleft clause. It is interesting to note that if the antecedent of WHAT is clearly mentioned in the clause/sentences it can be reversed, on the other hand when the antecedent of WHAT is an abstract element, it is not the case of clefting. See below:

33. *What he did* was that he went to the principal. (*wh*-cleft)
34. *What he did* was horrible. (nominal relative clause)
35. What he writes makes me happy. (nominal relative clause)
    The first(33) is a *wh*-cleft, corresponding to the plain version *He said that he didn't like the play* whereas (36-37) are NOT *wh*-cleft as there is no corresponding form as
    **He said very interesting/pleased me.*
    Another way to test this is to try for reversibility. (33) is reversible, but (34-35) are not(Angela Downing and Philip Locke ibid), see below:
36. That he went to the Principal was what he said.(33)
37. *Horrible was what he said. (34)
38. *makes me happy was what he said.(35)

10. THE PROBLEMS FOR THE L_2 LEARNERS: In Synthesis the clauses play important roles, in the sense that two sentences are combined into one using a relative clause. While learning regular Relative clauses, the L_2 learner is taught that the second identical noun/pronoun is replaced by one of RPs. Keeping this in mind the mistake he makes is that he places Nominal Relative pronoun after overt noun resulting in the ungrammatical expression. See the following examples:

39. I have the book(that/which) you brought for me.
40. *I have that you brought for me.
41. This is what you brought for me.
42. *I have the book what you brought for me.

In (38), the RP(regular) may be optional, when it precedes a noun, and (39), the RP is present but doesn't precede the noun hence ruled out. (40) is OK as the nominal RP doesn't precede a noun if it does, it results in an ungrammatical sentence as shown in (41). The data interpreted above reveals that when the learner comes to know that "what" cannot follow a noun and becoming over-conscious uses a regular RP in place of a nominal RP, shown in (39) and uses "what" in place of a regular RP as shown in (41).

The above examples reveal that the problem can be overcome when the learners are taught the use of"WHAT" along with the normal RPs (which, that, etc.) at intermediate level. Using the communicative and the task based exercises, the L_2 learner may be made to master this construction and to make the difference between the regular and nominal relative pronouns as far as its usage is concerned.

Conclusion

The present paper talked about the importance of using Nominal Relative Clauses and the difficulties the learners face using this construction. The syntactic and semantic aspects of Nominal Relative Clauses were discussed. It was emphasized that WHAT (merged with its antecedent) comes in all grammatical positions in the embedded sentences, whether the embedded sentence comes initially or medially or finally. It was also emphasized that the semantic range of WHAT affects the structure of the sentence, in the sense that it can occur in cleft and reverse *wh*-cleft sentences only when the antecedent of WHAT is overtly present in the clause/sentence, whereas, elsewhere it is not. It is suggested that using communicative approach and task-based exercises to teach such topics in context, the students can be made to be comfortable using Nominal Relative Clauses.

Works Cited

Azar, Betty Schrampfer. *Understanding and Using English.* New York: Pearson Education, 10 Bank Street, White Plains, 2002.

Bier, D., Johnson, S.; Leach, G.; Conard, S. and Finegan, E.. *Longman Grammar of Spoken and Written English.* Longman, 1999.

Crystal, D. *The Cambridge Encyclopaedia of the English Language.* Cambridge: Cambridge University Press, 1995.

Crystal, D. *A Dictionary of Linguistics and Phonetics.* Blackwell Publishing, 2008.

Ehrlich, Eugene. *English Grammar.* The McGraw-Hill Companies, 1991.

Greenbaum, Sidney. *English Grammar.* Oxford University Press, 1996.

Huddleston, R., Pullu, G.K., et al. *The Cambridge Grammar of the English Language.* Cambridge: Cambridge University Press, 2003.

Mala, Marcela. Syntactic and Semantic Differences between Nominal Relative Clauses and Dependent wh-Interrogative Clauses, in *Theory and Practice in English Studies.* 3(2005): Proceedings from the English Conference of British, American and Canadian Studies, Brno: Masarykova Univerzita, 2005.

Murphy, Raymond. *English Grammar in Use.* Cambridge: Cambridge University Press, 2004.

Swan Michael. *Practical English Usage.* Oxford University Press, 2002.

William Collins Sons & Company. *Collins Cobuild English Grammar.* Collins Publishers, The University of Birmingham, 1990.

Dramas of Girish Karnad: Reshaping the Mind through Myth and History

Dr. D.N. Sinha
Dr. Arvind Kumar Thakur

Girish Karnad is undoubtedly the most significant Indian English playwright who has profound concern for the neglected class of the society i.e. the downtrodden who were oppressed, exploited and insulted from time immemorial. Karnad's reinterpretation of the mythical past and oral tradition and his demystification of the dominant beliefs and practices are not only to raise the contemporary problems that Indian society is facing but also to make the society feel what man has made of man and to find out solutions for its betterment. And true literature serves the purpose of (शिवेत्तरक्षतये) *shivettarkshataye* social wellbeing.

In a country that claims to have survived till date on the strong pillars of culture while other cultures and civilizations perished as described by Iqbal :

Yunan, Misra, Roman sab mit gaye jahan se
Ab tak magar hai baki namon nisha hamara
kuch bat hai ki hasti mitati nahin hamari
Sadiyon raha hai dushman dauren jahan hamara

It is passing through the phase of cultural tensions more prominently after independence. Karnad's dramas are endeavours to explore the possibility of transcending the conflict to achieve wholeness, to use Arnoldian phrase "sweetness and light."

In *Naga-Mandala* four different stories are narrated on four levels. The flame story contains three other stories, each one of them inside the previous story. On the first narrative level, the flame story tells of an author whose plays were so boring that the audience often went to sleep. For this "crime" the author is condemned to death unless he manages to remain awake for one entire night before the end of that month. The night of this theatrical performance is precisely his last chance. We hear his repeated laments: "I may be dead within the next few hours."

The second and third narrative levels contain magical elements. The second is formed by the gossip-type tales that a group of personified flames tell each other when they gather at night, after their work has ended. The Flames choose to go to the same ruined temple where the author is bewailing his plight. When he sees them arrive, he hides himself behind a column from where he closely follows their stories. On the third narrative level, there is a tale told by one of the Flames who wants to be forgiven for arriving late. Her singularized tale is about a woman who knew a beautiful story but refused to tell it and share it with other people. One day, that story, taking advantage of the fact that the woman was sleeping with her mouth open, escapes and it was transformed into a young lady. And the song that accompanies it turns into her beautiful sari. The Story thus personified on the fourth narrative level relates the life of Rani, the main character of *Naga-Mandala.* The need for the story to escape illustrates the paradoxical nature of oral tradition, according to Karnad.

The central story is that of Rani, young Rani, recently married to Appana, is locked inside the house by her husband. He treats her as if she were a mere servant, and meanwhile he keeps and uses a concubine. An old blind woman, who is always carried around by her son Kappana, tries to help Rani by giving her a potion which, she says, will cause Appana to fall in love with her. Rani gives up that plan at the last moment, however, and pours the potion on the ant hill which happens to be the dwelling place of a King Cobra. The Cobra (a Naga) then falls in love with Rani. He enters the house through the drain in the bathroom at night and once inside takes on the appearance of Appana, the husband. Despite the disorientation and wonder that this new situation causes in Rani, their relationship is fruitful and results in Rani getting pregnant. As soon as Appana discovers her pregnancy, he informs the elders of the village in order that they may determine her guilt or innocence, since he and she had never had sexual intercourse. Rani proves her "innocence" by undertaking the Snake Ordeal, that is, by holding the King Cobra in her hand. Surprisingly, the Cobra, instead of biting her, "slides up her shoulder and spreads its hood like an umbrella over her head." The onlookers are awestruck, Rani is considered a goddess, and Appana can do nothing but accept her as his wife.

The four stories of *Naga-Mandala* are interconnected and the plot of the main one moves towards the liberation and fulfillment of Rani, the new Indian woman, through her relationship with the Cobra. The complete circles and the complementary intertwined triangles, which in this case are part of the mandala (circle) are symbols that in themselves represent unity.

Karnad questions the gender-based justice, which is favourable to men. Men are favoured because "the concept of ritualistic purity of the metaphysical tradition has structured the hierarchically vertical line-up of gods at the top, men below and women still underneath."

The play exposes male chauvinism and the oppression of women and the great injustice done to them by men and patriarchal culture. Woman in a traditional society is not even permitted to express her feelings of love to another man; she has to seal her heart within herself like a body within a grave. She is accused and punished whereas men doing the same crime escape from the accusation and punishment. Karnad, in his plays, has portrayed the harsh and realistic situation faced by women in India.

In *Naga-Mandala,* Rani has been portrayed as a helpless woman shut up in an old and huge house for most part of the day and the night. She has to undergo barbaric ordeals and through this Karnad makes a severe indictment of the male dominated Hindu society. In the Indian cultural context, specifically in Kundalini-Yoga, the snake is the image of vital energy, or the energy of the cosmos. Ajit Mookerjee says: "The Sanskrit word Kundalini means "coiled up." The coiled Kundalini is the female energy existing in latent form, not only in every human being but in every atom of the universe." Thus, the process of development in human beings consists in moving up this energy, coiled at the base of the spine, so that the seven centres of energy and consciousness (chakras) can be progressively opened. The initial state of this energy is described in this way in the Yoga Kundalini Upanishad. "The divine power, / Kundalini, shines / like the stem of a young lotus; / like a snake, coiled round upon herself, / She holds her tail in her mouth / and lies resting half asleep / at the base of the body" (Mookerjee 2001:10).

Myths and folk tales are sometimes rejected as being unreal but they have great roles to play in the shaping of man's emotional, intellectual and visionary personality. A balance between intellect and emotion is certainly a must because we cannot afford to part with either of them. So sometimes "willing suspension of disbelief" acts as panacea if our intellect is confronted with emotions. How joint family in which old women *nani* or *dadi* tell the children the stories serve the purpose of bringing integration in the family, the society and the country is a thing to be thought of as those stories are also replete with moral lessons and give us liberty to strengthen our critical acumen to judge what is right and what is wrong. Myths and stories enable us to sustain even in intolerable situations. Sometimes myths become so important that even if we make advancements in the field of science and technology and become rational and logical in our approach, we do not wish to part with those myths. The snake myth is very important in Indian culture. The earth is said to be situated on the *Sheshnaga.* Varanasi, the holiest and most ancient city of India is said to be situated on the *trishul* of Lord Shiva. Snakes are the garlands of the Lord. Lord Vishnu takes rest in the *Kshirsagar* on the *Sheshnaga.* Not only this but the *Sheshnaga* was made the *arni* during the churning of the sea from where fourteen items came out. In *The Mahabharta* there are a number of stories related to snake. During the war when Karna and Arjuna were facing each other, one snake came and requested Karna to take its help in defeating Arjuna but Karna refused. Myths are not always irrelevant but sometimes very relevant. If we are in utter dark and find ourselves unable to decide what to do and what not to do, myths and stories come to our rescue. These days the myth of *Bhasmasura* should be an eye-opener for some of our politicians who for petty gains encourage the anti-social elements and give them political patronage. They must learn from that myth that blessings to *Bhasmasuras* will ultimately damage their creators and will continue to harm the country as it is in their nature that they cannot do good :

> To do good aught never will be our task,
> but ever to do ill our sole delight.
>
> (*Paradise Lost, BK I,* p. 13)

Those myths and stories have great capacity to sustain the people. History is a witness that whenever man has fallen into deep distress and there is no way out, he takes refuse in myths and from them he gets sustaining power and strength. When people from Bihar and eastern UP were sent to the African countries by the British, they had romantic dreams of earning more and more but when they reached there, they found themselves cheated. We can easily guess what type of situations they were put into but they could sustain themselves because they had with them *The Ramayana, The Mahabharta* and *The Holy Koran.* Girish Karnad, too, tells about himself that when he received a scholarship to go abroad for further studies, he faced trauma because going abroad was a much rarer occurrence in those days and moreover he came from a large, close-knit family and was the first member of the family ever to go abroad. His parents were worried about him thinking if he would come back or settle there. Karnad was to choose either of the two to remain in India for the sake of his family or to utilize his talent, abilities and training to the maximum and then he chose the second option. His emotional situation finds its outset in a story in *The Mahabharta.* The story is that of King Yayati, who for a moral transgression he has committed, is cursed to old age in the prime of life. Distraught at losing his youth, he approaches his five sons one by one requesting each of them to lend him his youth in exchange for old age. After the four sons refuse, the youngest one yields to his enterprise, exchanges old age for youth and becomes older than his father. Karnad interprets the *Mahabharta* story. To him old age brings no knowledge, no self-realization, only the senselessness of punishment meted out for an act in which he had not even participated. Karnad accepts that while writing the play, he saw that myth only as an escape from his stressful situation. He is amazed even now at how precisely the myth reflected his anxieties at that moment, his resentment with all those who seemed to demand the sacrifice of his future. The myth enabled him to articulate to himself a set of values that he had been unable to arrive at rationally. Whether to return home finally seemed the most minor of issues the myth had nailed him to his past.

It is not that only Girish Karnad faced that type of a situation. Many youths are confronting this issue even today when they want to leave India for better prospect. When they are put into the two thorns of dilemma, myths are there to show them the path. Karnad is not an individual but a type.

Similarly History as an important subject is taught in the universities. The objective behind its teaching is not simply to give them informations of what happened in the past but also to make them aware of the future. By taking lessons from the past we can be aware of the future. By taking lessons from the past we can make our future. Historical events cannot be represented in History – the subject as it can be in literature. In literature it can act as objective correlative, an image, a metaphor, a simile or a conceit in order to target the modern situations in our society. In order to reflect the disillusionment right from the Nehruvian era upto Manmohanian era in which gradual erosion of the ethical norms that had guided the national movement and had instilled the golden image of the would be India after independence, the history of Muhammadbin Tughlaq, a fourteenth Century Sultan of Delhi is very apt. *Tuglaq* is a metaphor for the crisis of Indian politics. A perusal of the play will reveal that the issues of the unity of Hindus and Muslims, equality before justice, solving the problems on the table instead of facing people at the right place (for example Jantar Mantar) the irrational thinking even at the time of attack from outside, sometimes practically wrong decisions leading to chaos, alienation from public as well as from moral values, and many other situations present striking parallel between that time and this time.

The plays of Girish Karnad are great contributions to the society that they, at least, make the readers understand what is right and what is wrong. His messages are communicated in the forms of myths, history, folktales with new meaning and light.

Works Cited

Milton, John. *Paradise Lost.* Scott, Elledge, (*ed.*) New York: W.W. Norton & Company, 2005.

Babu, Manchi Sarat. *Indian Drama Today: A Study in the Theme of Cultural Deformity.* New Delhi: Prestige Books, 1997.

Chandar, K.M. *Mythifying a Folktale: Girish Karnad's Nagamandala.* Journal of Indian Folkloristics, 1999.

Cirlot, J.E. *A Dictionary of Symbols.* New York: Philosophical Library; Routledge & Kegan Paul, 1962.

Dharwadker, Aparna Bhargava. *Introduction, Collected Plays; Tughlaq, Hayavadana, Bali: The Sacrifice, Naga-Mandala.* Vol One by Girish Karnad. Oxford: OUP. vii-xxxvi, 2005.

Garcia Lorca, Federico. *The Authority of the Theatre, Playwrights on Playwrights.* (*ed.*) Toby Cole, New York: Hill and Wang, 58-61.

Karnad, Girish. *Performance, Meaning, and the Materials of Modern Indian Theatre.* Interview by Aparna Dharwadker, New Theatre Quarterly 11.44: 335-370, 1995.

Karnad, Girish. *Three Plays: Naga-Mandala, Hayavadana, Tughlaq.* Oxford: Oxford UP, 1999.

Karnad, Girish. *Collected Plays: Tughlaq, Hayavadana, Bali: The Sacrifice, Naga-Mandala.* (Play with a Cobra), Vol. One, Oxford: OUP, 2005.

Mendoca, Alex. *Circle of Reason.* A Supplement of Sunday Times of India 263, January: 4, 2003.

Vijay Tendulkar as a Social Critic: A Study of *Kanyadaan*

Dr. Sweety

If we talk about the modern Indian drama, the contributions of the playwrights like Mohan Rakesh in Hindi, Badal Sirkar in Bengali, Vijay Tendulkar in Marathi, and Girish Karnad in Kannad are remarkable.

Vijay Tendulkar is a prolific writer. Twentyeight long plays are to his credit. He has written several one-act plays as well as children plays. He often portrays socio-political problems in his dramas.

> I have written about my own experiences and about what I have seen in
> others around me. I have been true to all this and have not cheated my
> generation. I did not attempt to simplify matters and issues for the audience
> when presenting my plays, though that would have been easier occupation....
> My plays .... contain my perceptions of society and its value and I cannot write
> what I do not perceive
>
> (Vijay Tendulkar "Afterword," *Kanyadaan* 71).

In *Kanyadaan,* he depicts the conflict between the upper-class and the Dalit. He criticizes the politicians on the base that rather than removing the evil of class-distinction, they capitalize on it. He presents this evil as it is. He certainly arouses some questions in our mind but he does not bother to answer them. As a creative genius, he does not take side!. His *Kanyadaan* (*The Gift of a Daughter)* has been translated into English by Gowri Ramnarayan who is a journalist and writer. He translated from the original Marathi play. *Kanyadaan* is the first English translation of a major, award-winning Marathi play.

Kanyadaan is a family drama with strong socio-economic undercurrents. Set in the 1980s in the city of Pune, it asks some hard hitting questions about idealism, morality, parenting, discrimination and choices we make every day in our lives. *Kanyadaan* has the background of the twentieth century history of the struggle over the practice of untouchability and the immediate phase of the Dalit movement in Maharashtra and in the nation as a whole. It is a psychological study of the social tensions caused by casteism in India and the development of Jyoti's character from a highly cultured Brahmin girl into a hardened spouse of her Dalit husband. It gives expression to the suffering and exploitation endured by Dalits and looks at what it means to be treated as a lesser human being on account of one's so-called lower caste in contemporary Indian society. Dalits are often treated by the upper castes as an undesirable segment of society. By rejecting a part of the society (in the form of Dalits), the upper castes probably feel comfortable and secure in their self-identity. The play also reveals how caste violence gets transmuted into fresh rounds of violence against other innocent victims. Moreover, it looks at the disillusionment of those reformers who try to bridge the distance between the castes. Ironically, after this play, Tendulkar was branded as an anti-dalit playwright by some critics. Of course, he was also honoured with the Saraswati Samman. According to Tendulkar:

> The work which has been selected for the Saraswati Samman is not the story of a victory; it is the admission of defeat and intellectual confusion. It gives expression to a deep rooted malaise and its pains. (Collected Plays*:* 598)

Jyoti, the daughter of socialist leaders and reformers, Nath and Seva, is attracted to Arun, a Dalit, after reading his powerful poetry and hearing his politically charged speeches. Hers is a middle-class Brahmin family with idealistic humanitarian values. Nath is ready to sacrifice everything for the sake of his values and tries to inculcate those values also in his children, Jyoti and Jayaprakash. Jyoti stands in awe of her idealistic father and tries to follow him in letter and spirit. Motivated more by the ideals of a caste-free society and Dalit upliftment than by passionate love, she wishes to marry Arun and so announces her decision to her family. She admits that she does not even know him well:

> I don't know much about him. The little I know about him is through his poems. He asked me, I said yes, quite

> spontaneously. To tell you the truth, I have been learning something of him only since then. Not only getting to know him, but also getting to know about him. And sometimes he shows such a different side, that it strikes me, I don't know him at all. At times I feel I can trust him, but the very next instant I am left miles behind him. I ask myself – this thing that I want to do, is it the right thing . . . ?

Jyoti is haunted by doubts and is unsure about marrying him but her idealistic training helps her reach a decision:

> But right or wrong, what does it matter anyway? I made a commitment and now I can't run away.

However, it appears that she has made a commitment without giving it much thought. Although she soon begins to sense that her decision might be wrong and that Arun may not be the kind of person she thought him to be, it is now difficult for her to reconsider her decision.

> A conflict between ideal and reality thus makes her indecisive.

As the play moves on, the lights turn on her subjectivity as she tries to negotiate between ideal and reality. Both Seva and Jayaprakash try to persuade her to reconsider her decision. Seva says:

> Why not? . . . A promise given in a weak moment can certainly be reconsidered. If you find it difficult, we can tell him on your behalf that . . ..

But Jyoti would hate to go back on her decision and is supported and assured by Nath to go ahead. Nath sees a streak of his own idealism and will for social reform in Jyoti's decision and is pleased. He thinks that educated and socially aware girls like her ought to make such bold experiments to break the caste barriers. He tells his wife:

> Look, Seva, society cannot be transformed through words alone.We have to act as catalysts in this transformation. The old social reformers did not stop with making speeches

> and writing articles on widow remarriage. Many of them actually married widows. Why did they do it? That was also an experiment, a difficult experiment. But they dared to risk it.

In Jyoti he sees the potential to become another Christ to endure suffering for other people's sins. He therefore wants her to marry Arun. It would be expiation for the suffering and exploitation that all Dalits have undergone at the hands of the upper castes. The title of the play thus suggests a daughter's sacrifice, which Nath performs in the name of the "norms of civilized humanity."

He seems to think of her not as an individual with her own rights as a human being, but as a means to an end. At the same time, the play first romanticises Dalit identity, only to de-romanticise it soon after. In the process, Tendulkar boldly confronts the human reality of Dalit subjectivity, including its violence, cruelty and stupidity. The play de-romanticises Dalit subjectivity as an object of pity and compassion.

Both Seva and Jayaprakash feel that Jyoti cannot be happy with Arun, since he displays a marked proclivity to violence and stubbornness during his very first visit to their home. He is rude and probably feels intimidated by the higher caste and class status of Jyoti's family:

> If you see my father's hut you will understand. Ten of us, big and small, lived in that eight feet by ten feet. The heat of our bodies to warm us in winter. No clothes on our back, no food in our stomach, but we felt very safe. Here, these damn houses of the city people, they're like the bellies of sharks and crocodiles, each one alone in them!

We find here an implication of caste and class, so that caste is identified with class which may not be the case always. Arun presents before Jyoti the dismal and frightening details of his life of deprivation and expresses his doubts as to whether Jyoti will be able to live with him:

> Our grandfathers and great grandfathers used to roam barefoot, miles and miles, in the heat, in the rain, day and night . . . till the rags on their butt fell apart . . . used to wander shouting "Johaar, Maayi-bap! Sir-Madam, Sweeper!" and their calls polluted the Brahmins' ears.

But Arun is a shrewd person. He challenges Jyoti to try and live in his world as he knows Jyoti's temperament and is sure that she cannot say no to the challenge:

> Will you marry me and eat stinking bread with spoilt dal in my father's hut? Without vomitting? Tell me Jyoti, can you shit everyday in our slum's village toilet like my mother? Can you beg, quaking at every door, for a little grass for our buffaloes? Come on. Tell me!

It is a disclosure of the cunningness of Arun. He uses the condition of Dalits as a tool to achieve his selfish ends. Arun's description scares Jyoti, but his challenge strengthens her resolve to experience with him his kind of life, as her eyes are blinded by her father's idealism. But it is Nath who gives her the final push:

> I am on Jyoti's side. It is perfectly natural that the boy should have rough edges; they are the product of the circumstances he has endured. In fact it would be surprising if these peculiarities didn't exist. But just because he has them, it doesn't mean he's a bad fellow. . . . As a human being he has potential. He has intelligence, drive and creativity.

It is surprising that Nath perceives unmatched qualities in Arun, although he has not exchanged even a word with him so far. It appears that he is so keen on his Brahmin-Dalit marriage experiment that he highlights all that is good in Arun and refuses to see his violent streak and shoves the thoughts of Jyoti's future unhappiness away from his mind. The play raises a pertinent question: whether the knowledge, that a person is a product of certain circumstances, enables one to be happy with that person. In other words, a better understanding of Dalit experience may not provide adequate tools to accept Dalits in real life.

In Act II, we find that Jyoti and Arun have been married. They, however, do not have a home. Jyoti goes on staying with her parents while Arun puts up with his friends. Seva appears worried about Jyoti's changing attitude. She complains that Jyoti comes and goes as she pleases and does not care about her parents' concerns about her whereabouts. Seva has begun to be alarmed at the change in Jyoti and she attributes her carelessness to Arun's influence:

> This impertinence – it is not yours. We know very well who puts you up to it.
>
> Both Nath and Seva are worried about Jyoti. Jayaprakash feels that Jyoti is herself responsible for her situation as it was her decision to marry Arun. And then suddenly Jyoti announces her decision to leave Arun:
>
> I must tell you, Bhai, I must. I am fed up with him. Fed up! Fed up!

It is not hidden from Nath and Seva that Jyoti is subjected to violence at the hands of Arun, but she does not discuss her troubles with them. She thinks that she must own the responsibility of her decision:

> I must learn to live without tears. I mustn't even complain. It was I who made the decision, I have to find my own strength to bear this, alone.

Jyoti appears to be stubborn like Arun and does not want anyone to pity her. She refuses to accept the reality and, despite all the violence and suffering, she suffers at the hands of Arun, she hates to discuss her problems with her parents. Nath too is shattered when he hears of Jyoti's decision to leave Arun:

> Seva, let not this wonderful experiment fail! This dream which is struggling to turn real, let it not crumble into dust before our eyes! We will have to do something. We must save this marriage. Not necessarily for our Jyoti's sake . . . This is not just a question of our daughter's life, Seva, this has . . . a far wider significance . . . this experiment is a very precious experiment.

Nath is so blinded by his dream of an ideal, casteless society, that he fails to see the suffering and emotional harm Jyoti is going through. He is ready to sacrifice his daughter's happiness at the altar of his idealism.

Arun apologises to Jyoti and expresses his helplessness:

> When have I claimed that I am civilised and cultured like your people? From childhood I have seen my father come home

> drunk everyday, and beat my mother half dead, seen her cry her heart out. Even now I hear the echoes of her broken sobs. No one was there to wipe her tears. My poor mother! She didn't have a father like Bhai, nor a mother like you. . . .

Arun shows his helplessness to behave like civilised people and blames it on his upbringing. He tries to explain away his personal misconduct with the help of the suffering endured by his caste, but does not have the strength to change his behaviour. He declares that he is powerless, forgetting that if as a Dalit he wants to be free, he must believe that the given circumstances can be overcome. He thus articulates the central irony of the discourse of Dalit empowerment. Dalits should struggle for freedom and change but they have also to accept the responsibility that attends freedom:

> What am I but the son of scavengers? We don't know the non-violent ways of Brahmins like you. We drink and beat our wives.

He thus transmutes the humiliation received at the hands of society into violence against his wife. And it does not seem to him to be wrong, since he has seen his father do the same against his mother so many times. Arun claims to love Jyoti unconditionally, and offers to show his violence against her as an expression of love. Tendulkar, in this way, exposes here the not so uncommon reality of Indian homes, supposed to be united by bonds of love but concealing widespread violence. At another level, Arun represents the politically successful Dalit leaders who exploit the discourse of freedom and self-pity to promote their own interests and to harm others.

Arun is shown as a victim of the discourse of hatred towards upper classes often circulating among the victim castes. He hates Jyoti for being a Brahmin and avenges the violence of generations on her. He hates everything that is upper caste, including the idealism of Nath, which seems to him superficial and false. Arun's resentful behaviour can be understood with the help of Nietzsche's insight: Nietzsche names it as ressentment, the expression of "slave morality," which surfaces when natural impulses are denied expression. According to Kim Atkins:

> In the case of slaves, whose bondage effectively denies their will to power free expression, the suffering of bondage produces hatred and fear, but also resentment because slaves cannot act on their feelings.

Arun is also the victim of a similar oppression and hence he labels his oppressors, the upper castes, as bad and as a result himself as good. In On the Genealogy of Morals, Nietzsche looks back on the origins of the words "good" and "bad," and concludes in a satiric tone: "the enemy" as the man of ressentment conceives him - and here precisely is his deed, his creation: he has conceived "the evil enemy," "the evil one," and this in fact is his basic concept, from which he then evolves as an afterthought and pendant, a "good one" himself!

The weak uphold their weakness by claiming that whatever the strong did was evil, and attribute everything to Divine Providence and resign themselves to their fate as if it were a voluntary achievement and a meritorious act. They hate the strong for their power and strength.

Arun too cannot bring himself to respect Jyoti or at least treat her as an equal human being. It could, of course, be argued that Tendulkar has painted Arun in this light probably because he himself is not a Dalit and has a fixed stereotype of a Dalit in his mind.

Jyoti is influenced, as we have noted, by the discourse of reformist idealism and social equality fed to her by Nath since her childhood. She reveres her father and craves his approval in all the decisions she takes. Her actions are guided by the discourse in which her father believes and which he wants her to subscribe to. So she once again submits to Arun's requests and goes with him. And she is once again subjected to intense violence and economic exploitation. Arun is an idler and spends Jyoti's money on alcohol and even beats her mercilessly even when she is pregnant.

Arun has meanwhile written an autobiography, which becomes an instant hit with the Marxist critics. The gap between moral posturing and personal behaviour of a Dalit writer is acceptable to certain groups in the society. This means that the entire Dalit subjectivity has to be analysed in terms of the personal and interpersonal also. Nath happens to read the book and likes it, but when he comes to know from Seva how Arun has been treating Jyoti, he is disillusioned. Seva remarks:

> I will say that in this excellent book whatever the author has said about injustice and exploitation is hypocrisy of the first

> order. Because this man himself exploits my daughter. Like a shameless parasite, he lives on my daughter's blood and on top of that he gets drunk and bashes her up. Constantly he taunts her about her caste and about her parents, heaping foul abuse on them for being highborn.

Arun blackmails Nath into appearing for a public discussion of the book. Nath agrees to speak appreciatively of the book to prevent further misery for Jyoti. Jyoti, however, criticises Nath for failing to stick to his ideals and for inculcating impracticable ideas in his children.

> I was deeply offended by your hypocrisy. I thought: why did this man have to inject and drug us everyday with truth and goodness? And if he can get away from it at will, what right had he to close all our options?

Her disillusionment is complete after staying under Arun's influence for some more time. Arun is the champion of a kind of Dalit discourse which looks down upon everything that is high-class/caste, and he looks for hints of exploitation in each of their moves. Jyoti is at first shocked by Arun's changing behaviour towards her and fails to understand him:

> There is a savage beast in his eyes, his lips, his face... in every single limb. And bestiality is something which cannot be separated from him . . . Arun is both the beast and the lover. Arun is the demon, and also the poet. Both are bound together, one within the other, they are one.

But she realises later that his multifacetedness is where she can begin to know him. It is one Arun but made of all the contradictory things bound together. The play thus hints at the fragmentary nature of subjectivity and its lack of coherence, as against conventional assumptions of an essential, coherent and unified self. It brings home the insight that individual identity is not a free and self-transparent consciousness, or a stable essence.

Her father's final betrayal pushes her further towards Arun, and so she leaves her family for good. She tells her father:

> You made me waste twenty years of my life before I could discover this. I had to learn it on the strength of my own experience. I had to meet a man named Arun Athavale. Arun gave me what you had withheld from me. I must acknowledge my debt to him.

The ideas, which Nath instilled in Jyoti, should have been re-examined. Jyoti resents this fact and it appears that it is Arun speaking in her when she says:

> I am an untouchable, a scavenger. I am one of them. Don't touch me. Fly from my shadow, otherwise my fire will scorch your comfortable values.

These are very distinctly Arun's words. Arun is successful in exerting so deep an influence on Jyoti that she begins to believe that all upper-caste values are anti-dalit and that her parents could hate her for being a Dalit.

The play can be read, among other things, as a study of the construction of idealist subjectivity. For instance, Nath is caught between two discourses. One is the anti-dalit discourse which asks him to hate Dalits. He has struggled against this discourse all his life; he has tried to fight it tooth and nail and fashioned his life on the opposing discourse of equality and humanitarian values, treating all the castes as equal and trying to reduce caste hostilities through public intervention and personal example. He is delighted when he learns that Jyoti wants to marry a Dalit and he is ready to forego his daughter's happiness for the sake of what he considers to be the wonderful experiment of bringing together the two castes. But the same Nath is utterly disillusioned when he sees how his experiment has failed, bringing immense agony to Jyoti.

At such a weak moment, hatred against Arun overpowers him and compels to say those very things which he has always regarded as anathema:

> ... his visit has polluted this drawing room, this house and this day. ... It stinks. Seva – you know – you see – I feel like taking a bath, like cleaning myself! Clean everything! This furniture, this floor ... all this ... he had made them filthy, dirty, polluted!

> Why did I have to come into contact with a man like this? A man like this ... why?

He simply becomes "the Brahmin," whose house has been polluted by the visit of an untouchable. It is clear that the discourse of untouchability was always present in his consciousness; it had just been suppressed by the discourse of humanitarian concerns and equality, but it resurfaces when a Dalit gives him reason to vent his anger. Nath thus condemns Dalits on the basis of his experience of a single individual. Nath is anti-Gandhian in this respect because Gandhi would never go back to opposing his dearly held ideals, whatever the extent of his disillusionment. Nath's experiment seems to have been Gandhian, but it remains half-hearted and fundamentally inauthentic.

The same may be said about the hypocrisy of the higher castes in India, who conveniently switch roles in personal and public spheres, treating Dalits in a way that is most suitable for a particular occasion. They would speak eloquently and forcefully about Dalit upliftment but in their own homes they still treat them like dirt. Try as much as they can, they cannot shake off the age-old influence of the Varna system fed to them through generations. Tendulkar brings out the stubborn habits of perception among the upper castes as a result of which caste differences remain hard to erase. To some extent, Arun and Nath are the alter egos of each other; there is redemption for neither.

The title of the play, interestingly, does not suggest anything about caste. The concept of "kanyadaan" is taken from mainstream Hindu rituals ideology. It suggests the patriarchal arrangement of giving the daughter as a gift. This is a play situated in the confines of patriarchal institutional arrangements. There is a displacement from the title to the thematic of the play – a shift from gender and patriarchy to caste.

Through *Kanyadaan* Tendulkar probes deeply into the layers of Indian castes-psychology in presenting before us the complicated, conflicting and tense relationship between Indian middle class and socially outcaste and untouchable community. Social reformers have given thought to it from time to time and through a number of reform campaigns, donations, reservations, meetings, seminars, have tried to eliminate this bias, doubt and misunderstanding between the classes. But all these big efforts had little effect on the real conditions of the people. The so-called reform campaigns for the downtrodden people and talks of democracy and equality proved to be a mere show; and even today the disturbing rift between social classes of India can be clearly perceived.

Indianness is the sum total of the cultural traditions of India. It reflects the deep-seated ideas–political, economical, cultural and spiritual–that constitute the mind of India. *Kanyadaan* is a social play which reveals status/class differences of the characters. Indian society has an age-old tradition of hierarchy which dates back to the heyday of feudalism and imperial power. Choice of address/reference terms depends on power semantics, solidarity, social stratification and position in a social group, age and kinship.

Vijay Tendulkar's fame has crossed the boundaries of Marathi culture. His forte was that he voiced the silence of the common man. His ranking on the national as well as international stage for dramatics is indisputable. Tendulkar could bring in reality into dramatics and brought new authenticity to the depiction of the common man's life in Marathi Theater. Being an aestheticist he enjoyed beauty in all the little things he observed in his lifetime. He was a lover of modern fine arts, as also new thoughts and all novelty in life. He always welcomed modernistic thoughts, literature, art and artists who created them. He never intended to make any social changes or had any good or bad intentions against anybody. He never thought of saleability while writing, rather would consider what the society needs to contemplate on and assiduously worked towards presenting human feelings. This is how he became an eminent playwright in the history of Indian dramatics with his rebellious ideology.

He was therefore far ahead of his time. He was an activist of the *Seva Dal* party for some period and always tended towards and was at the forefront in social movements like the *Narmada Bachao Andolan* (a movement to save the people displaced by the Narmada dam project), cultural movements like *Granthali* movements that expressed freedom of thought, experimentations in dramatics, etc., he not only broke the picket fences of dramatics, but also gave a new dimension to script, dialogues, and backstage. Very few Marathi authors have such varied interests, or are so active and socialistic.

Delivering the prestigious Sri Ram Memorial Lectures for Performing Arts in 1997 in New Delhi, Tendulkar summed up his lifelong involvement in theatre as follows:

> What I like about those years is that they made me grow as a human being. And theatre which was my major concern has

> contributed to this in a big way. It helped to analyze life—my own and lives of others. It led me to make newer and newer discoveries in the vast realm of the human mind that still defies all available theories and logic. It's like an ever-intriguing puzzle or a jungle that you can always enter but has no way out. Not that I am any wiser than the fool I was when I entered the theatre. I still act like a fool and think like one; but there is a difference. Now I am aware of what I am doing while I do it. I am my own audience and the critic, if one may use the language of the theatre. Now I enjoy my foolishness and laugh at it; and of course the foolishness of others too, at times.

Tendulkar takes his onus on shoulder and attacks dirty caste politics of India. He takes the subject "Kanyadaan" not just to transfer females from one house to another or to discharge patriarchy burden but describes the caste shifting and prejudice of upper caste towards the lower caste and from lower to upper caste but these change within the internal character of Jyoti from higher caste to lower caste with her own will and in this way the projection of Jyoti in "Kanyadaan" is shifting of gender and patriarchy to caste and open the minds of common people and awaken them against rank corruption in Indian politics due to the opportunist politicians and their role. And in this way Tendulkar participates in the process of nation building and achieves a milestone in Indian writing in English and new drama.

As a keen observer of life Tendulkar presents the changing reality of contemporary society authentically and honestly in the play. His real and genuine concern for the oppressed and his awareness of social evils have originated from his true understanding of society. Tendulkar does not offer any solution to the problem but leaves it to the discretion of the readers. The treatment of the theme, characterization and the structure of the play reveals his artistic excellence. The play is widely appreciated for its technical experiments, textual compactness, sharp dialogue, skilful art of characterization and brilliant plot construction. On the whole, Vijay Tendulkar's Kanyadaan has become an artistic and creative treasure in the realm of Indian Drama in English.

Works Cited

Madge, V.M. *Vijay Tendulkar's Plays, An Anthology of Recent Criticism.* Delhi: Pencraft International, 2007.

Nayar, Pramod K. *Literary Theory Today.* New Delhi: Asia Book Club, 2006.

Ramnarayan, Gowri. (trans.) *Kanyadaan.* New Delhi: Oxford University Press, 1996.

Tendulkar, Vijay. *"Afterward" Kanyadaan.* Delhi: Oxford University Press, 1996.

Tendulkar, Vijay. *Kanyadaan.* Bombay: Oxford University Press, 2006.

Interview, "Vijay Tendulkar in conversation with Gawri Ramnarayan."

Chastity Demythicized in Karnad's *Naga-Mandala*

Dr. Anuradha Deepak

Indian English Drama, beginning in the early nineteenth century has walked a long tedious path to the present where it has received a breath of fresh air and life from such emerging dramatists as Asif Currimbhoy, Girish Karnad, Vijay Tendulkar, Mahesh Dattani etc. Among this new breed of playwrights, Girish Karnad is a name that strikes a chord of recognition for many. He has given many thought provoking and symbolist plays richly steeped in myth and local culture. A highly learned and intellectual person, Karnad makes his plays his mouthpiece to act as an impetus to thought regarding many of the contemporary issues plaguing man and society. He is a mature humanist and in an interview has said :

> .....the subject of any play has to be the human spirit.
>
> (Nimsarkar : 2009, p.15).

Like some other Indian dramatists, Karnad also has used myths, mythologies, legends and folktales to reflect upon contemporary Indian culture and social life. He weaves together timeless truths about human life and emotions contained in ancient Indian stories with the changing social modes and morals of modern life. His use of myths in the plays has displayed that:

> the ancient Indian myths can be harnessed to address the modern sensibility of loss of individuality.
>
> (*Boratti and Haritsa*: 2006, p.62 as quoted by Nimsarkar: 2009, p. 34).

The myths, legends and folk forms are reflectors of the racial and cultural unconsciousness and all ritualistic performances. M. Sarat Babu rightly says that Karnad uses:

> ......myths and folk form in his plays to exorcise socio-cultural evils. (2009, p. 238).

Karnad himself says:

> The energy of folk theatre comes from the fact that although it seems to uphold traditional values, it also has the means of questioning these values, of making them literally stand on their head.(2009, p. 34)

Naga-Mandala is a play inspired by popular myth and oral stories centering around the king Cobra "Naga." In this play, Karnad not only exposes male chauvinism, oppression of women, great injustice done to them by men and patriarchal culture but also stealthily deflates the concept of chastity.

Both fidelity and chastity are the values and beliefs transferred from individual to socio-cultural psyche with the inception of the civilization. It is one of the most powerful yet invisible cultural fetters that have enslaved women for ages since the dawn of patriarchy. Moreover, men have enacted the values and women have followed them meticulously. There has been enough literature, both oral and written, glorifying this enslaving value and deifying the women characters who observed it faithfully. *The Ramayana* in which Sita undergoes the fire ordeal to prove her chastity to Rama, has always been a cultural guide to Indians. The concept of chastity goes with, and gets its indispensable support from another morbid concept that sex is mean and sinful. Every mother along with father and other elders enslave their daughters to patriarchy by teaching them verbally and non-verbally that chastity is more important than life and that its loss which brings an unbearable social stigma is worse than death. If any brave woman violates these values, she is not only looked down upon but also culturally excommunicated.

Karnad is the play-wright who is outstandingly liberal in portrayal and development of women protagonists in his plays. He presents women in the social network in the backdrop of Indian social, cultural, patriarchal family life and social politics but at the same time he envisages the individual aspiration of women and their various roles such as mother, wife, lover, and so on. While performing their social roles in the family and society, Karnad's women take care of their desires and to achieve them find their own way.

Besides other aspects of women's personal roles as assigned by society, Karnad prominently discusses the most talked about concept of sexuality. He has a refined idea of sexuality and here Kakar's opinion about it is quite relevant;

> Sexuality ....is a system of conscious and unconscious human fantasies, arising from various sources, seeking satisfaction in diverse ways and involving a range of excitations and activities that aim to achieve pleasure that goes beyond the satisfaction of any basic somatic need. [1990, p. 21]

For Karnad, woman's sexuality and adultery is a "normal" human response, not something "sinful," as he has said in a conversation with Tutun Mukherjee. [Mukherjee : 2006, p. 43].

In the same conversation, Karnad relates :

> I used to know a married woman once who positively blossomed after she had an extra-marital affair. If womanhood finds fulfillment in love that happens to be outside marriage, why should that be considered wrong? Radha's love for Krishna was such.
>
> [*Mukherjee* : 2006, p. 43 as quoted by *Nimsarkar* : 2009, p. 20].

The treatment of female sexuality is thus central in the projection of women in some of his plays besides their other social roles. Karnad has thus supported extra-marital relationship and hence can be seen as an author who presents the character of married woman from within an unconventional perspective. Satyadev Dubey believes Karnad to be:

> the only play-wright in the history of Indian theatre to have treated adultery as normal and treated adulterous women sympathetically. (as quoted by *Collellmir*)

Naga-Mandala discusses issues about man-woman relationship, position and identity of a woman, about psychology and the impact of social and cultural modes on the feminine psyche.

> In fact, *Naga-Mandala* is a powerful portrait of the agony and anguish faced by both men and women in their development into adult roles and social adjustment in a society where the individual is given little space for self- development, awareness and independence as a being.
>
> [*Gupta* : 1999, p. 249]

Rani, the protagonist of the play is a character who has been shown to evolve from an immature naive girl into that of a confident and mature woman. She is a symbol of any woman who is unprepared to face life on her own once she leaves the protective threshold of her parent's home. In the beginning of the play, Rani is introduced as a young bride on the verge of a new life with her husband Appanna. Like any other girl, she too enters her life with a lot of expectations, desires and dreams but the harsh reality of life shocks and confuses her. Appanna locks her up in the house all alone only to return in the day for her bath and lunch. He spends his nights with his concubine ignoring altogether the needs and desires of Rani. Her situation proves that:

> man is the maker of outside world, and woman's duty is to make a house.
> [*Devi* : 1995, p. 19 as quoted by *Chatterji* : 2010, p. 3]

In the same context, M. Sarat Babu also writes:

> This solitary confinement of Rani by Appanna in the house symbolizes the chastity belt of the Middle Ages, the reduction of women's talents to house-work and the exclusion of women from enlightenment and enjoyment. [1999, p. 239]

Rani's husband Appanna represents the stereotypical image of a chauvinistic male as per the patriarchal dictates of society : dominating, cruel, selfish and callous. Naga on the other hand is a representation of the mature, caring and loving male, truly a myth in the rigid and tradition bound patriarchal society.

Gender discrimination is the basis of all kinds of domination and subjugation amongst the sexes. *Naga-Mandala* exposes the ugliness of a society where woman is considered "second sex," "other," "subject," "non-man." In the process of being socialized, women are taught to internalize the reigning patriarchal ideology where the male is considered "superior." A woman exists as having no identity of her own. A victim of "incompleteness" she craves for completeness in her relations, in love but usually finds none. In the conventional comparison of the man-woman relationship to the two wheels of a cart, both equally important, the female's reality is always that of the broken, fragmented wheel clinging to the other (male) for support and survival. This inequality and imbalance is clearly visible in the relationship of Rani and Appanna. Rani has no say in any matter. If ever she tries to speak or ask anything, Appanna responds with irritation and disregard:

> Look, I don't like idle chatter. Do as you are told, you understand ? [p. 28]

Naga-Mandala is a dramatization of folk-tales where the illusion has been transformed to embody the reality of issues. Karnad has reconstructed a myth by mixing mythical and magical combined with the contemporary social problems so that the spectators/readers should watch/read, think over the affairs and apply their reasoning power for understanding them. The myth of "Naga" is a folk-tale in local culture of Kerala where it represents prosperity, happiness and fertility. In *Naga-Mandala,* this myth explains the importance of love filling the emptiness of Rani's life with affection and care. A man in our society does not need to explain his reasons for gratification of his sensual pleasures but a woman's instinctual need is ignored, and their desire is considered a transgression of moral codes. The Naga in the guise of Appanna presents a choice for Rani, a choice to live a fuller and happier life. It is her expression of desire and also the fulfillment of her wish for love, her desire to live life fully and with satisfaction. If Appanna is the demon, Naga is the prince in Rani's life. A source of energy, the Naga represents the positive element. He is the cultural leader, and harbinger of a social change, generating a transformation not only in the character of Rani but also in the society at large. A representation of the true life force, Naga is the source as well as the preservation and regeneration of life.

Dr. G.A. Ghanshyam writes:

> Considered from a realistic point of view, Naga represents the modern, new woman's right to choice, the right to choose a life overcoming all obstacles to her happiness. It symbolizes the breaking of barriers, crossing of the lines that intend to imprison a woman and distance her from her surroundings as well asher own "self."
>
> (Submissive to Assertive : Metamorphosis of Rani in Karnad's *Naga-Mandala*)

The entry of Naga in Rani's life is the beginning of transformation in her character and attitude. She had been left to wither away in neglect and isolation. She did not possess even the right to tell her husband about her plight or ask him anything. The love, care and concern of Naga, however, makes her blossom like a beautiful flower. She even becomes bold enough to assert herself and further question him, though her love for him still makes her accept his decisions and advice:

> I was a stupid, ignorant girl when you brought me here. But now I am a woman, a wife, and I am going to be a mother. I am not a parrot. Not a cat or a sparrow. Why don't you take it on trust that I have a mind and explain this charade tome? (p. 51)

Rani's intentions are however, questionable regarding the difference in the behaviour of the Naga and Appanna. There are several reasons to believe that Rani deliberately ignores the difference between the two. Appanna is always rude, indifferent and inconsiderate where as the Naga is always affectionate and considerate towards her. But seen from her point of view as an individual and a woman seeking fulfillment in life, she stands justified. She definitely realizes that Naga is her love whose presence during night as Appanna has brought pleasure and security to her. The very moment of the Naga's arrival creates wonderful atmosphere around her as she describes:

> The smell of the blossoming night queen! How it fills the house before he comes! How it welcomes him! God, how it takes me, sets each fibre in me on fire! (p. 49)

The discovery of her self and the long subdued instinct for sex fulfillment are achieved in the company of Naga to such an extent that she forgets everything else. She deliberately ignores the reality of the difference between the two persons. Instead of tolerating humiliation, torture and imposing presence of Appanna, she prefers the loving company of the Naga who appreciates her beauty, comforts her and fulfills her sex-urge with respect and mutual understanding. In this context, Nimsarkar has stated :

> The fire in Rani is metaphoric; it is not the fire of sex but the strong desire of a woman aspiring for complete womanhood and family, what she ultimately feels to achieve in the life. (2009, p.135)

Rani travels from innocence to experience by the end of the play. But even this long route to experience does not reach its ultimate destination without a final ordeal for Rani. Hypocrisy underlines the dictates of a patriarchal society that is more favourable towards men and unduly harsh and cruel to the women. Rani's transformation, her shift from suppression to emancipation requires a final show of resilience of spirit and courage. She has to face trial before the village elders to prove her innocence. Following the advice of her beloved Naga, she takes up the Snake trial and speaks the truth:

> Yes, my husband and this king Cobra. Except for these two, I have not touched any one of the male sex. (p. 58)

Her submission that she has touched two persons, and acceptance of the adultery indirectly makes the elders also accept the human shape of the Naga and the supernatural power in her:

> Appanna your wife is not an ordinary woman. She is a goddess incarnate...
> You were the chosen instrument for revealing her divinity. (p. 59)

The situation does not end even here. The same villagers who were to test the so-called "chastity" of Rani, say to Appanna:

Spend the rest of your life in her service.You need merit in ten past lives to be chosen for such holy duty. (p. 59)

The biggest irony of Appanna's life is that he knows Rani is not "chaste" according to the social and patriarchal norms of chastity. He knows that he is not the father of Rani's child yet he can't prove it. Neither can he reject her. He is shocked and bewildered as he says :

> What I am to do?...Have I sinned so much that even Nature should laugh at me?...Let any miracle declare her a goddess. But I know! (p. 60)

In the context of all these situations, it can be said that Karnad presents a rebellious and open-minded outlook on the issue of female sexuality and chastity. He has demythicized and subverted the whole concept of "chastity"(that too framed specifically for females) showing Rani's boldness and acceptance of the Naga. The moment when the individual is capable of discovering his or her true essence is symbolically represented by her placing and keeping Cobra in her hair:

> This hair is the symbol of my wedded bliss. Live in there happily for ever. (p. 64)

In saving the Naga from being killed and allowing him to stay with her, she proves the realization of the power of her feminine desires over other social and moral duties. Yet her transformation is in agreement with her acceptance of Appanna as her husband. The playwright thus is unwilling to break the fragile balance of socio-cultural norms despite all his boldness to deflate the concept of "chastity." Any sensitive writer has to use a kind anaesthesia while operating on culture to remove the morbid tissue. Karnad has proved himself to be a sensible writer using this *cultural anaesthesia.*

(*Babu* : 2009, p. 236)

A.K. Ramanujan's views about the relevance of using folklore are worth quoting in this context:

> Tales speak of what cannot usually be spoken. Ordinary decencies are violated. Incest, cannibalism, pitiless revenge are explicit motifs in this fantasy world, which helps us face ourselves, envisage shameless wish fulfillments, and sometimes "by indirection find direction out."
>
> (1989, p. 258 as quoted by *Collellmir*)

Works Cited

Babu, M. Sarat. "The Concept of Chastity and Naga Mandala" in J. Dodiya (ed.). *The Plays of Girish Karnad.* New Delhi: Prestige: 2009.

Chatterji, Shoma A. *Women in Perspective : Essays on Gender Isues.* New Delhi: Vitasta: 2010.

Collellmir, Dolors. *Mythical Structure in Girish Karnad's Naga-Mandala.* http:www.publications.ub.es/revistes/bells15/documentos/71.pdf

Dodiya, J. *The Plays of Girish Karnad.* New Delhi: Prestige: 2009.

Ghanshyam, G.A. *Submissive to Assertive: Metamorphosis of Rani in Karnad Naga-Mandala.* http : www.creative saplings.com/ submissive to assertive.doc.

Gupta, Santosh, "A Story of Marriage and Love" in J. Dodiya (ed.) *The Plays of Girish Karnad.* New Delhi: Prestige: 2009.

Kakar, Sudhir. *Intimate Relations.* New Delhi: Penguin: 1990.

Karnad, Girish. *Three Plays.* Delhi: OUP: 1994.

Nimsarkar, P.D. *Women in Girish Karnad's Plays : A Critical Perspective.* New Delhi: Creative Books: 2009.

Isolated and Deserted Women in the Early Poetry of Tennyson

Dr. Rajni Singh

The mute and stifled female voice was denied freedom of self- expression since ages due to the long period of cultural and environmental conditioning. This poor status of woman had been stated with great rigour by progressive thinkers who wished to emancipate her from the helotage of a male-dominated world. The "Women Liberation Movement" gained momentum in the 19th century with progressive thinkers like Mary Wollstonecraft, Margaret Fuller, and John Stuart Mill who started a continuous agitation for women's rights on social, economic and cultural grounds. These agitators on behalf of fair sex tried to dismantle the structures that had been despised by the male-centered society. They recognized the inadequacy of male-centered ideologies and struggled for the spiritual, economic, social equality of women who had been sexually colonized and biologically subjugated. The progressive minds challenged the supremacy of the lordly male and affirmed the rights of woman to be treated intellectually and morally on the same footing as man.

Tennyson, the bard of Queen Victoria was fully aware of the changing roles of women but he never had the courage to openly challenge the male-dominated society and thus rigorously confines man and woman to their respective spheres. He presents his women in traditional framework. The typical Tennyson heroine is a meek and yielding creature, easily submissive and takes pride in her suffering.

In his long poetic career beginning from the year 1827-1885 Tennyson wrote a number of poems on women. Prominent among these are the poems written between 1830-1842 wherein the typical Victorian/ Tennyson women willingly drape themselves with all the expected feminine features without questioning or doubting the intentions of their male counterpart – Margaret (a lonely figure by choice); the two Marianas (deserted by their lover); Oenone (who is victim of her husband's infidelity); Lady of Shalott (who under a curse lives a secluded, unreal life, lit up and shattered suddenly by the lightning of reality) and the Soul in The Palace of Art that leads an isolated life are garbed with the virtues of modesty and self-effacement. All these women are the archetypes of the Good Angel but strangely many of them are isolated or deserted. They are purely traditional and feminine in nature and thus become a prey to their own emotions. They are literally the "other"/second class citizens and are supposed to exist in some kind of inescapable relationship with man.

"Margaret," a poem from Juvenilia published in 1830 is the first such woman. Margaret is a woeful and melancholic figure who has declared to stay alone due to some personal loss. Throughout the poem the emphasis is on the sweet pale face of Margaret and her tearful eyes. She turns a deaf ear to her lover's request to leave her ivory tower and come down. We do not know as to who lent her the dower of pensive thought and melancholy, her sorrow is without sound. She is presented as a person sitting all day in the feast of sorrow. Perhaps all the subsequent isolated women are an elaboration of this pale, sorrowful and melancholic woman.

Tennyson composed three poems in a row, "Mariana," "Mariana in South" and "Oenone" sometime during 1830-31. All these three poems are linked by a common subject, with the same prevalent mood and theme, revealing the agony of deserted women, sometime with the help of scenic parallel of desolation in Nature, sometime with a rich setting made desolate because of the distraught heart.

The image of a distraught, pining woman haunted Tennyson in different background. We have the first Mariana in the "moated grange" and the second Mariana in a Southern barrenness. In "Mariana" (1830) Tennyson projects a weary forsaken, forlorn young woman, who is heartsick with waiting in the moated grange. The poet starts simply with the words from *Measure for Measure,* "Mariana in the moated grange" which he uses as epigraph, and then proceeds to weave his mood piece around them.

Mariana lives all alone in a dilapidated house which gives a sense of generalized loss or decay. It is a building in ruins where "The rusted nails fell from the knots," "The clinking latch" is even un-lifted and "the broken sheds looked sad and strange." Mariana complains about her loneliness and dreariness of life. She weeps all the time, morning, evening and night. She is weary of life because her lover does not come back to her. She wants to put an end to her waiting. She wishes that only death can break the weary monotony and free her from her seclusion:

She only said, "My life is dreary,"
He cometh not, she said;
She said, "I am aweary, aweary,"
I would that I were dead! (11.9-12)

This hopeless cry of the abandoned woman echoes throughout the poem.

The poem is a series of pictures of the grange, the woman, and the country round the grange, making up a powerful evocation of the sadness of the house and of the woman who lives in it. For miles and miles there is the wasteland all around. What endures is that picture of black moss, black ferland-waters, black levels of sodden plain beneath the grey glint of dawn, the dance of motes in the sinking sunlight, the white curtain wavering beneath the setting moor, the poplar-shadow across the forsaken bed. The sordid landscape perfectly matches with the mood of Mariana. The detailed description of the lonely farmhouse is not of decay alone, but also of motion and life frustrated of their normal function which still retaining their potential vitality, precisely as Mariana herself is in her deserted, unloved state. It is destined for her to live in that house with doors that "creak" without being opened and to listen to the hateful sounds:

All day within the dreamy house
The doors upon their hinges creak'd;
The blue fly sung in the pane; the mouse
Behind the mouldering wainscot shriek'd. (ll. 61-64)

The fly and the mouse are symbols of domestic decay. The fountain has become "a sluice with blackened waters," and the imprisoned soul longs for "him." The horror of loneliness is indicated by the slowly changing hours of the day that bring no change to Mariana and little to the refrain:

Then said she, "I am very dreary,"
"He will not come," she said;
She wept, "I am aweary, aweary,"
O God, that I were dead! (ll. 81-84)

The four shorter lines, operating as an almost incantatory refrain, serve to gather up the implications of the imagery in the preceding lines and repeat, almost hypnotically the suggestion of loss, regret and weariness.

This vein of the lonely woman in "Mariana" is frequently exploited by Tennyson in "Mariana in South" published in 1832. The idea for the poem came to Tennyson during the same tour in which he conceived the idea of "Oenone" – his tour of the Pyrenees with Arthur Hallam, when the two were "journeying together... through the South of France...came upon a range of country just corresponding to this preconceived thought of barrenness." The melancholic musing of the heroine and the natural surroundings steadily build suggestions of loneliness, and distance from an active busy world. Like the lonely lady in Mariana, she too is trapped in a certain stillness, silence, seclusion ("one black shadow"), and emptiness ("An empty river-bed before"): "Nor bird would sing, nor lamb would bleat,/Nor any cloud would cross the vault" (ll. 37-38).

In the poem the mood and picture of external world is unified. The correspondence and interaction between the mind and its surroundings, between the situation and the subjective feelings comes out even more forcibly in the poem, where we have the troubled sleep in exhaustion produced by intense heat, with the dream of cool breezes and running brooks and the waking to consciousness of bare desolation:

> But day increased from heat to heat,
> On stony drought and steaming salt;
> Till now at noon she slept again,
> And seemed knee-deep in mountain grass
> And never heard her native breezes pass,
> And runlets babbling down the glen
> She felt he was and was not there.
> She woke; the babble of the stream
> Fell, and, without, the steady glare
> Shrank one sick willow sere and small (ll. 39-48)

The barrenness of the landscape depicts the strange hollow yearning in the lady. The poem constantly moves inward to what we call the heart: through the spacious expanse of field, road and sky. It penetrates further and further till it reaches the innermost nerve, the microscopic seat of the emotions, the centre of a power which for the individual can transform the whole exterior world. For Mariana, the beauty around her is poisoned by what is within her. At the end of every stanza echoes the heart-rending cry "...left alone,/ To live forgotten, and die forlorn" which strongly emphasizes the hapless state of the lady.

She is sick of the dreary surroundings, of her old memories, her loneliness, long waiting and lamentation. She finally bursts out in tears:

> And weeping then she made her moan,
> The night comes on that knows not morn,
> When I shall cease to be all alone,
> To live forgotten, and love forlorn (ll. 93-96)

The slight variations in the refrain aptly emphasize the persistent monotony and despair in the lady's life. Thus the psychological setting of "Mariana in South" depicts the strange uncanny horror of isolation and abandonment. Much of the effect of the two Mariana poems is dependent on the contrast between the carefully detailed, sensuous description of the physical world and the utter sterility of Mariana's emotional state.

"Oenone" published in 1832 was written on the inspiration of the Pyrenees which stood for Ida. In the poem Oenone tells of her grief at being deserted by Paris for the promise of Helen. She is a woman cheated in love. She symbolizes the deserted yet faithful wife. Oenone lives in the lap of Nature amidst mountain streams, under the shadowy Gargarus. She communicates with Mt. Ida, cohorts with its birds and beasts, and its caves are her hideout. She makes it her home because it is associated with happy and sad memories of the past. She in her bewilderment raves and roams over the hills and dales of her "Mother Ida" and complains about her loneliness:

> ...I alone awake.
> My eyes are full of tears, my heart of love,
> My heart is breaking, and my eyes are dim,
> And I am all aweary of my life. (ll. 29-32)

This sense of dejection and loneliness prevails throughout the poem. Oenone who was once "Beautiful browed" has now lost her charm:

> Her cheek had lost the rose, and round her neck
> Floated her hair or seemed to float in rest.
> She, leaning on a fragment twined with vine,
> Sloped downward to her seat from the upper cliff.
> (ll.17-21)

The golden apple of discord brings havoc to Oenone. She stays in the "wooden Ida" and desires to talk with the wild Cassandra, who had prophesied great discord and war. As an aggrieved wife she thinks of only one option, i.e. death – "Dear mother Ida, harken ere I die." This also is the refrain of her lament. The complaints in her wails are but an unburdening of her heart before she silences herself for ever. Tennyson makes her change her tone and mood in the end. The thought of dying helplessly, with Paris glorying in his new found love, becomes unendurable for her. Burning rage mounts within her as she imagines her husband and his paramour's shrill laughter breaking in on her "starless road of death." She declares that she will not die alone. The poem ends on her seething anger and revolt.

The vanity of Gods and man not only bring havoc to Oenone but also to Iphigenia, the daughter of Agamemnon. The poem "A Dream of Fair Women" was published in the 1932 volume. Iphigenia suffers much when the Greek fleet, on its way to Troy, is detained by contrary winds at Aules. In order to appease the Gods, Iphigenia is sacrificed to Artemis. She says:

> My youth...was blasted with curse:
> This woman was the cause. (ll. 103-104)

"This woman" is Helen for whom the ten year long war was fought. Iphigenia describes her death scene:

> My father held his hand upon his face;
> I, blinded with my tears,
> Still strove to speak: my voice was thick with sighs
> As in a dream. Dimly I could descry
> The stern black-bearded kings with wolfish eyes.
> Waiting to see me die.
> ...the bright death quivered at the victim's throat-
> Touched and I know no more. (ll. 107-112,115-116)

In "The Lady of Shalott" (1832), a poem based on the Arthurian legends, Tennyson depicts the life of a lonely young lady. She is as isolated as Mariana and Oenone though she has not been deserted like them, she is separated from the world and is imprisoned in an enchanted tower of Camelot under some curse, a curse about which she is not aware. Only a "whisper" has told her about it. The lady weaves away in seclusion at a web or tapestry, looking into a mirror to see the life that surrounds her tower, and then translating what she sees into the fabric before her, a reflection of a reflection. At the intrusion into the glass of the vision of Lancelot on his horse she recognizes the emptiness of her existence, cries aloud, and the mirror cracks as the web floats away. But she is unable to live in the world that she now attempts to enter. As her body floats down the stream to Camelot, Lancelot and his brother knights stare benignly but uncomprehendingly at her dead beauty.

At the beginning we find the lady leading a monotonous life, weaving beautiful patterns without looking at the world outside for the fear of the curse. But when she sees a glimpse of warm emotion in the mirror, she feels sick of her loneliness:

> Or when the moon was overhead,
> Came two young lovers lately wed;
> "I am half sick of shadows," said
> The Lady of Shalott. (ll. 69-72)

The lady grows weary of the mirror images. When she sees Sir Lancelot who represents life in its most attractive aspect, she leaves her web and her isolation to participate in life:

> In the stormy east-wind straining,
> The pale yellow woods were waning,
> The broad stream in his banks complaining,
> Heavily the low sky raining
> Over tower'd Camelot:
> Down she came and found a boat
> Beneath a willow left afloat,
> And round about the prow she wrote
> *The Lady of Shalott.* (ll. 118-126)

She comes down and in order to be recognized, writes her name on the boat. But before she reaches the first house in Camelot, she dies. The lady defies the spell when she turns around to the window to see Sir Lancelot riding by, and pays penalty of the curse by her death.

The lady of Shalott represents a typical Victorian woman leading an isolated life in the prison-like four walls. Her weaving of the magic web is the prescribed womanly work that a woman was supposed to do. In case she tries to seek a separate identity, as the lady does, the result is death. The moment she leaves her prison, she is doomed.

"The Palace of Art" pub. 1832 takes as its central symbol the figure of a lonely maiden in a tower or palace. The desert that surrounds the lady projects her emptiness and loneliness:

> One seem'd all dark and red – a tract of sand
> And someone pacing there alone. (ll. 65-66)

The narrator builds the soul withdrawn but "lordly pleasure-house," are treat for her to live in forever. Most of the poem is detailed description of the art adorning the building, which sounds rather like Xanadu as constructed by the architect of the Crystal Palace. At the conclusion of the poem the soul, like the lady of Shalott, shrinks from her solitude:

> "No voice", she shrieked in that lone hall,
> "No voice breaks through the silence of this world:
> One deep, deep silence all!" (ll. 259-261)

Her shriek, like the anguished cry of the Lady of Shalott, is the signal to leave the palace of lonely art.

The condition of women in the Victorian society has been realistically transmuted by Tennyson in these poems. The women in these poems are not complementary equals, they lack the strength, the vivacity and this is because the Victorian consciousness had difficulty in imaging women who possessed other than a narrow range of feminine qualities. Thus in this respect, Tennyson is part of his age. These lonely, suffering women of Tennyson can be put into two categories. In the first category we can place the sad melancholic young female deserted by their lovers and the second category comprises the lovely mothers languishing for their lost children. It was the poet's own sense of isolation which found its complete expression through these solitary female characters. Some personal sorrow or experience, which was gnawing at his heart, finds expression in these poems. Most of the poems based on suffering and lonely women were composed during 1830-31. It may be recalled that his mother was similarly distraught during this period. The estrangement this lady suffered was not because of the infidelity of her husband but because of the gradual distancing between the husband and the wife, brought about by his mounting ill-temper and fits of violence. The years from 1827 till Rev. Tennyson's death in 1831, seem to be particularly trying. For her it was not a physical desertion but an emotional one. Her faithful heart and loving nature suffered the gradual erosion of companionship and togetherness. That could be a reason for the composition of poems on deserted women.

On a personal level too, Tennyson had undergone all the suffering of a lonely man for the love of Rosa Baring and Emily. Life must have appeared a desolated wasteland to him. Moreover, the deaths of Arthur Hallam and his son Lionel had also aggravated the suffering and loneliness of the poet. In Tennyson loneliness is also a part of the romantic tradition which he follows. Thus these women may be called an unintentional diary of his psychological evolution.

Works Cited

Martin, Robert Bernard. *Tennyson: The Unquiet Heart.* London: Clarendon Press, 1983.

Ricks, Christopher. *Tennyson.* New York: Macmillan, 1972.

Tennyson, Alfred Lord. *The Poems and Plays of Alfred Lord Tennyson,* New York: The Modern Library, 1938.

Of Scholarly Writing and Creative Writing: A Satirical Approach

Dibakar Pal

Introduction

As you know well that Francis Bacon (1561-1626), the immortal essayist, wrote many essays namely Of Love, Of Friendship, Of Ambition, Of Studies, etc. The myriad-minded genius rightly pointed out that all the words of the dictionary can be the themes of essays one can write. But little has been done, in this regard since his death, in order to finish his unfinished monumental works. In fact Bacon's way of presentation, i.e., his unique individual style kindled the imagination already in me and encouraged me as well to write essays, in the light of creative writing, thus to get relief through Catharsis.

Abstract

Creative writing does not inform rather reveals. So it bears no reference. The present article is an outcome of creative writing meant for lay readers. As such, free style is the methodology adopted so that pleasure of reading can be enjoyed by the common mass. In this paper the basic differences between scholar and creator are discussed. A scholar is honoured everywhere but a creator gets hatred instead and thereby dies unfed, unwept, unsung and unknown as well. The paradox is that a Shakespearean scholar, doing research on the immortal creations of Shakespeare, is awarded a Doctoral Degree, but Shakespeare, the creator himself, had no formal education beyond school.

Source of the Idea

Boston University, USA asks to submit Scholarly Writing sample for admission in MA (English) and Creative Writing sample for admission in MA (Creative Writing). Now the question arises what is the difference between these two types of writings. How one can judge a writing either is the brain child of a scholar or a creator!

Who is a scholar? A widely read person is a scholar. But a creative writer (creator hereinafter) may not have such extensive study. Even without so-called formal education, an individual may be a creator.

A scholar makes brilliant result in the examination. In other words, score is the yardstick of a scholar. The more marks, the more scholar an individual is. On the other hand, a creator, generally, cannot make good result and even sometimes fails to qualify in the examination. Perhaps, failure renders an individual to be a creative writer. Thus, disqualification is his qualification.

A scholar has thirst for knowledge. But a creator feels to create something new. Both of them try to increase knowledge. A scholar continues his study to widen the horizon of knowledge. He can do anything to acquire knowledge. For that reason he undertakes painstaking endeavour to realize his ambition. A creator also starts his study like a scholar. But in the mid-way creativity disturbs his attention towards studies and leads him to do something new thus rendering him a diverted genius. And finally a creator fails in the examination due to lack of preparation. But a scholar makes brilliant result and paves his way towards temporal gain. However, both the scholar and the creator start with studies but the former finishes it while the latter leaves it. They say a scholar works hard, but a creator hardly works hard. This assumption is not correct always. A creator also toils much, may be, for classical return.

Everybody cares and respects a scholar. But a creator is ignored. He has innovative power. Imaginative faculty of mind agitates him much. So he is compelled to forget his mundane existence. Wild flights of fancy chase him from one galaxy to another. As a result, a creator fails everywhere in this world and becomes a laughing stock. He has business having no return at all. This is the sad story of a backward society. In an enlightened society creators are valued much. History is full of successful and respected creative writers. Writing of a scholar lacks imagination but is full of information. A scholar, in fact, is always guided by reference. But no reference is the preference of a creator since his writings are based mostly on hearsay. Thus creative writing is akin to and alias of hearsay writing. A scholar always pays attention for chronological and systematic representation of writings. But the talent of a creator is scattered.

In every sphere of life we expect consistency. We hate inconsis-tency since it has no exchange value. But consistency is the manifestation of artificiality already in man. On the other hand, inconsistency is the outcome of natural trait of an individual. The nature itself is inconsistent in its nature and behavior. For example, the sun rises in the east and sets in the west. But both sunrise and sunset do not happen at the same time. Everyday, the time of occurrence, changes. A man who, everyday, comes in time has to face much trouble. Every morning does not dawn to him at a particular point of time. So to reach in time he has to deprive himself from enjoyment and engagement from other events. As such to maintain continuity one has to face many hurdles which remain unknown to us.

Inconsistency faces no such troubles. Spontaneity is the alias of inconsistency. Inconsistency needs no practice. It is quite natural like a spring of the mountain. But one has to practice much to be a consistent artist, i.e., an artificial individual. A scholar, basically, is a consistent person. His consistency may not show equality always. In the worst case, he may be inconsistently consistent. Thus, whatever the case may be in the activity of a scholar, there must be an essence of consistency at least. But a creator is very whimsical. He is a vagabond. In fact a creator is an inconsistent individual by birth. He will, either be consistently inconsistent or, in most of the cases, he is inconsistently inconsistent. In real life, consistency has immense value. There is no substitute for consistency. In fact, consistency itself is its substitute.

A scholar has to mind many things. A creator has no such bindings. He writes of his own.

Innumerable and various thoughts, like the careless waves of the sea, flash in his mind's easel ceaselessly. His creation is the manifestation of inspired writing. He writes to get relief through catharsis. But a scholar experiences no such pain to get relief. Another school of thought disagrees with this doctrine. Writing either way creative or scholarly is an enjoyable experience. Even scholarly writers love doing their writing as they are creating something new of their own.

A creator reads little, thinks more and hears most. As such his writings are akin to hearsay writing. He argues that a scholar writes basing on his own experience. But hearsay writing is the outcome of many men's opinion. He hears and writes accordingly.

So he saves time and remains free from hazards of reading. Now if a scholar intends to write on what people say, firstly, he will read those books read by the mass and then he will write. It is a time consuming and painstaking venture. It is the credit of the scholar that he does not rely on third party's casual talks. A creator practices hearsay writing. He honours third party's opinion. He believes in democracy and thereby right to speech. But a creator seldom writes whatever he hears. For, he does not practice journalism. He hears, thinks over the matter and then writes in the light of literary essence. A scholar writes and gives references. Sometimes the length of references is more than the length of article itself. The scholar claims credit but fixes liability upon the references. Similarly, in hearsay writing prize goes to creator but punishment is imposed upon the public at large.

It is quite an interesting and safe game played and enjoyed by both the scholar and the creator.

A scholar may write scholarly notes on demand. But a creator cannot write on compulsion. In fact, the innovation of a creator cannot be regulated or controlled by demand and supply theory of economics. Appearance or disappearance of imagination obeys no rule at all. They are so whimsical rendering a creator bohemian in character. Thus bohemian whimsicality isolates a creator from reality.

A creator may be a scholar through extensive study. But a scholar may not be a creator. Creativity cannot be acquired by practice; rather it is a gift man gets by birth. Some critics disagree with this assumption. They contend that a scholar cannot be a creator within the strict boundaries of which he has to write scholarly articles. However, he also can interchange to a role of a creator with creative writing. Being a scholar doesn't come at the expense of losing creativity.

A scholar is a biased person. He, generally, is influenced by knowledge, i.e., other men's thoughts. Thus acquired knowledge kills his clarity of thought and thereby his originality. As such his innovative power is defeated by the giant knowledge. A scholar beats everybody's drum except his own. But a creator always beats his own drum. He seldom beats other person's drum. He is so undaunted and a confident person. Another school of thought argues that scholars depend on references to cite what has been done or known previously on a topic. Still, what is published would be his own interpretation of things. If scholars are not creative where would all the progress of science and technology come from?

This world is for scholar of scholar by scholar. So everywhere we see the infrastructure of manufacturing scholars. So creators are unwanted in a society that lacks in aesthetic essence. That's why only a scholar gets scholarship. Because scholars build the nation. If it is so, then another school of thought argues that creators are the ornament of a nation. Thus scholars are the builders of a building and creators are its decorators. So a scholar is a civil engineer but a creator is an architect. Thus scholars are a must for the nation. But creators are optional. Because, without architectural or aesthetic beauty a building can stand erect. So scholars are rewarded and creators die unfed. Thus to give scholarship to a creator is nothing but wastage of money. So society spends for scholars only. A scholar needs dollar. Conversely, dollar makes a scholar. However, if a scholar is a national scholar then a creator is a rational scholar.

But a creator is superior to a scholar. In fact where scholarship ends, creativity begins. For example, an aeroplane runs in the runway before take-off. Here running ends with the flight of imagination. A scholar gathers knowledge from books. He is a mobile library, a ready reference. But a creator learns gazing at the sky, observing a hill or horizon or ocean, i.e., nature is his teacher. As such, unobstructed view of the sky, robustness of mountain, distance of horizon, vastness and depth of ocean influence and perplex him much and he becomes indifferent.

A creator always feels to communicate what he feels. So he expresses simply so that everybody can realize what he says. But a scholar is a man of a complex mind. His allusion may not easily be understandable. Also he has no commitment to communicate his high thoughts. So the contribution of a scholar is the so-called "large still books" which remain unread.

Lord Buddha, Lord Christ, Prophet Mohammed, etc., were all creators. They had no so-called formal education. But they were naturally learned by birth. They appeared in this world with greatness already in them. They preached wise and immortal sayings to the world and saved the ailing humanity thereby. Thus, a creator is naturally learned. They say natural learning is good but sometimes it is at the cost of social unrest. More people kill each other on religious differences than on anything else.

A scholar, on the other hand, has to acquire knowledge. As such, a novice attends an Alma-Mater and becomes a scholar. So, a scholar is an artificial learned. For example, a duckling can swim. But a human baby cannot. It has to acquire the art of swimming.

In creative writing there must not be any influence of other schools of thoughts. But a scholar's writing is fully pregnant with different thoughts of his predecessors. So a 100% creator is seldom born. But 100% scholar is abundant in the world. There must be shadow of external influence that devours, like an eclipse, the spontaneity of a scholar.

Thus reading means to increase knowledge as well as invasion of other thoughts. A scholar considers the voice of a book final. But a creator values his own choice. So he declines to confess the sayings of a book, rather he likes to preach his own views without being influenced by the news of a book. As such a creator reads very cautiously lest he be influenced by other schools of thoughts. Now he who wants to be a scholar should be absorbed in studies freely without any tension but with great attention.

A scholar compiles a dictionary. He explains the meaning of the words which are chronologically arranged in a definite manner. But a creator interprets the meaning of any word from a different point of view. His way of representation has rare individual style.

This different angle of view and new light illuminates the dark avenue to reach an un-trodden destination. Thus this endeavour kindles the imagination of an inquisitive heart.

A 100% creator dies unfed, unwept, unsung and unknown as well due to lack of practical experience. A 100% scholar communicates only with another 100% scholar. As such his friends are numbered. In fact a scholar is a reserve personality. This theoretical assumption suffers from serious criticism. One cannot give numbers and it's grossly wrong to assign and thereby grade scholarship and creativity measuring through percentage scale. There is nothing called 100% on these issues like IQ measurement. Basically a bad scholar and a bad creator may die unfed and unappreciated while the good ones shine through no matter what path of writing they practice.

Degree of reference, in a scholarly writing, is the yardstick of measuring the talent of a scholar. The more reference the more scholar, the less reference the less scholar. Similarly no reference means no scholar. In fact a scholar lives with reference and dies with reference. He cannot think anything without reference. To him no reference is also a reference, like no politics is also a politics or no style is also a style or no statistics is also statistics or no expectation is also an expectation, or nothingness implies everything or no existence means staying elsewhere beyond our knowledge as well. Many would disagree with this high opinion.

On the other hand, reference is considered as the demerit of a creator. Scholarly writing is quite stereotyped. Also there should be room for diversity in scholarly writing as well.

All scholars, generally, use the same data of reference. As such scholarly writings may have similarities with each other. This is due to the so-called fact that great men think alike. In other words all roads lead to Rome. But creative writing differs with each other. They differ even on any definite topic. They think not alike. So they are not great. As such, they follow no rule at all, rather break the rules. But a scholar is strict in obeying established rules while he writes anything.

Research means to agree or disagree with the existing school of thoughts. If a researcher agrees, then further extension of idea crowns him with doctoral degree. But if he disagrees then, to be laurelled, he is liable to prove the wrongs of existing theory and must propose his idea with validity. A scholar seldom contributes but, generally, agrees with his predecessors. As such he mentions references in support of his claim. But a creator disagrees always. So he has no liability to site examples. Thus, a scholar when disagrees and pleads for new ideas becomes a creator.

A creator goes ahead with a hypothesis. He tries to establish it. If he fails, he modifies it and ultimately finds the truth i.e., the theory. So, he uses no reference at all. But his works are used as reference by the scholars to get Ph.D. Reference is a must to prepare a doctoral thesis. If any scholar does not give references then the reviewers will reject the thesis forthwith without examining in spite of having sufficient merit. The creator does not use reference and remains unrewarded. But giving of references is nothing but simply mentioning the name of the books or journals. It adds no contribution at all in the whole thesis. Yet the reviewers need it. Thus it is a severe punishment to a creator merely for a venial offence.

In school or college, during examination, the students do not give any reference while they write the answers. Also the teachers don't need any reference while they examine the answer scripts. The creator considers it as norms. To him a thesis is nothing but the answers of a problem defined. This is an agreed paradox of the critic. Yet, published scholarly literature is concise and needs to be focused and the reader should have the right to independently assess and verify what the author is presenting. So the transparency with references need not be seen as a demerit.

The creator respects the reviewers as learned. To him reviewers are always versatile genius having infinite wisdom. Their spectrum of knowledge is much wide both horizontally and vertically with diversification. He thinks that the reviewers are always busy to update themselves with latest knowledge. So he finds no justification to mention the reference, i.e., the source of knowledge to the highly knowledgeable critic-cum-reviewers.

Mathematicians deal with necessary and sufficient condition of any theory. They also mention the limitation of any idea. Similarly, if knowledge be the necessary condition to be a reviewer or critic then updating work is the sufficient condition and is a must for examination of any thesis. At this present age of fast development of technology and knowledge, a reviewer without updated knowledge, will merely become a novice or a marginal player who should not be burdened with the important task and responsibility of examining a thesis. But the funny thing is that the educational institutions engage such novices as examiner who naturally needs the references which they use as torch to illuminate the darkness and reach their unknown area of study and knowledge. Mathematicians are the most creative people ever. However to prove their theorems and formulae they have to stick to a rigid form of writing. Still, that enables them to communicate to a fellow mathematician in a language they understand. Sticking to rigid methods of presentation of information and loss of creativity are not synonymous.

A scholar copies and gives reference. When the number of reference is less it is called "plagiarism." Unfortunately, a novice scholar is blamed as a "plagiarist." But huge number of references crowns such a "plagiarist" a researcher. So little stealing is called theft but much stealing is called research. Thus, through stealing, he becomes an expert. Now the question arises – who is an expert? They say, an expert is one who complicates simple things. An expert, to prove his expertise, can convert complex into simple and simple into complex as well. He enjoys sadistic pleasure through complicacy. But a creator is free from all such allegations of plagiarism or expertise.

A good writer knows what to write and a great writer knows what not to write. Further, there are two types of writers. One finds pleasure when the reader understands his writing. But the other class likes to remain obscure. It is a fact that he who realizes any matter clearly can explain it lucidly. A scholar enjoys much when his writings remain not understandable to others. It may be the merits of a scholar but demerit or misfortune of a reader. But a creator enjoys immense and intense heavenly delight when the reader enjoys his feeling. He feels akin to the readers. Thus a creator wants to share his ideas and thoughts. But a scholar keeps safe distance, lest he should come close.

Further, there are two types of writings namely writing before reading and writing after reading. A scholar at first reads and then writes. But a creator writes without reading. He reads if he likes. He reads not if he likes not. Thus to him reading is quite optional. As a result the creation of a creator has three outcomes. The first outcome is similar to an existing school of thought. In this case he contributes nothing but wins the crown of a great man. For, great men think alike. So, without reading or knowing nothing a man becomes great through ignorance. This is quite a noble and warm feeling. In the second case the writing is dissimilar to others. Then it is called creation. In the third case the writing signifies nothing or quite rubbish. As such it is thrown into the dustbin. But the creator argues that the present scholars can't realize the inner meaning of his so called obscured matter. But the scholars of future must illuminate this dark assertion.

A scholar is a mature person. As such he is calm and humble by nature. But a creator is quite restless just like the spring of a mountain. A scholar dies of heart attack due to excessive pressure of facts, figures and theories. But a creator, generally, leads a long life due to absence of cares and anxieties as faced by a knowledgeable scholar. Obviously, there is exception to this fact.

A scholar becomes biased through reading. All his thoughts are channeled as per existing thoughts. He seldom deviates from the existing standards which he considers as unchangeable. He is afraid of deviation. To him deviation means demolition. Thus he is self imprisoned. Much study renders him a rigid character. The more study the more rigidity. Thus he becomes an orthodox or conservative like a communist. A communist is hurt if he is blamed for his strict discipline. In fact he suffers from and thereby enjoys holding instinct aroused from obsolete doctrines. But a creator is a flexible one. He appreciates that variety is the spice of life. He changes his opinion with the change of time. His change occurs very quickly. As such to him time never freezes. Thus a creator is moulded very easily. He says that there is no basic difference between the two sentences, viz., he may come or he may not come. He explains that he may come means, he may not come also. Similarly, he may not come means that he may come as well. The former expresses the affirmation and the latter being the negative one, i.e., it simply expresses the tendency of uncertainty instead of certainty of a concerned individual.

In an appointment letter of any job the statement of employer is either of two types namely (i) Appointment is hereby given to the concerned candidate. Or (ii) Appointment is hereby given to the candidate concerned. A scholar finds no difference between these two sentences. But the creator begs to differ. He argues that in the first case the word "concerned" is the adjective of the noun "candidate" who is a person of choice of the authority even in spite of having low profile. But in the later case it is just reverse. In fact, an ill motive plays behind such first type of appointment. Thus, the first category allegedly suffers from nepotism and the second one stands for fair selection. Because in case of second type the candidate is unknown till the selection process is completed. Rather the candidate is selected considering all factors. In the case of the first instance the candidate is known and selected already prior completion of selection process. Thus this interview is like a got up game whose Fate is already fixed. As such the interview is merely an eyewash and thereby a farce to obey the law just to disobey it thereby proving so-called obedience.

Criminology pleads that a criminal must leave at least a single clue. And it is identified from the clue it leaves. Here the clue is "concerned candidate" instead of "candidate concerned." Now it seems clear that in the first case the candidate was selected earlier before the selection process which was merely eyewash. But in the second case the candidate was unknown before selection and was selected observing to due formalities and maintaining transparency. Now an investigator can detect at ease the psychology of subconscious mind of the biased and partial interviewer. Also the biased interviewer while fails to offer appointment to their own candidate submits the report stating "NFS," i.e., none found suitable paving the way for future nepotism.

A good student does not write different things. But he writes differently. Similarly, the difference thus manifested by the creator has its uniqueness having quite uncommon and rare individual style. A scholar shows his highest aptitude as a critic. He is a judge of literary or artistic merit. He shows his expertise as a professional reviewer. Besides these a critic is also a fault-finder. But criticism becomes lively only when it is constructive and helpful. But the critical critic seldom bothers it. For, he warms his ego through sadistic pleasure. They say, he who can does, on the contrary, he who can't criticize. As such a critic is hardly seen to create something. The wearer knows where the shoe pinches. The barefooted critic has no shoe, thereby remains safe from pinching. But who will be so dare devil to find fault with a learned critic? Generally, a critic should describe the merit or demerit of any writing sympathetically. This helpful criticism encourages new writers to write more successfully. But novice writers die immature due to merciless criticism.

Tact of omission is an art of a creator. But this art becomes a dangerous weapon to the critics since they interpret as per their sweet will with far-stretched meaning. Sometimes the critic becomes interested to express more what the writer did not think at all. In many cases the critic opines the opposite view or completely a new one. The criticism becomes dangerous when the writer throws little light on any dark assertion, thus allowing the readers to enjoy liberal thinking. In such a case the critic enjoys the full liberty and jumps accordingly with full enthusiasm to explain an obscure matter. Here lies the merit and demerit of democracy. However, sometimes, to acquire cheap popularity, a critic becomes interested more in what is not told than told. Thus degree of scholarly criticism depends on the success of exaggeration, manufacturing of the untold and unheard doctrine as well.

The moralist believes in the principle, "Art for life's sake." The antithesis being, "Art for Art's sake" hankers after Aesthetic movement whose followers believe in the cult of beauty, or the enjoyment of beauty for its own sake. Perhaps the creator has equal respect to both the doctrines, the brainchild of the scholars. He believes in classical success instead of commercial one. It seems didactic fragrance destroys the classical essence of a writing.

In English grammar there are two types of articles namely definite and indefinite. Truth is always one. But lies are many. A teacher advises, speak the truth and never tell a lie. Thus definite article, "the" is used before the truth. But, indefinite article, "a" is used before a lie. The proverb goes many men, many minds. As such different critics explain a single matter differently and independently. Great men think alike. But in many cases the critics seldom think alike. As a result more than one meaning are found in the market on a single issue. Thus so many scholars deal with so many lies.

Wisdom is the glamour of a learned scholar. Through serious study, constant meditation and continuous experience he becomes wise. A creator becomes a scholar when he uses reference. Similarly, a scholar becomes a creator without using any reference. So a man may be 100% scholar or 100% creator or "cocktail" of both in different proportions.

Perhaps both of them dwell at the threshold of creativity and scholarship. They say if there would have been only creators then progress and scientific advancement wouldn't have reached where our world is now today. Though there are a lot many reference holding writers but all are not in the same boat. However, it seems, both the scholar and the creative writer are complementary to each other for the advancement of the civilization. Now it seems clear that Shakespeare is a creator but he who has read all his writings is a Shakespearean scholar.

They say where goodness ends, greatness begins. In fact goodness of a scholar renders a nation good; on the other hand, greatness of the creator converts a nation great. As such, a good nation salutes a scholar. But a great nation welcomes a creator.

Shakespeare in Business

Dr. Rashmi Kumari

> Let me tell you, Cassius, you yourself Are
> much condemn'd to have an itching palm
>
> —*Julius Caesar* by Shakespeare

Great writers are gifted with not merely powerful imagination but also incisive intellects. The greatest among the world writers, Shakespeare had both these gifts in great measure than any other writer known to mankind. Given to seeing life steadily and seeing it whole Shakespeare screened and scrutinized every subject he presented on the stage showing it from all sides, throwing the dramatic searchlight on every nook and corner in the multidimensional structure of his plays, be they comedies, tragedies, histories, or romances.

"To know the force of human genius, we should read Shakespeare" wrote essayist William Hazlitt. It's the genius revealed in the Bard's profound insights into human nature that has made him so extraordinarily successful for four hundred years.

While going through all these sentences pinpointing Shakespeare's genius on portraying human life so truthfully and so passionately, I began pondering over this very question – "Is Shakespeare relevant to today's globalised corporate world" or will studying his plays be an enriching experience in the cut-throat world of management?

And as I went on studying his plays one after another, I just got amazed to find how his plays are packed with essential insight into human psychology and the use and abuse of power. Shakespeare's shrewd understanding of palace politics and the strategies of warfare can just as easily be applied to the twists and turns of the corporate world. Whether it is looking at Henry V's amazing ability to motivate team facing almost certain defeat and turn the situation around or King Lear demonstrating the perils of poor estate management, Bard's management skill is just revealing and amazing. A bard can easily bridge the issues faced by a 16th century shopkeeper and a leader of a 21st century global enterprise.

Today, in our world barraged by entertainment options as never before Shakespeare remains an undisputed star of stage and screen. The growing number of executives find that time spent with the Bard is a sound investment and unpredictably enjoyable. The Bard boom has hit the boardroom. For business leaders find that Shakespeare's plays offer deft and gripping exploration of the world of power which remains as relevant today as they were in the 16th century. The lessons they teach are remarkably useful in today's tough corporate universe.

At first blush, it might seem that Shakespeare and modern management don't mesh. Shakespeare conjures up images of crazy princes, ugly witches, fallen kings and sulking guys in tights holding skulls of worthy corpses. The word management conjures up images of crazy prices, ugly deals, fallen CEO's and sulking guys in gray suits holding stacks of worthless options.

But the two do mesh, for business involves people, and people – fundamentally – don't change. The essence of business is thus remarkably constant.

While the accoutrements of corporate life are now dramatically high tech-dominated by e-mail, cell phones, the web, and PCs – the basics still hinge on human nature. Corporate affairs remain dependent largely on the strengths or fallings of the men and women who make up a company or organization. Ambition and greed have brought down many a man. Be it during the Bard of Avon's time in the seventeenth (17th) century or now as Rajat Gupta, former head of Mckinsey, is arrested for sharing boardroom secrets with billionaire hedge fund manager Raj Rajaratnam. Even the "occupy wall street" protests are a reaction to this. The darker side of human nature – greed, overreaching ambition, ravaging jealousy, dishonesty – is as likely to undermine or even destroy a business now as it was before the days of the Internet and pagers. And it is that darker side that Shakespeare understands so well.

Not all business recapitulates Shakespearean tragedy, of course. But neither do they habitually achieve the happy ending of the Bard's comedy. Success is difficult to achieve at any level. Many modern executives face a series of obstacles along their path that require intense understanding and careful handling. As Rosalind puts it in *As You Like It,* "How full of briers is this working day world." A study of Shakespeare can teach us, in our "working day world" how best to handle those "briers." For he offers the most penetrating insight into what makes people and organizations tick at every level.

"Speak on, but be not over tedious" says Burgundy in *Henry VI Part-I* and "all things are ready, if our minds be so" as Henry V declares at the outset of his adventure.

In *As You Like It* a rather melancholy Jacques lamented the following: all the world's a stage and all the men and women merely players; and one man in his time plays many parts. He gives advice with these words that we should take to heart. Playing these many parts will, at times, gain us the most traction as we make our vertical move. With Jacques' musings in mind, another of Shakespeare's characters, Polonius, from *Hamlet* gives his son Laertes some sound guidance as Laertes travelled off to school. This counsel establishes a baseline for young professionals and executives finding their way in the new, volatile and unpredictable corporate world.

What struck me, are five valuable business lessons from Shakespeare, embedded in a father's pearls of wisdom delivered to his son in one of Shakespeare's timeless masterpieces: *Hamlet* (Act-I, Scene III) Lines 59-80.

1. Give Thy Thoughts No Tongue

Basic as it may be as business lessons go, keep in mind the idea of thinking before you speak, it looms large when you are just starting to feel your way through your career. You must pick your battles wisely and with caution. Know your audience, when you have one, and cater to their needs; not your own. Remember, early on in your tenure at least to check your ambition at the door unless ambition is paramount in the jobs expectations.

2. But Do Not Dull Thy Palm With Entertainment of Each New Hatch'd, Unfledged Comrade

Stay away from misguided individuals in the workplace who thrive on negative gossip. Attempt also to steer clear of office politics and maintain constant focus on your objectives (once you actually know what those objectives will be). Do your job, but also be flexible when good opportunities present themselves. In the words of another language master, hip-hop mogul and prep revolutionist Pharrel Williams, think "boxlessly."

3. Give Every Man Thy Ear, But Few Thy Voice

Regardless of the person, be it the CEO or head custodian, practise active listening. Actually listen to the words and understand those words before you retort. Hard though it may be, try not to form your responses until you have let the speaker speak. That way you will continue to follow the speaker's intended message. Use what you hear by disseminating what is useful and what can be tossed aside as unimportant (at least right now). Make intelligent decisions about with whom you plan to share ideas and information; moreover be careful about the information you share.

4. Neither A Borrower Nor a Lender Be –

Depending on your role and responsibilities, be careful of the information you give to a manager, supervisor or CEO, especially if you care about credit, it may be wise to put your head down and work without ruffling too many feathers. And when you do dole out jewels and nuggets of wisdom, do not give away the farm. It is also crucial to remember that your personal life is personal. Be protective and vigilant. Stay away from cliques and group alignments.

5. This Above All: To Thine Own self Be True –

This particular comment by Polonius sums up the totality of his fatherly advice as well as a major component of realizing and maintaining power for a satisfying and lengthy career. Be true to yourself and your work and if you believe in hard work, fight for it intelligently with difference and without arrogance. Be clear about your role, responsibilities and objectives, and stick to them until your time comes. If your time does not come in your current job or career, be patient – it will. And most importantly, contrary to Shakespeare's true genius – do not deceive or lie, it will only hurt you later.

So, the issues fuelling the intricate plots of Shakespeare's four hundred year old plays are the same common yet complex issues that business leaders contend with today. Because Shakespeare's plays – portray the "The General Human Nature," something that never changes from century to century, or country to country, despite all the differences in knowledge, culture and emphasis.

Works Cited

Augustine, Norman and Adelman, Kenneth. *Shakespeare in Charge : The Bard's Guide to Leading and Succeeding on the Business Stage.* Talk Miramax Books.

Bloom, Harold. *Shakespeare: The Invention of the Human.* Open Marke (*ed.*) Harlow Essex: Logman-2001, ISBN:1-57322-751-X.

Spencer, T.J.B.(*ed.*) *Hamlet.* New Penguin Shakespeare Ser. London: Penguin, 1980.

Times of India. New Delhi, November 6, 2011.

Whitney, John O, and Packer, Tina. *Power Plays Shakespeare's Lessonni Leadership and Management.* New York: A Touch Stone Book, 2001

King Lear Revisited

Dr. Sarita Sinha

King Lear is generally regarded as the greatest of the four tragedies of Shakespeare, though some would, no doubt, express their preference for *Hamlet.* The real greatness of the play resides in the fact that it is not the tragedy of just an individual but rather of all humanity. It is a cosmic tragedy. In it there is a parent-child relationship, or more precisely, filial ingratitude which is a universal experience. But in the sequence of its event, it demonstrates the spiritual growth of Lear from the egoistical autocratic king to a humble person, who feels for the poor man in the street.

The purpose of this article is to analyse *King Lear* in the light of India's ancient *Rasa theory* in a fresh paradigm.

In the history of Indian aesthetic thought the concept of *Rasa* is the oldest one. *Rasa* theory became the most dominant literary theory of India after a long battle against the schools of *alankara, riti, vakrokti* and *auchitya,* and was adopted by the *Dhwani* School which ultimately emerged as the most powerful school of literary criticism in India.

Bharata was the first thinker to define the term *rasa* in his *Natyasastra.* He very emphatically states in the *Rasadhyaya* of *Natyasastra* that "no meaningful idea is conveyed if the *rasa* is not evoked."

According to Sanskrit *natya* theory every dramatic presentation is aimed at evoking in the minds of audience a particular kind of aesthetic experience which is described as *Rasa. Rasa* has no equivalent in word or concept in any other language or art of world hitherto known to us. The closest explanation can be "aesthetic relish."

We do come across the mention of the *Natyasutras* prior to Bharat's *Natyasastra,* yet it is only Bharata muni who gave a scientific codification of the concept of *Rasa.* Bharata says that *natya* is the imitation of life wherein the various human emotions have to be grammatically glorified so that the spectator may be able to relish the portrayed pleasure and pain as *Natya Rasa.* This *Rasa* experience entertains the spectator. Bharata tried to encode the multidimensional nature of *Rasa* in one sentence "*Rasyate anena iti rasah*" (NS 28).

Vibhavanubhavavyabhichari sangyogat rasa nishpattihi, is a famous sloka in Bharata's *Natyasastra* which explains how *rasa* is relished.

The aesthetic relish is produced by a combination of the determinants (*vibhavas*), consequents (*anubhava*) and transitory emotions (*vyabhicharibhavas*). This aesthetic relish, which is possible only through mental perception, is termed as "*Natya Rasa.*"

Vibhavas are the determinants, which is the cause of the birth of feeling. These are the stimuli such as the story, the stage, the actors, responsible for the awakening of the *sthayi,* i.e. the latent sentiments in the spectator. The *vibhavas* are of two kinds:

A. *Alambana* – It is the basic stimulus capable of arousing the sentiments.

B. *Uddipana* – *Uddipana vibhavas* are the enhancing stimuli, the environment in which the basic stimulus is located.

C. *Anubhava* (consequents) is the manifestation of feeling on the part of the actor. It consists of various gestures and glances, etc. of the actor.

D. *Vyabhicharibhavas* (transitory mental state) are the transient emotions which arise in the course of maintaining and developing the basic mood. These emotions are very strong. These *bhavas* are 33 in number. They arise to one *sthayibhava.*

Bharata classifies the *rasa* under eight categories and gives the corresponding *Bhavas* which give rise to the *rasa.* These are known as *sthayibhavas* or pervading stable emotion. These are *rati* (love), *hasa* (mirth), *shoka* (grief), *krodha* (anger), *utsaha* (heroism), *bhaya* (fear), *jugupsa* (disgust), and *vismaya* (wonder).

The corresponding eight *rasas* are *sringar* (amorous), *hasya* (humorous), *karuna* (pathetic), *raudra* (furious), *veera* (valorous), *bhayanaka* (horrific), *vibhatsa* (repugnant) and *adbhuta* (wondrous). These states of mind are inborn in every human heart and permanently exist in the form of latent impression in the mind, which is derived from real experiences of life or from inherited instincts. They spring into man's consciousness on suitable occasions when these are acted artistically on the stage or expressed in the poetry; gradually they lead the spectator to particular pleasure which Bharata calls *rasa.*

With a view to studying *King Lear* in the light of Bharata's *rasa theory* it is planned to take the last act of the play and analyse it within the framework of the doctrine concerned.

ACT V, SCENE I takes place in the British camp near Dover, where Regan and Edmund are talking about Goneril and Albany. Edmund complains that the duke of Albany is constantly changing his plans. At this Regan asks him whether he loves Goneril. She asks him not to be very intimate to Goneril as she cannot tolerate this. At this Edmund assures her that he has nothing but honourable sentiments towards her. At the same time Goneril and Albany enter. When Goneril sees Regan and Edmond together, she thinks that she would rather lose the battle than Regan, because Regan has come between her and Edmund.

After sometime Goneril and Regan depart. Edgar enters still disguised. He hands Goneril's letter, addressed to Edmund over to Albany and goes away. At the same time Edmund also enters with the intelligence of the enemy's strength and sends Albany to his army. Edmund is then left alone. He thinks now what he should do. He had sworn his love to both sisters, but they are so jealous that neither can be enjoyed if both remain alive. He decides to wait until the battle is over.

In this scene we find that Goneril and Regan are terribly jealous of each other. When Goneril finds Regan talking to Edmund, she becomes suspicious. Here the *vyabhicharibhava* of *shanka* mixed with *irshya* can be noticed in Goneril.

Ashraya: Goneril.

Alambana: Regan.

Uddipana: The sight of Regan and Edmund, sitting close to each other.

Anubhava: Her thinking, "I had rather lose the battle than that sister should loosen him and me."

ACT V, SCENE II takes place in the countryside near Dover, where Edgar places his father under the shadow of a tree. He asks him to "pray that the right may thrive" and then goes to the battle. But he returns with the sad news that Cordelia has lost the battle and both she and her father have been arrested. Hearing this sad news Gloucester is full of remorse and desires to end his life. But Edgar warns him that he should not be obsessed with such sinister thought of suicide and like a philosopher he utters the following word:

"Men must endure their going hence, even as their coming hither: Ripeness is all."

He means to say that a man must wait for death just as he waits for birth. Gloucester seems to be convinced.

In this scene the *vyabhicharibhavas* of *shoka* and *nirveda* are found in Gloucester when he says, "no further Sir, a man may rot even here."

Ashraya: Gloucester.

Uddipana: The news of cordelia's defeat and the consequent arrest of Lear and Cordelia.

Anubhava: Gloucester's decision to commit suicide.

ACT V, SCENE III takes place in the English camp near Dover. Lear and Cordelia are led as prisoners. Edmund sends them away and secretly instructs a gaoler to hand Cordelia in such a way as to let it appear that she herself has committed suicide out of sheer despair. At the time when they are being taken, Cordelia is very sad for her father but the king is happy because he will have his beloved daughter's company in the prison. He tells that they will pass their days happily by praying and singing together like birds in a cage. They will tell old tales and talk of the mystery of things as if they were God's spies.

After their departure Albany, Goneril and Regan enter. Albany congratulates Edmund on his victory and requests that the two prisoners should be delivered to him. At this Edmund tells him that he has sent Lear and Cordelia away to a prison because the king's age and title still have charm to win over common people and include their own soldiers to rebel. Albany is not pleased by this. He tells Edmund that in this war, Edmund is his subordinate, not his brother or social equal. Hearing this, Regan comes forward and submits herself to Edmund as her lord and husband, Regan's shameful surrender is denounced by Goneril. But Albany arrests both, on the charges of high treason and at the same time he exposes the liaison between Goneril and Edmund. Edmund throws down his gloves as a symbol of challenge. In the mean time Regan grows sicker as a result of poison administered to her by her sister Goneril and she is led away. The herald sounds a trumpet and in response Edgar appears in disguise. Edmund and Edgar fight and Edmund receives a deadly wound and falls down. Goneril cries out that Edmund is unfairly beaten. Albany sternly cries and asks her to be silent and upon her refusal, he throws at her the letter sent by her to Edmund, asking him to murder Albany. At this she goes out saying "Ask me not what I know."

Edmund, who has been mortally wounded, now admits Albany's charges of treachery and confesses that by a turn of fortune's wheel, he was just now so high but is here laid low in death. "The wheel is come full circle, I am here." On seeing his brother's plight, Edgar reveals his identity. He is then warmly embraced by Albany when he tells the whole story of his and his father's miseries including the services of banished Kent. As Edgar concludes, an attendant enters with the views that Goneril has killed herself with a knife and that Regan has died of poison given by her sister.

At the same time Kent enters and asks for the king and Cordelia. At this Edmund says that he has already issued orders for the execution of the king. Now Edmund wants to save their lives, but Cordelia has already been hanged.

Lear enters with the dead body of Cordelia in his arms. The king still attempts to see the symptoms of life in her body. He is unable to recognise faithful Kent and knows not what he says. He calls all of them traitors and murderers of his beloved daughter. Meantime a messenger brings news that Edmund has died. Albany then announces that he will resign absolute powers to King Lear for as long as he lives. But Lear dies of an excess of grief caused by Cordelia's death. Albany then asks Edgar and Kent to govern with him. Kent refuses. He is so full of grief. He says that he must soon follow his master, Lear. Edgar praises the old Kent: they who are young "shall never see so much nor live so long." Thus the play ends here on a highly pathetic note.

With a view to applying the theory of rasa to this scene we can divide it into three clear-cut parts. In the first part where Lear and Cordelia are lost in a make-believe world of simplicity and plainness in the prison, free from all intrigues and waywardness of the court-life, we have an experience of *vatsalya rasa.* Its *sthayibhava* is *vatsalya* or loving affection in the heart of Lear for his daughter Cordelia. The allusions to telling of old tales, praying and singing serve as *uddipana vibhava* and Cordelia's sincere concern and Lear's attempt to console Cordelia by saying that Goneril and Regan will not be able to separate them (i.e. Lear and Cordelia) can be regarded as the *sancharibhavas* for the purposes of *rasa* evoked here.

The second section of the scene, dealing with the love-affair of Goneril and Regan on the one hand and of Edmund on the other and its evil consequences provides an example of *sringara-rasabhasa.* The *sthayibhava* here is the illegitimate *rati* (erotic feeling) felt by Goneril and Regan for Edmund. Thus Edmund is the *ashraya* here and the two rival sisters are the *alambana.* Goneril's administration of poison to her own sister and Regan's (who is a widow), shameless declaration of Edmund's mastery over her "place and person" in the presence of Albany and Goneril and Albany's exposure of his wife's secret love-affair with Edmund through the love-letter addressed to her paramour all serve as *uddipana vibhavas.* The death of Regan and Goneril and Edmund's fight with Edgar and his resultant death further inflame the inherent *sthayibhava* of the evil erotic love; these incidents are not pathetic at all though they appear to be so. With the help of these *sancharibhavas* the *Rasabhasa* grows and reaches its fruition in the form of our revulsion or *jugupsa.*

The third part of the scene, dealing with Lear's response to the dead body of Cordelia who has been hanged produces *karuna rasa.* The *sthayibhava is karuna* or *shoka* and Lear is *ashraya* here. The dead body of Cordelia serves as *uddipana.* Lear's pathetic speech, expressing his unbelief and shock of his hysterical behaviour and his fainting serve as *sancharibhava* and his death is the *anubhava* here.

It appears that the most comprehensive and representative literary theory of India is the *rasa* theory which can be applied to all literatures of the world but unfortunately in spite of its dynamic nature it has remained mostly in India without shedding much light in the international arena. Therefore an attempt has been made to enable the people to become aware of such unique literary theory that can be applied to any works of art.

Works Cited

Bhannudutta. *Rasatarangani.* Varanasi: V.P. Samvat, 1924.

Keith, A.B. *The Sanskrit Drama.* Oxford at the Claren, 1924.

Mishra, Hariram. *Theory of Rasa in Sanskrit Drama.* Sagar: Vindhyachal Prakashan, 1964.

Pandey, K.C. *Abhinav Gupta, Historical and Philosophical Studies.* Varanasi: CSS Office, 1963.

The Grapes of Wrath and *Kanthapura*: A Comparative Study

Dr. K.B.S. Krishna

In the first half of the 20th century, two novels were published around the same time on almost diametrically opposite sides of the globe. These two novels share so many similarities that they seem bent on proving Rudyard Kipling's (1865-1936) statement in his "The Ballad of East and West" that "East is East and West is West and never the twain shall meet" (54) is wrong.

Raja Rao's (1908-2006) *Kanthapura* (1938) was published at around the same time as John Steinbeck's (1902-68) *The Grapes of Wrath* (1939). Considering that both novels were written at a period when the authors' countries were going through a difficult period, it is probably not too surprising that the themes are similar. The U.S. was working its way out of the great depression, and the people were naturally nervous. This apprehension and the economic situation form the setting for Steinbeck's novel. *Kanthapura*, meanwhile, was written when the Indian freedom movement was at its peak, and almost all the Indians were the followers of Mahatma Gandhi (1869-1948). The nationalistic fervour forms the backdrop for this novel.

However, it is surprising that the similarities between the two texts are not limited to the theme, but extend to the plot, characters, setting, and style. This paper will look at how this is done.

Plot-wise, *Kanthapura* describes the coming of the freedom movement to Kanthapura, a small village in South India. However, the novel is not only about the political struggle that takes place, but also about the social exploitation of the Indian labourer by the British, and their realisation of this, leading to revolt. The way this social struggle is depicted in the novel is similar to Steinbeck's Pulitzer Prize winning novel, *The Grapes of Wrath*.

Both the novels are similar in the sense that they start off by describing the way exploitation takes place, and then come up with a hero, who although seemingly beaten at the end, had meanwhile inspired others to take up the fight. In *Kanthapura* life on the Skeffington coffee estate is described in detail. The labourers come from all over south India with hope and are at the mercy of the estate owner, an Englishman – who is called in the novel as the "Red Man." The way they come to the land is described in poetic detail, and at the same time highlights the hopes and expectations they had:

> [...] coolies from below the Ghats that talked Tamil or Telugu and who brought with them their old men and their children and their widowed women-armies of coolies marched past the Kenchamma Temple, half-naked, starving, spitting, weeping, vomiting, coughing, shivering, squeaking, shouting, moaning coolies – coolies after coolies passed by the Kenchamma Temple, the maistri before them, while the children clung to their mothers' breasts, the old men to their sons' arms, and bundles hung over shoulder and arm and arm and shoulder and head; and they marched on past the Kenchamma Temple and upto the Skeffington Coffee Estate – coolies from below the Ghats, coolies, young men, old men, old women, children, baskets, bundles, pots, coolies passed on – and winding through the twists of the Estate path – by the Buxom-pipal bend, over the Devil's Ravine Bridge, by the Parvati Well Corner – they marched up, the maistri before them, the maistri that had gone to their village, and to the village next to their village, and to the village next to that, and that is far away, a day's journey by road and a night's journey by train and a day again in it, and then along the Godavery's banks, by road and by lane and by footpath, there he came and offered a four-anna bit for a man and a two-anna bit for a woman, and they all said, "Is there rice there?" and he said, "There is nothing but rice around us;" and they all said, "That is a fine country, for here, year after year, we have had neither rain nor canal-water, and our masters have left for the city." (50-51)

The exploitation is financial as well as emotional and physical, as he not only give the labourers enough wages but also physically abuses them by raping the women, etc. As the narrator points out "[...] but he will have this woman and that woman, this daughter and that wife, and every day a new one and never the same two within a week" (60).

However, in *The Grapes of Wrath* this sort of exploitation is not depicted. Similar to the labourers in *Kanthapura*, here also the workers come all the way from Oklahoma due to being displaced from their land to work on the cotton farms in California with lots of hope. But their hopes are dashed. However, they are not paid adequate wages, and treated as a lower class.

Exploitation generally results in uprising. However, while in *The Grapes of Wrath,* the uprising is initiated by the labourers themselves, realising the poor conditions they are toiling under; in *Kanthapura,* the uprising is initiated by someone who is outside the estate – Moorthy, who had come under the influence of Gandhi.

Although the revolt is started by the labourers, they have a leader or a motivator in Jim Casy in *The Grapes of Wrath.* Casy is a priest, who travels along with the Joad family. He dies soon after, but he already has followers, who are willing to take the responsibility of continuing the struggle. A parallel to this is the character of Gandhi in *Kanthapura.* Gandhi is, however, never shown directly in the novel. He has an overpowering influence on the society, while remaining in the background. The struggle is carried out by the followers of Gandhi, but unlike in *The Grapes of Wrath,* where we actually are shown the way. Jim Casy motivates others to take up the struggle, here we are not shown the way. Gandhi influences people like Moorthy to take part in the struggle.

As for characterisation, Gandhi and Casy are shown as being almost divine. In *Kanthapura,* the old woman narrator – Achakka, always refers to Gandhi as God. Also, the village bard Jayaramachar who is invited on the occasion of the consecration of the Shiva Linga, brings in Gandhi in his narrative in a bid to keep in touch with the times, and compares him to the Hindu Gods, Rama and Krishna. "Today," he says, "it will be the story of Siva and Parvati." And Parvati in penance becomes the country and Siva becomes heaven. "Siva is the three-eyed," he says, "and Swaraj too is three-eyed: Self-purification, Hindu-Moslem unity, Khaddar." And then he talks of Damayanthi and Shakunthala and Yashodha and everywhere there is something about our country and something about Swaraj. (16)

In *The Grapes of Wrath,* Jim Casy is given the initials of Jesus Christ – "J" and "C." This is not done unconsciously. Steinbeck does this consciously as can be seen in the way he depicts the character of Casy – as being a martyr.

> Casy stared blindly at the light. He breathed heavily.
> "Listen," he said. "You fellas don't know what you're doin':"
> You're helping to starve kids."
> "Shut up, you red son-of-a-bitch."
> A short heavy man stepped into the light. He carried a new white pick-handle.
> Casy went on: "You don't know what you're a-doin'."
> The heavy man swung with the pick-handle. Casy dodged down into the swing. The heavy club crashed into the side of his head with a dull crunch of bone, and Casy fell sideways out of the light. (354)

In *The Grapes of Wrath,* Tom Joad is inspired by Jim Casy, the preacher, to take up the fight for the cause of the Oklahoma workers, who have been deprived of their land, and now are being exploited by the Californian farmers. Similarly, in *Kanthapura,* Moorthy is inspired by listening to the speeches of Mahatma Gandhi, (which is not shown directly in the novel, but described by the other characters of what has taken place), and takes up the assignment of solving the problems of workers in the Skeffington coffee estate.

However, there are differences in the depiction of the characters of Tom and Moorthy. While Tom is also one of the exploited labourers, Moorthy is not a labourer, but an educated Brahmin youth who is touched by the plight of these workers, and fights for their betterment against the establishment. Moorthy is referred to by the old woman narrator as being a divine figure – a Hanuman to Gandhi's Rama; whereas, Tom is never depicted as anything but human, and at best an apostle. The narrator – who, here, is a third-person-narrator – too, never refers to him in the way Achakka refers to Moorthy, as being divinely.

Both Tom and Moorthy, however, are racked by self-doubts. Moorthy's obvious discomfort when faced with the problem of partaking of milk in the house of an "untouchable."

> But as he goes up the steps something in him says "Nay" and his hair stands on end as he remembers the tumbler of milk and the pariah home, and so he calls out, "Rangamma, Rangamma!" and says he has for the first time entered a pariah house and asks if he is permitted to enter; and Rangamma

> says, "Just come the other way round, Moorthy, and there's still hot water in the cauldron and fresh clothes for the meal." So Moorthy goes by the backyard, and when he has taken his bath and clothed himself, Rangamma says, "Maybe you'd better change your holy thread," but Moorthy says, "Now that I must go there every day, I cannot change my holy thread every day, can I?" (79)

is akin to the doubts that keep on assaulting Tom about whether he is right in doing whatever he is doing.

> "Lookie, Ma. I been all day an' all night hidin' alone. Guess who I been thinkin' about? Casy! He talked a lot. Used to bother me. But now I been thinkin' what he said, an' I can remember all of it. Says one time he went out in the wilderness to find his own soul, an' he foun' he didn't have no soul that was his'n. Says he foun' he jus' got a little piece of a great big soul. Says a wilderness ain't no good 'cause his little piece of a soul wasn't no good 'less it was with the rest, an' was whole. Funny how I remember. Didn't think I was even listenin'. But I know a fella ain't no good alone." (383)

Of course, these doubts on the part of either Tom or Moorthy cannot be taken as hypocrisy, but should be understood taking into account the way in which each had been brought up – Moorthy in a conservative Brahmin household, and Tom in a house where familial bonds are given precedence over helping/aiding "outsiders."

Tom and Moorthy influence people to follow them, and are in that sense charismatic leaders. While Moorthy is able to convert almost the whole village on to his side, Tom at the end of the novel has a couple of converts in his mother, and his sister, Rose of Sharon. It is interesting to note that at the end of both the novels the protagonist is significantly absent. Tom goes away into hiding at the end of *The Grapes of Wrath,* and in *Kanthapura,* Moorthy is imprisoned. (They are let out after the Gandhi-Irwin pact, but Moorthy, at the end of the novel, has not yet returned to the village.)

But the symbolic end of the novel, *The Grapes of Wrath,* suggests the coming together of the whole society of "Okhies" to fight against the injustice meted out to them.

> For a minute Rose of Sharon sat still in the whispering barn. Then she hosted her tired body up and drew the comforter about her. She moved slowly to the corner and stood looking down at the wasted face, into the wide, frightened eyes. Then slowly she lay down beside him. He shook his head slowly from side to side. Rose of Sharon loosened one side of the blanket and bared her breast. "You got to," she said. She squirmed closer and pulled his head close. "There!" she said. "There!" Her hand moved behind his head and supported it. Her fingers moved gently in his hair. She looked up and across the barn, and her lips came together and smiled mysteriously. (416)

This symbolic act of giving milk to a stranger suggests the coming together of the oppressed and thus offers hope for a better future for the "Okhies," and this is similar to the way *Kanthapura* ends – although there is destruction all around, as in *The Grapes of Wrath*, the novel ends on a note of hope that freedom is round the corner.

> They say the Mahatma will go to the Red-man's country and he will get us Swaraj. He will bring us Swaraj, the Mahatma. And we shall all be happy. And Rama will come back from exile, and Sita will be with him, for Ravana will be slain and Sita freed, and he will come back with Sita on his right in a chariot of the air, and brother Bharatha will go to meet them with the worshipped sandal of the Master on his head. And as they enter Ayodhya there will be a rain of flowers. (183)

Along with the thematic similarities, both novels experiment with the manner of telling the story too – *The Grapes of Wrath* uses the technique of alternating between the Joad story and an essay like chapter depicting other people who have moved on from Oklahoma, thereby showing that the Joads are not alone in their problems; in *Kanthapura* the story is related as if the sentences are transcribed from a south Indian language.

Kanthapura, thus, is similar in many ways to *The Grapes of Wrath;* in the sense that they start off describing the way the exploitation takes place, and then come up with a hero, who although seemingly beaten at the end, had meanwhile inspired others to take up the fight.

The similarities between these two novels show that people and their problems, aims, hopes, and their striving for their achievement are the same irrespective of where the people come from.

Works Cited

Amis, Kingsley. *Rudyard Kipling and his World.* London: Thames and Hudson, 1975.

Cunliffe, Marcus. *The Literature of the United States.* Middlesex: Penguin Books Ltd. 1970.

Iyengar, Srinivas, K.R. and Prema Nandakumar. *Indian Writing in English.* New Delhi: Sterling Publishers Private Limited, 1962.

Rao, Raja. *Kanthapura.* Delhi: Orient Paperbacks, 1970.

Spiller, Robert; William, Thorp, E., Thomas, E., Johnson, H., Henry Seidel Canby, Richard; M Ludwig. *Literary History of the United States.* New York: The Macmillan Company, 1946.

Steinbeck, John. *The Grapes of Wrath.* 1939. Middlesex: Penguin Books, 1972.

English Poetry: A Journey from Obscurity to Ambiguity

Rajesh Kumar

> The machinations of ambiguity are among the very roots of poetry. (Empson, W. *1955: 21)*

Meaning, particularly in literature, is a three-dimensional concept – the meaning of a word, of an utterance, and of a text. Possible meanings of words contribute to the meaning of utterance, which is an act performed by the writer. The relationship however is not that simple and straight, as the utterance may, in turn, condition the meaning of the word. Finally, the two together contribute to the meaning of the text. Meaning of a text – what it is and what it is not – has been a problematic area of practical criticism, and this has been the inspiration behind several schools of criticism. The emotive elements of language make it "vague, protean, fluctuating phenomena," something that we accept in literature but refuse to do so in sciences. The lyric, oriented toward the first person, is intimately linked with the emotive function; epic poetry, focused on the third person, strongly involves the referential function of language. The traditional model of language was confined to three functions – emotive, conative, and referential – and the three apexes – the first person of the addresser, the second person of the addressee, and the third person (Buhler, 1933).

> ... the literary work has two poles, which we might call the artistic, and the aesthetic: the artistic refers to the text created by the author, and the aesthetic to the realization accomplished by the reader. From this polarity it follows that the literary work cannot be identical with the text, or with the realization of the text, but in fact must lie halfway between the two. The work is more than the text, for the text only takes on life when it is realized, and furthermore the realization is by no means independent of the individual disposition of the reader – though this in turn is acted upon by the different patterns

> of the text. The convergence of text and reader brings the literary work into existence, and this convergence can never be precisely pinpointed, but must always remain virtual, as it is not to be identified either with the reality of the text or with the individual disposition of the reader. (Iser, 1988:189)

It is reasonable to presuppose that author, text and reader are closely interconnected in a relationship that is to be conceived as an ongoing process that produces something that had not existed before. For some, meaning of a text is the author's intention; for others meaning of a text is what the text means, not what the author intends; and for yet others meaning of a text is what the reader understands, not what the author intends or what the text means.

> There are three possibilities. It might be found in using the text as evidence of writer's intention: what is significant is what the writer means by the text. Alternatively, one might take the view that the text signals its own intrinsic meaning, whatever the writer might have intended: what is significant is what the text means. Or, thirdly, one might say that what is significant is what a text means to the reader, whatever the writer may have intended, or whatever the text itself may objectively appear to mean. (Widdowson, 1992: viii)

Meaning for Saussure is based on differences – "language is a system of differences" and the meaning of an element depends on how it differs from other elements of the system that can replace it on the paradigmatic scale. Deconstructionists attempt to deconstruct the author's intention by reversing the process of creation. I.A. Richards (1929) warns against individual readings into the poem and talks about respecting the autonomy of the poem. Cox and Dyson (1965) appear to believe that poems have their own independent existence. The New Criticism locates literary meaning in the formal features of the text, rather than in the author's intention or the reader's response. By implication,

> "meaning [is] the property of the poem itself as an autonomous artefact and [is] in principle recoverable from the text, totally and intact" (Widdowson, 1992).

Nowottny's "unarguable" dimension of language and Wimsatt's "explicit meaning" imply that all words have stable and stateable meanings. Reader Response School of Criticism believes that no piece of language has a meaning unless it has been understood by a reader. The only meaning that a text can have is what is read into it by the reader.

> Traditionally, the role of the reader has been seen as animator
> of the text and as a disposable machinery of extraction, whose task is simply to activate meanings deemed to be in the text, but who takes no initiative to engage creatively with the text (Widdowson, G. 1992).

This rather passive role of the reader has been challenged by Fish (1980) and Freund (1987) – "*You do not read meanings out of a text but into a text.*" This three-dimensional picture of meaning – writer's meaning, reader's meaning, and the meaning of the text – would have been easily accepted without debate, if all the three dimensions had been the same. Not only this, different readers generate different meanings in the same text. Though it would be too much to question the legitimacy of what textual critics have done by focusing on the text, and the text only; it is more than apparent that the inspiration behind this was the natural human tendency to streamline things and smother any discordant note. The objection against allowing the readers to have several different interpretations of the text is not philosophical but a practical one.

> A poem is free of an author's intentions and his experiences, and of a reader's responses, because these are variable, irresponsible, undiscoverable, demonstrably erroneous, etc., while the poem remains stable. We cannot locate the poem in the author's state of mind at the moment of creation because this is inaccessible and may be changed by the act of writing ... we cannot allow the poem to reside in the individual reader's experience as he reads, because that would be tantamount to saying that there are as many poems as there are occasions of reading, whereas we know very well that there is only one poem. (Bradbury and Palmer, 1970: 178-79)

It is clear that the objection is more of a pragmatic nature than of a philosophic one. Readers should not be allowed to be differently affected by the "reality" of a particular text because their responses are "variable, irresponsible, and undiscoverable" which is ample evidence of the fact that there was no love lost between the text and these textual critics, rather they were afraid to allow the readers to spin millions of individual webs of interpretation to come out of which will be a Herculean task for the critics. The fact of the matter, as it appears to me, is that:

> The literary text activates our own faculties, enabling us to recreate the world it presents. The product of this creative activity is what we might call the virtual dimension of the text, which endows it with its reality. This virtual dimension is not the text itself, nor is it the imagination of the reader: it is the coming together of text and imagination. (Iser, W. *1988:191*)

This discordance between the intention of the author, the text and the response of the reader as well as between various interpretations of the same text by different readers may be understood in terms of the fluctuating relationship between signifier and signified. In Derrida's view of language the signifier is not directly related to the signified. There is no one-to-one set of correspondence between them. Signifiers and signified are continually breaking apart and reattaching in new combinations, and one never arrives at a final signified which is not a signifier in itself. Derrida argues that when we read a sign, meaning is not immediately clear to us. Signs refer to what is absent, so in a sense meanings are absent, too. Meaning is continually moving along on a chain of signifiers, "*and we cannot be precise*" about its exact "location," it is never tied to one particular sign. (*Sarup*, 1993)

I would rather use *"and we cannot be precise"* – literature defies precision. A great work of art cannot be reduced down to a precise, neat and systematic explanation; it is achieved by a subtle use of language that induces different meanings in different minds. Nowottny says that the structure of a poem is not *"discontinuous with linguistic process in ordinary life,"* however, she accepts that the language of poems is *"more highly structured"* than *"language outside poems."* One characteristic of a poem is that it fashions the language in such a way as to give poignancy to words which cannot be explained but experienced only. When readers try to explain this unexplainable, they read different meanings in the same text. In a poem, the function of language is not referential but representational.

> Whereas with reference language is dependent on external and actual context, with representation, context is internal, potential, and dependent on language: it takes shape in the verbal patterns of the poem. These ... provoke the reader into divergent interpretation ... . (Widdowson, 1992: 33)

Reading a literary text is a creative process that is much more than a mere perception of what is written "there." Part of this creativity, to me, is lexical in nature. Reading literature gives us the chance to formulate the unformulated. Gaps or blanks in literary texts created by Derridean binary oppositions like presence/absence stimulate the reader to construct meanings which would not have otherwise come into existence. The techniques frequently used by the poets to create these gaps or blanks is that of sincere lying, non-linear progression of events, the art of distancing and back and forth movements of rhythm and tone eventually evincing a keen bend towards "purposeful distortion," which lends words and phrases more than one possible meaning. The possibility of this plurality of interpretation makes a poem ambiguous.

It would be worthwhile to carefully state the parameters set for this paper whereby "ambiguity" means not the multiplicity of meaning caused by phonological, morphological or syntactic ambiguity but a multiplicity of meaning caused by a word having two or more than two relevant connotations that keep on changing from time to time, from text to text, and from reader to reader: co-text and context become very significant here. Ambiguity has rightly been argued to be a purely mental phenomenon that takes place in the mind of the reader, however, that is caused by some linguistic features – and that linguistic feature for the purpose of this paper is the connotative aspect of English vocabulary.

It is also essential for the purpose of this paper to distinguish ambiguity from obscurity which is the case of a word having more than one acceptable, but stable and stateable, meaning that call upon the reader to choose the relevant one. Potentially ambiguous words possess distinct, disparate but clear meanings all of which are relevant as alternatives in a given context, although there is always an uncertainty as to which one is the more appropriate. Lack of clarity lies at the pragmatic level where the intended meaning is not clear to the reader. Ambiguity is an intrinsic, inalienable character of any self-focused message, briefly a corollary feature of poetry. Not only the message itself but also its addresser and addressee become ambiguous (Jakobson, 1988).

In the case of obscurity, on the other hand, lack of clarity occurs at the semantic level itself. Faced with ambiguity, the reader asks, "Which one is the intended meaning?;" faced with obscurity, he asks, "What is the intended meaning?" Obscurity is, therefore, different from ambiguity, though it can provide the latitude for ambiguity to occur in. Most of us, I think, will agree that 17th and 18th century poetry may be obscure because the reader faces the difficulty in finding "what is the intended meaning," but not as ambiguous as modern poetry wherein he undergoes the trauma of deciding "which one is the intended meaning." This may partly be significant to show how English poetry has been on the move from obscurity towards ambiguity.

Heavy borrowing from different sources, particularly of words that led to an unequalled profusion of synonyms, is a characteristic of English that distinguishes it from other languages.

> The Latin element in Modern English is so great that there would be no difficulty in writing hundreds of consecutive pages in which the proportion of words of native English etymology ... would not exceed five percent of the whole.
>
> (Bradley, 1904: 63)

It is a matter of common knowledge that traditional education and literacy had been the prerogative of a particular class of British society, and the poets had that particular class in mind while writing. So much so that there may be seen a clear distinction between language being used in poetry and that being used by the common folk.

> ... a similar historical process began in English in the seventeenth century, when literary and colloquial norms were set apart by the conscious creation of a literary standard.
>
> (Adamson, S., 1989: 207)

Though English replaced French as the official language in the later middle ages, and Latin as the language of scholarship during the Renaissance in successive stages, the substitution was not a single act. In both the cases the English that substituted French or Latin was heavily influenced by the language it substituted (Baugh, 1959). Prescriptive grammarians and lexicographers of the 18th century turned to Latin for their models of correct usage. There was a widespread belief among writers that the propagation of Latinized forms would "fix" the diversity and changeability of speech forms, and place English on the rational foundation of universal grammar.

A reading of English poetry down the ages reveals that words of foreign origin tend to be used more frequently in the poetry of 17th and 18th century in comparison to that of the 19th and 20th century poetry. It can also be safely assumed that modern poetry is by and large more ambiguous than 17th and 18th century poetry. Modern poets, like modern men, look at themselves in relation to others or others in relation to themselves. Life for them since Einstein is no more absolute but relative; it is not possible for them to look at life in isolation like 16th century lyricist, for example. The primacy of the metaphoric process in the literary schools of romanticism and symbolism has been repeatedly acknowledged, but it is still insufficiently realized that it is the predominance of metonymy which underlies and actually predetermines the so-called "realistic" trend, which belongs to an intermediary stage between the decline of romanticism and the rise of symbolism and is opposed to both (Jakobson, 1988). Modern poetry tries to transform the sign back into meaning: its ideal, ultimately, would be to reach not the meaning of words, but the meaning of things themselves. This is why it clouds the language, increases the abstractness of the concept and the arbitrariness of the sign and stretches to the limit the link between signifier and signified (Barthes, 1957).

The reasons may be many, but the one that I propose to be the case is an apparent journey from the classical to the colloquial. The substitution of classical by the colloquial that started during the latter half of the 17th century was completed by Wordsworth's democratic humanism which demanded that literature must leave the territory of the literate elite and occupy the common ground shared by both the poet and the audience. Gradually Latin got "frozen" as the language of education and books. Today its creative use is confined to a diminishing elite whose classical education gives them a working knowledge of Latin roots and derivational morphology.

The failure of the classical vocabulary to get integrated into the colloquial standard has had important consequences for the semantic structure of English. There are systematic differences found in meaning between classical and colloquial terms which can be attributed to their dichotomous learning conditions. Colloquial terms are learnt communicatively in the context of actual experience and hence are interpreted by reference to a wide range of experiences with which they are associated. Classical terms, on the contrary, are learnt in academic context devoid of any real life association and hence are interpreted by reference to a prescribed definition. They "fall upon the facts like soft snow, blurring the outlines," smothering any possibility of multiplicity of interpretations.

To support my line of argument I would take a classical-colloquial pair *"parsimonious-mean"* as an example. Longman Dictionary of Contemporary English (1998) defines *"parsimonious"* under a single entry as *"extremely unwilling to spend money,"* while it defines *"mean"* under multiple entries as *"have a particular meaning; intend to say something; say which person or thing; intend to do something; say something seriously; result in something; involve doing something; show something is true or will happen; unkind or nasty; unwilling to spend any money or share what you have with other people; cruel and bad tempered; average; poor or looking poor; and belonging to a low social class."* The word *"preserve"* too is defined under three entries as *"to save something or someone from being harmed or destroyed; to store food for a long time after treating it so that it will not decay; and to make something continue without changing,"* whereas *"keep"* is defined under thirty entries as *"not give back; not lose; not change/move; make somebody/something not change/move; do something repeatedly; delay somebody; store something; look after; protect; and celebrate something"* (Longman Dictionary of Contemporary English, 1998).

The two examples, though by no means exhaustive, demonstrate my contention clearly that colloquial words have greater connotations than that of the classical ones. It is this fluidity or indeterminacy of meaning associated with the colloquial vocabulary that makes readers have divergent interpretations – the hallmark of ambiguity. Moreover,

> ... [classical terms] have connotations of conceptual clarity and emotional neutrality, while the ... [colloquial terms] are associated with physical reality and subjective response. In the most general terms, the ... [colloquial] vocabulary is associated with an experiential mode of reference, the ... [classical] vocabulary with a noetic mode. (Adamson, S., 1989: 214–15)

This dichotomy further strengthens the idea that colloquial terms do have greater scope of plurality of interpretations and their greater frequency in modern poetry leads to greater ambiguity. The movement from classical to the colloquial vocabulary in English poetry can be seen as a movement from the monosemic to the polysemic, from the noetic to the experiential. The relatively monosemic nature of the classical items allows it to stand as an abstract statement of the semantic content, whereas the more polysemic colloquial items are open to scrutiny for alternative meanings leading to greater ambiguity.

Works Cited

Adamson, S. *With Double Tongue: Diglossia, Stylistics and the Teaching of English in Reading, Analyzing and Teaching Literature.* Mick Short (*ed.*), London: Longman, 1989.

Barthes, Rolland, *Mythologies,* Paris: Seuil, 1957.

Baugh, A.C. *A History of English Language.* London: Routledge and Kegan Paul, 1959.

Bradbury, Malcolm, and Roy Palmer. (*eds.*) *Contemporary Criticism.* London: Arnold, 1970.

Bradley, H. *The Making of English.* London: Macmillan, 1904.

Buhler, K. (1933), Die Axiomatik der Sprachwissen-schaft in *Kant-Studien.* 38. Berlin: 19-90.

Cox, C.B. and Dyson, A.E. *The Practical Criticism of Poetry: A Textbook.* London: Edward Arnold, 1965.

Empson, W. *Seven Types of Ambiguity.* New York: Penguin, 1955.

Fish, S. *Is There a Text in This Class?.* Cambridge: Harvard University Press, 1980.

Freund, E. *The Return of the Reader: Reader-Response Criticism.* London: Methuen, 1987.

Iser, Wolfgang. *The Reading Process: A Phenomenological Approach in Modern Criticism and Theory: A Reader.* David Lodge (*ed.*), London: Longman, 1988.

Jakobson, R. *The Metaphoric and Metonymic Poles in Modern Criticism and Theory: A Reader.* David Lodge (*ed.*), London: Longman, 1988.

Lodge, David(*ed.*). *Modern Criticism and Theory: A Reader.* London Longman, 1988.

Longman Dictionary of Contemporary English. India: Thomson Press Ltd., 1998.

Richards, I.A. *Practical Criticism.* New York: Harcourt Brace and Co, 1929.

Sarup, M. *An Introductory Guide to Post-Structuralism and Postmodernism* Edinburgh: Pearson Education Limited, 1993.

Short, Mick., (*ed.*). *Reading, Analyzing and Teaching Literature.* London: Longman, 1989.

Widdowson, G. *Practical Stylistics.* Oxford: OUP, 1992.

Wimsatt, W.K. *The Verbal Icon: Studies in the Meaning of Poetry.* London: Methuen, 1970.

Indianness as Reflected in the Short Stories of Ruskin Bond

Dr. Shrikant Singh

Indianness is as complex and elusive a concept for an Indian mind to grasp as it is to a foreign mind. Different writers both Indian and foreigner, have made different approaches to discern the true spirit of India and have drawn different almost contradictory facets of Indian phenomena. John Richardson, for instance, found the Indians as the "sweetest people in the world" and India as "heaven's neighbouring state." V.S. Naipaul found India world's largest slum with ever receding degrees of degradation. Ruth Prawar Jhabvala's India is made of heat and dust and is full of flies and mosquitoes. Such perceptions are bound to remain superficial. This country is a land of such contradictory elements that any statement will be a case of oversimplification.

During the colonial rule many British writers such as Rudyard Kipling, E.M. Forster, L.H. Myers and John Masters wrote about the myths and mystery of India but their efforts remained only peripheral. Kipling tried his best to know India but for him it was no more than a land of fairs, Sadhus, Sanyasins and mullas of different faiths. E.M. Forster in his *A Passage to India* highlights some important facets of Indian reality but he too fails to solve the riddle and mystery of India. In John Master's novel the Englishmen are everywhere and the hero is trying to establish order, peace and justice in the state of anarchy and lawlessness. To L.H. Myers also India appeared a muddle. Their collective conclusion about India finds best reflection in the words of Forster:

> How can the mind take hold of such a country? Generations of invaders have tried but they remain in exile.
> (Forster : 135)

The problem with all these foreign writers was that they tried to discover India through the coloured spectacle of a foreigner, they could not accept it as it was. Ruskin Bond's case is different from all those writers and is best reflected in the words of Mulk Raj Anand:

> ... you have no sense of superiority over the Indians around you,
> so your novels and stories seem to have emerged from within Indian Homes.
> And your heart is in the mountains with your inborn love for nature. (Anand : 1995: 34-35)

The image of India presented by different Indian writers is also different in view of their varying psyche and interests. Mulk Raj Anand, Bhabani Bhattacharya and Kamla Markandeya expose India's social problems. R.K. Narayan has chosen comic stance and enjoys idiosyncracies of man in his day to day life. Raja Rao is moved by Vedantic India. Manohar Malagonkar and Nayantara Sahgal assess Indian history and politics respectively. Arun Joshi and Anita Desai are also in search of their roots in India. A suspicion, sort of restlessness and despair is palpable in their India whereas Bond's India lives and breathes in the hills. To him trees, mountains, rivers have special appeal and have as much beauty and as many problems as we human beings have. He is neither attracted by the glitter of everexpanding cities nor is he unduly moved by the ever present social problems.

When the British left India, Bond faced the trauma of loss of identity. He went to the UK to brush up his career as a writer. But soon after he felt nostalgic and India began to haunt him. In a way he, for the first time, experienced the true feel of India:

> The gulmohar trees in their fiery summer splendour, barefooted boys riding buffaloes and chewing sugarcanes ... the scent of wet earth after the first rain and most of all, the easy going pleasure of his Dehra friendship.
>
> (Bond : 1997 : 132)

Human touch is the soul of Indian culture which Bond realised when he was in New Jersey:

> The loneliest period of my life constituted of two years I spent in New Jersey, where I lived with relatives. They were

> not unkind to me but we did not really love each other ... and yearned for all I had left behind India.
>
> (Bond : 1998 : XIII)

Bond lived there for a brief period but he felt himself alienated soul, a foreigner in the crowd of his own creed, a sharp contrast of what was India.

In India there are no strangers. People meet and inquire about each other without being understood. They touch each other out of love and regards – whereas people in the Western countries are reserved, constrained, and highly individual. The warmth of human relationship is a typical characteristic of Indian culture. In India people of various sects and creed live in peace and harmony. They respect others' views and faith. Such broad concept of individual liberty made this country truly democratic.

It is a fact that in spite of longing for their motherland hardly a few ventured to return to their country. It is Bond who followed the call of his conscience and returned to India to merge his own self with its soil. Highlighting Bond's adaptation of India P.K. Singh says:

> Bond's writings give the true flavour of the Indian soil ... he gives his readers the true feel of Indian life he has seen and lived. His European blood seemed to be fully naturalised with the Indian spirit. (Singh : 1995 : 7)

The India Bond loves is not one which makes headlines but the one that comprises the goodwill and humour of common people, a tolerance of all people and customs, non-interference in the private life of others, a philosophical acceptance of hardships, love and affection especially in children. His stories move around the rural or middle urban class. People are farmers, small shopkeepers, grass cutters, postmen, tonga drivers, school teachers or retired officials etc. They truly embody Indian spirit of universal love and fraternity. Glamour and competition, the two prime facets of western culture have not yet violated the sanctity and peace of their life. Love of humanity sits at the centre of their heart.

The other picture of Indian life presents cheerful, easy-going, fun-loving children. Boys and girls are not matured under heavy pressure of materialism. Vijay, Bishnu, Suraj, Arun, Satish, Rusty and many other boys of his stories go to school but they have enough time to wonder about the slopes and attend to their fields and cattle. Satellite channels have not snatched away their social delights. Occasionally they enjoy cinema, cheat and circus too. Their social belongingness is still very high.

Bond's writings including his stories are the evidence of his firm belief, like those of other Indians, in the immortality and transmigration of soul. The truth that physical body perishes and mixes with dust from which it springs is reflected in his stories. The heroes in their soliloquies frequently contemplate about the eternity of soul and nature. Realisation of life and death comes naturally as parts of experience and instinct of Indians, they know that life goes far beyond the known limitations of time and space. Meeting of two strangers and their getting close are also understood to be a matter of accumulated consciousness or pre-birth impressions which every child carries with him. In the story *The Room of Many Colours*, Rani believes that the snake living in the root of the banyan tree was none other but her own prince. As a result she is full of concern for the safety of the snake. Rani blurts out:

> You don't understand, Master Bond. Princes, when they die, are born again as snakes. (Bond: Collected Fiction: 244)

For Bond as for Indians, nature is not just fascination towards the landscape and flora and fauna of the Himalayan region that we come across again and again in his love-stories, it is something far deeper and much profounder. His concern for ecology, love for trees and mountains, for rivers and brooks, becomes a living faith. He says:

> Hinduism comes closest to being a nature religion. Rivers, rocks, trees, animals and birds all play their parts both in mythology and everyday worship. This harmony is most evident in remote places like this, and I hope it does not lose its unique character in the ruthless urban advance.
>
> (Rains in the Mountains: 234)

Bond's compassion and understanding of the wild animals and particularly man's close relationship with them is part of Indian's vision of life. For example, his story *Tiger, Tiger Burning Bright* is in fact not a short story about one tiger but about all tigers and all wild animals. In fact it is a story about the harmony in forest. Similarly in a number of stories of Bond, the river, and the trees and mountains come to life and become active participants. The long story *Sita and the River* illustrates how man pitted against the fury of devastating flood accepts the river as synonymous with gods.

Depiction of Indian festivals and seasons imparts a powerful realism to Bond's short stories. All the places – streets and lanes, bazaars and railway platforms, theatre and garden – have been portrayed in native colour. In the story *The Kitemaker* one can find Mahmood Ali, the kitemaker sitting under old banyan tree and contemplating on the glories of bygone days with half shut eyes anywhere in this land. Likewise in the story *The Blue Umbrella* a girl named Binya running after her cow Neelu can be easily traced on the slopes of the hills. In the story *Panther's Moon*, Bishnu represents every school boy in the hills who walk miles daily to reach his school amidst the lurking fear of a panther, persons like Dhukhi spending the whole day on his haunches and trimming the garden hedge, Vishnu serving tea in cinema halls, Daya Ram losing his small money bag in the train, Masterji grappling money by leaking question papers reflect various shades of Indian life.

Bond's stories also reflect religious diversity of India and people's deep faith in religion. If Vishnu propitiates Ganesh, Sita (*Sita and River*) adores Lord Krishna. His faith in Krishna is so deep that Vijay, the simple boy of the village, who saves her life becomes the blue god. Bond's stories reflect his deep understanding of the motif behind Indian myths. He knows that in this land people are by nature very grateful, a man becomes god if he helps and protects others. Religion, for Indians, is not merely a mode of ritualistic worship, it teaches the art of living with full conformity with nature. Bond rightly describes Hardwar and Rishikesh as the spiritual seats of India. India to him is Goethe's "the humanisation of the whole world," it is *Basudhaiva Kutumbakam,* it is non-violence and tolerance of Lord Buddha and Lord Mahaveera, it is sthitpragyata of *The Gita,* it is deep yogic system of Patanjali, it is the *sunyavad* of Nagarjuna, values of Ekalvya, the myth of Bhasamasura, the ideals of Rama and Krishna, the deep spiritual experience of the Kumbhmela it is as much the mountains and hills as much their thrills. Directly or indirectly Ruskin Bond's stories reflect all these and a temporal change he deliberately ignores because he knows what endures.

Works Cited

Bond, Ruskin. *Scenes from a Writer's Life.* New Delhi : Penguin Books India Pvt. Ltd., 1997.

———, *The Lamp is Lit.* New Delhi : Penguin Books India Pvt. Ltd; 1998.

———, *Collected Fiction.* New Delhi : Penguin Books India Pvt. Ltd., 1999.

———, *Rains in the Mountains.* New Delhi : Penguin Books India Pvt. Ltd., 1993.

Forster, E.M. *A Passage to India.* Harmondsworth, England: Penguin Books Ltd., 1961.

Singh, P.K. (*ed.*) *The Creative Contours of Ruskin Bond.* New Delhi: Pencraft International, 1995.

Women in Love: A Critical Perspective

Dr. Rajiv Ranjan Dwivedi

As a sequel to the novel, *The Rainbow, Women in Love,* in a series of controversial works which precede and succeed this novel is an evocative creation which amply manifests Lawrencian profound philosophy of blood and flesh and establishes the varied personal relationships based on it. *Women in Love* of the title are Ursula and Gurdun, the two sisters who struggle with their own feelings, attitudes, and desires about themselves, love and men. The violence and passions, which lay beneath the surface of the characters' egos and how they allow their hidden desires to spontaneously display themselves. Multiple strands of personal relationship such as love, its domination or submission, defeat or victory, of female vs. male etc. typically surface the plot of the novel.

The story of Ursula of *The Rainbow* continues in *Women in Love.* She has now become a school teacher and lives with her parents in Beldover. Gurdun, a sculptress with a growing reputation, has returned home to take a break from the metropolis. Ursula forms a relationship with Rupert Berkin, a school inspector, while Gurdun enters into a relationship with Berkin's friend, Gerald Crich, whose family runs a local colliery. *Women in Love* is a novel written at the time of war. At that time Lawrence was haunted by the horror and ugliness of the war and thus the book is underpinned by violence. *Women in Love* enacts Lawrence's vision of death. It contemplates the end of culture and the physical and spiritual breakdown in individuals who accompany it. This is further observable in a number of little deaths: the death of the mind, the death of the body and the death of the soul. The paper attempts to focus on these metaphors and unfold their implications with textual and intertextual justifications and thereby critically examine the space of human ethos in the novel.

While reflecting on the pertinent issue of death and disintegration, H.M. Daleski opines that they are repeatedly used in the novel with negative connotations:

> Gerald's work in the mines and Gurdun's art are revealed as "disintegrative" as an abuse of organic life; and the black sensuality of their relationship is productive of the violence which, in the novel, is seen as an inevitable concomitant of process of "dissolution."(181)

However, for Colin Clarke this integration is more positive than negative:

> The process of dissolution is positive quite as often as not, or positive-negative. For the coming into being of the true and original individuality of the blood entails a disintegrating, or dissolving, of the dreary individuality of the ego.(Clarke, 219)

Thus we see that disintegration is positive when Ursula declares that to die is to move on. But to live mechanized and cut off within the motion of the will, to live as an entity absolved from the unknown, that is shameful and ignominious. Though this disintegration is nauseating and painful, it is a sign that:

> human spirit is in contact with the rhythms of living and dead. On the other hand, the incapacity to dissolve is seen as a mark of isolated and mechanical state. Thus the disintegration or death in *Women in Love* is one which is before the revival of the true self.(220-221)

Adding to the cyclic and renewable nature of this death and disintegration the following passage can be seen as amply justifiable:

> the metaphorical entanglement of tropes of race, eros and death in *Women in Love* is extraordinarily dense. To understand these metaphors we need to appreciate the contradictions actively at work within them, most importantly the one that brings life close to death, merging creation, fulfilment and dissolution.(Stevens, 50)

So, this disintegration represents Lawrence's symbol of the phoenix and suggest the possibility of life after death.

The African fetish statue of a woman that Birkin sees is important because it tells him about the history of civilization and his own future. This statue haunts Birkin because it suggests an extreme physical sensation beyond the limit of mental consciousness:

> He remembered her: her astounding cultured elegance, her diminished, beetle face, the astounding long elegant body, on short ugly legs, with such protuberant buttock so weighty and unexpected below her slim long loins. She knew what he himself did not know. She had thousands of years of purely sensual, purely unspiritual knowledge behind her. It must have been thousands of years since her race had died, mystically: that, since the relation between the sense and the outspoken mind had broken, leaving the experience all in one short, mystically sensual. Thousands of years ago, that which was imminent in himself must have taken place in these Africans: the goodness, the holiness, the desire for creation and productive happiness must have elapsed, leaving the single impulse for knowledge in one sort...in disintegration and dissolution, knowledge such as the beetles have. (*Women in Love,* 167)

It is a mistake to overlook what Birkin calls "the astounding cultured allegiance" of the statue and assume that he is evoking a work of art. Lawrence has learnt from his reading of Leo Frobenius's *The Voice of Africa* that long before the coming of Europeans there had existed great city states in Africa which had produced highly sophisticated works of art and established a tradition of fine craftsmanship. A slow decline, not a cataclysm, finished off this civilization, and it is the nature of this decline that Birkin tries to conjure up as he contemplates what the statue symbolizes for him.

Lawrence, in the novel, expresses his belief in the duality of blood and brain. Birkin represents Lawrence's ideal self. He symbolizes an integrated human being who has polarized the two centres of consciousness, that is, the mental and the blood consciousness. Thus he is able to live positively and in harmony with nature. He is the glorified male, the eternal male for whom Ursula has waited and whom she finally accepts. Unlike Birkin Gerald is not able to polarize the mind and the blood. He is an image of the modern industrial man who is unable to harmonize with nature. He fails to establish the deeper harmony in his relationship as his approach to life is purely mental. He cannot experience the satisfying fullness of sense-life as he must analyze sensation. Even Gurdun is the victim of an intellectual, analytical attitude to experience. She is fascinated by the intelligence of Loerke, the typical modern artist with his mechanical sensibility and sterile wit.

The novel also strongly projects Lawrence's ideal sexual relationship between man and woman. This is done through a comparison of the relationship of Birkin and Ursula and that of Gurdun and Gerald. Gurdun and Gerald represent the modern instinctual woman and man. They are unable to maintain a happy relationship. In the novel Berkin has established his own intellectual theory of sexual harmony and asserts that the sexes must fulfil each other. He puts this theory to test through Ursula. Birkin harps on the wastefulness of modern civilization that has been caused by the loss of old male principle of domination. He believes that this could be resorted by going back to a life of pure sensation, "mindless, utterly sensual" and thus while the relationship of Gerald and Gurdun miserably fails and Gerald dies, the relationship between Birkin Ursula is successful. Thus Ursula and Birkin are able to achieve the pure duality of polarization. As noted earlier, Birkin is Lawrence's ideal self, he is the mouthpiece of Lawrence's philosophy of sexual harmony and education, alienation of man in modern life and means to overcome that alienation.

Lawrence believed that the alienation typical to modern life could be overcome through a fusion of man with man, man with woman and man with nature. The relationship of Birkin and Ursula replicates Lawrence's philosophy about fusion of man and woman. His emphasis on the fusion of man with man is evident in the last page of the novel when Birkin says to his wife that "You are all women to me. I want a man friend as eternal as you and I are eternal." (WIL,106, all the subsequent references from this text are referred to as WIL.) In real life too Lawrence had hoped that he had found such a friend in Middleton Murry whom he first met in July 1913. However the relationship failed as Murry fled in alarm of an incomprehensible and undefined intimacy.

The multifaceted aspects of dying culture are depicted in the very first chapter of the novel. The concept of the disintegration of the modern society and the break of the bond with nature of the industrial man in *The Rainbow* is enlarged to become a major theme in *Women in Love.* In the novel, Gerald is the main symbol of the industrial man. Ted Brangwen and his disintegrated lifelessness of soul are recalled in Gerald Crich, another industrial magnate. Kenneth Young in this regard opines:

> The book is again about emptiness of soul which Lawrence saw as the outstanding characteristic of his time; but now it is seen throughout society, from the minors, through the Bohemian, arty circles...the house party society...and the industrialists. (25)

This last group is represented by Gerald and his father, and in a perverted form, by Loerke. The father wanted to run the mines on love but he found that as he "triumphed in the world, he became more and more hollow in his vitality, the vitality was bled from within him, as by some haemorrhage" (WIL,123), and he was unable to anyone, including his wife who then withdrew from society. The father has failed at life and realizes this on his deathbed. He attempts to make his life worthwhile by giving the child, Winifred a chance to live, in a Lawrencian sense of the word, knowing beauty and expressing herself in her art.

During the father's illness Gerald takes over the mines. He becomes a willing victim to the machine. The colliery then becomes like a great machine that takes everyone captive:

> He was the stream of the minors flowing along the causeways from the mines at the end of the afternoon, thousands of blackened, slighted distorted human beings with red mouths, all moving subjugate to his will. He pushed slowly in his motorcar through the little market top on Friday nights in Beldover, through a solid mass of human beings that were making their purchases and doing their weekly spending. They were all subordinate to him. They were ugly and uncouth but they were his instruments. He was the God of the machine. (125)

Growing industries in the early twentieth century have been the most enervating factor for writers including Lawrence. Industrialism is the greatest enemy for Lawrence for the kind of society it produces.

It is at the centre of all the narrative profundity of his novel and many a serious and sensitive concern giving birth to philosophical offshoots owes to such development at his time. For him, "the industrial problem arises from the base forcing of all human energy into a competition of mere acquisition." (Spilka, 163). It is a condition of mind rather than the physical condition of the society. This desire for power and the competition for acquisition are portrayed through Gerald.

Gerald likes the power of the managing job. For him, the central purpose of life was to "be all." In *The Rainbow*, Lawrence created his perfect society, one near nature and instinctual life. In such a society men did not work for money; in the perfect society work is simply a natural part of living. However, in *Women in Love*, the society is ruled by intellectualism. For Gerald, far removed from the perfect society, work has become the central purpose of life, the "be all." In his position of authority, Gerald finds a part of the system, a system that works as machine. "It was like being part of a machine. He himself happens to be a controlling, central part, the masses of men were the parts variously controlled." (WIL, 219). This is the image of mechanization of human life, the inevitable consequence of industrialism and intellectualism. Gerald has been caught up in the system, and can no longer appreciate non-mechanical beauty. He sees himself as only a part of a massive machine and he sees other men as mere objects, "parts variously controlled." He is completely captive to the machine.

Infact, this tendency to lose one's ability to feel and yet to stay mentally alert is what Lawrence says has happened in our mechanized society. Gerald is captive, and both he and mistress, Gurdun, must turn to sensation because they are incapable of real emotion. Their centres of feeling are dried up. Gurdun, a woman produced by our mechanized society and incapable of real feeling, finds the pervert Loerke mentally attractive and it is logical that she turns to him from the entirely unsatisfactory physical battle with Gerald. He can satisfy the needs by conversing about ideas and art of her mental consciousness by conversing about ideas and art. Even Loerke is entangled in the mechanical society. He is creating a fresco for a factory. He tells Gurdun "Art should interpret industry as art once interpreted religion." (221)

For Lawrence industry is the new religion of the masses. Under Geralds guidance the mines have modernized with the help of new cutting machines ironically called iron men. The men are forced into working conditions that are tightly organized:

> "The joy went out of their lives; the hope seemed to perish as they became more and more mechanized. And yet they accepted the new conditions. They even got a further satisfaction out of them. At first they hated Gerald Crich...but as time went, they accepted everything with fatal satisfaction. Gerald was their high priest, he represented the religion they really felt...there was a new world, a new order, strict, terrible, inhuman, but satisfying in its very destructiveness, the men were satisfied to belong to the great and wonderful machine, even while it destroyed. It was what they wanted." (223).

This has resulted in the detrimental dependence of society on machine and getting subjugated under it. The advent of industries in the name of the development and growth of society had also upset Wordsworth with his reaction: "And much it grieved my heart to think, what man has made of man. Gerald has been taken captive by the urge to power and the miners have accepted the machines as their religion."

The mechanical nature of the society, however, and not the machines themselves, is mainly responsible for the harms and damage done to men. Gerald thinks of himself as the god of machine. He insists that society is mechanical and even thinks in terms of Mechanical, disintegrated, amorphous: these are the continuing key words to describe the effect of the industrial priorities on individuals and on the whole society. In this condition of mind, rather than industry as such, which is seen as having led to the ugliness of an industrial society, on which Lawrence is always emphatic... (*Spilka,* 164)

Thus the mechanical character of the society is the corrupting factor of men with its catastrophic nature killing the elements of humanness and freezing the life out of mankind. The roots of perpetual image of death and destruction depicted in Women in Love can also be explored in mechanical progress looming large on the twentieth century civilization. However, as pointed earlier, this destruction is a positive sign. In *Lady Chatterley's Lover,* the civilization like the phoenix, would rise from the ashes and would attempt to revive the blood consciousness of the early Brangwens.

Works Cited

Daleski, H.M. *The Forked Flame: A Study of D.H. Lawrence.* Northwestern: University Press, 1965.

Clarke, Colin. *The Rainbow and Women in Love: A Casebook.* London: Macmillan, 1969.

Lawrence, D.H. *Women in Love,* Wordsworth Classics, 1999.

Stevens, Hugh. *Sex and the Nation: The Prussian Officer and Women in Love.* The Cambridge Companion to D.H. Lawrence, (*ed.*) Anne Fernihough, Cambridge: Cambridge University Press, 2001.

Williams, Raymond. "Lawrence's Social Writings", *D.H. Lawrence: A Collection of Critical Essays.* (*ed.*) Mark Spilka, New Jersey: Prentice-hall, 1963.

Young, Kenneth. *D.H. Lawrence.* London: Longmans Green and Co., 1952.

A Spotlight on an Indian English Poet

Dr. Bhushan Singh

Dr. Amarendra Kumar, a bilingual poet of North Bihar, writes in such a fashion that it reverberates the rhythmic tone of his poetic sensibility. His writings, especially poetry, is the outcome of his overall experiences that he has shaped through various volumes of creation. He still takes much pains in penning down his insatiable passion for fiction and poetry risking his life, likely to meet an imminent end. Having a weak bony body with frequent memory slips, he still depicts his compassionate vision of life with a passionate identity with suffering humanity. Not only that, he has not concealed anything in revealing his true inner feelings through images and symbols about the mundane world with harsh realities of life and death and about flashes of spiritual illumination through torment and doubt.

Born and brought up in the countryside, he received his early education at village schools living with his physician father. A deep impact of his father's literary leanings made him familiar with Hindi and English fiction, drama and poetry at the early school stage itself. His inclination towards literature developed slowly and steadily through his father's scholarly pursuit that later on turned him into a writer of versatile genius. His subtle observation of birds, bees, beasts, insects and even the tiny grass blades reminds us of his Wordsworthian outlook in the whole frame of his creative endeavour. He finished his college and university education from Patna University itself with no distinction of academic excellence. Though he did his Ph.D. on the topic titled *William Sansom's Art as a Short Story Writer: A Critical Study* under the scholarly guidance of Dr. R.K. Sinha who was a great teacher and academician of international repute.

Influenced by Marxist theory and ideology of socialism, he could not prevent himself from engaging in student politics without being an active member, though he didn't pursue politics in right earnest. His active participation in that field came to a halt all on a sudden when he started his career as a teacher in Bihar university service. But his deep sense of dedication to duty with a philosophical approach of thought and feeling made him a hero as a great classroom performer. He was a duty-bound professional who rarely skived any lecture in his long teaching career. His fascination for reading and writing books and relishing them completely cut him apart from all worldly activities in the true sense of the term. But he was a seminarist lecturing and presenting research papers in the country at many university centres during his university service. That his research articles on the short stories of William Sansom were published in India and abroad exclusively marks his analytical mind and art in true perspective. He spent much of his life in the small cabin of his house in a suburban town, Hajipur, composing verses or writing short stories except a few years of foreign assignment that he got as a university professor in Dhamar university, in the Republic of Yemen.

One of the simplest qualities that he has as a man is his gentlemanly behaviour with a sense of humility and submissiveness. Not only does he entertain the people but also meets, greets and talks with them in a natural way expressing his views on humanity, society and the direction in which he saw the world going fast. Having a saintly soul he leads a lonely life away from the din and bustle of town life, unfamiliar to the common masses. He broods over a variety of subjects imaginatively to give an aesthetic design to his innovative ideas and jots them down for timely publication throughout the year. The sole aim of writing is nothing but his passionate urge for aesthetic pleasure that he rejoices the most in a meditative mood. In his creative work, however, he sublimates it and is often torn between a passionate love for life and an intense desire for death.

His passionate interest in the classical Indian dances, mainly in Bharat Natyam and in other dance-forms as well survived and continued to move him to artistic articulation, particularly in poetry. Truly speaking, dance was food of life for him deeply rooted in his flesh and blood that inspired him to dedicate a book of poetry *Sound and Shell* to a great dancing star and film actress Mrs Vyjayantimala Bali. His intense love and longing for this art-form culminates in his evocation of the verbal music of life and literature. The deep impression of Miss Vyjayantimala's Bharat Natyam dance in Madras in 1959 kindled a flame of aesthetic spirit in Kumar to compose a few lines of deep delight through musical transmutation. In the opinion of Prof. Ramjee Roy, "The poem captures in poetic phraseology the eternal dance drama of the Divine Maker and seeks to discover dance as a divine frenzy through which the body beautiful explores the art musically and artistically."

As a visionary artist, he has been passing through a traumatic doubt about the existence of a good and kind God. Spiritual dilemmas gripped his delicate poetic sensibility so hard that it finds its utterance in both his poetry and fiction. Still he realizes the ambiguous and complex nature of divine force that is very difficult to apprehend, almost beyond the power of expression.

In the present day poetical scenario, the trend of writing poems is to express the feeling and emotion in a short and suggestive manner with free verse form, but Kumar did not get rid of the traditional device of rhyme and rhythm and lengthy verse form of complex texture of expression. Most of his books of poetry that appeared consecutively after 1980 namely *The Real Episode* 1981, *Sound and Shell* 1986, *Stage Dilemma* 1988, *Song/Anti-song* 1996, *Poetry Time Here* 2010 and *Voice Modulations: Poems* 2012 evoked through artistry and imagination a vivid impression of reality related to the trauma of cruelty to man and the eruptive, destructive fury of nature. Choosing a number of subjects to do the threadbare analysis by manipulating the enormous potential of tone, temper and technique has been his prime job of writing in a contemplative and compassionate way. The concluding lines of "O My Daughter:"

> Better I or she were stillborn,
> Or denied the suck of oxygen milk,
> Better never born at all...
> Anything better than this roasting
> In a blast furnace
> to forge a hand of steel
> for the Kanyadaan...

ironically hint at the prevailing trauma of fathering a daughter and giving her in marriage in the form of Kanyadaan. It sarcastically focuses on the pangs of misery and helplessness of a father and the travails of the procreative mother. Obviously, the art and craft involved in giving form to the agonizing feeling is superb in encompassing the Indian social situation and human relationship. One of his poems of almost the same kind "The Desert Sun" tells a pathetic tale of poor fathers or relations who go out for marriage negotiations for their daughters or sisters with little money for the dowry gift. The poem ironically presents the pitiful condition of the human predicament in the diabolic drama of dowry devil where "the boy-band's bumper crop/the girl-side's gloom and doom" speaks a lot about the present day prevailing system of marriage in Indian society. The "heatwave" of the sun is felt naturally and sarcastically to expose the bitter truth of real life situation in a tangible manner.

Almost all his religious poems such as "Lord Buddha," "Lord Venkateshwar," "Great Buddha Statue," "Ganga," "Narayani," etc. echo the music of the eternal truth and beauty of divine illumination and spiritual visions of faith and grace. They give his thought and feeling an adequate form through images and symbols, rhythm and diction with a touch of freshness. Most of his poems deal with contemporary problems and social situations like terrorism, poverty, politics, love, marriage and sex, and mock at or satirize crippling rituals and unpredictable calamities of Nature. These poems paint the cultural, social, economic and political pictures of the globe with multiple shades and colours.

Taken from his book of verse *Stage Dilemma*, "The Martyrs Memorial," a patriotic poem, is included in Bihar Intermediate syllabus of Supplementary Reader of *Rainbow* II for class twelve students. The poem sings the song of seven young martyrs who by their fearless passionate daring to hoist the national flag on the Secretariat at Patna sacrificed their lives to win freedom from the British regime. The unforgettable act of these true sons of the soil leaves an imprint of heroic feat of self-immolation and self-sacrifice on the altar of the motherland.

Apart from producing six books of verse, Kumar wrote two books of short stories titled *Passionate Pilgrim* 2006 in English and *Kachcha Bela* 1993 in Hindi that present the moving picture of human psyche in a forceful way. His first book of Hindi poetry *Avartan* came out in 2010 just after the publication of *Poetry Time Here* that exposes his personal, social and spiritual dimensions with a notable inventive skill. He has an equal hold on both versions of delicate writing. His style is, no doubt, ambiguous and obscure but the very approach is logical and genuine. What he perceives is accurately transmuted into suitable idioms and phrases of his choice to make it more touching and engrossing. The way he presents his innovative ideas and emotions contextually in both longer and shorter forms of writing casts a larger focus on his mind and work as well as his creative life.

His later poetic work *Poetry Time Here* is planned as a Joycean epic of discovery and development, of the evolution of his sensibility and expressive medium.

Diction, style, verbal music and imagery have their full form evolved through permutations and combinations of themes and artistic devices. Savage violence, terrorist or extremist, or of any other brand, and the indifference of the established poets, writers and critics to his small body of work have exercised his creative faculties to a pitch of intensity, recurrently, often a bit bitterly but nevertheless it reveals his deeper feeling that he tries to conceal by ironic phrasing or expression, with a certain degree of objectivity.

Like James Joyce he embraces the whole world, but though he is a bit innovative, he is basically Shakespearian and Yeatsian in sensibility and style. Thus, he is closer to the springs of the living world than to the conceptions and realizations of spiritual illumination in literature, art and philosophical thought. Besides, he can hardly imagine a poet being unpoetic, businesslike, callous and cruel in his real life and therefore it is not unwise to conclude that he lives poetry as much as he writes and produces it.

But the bright side of life – its instinctive joys, emotional attachments, creative delight in terms of verbalization – also gets him involved with a singular intensity of emotional and intellectual focus on it, so that he sings a paean to the beauty and joy of life in his extensive portrayal of it in verse and fiction writing. On the creative level, he is an acutely word-phrase-conscious person who delights in manipulating music to shape out the subtle rhythm of his feelings and thoughts. He is often accused of being a little too fond of alliterative expression and exploitation of other musical devices to serve his expressive ends, but the implications and resonances of irony beneath the textual exterior articulate his complex poetic sensibility in a sensitive and evocative manner. He is nothing if he is not an ironist.

Works Cited

Kumar, Amarendra. *The Real Episode.* Patna: Bachaspati Printing Press, 1981.

————, *Sound and Shell.* Patna: Vaishali Press, 1986.

————, *Stage Dilemma.* Calcutta: Writers Workshop, 1988.

————, *Kachcha Bela.* Patna: S.K. Printers, 1993.

————, *Song/Anti-song.* Hajipur: Indu Printing Press, 1996.

————, *Passionate Pilgrim.* Patna: Literary Research Centre, 2006.

————, *Avartan.* Patna: Rashtriya Press, 2010.

————, *Poetry Time Here—Poems: Perspective.* Patna: Balaji Graphics, 2010.

————, *Voice Modulations: Poems.* Patna: Novelty & Company, 2012.

Women at the Centre in the Novels of Anne Tyler

Dr. Ramesh Kumar Sharma
Dr. Thirupa Thi Reddy Maru

What's a family if not a trilogy – father, mother, child(ren) – where the mother, the woman, is positioned at the centre of things both chronologically and genetically. So too in the fictional families of Anne Tyler, it is the woman, more often than not, in the role of a mother, who makes or mars the peace and stability, nay the very premise of the household. It is she who can be regenerative and therefore nurtures as she adapts and moves through life, capable of enduring hardships and difficulties; and it is she who can be rigid and therefore make the family suffer because of her narrow view of life, and can even destroy the domestic balance.

Tyler's women, however, cannot be so easily categorized and pigeonholed; they are as multifarious and as polyphonous as they are numerous, though superficially they do share a few basic characteristics. For most of the women characters, marriage, at least the semblance of marriage, is assumed even if the marriages do not often seem to be sensible choices; only a few of them pursue education and professions and show little interest in things intellectual; over and over again they are forced to rely on their men for support; and, as Evans (1993) points out, the women characters who appear in Tyler's novels are "shockingly alone" (90); and well-neigh homely, wifely wives too.

The Tyler women range from proper and moneyed Roland Park matrons to sharp streetwise characters; from just adolescents to past middle-agers; from the phobic and anorexics to the vicious and maligning – the breadth and depth is truly awesome. There are left-behinds and those who leave, hangers-on and takers-on, alienated and alienating, superstitious and witchlike, and the differences are wrought so subtly that the distinctions need magnification and detailing.

Tyler's first novel, *If Morning Ever Comes*, has many of her women prototypes: there is Ellen Hawkes who is tough and rigid, cold and distant. Perhaps her husband, Dr Phillips Hawkes, would not have moved out with Lili Belle Mosely, had she said but one word: "He was just wanting her to ask him. But she did not" (126). Her refusal to talk or interfere becomes the predicament of her life – when she heard of the birth of her husband's illegitimate child, she "clamped her mouth shut and said it was his lookout" (117); when Ben Joe turns to his mother for explanation of the unexpected return home of his married sister she gives another hands off reply: "What's done is done; and it's none of our affair" (19). Later in the novel Ellen lectures Ben Joe when he tries to encourage Joanne to reconcile differences with her husband Gray: "And it's her own business, Ben Joe – nothing we have any right to touch. I don't want to hear about your meddling in it" (55). Her attitude has been, perhaps, conceived as a childish denial of reality in order to face the harshest reality of her life – her husband's going off; perhaps she suffers from foolish pride, refusing money from the alienated Phillips; but perhaps and more discreetly, she is the reflection of an independence that was unconventional for a small town southern woman in the 1960s. At a deeper level, however, Ellen evinces a strange trait running through the sub-text of Tyler's family stories – women take no decisions, and if they do they are inconsequential. So Ellen resigns herself to her lot in life and regularly has Tom Collins over after supper, sipping drinks and incongruously leafing through *Ladies Home Journal*.

Tyler's women, though performing universally expected roles, perform them in the most unexpected ways. Within the grooved age-old history of male-authored plots Tyler creates new meanings by fiat and bypass. As Joanna Russ (1972) points out with polemical flair that plots are reserved for men, it is they who are heroic, adventurous, worldly wise and more, and plots involving women are impoverished and ununique. Nancy Miller (1980), Patricia Meyer Spacks (1990) Rachel Blau du Plessis (1985), have also shown how, across different periods and national traditions, female action is curbed and contained by the ubiquity of the love plot. But Tyler differs and casts her women in different moulds that disturb the well-laid plans of even a male-protagonist narrative. Thus, in *If Morning Ever Comes* Ben Joe lacks the power traditionally held by men of the house. Though he dreams of running and thus ruling the Hawkes's household, he is a mere stranger to it living in New York and being provided for rather than providing, "Enclosed," writes Jennifer, his sister, "is next month's check for your expenses, etc. I hope you will remember to send a receipt this time as it will make my book-keeping neater" (14).

The young Jennifer assumes adult responsibilities early and her orderly household management makes her sound like an early version of Rose Leary in *The Accidental Tourist* who kept her groceries in alphabetic order. But beyond stray parallels the Tyler women are each unto her own. In this first novel there are three generations of women under one roof – grandmother, mother and daughters – besides Shelley Domer, Ben Joe Hawkes's fiancee, and Lili Belle Mosely, the dowdy but warm mistress of Phillip Hawkes; and there are three curious men – Phillip the absentee and then dead husband, Ben Joe the turned-way son, and Gary the once-estranged-wanting-to-patch up husband of Joanne. The women are practical and forward-looking, the men either absconding or ineffectual. Even Ben Joe, the so-seeming protagonist is but a dreamer, and his dreams always are underlined by failure as the tentative, conditional title suggests "that irritable alertness that characterizes the consciousness in the hours before dawn" (Voelker, 17). The dawn is reality and the consciousness is of his impending anonymity which does not plague the women around him for they live nearly contented lives in the cocoons they have woven round themselves.

In *The Tin Can Tree* there are again women who live together but this time they are not family, and yet there exists more sympathy between them for they peer into one another's personal lives. This second novel is not ambivalent, indecisive, arbitrary, like the first, and neither does the ordinary non-tragic define the lives of the characters. Tragedy, the death of the six-year old Janie Rose, and its relation with the inmates of the Pike's extended household is the moment that occasions, and around which, the plot is constructed. The narrative follows the actions and words of the house's survivors in the days following Janie Rose's death; the odd and asymmetric shakings out of grief, and the way it surfaces delineates the characters.

The women include Mrs Pike, the mother of Janie Rose, Joan Pike, a cousin, the two potter sisters Faye and Lucy, the black woman Missouri and her daughter Lily. The potter sisters live shuffled lives and temper their reclusiveness with an intense hunger for news of their neighbours. To participate in the goings-on around them they cast a light on others and trace a shadow of them a silhouette on paper taped to the wall. They themselves are only shady presences who are used as the darker shades to lighten the foreground of the narrative. Mrs Pike is so hit by the tragedy that she forgets to live till Missouri reminds her of her obligation to her living child, Simon. Joan Pike is the only fully realized character, and she is also the most unsettled. She keeps her suitcases packed and is always on the verge of leaving. Her affair with James is tragic, for he cannot give her the full attention she desires.

Tyler's women in *The Tin Can Tree* disrupt the traditional narrative patterning and despite the strong men present the women who are able to disorder, rupture and disorient the coherence and linearity of the story. The men, James particularly, try to control and master the messiness of the reality and patch the tragedy of Janie Rose's death, but the women in the novel subvert the closure, logic and fixed authoritarian points of view. The end is the reclaiming of Simon by Mrs Pike and her awareness that the family goes on. We wonder what the story line would have been if it had not been Janie Rose who died but Simon!

It is in her third novel, *A Slipping Down Life* that Tyler creates her first woman protagonist, and with the exception of the last page, the entire narrative is told from the point of view of a single character, Evie Decker. Tyler exhibits a patriarchal mastery in her plot construction, hence there are no flashbacks or other complicated narrative structures, and only a handful of other characters to undermine the linearity. Unlike stories by women, Tyler does not take it "as axiomatic that the structure (of her story) . . . is cognate with social structure" (Homans, 5). Here is a novel that moves in a straight line and expands on woman's capaciousness rather than mourning its constraints.

Evie is no Cinderella, Snow White or Sleeping Beauty, nor is she a Medusa or even Medea; she displays heroism in her womanliness, and looks forward rather than back, moving into unknown territory, striving to fashion new stories of action and freedom. She loves Casey to distraction, so much so that she distorts herself without a qualm. Her love changes her from a passive, unpopular teenager, watching life pass her by, to someone who speaks her mind and asserts herself. And as she becomes more assertive, her sense of middle-class propriety comes to the fore. She wants to marry not to run off. More and more she becomes the decision maker, and Drum reluctantly goes along after mounting only a token protest. And finally a stage comes when Evie needs not even to tell Drum about her decisions – not even when she decides to leave him and move out of their tar paper shack for good, for she has learnt never to "back down on things" (198).

A Slipping Down Life is really a coming of age novel, as Evie faces poverty, pregnancy and infidelity, and the death of her father, she develops. Instrumental in her maturation is Mrs Simmons the librarian with whom Evie works. She becomes a kind of mother substitute from whom Evie begins to internalize the organized atmosphere and the literal indifference of the books. However, Clotelia is the closest that Evie has to a maternal presence in the house. She is a housekeeper but is much more perceptive and aware of Evie's situation than her father. It is she who passes on the housewifely love to Evie, and it is she who comes to keep Evie company the night her father dies. She is not the motherly sort but still she is willing to help Evie with child care.

The novel is about Evie, perhaps the only one in which the story centres on a woman protagonist. It is all about growing up where Evie moves beyond her juvenile angst and slips down into a life of adult responsibility. As she moves ahead she is "scared" both literally and metaphorically. Her literal scaring is an act of mimesis as she looks into a mirror to carve "Casey" on her forehead. According to Irigaray (1985): "To play with mimesis is thus, for a woman to try to recover the place of her exploitation by discourse, without allowing herself to be simply reduced to it . . . It also means "to unveil" the fact that if women are such good mimes, it is because they are not simply absorbed in this function. They also remain elsewhere" (76). Evie at once imitates the dominant discourse, here Casey's name, and yet diverges from it by writing "Yesac," thus writing from her so called "marginal existence." Very subtly has Tyler used the looking glass trap to examine a woman's identity which is often distorted when she gazes into the mirror. Sandra Gilbert and Susan Gubar (1979) caution women to beware of this "trap" of the "Kings" voice that resides in the mirror, which actually is not their true self but one they have internalized at their own expense (37)." At the same time Virginia Woolf (1986) points out in *A Room of One's Own* that sometimes the women become the embodiment of the mirror itself:

> Women have served all these centuries as looking glasses, possessing the magic and delicious power of reflecting the figure of man at twice his natural size (35).

Thus the distortion of Casey is gradually magnified. Rose Quiello (1994) gives another interpretation by suggesting that the carving of Casey's name on Evie's forehead proclaims her desire in an inexorable way – metonymical of a desire that cannot be negated. For the first time in her life, Evie's body serves her own desires (53).

Graphically imaged in her scars are the psychological underpinnings of a woman who was finally able to begin to represent her repressed desires. Tyler clearly locates the source of woman's pain in her heroines' scars, but the scars simultaneously become a fictional hallmark which symbolizes women's empowerment. Evie runs her fingers across her scar whenever she is about to contradict public authority. On the narrative level, when Evie "scars" herself and is being carried to the ambulance, the still point becomes an epiphanic moment of movement and self-growth. The moment is crucial and enlightening for her as she insists: "While I was walking through the crowd with the police officer, I kept thinking of my name:

> Evie Decker, me. Taking something into my own hands for once. I thought, if I had started acting like this long time ago my whole life might have been different" (128).

Her very act of "difference" arouses suspicions in others regarding her being "normal."

In many of her novels, and particularly in *A Slipping Down Life* "the definition of normal demonstrates how Tyler's fiction creates a fertile field for reframing what constitutes "normality" – a field where she blurs the outlines between madness and sanity" (Quiello, 56). Phyllis Chesler (1989) underscores Tyler's attempt to redefine "normal" female experience, asserting that Freud's psychoanalytic theories, forced women into prescribed roles that "normal" behaviour, according to Freud, consisted of female passivity and dependency (xxxv). Evie is therefore abnormal in her rebellion, but this is true of other Tyler heroines too who are able to recast their moments of "madness" into moments of self-representation. And here, once again we see politics in the way Tyler has fashioned women. Their re-imagining and re-description of their lives carries an aesthetic, moral and political force. Of course, much of Tyler's fiction is not feminist in any strict ideological sense, nor should its value be assessed in such a light. But it exists by default, says Rita Feiski (2003) "in the aftermath of the women's movement, which has created endless eddies and currents that flow in often surprising and unexpected directions" (109).

In *Earthly Possessions* we have a replay of the earlier women role models but the story line takes them in different directions though through similar family myths. Here again is the mother of the protagonist and the mother-in-law and it is the latter who is responsible for the protagonist, Charlotte Ames' evolution. Clearly, the vivacious Alberta Emory is the antithesis of Lacey Ames, Charlotte's sullen mother, and she represents the full, breezy life Charlotte longs for, as Mary had in *Celestial Navigation.* The indomitable Alberta's days brim with change and complication that delight rather than confound the free spirit. Charlotte withers in the jail that is her parent's house, "stale, dark, ancient . . . in which nothing had moved for a very long time" (12). Charlotte says of Alberta, "I loved her. I hung on everything she told me . . . I wished she would adopt me. I longed for her teeming house and riches ... (and) eventfulness" (64). Compared to Alberta, Lacey Ames, Charlotte's mother is a deathly statis. Therefore, it is not hard to accept why Lacey's house is so stale and stagnant and so is her family life; Lacey lacks a firm sense of herself and when women are weak the family edifice crumbles, goes down in shambles.

Lacey has never been a "self," predominantly she defines herself as someone's daughter, wife or mother, and so develops a poor self esteem. She manifests the problem which Nancy Chodorow reveals typically beset middle class women in her struggle for individuation. So grooved do such women become in the other's perception of themselves that they discourage the breaking of dependence and the children, especially the daughters, grow up inheriting the legacy of low self esteem. This is exactly what conspires with Charlotte. She grows up and raises her family in the same house where her mother had been raised and where she had raised her family being first her father's daughter and later a travelling photographer's wife. Lacey sees herself as indistinguishable from her husband, so that their life "shrunk and dwindled" (11).

Alberta, on the other hand, takes control of her own life and can therefore direct the life of her family. Her son Saul, a boarder in the Ames's house and then the town minister, and Charlotte's husband, is settled and sedate, and chains his wife to the home of her youth. Charlotte is never able to have her own house and thus "home," no family that is of her making. Like her mother, Charlotte finds it difficult to claim herself. She runs her father's photography studio for seventeen years, longer than he runs it himself, but persists in seeing it only as a temporary position. She is a daughter, mother, wife, an actual livelihood bears no legitimacy for her. Jake Simms, Charlotte's bank-robber captor, uncannily sums up the weakness the two restive travellers share: "Any time you see someone running, it's their old, faulty self they're running from or other people's notion of their faulty self" (157). Charlotte's notion of her "temporariness" gives her an objective perspective which makes her live her life through, despite her own sense of dislocation she is able to relocate herself. And Alberta is the agent who indirectly moves her to a broader vision.

Like Lacey Ames and even Alberta Emory, Pearl Tull in *Dinner at the Homesick Restaurant* challenges societal prescriptions for maternal behaviour. In a painful scene in which Cody (Pearl's son) recounts memories of his childhood, his harboured angst surfaces on the day of his mother's funeral:

> "You think we're a family," Cody said turning back. "You think we're some jolly, situation-comedy family when we're in particles, torn apart, torn all over the place, and our mother was a witch," . . . "A raving, shrieking unpredictable witch," Cody told Beck (his father, who had abandoned him when he was a small child). "She slammed us against the wall and called us scum and vipers, said she wished us dead, shook us till our teeth rattled, screamed in our faces. We never knew from one day to the next, was that alright?" (221)

In the character Pearl, Tyler provides us with the ultimate breakdown of the woman as mother showing yet another dimension of deviant female behaviour. However, here Tyler is daring enough to expose the dark side that emerges from Pearl's tremendous rage and frustration and to show the destructive consequences of that rage. The sweet qualities of motherhood which are mythically perpetuated are blown apart. Tyler explodes the "apple pie" myth of motherhood and purposefully demonstrates what happens when women are ignored. In Pearl we see another aspect of the rage of the hysteric who breaks out of the conventional mode and expresses feelings that can no longer be contained to satisfy social practice.

So whether the woman is flying over culture, or under it, she is, according to Sherry Ortner (1974) "both under and over (but really outside of) the culture's hegemony" (85). Gilbert and Gubar (1979) press forward Ortner's thesis: "If we define a woman . . . as indomitably earthly yet somehow supernatural, we are defining her as witch or monster, a magical creature of the lower world who is a kind of antithetic mirror image of an angel" (26). Gilbert and Gubar go on to speculate that the "witch-monster-mad-woman becomes so crucial an *avatar* of the (woman) writer's own self. From a male point of view, women who reject the submissive silence of domesticity have been seen as terrible objects – Gorgons, Sirens, Scylas, serpent-Lamias, Mothers of Death or Goddesses of Night. But from a female point of view the monster woman is simply a woman who seeks the power of self-articulation (79). However, for all Pearl's and Lacey's apparent rejection of their children, Tyler treats these women affectionately, understanding the tragedy in their inability to participate in the circumscribed realm of motherhood and domesticity, and their subsequent need to protect themselves from it and retreat from it. As Gullette (1990) says, "Tyler saw that motherhood was not in every case a happy instinct, a gift of the life course. For some it comes as a curse" (110). Tyler understands that marriage and motherhood are often symbolic of structures designed to imprison women. Consequently, hysteria offers her protagonists a real way of escaping a constrained life.

Evie Decker, whose "scars shone like snail tracks," finds her counterpart in the character of Muriel Pritchett in Tyler's novel *The Accidental Tourist.* On the surface, these two characters seem antithetical. Muriel's means of expression and her outspokenness are vastly different from Evie's initial tortured attempts to speak, yet both use language as a mediating agency which enables them to challenge the dominant ideology. In the scene where Macon, who has gone to Muriel's apartment to leave a note declining her dinner invitation, is persuaded by Muriel to spend the night. The precise narrative moment where oppositions converge in the image of Macon's head on Muriel's abdomen after they have made love, graphically summarizes and extols the dialectic features of language which frame the scene. The following passage warrants a close examination:

> Then (Muriel) came over to the bed and lifted the quilt and slid under it. "I just want to sleep," Macon told her. But there were these folds of silk. He felt how cool and *fluid* the silk was. He put a hand on her hip and felt the *two layers* of her, *cool* over *warm.* He said, "Will you take this off?" She shook her head. "I'm bashful," she whispered, but immediately afterward, *as if to deny that,* she put her mouth on his mouth and wound herself around him . . . She sighed in her sleep and lifted his hand and placed it on her stomach. The robe had fallen open; he

> felt her *smooth* skin and then a *corrugated* ridge of flesh jutting across her abdomen. And it seemed to him, as he sank back into his dreams, that she had as good as spoken aloud. About your son, she seemed to be saying: *Just put your hand here, I'm scarred, too, We're all scarred, You're not the only one.*

Muriel, here, takes it upon herself to fuse polarities. The semantic field of the passage is explicitly polarized ("two layers of her," "cool/ warm," "smooth/corrugated"), and leads to a reflection of the two gender identities at play. Figured in the binary oppositions of this "touching" collaborative moment is the possibility of creativity.

Here, Tyler plays not only with the notion of biological reproduction (Muriel's abdominal scars are the direct result of her having given birth to her son, Alexander), but also with the reproduction of a feminine discourse. Muriel's gesture of coexistence in *The Accidental Tourist,* like Evie's gesture of defiance in *A Slipping Down Life,* becomes what Margaret Homans (1986) has described, in *Bearing the Word,* as a "literal transgression" against a linguistic boundary (5). Underlying Homan's argument, Muriel's and Evie's scars speak for them and "bear the word" in the aphonic message of the hysteric. Muriel's gesture is doubly subversive because she makes her argument by negation. It is based on "lack" as the scene marks an auditory lack of enclosure. Moreover, the framing observation is that the scene sets up the union of the two extremes touching. In her immense capacity to love and create, Muriel succeeds in assimilating herself into Macon's experience. She cures using no sedatives or pain-killers – Muriel cures by touching, in both the literal and the symbolic sense. Her silence is ambiguous: "... she *seemed* to be saying *Just put your hand here. I'm scarred, too*" but her body – just like Evie's – speaks boldly and clearly.

Tyler's women refuse to conform to traditional rules of discourse, and so they often find themselves involved in a battle of words with their male counterparts. At one point Alicia (Macon's mother) in *The Accidental Tourist* tells Julian: "All I have ever had is daughter-in-laws." Macon "automatically" corrects her and says: "Daughters-in-law Mother," but Alicia, who remains impervious to Macon's censoriousness and refuses to give Macon the satisfaction of repeating his corrective, then responds: "And didn't manage to keep them long either." Muriel, too, defies Macon's paternal attempt to encase her text (her life) by challenging his regulatory practices. Muriel, who "doesn't even speak proper English," who keeps confusing "simplistic" with "simple" and "nauseous" with "nauseated," and who "seemed (to use) words as a sort of background music," forges new texts with her frequent malapropisms, and breaks the hold of language by affirming the flexibility of linguistic constructs. Tyler presents us with women who, bound together by their remoteness from a social norm, cannot be contained in the paternal system of order and culture.

If Muriel can manipulate language, implicit in that ability is the power to create. Sandra Gilbert and Susan Gubar write: "Finally the fact that the angel woman manipulates her domestic/mystical sphere in order to ensure the well-being of those entrusted to her care reveals that she can manipulate; she can scheme; she can plot stories as well as strategies" (26). And if Muriel *can* manipulate language, she then has the "dangerous mobility" of the hysteric that Cixous and Clement describe in *The Newly Born Woman* (1975):

> Societies do not succeed in offering everyone the same way of hitting into the symbolic order; those who are, if one may say so, between symbolic systems, in the interstices, offside, are the ones afflicted with a dangerous mobility. Dangerous for them because those are the people afflicted with what we call madness, anomaly, perversion, or whom we even label, says Mauss, "neurotics, ecstatic, outsiders, carnies, drifters, jugglers, and acrobats." ... And more than any others, women bizarrely embody this group of anomalies showing the cracks in the overall system (7).

Muriel's life is framed by an interest in a different value system, and her interests become more and more subversive. She cares about what she enjoys doing and cannot be bothered with factual information:

> (Muriel) was inconsistent with Alexander to the point of *pure craziness* – one minute overprotective, the next callous and offhand. She was obviously intelligent, but she counteracted that with the most global cases of superstition Macon had ever witnessed.... .She believed in horoscopes and tarot cards and Ouija boards. Her magic number was seventeen. In a previous incarnation she'd been a fashion designer, and she swore she could recall at least one of her deaths ... She was religious in a blurry, nondenominational sort of way and had no doubt

> whatsoever that God was looking after her personally – ironic, it seemed to Macon, in view of how she'd had to fight for every little thing she wanted.

Refusing to allow themselves to be frozen into predictable postures, Tyler's heroines opt for the unpredictability and the suggestion of chaos associated with the supernatural world.

In retrospect, *Earthly Possessions* seems to be a first step in Tyler's changing narrative aim. That novel centres on the identity and the difficult self-determination of Charlotte Ames. Webbed in by the demands of many helpless family members and parishioners from her husband's church, Charlotte has decided to leave her husband. Marriage seems the reason for her draining life, even though Tyler is careful to leave Charlotte's relationship with Saul shadowy; the novel suggests that Saul is not intentionally at fault. Ironically, at the moment of her decision to leave him, as she stands in line to draw money out of the bank, Charlotte is taken hostage by Jake, a bank robber. Working, as she often does, to equate narrative line with metaphor, Tyler here makes Charlotte a hostage of both the gunman and her own life. She may as well go with the armed young robber; she has no personal volition anyway.

Works Cited

Cixous, Helene and Clement, Catherine. *The Newly Born Woman.* (*tr.*) Betsy Wing, Minneapolis : University of Minnesota Press, 1975.

du plessis, Rachel Blau. *Writing beyond Ending* : *Narrative Strategies of Twentieth Century Writers.* Bloomington: Indiana University Press, 1985.

Felski, Rita. *Literature after Feminism.* Chicago : University of Chicago Press, 2003.

Gilbert, Sandra and Susan Gubar. *The Madwoman in The Attie* : *The Woman Writer and The Nineteenth Century Literary Imagination.* New Haven : Yale University Press, 1979.

Gullette, Margaret Morganroth, "Anne Tyler: The Tears (and Joys) Are in the Things" in Ralph Stephens (*ed.*) *The Fiction of Anne Tyler.* Jackson: University Press of Mississippi, 1990.

Irigaray, Luce. *This Sex Which is Not true.* Catherine Porter with Carolyn Burke, Ithaca : Cornell University Press, 1985.

Miller, Nancy. *The Heroine's Text : Readings in the French and English Novel 1722-1782.* New York : Columbia University Press, 1980.

Ortner, Sherry, "Is Female to Male as Nature is to Culture?" in Michelle Zimbalist Rosaldo and Louise Lamphere (*ed.*) *Women, Culture and Society.* Stanford : Stanford University Press, 1974.

Quiello, Rose. "Breakdowns and Breakthroughs" in Dale Salvak (*ed.*) *Anne Tyler as Novelist.* Iowa City : Iowa University Press, 1994.

Russ, Joanna, "What Can a Heroine Do? Or Why Women Can't Write" in Susan Koppelman Cornillon (*ed.*) *Images of Women in Fiction : Feminist Perspectives.* Bowling Green, OH : Bowling Green University Press, 1972.

Spacks, Patricia Meyer. *Desire and Truth : Functions of Plot in Eighteenth Century English Novels.* Chicago : University of Chicago Press, 1990.

Tyler, Anne. *The Tin Can Tree.* New York: Berkley Books, 1983.

————, *The Accidental Tourist.* New York: Berkley Books, 1986.

————, *If Morning Ever Comes.* New York: Berkley Books, 1992.

————, *A Slipping Down Life.* New York: Berkley Books, 1992.

————, *Earthly Possessions.* New York: Berkley Books, 1993.

Woolf, Virginia. *The Essays of Virginia Wolf .Vol. I, 1901-1912* (*ed.*) Andrew McNeile, London : Hogarth Press, 1986.

Khalil Gibran: A Model of Émigré Literature

Dr. Vijay Shankar Prasad

Khalil Gibran has been regarded as "The Messiah" by Osho Rajneesh. His commentaries in fortyseven special lectures on Gibran's masterpiece, *The Prophet* run over more than six hundred pages. Gibran's philosophy and mysticism have drawn attention of scholars worldwide. His writings make a remarkable place in world literature and he holds a unique place as the leading representative of Arab American literature. The purpose of my paper is to present Gibran as a model of émigré literature or literature in diaspora (exile). Émigré, in French history, is a refugee, usually royalist, who fled the French Revolution and took up residence in a foreign land. The émigrés comprised all classes, but were disproportionately drawn from the privileged. Later the literature written by the migrants became known as émigré literature. Generally Britain and America were most sought after destinations of the émigrés from different countries.

The traces of Arab American literature may be found in the late 1800s, when Arab immigrants first began to arrive in North America in significant numbers from the Syrian province of the Ottoman Empire, primarily from what is now present-day Lebanon. The 1910s saw several literary societies and journals and in 1920 the literary organization Al Rabita al Qalamaiyya (the Pen League) was established by Kahlil Gibran, Ameen Rihani and others. These authors wrote in both Arabic as well as English. They produced the Mahjar (émigré) school of Arab-American writing. These writers had impact on Arabic literature, yet they were conscious of serving as bridges between East and West. They made humble attempt to create philosophical meeting points between Arab and American ideologies and contexts. Arab-American literature of this period often reflected a strong grief and acute sense of alienation and, sometimes, rootlessness also experienced by the writers.

Gibran (1883-1931), Lebanese American Christian poet, philosopher and painter was an Arab Émigré and is usually considered one of the founders of the genre of Arab American Literature. While Gibran is most familiar to U.S. readers, Ameen Rihani is considered by all the "father of Arab American literature." Although the voice of Gibran's early rebellion was at times the cry of an *émigré* artist, as he grew in confidence, his expression became the roar of an artist tempered by "the harsh discovery of a freer way of life."

America is, in some ways, entitled to claim Gibran for one of her own sons as much as his native Lebanon. For he spent only the first twelve years of his life in Bisharri in Lebanon, the village where he was born in 1883, before emigrating with his family to the United States in 1895. Apart from two brief return visits to Lebanon and a two-year studentship in Paris, he lived out the last two-thirds of his life, including virtually all of his adulthood entirely on American soil. He died in New York at the age of 48.

Gibran's mother Kamila, a daughter of the village priest, supported her four children in Boston as a seamstress. And although she was not educated, she encouraged her son's artistic and literary talent he displayed from an early age. She even told him that she envisioned him becoming a great man one day.

In America, Gibran met Mary Haskell, a wealthy woman and the principal of a private school in Boston. She was impressed by his talent and interested in his work. One of the questions she asked Gibran was, "Why do you draw the bodies always naked?" to which the young artist replied, "Because Life is naked. A nude body is the truest and the noblest symbol of life. If I draw a mountain as a heap of human forms, or paint a waterfall in the shape of tumbling human bodies, it is because I see in the mountain a heap of living things, and in the waterfall a precipitate current of life."

Less than twenty years after his emigration to the New World, the youth from Bisharri found himself moving among the elite literary and artistic circles of America, where he would seemingly slip on new personae – masks that enchanted, fascinated, and sometimes beguiled his American acquaintances. What attracted Gibran was the real America, the abode of universities, research centers, laboratories, charitable foundations, and above all, the land of the free and of true democracy, especially meaningful to one who had emigrated from an Arab homeland that moved in the shadow of the Hamidian regime and Ottoman oppression.

Although a romantic himself and suffering from nostalgia for his tiny Lebanon, Gibran embraced the American transcendentalists like Whitman, Emerson, and Thoreau. His works bear the influence of their ideas of self-reliance, reincarnation, and the presence of a greater self that each individual is able to grow into. Gibran was among a younger generation of Arab-American writers who contributed to the ongoing Arabic literary renaissance. This movement had started by the end of the 19th century with revivalist figures in the Arab world like Butrus Al-Bustami, Kahlil Mutran, and Al-Aqqad, among others who were attracted to Western poetry and particularly English romanticism.

Gibran started to contribute to *Al-Mohajer* (*The Immigrant*), a prominent Arabic-language newspaper in New York. Its publisher, Ameen Goryeb, had met Gibran and was impressed by his prose poems recorded on his notebook. Gibran's column had a popular appeal and was entitled *Tears and Laughter,* the pieces of which later formed the basis of his book *A Tear and a Smile.*

Gibran continued to give talks to the Syrian audience in New York which welcomed him as a writer and also as a spokesman for their causes, especially Arab nationalism and Syria's independence from the Ottoman Empire. Gibran, indeed, was an advocator of Syria relying on herself and her resources to solve her own problems as well as unity among his people rather than sectarian divisions.

In 1923, Gibran's most famous book *The Prophet* was published and immediately received favourable reactions. Gibran knew it was his greatest achievement and the most important book he ever wrote. He had kept the manuscript for years before he had it published, seeking further moments of inspiration. He planned it to be the first of a trilogy; the second book was to be *The Garden of the Prophet* (edited and published in 1933 after Gibran's death) and the third, *The Death of the Prophet,* was left a fragment. Three years after *The Prophet* and at the height of Gibran's success, *Sand and Foam* was published in English. It is a book of beautiful sayings (322 of them) accompanied by seven illustrations by Gibran. *Sand and Foam* was followed a year later by another collection of aphorisms under the title of *Kalimat Jibran* (translated as *Spiritual Sayings).*

In 1928, the longest book Gibran ever wrote, *Jesus, the Son of Man* was published. It is widely acclaimed as his second most important book, after *The Prophet.* It portrays the life of Jesus and its human rather than supernatural aspect, and reflects Gibran's inspiration by the teachings of Christ. Then *The Earth Gods* came out in 1931. It is a dialogue in free verse between three titans on the human destiny. Gibran also wrote a play in English, *Lazarus and his Beloved* and *The Blind,* but it was not published in his lifetime.

As Gibran's interest shifted to mysticism and primitivism, his writings returned again and again to the beauty and purity of nature. He romanticized nature and found in it an inspirational power for his poetry. His poetry is nostalgic of the magnificent scenery of his childhood. It portrays him rejoicing in peace and freedom among the immortal cedars of Lebanon. Yet, inspired by Rousseau's ideas on the innocence of the natural man as opposed to the man corrupted by civilization and materialism, Gibran repeatedly points out to the contrast between the natural world and the human world. In the former there is peace, harmony, and innocence whereas in the latter there is chaos, injustice, and sorrow.

Gibran's writings are known for their prophetic tone against the evils that reigned in his beloved homeland at the time and against other evils that bring humanity to decadence. His message, however, is a healing one. He asserts that this modern world, corrupted by conventions, oppression, and hatred is redeemable through love, good will, and freedom.

Inspired by his own experience as an immigrant writer, Gibran aimed at uniting East and West and creating an intercultural reconciliation that transcends the barriers of language, religion, and politics. In 1925, at the height of his success in America, he was invited to become an officer of the New Orient Society in New York, which was dedicated to the promotion of East-West understanding. Among the contributors to its quarterly journal was the American author Claude Bragdon, who once asked Gibran for his impression of America. His reply was as follows:

> Conceive of the world as a rose-bush in a sky-garden, with races and civilizations for its blooms. Some flourish, from others the petals are falling, here one is withered, and just beside it, where once was a great red-hearted blossom, only an empty stalk remains to tell the tale. Now on this rose-bush America represents the bud just pressing at its sheath, just ready to blossom: still hard, still green and not yet fragrant, but vigorous and full of life.

Gibran considered himself as a spokesman of both cultures. He admired America's achievements and its values of individualism, dynamism, and freedom. On the other hand, he praised the Arab's contributions to the world, but advised them to evade the past and build one's own future, and to adapt the good aspects of Western civilization instead of blind imitation. Gibran appealed to the new generation of Arab Americans to be proud of both their Eastern and Western background.

The Prophet is Gibran's literary and artistic masterpiece. It remained during the 20th century America's bestselling book, after *The Bible.* Till the last century, it had sold more than 9,000,000 copies in North America alone. It has been translated into at least forty languages and has become one of the greatest classics of our time. The book presents Gibran as a writer of prophetic vision who shares his spiritual sensitivities with his readers. It portrays the journey of a banished man called Almustafa, which in the Arabic language means the chosen one. As he prepares to go back to "the isle of his birth," he wishes to offer the Orphalese, the people among whom he has been placed, gifts but possesses nothing. About the book Osho declares:

> THE PROPHET belongs to the category of a very small number of books which are not dependent on your action, your intelligence, on you; on the contrary, they are possible only when you are not, when you allow them to happen, when you don't stand in the way... In my experience, books like THE PROPHET are holier than your so-called holy books. And because these books are authentically holy, they have not created a religion around themselves. They don't give you any ritual, they don't give you any discipline, they don't give you any commandments. They simply allow you to have a glimpse of the same experience which happened to them.

As a wise sage and man of great vision, Almustafa teaches moral values, the mysteries of life, and timeless wisdom about the human experience: marriage, children, friendship, pleasure, death. He, for example, calls for balancing heart and mind, passion and reason. At the end of the book Almustafa closes his farewell address saying: "A little while, a moment of rest upon the wind, and another woman shall bear me." This image reflects a romantic vision of eternal rebirth, reincarnation, and continuity of life. Bushrui remarked that the secret of the book's success is "Gibran's remarkable ability to convey profound truths in simple yet incomparably elegant language."

The book apparently also draws on Gibran's readings, thoughts, and contemplations through the years. It is inspired by Biblical literature, Christian and Sufi mysticism, Buddhism, Hinduism... But we can also trace the influence of the romantics and transcendentalists. Gibran himself declared that *The Prophet* wrote him instead of writing *The Prophet.* Behind Almustafa's global vision of a harmonious universe healed by the power of love and unity, there is an underlying theme of the unity of all religions and the essential oneness of humanity.

First published in 1912, *The Broken Wings (Al-Ajnihah al-Mutakassirah)* is one of Gibran's early experimental works through which he sought to reform the Arabic literature and culture. In a manner unknown in traditional Arabic writing, it is free from rhetorical flourishes but more importantly, it debates the issue of the oppressed Arab woman in the Middle Eastern society of the late nineteenth and early twentieth centuries. Written in the tradition of "Romeo and Juliet" and based on oriental settings and images it is inspired by his own first love and bitter experience in his home village Bisharri.

The Broken Wings gives the taste of the bittersweet, of the beauty and pain of young love. It is an alive and profound story characterized by beautiful prose and evocative imagery, a tale of passion doomed by the restrictions of society and the power and greed of the clergy. His criticism is especially harsh when it comes to the heads of religion whom he accuses of maintaining the oppression of women. He says: "the Christian Bishop and the Moslem imam and the Brahman priest become like sea reptiles that clutch their pray with many tentacles and suck their blood with numerous mouths." Gibran sympathetically describes women in his native Lebanon as victims of a despotic patriarchal system. They are prisoners of social expectations and are treated as a commodity to be purchased, like in the case of Selma whose function was to take her father's riches to a husband who treated her like another possession. In *The Broken Wings*, Gibran is not just a story-teller but a culture analyst and a reformer who seeks to correct the wrongs.

A Tear and a Smile (Dam' ah wa-Ibtisamah), first published in 1914, is an anthology of Gibran's youthful writings in the Arabic-speaking éemigré newspaper. It is a collection of 56 poetic prose pieces. The language of the poems, stories, and parables is really splendid and it has poetic beauty. A mixture of tears and smiles, mourning and celebration of a wounded lover and solitary poet, the book shows that tears seem to be much more abundant than the smiles. The poet passes his life in agony and longs for his beloved, but is forced to accept that human life is a world of suffering and the way out is spirituality.

The Madman is a volume of illustrated parables and aphorisms, mostly in a tone that is ironic and rebellious against humankind. The book expresses the sense of alienation that Gibran had experienced during his thirty five years: a Christian from a predominantly Muslim region; the offspring of a broken marriage; a Lebanese *émigré* in America; and an artist living in a materialist society. To be an emigrant is undoubtedly to be an alien, but to be an emigrant mystical poet is in many ways to be thrice alienated. It was geographical alienation as well as estrangement from both conventional society and the world of spatio-temporal existence. Often Gibran was gripped with a triple longing; a longing for his homeland; for a more just and tolerant society; and for a higher world of spiritual union – a triple longing which fired his creativity. Indeed, in *The Madman* Gibran offers a self-commentary on the condition of being an artist.

Gibran's other writings have attracted less attention but they are by no means less important. "The Procession" by Gibran is a long ode in classical Arabic. Two metaphorical characters, Age and Youth, analyze the human society with its laws and aspirations, and embrace the fullness of the self in nature. *Sand and Foam* is a book of captivating and inspiring aphorisms and parables, all in Gibran's beautifully cadenced language. *Spirits Rebellious* is an early collection of four short stories: "Rose-Al Hani," "The Bridal Couch," "The Cry of the Graves," and "Khalil the Heretic." They all portray people who defy authority and social tradition in Lebanon. It represents a scathing attack on the abuse of religious power.

To sum up, more than a model of émigré literature Gibran is also a model of world literature. He has shown a mysterious power to synthesize the best of Christianity and Islam. And perhaps most important of all, amongst the literature of the twentieth century, with its fashionable emphasis on cynicism, anxiety and despair, his works stand out like a beacon of hope and compassion. Gibran as the man of letters is the embodiment of peace, spiritual values and international understanding the modern world is craving for.

Works Cited

Bushrui, Suheil B. "Khalil Gibran of America," *The Arab American Dialogue.* 7.3 1996.

Claude Bragdon, "A Modern Prophet from Lebanon," *Khalil Gibran: Essays and Introductions.* (*eds.*) Suheil Bushrui and John M. Munro, Beirut: Rihani House, 1970.

Daoudi, M.S. *The Meaning of Khalil Gibran.* Secaucus: Citadel Press, 1982.

Gibran, Khalil. *The Prophet.* New York: Knopf, 2000.

Gibran, Khalil, *The Broken Wings.* (*tr.*) Anthony R. Ferris, New York: Citadel Press, 1957.

Jayyusi, S.K. *Trends and Movements in Modern Arabic Poetry.* 2 vols., Leiden, E. J.Brill, 1977, vol.1, p. 70.

Naimy, Mikhail. *Khalil Gibran: A Biography.* Beirut: Khayats, 1964.

Waterfield, Robin. *Prophet: The Life and Times of Khalil Gibran.* New York: St. Martin's Press, 1998.

www.oshorajneesh.com/download/...The_Messiah_Volume_1.pdf.

Literary Intertextuality and Issues of Existence

Dr. Tanjeen A. Khan
Dr. G.A. Ghanshyam

Literary theories are recent development in the field of literary studies. With these theories literary study has moved from a position, which viewed literature as a "natural" phenomenon to a more questioning approach, which now interrogates many aspects, which were previously considered unquestionable, self evident or natural. It is in the common sense that work owes its origin and refers to other works. No one can claim that writer is entirely original and a writer is the original author of a work. A writer is not creator of the genre and the language he uses; he owes to his predecessors, and is only carrying forward his literary response. The production of literature is a socially mediated form of behaviour rather than a personal or an impersonal instinctive reaction to the world. Moreover, many or perhaps most writers have to work their way through an apprenticeship in which they consciously imitate or borrow from predecessors whose work they admire, though of course, a real writer does not stop there. Not only have they borrowed from the texts but from the myths, history and their own social milieu. Sometimes it becomes a habit of the readers to underrate the role of other texts (society, myth, culture and history) in shaping a new work and to overrate the originality of an individual artist. An unconscious search for new in a new work takes place in readers' mind. But the fact is that the underlying tradition and the basic assumptions are changing very slowly, even revolutionary literature, which are said to be different, has more similarities than differences from the orthodox or traditional writing that precedes it. The path breaking new work puts out only a little from the mainland of the already said, the already written. Debates have taken place on the relationship between authors and work in the late 1940s and the early 1950s and remarkable radical shifts have occurred since the 1960s. These have challenged traditional assumptions regarding the author as the originator or producer of the literary work and questioned the author's authority over the text. Barthes and others have theorized this process and the term frequently applied to it is "Intertextuality:"

> The intertextual in which every text is held, it itself being the text between of another text, is not to be confused with some origin of the text to try to find the "sources", the "influences" of a work, is to fall in with the myth of filiation; the citations which go to make up a text are anonymous, untraceable, and yet already read; they are quotations without inverted commas.
>
> —(Barthes, "From Work to Text," 288-289)

As a critical term, intertextuality is generally dated from Julia Kristeva's use of it in "Word Dialogue and Novel," published in 1966. This essay is primarily a recapitulation of Bakhtin's concept of the dialogic nature of the novel, and thereby, itself an illustration of intertextuality. According to Kristeva in this essay, "Bakhtin was one of the first to replace the static hewing out of texts with a model the "literary word" as an intersection of textual surfaces rather than a point (fixed meaning), as a dialogue among several writings; that of the writer; the addressee (or the character), and the contemporary or earlier cultural context, "by introducing the status of the word as a minimal structural unit, Bakhtin situates the text within history and society, which are then seen as texts by the writer, and into which he inserts himself by rewriting them" (Kristeva 3). She further adds, "we must first define the three dimensions of textual space where various semic sets and poetic sequences function"(Kristeva 3). These three dimensions or coordinates of dialogue are writing subject, addressee, and exterior texts. The word's status is thus defined horizontally (the word in the text belongs to both writing subject and addressee) as well as vertically (the word in the text is oriented towards an anterior or synchronic literary corpus. "Any text is constructed as a mosaic of quotations; any text is the absorption and transformation of another" (Kristeva 3). "Kristeva, views any given work as part of a larger fabric of literary discourse, part of a continuum including the future as well as the past" (Ross, Murfin 176).

When we read a text, consciously or unconsciously we place it in wider frames of reference of language and knowledge than those to do with a particular author, period or set of literary criteria. In a sense, we "cover" the text with a multiplicity of discourses drawn from our own culture and experience, which will vary according to time, place and the individual reader. Some stories serve as a kind of allegory for literary production and consumption, and illustrate the concept of intertextuality through fictional discourse. In a sense, all texts undergo a process of "rewriting" as they are reread, reproduced. Reading and interpretation following the palimpsest metaphor be thought of as transcription. Views of Roland Barthes and others may throw a more illuminating focus upon it.

In S/Z (1970) Barthes deconstructed Balzac's short story "Sarrasin," seeking to "de-originate" the text to demonstrate that it reflects many voices, not just that of Balzac. For Barthes, writing did not invoke an instrumental process of recording pre-formed thoughts and feelings (working from signified to signifier) but was a matter of working with the signifiers and letting the signified take care of themselves. "Barthes sees the text as a "network" both in turns of its internal structures of meaning and also in the ways in which it combines with the external frameworks in which it is situated." (Webster 99) Webster further writes defining intertextuality, "Instead, a text consists of multiple writings, and writings, which are drawn from a range of discourses, already in circulation in one form or other." (Webster 99)

Theorists of intertextuality problematize the status of "authorship," treating the writer of a text as the orchestrator of what Roland Barthes refers to as the "already-written" rather than as the originator, "a text... is a multidimensional space in which a variety of writings, none of them original, blend and clash. The text is a tissue of quotations drawn from innumerable centres of culture." (Barthes, "The Death of the Author" 146) The writer can only imitate a gesture that is always anterior, never original. His only power is to mix writings, to counter the one with the other, in such a way as never to rest on any of them. It is clear with the views of Barthes and Kristeva that intertextuality can occur at many levels:

> It is a broad area of study and it makes different meanings to different people, ...it could be used by a "poststructuralist" to suggest that a work of literature can only be recognized and read within a vast field of "signs" and "tropes" that is like a text and that makes any single text self-contradictory and undecidable.
>
> (Ross, *Murfin* 176)

All this is good in the sense that scholars now realize that a text cannot be studied in isolation. It belongs to a web of texts, which are (partially) present in the mind of the author. These are positive gains from the use of the term intertextuality. But there is a downside. The frequent use of the term is threatening to blunt the scholarly enterprise by lumping together a whole variety of approaches and calling them intertextuality. Even worse, it can sometimes be used to make vague and tenuous echoes sound credible. However, if intertextuality is best used as an "umbrella" term, then it requires subcategories to indicate the individual scholar's particular interest or focus.

Hamlet is a text which is constantly being reinterpreted: the limits of its meaning cannot be determined because the contexts in which it is read, performed or written about are always subject to change. In this sense, the multiplicity of meanings and the range of interpretations available ensure that literary studies and criticism are endless activities. Work like *Rosencratz and Guilderston are Dead* a response to *Hamlet.* Its central theme is the contrast between the constant bafflement which characterizes ordinary experience and the much greater understanding of events enjoyed both by the people in literature to whom they happen and the reader or spectator who is given privileged access to them by the traditional text. But it is also a presentation of the experience of everyman. In the same series, in 1972, in a play *Horatio's Version,* Alethea Hayter applied the concept of intertextuality to the plot of *Hamlet,* perhaps without quite realizing how useful an illustration she was providing for the concept of the French critics who invented it. The action of the *Horatio's Version,* like that of Perry Portac's *Hamlet Part-II* takes place after Shakespeares's play has ended, and looks at what might have happened afterwards. Horatio is, as Hamlet knew he would be, scrupulous in ensuring that the truth is told about the events leading up to the accumulation of dead bodies on and off the stage with which the play ends. The court of enquiry in which he refutes the version put forward by Osric and other former servants of Claudius show Horatio at his best, and is a splendid piece of imaginative reconstruction on Alethea Hayter's part.

In the same way Emma Tenent's *Tess* experiments with various kinds of such infringement. In this novel, several beautiful women whose lives follow the same pattern of betrayal and murder, are grouped into what may be termed the Tess category. Some of these women are real, others imaginary. Yet Tenant alludes to all of them as though they could all inhabit the same world, by doing this she blurs a major distinction on which conventional understanding of literature rests. The alert reader finds that he has to continually realign his perspective. At one instance he comes across a Tess from real life, like the actress who played the role of Tess Durbey field; and at another instance an imaginary character called Tess from Hardy's; both of them are described as having been subject to chauvinistic treatment. A movie in Indian celluloid "Lajja" with the castings of Rekha, Madhuri Dixit, Manisha Koirala and Mahima Chaudhury has the same theme and more or less all the women in same way or the other had the same urge against male-chauvinism.

One of the best illustrations of what intertextuality means in practice can be found in James Joyce's *Ulysses*. By presenting the reader with an alternative version of reality on to generations of readers. Joyce's novel calls into question the validity of accounts of experience couched in the established genres of the heroic epic. At the same time, the novel cast doubt on the value system on which the original work is constructed. Although Joyce did not have the Kristevan concept of intertextuality in mind when he wrote *Ulysses*, his rewriting of myth fulfils the basic ambition of intertextuality by ensuring that *Odyssey* can never be read in quite the same way again. Writing becomes in this context, primarily a reflection on literature itself and an invitation to the reader to think more of the account which novels, plays and poems have given experience in the past. Joyce's *Ulysses* (1992) deals with the events of one day in Dublin in June 1904. The principal character is Stephen (the hero of Joyce's novel *A Portrait of the Artist as a Young Man*), so is itself intertextual in a way. The various chapters roughly correspond to episode of Homer's *Odyssey*; Stephen representing Telemachus, Bloom as Odysseus, and Molly as Penelop.

A number of interpretations rose and fell in the waters of a great poem *The Waste Land*. This "master text" of English modernism indicates the ways in which a particular story or myth can be repeated in different ways. The poem is landmark for a modern reader. But to the uninitiated reader the poem may seem chaotic. Only those with some knowledge of Dante, Jacobean drama, Buddhism, mythology and the works of Sir James Frazer, can appreciate its movement. Such intertextual texts cover the multiplicity of discourses drawn from our own culture and experience that will vary according to time, place and to the individual reader. To quote Bloom in this context will be relevant:

> T.S. Eliot's poem *The Waste Land* or James Joyce's novel *Ulysses* are good illustrations of texts which self-consciously rework eclectic ranges of literary and other discourses already in circulation which are to a greater or lesser extent recognizable, but which come to assume a quite different status as they are incorporated into new combinations and juxtapositions.
>
> (Bloom, *A Map of Misreading*,18)

Not only literature, but also myths have splendid feast for intertextual writers. Use of myths in exploring contemporary history and society is another area for intertextual connections. There are certain values and meanings which were created in actual societies and actual situations in the past which still seems to have significance because they represent areas of human experience, aspiration and achievement which the dominant culture neglects, undervalues, opposes, represses or even cannot recognize. The use of myth in socially constructed texts reinforces the strength of the very text and makes its main objective realized. A step further is the use of history to explore contemporary society that attracts intertextual researchers.

Thus, intertextuality is not only proceeding forward with a previous literary text but social and historical events may also form intertexts. Human existence, no doubt has a million theories but it can not be denied that literature has its life parallel to human civilization. Intertextuality, not confined to literature is a very vast term, defuses all the other critical approaches or in the contrary it can be said that it involves all the critical approaches. Mimetic theory with Historical, Psychological, Feminist and Structural approach following influences and sources, all can be reduced to a single term "intertext." Why the dismay and confusion of "isms" and "ists," let the writers and readers do their job using their own intertexts. Their aesthetic sense cannot be bounded to any one approach. The perception and reception may change with the individuals. A reader is free to interpret the play on his own terms, with his own experiences. In the faculty of Laws, Lawyers and Judges use different previous court cases and specific sets of legal documents to interpret testimony and evidence and it is customary to cite quoted works while writing a research paper, but in writing a novel, however, authors never cite previous texts that have addressed similar themes and adopted similar techniques. It is the task of a reader to interpret the text using different sources, making it meaningful. Thus, an attention to intertextuality takes us to our old literary exercises. It reminds us that literary workout is a continuous process and each writer drifts it a little forward. In the ongoing evolution of literary tradition, each writer believes that a previous text contains a space that requires to be filled. He also believes that he is equipped to fill it. Intertextual activities create a literary lineage, the image of a palimpsest, with each successive author competing to transpose his writing on a previous textual perspective. With this Bhaktin's "Carnival," "Barthes," "Death of the Author" and Kristevan "Intertextuality" is forever fixed as a landmark in literary studies.

Works Cited

Barthes, Roland. "From Work to Text", *Postmodern Literary Theory—An Anthology.* (*ed.*) Niall Lucy, Oxford, Blackwell, 2000.

————. "The Death of the Author." *Image-Music–Text Selected and Trans.* Stephen Heath, London: Collins, 1977.

Bloom. *A Map of Misreading.* New York: OUP, 1975.

Kristeva, Julia. "Desire in Language – Word Dialogue and the Novel." *Intertextuality and Dialogue.* 14, April, 2004.

Long, J. William. *English Literature its History and significance.* New Delhi: Kalyani Publishers, 2002.

Murfin, Ross. *The Bedford Glossary of Critical and Literary Terms.* New York: Macmillan Press Ltd., 1998.

Webster, Roger. *Studying Literary Theory – An Introduction.* London: Arnold, 1996.

Recreation of History and Deconstruction of Myths and Mythological Symbols in Dalit Literature

Dr. Alpana Gupta

Myth according to *Oxford Advanced Learner's Dictionary* means "a story handed down from olden times especially concepts or beliefs about the early history of a race, explanation of natural events, etc."

Indian history abounds in such myths. One such myth is about the division of society into four orders or *varnas*. According to this myth there are four main castes or *varnas* in the Hindu social order arranged in a hierarchy in the order of the tasks they perform. According to the *varnavyavastha* Brahmins (the priest caste) are highest in the social order, next come Kshatriyas (warriors), third place is taken by Vaishyas (the business class) and the fourth or the lowest place has been accorded to Sudras, supposed to perform the menial jobs such as leather tanning, scavenging, sweeping, shoe-making, disposal of sewage and cleaning of night-soil of upper castes, etc.

The fourth or the lowest rung of *varnavyavastha* is Sudras (Untouchables) or Dalits as they prefer to call themselves disapprove of the existing myths in Hindu scriptures. Dalits reject the history, myths and the God of the upper caste. They believe that *varnavyavastha* was developed by the Brahmins in order to maintain their superiority. And the recent spurt in Dalit literature has enabled them to voice their opinions forcefully. In fact, in their present literature they are trying to recreate history and redefine the existing myths. While reconstructing Hindu myths and mythological figures Dalits have presented them from a Dalit angle. They are questioning the institutions and ideologies that have placed them at the lowest rung of social order. Some such examples relate to some of the heroic figures in *the Ramayana* and *the Mahabharata*. Thus, they reject the Brahmanical ideology and depict the Hindu gods and goddesses and heroes such as Ram, Krishna as villainous and depict historical figures such as Karna, Shambuka, Bali, Ekalvya, Ravana, Surpnakha, etc. as heroic. The present paper is an attempt to discuss and show recreation of Hindu myths and mythological figures and a recreation of history and the rejection of Hindu gods in the poetry of dalit writers.

One of the most hated documents by dalits is *Manusmriti*. *Manusmriti*, the first document on jurisprudence in India by Manu, strictly prohibits Hindus of very low caste from going through *the Vedas* or even listening to their recitation. "Sudra," the untouchable is sermonized through a sloka that acts like a canon of Hindu ethics:

> *Ekameba tu sudrasya prabhu: karma samadishat*
> *eteshameba varbababg sushrusamanasuyaya*

Elucidating, the Lord has endowed the Sudra (untouchable) with only one Karma (action) to render the three upper castes with selfless service. He, further, defines the superiority of Brahmins in the next sloka:

> *Uttamangobdhawajaisthaya bramanushaiba dharanat*
> *sarbasaibasya sargasya dharmato brahman prabhu*

A Brahmin was born earlier than a Kshatriya (warrior) out of the mouth of Lord Brahma, creator of the universe. With Veda in hand, he proved to be the religious master of the globe. Kshatriyas (warriors) came out next from the arms of the same Lord. The Vaishyas were third in the row that sprang out of the thighs of this supreme creator. Finally, Sudras appeared from the feet of Brahma to espouse the cause of servitude (*Mishra 1*).

Manusmriti, a sacred Hindu text, defines the laws for untouchables. In chapter 10, page no. 242, lines 50-56, this is what Manu says about the treatment of the outcastes:

> These (castes) should live near mounds, trees, and cremation-grounds, in mountains and in groves, recognizable and making a living by their own innate activities. But the dwellings of "Fierce" Untouchables and "Dog-cookers" should be outside the village; they must use discarded bowls, and dogs and donkeys should be their wealth. Their clothing should be the clothes of the dead, and their food should be in broken dishes; their ornaments should be made of black iron, and they should wander constantly.

> A man who carries out his duties should not seek contact with them; they should do business with one another and marry with those who are like them. Their food, dependent upon others, should be given to them in a broken dish, and they should not walk about in villages and cities in night. They may move about by day to do their work, recognizable by distinctive marks in accordance with the king's decrees; and they should carry out the corpses of people who have no relatives; this is a fixed rule. By the king's command, they should execute those condemned to death, always in accordance with the teachings, and they should take for themselves the clothing, beds and ornaments of those condemned to death. (Doniger and Smith, 242)

Manu, the Brahmanical law-giver is thus, seen as an enemy by Dalits. Voices against this sacred text of upper caste were raised as early as the nineteenth century by Pandit Kondiram. But the real credit of opposing it vociferously goes to B.R Ambedkar who, in a movement in 1928 at the Mahad Conference of the Depressed classes, burnt it publicly. It was a very bold step on the part of dalits which shocked the upper castes. The *Manusmriti* has been criticized severely by several dalit scholars and researchers.

Waman Nimbalkar uses the image of burning in a reversed way in "Itihas" (history) which begins:

> O heirs of Manu! For millennia we have watched our own Naked evening. In half a dozen huts on the village Boundary our countless bodies have been burning, set afire by your feeble thoughts. (Nimbalker)

One more poet, Shashikant Lokhande, says that Hinduism tries to burden the low-caste people with the precepts of *Manusmriti*:

> When you try to heat the bread of your sweat or pull up The lungoti of your pain they slash at your buttocks, Your breast, your hand, they bind on your neck the Burden of Manusmriti. (qtd. in Paswan)

Daya Pawar, in "Ye Hemangi" (come, gold-skinned one) talks about demolishing *Manusmriti* by a collective rebellion:

> By the mixture of our blood
> Manu's wall will be demolished brick by brick.
> (qtd. in Paswan)

Dalits are also not ready to accept the Aryans as natives of India. They strongly believe that it is dalits who are the original inhabitants of India. Aryans invaded India, conquered and displaced them. A poet very strongly pours forth his anti-Aryan feelings in the following poem:

> Bhils, Gonds, Dravids, their Bharat was beautiful,
> They were the people, the culture was theirs, and the rule was theirs;
> The Aryans infiltrated all this, they brought their power to Bharat
> And Dravidians were suppressed...
> Brahmans, Kshatriyas, Vaishyas, all become owners
> Drinking the blood of slaves, making the Sudras into machines.
> The Brahmans, Kshatriyas and Banias got all the ownership rights.
> All these three call themselves brothers, they come together in times of crisis
> And work to split the Sudras who have become workers.
> (Baliram)

Deconstruction of mythological symbols is one of the strongest points of Dalit poetic strategies. As a result, the presentation of mythological figures like Rama, Vishnu, Arjuna, Drona and Krishna is weak, inhuman and selfish. But the characters like Karna, Vidura, Sambuk, Ekalavya, Ravana and Bali are portrayed as real heroes. The subversion of symbols is quite in keeping with the thoughts and views of Ambedkar about Hinduism. Dalits also feel that history has depicted these dalit heroes as weak whereas they want their heroes to revolt. The low caste heroes in the puranas such as Eklavya, Vidura, and Karna etc are believed to have served the Brahmins despite being victimized by them. Shambuk has been shown to have remained silent on his victimization. Dalits are today no longer to accept history as it is. Thus, dalits strongly feel an urgent need to reinterpret history as they believe that history in its present form is actually a high-caste version of history.

Sivasagar in his poem "History in Progress" subverts mythology and expresses his thoughts in the following words:

> With a smile on his lips
> Shambuka is slaying Lord Rama
> Ekalavya is cutting Drona's thumb
> With an axe
> Bali with his little feet
> Is trampling down Vamana
> Into the Infernal Region.
> With needles in his eyes
> And lead in his ears
> Manu, having cut his tongue is seen rolling on the graveyard
> Standing on the merciless sword of time
> And roaring with rage
> The chandala is seen hissing four hounds on Sankaracharya
> Oh....!
> The history is occurring today.
> In the most Chandala History. (*Sivasagar*)

In this respect, Dalits follow the precepts of Ambedkar as against the philosophy of Gandhi and Marxists.

Mahaswapna on the other hand condemns both history and the historians as pages scribbled down falsely incorporating shrewd talks:

> In the damned darkness termed history
> deception, chicanery and bigotry
> the silently exploded bombs of falsity,
> a faceless humanity that is forlorn
> Mem manushulam kadu, maku inkoka perundi
> We aren't Men, We We have another Name (qtd. in Mishra)

Basudev Sunani, a young poet from Orissa wants to rewrite history in the form of a painting depicting not a scene from the *Mahabharata* with the shlokas from the *Gita* but a painting which shows a downtrodden on his way to work:

I am thinking of
building a house of my own
and on the wall
an oil painting.
Shall I have a painting
of a boat in the sea?
A battle-field
behind the bullock cart
Where it is written
"Yada yada hi dharmasya....."
No, these are pictures
common to everyone's walls.
I will have for myself
a novel for familiar sight
Like the labour *Podu Majhi*
boarding a bus
with a tin bin and an aluminum pot
on his head
to lay bricks
and below that just *Podu Majhi*
as its title
When at last the historians
will excavate this place
In their dissertations
the historians will write;
It is proved
from an ancient oil painting that
the people of that time
were business like
and a *Podu Majhi* was their leader. (qtd. in Mishra)

Subversion of the established history and myth characterizes most of the Dalit writings; for example Hira Bansode in her famous poem *Yashodhara*[14] a masterpiece, compares "the darling of her heart" Yashodhara to "a dream of sharp pain, lifelong sorrow." (Bansode)

For Dalit poets, Shambuka, Eklavya and Bali are ancestors. They do not give any importance to the deities of the Hindus. Satish Chander, a Telugu poet, describes Ekalavya as the "Great grand-father to Dalits." In this respect Telugu Dalit poets are following the ideology of Ambedkar.

While Ekalavya, for example, was to be important for them as an illustration of what *varnashrama dharma* meant, they wanted him to do what the myths did not reveal him doing, revolt. Marathi dalit poets have condemned the fact that Eklavya being a Dalit, had to lose his finger. They would have liked him to revolt as expressed by Sashikant Hingonekar in "Ekalavya":

> If you had kept your thumb
> History would have happened
> somehow differently.
> But ... you gave your thumb
> And history also
> Became theirs.
> Ekalavya,
> Since that day they
> Have not even given you a glance.
> Forgive me, Ekalavya, I won't be fooled now
> By their sweet words.
> My thumb
> Will never be broken. (*Hingonekar*)

A Marathi Dalit poet, Tryambak Sapkale, demands the finger of Ekalavya, which be a fulcrum (guide) for him. Marathi poet, Tryambak Sapkale recreates history by employing the image of Ekalavya as an embodiment of moral strength and transparency:

> Round earth
> Steel Oar
> In my hand?
> But no oarlock?
> O you ideal disciple
> Ekalavya!
>
> Give me
> Your slashed finger
> For support. (*Sapkale*)

Afsar, a Telugu Dalit poet, declares that he wants to rewrite Indian history in the light of Dalit reality:

Now
I am writing this history
With Ekalavya's sliced thumb
The reasons you give may be right to you
But to me
They are lies higher than Himalayas. (Narasaiah, p. 50)

A Telugu Dalit poet Suryavamsi, who uses Ekalavya's thumb as a weapon to fight against oppressive structures of Hinduism:

You have Vishnuchakra with you
Be it so:
You maintain Arjun's Gandeeva
Bhim's mace, Drona's tuff of hair
Let them all be with you
You have Ram's arrow
Anjaneya's tail
And Parasuram's Axe
You have authority with you
Elegance with you
Let them be yours
But
We have only Ekalavya's sliced thumb with us
And this is enough
To fight you all. (*Suryavamsi*)

Waman Nimbalker expresses the suffering of Ekalavya in "Kavita" (Poem) which ends with a reference to Buddha and Ekalavya as an oath of resolve:

Gathering the sky in my eyes,
I cast my glance forwards,
—and so on to Tathagatha.
On the horizon I will erectˇ
The rainbow arch of mankind.
I am conscious of my resolve.
The worth of the blood
Of Eklavya's broken finger—
This is my loyalty.

I will not barter my word.
I stand today at the very end
Of the twentieth century. (Nimbalker)

In the following poem by Mahesh Pandya the poet shows how desperate he is to avenge Rama and Drona for having oppressed Dalits. "Uttar Gujrat ni Jivali," a Gujrati poem reads thus:

Let us go the village
O Jamni
I want to buy a gun
Gun? Why Jivali?
Are you mad?
Why do you need a gun?
Ali Jamni, you do not know
Poor Shambuk was meditating and practicing Vedas
And then?
Ram killed him mercilessly
Now I want to shoot Rama and also
I want to kill Drona
Who demanded
Ekalavya's thumb as
Gurudakshina. (Pandya)

The use of mythology, scriptures and Dalit icons such as Shambuk and Ekalavya is important to show the unjust behaviour of the upper caste gurus towards their low caste disciples.

In continuation of the theme of subversion of mythological symbols Yendluri Sudhakar in his poem "Low Caste Script" speaks of Rama as a killer:

Rama is not my savior. He is my slayer.
A burning throat can't sing a
Suprabhata Sloka. (Sudhakar)

Madduri Vijayasree in her poem "Alisamma" (a bold witness of the atrocities on Dalits in Karamchedu) refers to Rama's order by which Surpanakha's nose was severed:

Day before yesterday according to Sri Rama's order
I got my nose and ears severed (Vijayasree)
Thus Rama in the above poem has been presented as inhuman.

Dalit also condemn and disapprove of the great Hindu epics the *Ramayana* and the *Mahabharata* because for them the epics are not the symbols of the perfect king Rama but a reminder of the images of Karna and Ekalavya and Shambuk. These minor epic characters are archetypal symbols of suffering.

Waman Nimbalkar expresses the attitude towards the epics in general:

O Gods of Words!
You have created great epics—
Those eating gold, walking with the wind,
Wearing gold-bordered cloth—
Heaps of words were dampened
In leaves, flowers, fragrance,
The intoxication of Madira.
This dire, crushed life of the
Outskirts of the village
Never became the subject of your poetry. (Nimbalker)

Daya Pawar in his poem "Pay" (Legs or Feet) refers to the Rigvedic hymn of creation, the story of giving water to a donkey and the legend of Dyaneshwar, who produced the sacred Vedas from the mouth of a buffalo to show that these sacrosanct texts should not be confined to the high castes. The imagery of "Pay" present a pyramidical structure of Hindu culture crushing those on the bottom, and ends:

The legs of those born from the feet
Were sapped like green buds.
Everyone says: "the safety of the pyramid is worth fifty
Legs. O come on, bear a little pain."
They paint the pyramid's pinnacle.
Your name is not mentioned.
Someone cuts the ribbon.
The pitchers of Ganges water come and are poured

Into the mouth of a donkey.
If the water vessel is filled, they say,
Dyaneshwar's buffalo will come! (Pawar)

Dalit poets openly attack, abuse and rebuke the Hindu gods and goddesses. They do not take Rama and Krishna as definatory and argue that there is no historical or logical ground to prioritise a Vedic tradition.

The angry response of Keshav Meshram on the concept of God is illustrated in the following lines from "One Day I Cursed that Mother-Fucker God": "... one day I cursed that mother-fucker god/he just laughed mercilessly" (Meshram).

In another poem a poet puts a fight against Manu and attacks gods too:

To cut my thumb and give
Do you think I am a gullible Ekalavya
Do you think I am Shambuka
To bend my head and do penance
Do you think I am vali
To be knocked down with a foul arrow
I am the one who breaks the sinews of Manu
I hang colours
I peel the skin of gods who made me lame
(Narasaiah, p. 40)

Works Cited

Bansode, Hira. *Phiryad.* Pune: Samaj Prabodhan Sanstha. 1984.

Doniger, Wendy; Brian K. Smith. (tr.) *The Laws of Manu.* Delhi: Penguin, 1991.

Hingonekar, Sashikant. "Ekalavya." Gail Omvedt and Bharat Ratnakar, *An Alternative History, Wendy Doniger.* UK: Oxford University Press, 2010.

Lokhande, Shashikant. *Gaokushabaheril Kavita.* Aurangabad: Asmitadarsh Prakashan, 1973.

Meshram, Keshav. "One Day I Cursed that Mother-Fucker God," (tr.) Jayant Karve et al. *An Anthology of Dalit Literature.* (eds.) Mulk Raj Anand and Eleanor Zelliot, New Delhi: Gyan Publishing House, 1992, 118.

Mishra, Ashwini. *Voice of Dalit in South Asian Literature.* Sasnet.com, N.p., 8 July 2004. Web. 7 Feb 2011.

Narasaiah, G. Lakshmi. (*ed.*) *The Essence of Dalit Poetry: A Socio-Philosophic Study of Telugu Dalit Poetry.* Vijayawada: Dalit Sana Publications, 1996.

Nimbalker, Waman. "Itihas." (*tr.*) Graham Smith and Eleanor Zelliot, *Dalit Identity and Politics.* (*ed.*) Ghanshyam Shah, New Delhi: Sage, 2001.

———, *Poem* (Kavita). (*tr.*) Graham Smith, Vagartha, 1976, p. 12.

———, *Gaokushabaheril Kavita.* Aurangabad: Asmitadarsh Prakashan, 1973.

Omvedt, Gail. *Dalit Visions: Tracts for the Times.* New Delhi: Orient Longman, 2006.

Pandya, Mahesh. "Uttar Gujarat Ni Jivali." (*tr.*) Darshna Trivedi. *Dalit Literature: A Critical Exploration.* (*eds.*) Amarnath Prasad and M.B. Gaijan, New Delhi: Sarup and Sons, 2007.

Pantawane, Gangadhar. (ed.) Mulyavedh, *The Perception of Value.* Aurangabad: Asmitadarsh Prakashan, 1974.

Paswan, Sanjay; Pramanshi, Jaideva. (eds.) *Encyclopedia of Dalits in India.* Vol. 11. New Delhi: Kalpaz, 2002.

Pawar, Daya. *Kondwada*(Cattle Pen), Pune: Magova Prakashan, 1974.

Ramteke, Kamal, Singh Balirame, *Janata.* June 21 (1941).

Sapkale, Tryambak, "Eklavya." (tr.) Jayant Karve et al, *An Anthology of Dalit Literature.* (eds.) Mulk Raj Anand and Eleanor Zelliot, New Delhi: Gyan Publishing House, 1992.

Sivasagar. "History in Progress." (tr.) K. Purushottam, *Museinida.* Nov-Dec (2007): Web. 5 Jan. 2009.

Sudhakar, Yenduluri, "Low Caste Script." (*tr.*) MO, *A History of Telugu Dalit Literature.* Delhi: Kalpaz, 2008.

Suryavamsi, "No Better Murderer They Are." (*tr.*) G. Lakshmi Narasaiah, *Padunekkina Pata* (Sharpened Song). Vijayawada: Dalit Sana Publications, 1996.

Vijaysree, Madduri, "Alisama's Curse For You." (*tr.*) K. Suneetha Rani, *A History of Telugu Dalit Literature.* Delhi: Kalpaz, 2008.

Rabindra Nath Tagore's *The Home and the World*: From Feminity to Feminism

Nagendra Nathawat

When a woman inclines to learning there is usually something wrong with her sex apparatus.

— *FW Nietzsche*

Mother what is a feminist
A Feminist, my daughter
Is any woman now who cares
To think about her own affairs
As men don't think she oughter(Allice Duer Miller, 1915)

The concepts of feminity and feminism are applicable to women from male-centered and female-centered perspectives. Feminity is associated with traditional sex roles, traditional values, attitudes and aesthetics. Her natural role is fixed as a wife, as a mother and her place is at home and domesticity. She is a thing – an object – "femme fatale," "tota mulier in utero." She contains a number of feminine qualities such as passivity, docility, submissiveness, physical weakness, emotionalism, negation of virility, strength, vigour and assertiveness.[1] Physically, a woman is said to be seductive and dangerously sexual, mentally incompetent and sentimental and behaviourally unstable.

Feminism, on the other hand, is a way of looking at the world from a woman's experiences and points of views. A woman started asserting her social and political rights for equality. She protested against stereotypical sex roles, gender bias, job discriminations, compulsory heterosexuality, imposition of wifehood and motherhood, oppression and sexism. It gives recognition to a woman's power of independent decision – maker, intelligence and her status as an equal, as an individual, as a human being, as a person capable of contributing to social and national progress and development. It is a new consciousness of redefining her social and cultural role, a process of self discovery.

Home and the World (Ghare Baire) is the story of a young liberal-minded zamindar Nikhilesh, his educated and sensitive wife Bimala, and Nikhilesh's friend Sandip, a charismatic nationalist leader whom Bimala finds herself attracted to. A perceptive exposition of the difficulties surrounding women's emancipation in pre-modern India, and a telling portrayal of the chasms inherent in the nationalist movement. *Home and the World* has generated endless debate and discussion.

Bimala marches to self-discovery when she moves out of the house and becomes engaged with the outside world, taking part in the Swadeshi Movement by working with Sandip. She feels drawn to Sandip's passion and the attraction between the two becomes inevitable producing a love triangle. She begins to help Sandip even financially. In this case, she takes her own decision.

The novel ends with Bimala's experience as a feminist with what love is for the first time, which leads her to realize that it is her own husband Nikhil, who really loves her. The novel, inspite of these feminist undercurrents does not cross the traditional boundaries of love, womanhood and the institution of marriage.

There are several types of feminists depending upon their goals and aspirations. Social, radical, soft and lesbian feminists have become popular. Radical feminists question patriarchal structure and are accused of being anti family or anti-male. Rich (1983) proposes the concept of lesbian continuum and observes that it " embraces many more forms of primary intimacy between and among women including the sharing of a rich inner life, the bonding against male tyranny, the giving and receiving of practical and political support."[2]

Considered from these concepts, one finds that Rabindra Nath Tagore's novel *The Home and the World* charts the progression of Bimala, the heroine of the novel from feminity to feminism. Bimala's feminity, though self-imposed and an inheritance from her upbringing and family traditions is discernible in her stereotypical sex role as a dutiful wife, who early in the morning, would cautiously and silently get up and take the dust of her husband's feet without waking him; in her denigration for her dark features and in her complete devotion to her husband. At such moments she could feel the vermillion mark upon her forehead shining out like the morning star.

Bimala is totally immersed in her traditional role of wifehood. She justifies her devotion to her husband by saying that her husband loved her body as it were a flower of paradise. She feels that "to surrender one's pride in devotion is woman's only salvation."

> Her real joy, she thought was that her true place was at her husband's feet. (p.1)

Another example of her faithfulness to her husband occurs in the following activity of hers. Her husband Nikhil had passed B.A. and was doing M.A. at a college in Calcutta. He was also in deep love with her. Hence, he wrote her letters everyday. "I kept them in a sandalwood box and covered them everyday with the flowers I gathered in the garden." (p.1)

Indian traditional values for women dictate that they should worship their husbands. The patriarchal system demands that husbands be regarded as gods.

When Bimala takes dust from her husband's feet, the husband asks "What is that Bimala?" To which her answer is: "It was my woman's heart which must worship in order to love." (p.1 – under-lining mine). She has been raised in traditional Indian home thereby imbibing all patriarchal traditional Indian values about women.

Her physicality and seductiveness attracted her husband. Her husband loved her body as it were a flower of paradise. She feels that "to surrender one's pride in devotion is woman's only salvation." Her pronouncements are indicative of her complete obedience and subservience to her husband.

After her grand-mother's death she wanted to remain in the house as head of the house but her husband told her, "Are there not more precious things in life?" She wants to remain within the four walls of the house performing her duties of wifehood, motherhood and womanhood. Her thinking about her husband remark goes like this, "Men never understand these things. They have their nests in the outside world; they little know the whole of what the household stands for. In these matters, they ought to follow womanly guidance."

In Indian traditional homes, the mother-in-law and the sister-in-law are quite domineering. What intrigues a westerner is that the mother-in-law and sister-in-law inspite of being women assist in the furtherance of patriarchal system. Bimala's sister-in-law was jealous of her and called her a thief who had stolen husband's love. She also disapproved of new tangled finery. The many coloured garments with which her husband loved to adorn her aroused her jealous wrath. She commented, "Is she not ashamed to make a show – window of herself and with her looks too!." She found pettiness in all her activities. She once told her husband, "Women's minds are so petty, so crooked like the Chinese women..." Bimala's husband was not like other husbands. He replied, "Has not the pressure of society cramped them into pettiness and crookedness? They are but pawns of the fate which gambles with them. What responsibility have they off their own!"

Notice, though Bimala's husband is not like other husbands; he is not cruel, domineering, yet he does not blame social discourse and hegemony for this skewed view of women. He blames fate like a devoted Hindu Indian. He is a mixture of old Indian values and modernity. In Indian households, a husband is not allowed to meet his wife during day. Like a true Indian husband he could not break completely with the old-time traditions. They would not meet at any hour of the day they pleased.

Another quality in her husband was that he wanted to treat women equal to men. He used to say that man and wife are equal in love because of their equal claim on each other. But Bimala still wanted to be faithful, obedient and devoted to her husband. She says that she never argued the point of equality with her husband but her heart said that devotion never stood in the way of true equality.

What is most crucial about their relationship is that Bimala's husband was very eager to ask her to abandon purdah (veil) system. Further, he wanted her to interact with the outside world. He was of the opinion that a woman's job is not to remain within the four walls of the house but she should step out of the house. This he recommends not because of granting liberty to women but because movement in the outside world will augment their true love. He said to her:

> I would have to come into the heart of the outer world and meet reality. Merely going on with your household duties, living all your life in the world of household conventions and the drudgery of household tasks – you were not made for that! If we meet and recognize each other in the real world then only will our love be true. (p. 6)

But Bimala did not want to move out of the house. She did not want to mix with the outside world because she did not want to cause any pain to her husband's grandmother because she would not approve of her going out.

Nikhil, even being a Bengali zamindar, marries Bimala, a woman who is both of a lower status and of a darker complexion, which is contrary to his family tradition. Their love is idyllic and both are dedicated to each other.

Though Bimala is married to Nikhil and their marriage was arranged since she was a little girl, Nikhil believes that Bimala is free to make her own decisions to her life "I was married into a Rajah's house. When I was a child I was quite familiar with the description of the prince of the fairy story." (pp. 17-18). Therefore, she is very much dedicated to her husband, her marriage and most importantly her family values. Nikhil sometimes questions her view of him, that of a traditional woman. But as she steps out of the house to join Swadeshi movement, her role as a traditional Indian woman changes.

Later on when she comes in contact with Sandip, weans herself away from her traditional housewife role. She becomes more daring, more confidently brushes off her sister-in-law's criticism and moves out of the women's quarters in the outside world and easily converses with another man, Sandip, who is not her husband. She changes herself from the good housewife to an independent, more modern woman.

Egged on by her own husband to step out in the outside world and drawn towards the Swadeshi movement launched by Sandip, Bimala comes in contact with Sandip. Bimala is very much impressed by the firebrand personality and dynamism of Nikhil and his energetic speeches in support of Swadeshi goods and boycotting of everything foreign. She attends rallies organized by him and enthusiastically participates in his movements. After hearing Sandip at a rally, Bimala invites Sandip to visit their estate and suggests that he should make his party's headquarters at their house. Once empowered by the inside world, knowing her husband and home, she becomes engaged with the outside world by working with Sandip for the Swadeshi movement very actively. Bimala is drawn to Sandip romantically and she begins to question her marriage with Nikhil and discovers in Sandip those qualities she always looked for in a man, that is enthusiasm, ambition and a desire to face danger.

After coming in contact with Sandip her entire outlook on her life both at home and in the outside world changes. She is a changed woman. She says:

> I was no longer the lady of Rajah's house but the sole representative of Bengal's womanhood. (p. 31)

Sandip convinces Bimala to steal 6000/- rupees from Nikhil's treasury. While stealing that money, she argues that the money that belongs to Nikhil also belongs to her as it belongs to the country also. She thinks that it is her national duty to donate, to contribute to Swadeshi movement. Nikhil subsequently discovers Bimala's theft and contribution of that money to Sandip. He does not say anything to her but grants her freedom to choose, to decide and grow in her life.

Bimala, while developing her identity as a free woman is constantly going through inner conflicts. She learns to rationalize her mistakes. At the same time she is able to discover correct answers to some of her actions. After the theft of Rs. 6000/- she realizes:

> I could not think of my house as separate from my country. I had robbed my house, I had robbed my country. For this sin my house ceased to be mine, my country also was estranged from me. (p.144)

These lines show her repentance. Hence she wanted to replace the money by pawning off her jewellery. Amulya wants to give the box back but Sandip steals it and he himself gives the box to her. This act of Sandip makes her realize that he is a highly selfish man and he only thinks about himself. She also realizes that it is only Nikhil who loves her most. Bimala also realizes that Sandip is robbing the country and also encouraging others to do the same. Hence she abandons Sandip and his movement and comes back to Nikhil, as a more enlightened woman.

> She says after coming back to Nikhil, I now fear nothing – neither myself, nor anybody else. I have passed through fire. What was inflammable has been burnt to ashes, what is left is deathless. I have dedicated myself to the feet of him who has received all my sin into the depths of his own pain. (p. 199)

However, Bimala through her interaction with Sandip has known the truth of *Shakti* (female power) but her life with Nikhil is centered on the truth of conjugality.

The new *avatar* of Bimala is a mixture of modern and traditional woman. She becomes an icon of a new kind of feminism which recommends co-existence of women with those of men who are not against their freedom, personal growth, decision making powers and establishment of personal identity. Nikhil is that kind of man and hence Bimala returns to him to explore her identity further.

I would like to conclude this paper by the ideas expressed by Sudhir Kakar in his article entitled "Is an Indian woman a person" published in the *Times of India* dated 9 January, 2013 because his ideas are quite relevant for the theme of the present novel. India has a society that traditionally defines a person through her relationship rather than her individuality, a woman is a person when she is a mother, a daughter or a wife. Indian society is caught between the extremes of traditional and western perspectives on women. If a woman is not in a relationship, then she is considered an object or a commodity. After the gangrape of a medical student in Delhi on 16 December 2012, the youth of the country demanded justice and equality for women. We came across slogans like "My body, not your amusement Park." In the present novel, Nikhil considers Bimala his wife as a person and wants to give her all dignity and identity of an individual. But, Sandip on the other hand, uses her as a tool to further his aim of getting money and may be an object of satisfying his lust. Like a true Indian wife, Bimala realizes the truth and comes back to Nikhil before it is too late. The novel ends by presenting Bimala as a woman who balances her role as a new and traditional woman in a remarkable way.

Works Cited

Gupta, Sagar, M. "From Femininity to Feminism in the American Detective Fiction in the 1980's *Feminism and American Literature."* (*ed.*) R.K. Dhawan, New Delhi: Prestige Books,1966.

Rich, Adrienne. "Compulsory Hetero – Sexuality and Lesbian Existence", *The Signs Reader: Woman, Gender and Scholarship.* (*ed.*) Elizabeth Abel and Amily K. Abel, Chicago: University of Chicago Press, 1983.

Tagore, Rabindranath. *The Home and the World.* Penguin Group, 2005.

Notes

1. For some writers of feminism, femininity is both biologically and culturally determined whereas for others it is only a cultural trait. For example, Julia Kristeva defines femininity as marginality to the symbolic order. According to her, Mallarme is as feminine as Virginia Woolf because of his marginal relationship to prevailing masculine culture. Psychologist Jean Baker suggests that feminine traits such as emotionalism, vulnerability and intuition are not the weaknesses but may be regarded as strengths to the development of a new and better social development of a new and better social order.
2. Adrienne, Rich, "Compulsory Hetero sexuality and Lesbian Existence in *The Signs Reader: Woman, Gender and Scholarship*" (*ed.*) Elizabeth Abel and Amuily K. Abel Chicago: University of Chicago, Press, 1983, pp. 156-157.

Gender Issues in Indo-English Novels: A Study of Women Novelists

Dr. Shahnaz Begum

The Indian novel is a living and evolving genre and is trying to obtain a fusion of form, substance and expression that is recognizably Indian, yet bearing also the mark of universality. It may be argued that comparatively the novel written in the spoken languages of India is more enterprising, having a richer content and wider range than the novel written in English, but considering the fact that Indian writers of English fiction have been a part of the Indian diaspora, using English almost like a mother tongue, it has been easier for them to reflect the challenges and changes that have also been reflected in other Indian languages. These writers have given a fresh orientation to the socio-cultural issues of this country. The novel is by its very nature better equipped to deal with the social reality and, therefore, the most substantial contribution comes from fiction.

The last three decades have been particularly fertile in producing fiction pertaining to the perspective of the new generation, arising out of a keen interest taken in area-wise study of society, especially concerned with the marginalized sections. There have been major factors that have contributed to generation problems like poverty, illiteracy, population explosion and other kinds of public exploitation during this period. Other disastrous failures have been in areas of education, the empowerment of women and the Dalits. In spite of legislations, dowry deaths, bride-burning and the discrimination against the girl-child are more frequent than could be believed. The promise of 33% reservation in the legislatures is still a far-cry, the actual percentage of women in state legislatures and Parliament being a dismal 7.3%. Only recently have women's writings begun to receive special attention from the gender point of view. A lot of buried or censored writing by women has been unearthed by the efforts of Susie Tharu and K. Lalitha. Indian fiction writers in English have contributed to a new awareness of women's issues raising the gender consciousness at a more popular level. They share certain common concerns and visions of a democratic society where women's voices will be heeded and women's status upheld.

This paper aims to probe into the gender issue picked up by some important women writers who have effectively revealed the true state of Indian society when it comes to the treatment of women.

India is the third largest English using nation after the USA and UK, where about fifteen million users are experimenting with this language day and night. This is about five percent of the whole Indian population. Moreover, English has the status of an official language in the constitution. India also has a large network of print media with a pan-Indian circulation and is one of the world's three major book publishers in English. Together with this it also forms the primary language of inter regional interaction within the country and also of the country's interaction with the outside world. In many ways English has become assimilated into other Indian languages and vice versa. This has helped Indian English to acquire a cultural identity of its own.

To be writing in English is, therefore, a great challenge in itself. Raja Rao has aptly expressed this in the following lines:

> We cannot write like the English. We should not. We can write only as Indians.... the tempo of Indian life must be infused into our English expression even as the tempo of American or Irish life has gone into the making of theirs... (Sachidanandan, 1999).

It is difficult for the Indian writer in English to play on the association of words or to make use of the kind of rich cultural register available for the writers in other Indian languages. It calls for a thorough decolonization of English, a total recreation that infuses English with our native perceptions.

Indian writers born after independence inherited their self-perception from Western Orientalists and ironically we even began to compare our writers to the Western writers just to establish their greatness. But an effort to decolonize our thinking and evolve our own concepts rooted in our social milieu gives a fresh angle to our own creativity and isolates us from basking in borrowed glory. After all, a writer addresses his/her own immediate society and the people of his/her language, place and time.

The Indo-English fiction which came into its own only in the third decade of the twentieth century began to project the themes of patriotism, social justice, East-West confrontation, rural-urban conflict, family relations, etc. At this point of time, the entire scenario was dominated nevertheless by the Big three of Indo-Anglo fiction Narayan, Anand, Raja Rao, though a younger generation of bolder and more experimental novelists, several of whom were women like Kamla Markandeya, Nayantara Sahgal, Anita Desai, has taken over whose works promise a new sensibility and a vibrant richness.

The Indian novel has come to say and as long as that quest for novelty exists In human minds which often finds solace in the works of fiction for its unfulfilled dreams, the novel shall continue to be the most impressive form of art not only for its inherent freedom of movement but also for its evocative thought process that affects human life.

The last three decades have been particularly fertile in producing novels in the English language pertaining to the perspectives of the new generation arising out of a keen interest taken in area-wise study of society and specially concerned with the marginalized sections. There have been major factors that have contributed to generating social problems like poverty, illiteracy, population boom and other exploitative measures. "Other disastrous failures have been in areas of education and empowerment of women and Dalits..." (Naik & Narayan, 2001).

Of course we are faced with myriads of challenges and the novelist tries to reflect and even address these problems. But, when talking of women writers the gender issue is the main focus, because a meaningful discussion on women's writings today is part of the larger enterprise of empowering women and this can join hands with other transversal struggle for social justice in various fronts.

The Indian sub-continent is particularly faced with a conflicting situation arising out of the gender issue. It concerns half of our population which is responsible for nurturing and nourishing the generation. It is also responsible for bringing dynamic changes in the very fabric of our society. It is this section that has the full potential to steer the country to a better future – far from ignoble strife and unwanted bloodshed. Women are endowed with the quality of motherhood. They are by nature caring and affectionate, but unfortunately, they are at the same time the most deprived and marginalized section of society. From time immemorial they have been facing contradictory position in Indian society, sometimes hallowed as Devi and at other times flung to the lowest abyss of wretchedness. During the recent years there has been a gradual awareness and growing self-assurance among women not found earlier. The gender issue has been taken up by many novelists during the past three decades and has resulted in generating a mass awareness for the overall uplift of the fair sex. But the Indian women writers of the twentieth century have determinedly taken up their cause with full seriousness.

> The problems and predicaments peculiar to the Indian women found artistic expression in the Indian literature in English since the 1970s. In their creative writings, the women writers like Shashi Deshpande, Anjana Appachana, Mrinal Pande, Gita Hariharan, Indu K. Mallah, Arundhati Roy, Indira Mahindra, Namita Gokhale, Mrinal Pande and others started discussing openly the varied problems of women and questioning the gender-role expectations. The female protagonists in their writings evince sufficient vigour and courage to question the oppressive role of society, religion and culture, but yet they refrain from taking the paths suggested by the western feminists. They rather seek to find their own paths. (Renganathan, 2009:71-72)

This paper attempts to make a short analysis of the novels of some prominent women writers of the last three decades of the twentieth century with special focus on Shashi Deshpande's writings, to see from the gynocentric point of view the gender issue as tackled by her.

Shashi Deshpande has seven novels and five collections of short stories to her credit. She started out just like any other starry eyed young writer-in-the-making. Like innumerable potential women writers she began her work with national magazines such as *Femina* and *Eve's Weekly,* slowly branched out to more serious literature oriented magazines such as *The Illustrated Weekly of India, The Junior Statesman* and so on. She has also mentioned that writing is a gift, sometimes like a fountain that spouts out words. She is not without the writer's gene in her, her father being a great Kannada dramatist and Sanskrit scholar.

Shashi Deshpande basically reflects on the problems and concerns of the middle class Indian women. Her writings, rooted in the culture in which she lives, remain sensitive to the common everyday events and experiences, and they give artistic expression to something that is simple and mundane. Her feminism is peculiarly Indian in the sense that it is born out of the predicament of Indian women placed between contradictory identities: tradition and modernity, family and profession, culture and nature. Her art is intensely personal, not political. Her feminism rooted in the native environment tends to be humanistic and optimistic in its outlook. (*Ibid.* 72)

Human relationships form the core theme of Deshpande's novels. Her women characters are particularly conspicuous for their strength. Writes R.S. Pathak: "Deshpande's women characters have a strength of their own, and inspite of challenges and hostilities, remain uncrushed." —(Pathak, 1999: 194)

She depicts three types of women: the first is the mother figure, the traditional woman who believes that her place belongs with her husband and family. In fact she represents the traditional religious ethos and confirms the code of Manu that a woman is under her father's control in her maidenhood, her husband in her youth and her sons in old age. Their only satisfaction is that sometimes they have control over other woman as mothers in law or mothers. A few examples are Jaya's mother in *That Long Silence,* Indu's and Saru's mother in *Roots and Shadows* and *The Dark Holds No Terrors.* The second type of women is the bold and rebellious one, who is consciously inclined towards radical feminist ideology. Such women are, however, rare in Deshpande. A poignant example is Saru's friend Nilu in *The Dark Holds No Terrors.* She chooses to lead the life of a spinster. The third type of woman characterizes the woman in between and most of Deshpande's heroines belong to this category. This woman is neither traditional nor radical in her ideas and practice. She might walk out of her home in protest against her suffering, but gradually realizes that this is not the solution to her problems. Saru in *The Dark Holds No Terrors* broods over her agonies even after she escapes her marital home. Indu in *Roots and Shadows* leaves her husband to seek refuge in her ancestral home, but she is unable to accept her fate as any ordinary woman might do.

When they want to assume newer roles the women of Shashi Deshpande break the mental barriers, which they had initially built around themselves. They learn more about their real "I" and understand themselves better while exploring the sexual and other causes that had led to their marital discords. Dissatisfaction in the women's sex lives is cited as one of the important factors affecting the marital relations of the Deshpande protagonists. Three types of sexual aberration are shown in her three novels. In *The Dark Holds No Terrors,*

Saru explains her sexual relations with Manu, her husband, Saru finds in him a "protean monster" at night and a "dutiful husband" in the day. She says: "We're on different planes. He chooses his level. And I ... try to choose the one he would like to be on. It humiliates me." (1980:90) Neither the woman nor the man in Deshpande's novels tries to do something about their marital or sexual monotony. The woman tends to ignore the sexual roots of her marital discord but knows how to justify her escapades with other men. As we see that Saru tries to justify her affairs with her boss and her college classmate as the substitutes she had found for her unfulfilled marriage. But satisfaction is still elusive for her. In the case of Indu's affair with her cousin, we see a woman-in-guilt. Like Indu and Saru, Jaya in *That Long Silence* feels guilty of her aborted affair with Kama, her neighbour. Shashi Deshpande's protagonists might be considered as sexual profligates as they go off the track of tradition. But their extra-marital refuge fails them because their sexual freedom does not steer them out of their predicaments. Instead of helping them to confront the problem, they only postpone the problem. When their sexual escapades bounce back, they divulge their problems to their friends or relatives. For example, Saru confesses to her father about her marital crisis to save herself from it. Her father advises her not to run away but to face the problem. (Renganathan, 2009: 76)

The awareness of the self and the ultimate refuge in the self are deep rooted in the novels of Shashi Deshpande. The awareness of the self leads to the awakening of woman's consciousness. This awakening is very crucial to feminism as Elaine Showalter says, "How much easier, how less lonely it is not to awaken.... Yet we cannot will ourselves to go back to sleep." (Davis,1986: 179)

The determination to confront and accept the self is found in all the three female protagonists of Deshpande. The act of confrontation gives them the courage to decide things for themselves and increasingly leads them to a positivistic detachment from life. The refuge in the self guides them towards a deeper awareness of their predicament. A deeper awareness of the self leads to the understanding of its true nature. The self-realization in the heroines is psychological rather than metaphysical. Towards the end Saru refuses to call her predicament as "fate" and would rather call it as something she "had helped to happen." (Deshpande,1980: 62) for blaming only the patriarchy or only certain external causes for her predicament, takes her away from the fact that she had also to be blamed for being weak and allowing her predicament to happen. Ultimately the Deshpande's women choose to be themselves, accepting themselves in whatever forms they are.

Deshpande is a realist at heart. She creates real characters in plausible stories. Her portrayal of the middle class Indian women, their predicaments, their inner conflict and quest for identity, issues pertaining to their family relationships, marriage and sex, and their exploitation and disillusionment are all dealt with from a feminist point of view.

Deshpande may be called a feminist. When asked whether she would consider herself a feminist, Deshpande is quoted to have replied to Geeta Gangadharan:

> Yes I would. I am a feminist in the sense that, I think, we need to have a world, which we should recognize as a place for all of us human beings. There is no superior or inferior, we are two halves of one species. I fully agree with Simone de Beauvoir that the fact that we are human, is much more important than our being men and women. I think that's my idea of feminism. (Gangadharan, 1994: II)

In her short stories too Shashi Deshpande has sketched the emotional deprivation of Indian women. The woman, bereft of love understanding and companionship forms the centre of her novels and stories. She shows how the traditional Indian society is biased against women, but also recognizes the fact that it is often the women who oppress their sisters through centuries of indoctrination of the traditional values of society.

The themes of discrimination against the daughter, the silence of women and the lack of communication between the sexes are treated in depth by Anjana Appachana,(a novelist of Indian origin living in the United States)in her first novel *Listening Now* (1998). The book renders an entirely credible recreation of Indian life. Indian culture is shown transcendent in regional variation in discriminating against the daughter whether it is in Delhi or Lucknow or Bangalore. The son invariably gets first preference in everything, whether food or pocket money or education. Through-out her first novel we are reminded to pay careful attention to the voices of the women who speak in its pages.

A number of woman novelists appear on the canvas of Indian writing who try effectively to reveal the truth behind Indian social traditions when it comes to the treatment of women. Indu K. Mallah in her novel *Shadows in Dream Time* (1990) speaks of the social "sati" a widow is subjugated to even in modern India. She is considered as inauspicious, cut off from all social intermingling. She has to give up her colourful silk saris, shun the kumkum on her forehead and discard the flowers she used to adorn her hair with. The gruesome fact is that she is happy nowhere and feels that the only way to happiness is by joining her dead husband.

Then we come to the most recent writers among whom Arundhati Roy whose *The God of Small Things* (published 1997) has received wide publicity thanks to the Booker prize. Some elements of the personal life are present. Roy's narrative powers are impressive. The lush vegetation of the Kerala landscape is shown in contrast to the oppressive atmosphere of the village of Ayemenem. There are great descriptions of paedophilia and incest. There is also a relentless injection of local colour by using Malyalam words. But keeping these aside there is no dispute about the power of the book, which shows the cruelty of women who discriminate against their own daughters in favour of sons. It is a comprehensive protest novel which describes atrocities against the powerless: children, women and untouchables.

Other women writers have written about life in the upper strata of urban society. Conspicuous among them is Indira Mahindra whose *The Club* (1989) reflects life in upper class society and *The End Play* (1994) exposes the personal relationships in Modern India, revealing the power struggle in Indian joint family. Next prominent writer is Namita Gokhale who deals with the upper crust of contemporary Indian society in Metropolitan towns. Her novel *Paro: Dreams of Passion* (1984) is relevant. Of course the list does not end here but can be extended much further.

One more name that focuses on gender bias is Mrinal Pande. Her novel *Daughter's Daughter* (1993) is a study of Indian childhood. This novel is a loosely connected series of episodes, in which a little girl Tinu is shown growing up in North India shortly after India's independence. The picture of discrimination against the girl-child is based on facts and written in a straightforward lucid style.

Gita Hariharan in *The Thousand Faces of Night* (1992) has elaborated on the woes of barren Indian women, and the ill-treatment meted out to them irrespective of whether they are educated or illiterate. It also treats of the fact that Indian women exterminate their own talent in view of their husband's career and this is a great sacrifice on the part of the woman.

To conclude, one can say that patriarchal power is one among the many forms of power that tyrannize the whole human species and creates an unequal relationship among human beings. A conscious reading of women's writing today will have to deconstruct the text to bring out the contradictory ideologies that constitute it, lay bare the play of power and locate the zones of resistance built into it.

Works Cited

Deshpande, Shashi, *The Dark Holds No Terror.* Delhi: Vikas Publication, 1980.

Gangadharan, Geeta, "Denying the Otherness" (Interview), Indian Communicator, *Sunday Magazine.* 20 November 1994.

Naik, M.K.; Shyamala A. Narayan, *Indian English Literature 1980-2000: A Critical Survey.* Delhi: Pencraft International, 2001.

Pathak, R.S. *Modern Indian Novel in English.* New Delhi: Creative Books, 1999.

Robert Con, Davis, *Contemporary Literary Criticism: Modernism through Poststructuralism,* (*ed.*) London: Longman, 1986.

Renganathan, Mala, Indian Woman at the Cross Roads: A Study of Shashi Deshpande's Heroines, *Journal of Literature, Culture and Media Studies.* Number 1, Summer, June 2009

Satchidanadan, K., *Indian Literature: Positions and Propositions.* Delhi: Pencraft International, 1999.

Srinivasa Iyengar, K.R., *Indian Writing in English.* Bombay: Asia Publishing House, 1973.

Double Crossed and Thrice Subjugated Women in Bama's *Sangati*

Mrs. Babita Mehra

Dr. B.R. Ambedkar once said, "It is a sin to get birth in a country whose people are so caste ridden and prejudiced." These words of Ambedkar echo the pain suffered by him and his brethren belonging to the depressed classes in India. He was the first to use the word "Dalit" in preference to his own earlier term scheduled castes. But, the second wave of Marathi Dalit Movement, with the formation of Dalit Panthers in 1972 can be considered to be the real ignition to Dalit movement as it stands today. For them, Dalit is a symbol of change and revolution who believes in humanism, rejects the existence of God, rebirth, soul, sacred books that teach discrimination, fate and heaven. Because these have made him slave and a Dalit represents the exploited in the country. According to Dalit Panthers, "All scheduled castes, scheduled tribes, neo-Buddhists, labourers, landless and destitute peasants, women and all those who have been exploited politically and economically and in the name of religion are Dalits."

Dalit literally means trampled, squeezed, crushed or broken, or reduced into pieces. Therefore, Dalit is the most secular identity than any others. Originally it denotes a class, than a caste. Dalits really are a part of Indian counter-culture. The core of dalit consciousness is made of protest against exploitation and oppression. In short, the term dalit stands for change and revolution. The term "Dalit" gained its popularity in Tamilnadu in the 1990's. Before that in the 1990's, the Dalits were referred by the Tamil equivalent taazhtappattor (those who have been put down) or odukkapattor (the oppressed). In Tamilnadu, Dalit uprising is not confined only to the expression of Dalit literature. On the contrary, Dalit literature came about as part and parcel of anti-caste struggles, agitation for reserved places in the interest of social justice, and political protests for economic equality. In his introduction to Dalit writing in the India Today Annual issue of 1995, Raj Gauthaman says, "Dalit literature has begun to bring about a change to enable non-Dalits to deconstruct a traditional mindset which made them perceive Dalits as lower than themselves; and instead to see Dalits as equal rather than pitiful victims, to awaken the Dalits who lie asleep with in the conscience of all people of all castes."

Hindu religion is a natural religion which was not found by a single person. It is not based on a single text and it possesses no single church. At the philosophical or metaphysical level it sees the Ontological reality in terms of Prakruti-Purush dialects. So, in this context dalit women are not an exception. They are rightly seen as "thrice-subjugated as women, as Dalit women and as Dalit women who perform stigmatized labour." So, we can say that Dalit women are exploited not only physically but socially, politically and economically.

Bama, being a woman is one of the best known Dalit writers was born at Puthupatti in Tamilnadu. Fighting impossible odds she went through both school and college and is trained as a teacher who imparts values aimed at building self-esteem and social consciousness. Bama wrote *Karukku, Sangati, Kusumbukkaaran* and *Vanman.* She remarkably portrayed the sufferings of Dalit women, who are doubly marginalized-being a Dalit and being a woman. She also introduces, Dalit-feminist perspective through her book *Sangati.* Dalit feminism means redefining woman from the socio-political perspective of a Dalit and she also examined caste and gender oppression together. Bama says about Dalit feminism in an interview:

> All women in the world are second class citizens. For Dalit women, the problem is grave. Their dalit identity gives them a different set of problems. They experience a total lack of social status; they are not even considered dignified human beings. My stories are based on these aspects of Dalit culture...... the hard labour they have to do all their lives. Other problems are the same for all women. The Dalits particular caste.....more agony and hard labour can be attributed to them. Dalit women have to put up with a triple oppression, based on class, caste and gender. They die in order to live.

Sangati, which in Tamil means news, events and happenings, published in Tamil in 1994 and translated into English in 2004 by Lakshmi Holmstorm, is the second work of Bama. *Karukku,* her first work is about the self and the community is infact an autobiography whereas *Sangati* is the autobiography of a Dalit community. But it has interconnected anecdotes. It is the story of "Paraiya Christian Women," who come together to fight oppression. *Sangati* has no plot in the normal sense but on the question of conversion which happened in her grandmother's time. According to this the women of paraiyas only became Christians with the hope that their children would get free education in missionaries. Other Dalit communities remained Hindu. But this conversion also could not help them out because their children denied to go to school. Rather they preferred either to work or to play. After conversion also Dalits didn't have equality to God according to Christian system. But it is only Dalit women who are put to sweep the church while other castes' women stand outside. For this they are told that they will gain merit by sweeping the church and God will bless them specially for this. But Bama makes clear the resistance that emerges in the minds of Dalit women.

> See how they fool us in the name of God ! Why, don't these people need God's blessing too?

This short narration accommodates more than thirty five characters most of whom are female. But in the conventional sense there is no individual who may be tagged a hero or heroine. The narration is in first person, followed by the general comments of the grandmother and mother figures and lastly the comments by the author-narrator.

The plight of women is at worst in *Sangati*. They are presented as wage-earners as much as men are, but earning less than man do. The money they earn has to bear the financial burden of running the family, often singly whereas the men spend it as they please. The situation of Dalit women has been portrayed by Tersamma, a lower caste activist in a poem:

> We go to work for we are poor,
> But the same silken beds mock us,
> While we are ravished in broad daylight,
> Ill-starred our horoscopes are,
> Even our tottering husband hiss and Shout for revenge,
> If we cannot stand their touch[6] *(*Dietrich, 1990)

Exploitation of women didn't stop here. In the fields they have to escape from upper-caste men's molestations. (p. 35) At Church also "they must lick the priest's shoes and be his slaves while he threatens them with tales of God, heaven and hell." (p. 35)

Bama explores the theme throughout the book, i.e. hard labour and violence. She has written about the violent treatment of women by fathers, husbands, and brothers. She also elaborates the domestic quarrels which are not limited to the four walls but carried on publicly. She also explores psychological stress and strain which bound them to believe in spirit or peys. With the help of a character she attacks on patriarchy system and asked, "Why does the Pey (spirit) only possess women? It never seems to go for the men, even when they are on their own." In answer to this, with the help of another lady she explains, "It is the women who are polluted every month. It is when they are menstruating; they say the spirit will get at them. Men do not have this nuisance, you see." (p. 50)

She doesn't stop at that but show the mindset of Dalit women she further says, "And even among women, I have never heard of upper caste women becoming possessed or dancing in frenzy. The spirits always seem set on women from the Pallar, Chakkiliyar and koraver (all Dalit communities)." (p. 58)

In the use of language, Bama used her own dialect as the voices of many women speaking to and addressing one another as they share the incidents of their daily lives. Use of obscene words also shows the agony of Dalit women which is the root cause. She says that it might be the result of the internalizing of a patriarchy based on sexual dominance and power. Raakkamma is the character who used this language. When she was fed up with her husband's kick she shouted, "Disgusting man, only fit to drink a woman's farts! Why don't you drink your son's urine? Why don't you drink my monthly blood? And she lifted up her sari in front of the entire crowd gathered there."(p. 61) At first the author too is disgusted, but later realizes that for vulnerable battered woman who has to cope such behaviour day in and day out, such outrageous conduct and using four letter words, referring explicitly to body parts – are clearly a means of survival and escape. But she also has the vigorous aspect of her own language i.e. use of proverbs, folk songs and folklore. The special characteristics of this language are its closeness to songs and chants. She writes, "From birth to death, there are special songs and dances. And it is the only women who perform them. Roraattu (lullaby) to oppaari (dirge), it is the only women who will sing them. After betrothal ceremony, a song made by women to tease her bridegroom because he was darker than she was and he also went to school upto eighth, so he could read some English.

Handsome men, dark as a crow
More handsome than a blackened Pot
I have given you my promise
You who can read Ingilissu. (p. 77)

Beside all this humiliation, violence and their plightful situation Bama examines the differences between women, their different needs, the different ways in which they are oppressed. But throughout the book so many times she presented women empowerment and feminism. She also admires the women of her Dalit community for their courage, fearlessness, independence and self-esteem. She says:

> They have made us as useless as rotten eggs. Now, generation by generation we must start thinking for ourselves, taking decisions, and daring to act. Don't we sharpen and renew a rusted sickle? Just like that, we must sharpen our minds and learn to live with self-respect. (p. 104) Bama herself has faced so many problems due to male dominance. She says, "Being a Dalit creates a problem on top of that, being a Dalit woman makes it more difficult. The biggest problem of all, I realized, is trying to live alone as an unmarried Dalit woman." (p. 120)

She again says, "Why shouldn't a woman belong to no one at all but herself?" (p.121) She calls for an action and even recommends effective protest by all such women. "Even the ocean will support us, if we only dare." (p. 67) By the proverb she put more effect, "If a man sees a terrified dog, he is bound to chase it. If we continue to be frightened, everyone will take advantage of us. If we stand up for ourselves without caring whether we die or survive, they'll creep away with their tails between their legs." (p. 66) With the help of so many characters she has shown her will power and determination to change the society. "We must stand up for ourselves and declare that we too are human beings like everyone else. If we believe that someone else is going to come and uplift us, then we are doomed to remain where we are, forever." (p. 66)

Besides having so many plightful things in Paraiya Community, it also has so many special things to be copied. It has a positive picture like no dowry is required of them, widows are not discriminated against, and may remarry if they choose, the dalit women are also free not to wear tali which is symbol of marriage. Moreover this novel also throws light on the unity of these women. The book is rooted in everyday happenings: of working and singing together, preparing and eating food, living in joint families and bathing and swimming. Bama also have explained very beautifully the rituals specially the coming of age ceremony. She says:

> On a Friday morning, at earliest dawn
> She becomes a Pushpawati, so the elders said –
> her mother was delighted, her father too,
> the uncles arrived, all in a row – *(Chorus of Kulavai, p.17)*

A bethrothal ceremony is also very interesting where gifts are made by the groom to the bride, a group wedding of five couples at Church.

Lastly, before concluding she advises to bring forth the children in the manner that this injustice, violence and inequality will come to an end. She concludes with the effective and apt words "Women can make and women can break." (p.123)

Works Cited

Bama, Karukku. *Madurai: Ideas.* 1992, (*tr.*), Lakshmi Holmstrom, Chennai: Macmillan India 2000.

Chandra, Ramesh. *Phases of Dalit Revolt.* New Delhi: Commonwealth Publishers, 2003.

Dietrich, G. The Relationship between Dalit movements and Women's movement, Cases and Conceptual Analysis, Paper for the *IAWS,* Calcutta, 1990.

From the 1972 manifesto of the Dalit Panthers, quoted in Tamil "Dalit Peenterkal, Tamililakkiyam, Penkal," *Gail Omvedt.* Pondicherry: Dalit Panthers, Special Edition, Nov. 1994.

Gabriele, Dietrich. *Dalit Movement and Women's Movement: In Reflection on the Women's Movement in India.* New Delhi: Horizons India Books, 1992.

Gauthaman, Raj. "We have no need for haloes," *India Today Annual.* 1995, 96-98.

Pendse, Sandeep. "Sadhvi Ritambhara Va Jamatvad," *Stree-Uvach* 7th issue, Bombay: 1993.

Rao, Anupama. (ed.) "Introduction: Caste, Gender and Indian Feminism," *Gender and Caste.* New Delhi : Kali for Women and Women Unlimited, 2003.

Group Discussion as a Pedagogical Tool: Replacing the Banking Clerk Teacher

Dr. Rajan J. Barrett

In this paper I will be discussing a model of group discussion used for evaluation of entrants for Management Schools in India. Secondly, I will try to discuss them as a method of teaching and learning instead of a method of evaluation alone. This is for students of faculties like Arts, Humanities and other "non-competitive fields." Finally, I would also try to argue that the use of Group Discussion (GD) could be a means of moving away from the banking clerk teacher syndrome[1] to a dialogic system of learning/teaching. Thus, this makes the enterprise of learning more performative and self-actualizing.

The three skills that the G.D. focuses on: speaking, listening and situation handling[2] are perhaps the point at which the student becomes an actor and learns to act for him or her self as it is the withdrawal of the teacher which is an extremely important step in the growth of a student and more so in a class room in India where- in the students are made just mere objects (or assumed silent listeners). The teacher is the one who does all the action (speaking) and the students look towards the teacher for action and perhaps a performance.

Learning models of speech and thought implies learning formats of speech and thinking which also implies a reformulation of the individual self into a structured commonality which has to become an individuality. This is a learning experience in itself, and initially the student is often found struggling to make what they want to say fit into the model of speech. It is also the individual utterance and the group utterance that the student has to struggle with. It is no more the teacher's presumed ideology and thought and speech pattern which a student is using but s/he gets a chance to modify the speech and thought module to fit in with the knowledges and skills that s/he gets to the class.

The student gets an understanding of his/her own methods of thinking, and ability to observe the method of his/her thinking put into practice. This for me is a way of conscientizing the student. While it brings about some understanding of how thought and language operate and a reflection upon usage, it also gives power to the individual student to create and recreate the world and the self in his/her unique manner. What is more, it makes the student aware that s/he can use the tool to make arguments effectively for ideological positions. Thus s/he has recourse to a tool that is meant for learning the language continuously by an auto-corrective method of gaining insight into thought and language and altering or modifying the way s/he thinks and speaks.

Colin Peacock discusses the utility of GDs, keeping a younger school audience in mind[3]. It, however, lacks utility in an Indian college classroom as it is not geared for an adult learner whose situation and comprehension of his/her self is more complex. This complexity stems from the student's understanding of him/her self as a language using being and who can reflect on him/her self and the language learning process, no matter how minimally this reflection works. One has to keep in mind that the classroom in India is a space lacking homogeneity. This is seen at various levels. Linguistic competence in the L_1 might be good, but in English, which is the $L_{2,}$ poor. Economic differences exist at the college level, which also tell on the performance and the competence of English. In a country like India social and cultural backgrounds are connected with "backwardness" and someone from a higher caste may belong to a lower class. It may also happen that someone from a higher class and caste because of a conservative family, might be backward or resistant to studying English. Certain cultures in India would perhaps be averse to English, while others make it a point to learn the language as well as their own.

Though the notion of the module for thought and speech sounds like a reinvention of the "new critical" form and content wherein the thought and the articulation is like content and form, I would locate it as a kind of liberating tool that brings in a certain kind of ability to be more articulate and bring in ones experience, knowledge and background to the class room. Peacock's "whole class discussion" might be fine in a British classroom or a classroom made for a few students. In an Indian classroom one would perhaps have anywhere above (about) sixty students who have to be given the skills of the GD. It is not that the whole class does not get involved. However, to have a kind of randomness in the group discussion, as Peacock suggests, is hardly productive as no skill is taught/learnt systematically though perhaps acquired unreflectively. It does not suit a classroom of students who are adult learners and who have acquired a number of social and pragmatic skills without the English language and all they need to do is reflect on using these skills along with the English language, instead of their own. One has to give Peacock the benefit of doubt as he is perhaps dealing with an English speaking audience, wherein there is no problem of the colonial hang over and the notion of awe that the colonizer's language carries with it.

The utility of the GD reaches across languages and can be put to practice in different forms of social discourse, from the "chai" shop to the "classroom" or "office," while finalising transactions like marriage, purchase of property, or in local area board meetings or committee meetings. Most importantly, it would be a useful way of being aware of how one takes part in discussions of news, politics and self-understanding.

The point which needs to be stressed here is that the forms of social discourse like the debate or argument are different from the discussion. What normally starts off as a discussion often gets personal and violent largely because of the confusion between the concepts. Though often, people would claim they are discussing thing, they are not because they lose control of themselves and are not aware of how thought and speech are operating, and where the interaction (discussion) is heading. A discussion does not have to end up as a fight but does when confused with an argument or a debate. It seems necessary here to draw attention to the fact that a formal debate does not land up in the kind of mind lock of an "I am right and you are wrong" situation wherein personal abuse slowly becomes a kind of corollary to the form of discourse.

In a classroom the speech and thought modules give the student a short term skill to master. These skills are often taught and tested in the classroom itself, with a longer goal for the student to look forward to i.e. making him/ herself articulate when ever s/he speaks, using the same skill over a period of time. More importantly, it makes for "noise in the classroom"[4] where the students and not the teachers make meaningful noises, hear their own voices and actualise them. As the valuable "muting of the teacher"[5] takes place, the floor giving[6] (to the student) is also "confidence giving" (to the student).

It is this confidence giving which is most often lacking in the Indian systems wherein the student is made to sit and watch the antics of the teacher as s/he "puts on the act" which often is boring, sometimes intimidating (as the student is made to feel the awe of the teacher's knowledge), brahminical (as there is perhaps just one value system or point of view articulated, which is supposed to be the right or the correct one), and most importantly is good practice of skills of speaking, for the teacher (which s/he does not need) when in fact it should be a space to facilitate learning and practice of skills for the students. The GD appears to me to be a chance to change this scenario.

To look at the conventional teaching systems in which a teacher is the one who gives the orders, the teacher speaks, the student listens, the teacher acts and the students feel that they act through the teacher, the teacher is the subject and the students the object. Thus ultimately we are here teaching to control, not to liberate or make free. This is an ideology that is not articulated but it suits governments, managements and corporate houses (not to forget the management training institutes). Besides, the brahminical status of the teacher and the social power structure is not challenged at all as the teacher is always right as "the boss is always right," a rule to go up the corporate ladder. This puts to question all the notions of correctness that we as teachers of English indulge in, because our teaching is not to set free but is meant to discipline and conserve traditions successfully and subtly for the state and for the status quo in society to be maintained.

Sometimes, teachers are not aware that they are putting to practice the business of the state and are in keeping with the ideological practices that the state would like to instill into the students. Often it is traditional values that are inculcated and the tradition is not challenged or questioned by teacher or student. Thus no real unlearning takes place which implies no learning takes place either. Unfortunately little or no teaching and no learning actually takes place in most conventional classrooms in India, as the teacher is no better than a trained animal, with a little (or a lot of) finesse and tact.

It is true that a management training institute uses a technique that should actually be used in a classroom to bring in confidence and articulation among students. It is evident however, that the students who have been deskilled, or rather never skilled at all, have to approach a management training institute, so that they can learn the skills that an ordinarily efficient system of education should have made available to them. This puts to question all the practices that we as English teachers employ in our classroom with the banking system of education. The banking system of education is a system which is content based. The student is treated as a knowledge, bank and material is stored in this bank to be called for at any time. The examination in India is when this knowledge system is tapped thus giving an unduly high importance to the examinations and minimizing various language skills to suit the need of exams where knowledge bank is tested on a gigantic if not in large scale. Concepts, learning and skills thus take a subservient position to store content as knowledge.

It is not that the GD brings in social conscientization or make students avid learners, when they attend a course for an entrance exam to an MBA. Nor do I imply that the aims of an MBA are anywhere close to the social conscientization that Paulo Freire discusses, though for schools of Social Studies like TISS (Tata Institute of Social Studies, Mumbai) or IRMA (Institute of Rural Management, Anand) the level of social awareness and desire for social change becomes an issue. However, as a model to make a student articulate and to think it would help a student in another discipline (say like Political Science, or Sociology, or English literature etc.) start finding ways of thinking and articulating themselves.

The teacher's role in the GD

The teacher might be of some assistance as s/he may be able to express what is being said in a more cogent way. It may also be possible for the teacher to find a number of points clustered together so as to make the articulation difficult and complex. Though arts education is more complex and engaging than an MBA, clarity in what is being said is required not only in speech but in writing also. One has to be clear in what one says be it in speech or in writing as one has to confront the examinations and interviews where one's understanding of complex ideas is tested. Thus the speech module brings in a method by which one could articulate oneself effectively. The teacher's role here is more of a facilitator and an analyst analyzing the sentence structure, or the vocabulary or the expression and the content to give feedback after the GD is over. I do not use the method that Peacock uses wherein the teacher breaks into the group and becomes an appendage to the discussion. Peacock prescribes and suggests:

The normal procedure for such a context is for the teacher to choose a contentious issue for discussion (the amount of freedom that teenagers should be allowed for instance) and to throw the topic open for the whole class discussion. Your role as teacher may be initially as catalyst to get the discussion going, perhaps too as neutral chairperson (especially if the debate is fluent and lively), and perhaps, if debate flags as devil's advocate. You may have to try deliberately to bring quieter students into the discussion and sometimes you will have to repeat what one pupil has said so that the whole class can hear clearly what the contribution was. In the main you will find your role is that of a manager facilitator and occasional contributor. *Classroom Skills in English Teaching: A Self-Appraisal Framework* (London: Routledge) 1990, 38-39.

The students have to be on their own in the GD which makes them self-reliant and are forced to use the language and communicate. Thus the role of the teacher is more of a sounding board after the discussion when the teacher gives his/her feedback. The need of the teacher as chairperson or plodding a student on may be necessary in Peacock's case however, I do not stand theoretically with Peacock as that is a pedagogy of oppression. It is the presences of the teacher which seems more like an absence rather than a presence which makes the student venture out on his/her own. The teacher becomes a person who arranges for a discussion and learning to take place and becomes wraith like for a positive end, i.e. getting confidence into the students.

Often it does take time before a student opens up in a GD and learns to put his/her point across. But given time and perseverance the student would be able to manage. Thus a GD wherein the teacher is seated in the classroom lets the group discussion take place and watches the group dynamics from the outside is more effective as it makes the students in a peer situation take part in the group discussion. Peer pressure to perform thus seems a more powerful tool than a teacher goading a student on. The teacher is an observer here and s/he observes the speech, the body language, etc. and gives a feedback on them. Thus it seems a more market place kind of situation in which some action is taking place and is observed rather in a classroom where one is on ones best behaviour. However, a modicum of formality is maintained till the given time for a group is over. The teacher and other students are observers who will comment on behaviour at feedback time.

From the Market place to the Classroom

Often in a situation where there is little knowledge of the spoken language this model helps students overcome the fear of speaking because of the peers who are along with them and as they see them speaking, the resistance or the hesitance slowly disappears. The post-colonial edifice of English being the language of the elite and the colonizer seems to melt away with time and students begin speaking English in what ever way they can.

A case in point is the comparison between a student who does not have the colonial hang over and one who does. This is something that came to my notice in an M.A. class where a Persian student with about six months of exposure to English was more willing to participate as compared to the Indian students who had a Bachelor's degree in English. It was with great difficulty that the Indian students started opening up and speaking. The Persian student was also forced to speak in English both inside the class and outside because he had to communicate in a real market place to get his work done. Wrong English, problems of pronunciation etc. were not his problem while it turned out to be the problem of the rest of the class.

Though there is merit in the argument that the colonial hangover contributes to diffidence. One has to consider the systems which are the "monastery" and the "market place" approaches theorized by Tom Mc Arthur in his *Foundation Course for Language Teachers* (Cambridge: CUP) 1987, 93-96. It is perhaps the influence of the market place on the monastic which one has to keep in mind when one considers the GD as in the market place approach to learning a language:

The "marketplace" approach to language has always been dictated by simple necessity. If you want to barter, buy or sell, then you need to be able to communicate – somehow, anyhow – with potential contacts. . . . Anything that works is welcome: a go-between if possible, or gestures, pictures, your words or his words, your grammar or his grammar, or anybody's words or anybody's grammar, in order to strike a bargain. The system has always worked but is haphazard, and gives rise to trade jargons, pidgins and creoles that are socially frowned on, much as their users – sailors, soldiers, hucksters, whores, dockers, innkeepers and ultimately, slaves – were or are frowned on. These inter languages are vitally alive, however, and many a respectable and matronly modern language has something of this wild blood in its family line.

The "monastery" approach was different in every way – was, in fact, shielded from the hurly-burly of the world and its marketplaces. It abstracted its students, usually boys of an impressionable age, from the flux of everyday life and put them together in roughly homogeneous age groups for longer or shorter periods, their instructors taking on the role of stern fathers or older brothers (and, in fact, have often had the title of "father" or "brother"). The work of instruction was in the hands of a priesthood or brotherhood such as the priests of ancient Egypt, the scribes of Babylon, the brahmins of India, the mullahs of Islam, the monks of medieval Europe, the teaching brothers and sisters of later Catholic schools and missions, the one-sex staff of semi-monastic private boarding or day schools. Much of the life of such institutions was box like...(Cambridge: CUP 1987, 94).

It is important to consider that the model of GD, that I discuss, is taken from the market place and transported to the monastery. This is when one applies it to the teaching of literature and language in the classrooms which are semi-monastic and semi-brahminical there is a balance stuck between the monastery and the market place approaches to teaching. The practicality of the module is useful for academic purposes and is a tool that helps students overcome their inhibitions to the ghostly colonial status of English in a brahminical setting. What has to be envied is that it is students are good listeners in a brahminical setting. This is because in the monastic approach there is little distraction and the students had the ability to be trained and concentrate on a few things. In the market place however, listening becomes quite specific and may perhaps be lost. However, the GD takes care of this as it is one of the characteristics of a good leader. The GD makes sure however that this skill is not taken for granted.

Listening as a part of the process of empathy is good perhaps for a leader. A teacher too is meant to be a good leader. And if a teacher is empathetic then some amount of listening is possible. Teaching students to listen is another thing in itself. Sensitizing students to listening is an important part of education as with globalization and the aggressiveness that accompanies it, there is little chance that listening has. When aggressiveness and not assertiveness is at a premium it is listening which is important especially in a world of arts and culture where listening to the uniqueness of the other becomes important. This is perhaps where the GD has a larger socio-linguistic role. The GDs are often priced as personality development and being sensitive to the other and listening to the other is part of the socio-linguistic education that will make an impact on the lives of people perhaps for a long time. If one learns to listen in a GD or is sensitive to the issue there is an impact on the personality and behavior of the person. There would perhaps be also a change in his/her idiolect as s/he listens to others. This change would also be reflected in the society of the person concerned. Thus listening is a transformative and educative process which is dynamic and not passive as the traditional teacher would believe.

In this situation of the GD, where the student has to learn listening, it becomes an important skill that has perhaps never been taught or perhaps never been emphasized in the classroom, as the solo performer, the teacher, perhaps naively believes that the students are listening if not learning. One has to look at the answer papers to find that most of the students did not really listen and did not learn at all. Colin Peacock's insight here too has some relevance when he says:

They need help with communicating for a range of purposes and in listening intelligently and sensitively as a discussion develops. We should recognise as research in fact suggests, that young people appear to be more at ease with "listener-related" talk where the emphasis is on relating to other people (especially those of their own age group who they know well), than on situations that are "information-related," where they have to concentrate on communicating clearly and explicitly a "message" of some kind, especially when the setting is unfamiliar and perhaps formal. (Classroom Skills in English Teaching: A Self-Appraisal Framework; London: Routledge,1990, 42.)

Though what he says may hold true in British settings the task of listening is not easy especially when a student in the group wants to say something that s/he is preparing for. To formulate what one wants to say specially when one is given a formula perhaps is not so easy and may take time away from listening. Besides, the problem perhaps is also related to the Indian classroom where English is not the first language or L_1.

To me it seems that listening is a skill that students' attention has to be drawn to so that they are able to get what is called expression from others. There are students who are able to express themselves better because of their background and reading perhaps. Vocabulary and also the fumbling for words or expressions make students aware about their shortcomings and pitfalls and there seems to be a kind of an auto-correction mechanism. Because of the peer group, and the confidence they derive from learning to listen and articulate themselves together, it is possible that some kind of foray into the language is made. Wrong starts, wrong vocabulary, incorrect grammar and pronunciation are all acceptable in this marketplace approach to learning. Though one should not encourage the use of modern Indian languages in the GD often students do use colloquialisms. During feedback time this provides an opportunity for a teacher to give students the choice of using different alternatives to the word s/ he used. This in a small way helps the students build vocabulary and expression and also the student is made to learn what formal and non-formal use of language is. This certainly is a way of imparting new vocabulary, pronunciation, and grammar. It is advisable not to correct the pronunciation, because often the student listens and corrects him/her self listening to his/her peers. However, one finds quite often that a student is willing to learn the acceptable pronunciation after the GD is over. This is important because there is no imposition of the right or accepted pronunciation but a kind of desire to get to know an acceptable form of it. Besides, as the student learns to listen and use words, there is "the hands on experience" that s/he gets by trial and error of pronunciation. This to me seems more of a democratic way of learning and the students learn with joy. Listening as a skill is thus educative not only for content but to build up vocabulary and pronunciation and acquire the syntax.

Often prejudice of other communities, dogmatism because of caste, class, region and religion sometimes surface in the GD. This is thus a place of unlearning and relearning behaviour and thought. It is with fixity to only one way of understanding a concept that a student gets dogmatic. It is the business of the teacher to guide him/her out of this rigidity lovingly and understandingly as s/he confronts the student who in a classroom situation is willing to learn and unlearn. Here again the question of semantics and vocabulary comes into play as the sociolinguistic situation of the marketplace is re-examined in the classroom.

Thus the student learns to articulate a point, learns to think and formulate what s/he wants to say and does so in the least possible time. This is a skill that arts students need to learn as often both teachers and students alike are not able to come to the point and say what they want to because of the complexity of the matter or thought. The learners are thus made aware of the pedagogy and the method that goes into their articulation and this is a meta-pedagogical situation that they are made to reflect upon, and correct for themselves. In simple words it is for each learner to ask him/herself questions like: "How do I think?" and "How do I put what I think into words that I can get across to the others in the group and be understood without difficulty?"

Situation Handling is a skill that normally comprises about eight situations which are the introduction, the conclusion, handling a chaotic GD, handling a stagnant GD, handling a silent GD, letting another person speak, and knowing when and how to make a PREP (Point Reason Example Pont) and when to leave off and let another person continue. This situation handling would largely be included in the pragmatics of discourse.

The introduction is the first two to three minutes of the GD where the GD is shaped and given direction. The students are taught how to make an introduction, define key terms and give the scope of the discussion. They are also taught that the process of the introduction is different from making the actual introduction as first speaker. They are also advised to see that they speak in the first three to five minutes of the GD so that their presence is felt for the rest of the GD and they would have contributed in shaping the GD. These are pragmatic considerations and are useful tips for getting into a management school. However, the pragmatics of the GD in the classroom for the purpose of getting students to learn the language and participate creatively in the GD would also tell them how to be present in the GD at the introduction and right through so that their points of view shape the GD and give a direction to it. Thus participation is stressed upon in both the GD for testing and the GD for learning. In the second case it is important that the student is made aware that after a point in the GD hardly any one would consider, or let the speaker speak as his competence in the subject concerned has not been proved at the beginning of the GD.

If the students have to participate at all right through the GD then they have to contribute in different manners right through the GD adding different PREPs and counter PREPs as they are supposed to think and make the GD progress. When it often happens, that students have no new area to deal with the GD then it stagnates. Either the same PREP is mulled around in different words or the participants speak about the same broad area like economics, or technology etc. The students have to be made aware that to prevent a stagnant GD from taking place one has to give new direction to the GD by coming up with a new point or a new angle.

Often the situation is such that the GD is a silent GD that is because the participants have little knowledge about the subject. For the entrance one is told that one should ascertain whether all the participants in the group are unable to handle the topic and after that ask for a new topic. Here in an arts class one has to be sure that the topic is suitable or related to what the students have to learn or already learn or know what the topic is about. It could be that they have some knowledge about the topic and as the GD progresses more is got out of the discussion.

The question of letting another person speak in a management entrance GD would be only after one has had enough of chances to make preps for oneself. Here perhaps there would be more emphasis on getting all the members of the group speak so that there is a more comprehensive discussion that takes place. I would suggest however that those who can speak and do so comfortably should think of themselves and getting their point across, and slowly the others who are diffident to speak will feel encouraged as the second and third GD"s take place. Colin Peacock seems to corroborate my view when he says:

For the self-confident, extrovert child the mode offers, when interpreted in this form an opportunity to seize the limelight and dominate the debate. For the less confident child, on the other hand, there is the struggle to speak up and be heard and the embarrassment of becoming the focus of the whole class's attention. And obviously in a single lesson it is unlikely that all members of the class will be able to make a major contribution to the discussion. Classroom Skills in English Teaching: A Self-Appraisal Framework (London: Routledge) 1990, 39.

The pragmatics of body language and eye contact can be taught by the teacher as these are associated with emotional intelligence and the corporative principle. The extrovert child in India is the one who has had some kind of an English medium education, is normally form an upper class and/or caste. Often one has to tone such students down as they might have the language but are still not able to get the point across, or are not able to think and put things across cogently. However, they are also the potential quick learners who because they have the language and the social background would be able to master the skills in a few sessions.

It is handling of the PREP's which often are a problem to participants as they are sometimes conscious of violating the politeness principle. The teacher, when asked, has to explain how one maintains a balance between the politeness principle and sufficient individual participation and contribution to the GD. At what point to come in, when another person is making his/her PREP, and towards the end of the PREP when to let another person take over, are elements often discussed by the students. However, the teacher can only make suggestions but the student has to learn to come in and let another person come in by practice, perception, observation and skill.

Finally the teacher may have to brief the student about the conclusion and how one systematizes the various preps that have been presented, mention the significant ones and the names of the persons who make them. It is also important that the students have to be made aware that in the introduction and the conclusion one has to speak for the group, while in the body one has to speak for oneself. The formula for the conclusion could be drilled with a number of students practicing it if need be.

The Teacher as facilitator: Feedback and Participatory Learning

Unless there is feedback given there is only action without reflection. The feedback is an important part of the learning process as the student is made aware of the method of learning s/he is undergoing. This reflection is what accounts for a chance to improve performance on a practical level as one is able to improve slowly and consciously. The action-reflection-action is thus a constant feed- back system that becomes something that is taught subtly if not drawn attention to.

An individual feedback is important besides a general feedback on the topic and handling the topic. The individuality of each of the students is acknowledged and the record of his/her progress can be maintained so that the strengths can be built up and the weaknesses minimized. Here there is greater amount of conscious involvement and observation of the teacher as s/he is part of the audience and is an evaluator. The evaluation is done on a GD to GD basis, which accounts for a constant involvement of students and teachers. Perhaps the teacher is more like a teacher of the performing art like speech and drama, music or dance. The role of the teacher giving a feedback is quite different from a banking clerk teacher who dishes out the solutions and the content and is incapable of listening, observing and responding to the individual needs of a student in a short period of time. It is exactly like what would be called a performance text without a dramatic text. Each GD is a unique performance and there are no repeats. In a large sized Indian classroom the individual would probably find it a luxury to be given personal attention but it is possible to deal with large classes giving about ten to eleven students at a time a chance to actualize themselves and feel that they are aware of who and what they are and are part of their role as learners.

It is also important that the students who are observing the GD give their feedback also, as does the teacher. This contributes more to the meta-pedagogical situation as the same students go in for the next GD and are more aware of what they should or should not do/say. They participate in their own pedagogy and are capable of observing and correcting their peers and themselves. Often they would be aware at feedback time where they have slipped and thus are more able to perform better. Most Arts students find this rather difficult as it involves a lot of quick thinking, analyzing and verbalizing. However, when they are able to learn the technique, then they find that they are more effective and feel that they can be understood, which seems to be an auto-motivating force. It is now the tools of learning are no more the property of the teacher but in the hands of the students. It is like the language situation itself where in a teacher, who is threatened, is not really interested in letting the skill pass on to the student for fear that the student will then perhaps not require the teacher.

The role of the teacher in a GD is now, perhaps, brought to a minimum, and is made to facilitate the process of learning. It is as if the teacher is made to be a kind of a feedback system to assure the speaker /student that s/he is getting things right. At the same time, goading the student on to think by challenging him/her with situations, reasons and events that perhaps were not thought about. There is here a kind of a democracy established, wherein the student can challenge the teacher too with reasons that are different. This is what a teacher would welcome as a student is slowly trained to make a counter PREP as a skill, to show his/her ability to think and use the PREP.

The question of the teacher being always right does not arise here, as no one is expected to be right or that will amount to being dogmatic. The notion of correctness might be effective in pronunciation, vocabulary, expression or grammar but as far as the logical thinking is concerned it is the form of PREP and the counter PREP that are important to the teacher and the strength of both of them which should be valid. For the validity of an argument one has to remember that it has to be valid in all places across time. The student is made aware that s/he has to be able to present a proposition both for and against the point and is made to realize that there is a difference between a GD, debate, and an argument.

Notions of correctness as far as content is concerned are that one has to be sure not to make statements that are objectionable to race, gender, creed and colour. Though certain discussions might be specifically full of content or the topic is close to one of these this is an entry point for a lot of issues in arts and the humanities. Areas like political science, gender studies, race relations, history, linguistics, etc. can make an intervention and thus produce a lively dialogue among the students. It is not prejudice that comes across but discussing what one stands for in a civil and logical manner that makes communication possible.

The skill learnt here are modes of discourse and methods of using them appropriately. This would thus be within the area of pragmatics, and socio-linguistics rather than a pure literary understanding of modes of discourse or an advanced foray into discourse analysis. The meta-linguistic/literary function of language is what the teacher is probably using here as s/he is making the students aware that there are modes of discourse which have to be used appropriately according to the situation given.

This also is a kind of reiteration of dealing with discourse. This is because one is made to understand that there is a beginning middle and end to a GD which gets translated as introduction, body and conclusion, both for the discussion and for essay writing. This is thus a point of entry that a teacher can make so as to bring about awareness that there has to be some kind of order in even forms of written discourse. This most often might seem like an aside but perhaps gets noted as the student is in the arena. S/he is the performer and actor and thus needs to pay attention to the minutest detail of instruction that the teacher gives. The utility of the teacher is thus enhanced and the students will ask the teacher's intervention when s/he has a problem of dealing with a concrete method of dealing with the task of learning the language.

An important part of the GD is putting into practice and testing the politeness and the cooperative principles. This is an area which, when taught, is associated with the notion of an argument, a debate, and a discussion. This perhaps brings in the other, because the listening and the voice modulation, besides the body language are not meant to be aggressive. It is a socio-linguistic and pragmatic skill, which has to be taught gently as students have to be made aware of the concepts of aggressiveness and assertiveness. The subtle difference between the two and the way in which one puts one's point across not to appear aggressive, accounts for awareness of voice modulation which is loudness, tone and pitch – here again one has to teach the students the meaning of intonation and what are intonation patterns. (It does not mean that the teacher teaches advanced prosody but is aware of intonation and meaning and conveys the same to the student in a practical and effective manner.)

Here the student is taught: 1) how to make it possible to raise and lower the volume so that one is heard and yet keep a non-aggressive stance. 2) How not to let the tone give way to a sarcastic attitude, anger, disgust etc. 3) An important lesson that students of language learn is that it is the tone which often is insulting not what is said in words. So in a GD the students are taught not only to handle their feelings but also not to display a negative attitude through body language (the non-linguistic), intonation, pitch, and volume. Thus there seems to be an overlap in the socio-linguistic and pragmatics of language, along with para-linguistic features like intonation.

It might be necessary to state that the pragmatics of floor giving and floor receiving is also taught as both the body language and the voice modulation show. However, a practical difficulty that students encounter and are eager to know about is "When two people start together who backs off?, Is it a bad thing to back off and would points be taken away for doing so?" Here is the chance to bring back the politeness principle and the cooperative principle and also to remind students that this is a GD and one scores points by knowing when to let the other person speak and when not to. Often this question comes up when students are confronted with who speaks first in the introduction of the GD and then again they have to be taught how to make an introduction. The defining of key terms, the scope of the discussion and the formula of wishing every one at the beginning of the discussion, brings about the active participatory learning at various levels.

Just as the students are made aware of the introduction and the conclusion, where they have to speak for the group, they are also made aware about the conclusion, where in they have not only be listening right through the discussion but at the same time have what is called a filing cabinet memory. There is the skill of ordering and systematizing the ideas that are discussed in the discussion and crediting people for what they said. The skills learnt here again are sifting, sorting, organizing and importantly not to indulge in plagiarism. This is quite different from the ideational skills that are taught in the thought modules. This skill is a skill of listening, prioritizing, analyzing, making a judgment about how to organize things, which are complex skills but never the less important to learn.

Note

The banking clerk teacher syndrome is a term derived from Paulo Freire. The Banking System of Education is a system of education where the students are treated like banks. Knowledge is banked up in them and when desired it is extracted from them. There is little or no learning that takes place and thus the dialogić system of learning is more effective as the students are made to think and ask questions to the teacher, themselves and each other. The Banking Clerk Teacher is a term that Paulo Freire uses for a person, leader or teacher who gets lost in a system that has stopped thinking and being creative. It is a system where in the students are treated like knowledge banks and knowledge is deposited and withdrawn at will as opposed to this is the dialogic system of education wherein there is a questioning and interaction. Paulo Freire summarizes the orientation of the banking clerk teacher saying: "Education must begin with the solution of teacher-student contradiction, by reconciling the poles of the contradiction so that both are simultaneously teachers and students.

This solution is not (nor can it be) found in the banking concept. On the contrary banking education maintains and even stimulates this contradiction through the following attitudes and practices, which mirror oppressive society as a whole:

(a) the teacher teaches and the students are taught;
(b) the teacher knows everything and the student knows nothing;
(c) the teacher thinks and the students are thought about;
(d) the teacher talks and the students listen – meekly;
(e) the teacher disciplines and the students are disciplined;
(f) the teacher chooses and enforces his choice, and the students comply;
(g) the teacher acts and the students have the illusion of acting through the action of the teacher;
(h) the teacher chooses the program content, and the students (who were not consulted) adapt to it;

(i) the teacher confuses the authority of knowledge with his or her own professional authority, which she and he sets in opposition to the freedom of the students;

(j) the teacher is the subject of the learning process, while the students are mere objects." *Pedagogy of the Oppressed* (London: Penguin) 1970, 1993, 54.

At least one of the management training institutes uses the model that I am dealing with here or a variation of it.

"Many experienced teachers will quickly lose patience with the kind of lesson that has been described. In some classes, just as in traditional directive lessons, pupils are not prepared to accept the rules and conventions of this kind of formal discursive lesson. Opinions are shouted across the room with great gusto, sometimes in a simultaneous chorus. Few pupils seem prepared to listen to points of view that conflict with their own values and beliefs. Some are happy to escape altogether and retreat into a personal dream world untouched by the lesson's debate. At its worst such a lesson is a travesty of a discussion; it becomes an incoherent babble of opinions. Even at its best, when discussion is well organized and tolerant, with a large number of pupils participating, a sense of dissatisfaction remains." Colin Peacock in *Classroom Skills in English Teaching: A Self-appraisal Framework.* (London: Routledge) 1990, p. 39.

Muting the teacher is an important method of teaching as the teacher moves away from the group and seems as if not there and certainly is not available. This makes the students stand on their own feet and trip over, make mistakes, use jargon, colloquialisms, creoles, etc. but communicate and find confidence in communicating. The over anxious teacher, like the over anxious parent, rushes in to help delaying the process of learning. Thus muting is an aid to learning and is a skill of unlearning rather than learning.

Floor giving and floor receiving as we know are part of pragmatics. However, the Banking Clerk Teacher syndrome makes floor giving minimal as the teacher wants to prove his/her supremacy. The floor space of the teacher is much like the space of the actor who uses his/her space on stage. The audience space is taken up by the students. Seldom does the Banking Clerk Teacher relinquish his/her space so that students can be actors in the class. Perhaps there is controlled floor giving where in the student is made to answer questions or read. Though perhaps this is a pragmatic consideration of the teacher it leads to an imbalance in the performance of teaching/learning that is if there is less student participation and thereby no floor giving.

T.S. Eliot's Theory of Objective Correlative and the Concept of *Vibhava* in Indian Rasa Theory: Some Parallels and Affinities

Dr. V.B. Srivastava

There is no evidence to show that T.S. Eliot came in touch with Indian poetics though his *The Waste Land* and *Four Quaterts* contain direct references to Indian scriptures particularly the *Brihdaranyaka Upanisada* and *The Gita*. The paper is not intended to show that Eliot's theory of "objective correlative" contained in his essay on *Hamlet* was formulated under the influence of Indian poetics. It is only designed to establish that Eliot's theory of objective correlative may be found compatible with the theory of *vibhava* propounded in Indian *Rasa Shastra*. The theory of *vibhava* is first found in Bharata's *Natyasastra* who while explaining *Rasa Nispatti* wrote the following aphoristic lines – "*Vibhavanubhava-vyabhicari-samyogad rasa-nispattih*" (M.M. Ghosh, Tr. *Bharata Natya Sastra,* p.105). Here Bharata has used three key words *vibhava, anubhava* and *vyabhicari-bhava*. Many writers have written on Bharata's *Natyasastra* prominent among those being S.K. De, P.V. Kane, M.M. Sastri, D.R. Bhandarkar and R. Pischel. The subsequent critics like Bhattalollata, Shrishankuka, Bhatta Nayaka and Abhinava Gupta have given manifold interpretation to the word samyogad which helps generate Rasa. The theories which they propounded to substantiate their views on *rasanispatti* are called *utpattivada, anumitivada, bhuktivada* and *abhyuktivada* respectively. Besides them Udbhata, Rahula, Battatauta, Kirtidhara and Matrigupta are some other prominent commentators of *Natyasastra*. The most subtle interpretation was made by Abhinavagupta, an eminent philosopher and critic whose philosophised ideologies got assimilated in his criticism. Taking a cue from Shaivagam philosophy he formulated that the *nispatti* of rasa is based on *prakasaka-prakasya* relationship (Dictionary of Indology, p. 9). Smell already lies in a pitcher which comes out when water is poured in it. The pleasure is already intent in good poetry or a good piece of literature. It has to be manifested which takes place when its three constituents, i.e. *vibhava, anubhava* and *vyabhicaribhava* are synthesised and crystallised which finally culminate into the manifestation of *rasa*. The dominant emotion preserved in the heart of the reader evaporates in the form of *rasa* after reading *kavya* or watching a drama.

Eliot came in contact with Indian poetics when he was at Harvard University and got the opportunity to learn Sanskrit and Pali literature from George Santayana and Irvin Babbit. He also presented his doctoral dissertation on the topic entitled *The Mind and Heart in the Philosophy of Irvin Babbit.* He is not an innovator. Nor does he claim to have formulated any critical school. His ideas are spread over here and there in his stray essays which are of great significance. He has coined many catch phrases relating to the art of poetry. Objective correlative, unified sensibility and emotional equivalent to thought are such phrases. Whatever he has to say about the worth of poetry and its essence is not foreign to Indian rhetoricians. By *objective correlative* Eliot wants to say that emotion gets its forceful expression when it is related to some object. One may find the kinship of this concept in Indian theory of *vibhava*. Eliots's objective correlative gives an inkling to *alambana vibhava* because it states that emotion is adequately expressed when it is tagged to some visible external objects.

Eliot's theory of *objective correlative* has been outlined in his essay on *Hamlet.* In this essay he propounds the theory of objective correlative. He observes:

> The only way of expressing emotion in the form of art is by finding an "objective correlative," in other words a set of objects, a situation, a chain of events which shall be the formula of that particular emotion. (Selected Essays, p.145)

Eliot precisely means that no emotion can be properly expressed unless it is expressed through some concrete medium. Emotion cannot be expressed in a void. In order to express emotion in a convincing manner, it is necessary that it must have some object before it. The greatest difficulty with the Romantic poets was that often they expressed their emotion without any concrete object before them. This accounts for vagueness and obscurity in their poetry. Shelley's "Skylark" is an example. In this poem Shelley expresses his emotion without taking any cognizable object before him.

Eliot is correct in saying that emotion can be expressed forcefully when it is expressed through some concrete object. Let us take an example. If a teacher goes to class and asks his bearer to bring attendance register and the bearer makes delay in fetching the register, the teacher gets annoyed. The teacher gets cross with the bearer. He expresses his anger and annoyance by thrashing the register. Here we get a clear compatibility between the emotion and the object.

Eliot put forward the theory of "objective correlative" in the context of Shakespeare's tragedy *Hamlet* which he calls an artistic failure (*Hamlet*, p. 142). Eliot's argument is that in this tragedy there is no compatibility between prince Hamlet's emotion and the stimulus or excitant which arouses this emotion. Prince Hamlet had not seen even the face of his father. Whatever he learnt about his father came through the lips of Horatio who suggested that he should see the ghost of his father on his tomb at dead of night. When the ghost of Prince Hamlet's father appeared before him, prince Hamlet was stunned to note that he did not die of snake-bite as the rumour was afloat but he was killed by his younger brother Claudius who poured poison in his ear. The ghost also asked prince Hamlet to take revenge upon his uncle and forgive Gurtrude, his mother and leave her to the mercy of God.

This lack of incompatibility between emotion and object led Eliot to think that despite all dramatic craftsmanship *Hamlet* is an artistic failure. He felt that in order to attain artistic perfection it is necessary that there should be compatibility between emotion and object.

Eliot wanted to apply his theory of objective correlative to other forms of literature also. M.L. Rosenthal has considered Eliot of strictly modern age on account of this novel theory of objective correlative propounded by him:

> It is T.S. Eliot's method which makes him the most inescapable as of the age. (The Modern Poets, p.118)

From psychological point of view the theory of objective correlative seems quite sound and cogent. The psychologists of introspective school have proved that emotion is appropriated in proportion to the stimulus. If the stimulus is strong, the emotion will also be strong. If the stimulus is weak or feeble, the corresponding emotion will also be weak and feeble. In Jayasi's *Padmavata*, king Ratnasena learns about the exceptional beauty of princess Padmavati through the parrot Hiramana and becomes enamoured of her. In the same way in Sri

Harsha's *Naisadhacarita,* king Nala falls in love with Damayanti after listening to her beauty from a swan. According to Eliot, the emotion of Ratnasena and Nala is not justified. It is an account of inadequate stimulus. As the stimulus of prince Hamlet is misdirected, so the emotion of Ratnasena and Nala is also misdirected. In this way like *Hamlet, Padmavata* and *Harshacarita* may also be considered artistic failures.

What Eliot calls objective correlative is precisely vibhava in Indian poetics. In literature emotion is expressed in a controlled manner. It is not left unbridled. The poet who fails to do so cannot be called a successful poet. In the words of Bhamaha, "bad composition of poetry amounts to death." (*Kavyalamkara,* 1/2)

Eliot's notion of objective correlative is, in one way or the other, nearer to the concept of vibhava in Indian poetics. In the *Rasasutra* formulated by Bharata in his *Natyashastra,* it is said that rasa is only manifested whenever *vibhava, anubhava* and *vyabhicaribhava* are properly synthesised and crystallised. In Indian rasasutra, emphasis has been laid on the assimilation of *vibhava, anubhava* and *vyabhicaribhava.* It is the synthesis of all three forms that leads to the manifestation of rasa.

Vibhava is stimulant or the objective condition of producing an emotion. *Anubhava* is gesture. It means bodily expression by which the emotion is expressed. Thus the arch glances of a lady, her inviting smile, may be regarded as anubhava. *Vyabhicaribhava* is ancillary emotions. It means a series of diverse emotion that feed the lamp of a dominant emotion. (*History of Sanskrit literature,* p. 594)

According to Bharata *vibhava* plays dominant role in the manifestation of rasa. S.N. Das Gupta has very appropriately defined *vibhava. Vibhava* may be of two kinds – *alambana* and *uddipana. Alambana vibhava* means a person or persons with the reference to whom the emotion is manifested. It is the object that stimulates the excitant. *Uddipana vibhava* means the circumstances that have excited the emotion (excitants). Thus it is easier for a man to be attracted towards a woman of young age if they are thrown alone and there is a beautiful scenery before them, the moon peeping through the clouds, the fragrant breeze blowing, and the like. Any one of such circumstances may be regarded as *uddipana vibhava,* whereas both the man and the woman are *alambana vibhava* to each other. (*History of Sanskrit Literature,* p. 593)

In Indian poetics one comes across a more subtle analysis of vibhava as compared to Eliot's concept of objective correlative. Eliot simply says that emotion can be powerfully expressed through some object and that object may be a set of objects, a situation, a chain of events, but in *Rasasutra* one comes across a more subtle and deeper analysis of the concept of *vibhava.* The concepts of *uddipana* and *alambana* may be ellucidated as follows :

Shakuntala, pinning for the love of Dushyanta, strolls here and there in the forest waiting for the lover. She is love-sick and grief-striken. The sweet breeze that blows, the fragrance of the flowers, the roaming of clouds, the chirping of birds, the dancing of peacocks, the sound of a flowing spring – all these act to enhance the *viraha* of Shakuntala. They act as stimulants. They intensify the pangs of Shakuntala. In this sense, they are *uddipana vibhavas,* the object of excitant. This is to say the object which excites the viraha of Shakuntala is Dushyanta. Suddenly Dushyanta appears and embraces Shakuntala. Dushyanta is *alambana* here. In Eliot there is no such dichotomy. But so far as theory is concerned, he puts forward a sound theory that emotion requires some object before it to help it express forcefully. This object must be a concrete phenomena rather than an abstraction.

There is clear correspondence between Eliot's theory of objective correlative and Indian concept of *vibhava,* though the approaches to the problem are different. The two theories have different cultural orientations and hence if some affinities are found between them they may be called coincidental. The Indian grammarians were in the habit of going into details while examining any critical question as is apparent from the subtle analysis of *vibhava.* Eliot, on the other hand, remains on the surface. But both the Indian grammarians and Eliot seem to bring out the universal truth that art can be better expressed through some concrete medium or object. It matters little whether it is called objective correlative on *vibhava.*

Works Cited

Bhandarkar, D.R. *Indian Antiquary.* 1912.

De, S.K. *History of Sanskrit Poetics.* Calcutta : Firma KLM, 1960.

Eliot, T.S. *Selected Essays.* London: Faber & Faber, 1953.

Ghosh, M.M. (*tr.*) *Bharata's Natyashastra.* Vol. I, 2nd edn. Calcutta: Granthalaya, 1967

Kane, P.V. *Introduction to Sahitya Darpana.*

Pischel, R. *Gottinger Celehrte Anzeigen.* 1886.

Rosenthal, M.L. *The Modern Poets.* Oxford University Press, 2nd edition, 1966.

Sastri, M.M. Article published in *J.A.S.B.* 1910.

Srivastava, V.B. *Dictionary of Indology.* Delhi: Pustak Mahal, 2009.

Sastry, P. V. Naganatha. *Kavyalankara of Bhamaha.* New Delhi : Motilal Banarsidass, 1970.

Indian Sensibility in Dr Umeshwar's Poetry: A Critical Appraisal

Subodh Kr. Jha

Like all regional imbalances so obvious in the context of Bihar, the most prominent of which is economic, there are certain imbalances which are subtle enough to be immediately grasped. One such imbalance is manifest in the critical attention given to poetry written in English and that too especially in Bihar. One can say that this imbalance accrues from the lack of generosity on the part of the critics, maybe, because of some notorious misgivings about the poetic merit or talent in such "backward region" – backwardness made more intelligible to general disinclination to English language in this part. We, as students of Indian literature in English, have come to feel it more acutely when we compare some of our poets writing in this region to current reputations like that of Nissim Ezekiel, Kamala Das, Parthasarthi, Shiv K. Kumar and others and feel that one or two of them are writing as good as, if not better than, these poets. Dr. Umeshwar Prasad is one such poet who has provided four anthologies of his poems which have not received the attention due to them. These anthologies are *Confrontation* (1976), a collection of five poems, *Confrontation and other Poems* (1979), a collection of nine poems, *A Nailed Dream* (1984), a collection of two long poems and *Unemployed Hope* (1984), a collection of seventeen poems. No doubt, there have been random reviews and indifferent responses but they are either too smug, or too peripheral to be noticeable barring a few such as the one by Dr. P. Raja.

The present paper, therefore, is an attempt to redress this imbalance by taking up the poems of Dr. Prasad for "close" inspection. Here, it is in place to make it clear that mere use of English for our artistic expressions/emotional apprehension does not entitle us to compare our levels of competence with that of a Shakespeare, or a Donne or an Eliot. An objection to this stand may be raised: is this kind of limitation to critical endeavours practicable or proper in view of the active, also assimilative/integrative inter-cultural encounters and engagement in modern world today?

Proper and practicable, surely it is not. But for a strict critical relevance, it is hardly possible to controvert the process of development. One can hardly appreciate the literatures of different cultures, if one's appreciation is not firmly grounded in the understanding of one's own. And in this respect, any outside assistance, however hearty and boosting, slights the chance of self-reliance. Moreover, it is distortive and mischievous in terms of the motivation and intent – conscious or unconscious – within the framework of their understanding. It is a fact that a poet of Shakespeare's greatness has not been born to our culture; but it is also a fact that neither Kalidas nor Tulsidas has been born to theirs, i.e. English culture. The artistic heights inevitably differ in key with the culture and tradition. This needs to be kept in mind while evaluating an Indian poet writing in English.

Even greater an issue is the benevolent toil that the bringing of new talents or the forgotten ones into light entails. In course of Indo-English poetry what has happened is this. Some poets, ambitious enough, cultivated contact outside India and got the pat by way of recognition and came into currency, whereas others with modest ambition remained happy securing occasional berth either in Indian dailies or weekly. Not only this, things went on so far that these current reputations were pointed monitors who testify the fitness of the poem for publication. Such a practice is hardly tenable in a situation where everything is in the process of shaping or making, more so because the contemporaries can prove to be incompetent judges of their counterparts. If Mulk Raj Anand finds Raja Rao to be a "deviant," a trespasser into fiction, it is because the two novelists look at the same coin but to its different sides. The present evaluation is an attempt to redeem the characteristic critical feature or norm obtaining in Indo-English criticism.

No sensitive reader of Indo-Anglican poetry can write off Dr. Umeshwar's poems, provided they get access to them. Since Dr. Umeshwar was a senior University teacher of English literature, this had bearings on his poetic sensibility which is suitably educated. It is partly Donnesque – seeking to create a sovereign world of love. ("But we are very proud pair -/ two in one, one in two.") It is partly Keatsian – a world for dissolution into the moon – drenched dream. ("My dream dissolved./ Dissolved it is/ into me") or swooning into a luxury of sensations ("My blood ran riot/ when I felt my hand on your bulge of honey/ I so much yearned to rest it there/ till all time lapsed in my clasp".) It is partly early Eliotic – trying to dismiss the overwhelming question with a mordant aside ("I don't carry the cosmos on my back".) But despite these multiple voices, the poet's own is not wholly lost. In fact, Dr Prasad's poetry exhibits above all an authentically contemporary Indian sensibility. The authentic contemporariety is quite manifest in all of his poems. This is quite clear in the very first poem "Why do I write" in the anthology *Confrontation and Other Poems*:

> I write,
> not for asking –
> never for aping,
> absolutely not for pleasure
> or displeasure
> of a doctrinal don,
> Yes,
> I don't claim competence,
> for I have none.
> I have flaws to offer
> – my agonies
> and my roots
> And my rootlessness.
> ("Why do I write?" *Confrontation and Other Poems*, p. 2)

The rugged or blunt articulation sets the tone of the poems not only in this anthology but in other anthologies as well. It also establishes that Dr Umeshwar Prasad belongs to the Indian tradition of "Swantah Sukhaya" (for the pleasure of the self) but in his poetry he also gives us the feel of the "way of the world – rather Indian world – through his agonies. It is only a person with "roots" who can feel the agonies of "rootlessness" that threaten to destroy what our tradition or culture so venerates. The agonised Indian soul is quite manifest in his poem "Confrontation." No doubt the beginning is rather ironical and rugged, reminding one of John Donne – perhaps a subtle influence of teaching and enjoying Donne." However what he talks about is quite Indian:

> Civilized men and civilized women!
> Thank you for allowing me to speak;
> Thank you.
> But would you mind if I introduce myself?

I am the present
– the nerveless anonymity,
plucked from past,
torn from future,
– the unholy ghost,
The afflicted youth,
the filth of conscience,
the damned Romeo,
the unremedied Macbeth,
the blighted Desdemona
the cursed Shakuntala,
– persecuted for natural passion of life,
I confess, I have.
("Confrontation" in *Confrontation and Other Poems*; p. 3)

Apparently the poem is a dramatic dialogue between two representatives, one of the older generation and the other of the younger. It is the younger whose voice is resonant throughout the poem. In fact, it is his monologue. The very first line of the introduction gives away the mode of what Eliot calls "depersonalisation." Though the speaker of the poem is "I," it is dissolved into unit of time, i.e. present. The phrase "nerveless anonymity" has an inclusive valency in the sense it refers to both "I" and "the present," and thereby completes the chemistry, the melting into an impersonal examination. The poem stretches over the length of time even though the speaker professes a violent dissociation from past and future. The allusive mode may be taken as the influence of Eliot on the poet but what distinguishes Dr Umeshwar is the wonderful blend of the East and the West – again in the synthetic mode of the Indian tradition that quite easily assimilates what is good or what constitutes the essence. He confesses that he is struggling "to liberate" himself

from the unmeaningful crusts
You call values?
– that affronting, pulseless heaviness.
("Confrontation" in *Confrontation and Other Poems*: p. 4)

Obviously, Dr Umeshwar's emphasis is on the "essence" of value not on the rigid conventions or rituals that have gained in currency.

That is why he wants to "rape the conscience of humanity/ entrenched in passive contemplations" (Confrontation, p. 10) and prefers "leprosy" to good health:

> I am no Kalidas
> to hymn to rid of leprosy;
> I am in love with it
> really.
> At least it is no false star,
> and it keeps me on;
> I have chosen an island
> to be wedded to this throbbing pain:
> it alone mitigates my rusted muscles
> and feeds the tigers in my veins,
> but, would you mind if I make guesses about you,
> about how you raped to construct a thesis on anti-rape,
> about how you built up "bundhs" to blow off
> the refused froths of humanity
> – the mutilated lambs;
> about how you chanted
> in the last secular meet at the Church Gate
> The slogans of Communal hate;
> ("Confrontation" in *Confrontation and Other Poems*: p. 6)

It is important to note here that the genesis of "Confrontation" was Dr Umeshwar's confrontation with his Head:

> The poem is result of a highly strained dialogue between someone who thought was my boss for being the Head. And me reacting that in teaching profession there is little scope for the kind of colonial nomenclature. The so-called boss blew his nose and wrote to the Vice-chancellor alleging that I often come for "confrontation." You see the title is his and for that I am deeply obliged to that awkward moment. (A Dialogue with Dr Umeshwar Prasad)

However, the poem goes beyond the personal confrontation and presents an inclusive picture of the contemporary society–the hypocrisy prevailing in the society – the objective behind developing the mechanism of "bundhs," chanting "slogans of communal hate" at the "secular meet" and "constructing thesis on anti-rape." In such a social environment, the speaker's refusal to "hymn" like Kalidas to "rid of leprosy" is an attempt to remain honest with himself; and show the problems ailing him as well as the society. So, in his address to "Civilized men and civilized women," the speaker gives us the feel of the way of the world – rather Indian world – and talks about the evils of casteism and "private tutoring" in the context of pretentions or hypocrisy:

> You can't be civilized if you can't pretend
> Learn to pretend
> I offer to tutor you for Rs 100 a month;
> However, are you not my caste man?
> – I will safeguard your interest
> – The interest of civilization.
> ("Confrontation" in *Confrontation and Other Poems*: p. 7)

Obviously, Dr Umeshwar very convincingly portrays the contemporary society – society in which violence and corruption dominate. The sensitive Indian soul fails to compromise with this state of the society and so he shouts in an angry tone: "I want to rape the conscience of humanity." In fact, this attempt "to rape the conscience of humanity" remains the informing spirit of Dr Umeshwar's poetry.

The authentic Indian contemporariety is to be discerned in several poems such as the astringent "Elegy on Indo-English poetry" or in the truculent "Crowding Draught." However, it is more pronounced in the "Unemployed Hope" and "This Mafia Wind, Mother" (both in *Unemployed Hope*). The social undertone of the Unemployed – "unemployed hope" "unemployed fancies" – allows the poet to straddle the two worlds of subjective isolation and impersonal crowd.

"This Mafia Wind, Mother" begins on a note of evanescent quietness reminiscent of Eliot's "Marina." But by the time we come to the end of the poem we have taken the measure of controlled turbulence and subterranean violence nearly as fascinatingly menacing as in Keats's "The Magi." This should give a fair idea of the poetic competence of Dr Umeshwar when he is at his best.

"A Green Corpse" is another poem that celebrates the loss of genuine feeling in the contemporary world. The speaker in this poem finds little difference between the dead and the living and before the grave of the beloved, he says: "I fall in my own account/A Green Corpse." (Confrontation in *Confrontation and Other Poems*, p. 16). The reason why he thinks so is obvious: he has

> no song
> no dirges
> to sing at your grave
> to comfort your fretted soul
> and to caress the wounds
> I once inflicted on you.

("A Green Corpse" in "Confrontation" in *Confrontation and Other Poems*, p. 15)

The Indianness of Dr Umeshwar's poetry lies not only in the realistic presentation of the contemporary society but also in wonderful incorporation of folklore into his poems. His poem *Hoarded Nights* published in *Youth Age* (15th July 1983) is derived from the following lines in Magahi:

> Ratiya ke roz-roz
> Bangla par sutai
> Moro Jawani Bekar ge (Magahi folk song)

Now derived from these lines is the poem:

> Sleep and sit,
> And sit and sleep
> I through the hoarded nights
> Under this un-husband'd
> And breathless roof,
> Eager and expectant.
> A despairing pile sits
> On the untenanted bulge
> Of my unseed'd softness
> Clasping the furnac'd feel
> That my youth's a waste
> And my unmanipulat'd body
> A leafless, lean reed.

It is remarkable how Dr Umeshwar captures the restlessness of the newly wed wife who has to spend her nights alone and who is dying to be "husbanded." This leads to abject subjectivism that is manifest in Dr Umeshwar's poems. Take for example "A Nailed Dream" – a poem remarkable for its abject subjectivism but with protruding edges:

> Mine you!
> you slip away like glad moments:
> yours is the manner
> human expressions can hardly guess.
> You are my wild dream, an intimate fever,
> a bosom implication:
> You are the end of a deep quest
> that began I know-not when.
>
> ("Monologue," *A Nailed Dream,* p. 3)

The nostalgic feeling that these lines capture informs both the poems in the anthology entitled "A Nailed Dream." The phrases like "glad moments," "wild dream," "intimate fever" and "a bosom implication" lend sharp concreteness to the feelings. One cannot fail to notice the "uninhibited" nature of utterance. The same holds good to these lines from "Dream Queen:"

> But last night we spoke in largeness.
> Your eye reflected my mind;
> and your body sang my soul ....
> I loved you to repeat,
> But the cock shrieked,
> "Some other time," you whispered,
> And sank into the withdrawing night.
>
> ("Dream Queen," *A Nailed Dream,* p. 12)

The celebration of physicality is another remarkable feature of Dr Umeshwar's poetry – a fact which is well recognised by the poet himself. Dr Prasad candidly acknowledges this:

> "I have written this poem under the stress of a relentless, doctoring inspiration. When I re-read it, I was embarrassed by its un-feigning protruding edges, its abject subjectivism

for which I don't think, I should apologise. There are such moments in the life of a poet when he uses words to tease out such feelings which are shy of coming in the open – "Shy" but they have the urge to be themselves. And once they are there, they are unafraid of the Sun as they themselves are genuine fires, an echoing Sun." ("Proem," *A Nailed Dream*, p. ii)

Dr Prasad's poems, thus, seek to create a sovereign world of love ("But we are very proud pair- / two in one, one in two"). This world is very close to Donne, the pioneer of the Metaphysical school of poetry as well as to Keats and Eliot. However, this world imitates none of theirs. Many voices, no doubt, mingle in his poetry but the poet's own voice is never lost, it remains the most resonant, the most vibrant. In the preface (Proem) to *A Nailed Dream*, Dr Prasad refers to "in-built recalcitrance to gross materiality" and in the poem "Monologue," he averse that "things don't matter." This poem is indeed not in a world of alienation, nor are there human relations reduced to "thinghood."

If one agreed with dominant opinion of Anglo-Indian scholarship that Indian tradition is what lies immutably stacked in Vedanta one would say that the poet's admitted aversion to materiality is quite in the tradition. And so would be the other assertion in "Pre-Poetry" (*Unemployed Hope*): "the personal alone/makes the impersonal accessible to me." Even if we leave aside the question whether the statement does not really belong to a tradition – no less authentically Indian – that runs counter to the nihilistic abstraction in Sanker's absolute monism, we shall find more palpable evidences in some of these poems that testify to the poet's success in achieving, by strictly poetic means, a tense and hard-earned equipoise of spirit amidst diverse and interactive cultural pressures coursing through complexes of intense feelings, aspirations and cogitations.

Needless to say that like any healthy poet, Dr Umeshwar is a dualist. He is so even when he is seen to be valorising his own concentric self or "personal" in opposition to the "impersonal." The broken syllables in "the personal alone/make the impersonal/a-cce-ssi-ble to me" – broken beyond the normal or grammar and natural articulation – enact the difficulty of a desired reaching out to be the "impersonal," which is thus not at all slighted. The poet's experiments with hyphenated words may be a strategy of energising the impersonal or the other, as in poems mother themselves and just be/ the poem-ing

(Poem-ing 2). On the other hand, in "I have cherished to possess you/ in the manner I possess/ me (Dream Queen" in *A Nailed Dream*) one may notice an extreme case of alienation where there is a felt chasm between "I" and its shadowy other self, "me." And yet, by registering equivalence between "You" and "me" in which you is equally internalised, its polarity is nevertheless inviolate.

Works Cited

Prasad, Umeshwar. *Confrontation. A Collection ofFive Poems.* Muzaffarpur: Indian Sensibility Publication, 1976.

————, *Confrontation and Other Poems, A Collection of Nine Poems.* Muzaffarpur: Indian Sensibility Publication, 1979.

————, *A Nailed Dream, a collection of two long poems.* Muzaffarpur: Indian Sensibility Publication, 1984.

————, *Unemployed Hope.* a collection of 17 poems, Muzaffarpur: Indian Sensibility Publication, Muzaffarpur, 1984.

Raja, Dr. P. Hoarded Nights, *Youth Age.* (ed.) Mrs. Annsbel George, Vivekananda Nagar, Pondicherry : Geobel Publishing House, No. 3, 15th July 1983.

Raja, P., Book review of Prasad Umeshwar's Confrontation and Other Poems, *Youth Age,* (ed.) Mrs. Annsbel George, Vivekananda Nagar. Pondicherry : Geobel Publishing House, No. 3, 15th July 1985.

The Namesake and *Namesake*: A Generic Transformation from Text to Film

Dr. R.P. Singh

The Namesake (both the novel and the film) deals with the experiences of the community of expatriate Bengalis leading otherwise mostly unremarkable lives in the United States. It is a story of a name, which symbolises, search for identity and cultural identification. The protagonist, Nikhil "Gogol" Ganguli, along with his family struggles to find his identity in an alien land. In one way or other Gogol's life-story shows familiarity with the lives of the Indian Diaspora at large.

A debate is in the air over *The Namesake* as to which one is better, Jhumpa Lahiri's novel or Mira Nair's film adaptation of the book.

Jhumpa Lahiri, a celebrated writer and the year 2000 Pulitzer Prize winner for *The Interpreter of Maladies,* had taken long strides with the publication of the novel *The Namesake.* Lahiri's panache as a novelist is seen in the emotional portrayals of her characters. Search for identity, loss of sense of belonging, anguish of separation, and cruel demands of larger society that seek definitions, are the high points of her works. It also shows her familiarity with the lives of expatriates. However, the narrator in the novel held some limitations, which can't be recounted as narratorial flaw. It is something that often makes novel appealing, somewhat evocative and at times allows varied interpretations.

Mira Nair, an acclaimed Indian filmmaker, through her films has often taken into account the human lives and their relationships in a world where cultural boundaries lose colour. *The Namesake,* Nair's most remarkable film to date, is a screen adaptation of Lahiri's novel. The film is somewhat personal to Nair as the novel is to Lahiri. Both Nair and Lahiri share the emotional space peculiar to the people of Indian Diaspora.

The audio-visual felicity that comes with the cinema-form always has an added advantage. Mira Nair too has used this aesthetic form to bring to the screen the complex web of expatriate experience. Characters in the film as compared to the novel are profoundly carved out. The way this film has received applause shows Nair's expertise to transport thematic reality of the novel into triumph of visual world of film. Nair not only explores modern life and vicissitudes of change, loss, fear, conflict, and catastrophe with remarkable ease, but also paves way for the ties and bonds that overarch frustration and agony, desolation and identity-crisis, that creep in the lives of global families.

Film adaptation is based on a story, novel or any other work of art. (Bandi 2009: 11) Most of the films are based on novels. For they offer ready plots and stories for filmmakers. Adapting novels for films is a well-known phenomenon in the film industry. Both Hollywood and Bollywood have adopted many novels for their film scripts. To name a few: *Gone with the Wind* (1939: George Cukor), *Pather Panchali* (1955: Satyajit Ray), *Godan* (1963: Trilok Jetley), *Samskara* (1970: Pattabhi Rama Reddy), *The Godfather* (1972: Francis Coppola), *Train to Pakistan* (1997: Pamela Rooks), *The Namesake* (2007: Mira Nair) and so on. Recently, Christian Colson has adopted the novel *Q & A* (2005) by Vikas Swarup for the film *Slumdog Millionaire* (2008). This film adaptation has won eight Oscar Awards. The film adaptation process is the study of "Word to Image."

The Namesake is a realistic novel. Its story takes place in different places in India and the United States and depicts the life of an ordinary Indian family that emigrated to America. The novel begins with Ashima Ganguli standing in her kitchen. She is on the verge of her first pregnancy. She gives birth to a baby boy. Ashoke, the father, decides that the baby's name would be Gogol. Then after some years Sonia is born. Gogol has been uncomfortable with his name because it is neither Indian nor American. Ashoke gives Gogol a copy of *The Short Stories of Nikolai Gogol* on his fourteenth birthday. Gogol changes his name legally and chooses to call himself Nikhil. Gogol feels guilty when his father tells him about the train accident and his miraculous escape. In his early twenties, Gogol has had affairs with several American girls Ruth and Maxine before marriage. He takes seriously the warning of his parents that marriages of Bengali boy and American girls end up in divorce, and marries Moushumi which nonetheless meets the same fate. Meanwhile, he was informed that his father had had a massive heart attack and had died. At the end of the novel, Gogol opens the book and begins to read the story "The Overcoat" which had been read by his father at the time of the train crash.

The novel as well as the film describes the struggles and hardships of the Indian people immigrated to the United States. Ashima and Ashoke migrate to America and raise their two children Gogol and Sonia. Gogol has to struggle his awkward name.

He finally searches the true story behind the awkward name from his father, who later on faces a severe heart attack and dies. Thus, the novel as well as the film adaptation becomes a geographical as well as a psychological journey of two generations.

The Namesake – novel and film are realistic and are capable enough to concentrate any person's attention especially those who have lived long away from their native places. In fact, it is not the only story of the difficulties of the Indian emigrants but also the universal saga of the modern life.

The film has fifty-six characters in all. The film revolves around its hero Gogol (Kal Penn). Other major characters are Ashima Ganguli (Tabu), Ashoke Ganguli (Irrfan Khan), Maxine Ratliff (Jacinda Barrett) and Moushumi Mazumdar (Zuleikha Robinson). The minor characters are Sonia (actress: Sahira Nair), Ashima's Mother (actress: Tanusree Shankar), Ashima's Father (actor: Sabyasachi Chakravarthy), Ashoke's Father (actor: Tamal Sengupta), Mira Masi (actress: Gargi Mukherjee) and so on. Jhumpa Lahiri also acted in this film as Aunt Jhumpa. The film was produced under the UTV Motion Pictures and Mirabai Films. It is directed by its producer Mira Nair. The screenplay is written by Sooni Taraporevala. Excellent photography is done by Frederick Asc. The film is edited by Allyson Johnson.

The film requires traditional Indian as well as modern American costumes of two generations. This responsibility is carefully handled by Arjun Bhasin. Music of the film must have a pathetic note. There is need for the mixture of the Indian classical music along with the western tinge. The eminent musicians Nitin Sawhney and Linda Cohen carefully accomplish this delicate responsibility. The film also contains the famous old Hindi song, "Ye Mera Divanapan Hai" (this is my madness) composed by Shankar Jai Kishan.

The film contains visual description of high quality. We find proper use of camera. The visit of the Gangulis to the Taj Mahal and their conversation with each other at Agra is one of the unforgettable scenes of the film because they provide us with the emotions of nostalgia. Mira Nair has used the flashback technique wisely and skillfully. It is evident from the portrayal of the train accident.

The people of India as well as of other nations have well accepted the novel. Its film adaptation further made it famous and its popularity reached its peak. The film is produced in English, Bengali, Hindi and French. Along with many awards and nominations, the film won the prestigious International Film Festival Award of Bulgaria. Many leading newspapers, periodicals and film magazines have taken cognizance of its success.

Nikhat Kazmi reviews the film in the entertainment supplement of *The Times of India* March 24, 2007:

> India is an idea that lives in the heart and the mind, rather than a land-locked territory; and India is a style of upbringing and attitude that transcends territory. Great performances, an iridescent canvas and a topical theme: *The Namesake* is Mira Nair's tribute to her *janmabhumi.* Cinematic considerations must be made when a novel is to be successfully adapted to the film. Novel is a lingual medium while film is a visual one. Film provides an abundance of details to the spectators through major changes of light, inflections of colour, music, camera, physical expressions and so on. The reader has a far more control over the novel than the viewer does over the film. The novel and the film are different in terms of the structures, perception and the narrative. Hence, no one can really judge the relevance of the novel or film. It may be necessary to deviate from the original story while transforming novels into films. Film adaptation of *The Namesake* is not an exception to this.

Here are certain major deviations in the movie *The Namesake* which are in fact the creation of the film producer:

1. The novel begins with Ashima Ganguli standing in her kitchen. She is at the verge of her first pregnancy. The film begins with a train accident which Ashoke faces.

2. The novel carefully gives us the description of the Montgomeries who were the first neighbours of the Gangulis in the United States. In the film, such important events are omitted.

3. In the novel, Ashima sends letters to her relatives and friends. In the film, she sends the letters along with photographs.

4. The novel describes the Rice Ceremony of Gogol. The film describes the Rice Ceremony of Sonia.

5. The novel describes Gogol's relationship with Kim and Ruth. The film has omitted the important characters Kim and Ruth.

6. The novel describes premarital relations of Moushumi with her boyfriend Dimitri. The film has omitted the important character of Dimitri and instead gives us the character of Pierre.

7. The events in the novel are concentrated in Cambridge, Boston, Yale, New York, Ohio, New Hampshire and some scenes are related to India. The film is only centered in an around New York and some scenes are related to India.

8. The novel ends with an event when we find Gogol reading the short stories of Nikolai Gogol. The film ends with an important scene when we find Ashima practicing Indian classical vocal at Calcutta(Kolkata).

The film is warmly received by the viewers from all corners of the world. Indian people have now practically reached all the countries of the world. They peacefully try to assimilate themselves in the respective foreign societies. And at the same time they constantly remember their motherland and their culture. Lahiri has certainly depicted the culture conflict in her literary pieces. There is more to study the difficulties Indian people of India origin face in France, China, Germany, Russia, England, South Africa and the Arab countries.

Works Cited

Bandi, Raghu Ram. *Adapting Novels into Films.* Delhi: Prestige Books, 2009.

Kazmi, Nikhat. Rev. *The Namesake.* 24 March 2007<http://timesofindia. indiatimes.com/entertainment/movie-reviews/english/The-Namesake/moviereview/1802655.cms>.

Lahiri, Jhumpa. *The Namesake.* New Delhi: Harper Collins Publishers, 2006.

The Namesake. Dir. Mira Nair. Adapt. Sooni Taraporevala. Perf. Irrfan Khan, Tabu, Kal Penn, Zuleikha Robinson, Jacinda Barret, Sahira Nair and Ruma Guha Thakurta. FoxSearchlight Pictures, 2007.

Alice Munro as a Feminist Writer

Dr. Akhilesh Kr. Singh

Alice Munro, a Canadian writer, born in 1931 to a farming family, established herself in avant-garde of feminist writers. Feminism is a doctrine that advocates equal right for women in society. Munro points out:

> Because I am a feminist. Yes, I am that nut case who thinks that women can do the traditional male jobs just fine or, in some cases, even better. I am the one who is against gender discriminations such as unequal compensation of men and women for the same position with the same amount of training and experience, promotion difficulties, and even a matter of courage. I think that because of their natural maternal instinct women generally survive in a "grinder" of modern life much better than men do. Moreover, women are that magic force which keeps men going. We could be struck by a sad number if only we tried to count how many men lost their life battle and sunk straight to the bottom without a female encouragement.

From *Selected Stories* of Alice Munro I have chosen "Boys and Girls" because it spans her writing career and shows that although her style has developed, she still explores similar themes throughout her writing. In this story she deals with a woman's view of her surroundings and relationships, but the character is at a different stage of her life.

Feminism emerges as a concept that is based on a critical analysis of male privilege and woman's subordination within any given society. It opposes woman's subordination to man in the family and society. Feminism is a global and revolutionary ideology that is political because it is concerned with the question of power. A feminist is one who is awakened and conscious about woman's life and problems. The feminist apprehends certain features of social reality as intolerable and hence to be rejected if one is to transform the society for a better future. The concept of woman is of central importance in the formation of feminist theory. Themes explored in feminism and feminist theory include patriarchy, sexual objectification and oppression. In literary theory Feminism means challenging the patriarchal canons. Feminist theory studies structural inequality of women caused by systematic social injustice.

In the story "Boys and Girls," the central character, a girl, describes her life on a fox farm and her process of search for gender identity. From the vivid descriptions, the readers learn how the girl used to watch her father pelting the foxes. The narrator also proudly shares how she helps her father in the barn feeding the foxes, bringing water, and cleaning, watering dishes. The girl witnesses how on several occasions her mother persistently negotiates with her father about getting the girl to work in the house more. One day she secretly watched how her father shot one of the two horses for fox food. At the end of the story she let the second horse, Flora, escape, but the horse was still captured and butchered. Although the girl's younger brother announced proudly during the family dinner that it was his sister's fault that Flora got away, her father dismissed her with resignation and even good humour by saying that she was "only a girl."

Munro presents her characters through direct description and also shows them in action. In "Boys and Girls" the central character is a young girl who narrates the story about her life on a farm and about her search for gender identity. Through various episodes in the story we learn that the girl is courageous, physically strong, adventurous, and highly imaginative. Some of those qualities are typically masculine strengths and would be normally used to describe a male character. Feminism of Munro's central character is shown through her possession with those masculine qualities and with her exercising them in her everyday life. For example, every night when Laird, the girl's younger brother falls asleep, she arranges herself tightly under the bed covers and tells herself stories. According to the girl's memories, she "rescued people from a bombed building, shot two rabid wolves, and rode a fine horse spiritedly down the main street of Jubilee" (Barnet 254). The fact that those bedtime stories presented the opportunity for heroism, boldness and self-sacrifice, specks of the girl's courage, which is usually considered to be a male quality. The girl was also learning to shoot in reality, and although she could not hit anything yet, she practised definitely a masculine (male) hobby, which may have made her look manly in the eyes of the strangers.

From descriptions of the girl helping her farther to take care of the foxes, we conclude, that despite her young age she possessed enough physical strength to carry out jobs, which involve hard physical labour. One of the girl's jobs in summer was to bring water to the fox pens. Twice a day, after nine in the morning and then again after supper, she filled the drum at the water pump and trundled it down through the barnyard to the pens, parked it, filled her watering can, and went along the pens. She recalls sarcastically that Laird, her younger brother, "came too, with his little cream and green gardening can, filled too full and knocking against his legs and slopping water on his canvas shoes" (Barnet 255). As opposed to Laird, his older sister used her father's "real watering can," though she could only carry it three-quarters full. With great pride, the girl demonstrated to her father that she was capable of doing man's work and handling the real tools from the adult world.

Ironically, the girl perceived Laird only as a little boy, not seeing or not wanting to recognize a perspective of him eventually growing up and becoming a man. When one day the children's mother said to her husband, "Wait till Laird gets a little bigger, then you'll have a real help," the girl's entire nature furiously protested. She felt that no one "could imagine Laird remembering the padlock and cleaning the watering dishes with a leaf on the end of a stick, or even wheeling the tank without its tumbling over" (Barnet 256). In her opinion Laird was of "no help to anybody" because he usually swung himself sick on the swing, went around in circles, or tried to catch caterpillars. It was not until the girl turned eleven years old when she experienced her brother's physical strength. Once Laird and she were fighting, and "for the first time ever" she had to use all her strength against him. Even so, Laird still caught and pinned her arm for a moment, really hurting her. The farm worker Henry saw the fight and said, "Oh, that is where Laird is gonna show you, one of these days!" (Barnet 257). This was the first time when the girl realized that her brother, slowly but surely, began turning into a man. However, the feminist part of her character refused to surrender, saying that she "was getting bigger too."

From the two outstanding episodes we learn that the central character in "Boys and Girls" is not only courageous and athletic, but also adventurous. On the day the children's father is going to shoot one of the two horses, Mack, he sends them out of the stable to play around the house. The girl never saw her father shoot a horse, but she knew where it was done. Dying from curiosity, she leads Laird around to the front door of the barn, opens it carefully, and goes in.

The hay is low, and the children have to pile it up in one corner. Then the girl boostes her brother up and hoists herself. They find the knot holes in the barn walls and quietly watched Mack being shot. When Mack's legs stop kicking in the air and his muscles sink, the girl says in a congratulatory way, "Now you've seen how they shoot a horse" (Barnet 259). The procedure of shooting a horse is not something the girl wants to see, but as she admitted, "it was better to see and know as if a thing really happened" (Barnet 258). This confession characterizes the girl as a person of action and also communicates her need for being a center of attention. She does not want other people tell her how they saw a horse being shot; instead, she wants to watch the process herself so that she could tell about it.

Right after Mack was shot, the girl remembered how, when Laird was little, she had brought him into the barn and told him to climb the ladder to the top beam. When he did, she ran screaming to her father. Her mother leaned against the ladder crying while her father climbed up and brought Laird down. Both parents arrived at the conclusion that the girl simply was not watching her brother, and, of course, the boy was too little to know enough to tell. We find out from the narrative that the girl had done it not out of cruelty, but "out of a need for excitement and a desire for something to happen" so she could tell about it (Barnet 259). The life on the farm was safe and steady, and the girl carried out the same old chores day after day, year after year. It was the routine that the girl could not put up with, and it was a need for exciting adventure that inspired the girl to commit these two acts. Nothing can add more to an image of a feminist character than these two episodes where the girl basically acted as a leader. Both the times she told her younger brother exactly what she wanted him to do, and both times he obediently followed her orders. Here is another way to look at it: how often do we run into a traditional, non-feminist girl who wants to see a horse being shot and who puts her brother's life in danger for fun?

The same need for excitement along with unsatisfactory, boring reality boosts the young girl's immense imagination. The narrator lives in two worlds, imaginary and real, travelling back and forth in her mind between home and an exotic other place. The girl recalls how in her early bedtime stories she "rescued people from a bombed building, shot two rabid wolves, and rode a fine horse spiritedly down the main street of Jubilee." When the central character turns eleven years old, her fantasies undergo a substantial change. Now men rescued her and the stories were concerned with what the girl looked like. Even description of the fox pens was touched by the girl's vivid imagination that turned the entire animal area with a high guard fence into "a medieval town." The girl refers to her imaginary world as "recognizably mine" and is regretful of the real world, which does not present opportunities for courage, boldness, and self-sacrifice. As Carscallen writes, in Munro's writing "again and again we have the sense of a place or time or order of things standing apart from our own" (Carscallen 1). MacKendrick agrees with Carscallen by saying that "Munro's central characters often find themselves in circumstances where it seems that anything may happen," and that only these central characters "see the ordinary as extraordinary."(MacKendrick 115)

From another brief episode of meditation, we learn that the girl struggled to understand the reasons why her mother wanted her to help more in the house knowing that her daughter absolutely hated the housework. At first, the girl thought that her mother did it "simply out of perversity and to try her power," but after she matured a bit, she regretfully admitted: "It did not occur to me that she [mother] could be lonely or jealous" (Barnet 256). This sudden wisdom and sympathy appear in the girl's character not only due to her mature age, but also because she was a true female. On the basis of this episode we can say that females usually can explain the inner motives of human behaviour better than males can.

The word "girl" no longer seemed innocent and unburdened like a word "child." For the first time she realized that a girl was not, as she supposed, simply what she was; it was that she had to become. As the narrator says, "It was a definition, always touched with emphasis, with reproach and disappointment. Also it was a joke on me" (Barnet 257). She felt that people around expected a certain behavior from her, the kind of behaviour that is appropriate, typical, and socially acceptable for a girl.

During a few weeks when the children's grandmother stayed with the family, the girl got a third chance to feel directly a social pressure associated with the word "girl." The girl heard quite a few alarming things such as "Girls don't slam doors like that," and "Girls keep their knees together when they sit down." The worst the narrator hears is the response "That's none of the girl's business" when she asks some subject-related questions (Barnet 257). The girl continues to slam the doors and sit as awkwardly as possible, thinking that by such measures she keeps herself free. Given that much information, we can clearly see a conflict between regarding herself as the essential, and the social pressure to accept herself as a passive object.

Professor Blodget brings up an interesting nuance of the theme by pointing out that the word "girl" has been qualified twice in the story at its first and final usage by the word "only." Based on this, he suggestes that in "Boys and Girls" a state of becoming a girl "was accompanied by a sense of irrevocable separation and loss" (Blodget 35). By the fourth encounter with the hidden meanings of the word "girl," the girl's destiny is sealed in her father's final words "She is only a girl," which absolves and dismisses her for good. One is surprised by the ease, with which men can label girls, women, as "only girls" based just on one act of kindness. To the girl in the story, this label means a loss of not only her status as the father's helper, but also a loss of her individual identity and the freedom of choice. Blodget contributes greatly to this understanding of the story by a remarkable historic insight, where he explains:

> To be only a girl is rejection of a radical kind, for in the world of the rural Ontario farm in the late thirties and early forties aspirations that went beyond those of sexual stereotypes were not simply wrong, they were taboo. They are not corrected by anger, but by a more powerful method, by "good humor." The implication is that to be a girl is a destiny that carries with it a certain stupidity that cannot be corrected. (Blodgett 33)

Let us now analyze the indications in the text that foreshadow the internal changes occurring in the girl. After watching her father pelting the foxes on a regular basis, and especially after watching Mack being shot, the girl claims that she is used to seeing the death of the animals, and that she accepts it as a necessity by which the farmers live. However, the girl is surprised by a new sentimental feeling that fills up her heart. On the day she finds out that Flora is going to be shot, the girl feels a little ashamed. She recalls how "there was a new weariness, a sense of holding-off, in my attitude to my father and his work" (Barnet 260). By this slight bit of foreshadowing Munro gives us a clue that the seemingly masculine girl began slowly turning into a sensitive young lady. And surely, later on in the story the narrator leaves not even an iota of doubt in the reader's mind about the core changes that had occurred in her internal world. The girl describes how she decorated her part of the children's bedroom trying to make it fancy, and how she separated her section from the one of her brother. More importantly, the plot of her bedtime stories had also significantly transformed. Although the story might start off in the old way, "with a spectacular danger, a fire or wild animals," and for a while the girl might rescue people; then things would change around, and instead, somebody would rescue her. The significance of a twist here is that "somebody" was usually "a boy from our class at school, or even Mr. Campbell, our teacher" (Barnet 261). Perhaps the girl indicates somehow that she was romantically attracted to her teacher.

At this point the imaginary story is concerned with what the girl looked like – what dress did she wear and how long her hair was. By the time the girl worked out these details in her mind, the initial excitement of the story is lost. All these confessions only prove the original claim that the narrator is a "girl," which, among other things, means surrendering to a male savior. Being a girl also means having a soft heart and emotional personality. We can find a proof of this statement in the two episodes where the girl allows Flora escape and where she cries while her father questioned her about that positive gesture. According to the girl's own recollection, she could not understand why she disobeyed her father when instead of shutting the gate, she opened it as wide as she could. She claimed with confidence that she did not plan this in advance, or she did not decide to do this on the spot; she just did it. The irony of this situation comes to the surface when the girl tells us that she completely understands the interconnection of the chain of events she interfered. She knew that her father had paid for the horse, that the family needed the meat to feed the foxes, that the family needed the foxes to make their living, that her father would catch the horse anyway, and that all she did was that she created more work for him. Let us contemplate about the force that pushed the girl to free the horse. Obviously, the girl did not wish for the horse to die. But why? Perhaps the horse that was about to lose her life, reminded the girl of herself who was about to lose her freedom of self-concept and a freedom of choice. The fact that Flora broke free and ran away makes one think that she sensed the coming end. The horse ran away because she did not want to die. Flora's unwillingness to die symbolizes the girl's unwillingness to work in the house for her mother. To the girl, not only her freedom, but also her entire future would die with the death of the horse. Perhaps, that is why the girl feels so closely connected to the horse, and that is why the girl, led by her own subconscious, reflexively helps Flora escape.

At the very end of the story we see how emotional the narrator really is. During the family dinner Laird announced that his sister could have shut the gate but she did not do so. When the father asked his daughter if that statement was true, she nodded quietly, swallowed food with great difficulty, and began crying. A typical female reaction to the father's question, tears that flooded her eyes, illustrates the emotional aspect of being a girl. The society created certain rules of acceptable social behaviour for boys and girls, for men and women. From the early childhood, the boys are taught not to display their sensitivity; in other words, they are taught not to cry in public. By contrast, it is perfectly fine for the girls to cry in any place, at any time, for the reason whatsoever. According to Rasporich, the girl's final tears suggest compliance (Rasporich 38). The girl only commented that she was ashamed of her tears, of the mere fact of crying. Perhaps, her sensitive feminine nature confronted her feminist desire to stay strong as a man, and when the first finally won over, the girl burst into tears. A fear of punishment for letting Flora escape could be another possible reason for crying. Munro made her central character cry only once during the entire narrative, and she purposely saved this episode until (for) the end the story. By using this technique Munro made a powerful point – she revealed the conflict between the two parts of the girl's self: masculine and feminine.

In "Boys and Girls" Munro recorded the humiliated and anguished psychology of a child who was being conditioned by society to become a definition – a girl, which she perceived as a joke on herself. The characterization, symbolism, and theme are the three tools Munro uses to explore the process of self-discovery of a young farm girl. The child finds herself no longer free to help her fox-farmer father outdoors, but instead is forced to do the hated housework. The climax of the story occurs when the girl frees a horse that is about to be shot and by so doing demonstrates that she is "only a girl" as her father comments. The story pictures a contradiction between the girl's status as a real human being and her vocation as a female. Although there is no real resolution to the situation in "Boys and Girls" and it seems that the girl is conforming to social rules by adjusting her fantasies, she is partly victorious when she opens the gate in an attempt to rescue the fated horse. In the girl's opinion, the horse symbolizes freedom, and the death of the animal means the end of her own freedom and the loss of her identity.

Works Cited

Barnet, Sylvan, et al. *An Introduction to Literature.* 12th edn. New York: Longman, 2001.

Blodgett, E.D. *Alice Munro.* Boston: Twayne Publishers, 1988.

Carscallen, James. *The Other Country: Patterns in the Writing of Alice Munro.* Ontario: ECW Press, 1993.

MacKendrick, Louis K. *Probable Fictions: Alice Munro's Narrative Acts.* Ontario: ECW Press, 1983.

Rasporich, Beverly J. *Dance of the Sexes: Art and Gender in the Fiction of Alice Munro.* The University of Alberta Press, 1990.

Dialectics of the Opposites in Two of the Last Plays of W.B. Yeats

Dr. Swati Surbhi

In his reaction against the soullessness of the Naturalistic English plays, W.B. Yeats first gravitated towards the French symbolists, who equally failed to satisfy him. So he turned to the east in search of a suitable model of the type plays he wanted to write. It was a sort of revelation to him when he discovered the Japanese Noh Drama which, to him was "a distinguished, indirect, symbolic, aristocratic form." Built around a single action, it was extremely concise. The use of mask was a medium to depersonalize and universalize the characters. Ghosts and other supernatural agents interfered with man's actions. The ecstatic dance at the climactic moment made the play highly dramatic. Yeats adopted the Noh model for his plays and retained almost all its features in the plays of his middle, especially in the four plays for dancers. But he also knew that very few of his even "cultivated audience" would understand their literacy and mythological allusions; so he derived most of his allusions from the subjective European conventions, archetypal symbols, and from Irish myths and legends. But he hardly revealed their sources, for he desired his plays to be "mysterious, doing its work by suggestion, not by direct statement, a complexity of rhythm, colour and gesture." Although dance figures prominently in Yeats's last four plays, but other Noh features diminish gradually. Giving the reasons for modifying or dropping the conventions of the Noh in them he said that they seemed out of place on the newly founded Abbey Theatre. Why should musician or actor fold and unfold a cloth when proscenium curtain was there? Why carry to the stage drums, gong and flute when the orchestra was there? The plays under discussion, *The King of the Great Clock Tower* (1935) and *A Full Moon in March* (1935) imitate the Noh model in so far as "the climax in a dance, substitute suggestion for representation, but unlike Japanese plays, they are stage plays."

Yeats realized that his poetic plays, to be self-supporting, had to be popular with the audience. Accordingly, some of the items of the Noh, especially those unfamiliar and unintelligible to his audience, were dropped or modified in the plays of his last phase. *The King of the Great Clock Tower* and *A Full Moon in March* mark the highest point of Yeats's experiment with the form of dance drama. They were magnificently acted and danced, as he wrote Olivia Shakespeare. The polarizations of the opposites were successfully fused and elevated in the form. This marked a high degree of stylization. Though highly symbolic, they proved "most effective" theatrically.

The King of the Great Clock Tower was first written in prose, and published in 1934. Then it was rendered in verse and published in 1935. Again he rewrote it and published it as *A Full Moon in March,* as he was not satisfied with the plot. Giving the reason, he wrote:

> In *The King of the Great Clock Tower* are three characters, King, Queen and Stroller, and that is a character too many, reduced to the essentials, Queen and Stroller, and the fable should have greater intensity. I started a fresh and called the version *A Full Moon in March.*

Both the plays are quite similar in theme and intensity of presentation; the only difference is that the Stroller in the former is replaced by the Swineherd in the latter. As the King has been removed from *A Full Moon in March,* it is the Queen who orders for beheading the protagonist. F.A.C. Wilson rightly maintains:

> *A Full Moon in March* and *The King of the Great Clock Tower* have really no right to separate existence, but the high standard of his lyrics probably inclined Yeats to publish and preserve both.

Both the plays have simple and similar story line. The King recalls a year ago a woman walked into his palace and he married her without verifying her identity. She is mum and impassive all the time. A mystery surrounds her all the time. Equally mysterious is the arrival of the Stroller in the court, and his insistence on seeing the Queen he has praised in his songs without seeing. When the King says that the Queen is sitting on the throne in front of him, he bursts out impudently:

> Neither so red, nor white, nor full in the breast.
> As I had thought what matters for all that
> So long as I proclaim her everywhere most beautiful.

When asked to go away now that he has seen the Queen, he quotes god Aengus that prophesied:

> O listen, for I speak the very words –
> "On stroke of midnight when the old year dies,
> Upon that stroke, the tolling of that bell,
> The Queen shall kiss your mouth"

The King feels so outraged that he orders for beheading the impudent Stroller. When the severed head was brought and kept on the throne, the Queen who has maintained mysterious silence all along, begins to dance before it, and when she puts the head on her shoulder, it begins to sing of an erotic pleasure that the dead enjoy, that far exceeds the nuptial pleasure of men:

> All those living wretches crave Prerogatives of the dead that have Spring heroic from the grave Crossed fingers there in pleasure can Exceed the nuptial bed of man.

The Queen goes on singing and dancing. Then comes the climax. As soon as the tower clock strikes midnight, the Queen kisses the severed, the King draws the sword as if to strike the Queen, then lays it down at her feet, and kneels down in reverence. The play ends with an excellent song. All these climactic events are baffling and esoteric, and leave the audience dumb founded.

The main event of this play as well as of *A Full Moon in March* reminds the reader of the Biblical story of John the Baptist and the Dancer Salome. But Yeats acknowledges that its immediate source is Oscar Wilde's play *Salome* (1892), which presents a similar story of women's enraged cruelty. Yeats also cites an old Gaelic legend as another source, in which a certain man swears to sing the praise of a certain woman, his head is severed and the head sings.

Symbolically the Stroller's love for the Queen is spiritual. The Clock Tower represents time, and the midnight the moment of death and entry into heaven. Everything happens as if in a predestined manner. "On the microcosmic plane," writes F.A.C. Wilson, "the symbolism is of the liberation of each individual spirit after death, when man enters upon the joys of heaven." The songs in the play are the integral part of the play, they are integrated into the symbolic meaning of the play. At the stroke of midnight the temporal and the timeless are united; the opposites are reconciled. The severed head sings, the Queen kisses it and dances ecstatically as if impelled by some unseen force. It is the moment of annihilation as well as creation. The play through song and dance is elevated to the highest level of dramatic art.

The symbolic antagonism between the Queen and the stranger, the Swineherd is more sharply presented in the play *A Full Moon in March.* The King is dispensed with and the protagonist is a Swineherd. The direct conflict between the Queen and the Swineherd makes the plot of the play tighter. The virgin Queen, extremely beautiful and equally cruel proclaims that she will marry the man who satisfies her with his song. A Swineherd comes to take up the challenge even at the risk of his life. The Queen declares that she has punished many for their impudence. She is cruel as the winter of virginity. But the Swineherd is not deterred and declares that she will be won at full moon in March, as the beggars of his country said. When the Queen asks what she will get in return if she agrees to marry him, he simply says:

> A song the night of love
> An ignorant forest and the dung of swine.

The Queen feels greatly outraged and asks the captain of the guard to behead him, adding:

> All here heard the man and all have judged;
> I led him, that I might not seem unjust,
> From point to point, established in all eyes
> That he came .... not to sing but to heap
> Complexities of insult upon my head.

The Swineherd is beheaded. Then the scene climaxes into dancing and singing of the Queen, embracing the severed heads and kissing it, and the several head singing. This may be taken as the union of the self with its anti-self, growing out of love hate relationship.

According to Yeats's system, such intercourse or intersection between the opposites is essential for achieving unity of being, and self-sacrifice is the key to that unity. The Swineherd sacrifices his life for the desired union, and the Queen surrenders to the antithetical force represented by the Swineherd. From her proud position, and virgin cruelty she descends to the reproductive world of nature, represented by the child. She sings as if in self-defense:

> Child and darling, hear my song
> Never cry I did you wrong:
> Cry that wrong that come not from me
> But my virgin cruelty
> Greater my love before you came,
> Greater when I loved in shame,
> Greatest when there broke from me
> Storm of virgin cruelty.

The dramatic encounter between the Queen and the Swineherd may be worked out in terms of archetypal tale of a proud, disdainful princess ultimately marrying a filthy man. In the opinion of Mr. Wilson:

> The play is "ritual projection" of Yeats's metaphysical vision, which reconciles the antithesis of temporal and spiritual, male and female, war and love, as well as providing an analogue to or paradigm of poetic creation. There is a condescension on either side, the poet sacrifices his well-being for ecstasies of creation, while .... sacrifices her autonomy and ideal perfection as to "incarnate in the world of time."

In the opening line of *A Full Moon in March*, "Every Loutish Lad in Love" nature of love is illustrated in the line "crown of gold or dung of swine," love is absolute whether it is spiritual (crown of gold) or utter grossness (dung of swine). The Queen symbolizes spirituality, and the Swineherd carnality. In a vigorous, bitter verse, almost Rabelaisian, the playwright depicts the grossness of the Swineherd:

> Queen looks at me, look long at these foul rags,
> At hair more foul and ragged than my rags
> Look at my scratched foul flesh.
> Have I not come through dust and mire?
> My origin more foul than rag or flesh.

Swineherd's gross unwholesomeness may be taken to represent the fallen condition of man. The Queen represents purity and her infatuation for the Swineherd may be taken to suggest that divinity is still in love with humanity. In the musician's song that concludes the play the Queen and the Swineherd appear like Jack and Jill carrying pitchers where in "Time's completed treasure is which suggests that they are now above and beyond time." The solution to the problem of antinomies coming together is provided through the question and answer of the attendants. When the first attendant asks "why must those holy haughty feet descent?" the second one replies: "For desecration and the lover's night." Commenting on the highly symbolic nature of the concluding verses, Wilson writes:

> It is their symbolic meaning that makes them so impressive, and provides as completely satisfying a conclusion as the trick ending in Yeats's previous play. For to our surprise we see that in this resurrection it is the Queen who descends. Yeats's aim is to stress that "eternity is in love with the productions of time."

The consummation of virginity lies in its desecration just as that of the divine in its reconciliation with fallen inhabitants of this mundane world.

Works Cited

Bradley, Anthony. *William Butler Yeats.* New York: Fredric Ungar, 1979.
Wilson, F.A.C. *W.B. Yeats and Tradition.* London: Gollanez, 1958.
Yeats, W.B. *Collected Plays of W.B. Yeats.* London: Macmillan, 1960.
Yeats, W.B. *Cutting of an Agate.* London: Macmillan, 1919.
———. *Plays an Controversies.* London: Macmillan, 1927.

The Influence of Magahi on the English Speakers of Magah Region in Bihar

Dr. Awinash Kumar Sushil

English speakers of Magah generally pronounce school/sku:l/as/iskul/. The phonological errors made by them reveal that these are the outcome of interlingual interference as well as poor exposure to oral English. The basic differences between the sound systems of English and Magahi are also responsible for a large number of phonological errors. Magahi is almost phonologically written language; nearly every sound is consistently represented by a certain letter (or combination of letters) and every letter (or combination of letters) represents a sound. The number of Magahi letters and sounds shows a consistency, which is absent in English, English has 26 letters for writing and 44 sounds for speech. One letter (or combination of letters) represents different sounds at different places and more than one letter may represent one sound. There are five vowel letters for 20 vowel sounds and 21 consonant letters for 24 consonant sounds in English. This characteristic of English alphabet and its sound system confuse the English speakers of Magah region who expect their L_1 and L_2 (Hindi) features to hold good in English and tend to pronounce every word as they see it in the written form and so nearly all Magahi speakers fail to distinguish between certain differing English sounds when the ears of a native speaker perceive the distinction without effort. In other words wrong perception of English speech sounds leads to wrong production of speech sounds or substitution of one speech sound by another speech sound.

Regional lengthening of sound is used to show affection and intimacy. "Sir" and "Madam" are spoken as "respected sir" or "sir jee" or "respected Madam," "Shrimanjee," "Sarkar," "Hujur I will fall at your lotus feet" is also used. Since Magah region has been a feudel region so there is a feudal hangover from English and more respectability is shown than required by using Baboos and ornate and religious style. In some cases passive voice is used to show respect, as in "be seated" instead of "please sit down." "Aaw and Baitha" for "please come in, please sit down."

One says "please be seated, I am coming back very soon." One starts coming before going. In England one would say, "Would you mind sitting down for a while, I shan't be too long?"

Moreover, redundant sounds and words are used, such as "ine," unne," Court-fort, Court-kachhari, Per-panchayat. There are unnecessary pause between words and some words are unnecessarily added to English words such as, 'fort' and 'per' are added to court and panchayat.

The last sound of "teeth" and the first sound of "the" are dental in English but the speakers of Magahi language usually produce them as alveolar. They speak "f" as "ph." By mistake, the morpheme "s" is pronounced as /s/ in dogs, roads, girls, boys names, etc. The correct pronunciation of "s" is /z/ in these words as they are voiced sounds. Similarly "ed" in seated, decided, embedded, locked and laughed are never pronounced as /id/ and /t/. In other parts of India also seated is not pronounced as /si:ted/ decided as /disaidid/embedded as / imbedid/, laughed as /la:ft/ and locked as/lakt/.

Moreover code-mixing is common, for example, "Is Train late he/ hai." Only he/hai is Magahi word; two English words are used out of three words in this sentence and yet it is not an English sentence. Some English words are easier to understand than the words of Magahi.

Some English sounds also don't exist in Magahi language and so they are mixed, leading to breakdown in communication. In English /h/ sound in which; what, where, when, wherever, whatever and while and /b/ sound in bomb, comb, tomb, climb, lamb and limb are silent but English speakers of Magah pronounce them. They also use /r/ sound, although it is used only when it is followed by a vowel or as intrusive /r/, as in: There are boys (r-not pronounced). There are ants (/r/ is pronounced).

Thus, phonological errors made by Magahi speakers clearly demonstrate their learning difficulties at the phonological level. Their phonological difficulties can be explained in terms of following interlingual as well as intralingual factors:

1. The absence of near equivalent English sounds in Magahi.
2. Differences of sound distribution in English and Magahi.
3. Differences of sound values in English and Magahi.
4. False generalization based on English phonological features.
5. The lack of stress pattern (syllabic stress) in Magahi speech.
6. Poor exposure to spoken English.
7. Inadequate teaching of English pronunciation.

The last factor is quite significant so far as a remedial approach to phonological errors is concerned. Socially it, too, can be said that we (Magahi people) are not language conscious. If the people of this area go through any book then the substance of that book is important for them, not the language of the book due to which we find that some teachers of science tell their students that they should think only about the substance of any material. These teachers think that the meaning of a language is to convey the matter anyhow and for this they don't believe in the accuracy of language. They think that the responsibility to maintain the dignity of a language goes to the students of language and literature only, not to the students of other disciplines and so, they teach the students however, in English but they use bilingual method to teach science. I mean, teachers use the material which is in English medium but to make their points clear they use other dialects and distort the sound of English words.

There is a tendency among the speakers to imitate the pronunciation of the speakers who belong to the so-called prestigious stratam and areas since the teachers belong to the prestigious stratum and they, too, use the distorted form of a word so students, too, try to imitate the same pronunciation. As far as schools are concerned, the teachers of English are not well in English and they are not in the habit of speaking in English. It is because they are teaching in Hindi medium schools. Most of the English medium schools are being run as English medium but actually their faculty is not well in English then what can be said about the students. And so far as spoken English Institutes are concerned, no doubt they are working for the betterment of the English language but most of the Institutes have not well qualified faculty. One who can communicate in English can be the teacher of spoken English. It is the general qualification of most of the teachers of these spoken institutes. These institutes are in good position; it is because there is a need and craze for spoken English. Most of the learners, who learn spoken English, have not sound knowledge of English language. They are given some structures and are forced to speak English anyhow. For these institutes fluency is important; accuracy has nothing to do with a language; the meaning of a language is to convey the thoughts anyhow; there is no need of grammar and pronunciation in English. In some schools teachers do not exactly understand the process of teaching English. They divide their work into reading, writing, grammar, translation, dictation, composition and words. They feel fully satisfied if the students are kept busy during the whole period of teaching. They treat these related aspects of English as separate subjects. They fail to realize that all these are different means to an end. They never co-ordinate these different aspects. English has to be taught principally as a language of comprehension, rather than as a literary language. Since they have no hold over language and their guides, too, are incompetent so the speakers from these institutes and schools become satisfied after having the knowledge of some English words and some English sentences. Since their knowledge is superficial and they lack interest in English language so, their learning is always incomplete as far as the knowledge of pronunciation is concerned. It must be remembered that these types of speakers while looking for a word, consult only Hindi to English dictionary or English to Hindi dictionary. They hardly consult any English to English dictionary. They lack the knowledge of phonetic transcription so, for them the meaning of the word is important, not the pronunciation of the word. Daniel Jones' *English Pronouncing Dictionary is a peculiar thing for them.*

Owing to lexical borrowing, too, the English speakers of Magah problem. As we know that in this type of borrowing lexical items or words are borrowed from foreign sources. This is a very common thing for a language and one can say that all languages show a tendency to borrow words. Again the sociocultural factors play a crucial determining role in it. A language whose speakers come into close contact with those of other languages has a greater chance of borrowing lexical items so Magahi, too, has borrowed words from different languages in which English, too, can be included since they have no proper method for teaching pronunciation to the English speakers of Magah so, we find that the words of English are used in distorted form or in a form which is not acceptable.

A detailed analysis of phonological influence reveals that there is an impact of Magahi on the English speakers of Magah. However, it is not the only field where Magahi has its influence over English but in grammar, too, we find the impact of Magahi on the English speakers of Magah.

The grammatical errors by English speakers of Magah involve a wide range of grammar-based issues such as the correct use of verb forms and patterns, auxiliaries, articles, preposition, number, tense, pronoun, noun, phrase, word-order, etc. These errors relate to various aspects of English morphology and syntax. They arise from various sources: interlingual errors of interference from Hindi, interlingual errors within the target language, i.e., English, sociolinguistic context of communication, psycholinguistic or cognitive strategies and many other variables.

A careful interpretation of Magahi speakers reveals that many well-formed sentences are also erroneous because the speakers want to convey a different meaning through them. These sentences appear superficially well formed in terms of the rules of English grammar and use, but they cannot be interpreted normally in the context. These covertly idiosyncratic sentences have been compared with reconstructed sentences (the correct sentences) to determine the level and kind of idiosyncrasy. For example the following sentences from the speakers of English of Magah:

> Then I do so.
> Then comes the ragging period.
> I feel very happy.
> I stay there.

The above sentences appear to be perfectly well-formed grammatically but an interpretation of the context in which they have been used, shows that the speakers want to convey a past meaning and instead of using subject + verb[2] (past) structure, they have used subject + verb structure as they have still not internalized the simple past pattern. Let us now take the following examples:

> It has come.
> *(I aa gel he).*
> He has finished the work.
> *(U kam khatm kar del he.)*
> I have met another student.
> *(Hum dusar bidyarti se milalee he)*
> She has told me.
> *(U hamara kahalan he)*
> They have warned us.
> *(U sab hamanee ke chetayalan he)*

The speakers to convey past meaning reflecting their inability to use past tense structures correctly have also used the above sentences. Some more examples will further illustrate the point:

Ram: Shyam, where are you going?
(Shyam, kahan jai tha?)
Shyam: I was going to the market.
(Ham bazar jai thalee)
(Correct: I am going to the market.)
Mohan: what are you doing
(Ka karai tha)
Hari: I was writing a letter.
(Correct: I am writing a letter.)
(Ham Chhithi Likhee Thi).

Again, the above sentences cannot be normally interpreted and they require plausible explanations. The students use past continuous tense structures showing their lack of competence.

They also use simple past structure to convey a present meaning. All these covert errors have been included here along with the overtly idiosyncratic sentences which are superficially ill-formed in terms of rules of English grammar and usage.

English speakers of Magah region use a large number of Magahi structures while trying to communicate in English. When they do so, they think in Magahi and use words from English language, much as one would handle word for word translation. As English and Magahi differ considerably with respect to surface syntax, the use of Magahi structures results in interlingual errors. The following composition specimens illustrate this point. The literal translation of the sentences is given below each one of them:

He is sick since Friday.
(Sukarwar se beemar he/heth).
He is a doctor for five years.
(Panch baris se dactor he/hath).

The above examples show that Magahi speakers use Magahi structure (Subject + is/am/are + adjective/noun + for/since + noun) for English structure (Subject + has/have + been + adjective/noun +

for/since + noun). Because of the literal transfer of Magahi word "he/ hath" to English. There is no distinction in Magahi between has/have been or is/am/are. The following errors also show the retention of Magahi linguistic items in English:

He did not get a money.
[Source of analogy: unaka ego paisa n milalak: retention of ego (a)]
Met with my friend.
[Ham apan dost se milclee: retention of se with.]

Now take the following examples of omission errors:

He is good boy.
[U achchha laika he.]
It is very rich country.
[I bahut dhanee desh he.]
He is honest man.
[U imandar adeamee he/hath.]
He is idiot.
[U murakh he.]
Two pen.
[doo go kalam]
Some flower.
[tanee manee phool.]
Many poet.
[Baree manee kabee.]
Three part
[teen bhag.]

Above examples show omission of article by the English speakers of Magah on the basis of L_1 analogy. Some examples show error in number that indicates that speakers are transferring Magahi structures to English system.

The process of overgeneralization, too, is found in this case that refers to the process of creating deviant structures by the speakers by making false inductive generalization about the target language system on the basis of the restricted data to which they are exposed. It covers errors resulting from interferences between forms and functions of the language being spoken. Magahi speakers of English seem to make inductive generalization about English morphology and syntactic system on the basis of the data to which they are exposed. This data is restricted because of the lack of naturalness of the environment and lack of concrete referents and target language models. Magahi learner's exposure to English language is limited to the classroom with the teachers as the only target language model. Thus, English speakers of Magah overgeneralize and produce incorrect forms by analogy. The following examples demonstrate this point:

One of the important thing.
One of the big hotel.
One of the best place.

Overgeneralization is based on the exposure to structures like one thing, one hotel, one place, i.e. one takes singular form.

English speakers of Magah like other L_2 speakers of English try to reduce the linguistic burden by removing grammatical morpheme like noun and verb inflections, articles, auxiliary verbs, prepositions. The following examples make this point clear.

As he want.
My relative live there.
It cover.
He get up early.
His greed increase.
The government try.

The speakers do not use "s/es" in third person singular number in the present tense by generalizing the verb without "s/es" inflection for first, second and third person respectively. Thus, they remove the necessity of concord.

USA is rich country.
(Source of analogy: He is rich).
It is home utensil.
(Analogy: It is my home).
He was honest man.
(Analogy: He was honest).

An analysis of overgeneralization errors of our speakers also reveals that whenever there are both regular and irregular forms and constructions in English, speakers apply the rules that are used to produce the regular one to those that are irregular, resulting in errors of regularization. The following examples contain regularization errors:

> Wonderful sceneries. (Correct: wonderful scenery).
> We have to do some home works.
> (Correct: We have to do some home work).
> I like fruits. (Correct: I like fruit).
> All his works. (Correct: All his work).

In some cases the influence of Magahi on the English speakers of Magah is due to the ignorance of rule restrictions. There are many uses, which reflect the influence of Magahi on the speakers. The speaker's failure to learn condition under which grammatical rules are applied is responsible for this sort of influence. The speakers do not observe the restrictions of grammatical rules and apply them to contexts where that should not be applied. These rules restriction errors may be accounted for in terms of wrong analogy of the role learning of grammar rules. Our speakers commit a lot of rule restriction errors. The following rule restriction errors by our speakers are due to wrong analogy. The possible source of analogy is given below, each idiosyncratic sentence:

> Capacity of working decreases.
> (He has no capacity to work).
> He must know the English.
> (The English are wise).
> He asked to me.
> (He said to me).

The rote learning of grammar rules by Magahi speakers of English is also a major factor causing rule restriction errors. As the teaching of English in Magah is characterized by a heavy doze of prescriptive grammar, our speakers commit a lot of rote learning errors. The speakers make use of previously acquired rules in new situation without considering applicability or otherwise. The following examples illustrate this:

We were eaten together at a mess.
(Correct: We ate together at a mess).
It should be improve. (Correct: It should be improved).
He can be select. (Correct: He can be selected).

Furthermore, different professionals of Magah also misuse English. The journalists of Magah use "that" after statement and double inverted commas. An IAS officer usually writes "enclosed herewith." (Here "with" is redundant.) Period is used after minister, doctor and salutation in a letter. An engineer says, "I have constructed or built many houses" instead of I have got constructed or built up lots of houses. A judge also uses obsolete language. Dot is used after "Mr" in "Mr justice." A doctor would ask, "How many latrines have you passed? And how are you feeling?" and a patient would say, "I have sores on the path of my latrine." Now no dot or period is used in Mr, Mrs, Dr, Ph D, D Litt, MA, BA, IA, etc. but it is used by mistake by most of the people. However, it is not used in UNESCO and UNO. The English speakers of Magah do not use stress and intonation also correctly. Suprasegmental phonemes change meaning as in. I hate a woman, but the speakers of Magah don't care for them. They superimpose the intonation of their mother tongue on English, sounding at times, as if, they were singing "Biraha" (a folk tale in the form of a song) or speaking their mother tongue, not English.

The people of Magah are generally wedded to land and their voice is rough rather than soothing. It is generally said, "Rahalee Magah Bolalee "Re," Ihe La Tu Marabe Re" (I belong to Magah so I am using "Re" as vocative case. Will you beat me for this?) And so, due to tone or rhythm, too, it can be easily said that English is not a natural flow of language in Magah. It is unconscious rendering of the mother tongue. So, it sounds strange and artificial. However, there are some good speakers and writers of English even in Magah region.

Works Cited

Aryanee, Sampati. *Magahi Bhasha aur sahitya.* Patna: Bohar Rastra Bhasa Parishad, 2000.

Aryanee, Sampati. *Magahi Wyakaran Aaur Rachana.* Patna: Sandeep Publishing, 1992.

Bolinger, Dwight; Sears, Donald, A. *Aspects of Language.* New York: Harcourt Brace Jovanovich, Inc, 1981.

Jones, Daniel. *English Pronouncing Dictionary*. Cambridge: Cambridge University Press, 2006.

Prasad, Saryoo. *Magahi Phonology*. New Delhi: Concept Publishing Company, 2008.

Prasad, Shaileshwar, Sati. "Teaching of English in Bihar," *The British Lingua's Souvenir*. Patna: BAP Private Limited, 2002-03.

Rajimwale, Sharad. *Elements of General Linguistics*. New Delhi: Rama Brothers India Pvt. LTD, 2004.

Sinha, Sidheshwardhari, "Bihari English" *The British Lingua's Souvenir*. Patna: BAP Private Limited, 2002-2003.

Multilayered Social Messages in Girish Karnad's *Hayavadana*

Dr. Niraj

Girish Karnad's *Hayavadana* is a play having multilayered social messages. *Hayavadana* is based on Thomas Mann's story titled *Transposed Heads*, which in turn is based on the story in *Vetal Panchavimshati* but Karnad draws heavily on Thomas Mann's story. He uses the story to explore the theme of incompleteness, human destiny, a world of trangled relationships and struggle for perfection.

In the beginning of the play, Karnad presents the sub-plot of Hayavadana, a character representative of incompleteness in form. That is the main theme of the play both as prologue and as a story. Hayavadana is a man with the head of the horse. "Haya" means horse and "Vadana" means face. He has been trying to get rid of his head and become a complete man. His problem is alienation as well as incompleteness, the incompatibility of his head and body and his inability to find his society haunt him. He cannot join the world of Divine since he is rejected by his father; the animal is denced to him because he does not have his mother's advantage of having complete animal body, and the equine face makes him stronger among men. Bhagavata feels that it may be due to the error committed in the past birth but Hayavadana says that it has nothing to do with the last birth and further narrates his story. He says that his mother was a princess of Karnataka. When she came of age, her father wanted that she should choose her own husband. Hence the princes of different states in the world were invited and they all came from China, Persia, Africa but she did not like any of them. The last one to come was the prince of Araby. Hayavadana's mother took one look at the handsome prince sitting on the great white horse and fainted. His father at once decided that this was the man and all arrangements for the wedding were made. When Hayavadana's mother woke up and said that she would not marry the prince but the horse. No one could dissuade her. Ultimately, she was married off to the white horse. She married the horse and lived with it for fifteen years. When the stallion turned into a *gandharva* (a celestial being) after fifteen years, she refused to accompany him to the heavenly abode. Hence the enraged *gandharva* cursed her to be a horse. She happily galloped away, ignoring her horse faced yet human bodied child.

Chance or Fate seems to play an important role in *Hayavadana.* The first important character Hayavadana himself is the victim of fate. His mother, according to the story, was a princess who married a stallion instead of a human being. The offspring of a horse is likely to inherit the character of the progenitor. He gets the head of a horse and body of a man, a grotesque and incongruous figure. He is a victim of chance. His mother could well marry any of the princes who had come in the hope of getting her hand, but she felt a strong infatuation for the horse and she fainted as she saw "the great white stallion." No one could dissuade her. So ultimately she was married off to "the white stallion." Naturally Hayavadana comes to have a monstrous figure. Hayavadana is sore to find that he cannot fit in the society either of horses or of men. So he wishes to be complete – he cannot accept his fate. But is not in the power of man to reverse the course of nature. Therefore he is advised to go on pilgrimage in the hope that something unusual may happen again, to grant him completeness that he desires. He has made his efforts and is now convinced that his efforts will come to nothing. So now he has left himself to Fate. His past was determined by Fate and the future is to be built by Fate. Hayavadana is in search of identity and completeness of his physical body. There is also a struggle for perfection. Hayavadana all his life struggles for being a perfect (complete) man.

The story within the story starts when Bhagavata takes the reader to the city of Dharampura where two friends live. This is a triangular love story of Davadatta, Kapila and Padmini. Devadatta, an intelligent son of learned Brahmin Vidyasagar, was fair in colour, and Kapila the son of an ironsmith Lohita was dark in complexion but in physical strength he is unique. Fate has brought two persons of two opposite temperaments Devadatta and Kapita so close to each other that they are two bodies and one soul. Generally persons of same nature and taste become friends, but here fate plays strange tricks. Devadatta a poet as he is, has taken fancy to several girls, but Padmini has bewitched him – "It does look as though this sixteenth girl has really caught our Devadatta in her net." Devadatta tells Kapila – "I know this girl is beyond my wildest dreams. But still – I can't help wanting her – I can't help it." It is nothing but chance machinations of Fate, that he is hooked by a girl who is not an enchantress in the strict sense of the word. Padmini loves Devadatta for his intellect and Kapila for his physical strength. But the scale of love tilts towards Kapila. She dreams of a man that combines the qualities of both and fate drives her to join Devadatta's head with Kapila's body, all unknowingly. The incompleteness of human desire is symbolized by Padmini. Now she became the happiest woman on earth – "fabulous body fabulous brain – fabulous Devadatta." Devadatta has strange experiences "you know, I'd always thought I had to use one's brains while wrestling, or fencing or swimming. But this body just doesn't wait for thoughts, it acts!" For sometime Devadatta remains a blend of himself and Kapila. Padmini becomes the happiest woman on earth. But soon the heads of Devadatta and Kapila govern their bodies and they become the original selves which again drives Padmini to madness for the ideal of her dreams. She sends Devadatta away to the fair to get a chance to meet Kapila in forest. When Devadatta meets Kapila and Padmini together in the forest, he is not surprised. He still wants to take a chance to live with Kapila and Padmini in a new mind set, which as he proposes to live like Pandavas with one Draupadi, but Kapila dismisses his idea without giving a chance to Devadatta to speak out his mind.

Devadatta	:	Tell me one thing. Do you really love Padmini?
Kapila	:	Yes.
Devadatta	:	So do I.
Kapila	:	I know (silence) Devadatta, couldn't we all three live together – like the Pandavas and Draupadi?
Devadatta	:	What do you think? (Silence. Padamini looks at them but doesn't say anything.)
Kapila	:	(Laughs). No, it can't be done.
Devadatta	:	That's why I brought this. (Shows the sword.) (60)

Thus the two have no option but to put an end to their lives of rivalry. The two friends die together and Padmini performs sati like a true *pativrata.* Karnad wants to convey that the world is indifferent to the desires and frustrations, joys and sorrows of human beings. Padmini says to Bhagawata:

> "My son is sleeping in the hut. Take him under your care. Give him to the hunter who lives in this forest and tell to them it's Kapila's son. They loved Kapila and will bring the child up. Let the child grow up in the forest with the rivers and the trees. When he's five, take him to the Revered Brahman Vidyasagara of Dharmapura. Tell him it's Devadatta's son" (62).

According to Girish Karnad, it is true that a man is bound by the inheritance, yet he will struggle hard to go as close to the ideal as he can, as Darwin has said truly, that man will continue to evolve, no matter in what circumstances he is. Hayavadana, has been struggling for completeness, for perfection, he continues his struggle till he becomes a complete horse. Padmini dreams of a lover who is a blend of Devadatta and Kapila, hopes that her son would be a happy combination of her two lovers. She wants her son to have a perfect figure having both intellect and physical strongness. This story deals with the theme of mankind's aspirations to acquire both physical satisfaction and intellectual excellence. The story focuses on the issue of the child whose legal father is a scholar but the real father is someone else, who symbolizes physical strength. The theme is not a new one rather it has been discussed in an ancient Sanskrit text *Kathasarita-sagar* and in Thomas Mann's *The Deposed Heads.* In the ancient text the solution of the problem is that since the head governs the body therefore, the father of the child is the scholar, but Thomas Mann disagrees with this and he says since blood is more powerful than the intellect therefore the child is of Kapila, the physical strength. The modern science favours the latter as it is the DNA test that decides the fatherhood of the child. But here Girish Karnad has mingled the two. When Padmini performs *sati,* she hands over her child to a person Bhagavata, asking him to take the child to the village and declare that the child is the son of Kapila. After the child becomes five years old, he should be taken to his grandparents living in the town and they should be told that the child is the son of Devadatta, the man who symbolized intellectual excellence.

Karnad's six plays out of nine are based on ancient myths, legends, and traditions. This shows that he is deeply rooted in Indian culture in which myths and legends are inseparable from life. He uses myths and legends with a view to making them a vehicle of a new vision. By employing myths, he shows the absurdity of modern life with all its elemental passion and conflicts and man's eternal struggle to attain perfection. *Hayavadana* is a play having many social messages to give us. In both the stories there is the theme of incompleteness, and a struggle for perfection. Hayavadana as well as Padmini are representatives of incompleteness and they struggle for perfection. Both are the victims of destiny and they are in search for identity. Through the story Karnad wants to convey how people in the present time are restless and they think themselves incomplete and struggle for perfection. They are prey in the hands of their destiny. He also draws our attention towards the problem of human identity in a triangular relationship. Kirtinath Kurkoti says:

> Karnad's play poses a different problem, that of human identity in a world of trangled relationships.

U.R. Anantha Murthy in his *A Note of Karnad's Hayavadana,* comments about the theme of incompleteness in a comic mode. S. Sharma says:

> completeness is a humanly impossible ideal as suggested first in the story of *Hayavadana* and later in the transposition of head.

According to Krishna Gandhi:

> in *Hayavadana,* the theme of the play is an old one ...man's yearning for completeness, for perfection. It is this yearning which makes people restless in their ordinary existence, and makes them reach out for extraordinary things....

Thus *Hayavadana* is a play having different themes which in turn brings out multilayered social messages. This story tells us how people yearn for completeness and this yearning makes them restless in their ordinary existence.

Works Cited

Chakravartee, Vanthishi, "Myth and Reality in Hayavadana and Nagamandala" in Tutun Mukhrejee (*ed.*) *Girish Karnad's Plays: Performance and Critical Perspectives.*

Dharwadker, Aparna. Interview with Girish Karnad. "Performance, Meaning and Materials of Modern Indian Theatre." *New Theatre Quarterly*. Vol. XI, No.44, Nov.1995.

Goel, Savita, "Folk Theatre Strategies in Hayavadana" in Jaydip Singh, Doliya (*ed.*). "The Plays of Girish Karnad: Critical Perspectives."

Karnad, Girish. *Hayavadana.* Calcutta: Oxford University Press, 1982.

Mukherjee, Tutun. "In His Own Voice : A Conversation with Girish Karnad." *Girish Karnad's Plays : Performance and Critical Perspectives.* ed. Tutun Mukherjee. New Delhi : Pencraft International, 2008.

Naik, M.K. "A Study of Hayavadana" in Tulam Mukherjee (*ed.*). *Girish Karnad's Plays: Performance and Critical Perspectives,* 2005.

Raykar, Meenakshi. *An Interview with Girish Karnad.* New Quest.

Colonising the Child-Mind: A Study of Colonialist Designs through Pamphlets of the Great Exhibition

Dr. Shilpa D. Bhat

This article seeks to discuss the historical event of "The Great Exhibition" that was held in 1851 and a pamphlet that was specifically written for children by an anonymous writer. The event and the text, together highlight the fact that the pamphlet was an attempt to inform children about the various colonies of Britain. The event managed to denigrate the colonised countries and their inhabitants through the use of exhibits and animals that were perceived to be symbolizing India commercially and culturally, as a land with strange communities and society. Other colonized nations of the world particularly African, were also portrayed as dark regions needing light from the English. However, this paper will analyse the pamphlet and objects referring largely to India. The inhabitants of these regions as wells as the natural resources were on display, done up colourfully to act as reminders of the white superiority. "The Great Exhibition" was not an ordinary event and was referred to in several literary works. There was some correspondence between the aims of the Exhibition and children's literature being produced during the period.

Louise Purbrick's seminal work *The Great Exhibition of 1851*, discusses in detail how the Exhibition was seen as symbolizing Industrial Progress. The author states that:

> Accounts of the exhibits, both official and popular, also delivered a modern political version of imperial relationships in which British superiority over Africa and Asia was represented as an effect of industrial skill rather than the result of military conquest or commercial subjugation. (4)

Africa and Asia were the centres of attraction in the Exhibition. Historically, it is known that the two continents were ravaged by the imperialists. Devastation took place directly in the countries while the spoils were displayed as conquered objects of triumph in exhibitions. As Greenblatt points out, cultural forms, stories and games become part of the power question and the "way in which literary texts or forms can be co-opted to serve as tools in the construction of power is a central focus for new historicist work" (quoted in Brannigan 57).

On October 11th, 1849, the "Illustrated London News," carried Prince Albert's speech at the Lord Mayor's Banquet in London. The crux of the speech was that the globe was becoming a smaller place on account of modern science and technology. It was a realisation and an acknowledgement of the fact that "speed" had become a characteristic feature of the modern age. Everything he expressed suggested that the face of the world had undergone extraordinary changes and therefore, there was this need for people from various parts of the world to live amicably and share the benefits that contemporary science had granted.

Like a visionary, Prince Albert – husband to Queen Victoria and titled "Prince Consort" (Harlow and Carter 332), ventured to announce the organisation of "The Great Exhibition." It was a momentous occasion, an ambitious plan – a great task to accomplish. The event turned out to be a grand landmark in history for it led to the coming together of people from various parts of the world. There was a showcasing of the inventions that science had made. Alien cultures and people assembled to partake of this unique celebration, and so it was also a funfair apart from being a World Trade Fair. The speech that Prince Albert made suggests that he embarked upon this project because he felt that all the nations of the world could come together for "the realization of the unity of mankind." Did this really happen? What was this epoch-making event really like? What made it acquire so much popularity? And in the context of imperialism and with especial reference to India, was equality really even a possibility?

The "World Fair," as it was sometimes referred to be a historical episode. Whether it really was an equal opportunity for all countries represented and whether the colonized nations were able to talk about themselves, their problems and make their voices heard is a signicant query. If not, then the visionary ideals that Prince Albert had conceived and expressed in his speech arouse suspicion and examination.

Exhibitions have always been seen as a way of enhancing knowledge. They are platforms that enable the display of objects of curiosity. Adults see it as a prospect of introducing to their children as aspect of the world that would not only delight but also supplement their knowledge. Display of animal objects further generates the idea of fabricating stories through connecting the object and its place of genesis and why and how to get there. "The Great Exhibition" was meant to be not just a display, but also a motivation for imperialism. It turned out to be the starting point for conducting of such events every year and sought to target a wide audience. It was education of the practical kind, for it was an opportunity for the colonial people – adults as well as children to see the colonised as specimens on display and get to know of the astonishing commodities that adorned the exhibition which came from the colonies.

It would be essential to understand the historical significance of "The Great Exhibition," which was intended to make the people of England aware of their nation's colonial accomplishments. Along with the adults, there was a creation of "space" to accommodate children through imaginative use of beasts. The event was inaugurated on May 1, 1851, at the Crystal Palace specially constructed for this purpose at Sydenham Hill, England (Harlow and Carter 332). The palace, designed by Joseph Paxton, covered 19 acres of land and was made with glass, iron and timber. There were 14,000 exhibitors from different parts of the globe and the display tables ran up to more than eight miles (Harlow and Carter 332). The specialties of different colonies were made known to the public. It was an occasion not just to perceive trade and commercial relations, industry and economics that upheld the imperial banner but also a chance to have a glimpse of the ethnographic "realities" of faraway lands. It was supposed to be as much recreational as educational. The exhibition and the exhibitors were universally lauded. Queen Victoria records in her diary that the "World Fair" "had quite the effect of fairyland" (qtd. in Harlow and Carter 137). The word "fairyland" clearly highlights the idea of fancy. The fair catered to imagination. If adults could see it as a "fairyland," children who are believed to inherently and naturally curious would be completely mesmerized by the event.

The event had gained wide publicity and had attracted the attention of people. It was an occasion for them to "see" for themselves and judge what the imperialist undertaking had done to their country's economy. It was a moment to confirm the widespread opinion that going to the East meant garnering pecuniary blessings. The general public had to be aware of this and children had to be inspired. The public thronged to the exhibition because that was how it was advertised. The multitudes of people in the city had increased so much that in a span of 140 days (Harlow and Carter 333), nearly 6 million people (MacKenzie 101) had visited the exhibition.

The popularity of the exhibition was such that Alfred Lord Tennyson wrote a poem, "Opening of the Indian and Colonial Exhibition by the Queen," in the year 1886 at the request of the Prince of Wales. Through this poem, he tried to imply that everything exhibited was something that the British could consider their "own:"

> Works of subtle brain and hand,
> And splendours of the morning land,
> Gifts from every British zone;
> Britons, hold your own! (63)

"The Great Exhibition" was in reality a eulogy of the colonial project – an announcement that the Empire had accrued immense financial profits from its victories abroad. It was a declaration made universal to assert its invincibility. Since the Fair was a colourful celebration of imperial triumph and was meant to reach the masses that invariably included children, it had to fascinate this group too. The objective was not merely regaling them but also educating them about the colonies in a practical fashion.

Interestingly, during "The Great Exhibition," an anonymous pamphlet entitled "Prize Book" for children was circulated widely. It provided brief accounts of different colonies and their attractions with illustrations. All the subjugated countries have been encapsulated and ridiculed wherever possible.

The introduction to "The Great Exhibition" in the pamphlet echoes the ideas of Prince Albert's speech – that the people from different nations would get an opportunity to interact with one another, "and be joined in love and trade" (Prince Albert). Too utopian in its implications, the two words "love and trade" seem to be juxtaposed uneasily with each other. The descriptions are called, "pretty stories," followed by descriptions of objects from different nations. The impression one gets after going through the pamphlet is of the whole world being laid bare for the benefit of the English public's knowledge. And knowledge, as we know is power.

The passages alluding to the colonies of the British very plainly disparage their people and their culture but praise their resources. It encouraged travelling to those "curious" colonies either for trade prospects or for the possibilities of converting/reforming the "natives." The end was therefore political, economic and "ethical." The text, therefore, is like a globe, flattened and made palatable to the English people and more specifically to children.

When it comes to talking about India, the author states that the "Hindoo stuffs" are too thin to feel and, "made from rejected cotton husks," and all through the passages on India, the word "poor" occurs very often. It is to be observed that the European goods have been described, as a matter of "fact" and England has been praised to the skies. The anonymous pamphlet states:

> What a many thousand contributions have come from foreign countries, yet even a greater number have been sent in from all parts of our own dear islands, England, Ireland, and Scotland.... The English people are celebrated for their industry and perseverance.

The ratio of appreciation has been carefully adjusted to provide more weight to the possessions and wealth of England. The contrast between Britain and the colonised countries is glaring. While Britain has been described as practically flawless, the colonised countries and people have often been referred to derogatorily. After discussing the goods of trade from India, the author proceeds to provide a judgment about the people that, "(t)hey would lead rather a sorry life, were it not that their tastes were so extremely simple, and their wants so few." The dwelling places of the Indians are seen as "gypsy encampments" that appear "strange" to the Europeans.

The author makes a clear distinction between the kings and the common people of India in keeping with the idea of "Oriental Despotism." The "eastern grandee could formerly do anything he chose" implying that the Indian kings were absolute tyrants who would have continued so, but for the invasion of the British that had completely altered this situation. Now it was the British "who could do anything they chose" if they so desired. The word "formerly" stresses that the days of the Indians ruling their own country had gone, and that it was a thing of the past.

It is interesting to note that the same word has been used to point at Egypt which "was formerly, a mighty empire, and had rich and haughty kings." However, when referring to the United States, the author mentions that it was "formerly" occupied by several tribes like the Red Indians, most of whom were barbarians and that [L] ong ago, the United States belonged to the English, but because the natives grew stronger and could no longer endure foreign invasions, the English had to grant them independence.

A comparison of these terminologies makes it plain that the people of India and Egypt were considered poor and weak. In contrast, the American inhabitants, who after all were largely of European stock turned out to be powerful enough to be able to oust the English. The one who was tougher in militarism and endurance was the one who won the colonial struggles and the outcome nearly always had a sense of the excitement of unpredictability. To make their sway over India enduring, the English used several ways to make colonisation a popular job among her citizens. To persuade several people at once to help in expansion and administration was not simple. The idea had to be given sufficient time to grow in their minds; and this could happen on a grand scale only if the rewards of taking up the risky journeys were explained in tempting terms.

The account of India in the "Prize-Book" suggested to the attendees of the exhibition, that the Indian people were in dire need of a drastic change in their distressed lives. The suggestion was tempting and opportunities seemed to be manifold because of the vastness of India and its huge population. The reference to religion in the pamphlet and the social custom of "Suttee" shows that the British were interested not just in trade and commerce but in the other aspects of the Indian society as well. The pamphlet therefore tried to give a glimpse into the cultural aspects of India. However, the prime interest was the wealth of the country. The presentation of India in the pamphlet is as a land of contradictions – the positives are all appropriated by the English, the negatives constitute the "native" people, their religion and culture which are seen as despicable and difficult to reform.

Animals have always been significant in indoctrinating ideals as desired by the adults. During the colonial period, the imperialists found stuffed animals generally found in the commonwealth countries as useful objects to attract attention of children. Janie Hinds, in her paper "Deb's Dogs: Animals, Indians, and Postcolonial Desire in Charles Brockden Brown's Edgar Huntly," states that "As early as Aristotle's Historia Animalium, species were seen to have physical features in common, yet even medieval bestiaries used nonhuman species primarily to allegorize the human condition (qtd. in Hinds 327);" suggesting that animals reflect the essential dilemmas, philosophy and desires of human existence and the fact that they are not "humans" helps to see the situation objectively. This feeling of "otherness" when perceiving animal stories, animal objects is crucial. When there are animal objects or toys that are animals the feeling of possessing them is common among children. We do know that animal stories, most of them, have human voices and language attributed to them. Their talking quality brings them closer to humans and their bodies, alienate and form the outstanding difference from human beings. In the quest for lands and wealth, during the colonial period, animal bodies became cites of colonial and political ideology.

In exhibitions, animal objects became triggers to imagine and register the connection between the imperialists and the colonized and this came across through the pamphlet circulated during the period. The objective of the animal objects was to advertise the colonial agenda widely and emphatically. They did become symbolic extensions of the imperial aspiration. The organizers and founders of this event took advantage of this fact and the concept was translated into reality. The animals, therefore, were used as advertisers and reminders of India as a prospective colony. Of course, the English didn't come to India just to "see" the wild animals. It was invariably to make money. The figures of the animals were used to attract the attention of the public towards the outlying regions of the British Empire. The Exhibition therefore, became a very significant platform to perpetuate imperialism.

Works Cited

Brannigan, John. *New Historicism and Cultural Materialism.* New York: St. Martin's Press, 1998.

Edgar, J.G., "J. G. Edgar: The Colonial Museum." *Kingston Annual for Boys.* London: 1863.

Harlow, Barbara and Mia Carter, (*eds.*) *Orientalism and Imperialism: A Documentary Sourcebook.* US: Blackwell, 2000.

Hinds, Janie, "Deb's Dogs: Animals, Indians, and Postcolonial Desire in Charles Brockden Brown's Edgar Huntly." *Early American Literature.* Project Muse, Vol 39, No. 2, 2004, 323-354.

James, Lawrence, "The Bond of One Spirit: The Public Face of Empire 1919-1939." *The Illustrated Rise and Fall of the British Empire.* (*Ed.*) Arianne Brunette. New York: St Martin, 1999. MacKenzie, John M., *Propaganda and Empire: The Manipulation of British Public Opinion, 1880-1960.* London: Manchester UP, 1984.

Morgan, John S., *Aesop's Fables in the Executive Suite.* New York: Van Nostrand Reinhold Company, 1921.

Prince Albert, "The Great Exhibition." Lord Mayor's Banquet, London. 11Oct. 1849. Aug 30 2011. <http: www.ringmar.net /joomla index. php?option=com_content&view=article&id=825:prince-albert-on-the-great-exhibition&catid=98:wonders-of-technology & Itemid= 142.

Louise Purbrick. *The Great Exhibition of 1851.* Manchester: Manchester University Press, 2001.

Ritvo, Harriet, "Learning from Animals: Natural History for Children in the Eighteenth Vand Nineteenth Centuries." *Children's Literature.* Project Muse. Volume 13, 1985, 72-93.

Stearn, William T., *The Natural History Museum at South Kensington : A History of the British Museum (Natural History) 1753-1980.* London: Heinemann, 1981, 40-45.

Tennyson, Lord Alfred, "Opening of the Indian and Colonial Exhibition by the Queen (1886)." *Empire Writing: An Anthology of Colonial Literature 1870-1918.* (*Ed.*) Elleke Boehmer. New York: Oxford UP, 1998, 63-64.

The Worlds Fair, 1851, 3 Oct 2006, a. http://www.gutenberg.org/ files 14092/14092-h/14092-h.htm

Note

1. Prince Albert delivered the following speech at "The Lord Mayor's Banquet in London on October 11, 1849 which appeared in "The Illustrated London News." In the speech he envisioned the organisation of "The Great Exhibition of 1851." (The bibliographical details of the same are at the work cited at the end of the chapter.) I conceive it to be the duty of every educated person closely to study and watch the time in which he lives; and as far as in him lies, to add his mite of individual exertion to further the accomplishment of what he believes Providence to have ordained. Nobody, however, who has paid any attention to the features of our present era, will doubt for a moment that we are living at a period of most wonderful transition which tends rapidly to the accomplishment of that great end to which indeed, all history points – the realization of the unity of mankind. Not a unity which breaks down the limits and levels the peculiar characteristics of the different nations

of the earth, but rather a unity, the result and product of those very national varieties and antagonistic qualities. The distances which separated the different nations and parts of the globe are gradually vanishing before the achievements of modern invention, and we can traverse them with incredible ease; the languages of all nations are known and their acquirements placed within the reach of everybody; thought is communicated with the rapidity and even by the power of lightning.

On the other hand, the great principle of the division of labour, which may be called the moving power of civilization, is being extended to all branches of science, industry and art. Whilst formerly the greatest mental energies strove at universal knowledge, and that knowledge was confined to a few, now they are directed to specialities, and in these again, even to the minutest points; but the knowledge acquired becomes at once the property of the community at large. Whilst formerly discovery was wrapt in secrecy, the publicity of the present day causes, that no sooner is a discovery or invention made, than it is already improved upon and surpassed by competing efforts: the products of all quarters of the globe are placed at our disposal, and we have only to choose what is the cheapest and best for our purposes, and the powers of production are intrusted to the stimulus of competition and capital.

So man is approaching a more complete fulfilment of that great and sacred mission which he has to perform in this world. His reason being created after the image of God, he has to use it to discover the laws by which the Almighty governs His creation, and, by making these laws his standard of action, to conquer nature to his use – himself a divine instrument. Science discovers these laws of power, motion and transformation; industry applies them to raw matter, which the earth yields us in abundance, but which becomes valuable only by knowledge; art teaches us the immutable laws of beauty and symmetry, and gives to our productions forms in accordance with them.

Gentlemen, the Exhibition of 1851 is to give us a true test and a living picture of the point of development at which the whole of mankind has arrived in this great task, and a new starting point from which all nations will be able to direct their further exertions.

Performance, Vernacular Cosmopolitanism and Sociolinguistics in Montreal

Kaustav Kundu

Quebec's legislated shift in 1977 to a monolingual French culture affected attitudes to and usage of both standard and vernacular languages in Montreal, the province's largest city. Multilingual, multicultural cities frequently put their visitors and inhabitants into situations where they have a choice about how they perform a variety of sociopolitical identities in language, a choice that instantly invokes creative performativity and undermines authenticity. The tensions between authenticity and performativity are regularly tackled in translation: the literal/free distinction is just one name for it. Vernacular cosmopolitanism might be another way to frame this view of multilingual contact and performance. An examination of language contact that looks at a literary and a sociolinguistic examination of the same contact zone reveals how these tensions play out across disciplines, with literature invoking the freedom of inauthenticity, while sociolinguistics fixes a scientific "truth."

Statistics Canada figures from 2006 for mother tongues/home languages list French (49.8% of the population, around 900000 people), English (17.6%), Italian (16%), Arabic (14%), Spanish (12%) at the top. At the bottom (in the "Other" category) one finds Yiddish, between the world wars the third most common language spoken there, but now on a precipitous decline with only 8500 speakers (Lazarus). Mohawk, the most "local" aboriginal language is perhaps on the rise again after near-extinction (Hoover). The fates of Mohawk and Yiddish reveal how language can shift under political pressures.

Despite this richness of available languages, Sherry Simon, born and raised in Montreal's Jewish community, notes that she "grew up in a city as segregated as colonial Calcutta" (xi). For those anglophones, like her, who stayed after the passage of the 1977 Charter of the French Language (Bill 101)[1] moved the linguistic balance towards French, life became increasingly a life in translation: "Translingual poetics, creative interference," "non-translation," "translation," and "translation without an original," are some of the techniques that drive writing in both English and French (15). In a Montreal shifting from Anglo to Franco, non-francophones suddenly found themselves forced to rearrange their identities to accommodate new linguistic demands in a province that resolutely aspired to be monolingual. For some, such as the famous Jewish novelist Mordecai Richler, the move was both retrograde and bordering on anti-Semitic. His response, first published in the *New Yorker*, caused a furor. He saw his home city turning foreign, while Quebec nationalists saw him as a symptom of the Anglo-colonization that had held them back since the Conquest of 1759. For others, the changes were liberatory. Simon notes a trend "toward cosmopolitanism among Québéco is writers and translators. Pierre Anctil, who is not Jewish, translates Yiddish writers into French. Jacques Brault started out as a nationalist writer but blossomed into an experimenter, writing about and under the influence of European and Asian writers. Michel Garneau does controversial translations of Leonard Cohen and William Shakespeare into French" (Black). For many, then, to become bilingual was to become cosmopolitan, an identity unavailable to the dominant Anglophone majority outside Quebec. As Simon points out, "The New Anglo is only possible because this is [now] a French city" (qtd. Black).

Leonard Cohen, like Simon and Richler, a member of the large Jewish community in Montreal, published *Beautiful Losers* in 1966, just as the "Quiet Revolution" asserting Quebec nationalism turned violent. The novel is narrated, in part, by a self-described folklorist, known only as I – working on a mythical Aboriginal group, the A–, who are certainly connected to the novel's title: "There is no record that this unfortunate people ever won a single battle, while the songs and legends of its enemies are virtually nothing but a sustained howl of triumph" (5). He is obsessed with the Blessed Kateri Tekakwitha, a historical Mohawk convert who died in Kahnawake, just outside Montreal, in 1680. The novel is set in a Montreal "of rival francophone nationalist groups and of bomb attacks on mailboxes and statues and other symbols of Canadian federalism, the Montreal that in 1966... saw bomber Paul Joseph Chartier travel to Ottawa and accidentally blow himself up in a parliamentary washroom and in 1968 saw a separatist cell kidnap and murder Quebec labour minister Pierre Laporte (Davey 13). The novel grapples with Gayatri Spivak's question of how to "unlearn our privilege as our loss" (Landry 5) in a city that was rearranging its elites, as the English-speaking financial elite lost to the French-speaking majority in the province. Cohen was asking how to be a beautiful loser. Unlike Richler, he did not choose sides;

he turned, in fact, to one of the least authentic forms of translation described by Simon, "translation without an original."

The narrator, identified only as I, recounts his mixed feelings for a powerful older man, identified only as F, of whom he remarks, "I hear his phony voice, the slight Eskimo accent which he affected after a student summer in the Arctic" (27). The point I want to stress here is that those who do affect accents normally choose a prestige accent like Parisian French or Standard Southern British – one that will be recognized as marking the speaker as a member of an elite. In Canada then, as now, English-speaking Inuit are rarely heard outside the North. So why would anyone affect an accent that no one would be impressed by, or indeed, even recognize? I want to read the feigned accent as marking Cohen's *refusal* to see the use of *any* language, here Quebec French, either as a mark of authentic identity or as a rationale for violent revolution. The true cosmopolitan is fluent and without a heavy accent in whatever language she speaks. An accent that no one recognizes picked up after a summer reeks of anti-cosmopolitan inauthenticity. Frank Davey argues that various characters in the novel are, in fact, usually not speaking English, the language the novel is written in: Catherine Tekakwitha, a famous Mohawk convert and the French priest speak Mohawk and French together and much of the novel recounts verbal encounters that must have taken place in French. Thus the novel when composed in English was a translation without an original – another mark of inauthenticity. F appears to be a Roman Catholic francophone nationalist who comes to see the problems with nationalism, while I the narrator, is likely an anglophone able to pass as francophone. He concludes that the novel ultimately rejects the linguistic nationalism still driving Quebec politics in favour of an identification with the beautiful losers of the title, symbolized by such figures as F as an old man, raving in the last stages of syphilis, the blind African American jazz pianist Ray Charles, and the Blessed Catherine Tekakwitha. These varied figures cannot be consolidated into any sort of homogeneous authenticity, something that the novel disavows.

The shift to a feigned but unrecognizable accent highlights the performative in Judith Butler's sense of it as laid out in *Excitable Speech: A Politics of the Performative*:

> The question here is whether the improper use of the performative can succeed in producing the effect of authority

> where there is no recourse to a prior authorization; indeed, whether the misappropriation or expropriation of the perform-ative might not be the very occasion for the exposure of prevailing forms of authority and the exclusions by which they proceed. (158)

Her answer to this question appears to be "yes" as she concludes that "speaking words without prior authorization and putting into risk the security of linguistic life" is the "insurrectionary speech that replies to injurious language" (165).

F's feigned unrecognizable accent marks his refusal of his own ethno-linguistic identity and of linguistic authenticity in general and forges an alliance with the subaltern represented here by Tekakwitha and Ray Charles, the descendent of slaves. But the accent is one gained not in the service of authenticity over the lifetime of scholarship that I, engages in, but in one summer in the service of superficiality: F's watchword is "stop bravely at the surface" (4). Thus the subaltern is refused – or released from – the usual heavy weight of authenticity, an authenticity derived from isolation from other languages, not to mention from modernity. The Romanticization of the authentic folk, speaking a language steeped in antiquity, serves to counter the standardized languages of hegemonic power F, a former Member of Parliament, certainly spoke such a powerful language – but he refuses to move to its opposite, as his feigned accent (and later, syphilitic ravings) make clear.

The authenticity of the subaltern vernaculars has been central to both dialectology and to sociolinguistics, however. Sociolinguistics, founded in reaction against both elitist standardization and folklorizing dialectology in the 1960s, turned from the rural "oldest living inhabitant" to, with William Labov, the study of young male urban speakers, most famously those of African American Vernacular English (AAVE). Indeed, his *The Social Stratification of English in New York City*, the foundational work of the new field of variationist sociolinguistics, was published in the same year as *Beautiful Losers.* However, recently, sociolinguistics has been rethinking its grounding tenets. In a set of short papers published in the *Journal of Sociolinguistics* in 2003 under the heading "Sociolinguistics and Authenticity: An Elephant in the Room" Penelope Eckert, Mary Bucholtz and Nikolas Coupland consider how the figure of the "Authentic Speaker" – the figure that grounds the field – has held up over time. Eckert describes this figure – "This spontaneous speaker of pure vernacular" – as "the dialectological poster child" who provides "our direct access to language untainted by the interference of reflection or social agency" (392). She further describes the vernacular as "the central naturalizing concept of sociolinguistics, defined as the individual's most natural speech, learned early in life and forever "fixed" in the speaker's ingrained patterns thanks to a critical period for language – and dialect – acquisition. These ingrained patterns are produced most regularly in spontaneous speech, which, by virtue of its naturalness, is the source of regular linguistic change" (394). Any conscious or self-conscious linguistic monitoring or playfulness is thus regulated out of the field, which suddenly starts to look a lot like folkloric dialectology.

To focus on how sociolinguistics has dealt with Quebec English is instructive. Montreal had a population of 3.6 million in 2006. The rate of bilingualism moved above 40% in 2001, and, it seems, will continue to increase. Quebec anglophones reported 68.9% bilingual; francophones around 35.8 (2006 data). However, younger francophones in the province report a rate of over 53%. Allophones (those whose first language is neither English nor French) report a bilingualism rate over 50% – this group is now trilingual, at least (Canada, Statistics Canada). In other words, unlike in the past, there is a lot of language contact, with most people in the city speaking at least two languages in any given day. Linguistic contact also takes place in people's head, where, because they are speaking more than one language, meanings can shift and borrowings go unnoticed or grow familiar over time.

Some sociolinguists can and do ignore this contact, strictly designing it out of their "empirical" studies of "actual" language. They are only interested in speech, not writing, and only interested in spontaneous speech, rather than any speech that shows signs of reflection – which includes speech marked by wit or style. For example, Shana Poplack, James A. Walker and Rebecca Malcolmson in "An English "like no other:" Language Contact and Change in Quebec" (2006) found only four loanwords in the spontaneous speech of their informants – 185 anglophones born and educated in Montreal and Quebec City: *metro,* for subway, *Québécois(e)* for Quebecker, *cegep* (short for *Collége d'enseignement général et professionel*) and *stage* (internship, or work term). Poplack et al's conclusion is that the borrowed forms they find are extremely rare and used "with full speaker awareness" (210). They remark, dismissively, "This is hardly the kind of bilingual language use that can be expected to lead to contact-induced change" (210), as if only structural change was of interest. (This is where the disciplinary divide falls between "scientific" language study and, say, the literary or political study of language.) Further the interviews were done in the informants' homes and "all fieldworkers were native speakers of Canadian English and most were members of the respective communities in which they collected data" (192). Thus, the idea that conversations might happen between those with different mother tongues is excluded, as if Quebec English was only the English spoken by anglophones in spontaneous conversation with other anglophones, all born and educated in either Montreal or Quebec City. What Bruno Latour calls "the work of purification" is clearly going on in sociolinguistics.

To conduct such interviews in the home ignores the different effects of place on language use documented by Patricia Lamarre et al.: "Within institutional settings, language practices tend to be more conservative. Informal settings, such as cafes and large public events, as well as spaces less clearly identified with a language "community," are more likely to be characterized by bilingual and multilingual practices. Our observations clearly indicate the complexity of the language practices of young Montrealers and the need for a dynamic approach to the study of language use. We propose an approach that follows individuals through the different settings and social networks they traverse in the course of a day, as well as one that takes into account the power relations underlying interactions" (Lamarre et al.).

The study by Poplack also "excludes "established" loanwords, including cognates, here defined as French-origin words attested in the *Canadian Oxford Dictionary* (Barber 2004), prior to the birth of the informant" (207n). Thus they miss the creative meanings and differing frequencies that evolve in these loanwords because of contact. One simple example of a cognate that has different meanings in English and French is nation. *Nation*: in English it means Canada, and in French it means Quebec.

Sociolinguistics appears to retain its scientific credibility at the heavy cost of ignoring the politics underlying particular words. Quebecois is one of the French words that the study discovered in spontaneous use by its informants, but what exactly did they mean by it?

Canadiens once used to refer to French Quebeckers and survives in the name of the NHL hockey team, the Montreal *Canadiens* (in

French, *les Canadiens de Montréal*). This word has, as Pierre Coulombe explains, been replaced by others:

> Why did the appellation Canadiens give way to French Canadians if not because Confederation failed to respect their identity? Why did the French Canadians of Québec then begin to identify themselves as Québécois, if not because they saw Québec as the only place where they could be themselves? Why do the Québécois of French origins today increasingly designate themselves as Franco- or French-Québécois if not because the budding Québec citizenship does not succeed in recognizing their identity? (1995, 135)

Here is a slightly less sympathetic comment on the same struggle over meaning:

> To deflect any charge of racism, separatists have had to insist that the Quebecois included everyone in Quebec, when it is obvious that it is made up of Quebec "French-Canadians" – the so-called pure laine descendents of the early settlers from France" (*Gazette* 8 Dec 1993 B1).

Interestingly, these expressions are used neutrally or positively even in the English-language newspaper, the Montreal *Gazette*: "Parent is pure laine, vieille souche, and has shown herself time and again to be kind of godmother the Quebec women's movement needs" (*Gazette* 7 May 1990 C1). Indeed, they are even used playfully, and these usages mark the expression as assimilated and the user as making a strong political statement about his or her identity as an Anglo-Montrealer who speaks and accepts French. A rock music review notes that a particular group's appeal is to "male white trash de vieille souche" (*Gazette* 22 Mar. 1990 D16) without missing a beat and another reviewer comments on the dancing of les Grands Ballets Canadiens this way: "when it comes to a pure laine classical work like Giselle, they turn slipshod" (*Gazette* Nov. 12 1990 B7). These writers are New Anglos, performing their identities as bilinguals. They are adopting and adapting the linguistic features of contact in a fashion that permits them to move between languages leaving only a trace. Significantly, this is how Jacques Derrida moved words between English and French (not to mention other languages), allowing the trace to be visible, but inaudible (as in his mis-spelling of *différance*) and using other playful shifts to emphasize that translation can never be perfect, nor language ever fixed. Srivinas Aravamudan has described what he called Guru English as "a perfect example . . . of transidiomaticity" (9) and continues:

> The notion of certain languages and discourses as constituting a transidiomatic environment allows us to understand how they might have considerable appeal with multiple audiences without necessarily having to posit the particular medium of communication as a coherent foundation. (9)

Guru English, he notes "presents itself as already translated" although this certainly doesn't preclude further translation and interpretation. Language emerges into world of play in all of the varied senses of this word. In ignoring play, including feigned accents, the work of linguistic purification is done by much sociolinguistic methodology. The other issue that this work reveals is the ways in which the careers of frequent-flying cosmopolitan academics is anchored by their construction of the authentic vernacular speaker as fixed in a particular language, social class and territory. As Nicholas Coupland points out, the "traditionally conceived authentic speaker was a liberal, idealized socio-political construct designed by sociolinguists to supplant a hegemonic idealized alternative – the speaker imbued with the establishment's authentic values" (415). He notes that this move had considerable effect; however, in late modernity, authenticity – whether establishment or vernacular – is harder to come by. With the destabilizing of the social structures that formerly underpinned these constructed authenticities and their related speech norms, sociolinguistic theory and literary theory will become more complex. The desire for authentic identifications will not vanish, but won't come quite so "naturally" – rather, speakers will more consciously perform their identities, like F, and communities will move to refashion their authenticity in ways that are self-referential, self-conscious, and even self-mocking. Montreal, certainly, is no longer segregated like colonial Calcutta and neither is Kolkata.

Works Cited

Black, Barbara. "Choice Words from Sherry Simon," *Concordia Journal* 7 Dec. 2006.

http://cjournal.concordia.ca. Accessed: 29 Sept. 2007.

Charter of the French Language in Quebec. http:// www.olf.gouv. qc.ca english/charter index.html#t1 status. Accessed: 29 Sept. 2007.

Cohen, Leonard. *Beautiful Losers.* Toronto: McCleland and Stewart, 1966.

Coulombe, Pierre, A., *Language Rights in French Canada.* New York: Peter Lang, 1995.

Coupland, Nikolas. "Sociolinguistic Authenticities." *Journal of Sociolinguistics* 7, 2003: 417-31.

Davey, Frank, "*Beautiful Losers*: Leonard Cohen's Postcolonial Novel." *Essays on Canadian Writing* 69, 1999: 12-23.

Fee, Margery, "French Borrowing in Quebec English." *Focus on Canadian English.* (*Ed.*) Matthias Meyer. *Anglistik: International Journal of English Studies.* 19.2, 2008:173-88.

Hoover, Michael L., "The Revitalization of the Mohawk Language in Kahnawake." www.brandonu.ca/library/CJNS/12.2/ hoover.pdf. Accessed 30 Sept. 2007.

Lamarre, Patricia, Julie Paquette, Emmanuel Kahn, and Sophie Ambrosi, "Multilingual Montreal: Listening in on the Language Practices of Young Montrealers." *Canadian Ethnic Studies Journal,* 34.3, 2002: 47-61.

Landry Donna and Gerald Maclean, (*eds.*) *The Spivak Reader.* London: Routledge, 1996.

Latour, Bruno, *We Have Never Been Modern.* (*tr.*) Catherine Porter. Cambridge: Harvard UP, 1993.

Lazarus, David, "Use of Yiddish Declining in Canada." *Canadian Jewish News* 21 Feb. 2008. www.cjnews.com. Accessed: 30 Sept. 2007.

Levine, Marc, *The Reconquest of Montreal: Language Policy and Social Change in a Bilingual City.* Philadelphia: Temple UP, 1990.

Martin, Paul William. "Reproducing Culture(s): The Politics of Knowledge Production and the Teaching of the Literatures of Canada." Diss. Comparative Literature, University of Alberta, 2002.

Poplack, Shana, James A. Walker and Rebecca Malcolmson, "An English "like no other:" Language Contact and Change in Quebec." *Canadian Journal of Linguistics/ Revue canadienne de linguistique* 51. 2/3 2006: 185-213.

Richler, Mordecai, *Oh Canada! Oh Quebec!: Requiem for a Divided Country.* Toronto: Penguin, 1992.

Simon, Sherry, *Translating Montreal: Episodes in the Life of a Divided City.* Montreal: McGill-Queen's UP, 2006.

Srivinas, Aravamudan. *Guru English: South Asian Religion in a Cosmopolitan Language.* Delhi: Penguin, 2007.

Note

1. The passage of the Charter of the French language (Bill 101) in 1977 is at the centre of social, economic, political and linguistic changes that have brought many members of a traditionally isolated monolingual and elite English-speaking community into regular contact with French. See Charter.

Structure in the Novels of Anais Nin: A Modern Approach

Dr. P.K. Sinha

> It is a curious anomaly that we listen to jazz, we look at modern paintings, we live in modern houses of modern design, we travel in jet planes, yet we continue to read novels written in a tempo and style which is not of our time and not related to any of these influences. The new novel could be born of Freud, Einstein, jazz and science. *(The Novel of the Future,* p. 29)

The twentieth century authors experimented with the form and structure of their work. In the process they set many a new trail. They expressed the relationships in time and space, and also among the distinctly modern characters. The modern novel, Anais Nin suggests, is based on Freud, Einstein, jazz and science. Modern fiction differs from the fiction of nineteenth century with regard to "story" or "plot" or "character," as in the works of painters, sculptors, composers, playwrights and poets. Here, the characters are not the traditional ones; they may seem perverse or fantastic. They may express themselves through the streams of highly poetic language, or confusing patterns of narration. They may become frustrated, hostile or defensively contemptuous. This shift in structure is mainly because psychology and sociology, now-a-days, play a great part in our life. The present-day analysis of human behaviour is heavily indebted to psychology and sociology. This situation compels the modern novelists to abandon the surface and to invent new ways in order to penetrate the inner reality of his subject. As a consequence, the treatment of characters becomes "abstract" and "dehumanized." This dehumanization is a drive towards abstraction, which has characterized all the arts of the modern age. When humans feel uneasy, oppressed, overwhelmed or terrified by their natural or human environment, artists tend to abandon realism. They go for exaggeration or distortion, and ultimately abstraction. In this effort, images of the world are signified, purified and reduced to essences; and these reduced images provide a sense of comfort. Modern artist is also attracted by the revelation of dreams, in which the dreamer is released from all limitations of time, space and personal identity. Einstein's theory of relativity has laid significant influence upon the novelists of the modern time. Now, we find notable changes in their approach to time and space. This new novel or the modern novel is being created by writers like Djuna Barnes, Andre Gide, Vladimir Nobokov, Allain Robbe Grillet, Gertrude Stein, Carlos Fuentes, John Hawkes, Raymond Roussel, Hermann Broch, Virginia Woolf, Charlotte Bronte, Emile Bronte and many others. Leon Edel remarks:

> ...that whereas all artists utilize personal experience, in the psychological novel the traditional process of projecting the inner experience into an imaginative narrative dealing with the external world was not carried out. Those novelists sought to retain and record the "inwardness of experience."

Anais Nin also belongs to this tradition. She describes her novels as "dramas as unconscious lives them." She, too, like the authors of today, experimented with the structure of her novels. She invented the abstract character. The abstract or non-representational ideals for the structure are needed for the totality of vision. Though Nin's continuous novel *Cities of the Interior* is thematically conventional because of her interest in human personality, it is extraordinarily original in terms of style and structure. The cities are private and symbolic. They exist as objectifications of the psychic states of characters in the novel. When Lillian comes to Mexico, there is a description:

> She had landed in the city of Golconda, where the sun painted everything with gold, the lining of her thoughts, the worn valises, the plain beetles, Golconda of the golden age, the golden aster, the golden eagle, the golden goose, the golden fleece, the golden robin, the golden rod, the golden seal, the golden warbler, the golden wattles, the golden weddings, and the golden fish, and the gold of pleasure, the goldstone, the golden thread, the fool's gold.
>
> With her first swallow of air she inhaled a drug of forgetfulness wellknown to adventurers.

> Tropic, from the Greek, signified change and turning. So she changed and turned, and was metamorphosed by the light and caressing heat into a pool of silk.

In the above excerpt from the novel, the city of Mexico is transformed into a complex and intensely rendered symbol of Lillian's attempt to evade the confrontation with herself and her past life. The structure of *Cities of the Interior* is highly suggestive of the freedom that can be discovered, and accordingly the characters attempt drives for it.

Nin's other novel *Collages* also contains the fluid concept of personality. It embodies an original approach to the spatialization of time in a continuous present. But, in this novel the motion is circular. This movement without advance creates an intensification of the atmosphere, theme and images of the book. *Collages* consists of nineteen short episodes which are self-sustained. The materials are provided by three sources: settings, characters, and themes; each source maintaining considerable variety. The settings include Vienna, Mexico, Holland, Malibu and Downey, California; Haiti, France, England, Morocco, Acapulco; Japan, Germany; Russia; New York City. These settings have been decorated with rich colours and textures.

The characters are as diverse as settings. No detailed portrayal is there. The characters are swiftly sketched. There is Leontine, whose father was a revolutionary in Haiti. He is a buoyant black singer. There is a poignant old man, more a seal than a human being, who finally goes off to die on a rock ledge with animals whom he loves; Henry, a fabulous chef; exotic Lisa, a deliriously mad actress who calls herself Nina Gitano and who is in love with an imaginary man named Manfred; a "Toulouse-Lautrec-figure" awakened from her dream of Acapulco with a cigar-flavoured kiss from the ashcan painting period of her childhood; Nobuko, who everyday selects her kimono to be in harmony with season; Varda, the creator of exquisite airy collages of women collected from "all the legendry textiles of the world," but whose "daughter stubbornly wore Varda's torn shirts, discarded sweaters and went out with boys who were more sullen and mute with herself;" the betrayal of a French Consul, who invents a new love for herself – long-dead hero of Islam, Shumla, whose "valour made the modern world seem tame and fearful." Each of these brave and touching figures comes imbued with an aura of place and time. Each of them has created self-sustaining world of fantasy around her or him.

These nineteen episodes or vignettes have varied themes. This variation in themes is due to the rich creative power of Nin. In some of the vignettes love is essential between man and woman and it is universally essential for each and every person regardless of age. Moreover, those who are bereft of love can easily summon forth the excitement and pleasure of companionship and passion from imagination. This phenomenon points to the vital role of creativity in every life. It may be the charm and power of make-believe – the force of fantasy in inventing new personalities and life for oneself, or specific artistic creativity, such as represented by various characters. Another recurrent theme is the absolute necessity of freedom from restrictions of emotion, feeling and imaginative creation.

The juxtaposition that *Collages* contains is that art and life are indistinguishably entwined. The idea that dream and imagination can enrich daily life through compensation, through revelation and through prophesies is conveyed through various images. Nin dramatizes the interlocking creative powers of art and life. At the same time she finalizes the circular shape by ending the book with the same passage with which it opens:

> Vienna was the city of statues. They were as numerous as the people who walked the streets. They stood on the tip of the highest towers, lay down on the stone tombs, sat on horseback, kneeled, prayed, fought animals and wars, danced, drank wine and read books made of stone...

Novels of Anais Nin belong to the world which she describes as "almost in opposition to our surface world. It is first of all ruled by flow." Like Proust, she uses emotion and memory as determining principles of her selecting and positioning of episodes and paragraphs. As a result, episodes lack the chronological order. In *Ladders to Fire,* Lillian's unsatisfying teenage sexual encounter should be the first episode in a chronological novel. But, it is not so. It appears at the high point of the heroine's sexual frustration just near the middle of the novel. In *Seduction of the Minotaur,* Lillian sees a child on a bus trip. She is moved by seeing the child and makes a voyage back to her own childhood. At this stage Nin avoids the end-up passage, as such we find the passages ending with elliptical marks: "It was her piano Jay had left out in the rain to be ruined...," "Other Gerards will appear"... She has used questions and these also have the same function: "How could Jay have vanished with the father?"... "Will you be here tomorrow, Rango?" These short passages leave behind a sense of inconclusiveness: "a tale without beginning or end which encloses all things and relates all things."

In *Four Chambered Heart,* Djuna attempts to find "an individually perfect world." As she knows that such a world does not exist on land, she cuts herself off from the real world. She goes to live on a barge in a river. With the passing of time, she discovers that even in the dream (the barge) her search is futile. This discovery is an indication of her growth in self-awareness. She leaves the barge and comes back to the shore. This novel also takes the form of a voyage in order to establish that self-awareness can be achieved through these ways too.

In her novels, Nin makes frequent use of metaphors as a tool for creating order, as she believes: "metaphorical language... can be in the novels as in poems the basis of structure." In the first part of *Winter of Artifice,* the falsity of external appearances is presented through the images taken from the theatre. Djuna and her father play "roles." In her diary Djuna creates "her double." Her father wears a "mask." When they cannot communicate, they are "gesticulating in space." The novel ends with metaphors:

> At last she was entering the Chinese theatre of her drama and could see the trappings of the play as well as the play itself, see that the settings were made of the cardboard of illusion. She was passing behind the stage ...She could see the strings which rule the scenes, the false storms and the false lightening.

Nin started her novels with first person narration in *House of Incest* and ended with the third person narration in *Collages.* It shows the structural growth in her writing – from closed structure to the open structure, which suggests more mobility and life. Here she stands with James Joyce, who, in *A Portrait of the Artist as a Young Man,* dramatizes the growth of the artist from the first person to the third person narration.

The artists or the heroines in Nin's novels are changing as their roles are changing. They move as they have been made to. Their mobility in nature and their changing appearance make them fit and capable to achieve their purpose. They are involved in a struggle.

This struggle is not between the heroines in the novels and their outer world; it is between their various selves. Nin says in her study of Lawrence:

> Lawrence does not create what we generally understand by a "character," that is, a definitely outlined being who bears a resemblance to those we know. He does not give us such a clear outline because the personages in his book are symbolical; he is more preoccupied with the state of consciousness and with subconscious act, moods and reactions.

The above explanation about D.H. Lawrence is applicable to Nin's writings also. The personages in her fiction are always symbolical. They cannot act according to a set pattern, because they are archetypal and it is a modern device of writing fiction. Nin writes:

> There is a purpose and form behind my partial, impressionistic, truncated characters. The whole house, or the whole body, the entire environment, may not be there, but we know from modern painting that a column can signify more than a whole house and that one eye can be more than two at times.

In her fiction, Nin portrays the hidden self of her characters. She portrays her characters quickly and repeatedly at certain highly significant moments. During the time of extreme pressure or crisis when defenses are weak, true feelings burst through the protective facade of the persona. Her characters are caught in a series of revelation. For example, in *A Spy in the House of Love* we find that the character of Sabina is portrayed through super-imposed images of swift glances. Nin concedes that her characters are abstract. According to her, "To abstract" means "to extract the essence of the subject eliminating whatever merely renders the surface." She selects the details about a character that are most expressive, the most telling, restricting these to a small number; then she composes patterns and variations upon the details that she has selected.

Sabina's swirling cape, so admired by other women, suggests the costume of a spy in melodramatic fiction or film; it is glamorous and mysterious, but, above all the cape expresses her need for concealment:

> A spread out cape was the bed of nomads; a cape unfurled was the flag of adventure. Now she was dressed in a costume most appropriate to flights, battles, tournaments. The curtain of the night's defenselessness was rising to expose a personage prepared. Prepared, said the mirror; prepared, said the shoes; prepared, said the cape.
>
> She was not surprised when she looked out of her window and saw the man who had been following her standing at the corner pretending to be reading a newspaper.
>
> It was not a surprise because it was a materialization of a feeling that she had known for many years; that of an eye watching and following her throughout her life.

Here is the power that travels from the deep interior city and goes up. On the other hand Lillian's choked energy and unrealized capacity for passion are expressed by her way of dressing:

> Tumult in orange, red and yellow and green quarreling with each other. The rose devoured the orange, the green and blue overwhelmed the purple. The sport jacket was irritated to be in company with the silk dress, the tailored coat at war with the embroidery, the everyday shoes at variance with the turquoise bracelet. And if at times she chose a majestic hat, it sailed precariously like a sailboat on a choppy sea.

The revealing gestures, the unexpected tone of voice, the angle of head, and the choice of an unusual word reveal truths to the sensitive observer. Nin had been adjusted to these half-tones; as such she brought a highly original approach to the art of characterization:

> I am not writing case histories .... Psychoanalysis is merely the basic philosophy of my work. I accept its promise, that it is the unconscious which rules and shapes our lives. I am making a new art of story-telling, not stories told as case histories, but stories told with a new vision of the unfolding of the character.

Presentation of symbolic materials depends upon this poetic vision. Since there is a difference between a case history and a literary history of frustration, her characters and incidents are always born of theme. They are never manipulated to support an extreme scientific law.

Nin always attempted to externalize the inner conflict. She selected the women characters, looking for a "woman at war with herself." This is the unifying theme of her work, from which all the characters emerge. In order to develop this theme, "it is necessary to return to the origin of the confusion, which is woman's struggle to understand her own nature."

There are four main characters in Nin's novels and they are female characters. Each character portrays one aspect of the heroine. Each of these characters acts according to one of the basic patterns associated with the theory of four elements. Sabina, dressed in red and silver... "evoked the sounds and imagery of fire engines." She personifies the restlessness and feverishness, and therefore evasion and flight are her characteristic activities. She is the modern choleric character. Stella is a cool and withdrawn, elusive and pale character. She lives in a white world: ivory satin bed, white nightgown, white rug-splendor, satin and space. She is the cool dreamer, a modern phlegmatic character. Lillian is "always in a state of fermentation." She is always seeking males for satisfying her desires, as she is never satisfied. She represents the sanguine temperament. She requires more than the usual measures of sexual satisfaction. The fourth character, Djuna is also reticent like Stella, but her reticence leads her to "muse" rather than withdraw. She is Hamlet-like. She describes herself as a pale watcher. She represents the melancholic temperament. These various characters represent the different states of the mind of women. Here, we find a polar effect like Ben Jonson who uses the theory of four humours for making his drama more effective and psychologically true.

These characters are symbolic of a specific complex. They represent particular type of behavior. Sabina is schizophrenic. She has a mind always bordering the crime and punishment. Lillian has over-developed libido; she is extrovert. On the opposite, Djuna is introvert and sexually frigid. Stella has a "screen face" but an unimpressive body. She vacillates between pleasure and pain. She is a female character, but a sort of phlegmatic or masochist. She represents man as well woman. The depersonalizing effect is evident in all these four characters.

Nin's characters are often without a "local habitation and a name." All characters are artists: musician, dancer, and painter; they are all women; they do not have second names. There is rare description of their faces or bodies, though their clothing is carefully described. The reader often does not know where or with whom they live. These characters possess a fluid quality. It is always uncertain when and where they will turn up. Nin, like Beckett, cares for only those details which are closely related to a character or situation. It is psychological rather than real that Nin is interested in.

Since Nin is more interested in psychological states rather than in social scenes, her characters are excessive in their reactions and responses; they are not average. In reply to a question, "Do people really swing from one extreme emotion to another in so short a span?" she says, "we know that poets do." Her characters are artists because an artist embodies the exaggerated feelings of the common man, colouring them with his poetic personality. Subscribing to the archetypal concept, she recognizes the poetic significance of stereotype. She is in search of a comprehensive form of art. She tries to fuse the prose and poetry along with a literary synthesis of the other media:

> The craft of writing can include all the others. A writer can possess the eye of a painter as Proust did; the ear of a musician as Joyce did; the rhythm of a dancer as Isabel Bolton's prose has in Do I Wake or Sleep. He can possess the antennae of a clairvoyant, as Isaac Dinesan did in her book on Africa; the prophetic quality of a fortune-teller as Huxley did in Brave New World. He can have the sense of form of a sculptor.
>
> The knowledge of textures of a dress designer, an eye for scenic arrangements of the stage director. He has to be an architect to house his characters, an etymologist, a botanist. He needs all the arts and sciences to reveal all the aspects of man.

Like Henry James, she too, characterizes through environment. Djuna lives in a house in which there is a "sealed room:" "Even in the bathroom there were no medicine bottles on the selves proclaiming: castor oil, cold cream. She had transferred all of them to alchemist bottles, the homeliest drugs assumed the air of a philtre." These cosmetics and clothes are the index of the character. Lillian appears as a "tumult in orange and yellow and green quarreling with each other." To Stella, "hats demanded that role be played in its maximum perfection. So each time she had reached into joyous hat exhibit, looked at the treasured hats, she took again the little skull cap, the unobtrusive page and choir boy cap."

As all characters in Nin's novels are symbolic, all physical descriptions applied to characters indicate a psychological event. Her characters and their manner of acting resemble "Branensi's bird in space." The artist is interested in neither the bird nor the space but in interaction of the two – the flight. She strives for the similar effect, and not for a record, not for a photograph, nor for the illusion of life but for the impression of struggle, for which she eliminates unnecessary external characteristics and reshapes the "body" so that they can take a voyage into the cities of the interior and find out the self.

This development of character is presented in a beautiful way. The struggle of Lillian is marked in *Ladders to Fire,* which is resolved after a long suffering from her sexuality in *Seduction of the Minotaur,* where she finds an Eve-figure and accepts it in a creative spirit. Though her sexual desire is not very aggressive in nature, she has the normal female desire to be conquered: "Deep down, what her nature wanted was to be made to yield." But, she cannot perform the normal female role due to fear; fear that a male will not allow her to achieve her female expression because of his inadequacies; and fear that she, too, is inadequate as her nature is not a satisfying one. This fear is due to her lack of self-awareness. She, as a passionate woman, is forced to work like the unhappy, aggressive masculine warrior, or the unhappy dominative protecting guardian of others.

In terms of her development and transformation of her heterosexual relationships, her first lover is an unnamed male, whom she goes to see by a bicycle. Though both are coming to the meeting place from equidistance, she drives her bicycle very fast and reaches earlier. This is due to her fear that is transformed in pedalling her bicycle faster. She accuses herself of playing Romeo instead of Juliet, while coming earlier and waiting for her lover: "she had leaped, she had acted Romeo, and when woman leaped she leaped into a void."

Her second sexual relationship is with "a pale, passive, romantic, anaemic figure, garbed in grey and timidity." His name is Gerard. She chooses him because though she feels herself over-active, she has distrust of both – male and female alleviates. Again, she leaps into a void; she is forced "to play the lover alone, giving the questions and answers too." She is unable to see the nature and blames herself; "I did arouse his love – and she began to make a list of self-accusations." Since this time she was "the aggressor, she was wounded." "Lillian now becomes belligerent and defensive in addition to being aggressive." This way, she represents the modern woman who is incapable of performing her essential functions "because of her tendency to imitate man and adopt his goals."

Lillian's relationship with her husband also is imbalanced and incomplete. She feels that her husband is a child and therefore she plays a matriarch. Like Sabina, she feels that her husband has not accepted her as the woman she has become, rather he is in love with the woman she was, when she married her. Nin dramatizes this feeling of Lillian by introducing Poe-esque episode of the man who is discovered cohabitating with the dead body of his wife. As she cannot bear this "odor of death, image of death, created by her husband," she leaves her husband and her family.

Lillian meets Jay in a hotel. He also cannot satisfy her because he is as free and fickle as her husband was constant. His relationship is based on the appetite of a child. He wants her as a mother instead of a lover: "His taking of her was not to take or master her. He was lover inside of the woman, as the child is inside the woman." Her husband performed inadequate sex because he always remained "outside of her," he had been only able to "visit" and not to "fuse;" on the other hand, Jay is unsatisfactory because instead of "mastering" her he wants to lodge inside her. He gives her "the feeling of physical intermingling as she had with a child."

Lillian is still dissatisfied and thus disillusioned with these relationships, yet she does not sink or surrender like Sabina or Stella. She still believes that there is a "deeper truth ... She did not know what it was." The deeper truth is that she has disguised her real self in male, dressing in male clothes, and this is why her relationships are doomed. She feels disappointed with these relationships; she further attempts to find her real self by turning to homosexual relationship.

Lillian's relationship with Sabina or Djuna is not of lesbian nature. From these female friends, she tries to extract that particular female quality that enables them to enjoy their relationships satisfactorily with males. Djuna speaks about Lillian: "she wants something of me that only a man can give her. But first of all she wants to become me, so that she can communicate with man. She is doing it through me."

Djuna is the essence of "femininity" and Lillian learns from her the "pleasure of capitulation," which she has lost as a warrior, as "in war, the conquest was imperative." Sabina "has no roots," whereas Lillian "is strangling in (her) roots." She learns freedom and mobility from Sabina; and she learns the ability to delight in erotic adventures.

Though Djuna and Sabina attempt to discover Lillian's "dormant" and disguise female self, Lillian is not able to get her identification. She is still possessed by the "demon doubt and the monster fear:"

> A complete house-wrecking service. Every world, smile, act, silver jewel, lying on the floor, with the emerald green dress, and even Djuna image of Lillian to which she had often turned for comfort, that too lay shattered on the ground. Nothing to salvage. A mere pile of flaws. A little pile of ashes from a bonfire of self-criticism.

This war of Lillian is resolved in *Seduction of the Minotaur.* In the first part of the novel "Solar Barque," Lillian reintroduces her old problems in relationships with other inhabitants of Golconda. In the second part *Seduction of the Minotaur,* she solves the problem through her conversation with Dr. Hernandez, who plays the role of her conscience.

Lillian tries to avoid Dr. Hernandez; she opposes the doctor when he starts probing her motive of coming to Golconda. But, the doctor does not disappear and explains the theory of Karma; he tries to convince that roles played in the present are the re-enactment of some unresolved past conflict: "You are a fugitive from truth, only the backdrop has changed." The doctor purposely explains the four episodes. While attempting to free the American prisoner, she re-enacted the role that she had played with her husband – the role of a liberator and manipulator; her relationship with the anaemic Michael represents her relationship with the passive Gerard; while mothering the child Lietta, she re-enacts her relationship with her own children; her relationship with the young Fred corresponds to that with Jay – the man-child; and her relations with the half-men are due to the fear that she cannot respond positively to a positive man. Finally, she realizes her confusion of the maternal and sexual instincts; she becomes free from these preoccupations; she feels liberated and proceeds for two things: she "will drink her last cup of flowing gold; second, she will seek out the doctor;" and she wants to follow him as "he wanted her to talk." Now she is able to recognize her body and her sexual appetites. On the other hand, while she wants to see the doctor she expresses her willingness to accept her conscience. Ultimately, she returns to her village to "pack her unearthed treasures."

As she walks to meet the doctor, she feels "more aware of her body," aware that it has become "a firm, elastic, balanced body, free in its movements." While she has been waiting for the doctor who is detained by the "natives," the lights go out for a second; but she does not fear any more. Shortly after, she learns that the doctor is dead. This news does not affect her negatively because now she has invented her conscience and knows her impulse. Since, she has learned to fuse the conscience with impulse, she is now a whole woman; she no longer needs either the code or the judge. "The Last Cup of Gold" and the doctor's death symbolize Lillian's new ability that she has acquired – to fuse her two extremes: conscience and impulse. She realizes that the fear that resulted in her role of half-male and half-female was the Minotaur. She also realized that the male-role prevented her in achieving congenial and healthy relationships with males. Now she is whole; she can see the things with a clear vision: "The time was past when her body could be ravished from her by visitations from the world of guilt." Now she claims: "We do not see things as they are, we see them as we are."

In *Ladders to Fore,* Lillian is completely involved in the events on her personal level as being a part of the events. In "Solar Barque," the first section of the novel *Seduction of the Minotaur,* she participates, but with a developed insight of being a spectator of the dramas in which she is involved; whereas in the second part, she becomes a commentator, as being quite able to observe the scenes objectively. She has developed herself, transformed herself; she can now juxtapose her former problems with her newly acquired knowledge; she can draw conclusions now. She, as a protagonist, works like a participant, spectator, and finally a commentator.

Works Cited

Edel, Leon. *The Modern Psychological Novel.* New York:1964.
Nin, Anais. *Seduction of the Minotaur.* Denver: Alan Swallow, 1966.
———, *Realism and Reality.* New York: Alicat Book Shop, Outcast Series No. 6, 1946.
———, *Collages.* Denver: Alan Swallow, 1964.
———, *Seduction of the Minotaur.* p. 5.
———, *Winter of Artifice.* Denver: Alan Swallow, 1961.
———, *D.H. Lawrence: An Unprofessional Study.* Chicago: Swallow Press, 1964.
———, *Realism and Reality.* p. 13. Spencer, Sharoon. *Collages of Dreams: The Writings of Anais Nin.* New York: Harcourt Brace Jovanovich, 1981.

About the Contributors

Dr. Sister M. Carol A.C. is Professor and Head (Retired), Department of English, Patna Women's College, Patna University, Patna, Bihar, India.

Rajan J. Barrett is Lecturer, Department of English, M. S. University of Baroda, Vadodara, Gujrat, India.

Dr. Shahnaz Begum is Associate Professor, Department of English, Magadh University, Bodgh Gaya, Bihar, India.

Shilpa D. Bhat is a Research Scholar, Department of English, Gujarat University, Ahmedabad, India.

Maria Blaszkiewicz University of Warsaw, Poland.

Dr. Ádám Bogár is independent scholar from Budapest, Hungary.

Dr. Anuradha Deepak is Associate Professor of English, K.L.P. College, Rewari, Haryana, India.

Dr. Shanker A. Dutt is Professor of English, Patna University and Chairman, Bihar Sangeet Natak Akademi, Patna, Bihar, India

Dr. Rajiv Ranjan Dwivedi is Assistant Professor, University School of Humanities & Social Sciences, Guru Gobind Singh Indraprastha University, Delhi, India.

Dr. G.A. Ghanshyam is Professor of English, Govt. M.L.S. College, Seepat, Bilaspur, Chhattisgarh, India.

Dr. Gunjan is Assistant Professor of English (Ad-hoc), Bihar National College, Patna University, Patna, Bihar, India.

Dr. Alpana Gupta is Guest Faculty, MNIT, Jaipur, Rajasthan, India.

Subodh Kumar Jha is Assistant Professor and Head, Department of English, S N Sinha College, Jehanabad, Bihar, India.

Dr. Harish Kumar Khanna is Assistant Professor of English, PDM College of Engineering, Bahadurgarh, Haryana, India and King Salman Bin Abdul Aziz University, Kingdom of Saudi Arabia.

Dr. A.A. Khan is Professor of English, Govt. D.T. College UTAI, Durg Chhattisgarh, India.

Dr. Tanjeen A. Khan is Assistant Professor and Head, Department of English, Bhilai Institute of Technology, Raipur Chhattisgarh, India.

Dr. K.B.S. Krishna is Assistant Professor of English, Central University of Himachal Pradesh, Dharamshala, Himachal Pradesh, India.

Dr. Amarendra Kumar is Professor of English (Retired), R.N. College, Hajipur, Bihar, India.

Dr. Ashok Kumar is Professor of English, B.N. College, Patna University, Patna, Bihar, India.

Dr. Satyendra Kumar is Assistant Professor of English, Atma Ram Sanatan Dharma College, University of Delhi, India.

Rajesh Kumar is Executive Director, The Academic Resource Unit (TARU), Digantar, Jaipur, Rajasthan and Former Associate Professor of English, Sana'a University, Republic of Yemen

Dr. Tribhuwan Kumar is Assistant Professor of English, SRM University, NCR Campus, Modinagar, Ghaziabad, Uttar Pradesh, India.

Dr. Rashmi Kumari is Assistant Professor of English, L.N. College, Bhagwanpur, Vaishali, BRA Bihar University, Muzaffarpur, Bihar, India.

Kaustav Kundu is Research Scholar, Department of English, University of Calcutta, Kolkata, West Bengal, India.

Leni Marlina is English teaching staff at State University of Padang (UNP), Indonesia since 2006. She is currently on study program of Master of Writing and Literature at Deakin University, Australia by having scholarship sponsored by Indonesian Government (DIKTI scholarship).

Dr. Thirupa Thi Reddy Maru is Lecturer in English, College of Education, Omar Al-Mukhtar University, Al-Gubba, Libya.

Mrs. Babita Mehra is Assistant Professor, K.L.P. College, Rewari, Haryana, India.

Dr. Suresh Nath is Principal and Head (Retired), Postgraduate Department of English, P.G. College, Sikandrabad, Uttar Pradesh,

India.

Nagendra Nathawat is Assistant Professor of English, Modi College, Laxamangarh, Sikar, Rajasthan, India.

Dr. Niraj is Research Scholar, Department of English, Patna University, Patna, Bihar, India.

Dibakar Pal is a Civil Servant in India & Independent Researcher.

Prof. Sidheshwar Prasad is the Former Governor, Tripura, India.

Prof. Shaileshwar Sati Prasad is Professor and Head (Retired), Department of English, Patna University, Patna, Bihar, India.**Dr. Vijay Shankar Prasad** is Lecturer in English, Omer Al-Mukhtar University, Al-Gubba, Libya.

Mr. Rohit Ranjan is an Independent Researcher & Filmmaker, Patna, Bihar, India.

Dr. Ratri Ray is Professor and Head (Retired), Department of English, Patna University, Patna, Bihar, India.

Dr. R.P. Roy is Associate Professor and Head, Department of English, B.N. College, Bhagalpur, Bihar, India.

Prof. R. Saraswathi is Dean of Humanities and Chairperson, P.G. Board of Studies, Department of English, Acharya Nagarjuna University, Nagarjuna Nagar, Guntur, Andhra Pradesh, India.

Dr. Awadesh Kumar Sharma is Professor of English, Central University of Jharkhand, Ranchi, Jharkhand, India.

Amiya Bhushan Sharma is Professor of English (Retired), Indira Gandhi National Open University, New Delhi, India.

Dr. Kedar Nath Sharma is Professor and Head (Retired), Department of English, Patna University, Patna, Bihar, India.

Dr. Indu Bhushan Sharma is Associate Professor of English, S. Sinha College, Aurangabad, Bihar, India.

Dr. Raj Kumar Sharma is Senior Lecturer in English, Simdega College, Simdega, Ranchi University, Ranchi, Jharkhand, India.

Dr. Ramesh Kumar Sharma is Lecturer in English, College of Education, Omar Al-Mukhtar University, Al-Gubba, Libya.

Dr. Samir Kumar Sharma is Associate Professor of English, Bihar National College, Patna University, Patna, Bihar, India.

Jonathan S. Shaw is Principal of St. Columba's College(Retired), Hazaribag. Professor of English, University of Aden and Professor of English, University of Sana'a, Republic of Yemen.

Dr. Gokul Singh is Professor of English and Principal (Retired), S.K.R. College, Barbigha, T.M. Bhagalpur University, Bhagalpur, Bihar, India.

Dr. Ram Bhagwan Singh is Professor of English(Retired), Ranchi University, Ranchi, Jharkhand, India.

Dr. Bijay Bahadur Singh is Associate Professor and Head (Retired), Department of English, College of Commerce, Patna, Bihar, India.

Dr. Radha Mohan Singh is Professor of English and Dean Faculty of Humanities, Patna University, Patna, Bihar, India.

Dr. Rajni Singh is Associate Professor, Department of Humanities and Social Sciences Indian School of Mines, Dhanbad, Jharkand, India.

Dr. Shrikant Singh is Associate Professor and Head, Department of English, Nav Nalanda Mahavihara, Deemed University, Nalanda, Bihar, India.

Dr. Bhushan Singh is Head of the Department of English, P.R. College, Sonpur, Bihar, India.

Dr. R.P. Singh is Assistant Professor of English, D.A.V., P.G. College Siwan, Bihar, India.

Dr. Akhilesh Kr. Singh is Assistant Professor(Guest-Faculty), P.G. Department of English, B.N. College, Patna, Bihar, India.

Dr. Ashok Kumar Sinha is Professor of English(Retired), Patna University, Patna, Bihar, India.

Prof. Sidheshwar Dhari Sinha is Dean and Head (Retired), Department of Education, Ranchi University, Ranchi, Jharkhand, India.

Prof. Sudha Sinha is Professor and Head(Retired), P.G. Department of English, and Patna Women's College, Patna University, Patna, Bihar, India. Visiting Professor, LNMI, Patna, Bihar, India.

Dr. B.P. Sinha is Dean, School of Languages Central University of Jharkhand, Ratu Lohardaga Road, Brambe, Ranchi, Jharkhand, India.

Dr. Sarita Sinha is Assistant Professor of English, Department of English, Sri Arbind Mahila College, Patna, Bihar, India

Dr. Sunita Sinha is Associate Professor of English, Women's College, Samastipur, Lalit Narayan Mithila University, Darbhanga, Bihar, India.

Dr. D.N. Sinha is Associate Professor of English, Bihar National College, Patna University, Patna, Bihar, India.

Dr. V.B. Srivastava is Assistant Professor of English, R.M. Collect Sasaram, Bihar, India.

Dr. Swati Surbhi is P.G.T. English, S.S. High School, Ormanjhi, Ranchi, Jharkhand, India.

Dr. Awinash Kumar Sushil is Guest-Faculty, Department of English, B N College, Patna University, Patna, Bihar, India.

Dr. Sweety is Associate Professor of English (Professional Communication), Department of Applied Science and Humanities, IIMT College of Engineering, Greater Noida. Uttar Pradesh, India.

Dr. Arvind Kumar Thakur is Assistant Professor of English, D.S. College, Katihar, Bihar, India.

Dr. Quan Wang is Associate Professor of English, Beihang University, Beijing, China.